ABRAHAM LINCOLN: His Speeches and Writings

Meserve No. 82. A photograph made by Mathew B. Brady on February 9, 1864. Victor D. Brenner used this photograph in making his design for the Lincoln penny. The original glass negative is in the Meserve Collection.

ABRAHAM LINCOLN:

His Speeches and Writings

EDITED WITH CRITICAL AND ANALYTICAL NOTES

BY

Roy P. Basler

PREFACE BY Carl Sandburg

DA CAPO PRESS

Library of Congress Cataloging in Publication Data

Lincoln, Abraham, 1809-1865.
[Selections]
Abraham Lincoln, his speeches and writings / edited with critical and analytical notes by Roy P. Basler; preface by Carl Sandburg.
p. cm.
Reprint. Originally published: Cleveland: World Pub. Co., 1946.
Includes bibliographical references (p.) and index.
ISBN 0-306-80404-2
1. United States—Politics and government—1815-1861—Sources. 2. United States—History—Civil War, 1861-1865—Sources. I. Basler, Roy Prentice, 1906- . II. Title.
[E457.92 1990a] 90-3582
973.7′092—dc20 CIP

This Da Capo Press paperback edition of *Abraham Lincoln: His Speeches and Writings* is an unabridged republication of the edition published in Cleveland, Ohio, in 1946.

Second Da Capo Press edition 2001
ISBN 0–306–81075–1
ISBN-13 978-0-306-81075-6
Published by Da Capo Press
A Member of the Perseus Books Group
http://www.dacapopress.com

5 6 7 8 9 10 09 08 07

To my Father

CONTENTS

PREFACE *by Carl Sandburg* xvii

INTRODUCTION *by Roy P. Basler* xxiii

LINCOLN'S DEVELOPMENT AS A WRITER 1

SELECTIONS, WITH NOTES:

To the People of Sangamo County: Political Announcement, March 9, 1832 53

Announcement of Political Views in *Sangamo Journal*, June 13, 1836 58

Letter to Colonel Robert Allen, June 21, 1836 59

Letter to Miss Mary Owens, December 13, 1836 60

Speech in the Illinois Legislature, January 11, 1837 63

Letter to Miss Mary Owens, May 7, 1837 73

Letter to Miss Mary Owens, August 16, 1837 75

The Perpetuation of Our Political Institutions: Address Before the Young Men's Lyceum of Springfield, Illinois, January 27, 1838 76

Letter to Mrs. O. H. Browning, April 1, 1838 85

The Sub-Treasury: Speech at a Political Discussion in the Hall of the House of Representatives at Springfield, Illinois, December [26], 1839 90

Letter to John T. Stuart, January 20, 1841 113

Letter to John T. Stuart, January 23, 1841 115

Letter to Joshua F. Speed, June 19, 1841 116

Letter to Miss Mary Speed, September 27, 1841 121

Letter to Joshua F. Speed, January 3, 1842 124

Letter to Joshua F. Speed, February 3, 1842 127

Eulogy on Benjamin Ferguson, February 8, 1842 128

Letter to Joshua F. Speed, February 13, 1842 130

Temperance Address Delivered Before the Springfield Washington Temperance Society, February 22, 1842 131

Letter to Joshua F. Speed, February 25, 1842 141

Letter to Joshua F. Speed, February 25, 1842 143
Letter to Joshua F. Speed, March 27, 1842 144
Letter to Joshua F. Speed, July 4, 1842 146
A Letter from the Lost Townships, August 27, 1842 148
Correspondence About the Lincoln-Shields Duel, September 17, 1842 156
Memorandum of Instructions to E. H. Merryman, Lincoln's Second, September 19, 1842 159
Letter to Joshua F. Speed, October 5, 1842 161
Letter to James S. Irwin, November 2, 1842 163
Letter to Samuel D. Marshall, November 11, 1842 164
Letter to Joshua F. Speed, March 24, 1843 165
Letter to Joshua F. Speed, May 18, 1843 167
Letter to Williamson Durley, October 3, 1845 169
Letter to Henry E. Dummer, November 18, 1845 171
Letter to B. F. James, February 9, 1846 173
Remarkable Case of Arrest for Murder, April 15, 1846 175
Letter to Andrew Johnston, April 18, 1846 184
Religious Views: Letter to the Editor of the *Illinois Gazette*, August 11, 1846 186
Letter to Andrew Johnston, September 6, 1846 189
My Childhood Home I See Again, 1846 190
The Bear Hunt, [1846] 193
Letter to Joshua F. Speed, October 22, 1846 196
Letter to William H. Herndon, December 12, 1847 199
Resolutions in the United States House of Representatives, December 22, 1847 199
The War with Mexico: Speech in the United States House of Representatives, January 12, 1848 202
Letter to William H. Herndon, February 1, 1848 217
Letter to William H. Herndon, February 2, 1848 219
Letter to William H. Herndon, February 15, 1848 220
Letter to Usher F. Linder, March 22, 1848 221
Letter to David Lincoln, March 24, 1848 224
Letter to David Lincoln, April 2, 1848 224
Letter to Mary Todd Lincoln, April 16, 1848 226
Letter to Mary Todd Lincoln, June 12, 1848 228
Letter to Mary Todd Lincoln, July 2, 1848 229
Letter to William H. Herndon, July 11, 1848 232

The Presidential Question: Speech in the United States House of Representatives, July 27, 1848 233
Letters to Thomas Lincoln and John D. Johnston, December 24, 1848 250
Letter to William H. Herndon, January 5, 1849 252
Letter to C. U. Schlater, January 5, 1849 254
Letter to C. R. Welles, February 20, 1849 254
Letter to Joshua F. Speed, February 20, 1849 256
Letter to Abram Bale, February 22, 1850 258
Letter to John D. Johnston, January 12, 1851 259
Letter to Andrew McCallen, July 4, 1851 260
Letter to John D. Johnston, November 4, 1851 261
Letter to John D. Johnston, November 9, 1851 263
Letter to John D. Johnston, November 25, 1851 263
Eulogy on Henry Clay Delivered in the State House at Springfield, Illinois, July 6, 1852 264
Fragments: On Slavery, [July 1, 1854?] 278
Letter to J. M. Palmer, September 7, 1854 279
The 14th Section: An Editorial in the *Illinois Journal*, September 11, 1854 281
The Repeal of the Missouri Compromise and the Propriety of Its Restoration: Speech at Peoria, Illinois, in Reply to Senator Douglas, October 16, 1854 283
Letter to E. B. Washburne, December 14, 1854 325
Letter to E. B. Washburne, February 9, 1855 326
Letter to Owen Lovejoy, August 11, 1855 328
Letter to George Robertson, August 15, 1855 330
Letter to Joshua F. Speed, August 24, 1855 332
Letter to Isham Reavis, November 5, 1855 337
Letter to R. P. Morgan, February 13, 1856 338
Frémont, Buchanan, and the Extension of Slavery: Speech Delivered at Kalamazoo, Michigan, August 27, 1856 339
Letter to Julian M. Sturtevant, September 27, 1856 346
Sectionalism, [October 1?], 1856 347
The Dred Scott Decision: Speech at Springfield, Illinois, June 26, 1857 352
Letter to E. B. Washburne, April 26, 1858 366

Letter to E. B. Washburne, May 15, 1858 368
Letter to Jediah F. Alexander, May 15, 1858 369
Letter to E. B. Washburne, May 27, 1858 370
Letter to Samuel Wilkinson, June 10, 1858 371
A House Divided: Speech Delivered at Springfield, Illinois, at the Close of the Republican State Convention, June 16, 1858 372
Letter to Joseph Medill, June 25, 1858 382
Letter to James W. Somers, June 25, 1858 384
Speech in Reply to Douglas at Chicago, Illinois, July 10, 1858 385
Speech in Reply to Douglas at Springfield, Illinois, July 17, 1858 405
Letter to John Mathers, July 20, 1858 424
Letter to Henry Asbury, July 31, 1858 425
Fragment: On Slavery, [August 1, 1858?] 427
Letter to Henry E. Dummer, August 5, 1858 427
First Debate, at Ottawa, Illinois, August 21, 1858 428
Fragment: Speech at Edwardsville, Illinois, September 11, 1858 469
Letter to M. P. Sweet, September 16, 1858 475
Verses: To Rosa, September 28, 1858 476
Verses: To Linnie, September 30, 1858 477
Fragment: On Slavery, [October 1, 1858?] 477
Letter to J. N. Brown, October 18, 1858 478
Last Speech in Springfield, Illinois, in the Campaign of 1858, [October 30, 1858] 480
Letter to Henry Asbury, November 19, 1858 482
Letter to Doctor C. H. Ray, November 20, 1858 482
Notes of An Argument, [December ?], 1858 483
Letter to James T. Thornton, December 2, 1858 485
Letter to Lyman Trumbull, December 11, 1858 486
Letter to H. L. Pierce and Others, April 6, 1859 488
Letter to T. J. Pickett, April 16, 1859 490
Letter to Salmon Portland Chase, June 9, 1859 491
Letter to Salmon Portland Chase, June 20, 1859 492
Agriculture: Annual Address Before the Wisconsin State Agricultural Society at Milwaukee, Wisconsin, September 30, 1859 493
Written by Lincoln in the Autograph Album of Mary Delahay, December 7, 1859 505

Letter to William Kellogg, December 11, 1859 506
Letter to G. W. Dole, G. S. Hubbard, and W. H. Brown, December 14, 1859 507
Letter to J. W. Fell Inclosing Autobiography, December 20, 1859 510
Fragment: The Constitution and the Union, [1860?] 513
Letter to M. W. Packard, February 10, 1860 514
Letter to O. P. Hall, J. R. Fullinwider, and U. F. Correll, February 14, 1860 515
Address at Cooper Institute, New York, February 27, 1860 517
Letter to Mark W. Delahay, March 16, 1860 539
Letter to F. C. Herburger, April 7, 1860 541
Letter to Lyman Trumbull, April 29, 1860 542
Letter to George Ashmun, May 23, 1860 543
Letter to Samuel Haycraft and Autobiography, May 28, 1860 544
Letter to Charles C. Nott, May 31, 1860 545
Short Autobiography Written for the Campaign of 1860, June [1?], 1860 547
Letter to Samuel Galloway, June 19, 1860 555
Letter to Abraham Jonas, July 21, 1860 557
Letter to George Latham, July 22, 1860 559
Letter to Charles C. Nott, September 22, 1860 560
Letter to Mrs. M. J. Green, September 22, 1860 561
Letter to Miss Grace Bedell, October 19, 1860 561
Letter to George T. M. Davis, October 27, 1860 563
Letter to H. J. Raymond, November 28, 1860 564
Letter to William Kellogg, December 11, 1860 565
Letter to John D. Defrees, December 18, 1860 566
Letter to A. H. Stephens, December 22, 1860 567
Farewell Address at Springfield, Illinois, February 11, 1861 568
Speech at Indianapolis, Indiana, February 11, 1861 571
Address to Germans at Cincinnati, Ohio, February 12, 1861 572
Address to the Senate of New Jersey, February 21, 1861 574
Address to the Assembly of New Jersey, February 21, 1861 575
Address in Independence Hall, Philadelphia, February 22, 1861 577
First Inaugural Address, March 4, 1861 579
Reply to Secretary Seward's Memorandum, April 1, 1861 590

Letter to Colonel E. E. Ellsworth, April 15, 1861 592
Letter to Colonel E. E. Ellsworth's Parents, May 25, 1861 593
Message to Congress in Special Session, July 4, 1861 594
Proclamation of a National Fast-Day, August 12, 1861 610
Letter to Governor Beriah Magoffin, August 24, 1861 611
Letter to O. H. Browning, September 22, 1861 613
Letter to Major [G. D.?] Ramsay, October 17, 1861 615
Annual Message to Congress, December 3, 1861 616
Letter to Mrs. Susannah Weathers, December 4, 1861 635
Telegram to General D. C. Buell, January 4, 1862 636
Letter to General D. C. Buell, January 6, 1862 636
Letter to General A. E. Burnside, January 28, 1862 637
Letter to General G. B. McClellan, April 9, 1862 638
Letter to the Senate and House of Representatives, April 16, 1862 640
Letter to General G. B. McClellan, May 9, 1862 641
Telegram to General G. B. McClellan, May 28, 1862 643
Telegram to General G. B. McClellan, June 28, 1862 644
Telegram to General G. B. McClellan, July 1, 1862 645
Letter to General G. B. McClellan, July 2, 1862 645
Telegram to General G. B. McClellan, July 3, 1862 646
Telegram to General G. B. McClellan, July 5, 1862 647
Letter to General G. B. McClellan, July 13, 1862 647
Letter to Cuthbert Bullitt, July 28, 1862 648
Letter to John M. Clay, August 9, 1862 651
Letter to Horace Greeley, August 22, 1862 651
Telegram to General G. B. McClellan, September 15, 1862 653
Testimonial for Doctor Isachar Zacharie, September 22, 1862 654
Letter to John Ross, September 25, 1862 654
Meditation on the Divine Will, September [30?], 1862 655
Remarks to the Army of the Potomac at Frederick, Maryland, October 4, 1862 656
Letter to General G. B. McClellan, October 13, 1862 657
Telegram to General G. B. McClellan, October 24, 1862 659
Telegram to General G. B. McClellan, October 27, 1862 660
Letter to General Carl Schurz, November 10, 1862 660
Letter to Samuel Treat, November 19, 1862 663

Letter to General Carl Schurz, November 24, 1862 664
Annual Message to Congress, December 1, 1862 666
Letter to Miss Fanny McCullough, December 23, 1862 688
Final Emancipation Proclamation, January 1, 1863 689
Letter to General J. A. McClernand, January 22, 1863 692
Letter to General Joseph Hooker, January 26, 1863 693
Letter to Governor Andrew Johnson, March 26, 1863 694
Letter to General Joseph Hooker, May 7, 1863 695
Letter to Isaac N. Arnold, May 26, 1863 696
Telegram to General Joseph Hooker, June 5, 1863 698
Letter to Erastus Corning and Others, June 12, 1863 699
Telegram to General Joseph Hooker, June 14, 1863 708
Response to a Serenade, July 7, 1863 709
Letter to General U. S. Grant, July 13, 1863 710
Draft of Letter to General G. G. Meade, July 14, 1863 711
Letter to General H. W. Halleck, July 29, 1863 713
Letter to General N. P. Banks, August 5, 1863 714
Letter to Mary Todd Lincoln, August 8, 1863 716
Letter to General J. A. McClernand, August 12, 1863 717
Letter to J. H. Hackett, August 17, 1863 718
Letter to James C. Conkling, August 26, 1863 720
Letter to James C. Conkling, August 27, 1863 725
Letter to General H. W. Halleck, September 19, 1863 726
Proclamation for Thanksgiving, October 3, 1863 727
Telegram to General G. G. Meade, October 8, 1863 731
Letter to General H. W. Halleck, October 16, 1863 731
Letter to J. H. Hackett, November 2, 1863 732
Letter to E. M. Stanton, Secretary of War, November 11, 1863 733
Address Delivered at the Dedication of the Cemetery at Gettysburg, November 19, 1863 734
Letter to Edward Everett, November 20, 1863 737
Proclamation of Amnesty and Reconstruction, December 8, 1863 738
Letter to Crafts J. Wright and C. K. Hawkes, January 7, 1864 742
Letter to General N. P. Banks, January 31, 1864 743
Letter to E. M. Stanton, Secretary of War, March 1, 1864 744
Letter to Governor Michael Hahn, March 13, 1864 745

Letter to E. M. Stanton, Secretary of War, March 15, 1864 745
Memorandum for Mrs. S. W. Hunt, April 11, 1864 747
Address at a Sanitary Fair in Baltimore, April 18, 1864 748
Letter to General U. S. Grant, April 30, 1864 750
Speech at a Sanitary Fair in Philadelphia, June 16, 1864 751
Letter to William Dennison & Others, a Committee of the National Union Convention, June 27, 1864 753
Letter to Horace Greeley, July 15, 1864 754
Address to the 164th Ohio Regiment, August 18, 1864 755
Address to the 166th Ohio Regiment, August 22, 1864 756
Letter to Mrs. Eliza P. Gurney, September 4, 1864 757
Letter to General U. S. Grant, September 22, 1864 758
Letter to Henry W. Hoffman, October 10, 1864 759
Response to a Serenade, October 19, 1864 760
Proclamation of Thanksgiving, October 20, 1864 761
Telegram to General P. H. Sheridan, October 22, 1864 763
Response to a Serenade, November 10, 1864 763
Letter to General W. S. Rosecrans, November 19, 1864 765
Letter to Mrs. Bixby, November 21, 1864 766
Story Written for Noah Brooks, December [6?], 1864 772
Annual Message to Congress, December 6, 1864 773
Letter to General W. T. Sherman, December 26, 1864 789
Letter to General U. S. Grant, January 19, 1865 790
Terms for General R. E. Lee's Capitulation, March 3, 1865 791
Second Inaugural Address, March 4, 1865 792
Letter to Thurlow Weed, March 15, 1865 794
Address to the 140th Indiana Regiment, March 17, 1865 794
Telegram to General U. S. Grant, April 2, 1865 796
Last Public Address, April 11, 1865 796
Telegram to General Godfrey Weitzel, April 12, 1865 802

SOURCES AND BIBLIOGRAPHY:

Sources of Text 805
Works Cited in the Notes 818

INDEX 823

ILLUSTRATIONS

Brady Profile of Lincoln, February 9, 1864. *Meserve Collection, No. 82* — *Frontispiece*

Cooper Institute Portrait of Lincoln, by Mathew B. Brady, February 27, 1860. *Meserve Collection, No. 20* — 126

Photograph of Lincoln, by Alexander Hessler, June 3, 1860. *Meserve Collection, No. 26* — 414

Inaugural Photograph of Lincoln, by Mathew B. Brady, February 23, 1861. *Meserve Collection, No. 68* — 446

Photograph of Lincoln, by Mathew B. Brady, February 9, 1864. *Meserve Collection, No. 85* — 670

Last Photograph of Lincoln Made in Life, by Alexander Gardner, April 10, 1865. *Meserve Collection, No. 100* — 702

Facsimile of the Hooker Letter — 844

THE PHOTOGRAPHS of Lincoln which illustrate this book are from the Collection of Frederick Hill Meserve. Mr. Meserve, whose prodigious research in Lincoln likenesses dates back to the turn of the century, is regarded as the leading authority on the subject. Arranged chronologically, these photographs record Abraham Lincoln, the man, during the momentous last five years of his life.

There has been no touching-up or removing of blemishes in order to make more perfect pictures. The original photographs in the Meserve Collection have been copied with absolute fidelity.

THE FACSIMILE of Lincoln's letter to General Hooker, which appears on page 844, is used by permission of the owner of the original letter, Mr. Alfred Whital Stern of Chicago. It was made from a half-tone reproduction issued by R. R. Donnelley & Sons Company for the Chicago Caxton Club.

PREFACE

"He has a style his own," has often been the comment on a writer or speaker. When it was said of Walt Whitman it meant that any imitation of his style, so distinctive was it, could at once be seen as mimicry. One result of this was many parodies.

And though we sometimes meet the expression, "a Lincolnian style," it has no strict meaning as in the case of Whitman. Lincoln had many styles. It has been computed that his printed speeches and writings number 1,078,365 words. One may range through this record of utterance and find a wider variety of styles than in any other American statesman or orator. And perhaps no author of books has written and vocalized in such a diversity of speech tones directed at all manners and conditions of men.

This may be saying, in effect, that the range of the personality of Abraham Lincoln ran far, identifying itself with the tumults and follies of mankind, keeping touch with multitudes and solitudes. The freegoing and friendly companion is there and the man of the cloister, of the lonely corner of thought, prayer, and speculation. The man of public affairs, before a living audience announcing decisions is there, and the solitary inquirer weaving his abstractions related to human freedom and responsibility.

Perhaps no other American held so definitely in himself both those elements—the genius of the Tragic—the spirit of the Comic. The fate of man, his burdens and crosses, the pity of circumstance, the extent of tragedy in human life, these stood forth in word shadows of the Lincoln utterance, as testamentary as the utter melancholy of his face in repose. And in contrast he came to be known nevertheless as the first authentic humorist to occupy the

Executive Mansion in Washington, his gift of laughter and his flair for the funny being taken as a national belonging.

Thus Lincoln, by plain reasoning, would overcome, or by a story of pointed humor would reduce the opponent's position to absurdity, and this was often his aim and method as a writer and speaker.

How he moved and spoke as a part of the human comedy became vivid mouth-to-mouth folklore while he was alive, and his quips and drolleries went beyond his own country to lighten the brooding and speaking figure of Lincoln in the human tragedy. And so began the process by which he was internationally adopted by the family of Man.

Not yet has there been compiled and annotated a complete collection of the speeches and writings of Abraham Lincoln. No definitive work in this field has as yet come into existence. If there were such a work it would be heavy to use, it would be loaded with repetitious material, it would be cumbersome, definitely lack convenience, certainly not a handy volume. Of course such a complete and definitive collection of Lincoln utterances is wanted and needed. There are those students of Lincoln who give themselves the assignment of reading every last available word written or spoken by Lincoln. The statesman and politician, the executive, the humorist, the literary artist, the great spokesman of democracy, the simple though complicated human being Abraham Lincoln, is best to be known by an acquaintance with all that he wrote and said. For large masses of people however this won't do. They must live and work and time counts and in small houses room, just plain cubic space wherein to keep things, has to be considered. Therefore, says Mr. Roy P. Basler, why not one book, a single volume, holding the best and the most indispensable of Lincoln utterance? In having read this book, who is to stop you from going farther, if you are interested?

Basler is out of Missouri, the Show-Me State, born in St. Louis November 19, 1906, a graduate of Central College, Missouri, a high school English teacher (1926-28) in Caruthersville, Missouri, in the southeastern heel of that state, often designated as "Swamp-East Missouri." A terrain it is where during the War of the 1860's nobody could always be sure just who to shoot. Should you sometime visit the battle area around Vicksburg they can show you a hill held by Missouri Confederate troops attacked by Missouri Federals. Roy Basler as boy and youth grew where he heard and saw many sides of the argument and elemental passions that brought on the war. The vernacular and slang of Lincoln's southern Illinois and Kentucky soil are native and familiar to Basler.

It didn't hinder him any to go down to North Carolina and work for a Ph.D. at Duke University, there meeting Jay B. Hubbell, Professor of American Literature, a scholar and seeker. Their conversation one hot summer evening in 1930 "drifted around," says Basler, "to Lincoln's literary style and the numerous treatments of Lincoln in fiction, poetry, drama, letters, diaries." From this talk burgeoned and developed Basler's doctoral dissertation, *Abraham Lincoln in Literature: the Growth of an American Legend.* Also at Duke, Basler married a South Carolina girl of whom he says, "Without her help and sympathetic understanding of my aims and endeavors, I couldn't have gone through with the labors required." As a family the Baslers have arithmetical balance—two boys, two girls; and a handsome, vital group they are singing "The Arkansas Traveler" and "Whoa Mule Whoa."

In colleges at Sarasota, Florida, and Florence, Alabama, Basler taught English and American literature, twelve months in the year for the most part, largely to Southern students though his classes always had young folk from Northern and Western states. His years of final painstaking labors on this present book have been at the University of Arkansas at Fayetteville, from which place he wrote to his loyal and indefatigable Chicago friend Ralph Newman of the Abraham Lincoln Book Shop: "I suppose that it would be a pleasure to teach Lincoln, Emerson, Melville, Walt Whitman and Mark Twain, to college students anywhere; but I doubt that it could be any more fun than it is in the South, where although we still have our Bilboes we have also our Lister Hills and our J. W. Fulbrights ("Bill" Fulbright is a hometown boy here in Fayetteville). The America that means most to me is less her rocks and rills, etc., than her Jeffersons and Lincolns. I use the plural advisedly in speaking of those nonpareils, for when a Southerner can go to Chicago and meet an Oliver R. Barrett, or a Middlewesterner can go to Durham, N. C., and meet a Jay B. Hubbell he learns that what was Jefferson, and what was Lincoln, still is and will be."

Throughout Basler kept asking, "Where is the original?" as to this speech or letter of Lincoln's. From the Library of Congress and the National Archives in Washington, D. C., from the Maine Historical Society, from the Huntington Library in Pasadena, California, from coast to coast in their various repositories, Basler got photostatic copies of Lincoln's manuscripts. To Springfield, Illinois, he journeyed for consultation with Paul M. Angle, then Librarian of the Illinois State Historical Library and Secretary of the Abraham Lincoln Association. Then to Chicago for sessions with Oliver R. Barrett, an attorney-at-law and antiquarian, who since a boy in the 1880's has been gathering Lincoln manuscripts and now owns an immense collection that includes every type and period of Lincoln document and handwriting. Having seen Angle and Barrett, it might be further said that Angle and Barrett probably know more about the characteristics, quirks, oddities and quiddities of Lincoln's handwriting than did Lincoln himself when alive. Lincoln was an exact man, careful, scrupulous, but he was independent and quizzical at times with dashes and commas, with spellings, with the shapings of certain letters. The troubles and manifold chores of Basler in this field will interest the reader of the "Introduction." His list of titles and source of texts in the "Bibliography and Sources" indicate Basler's persistent labors in following up his question, "Where is the original?" Each letter, speech or state paper of Lincoln herein printed exists now in some place where you can see it, if you like. From these originals Basler makes his book. What slight or minor changes he has made in the text he consulted and copied, he tells you. Those slight changes are for your convenience. What we have herein is more than another compilation for it is also a new and interesting study of Lincoln as writer and speaker.

Basler's book, *The Lincoln Legend*, published in 1935, is one of the most able studies we have of the man and myth, the beliefs and the make-believes, that give Lincoln a place among the foremost voices of our modern world. We have become a global humanity. Lincoln used the phrase, "The Family of Man." He saw the Family as a unity. He hoped to see it move toward closer unity and wider freedom—everywhere.

Basler has gone through the body of Lincoln utterance and his selections from it in a very peculiar time, a global war time and that war interwoven with many civil wars, a war in which the American Union of States issued as a colossal and decisive force among world powers. What have we to learn from Lincoln in this time when unprecedented and incalculable forces are to operate on our future, when the mind of man and his will and vision must meet the challenge of what is termed AA1, the Year One of the Atomic Age, when we hear the oft-recurring question, "What would Lincoln do now?."

And now comes Mr. Basler to lay before you the best writings and speeches of Lincoln for you to find what of Lincoln is usable for these terrific history-shaping years.

As a writer and speaker Lincoln had several styles and used them according to what events and occasions demanded. Plain talk, blunt and utterly lucid statements, these are to be found in plenty throughout his writings and speeches. Then again you may find him employing a prose that is cadenced, sonorous, masterly and having its relation to certain masterpieces of literature that had become part of him.

You will find Basler's "Lincoln's Development as a Writer" a scholarly treatise worth careful reading. You will find you can come back to it with renewed interest after you have read his selections from Lincoln. He tells us how Lincoln developed, how he changed and grew as a speaker and writer.

His book is honest and able. It is meant for human service in these our years of tumult and change. It can challenge your hope and imagination about America and the wide flung Family of Man around this new small global world of ours. Yes, truly it can challenge you unless it should be that you are dead from the neck up and heart wooden.

CARL SANDBURG

Flat Rock, North Carolina

INTRODUCTION

The editor has attempted in this volume to give readers a full and accurate text of Abraham Lincoln's most important works. Three considerations have guided his choice of selections: literary significance, historical importance, and human interest. In few instances, it is believed, will the reader fail to find any authentic piece which merits inclusion for all of these considerations, although numerous items of an interest chiefly historical, and perhaps a few of some slight literary significance, may be missed by the Lincoln specialist. Since the editor believes that the reader can best do his own abridging and extracting, all selections are complete.

The text of more than three-fourths of the selections has been edited from the original manuscripts or from photostatic copies of the originals. The text of other selections, for which no manuscript is available, has been edited from the original printed version or from a later printing which Lincoln corrected or authorized. In a few instances two or more printed texts, each having its own particular significance, have been collated. The editor regrets that he has been unable to obtain access to the original or to a photostatic copy of thirteen of the selections. Since each of the thirteen is an item of considerable interest and importance to a volume which attempts to present the best of Lincoln's writings, he has reproduced them as edited by Nicolay and Hay in the *Complete Works of Abraham Lincoln*. The source of text for each selection will be found listed under "Sources."

The volume had its inception several years ago when the editor had occasion to consult a number of manuscripts and found to his amazement that Nicolay and Hay had in some instances so emended or miscopied Lincoln as to leave either something less or something more than Lincoln had written. The extent to which their editorial labors took them included changes in diction, punctuation, sentence structure, and paragraphing. No doubt the sense of propriety which motivated Secretary John Hay in changing Lincoln's phrase "better posted" to "better informed" in the "Letter to Henry W. Hoffman," October 10, 1864, remained with him in later years. That Hay felt his superiority to the "Tycoon" in matters pertaining to literary style is obvious from the tone of comments scattered throughout his Diary—comments which sometimes reveal a strangely inept sense of values in disparaging Lincoln's rhetoric. Furthermore, the conception of guarding a national tradition may have motivated both men in their desire to leave nothing rough or uncouth in grammar and rhetoric that would be incompatible with the memory of the great man.

The resolution which grew therefore, in the present editor's mind, was to edit a volume of Lincoln's best writings *just as Lincoln had written them.* The difficulties in the task were minimized by ignorance, and the work was begun with the assembling of a large number of photostatic copies of manuscripts from widely scattered sources, to be transcribed into a typed script. Then appeared the problems which eventually became so numerous as to necessitate the drawing up of a list of rules for emending Lincoln's punctuation so that it would conform to printing practice with a minimum of misrepresentation. Of these rules, some were adopted with reluctance. To abandon Lincoln's characteristic dash at the end of a sentence seemed both more than called for and less than representation, but on the advice of other students of Lincoln and in the interest of general uniformity between pieces taken from manuscript and pieces taken from printed sources the manuscript dash had to go. Likewise, the double period which Lincoln occasionally used after the initial in signing his name, and the two short dashes, one above the other, which punctuated certain abbreviations, and the apostrophes which Lincoln sometimes dropped to the position of commas, were normalized.

Less difficulty was encountered in deciding what to do about careless grammar, diction, capitalization, and bad or obsolete spelling. The obvious choice was to leave it as Lincoln had written it. To record only what the eye could see seemed simple enough. With Lincoln's handwriting being what it was, however, the trouble was to know what one saw. In his hurried scrawl, within the same paragraph, would appear *territory*, *teritory*, and *terrtory*, or *slavery, slavey, slavy*. Obviously Lincoln knew how to spell both *slavery* and *territory*. Then, should all be made standard in print? Also there were the words containing *a* and *e*, and often Lincoln's *a*'s were left not merely open after the loop but identical with *e*'s, and his *e*'s cropped up looking precisely like *a*'s in instances where there could be no doubt of his intention to write *e*. As in the handwriting of many persons, Lincoln's *i* and *e* were also frequently identical except for the dot, and the dot was often inadvertently omitted. And an occasional *n* would be, so far as the pen stroke was concerned, an indubitable *m*, or an *r* would be indistinguishable from an *n* or an *s*. One debates a long time about these things and occasionally asks and disagrees with the opinion of others. Recognizing Lincoln's early habit of dropping apostrophes to the position of commas and occasionally writing an *s* and an *r* identically, the editor had a hard time deciding that the line in "The Bear Hunt" which has heretofore been printed as "And Mose' Hill drops his gun," should read "And more, Hill drops his gun." Then there was the embarrassing word, "seaman," in the last sentence of the "Response to a Serenade," November 10, 1864: "And now, let me close by asking three hearty cheers for our brave soldiers and seaman . . ." The editor is confident that most readers who undertake to examine a photostatic copy of the "Response" will offhand be sure that Lincoln wrote *seaman* rather than *seamen*, and yet if they will also examine a number of other *a*'s and *e*'s in the same photostatic copy and in a number of others, he is satisfied that their opinion will soon waver, and that eventually they will find a dozen or more instances in which they cannot distinguish an *a* from an *e* except that they know how the word is spelled and presume that Lincoln also knew how to spell it.

But there is the next question. How far is an editor justified in assuming that Lincoln knew how to spell? The notion that Lincoln was usually a poor speller will vanish after a few hours spent with his manuscripts. And likewise, lest one give the impression that Lincoln's script is often illegible, it should be said that Lincoln's handwriting is normally far easier to read than that of most literary figures whose script has been perused at length by the editor. The question has been answered, but not always to the editor's complete satisfaction, in each of a hundred or more instances in this volume.

Lincoln's capitalization is sometimes inconsistent, but in addition Lincoln employs certain capital letters which are indistinguishable from lower-case forms except in size, and size tends to become indefinite in the hurry of composition. The editor's best judgment has been used in each instance of uncertainty, but he recognizes that there is room for disagreement.

With printed sources, the difficulties were less numerous, but in many instances more complex. Most of Lincoln's early speeches were not too carefully printed in the newspapers of the day. It is charitable to remember that the typesetters and editors of that day had to deal with the same sort of manuscripts that we have been discussing, or had only a reporter's script. In any event, there are errors and dubious sentences. Usually, it is best and safest to stick to the source, except for the correction of obvious typographical errors and omissions, and this has been done. For certain speeches, however, there are several printed sources. Collation then is in order, but which punctuation to choose out of two or three possibilities is never easy to decide. When a later printing authorized by Lincoln appeared, presumably corrected over the earlier, it would seem obvious that the later should be adopted in all things, but this is not always the case. One sentence in the "House Divided Speech" will illustrate the difficulty. The first printing was done from Lincoln's manuscript, and reads, "I believe this government cannot endure, permanently half *slave* and half *free*." The Sycamore edition, one of the earliest pamphlet printings, adds a comma after *permanently*. In his "Letter to Hall, Fullinwider, and Correll," February 14, 1860, Lincoln quoted the sentence thus, "I believe this government can not endure permanently, half slave, and half free." The shift in emphasis achieved by the change in punctuation is obvious, and the editor thinks deliberate, in Lincoln's effort to play down the implications drawn by so many readers from the original statement balanced on the comma which follows *endure*. Finally, in the official edition of the *Debates*, the sentence appears without internal punctuation. Did Lincoln give up trying to punctuate it internally, for political reasons, leaving the reader to place the emphasis where he would, or did Lincoln's editors simply abandon the comma at their own discretion? And which, finally, is the best reading? The editor has chosen the first because he believes it represents what Lincoln wanted to say with the emphasis Lincoln originally desired it to have.

A final word about Lincoln's punctuation will give the reader at least a clue to the motivation of choice in instances such as the one mentioned. Lincoln's manuscripts show him punctuating for pause and emphasis as one accustomed to speak rather than to write for print. He breaks sentences into clauses and phrases sometimes to the point of fragmentation. Likewise, his liberal use of italics to point his emphasis is the use of a speaker trying to carry inflections of voice to the written word. The speeches which he wrote out, and which were set in type from manuscript, thus show a remarkable similarity in punctuation to those taken down by newspaper reporters who caught the inflection and phrase groupings from the platform and to a certain extent carried them over into their text. For this reason most speeches which were merely reported are not noticeably at variance in style with those written out for publication by Lincoln himself, and, in the editor's opinion, are often better representations of Lincoln's pauses than the later revised editions published in the *Debates*, or the revisions of revisions to be found in the *Complete Works of Abraham Lincoln*. That there is room for difference of opinion in such matters must, of course, be recognized.

In retrospect, the editor's opinion of Nicolay and Hay is considerably mellowed by his own experience. Their task and accomplishment were immense. Their editorial performance leaves much to be desired, but an understanding of the difficulties which beset them banishes all desire to carp at their achievement. Until a truly definitive edition of Lincoln's complete works appears, it is hoped that the present volume may supply the reader with a superior text for Lincoln's best writings, and afterwards may remain a serviceable single volume of selections.

The following rules have been observed to the best of the editor's ability.

Bracket all editorial suggestions.

For a printed source—keep it as it is except for correction of typographical errors, and normalizing of spacing and type face in headings, salutations, closes, and signatures.

For a manuscript source:

Dash at end of sentence—change to period.

Dash in heading or close of letter—let it stand.

Double dash, one above other, after abbreviations—change to period.

Double period after initial—reduce to period.

Period omitted at end of sentence—let it stand.

Period omitted after abbreviation—let it stand.

Comma or period omitted in letter heading—let it stand.

Comma used for apostrophe—raise to apostrophe.

Apostrophe inadvertently omitted or incorrectly used—let it stand.

Misspelled word—let it stand and [*sic*], but do not quibble over *i* or *e*, *a* or *e*.

Obsolete and variant spelling—let it stand.

Word blurred or obliterated in manuscript—bracket as in *Complete Works of Abraham Lincoln.*

Inadvertent omission—insert omitted word followed by a question mark and inclose in brackets.

Any other error—let it stand and [*sic*].

Print single underscoring in italics and double underscoring in small capitals, except in letter heading, salutation, or signature.

Normalize spacing in all headings, salutations, closes, and signatures.

The editor wishes to acknowledge that a very large share of the labor in editing the selections has been done by his wife, Virginia Anderson Basler. Hardly less than her assistance has been that of Mr. Harry E. Pratt, formerly Executive Secretary of The Abraham Lincoln Association, who very early in the project laid open the Association's files and continually gave invaluable suggestions. Mr. W. E. Barringer, successor to Mr. Pratt in the Secretaryship of the Association, has also been helpful. Mr. Oliver R. Barrett of Chicago, whose wealth of manuscripts is matched by his wealth of generosity and sound advice, has been indispensable to the making of this volume. Mr. Paul M. Angle, formerly Librarian of the Illinois State Historical Library and now Director of the Chicago Historical Society, has made available the library's large collection of manuscripts and offered pointed critical comments which have contributed largely to whatever quality the volume may have. Dr. Louis A. Warren, Director of the Lincoln National Life Foundation, has likewise opened the resources of his institution.

In addition to these without whom the work could not have been undertaken, the editor wishes to express his indebtedness to Mr. Carl Sandburg, and to Professor Jay B. Hubbell of Duke University for reading the introductory sketch of Lincoln's development as a writer. Among the many people who have lent their assistance, the following persons deserve the editor's special thanks: Miss Margaret Flint and Mr. Jay Monaghan of the Illinois State Historical Library; Mr. D. W. McClellan, Mr. St. George L. Sioussat, Miss Lucy Salamanca, Mr. C. Percy Powell, Mr. James B. Childs, Mrs. Amelia Baldwin, and Mr. H. S. Parsons—all of The Library of Congress; Mr. P. M. Hamer of The National Archives; Mr. Otto K. Bach of The Grand Rapids Art Gallery; Mr. George B. Utley of The Newberry Library; Mr. McKendree L. Raney and Miss Gladys Sanders of The University of Chicago Libraries; Mrs. Herbert A. Kellar of the McCormick Historical Association; Miss Mae Gilman of the Maine Historical Society; Miss Marie Hamilton Law of the Drexel Institute Library; Mr. Paul North Rice of The New York Public Library; Mr. William Reitzel of The Historical Society of Pennsylvania; Mr. Allyn B. Forbes of the Massachusetts Historical Society; Mr. G. V. Fuller of the Michigan Historical Commission; Mr. Henry V. Van Hoesen and Miss Edna M. Worthington of the Brown University Library; Miss Norma Cuthbert of the Henry E. Huntington Library; Mr. R. Gerald McMurtry of Lincoln Memorial University; Miss Brenda Richard of the Missouri Historical Society; Mr. Raphael

Semmes of the Maryland Historical Society; Miss Frances B. Wells of the Maryland State Library; Mr. A. J. Wall of The New York Historical Society; Mr. C. C. Williamson of the Columbia University Libraries; Miss Miriam L. Colston of the New York University Library; Miss Sudie J. Kinkead of The Filson Club, Louisville; Miss Edith H. Rowley of the Allegheny College Library; Mr. F. Lauriston Bullard of Boston; Mr. Thomas I. Starr of Detroit; Mr. William H. Townsend of Lexington, Kentucky; Mr. Sherman Day Wakefield of New York; Mr. J. Friend Lodge of Philadelphia; Mr. Ralph G. Lindstrom of Los Angeles; Mr. A. L. Maresh, Jr., of Cleveland; Mr. Philip Van Doren Stern of New York; the firm of Gabriel Wells, New York; Mr. Louis W. Bridgman of Madison, Wisconsin; Mr. Percy E. Lawler of the Rosenbach Company, Philadelphia; and Miss Myrtle Emerson of State Teachers College Library, Florence, Alabama.

ROY P. BASLER

LINCOLN'S DEVELOPMENT AS A WRITER

LINCOLN'S DEVELOPMENT AS A WRITER

I

Concerning Lincoln's early life, the facts which he considered significant enough to relate in his autobiographical sketches written in 1859 and 1860 are still those which most concern a student of his writings, and there seems to be little need to do more than refer the reader to them among the selections in this volume.

A word of caution should be sufficient to prevent one's falling into the common error of supposing—as Lincoln did—that this period is notable only for its barrenness. A certain type of biographer has made much of the hardships, poverty of educational opportunity, and undistinguished culture of the frontier settlements in which Lincoln grew up; and in reaction, another type has attempted to glorify the same environment as the paradise of opportunity for virile American genius. In any event, Lincoln's early life sufficed to provide him with a great store of practical knowledge and a deep understanding of and sympathy with the people among whom he would live most of his life. This knowledge and understanding provided a firm footing which served him more dependably than an elaborate schooling served many of his contemporaries.

Anyone inclined toward the various types of "progressive" education which are sponsored today by the pedagogically elite—with their emphasis on "social living," "cooperative endeavor," "discussion-action," and "learning by doing," might, in fact, conclude that Lincoln's early educational advantages were nonpareil. He learned the fundamentals of farming, surveying, business, and politics by doing them, and his need directed the acquisition of manual and mental skills in what "progressive" educators today might call "meaningful situations." In short, he received an abundance of the practical kind of well-rounded education which it is becoming customary in the twentieth century for financially favored urban parents to send their children hundreds of miles, with hundreds of dollars, to get.

What is perhaps more important is the personal philosophy of education which Lincoln developed during these years, and which he did not materially alter during his mature life. It is summarized in the succinct and homely adage, "a man is never too old to learn." Of his several expressions which state this attitude, one of the best is the following piece of advice on studying law, written in 1858:

> When a man has reached the age that Mr. Widmer has, and has already been doing for himself, my judgment is, that he reads the books for himself without an instructor. That is precisely the way I came to the law. Let Mr. Widmer read Blackstone's Commentaries, Chitty's Pleadings, Greenleaf's Evidence, Story's Equity, and Story's Equity Pleadings, get a license, and go to the practice, and still keep reading. That is my judgment of the cheapest, quickest, and best way for Mr. Widmer to make a lawyer of himself.

And also, Lincoln might have agreed, it is the best way for one to grow in general intellect.

In keeping with this philosophy is the constant development in Lincoln's whole personality throughout his entire life. If there is one incontrovertible theme that runs throughout the biographical sequence of facts, opinions, and legends concerning Lincoln, it is that as a personality he never ceased to grow in a unique pattern, which was both organically logical and objectively adaptable. There is only a half-truth in the famous statement of Charles Francis Adams, Jr., that "during the years intervening between 1861 and 1865 the man developed immensely; he became in fact another being. History, indeed, hardly presents an analogous case of education through trial." Lincoln did grow between 1861 and 1865, but in no essential did he become a *different* being. The failure of numerous biographers to bridge the gap between his early life and his presidency might have been avoided had they given as much attention to his writings as to the minutiae of his daily living.

Something should be said of his schooling and study during his boyhood years. His own testimony that he went to school "by littles" which in "the aggregate did not amount to one year" has been accepted by some as a statement indicating relatively slight acquisition of knowledge or skill. Actually, this means that Lincoln attended school for several years, short terms of two or three months being the general rule, and many school terms averaging less. Need one be reminded that even yet in the United States in certain areas it would require three years of schooling to accumulate an "aggregate" of twelve months? Or, that if concentrated attention on the skills of learning—all the frontier school concerned itself with—be considered, then four or five grades, and perhaps more, of a modern curriculum would be required to furnish the equivalent of Lincoln's twelve months? One year, by littles, of learning to read, write, and cipher enabled Lincoln to acquire the basic tools which he used and kept sharp until he could at twenty-three study Kirkham's *Grammar*, a difficult textbook, and within a few months write with a clarity that few college graduates ever achieve today. This fact need not startle us when we consider that although undeniable advancement has been made in the manner of education, the essentials of logic and rhetoric and the basic skills are still matters which one *learns* rather than *is taught.* The intellectual avidity of the child is more important than methods of instruction, and good books, with the opportunity and desire to master them, need little from a teacher when in the hands of an exceptional student.

The textbooks which Lincoln studied probably provided as good an opportunity for learning the essentials and the graces of expression then, as the best modern textbooks do now. Dilworth's *A New Guide to the English Tongue*—the leading elementary textbook of the day, with lessons in spelling, grammar, and reading; tables of homonyms; exemplary fables and recommended prayers—is in spite of its stilted precepts, pedagogically sound. *The Kentucky Preceptor* and Scott's *Lessons in Elocution*, with well-chosen selections of prose and poetry, might be criticized as too mature and difficult for the slow-to-average child, but are excellent collections for a child intellectually alert. A careful examination of these and other textbooks which Lincoln studied both in and out of school will not impress anyone with Lincoln's poverty of opportunity for the study of grammar and rhetoric. It is safe to say that few children today learn as much through twelve years of formal schooling in these two subjects as one finds in the several textbooks which Lincoln is supposed to have studied.

Thus, one may conclude that Lincoln came to his study of Kirkham's *Grammar* in 1831-32 as an advanced student, ready to form a permanent habit in writing. This was his own testimony, allowing for modesty, in 1860, when he wrote in his "Autobiography": "After he was twenty-three and had separated from his father, he studied English grammar—imperfectly, of course, but so as to speak and write as well as he now does." That this was no idle claim, the student may determine by analysis of the earliest selections in this volume. Noting the possible but unlikely truth of the tradition that his friend Mentor Graham assisted him in composing the announcement, "To the People of Sangamo County" (1832), the student will, nevertheless, recognize predominantly the certainty and deliberateness in style which marked Lincoln's mature writing.

By his twenty-eighth year Lincoln had acquired the facility in fundamentals of rhetoric which marks all his later work. "The Perpetuation of Our Political Institutions" (1838) contains many passages comparing favorably with more famous paragraphs often admired in his later speeches. Other speeches of this early period show similar facility, and if they err, it is in the excessive use of rhythm and trope. Lincoln's taste improves much thereafter, as his literary stature increases; but the very sins of his early public style, subdued, become the virtues of his mature public style. His private style as revealed in his early letters is constant throughout his later letters in its idiomatic, loosely deliberate, and colloquial effectiveness.

But even his worst rhetorical blandishments in his early speeches exemplify his deliberate seeking for effect. There is, for example, the concluding paragraph of "The Sub-Treasury" (1839), a campaign speech in which Lincoln attacked the Sub-

Treasury and defended the National Bank. The fact that his audience loved such rhetoric perhaps made the performance expedient, for certainly the speech as a whole, though a tight bit of reasoning, could hardly have been inspirational and needed some political fireworks as a tail-piece.

Aside from textbooks, the efforts of biographers have uncovered a good many books that Lincoln indubitably read before 1831, but the list is undeniably spare, perhaps largely because the records of his life prior to this date are poor at best, and because books were without doubt scarce in his younger life. Among other works, Lincoln read *Arabian Nights*, Ramsey's *Life of Washington* (the book damaged by rain and paid for with two days' labor topping corn, as first narrated by John L. Scripps in his campaign biography), Grimshaw's *History of the United States*, Aesop's *Fables*, Bunyan's *The Pilgrim's Progress*, Defoe's *Robinson Crusoe*, Weems's *Life of Washington*, and the King James Bible. In so far as his early reading may have influenced his later style as a speaker and as a writer, the two most significant of these are the *Fables* and the Bible. His technique in telling stories to enforce a truth and his fondness for rhythmic parallelism and balanced structure may have derived chiefly, though not entirely, from these two sources.

II

Lincoln went to New Salem, Illinois, in July, 1831, and during the next six years his intellectual horizon extended rapidly. Apparently it was during the first year that he began his study of grammar, possibly as tradition has it, under the tutelage of his appropriately named friend, Mentor Graham; for he composed and published on March 9, 1832, his political announcement, "To the People of Sangamo County," his first writing of importance, so far as is known. Just how much Mentor Graham had to do with this composition is not certain, but what is certain is that the announcement was ably written, and that the few letters written by Mentor Graham which are preserved in the Herndon-Weik papers do not even suggest a competence in grammar or rhetoric sufficient to account for any material assistance that

Lincoln may have had in writing this piece. With whatever assistance, Lincoln continued his study and reading and in the fall of 1833 mastered the rudiments of surveying in order to work for the county surveyor, John Calhoun.

In addition to the schoolmaster, Graham, Lincoln had for friends a number of well-educated people whose libraries and conversation were educational gold mines. Among these was Jack Kelso, whose love for and knowledge of Shakespeare and Burns became a legend to a later generation. If Lincoln's fondness for these poets had not developed before this time as a result of his early reading, possibly his reading and discussion of them with Kelso may have served to fix a literary preference that remained strong until his death.

Without attempting to give an inclusive list of books that Lincoln read during his residence at New Salem, one may note that accounts of this period agree in portraying him as ransacking the private libraries of his friends, though they do not always agree as to the specific books read. William H. Herndon's biography has Lincoln running a gamut from newspapers and the sentimental novels of Caroline Lee Hentz through Thomas Paine, Voltaire, Volney, and Rollin, to Burns and Shakespeare. It is unlikely that Lincoln acquired a fondness for the novels of Mrs. Hentz during this period, since the earliest was not in print until 1846, and most of them were published in the fifties; but that Thomas Paine in particular may have been one of Lincoln's favorite authors seems not improbable. In philosophy, no other writer of the eighteenth century, with the exception of Jefferson, parallels more closely the temper or gist of Lincoln's later thought. In style, Paine above all others affords the variety of eloquence which, chastened and adapted to Lincoln's own mood, is revealed in Lincoln's formal writings. From reading such as this, rather than from the instruction of a frontier schoolmaster, Lincoln derived his most important literary education. Aside from general reading during this period Lincoln studied law, borrowing books from his friend, John T. Stuart, and purchasing a copy of Blackstone's *Commentaries* at an auction in Springfield.

Lincoln's writing was apparently not confined at this time to letters, legislative bills, and political speeches. Herndon refers to a predilection for scribbling verses which began when Lincoln was a youth in Indiana, and expresses the opinion that it is just as well none are extant. Perhaps during this period also Lincoln began a practice of writing pseudonymous political letters to the *Sangamo Journal*,* which he continued until 1842, when one of them resulted in a challenge to a duel. The problem of assigning pseudonymous or anonymous letters and editorials to Lincoln is, however, a dangerous one, and requires more careful study than has sometimes been given to it. Of these writings one may say that Lincoln's authorship has not been finally established for any except those included in this volume. Several political letters which appeared in the *Journal* in 1837-1838, signed variously "Sampson's Ghost," "Old Settler," and "A Conservative," seem certainly to have been written by Lincoln, but in no instance do they add to his literary accomplishment. In racy idiom, satire, and humor they are distinctly inferior to the second "Rebecca" letter, which will be discussed later.†

Lincoln's move from New Salem to Springfield in April, 1837, brought a further extension of his social and intellectual horizon. Springfield became the State Capital in 1839, Lincoln having largely directed the legislative maneuvering that deprived Vandalia of this distinction. But before this event Springfield was a thriving town in its own right, containing among other advantages "a State Bank, land office, two newspapers . . . the Thespian Society, the Young Men's Lyceum, a Colonization Society and a Temperance Society."‡ To the Young Men's Lyceum on January 27, 1838, he delivered the address previously mentioned, which was his first considerable literary effort, though he had a year earlier delivered before the Legislature a speech

* The name of this newspaper was originally *Sangamon Journal* (1831-1832), but was shortened to the colloquial *Sangamo Journal* (1832-1847), and became *Illinois Journal* (1847-1855), and finally *Illinois State Journal* (1855 to date).

† For a discussion of these pseudonymous letters see Glen H. Seymour, "'Conservative'—Another Lincoln Pseudonym?" *Journal Illinois State Historical Society*, July, 1936; *Bulletin*, The Abraham Lincoln Association, No. 50, December, 1937; Roy P. Basler, "The Authorship of the 'Rebecca' Letters," *The Abraham Lincoln Quarterly*, June, 1942.

‡ Harry E. Pratt, *Lincoln, 1809-1839*, p. lviii.

defending the State Bank, which is significant for its logical analysis and close argument.

"The Perpetuation of Our Political Institutions" is resoundingly conservative in its treatment of the theme of law and order, swelling deeply with moral and patriotic fervor but completely ignoring the greatest moral issue of the day—the abolition of slavery. In the set of "objections," which Lincoln together with Dan Stone drew up in March, 1837, opposing resolutions passed by the Legislature in support of slavery, Lincoln stated carefully "that the institution of slavery is founded on both injustice and bad policy, but that the promulgation of abolition doctrines tends rather to increase than abate its evils." The position taken in these conservative "objections," Lincoln maintained until he was elected President. On the whole the "Lyceum" address probably represents Lincoln's personal ideas during this period fairly accurately, and as such it must be judged, though inferior when compared with his later expressions, of great interest for its ideas as well as for its rhetoric. Herndon certainly underestimates it as "highly sophomoric," but comments that it created for "the young orator a reputation which soon extended beyond the limits of the locality in which he lived."

In his early speeches Lincoln reveals himself clearly as the intellectual and spiritual child of the romantic era no less than Emerson, Thoreau, Whitman, Whittier, and Lowell, as well as William Ellery Channing, Theodore Parker, William Lloyd Garrison and many lesser lights. The philosophical ideas that animated American thought from the time of the American Revolution to the Civil War were perhaps no less potent in Springfield than in Boston. Among the ideas which run through both "The Perpetuation of Our Political Institutions" (1838) and the "Temperance Address Delivered before the Washington Temperance Society" (1842) are the concepts of human perfectibility and the progressive improvement of human society through education; the exaltation of reason, of "all conquering mind," as the human attribute through which progress may be achieved; and the ideal of liberty, equality, and brotherhood. These concepts composed the essential humanitarianism of Thomas Jefferson, which consistently held men above things. Likewise they were the essentials of Lincoln's philosophy, though subdued by the innate conservatism that held him aloof from the radical reformers of his day.

It is clear in "The Perpetuation of Our Political Institutions" that the fundamental theme of the "Gettysburg Address," which was later to be woven out of these very concepts, was essentially in 1838 what it was in 1863, the central concept of Lincoln's political philosophy. Lincoln thought of American democracy as an experiment in achieving human liberty, relatively successful though far from completed, and threatened most by the mobocratic spirit and the failure of the citizens to observe and preserve the duly constituted authority of government. One sentence from this early speech contains the essential germ of the "Gettysburg Address." Speaking of the founders of American political institutions, Lincoln said, "Theirs was the task (and nobly they performed it) to possess themselves, and through themselves us, of this goodly land, and to uprear upon its hills and its valleys a political edifice of liberty and equal rights; 'tis ours only to transmit these—the former unprofaned by the foot of the invader, the latter undecayed by the lapse of time and untorn by usurpation—to the latest generation that fate shall permit the world to know." In 1863 he was to say, "It is rather for us to be here dedicated to the great task remaining before us . . . that government of the people, by the people, for the people, shall not perish from the earth."

Curiously woven into the texture of these essential concepts is Lincoln's belief in the "doctrine of necessity," which he defined as the "belief that the human mind is impelled to action, or held in rest by some power, over which the mind itself has no control." Like several of the early nineteenth century romantics, Lincoln made a correlation of his belief in "necessity" and his belief in human progress and perfectibility. William Godwin's "doctrine of necessity," which so deeply influenced Coleridge, Wordsworth, Shelley, and others among the English romantics, was such a correlation of necessitarianism and perfectionism. Godwin himself began as a Calvinist, came under the influence of Condorcet, Rousseau, and others of the French school, and eclectically concocted his own philosophy from the concepts of his masters by correlating the "doctrine of necessity" with the romantic doctrine of human perfectibility rather than with Calvin's doctrine of human depravity.

Although Lincoln probably had not read Godwin's *Political Justice*, Godwin's theories along with those of Rousseau may have come to him as to many, in the never ending succession of ripples in popular thought created by the original intellectual splash produced by the writings of those worthies. It is just as possible that Lincoln made somewhat the same correlation in his own thinking without benefit, either at first or second hand, of Godwin's philosophy. In any event, necessitarianism and perfectionism were inextricably woven into Lincoln's personal philosophy during these early years and remained strong with him until his death.

Though Lincoln's writings are few between 1838 and 1842, these were otherwise busy years during which his legal practice was growing, his political leadership of the Illinois Whigs was becoming firmly established, and his social position was gradually elevated. He courted the Kentucky belle Mary Todd, jilted her, suffered terrific hypochondria, recovered, and re-established his position as favored suitor to marry her November 4, 1842.

III

The year 1842 is one of considerable literary significance. Lincoln's remarkable friendship with Joshua Speed, apparently the only intimate personal friendship of Lincoln's life, is recorded in an interesting series of letters. The "Address before the Washington Temperance Society," already noted, was delivered on Washington's birthday. A "Eulogy on the Death of Benjamin Ferguson," delivered before the same society on February 8, displays a solemn rhythm and elegiac diction not matched in literary effect by anything he had written prior to this time. But most interesting is Lincoln's participation in a series of pseudonymous political satires published in the *Sangamo Journal* during August and September. The second "Rebecca" letter, the only one of the series which Lincoln wrote, reveals a bent indicative of a wider scope in his literary possibilities than he had shown before. The fact that he afterwards eschewed such literary activity, perhaps largely because of the unpleasantness which followed, does not diminish the letter's significance to the student of Lincoln's growth as a writer. It displays an ability to portray character, a skill in handling dialogue, a realistic humor, and a biting satire, which mark him at this time the potential equal of his Southern contemporaries, Augustus Baldwin Longstreet and Johnson Jones Hooper, if not of the later Mark Twain.

Lincoln's literary activity during the next four years is relatively slight in significance, except for his writing a series of poems. During the political activity of the campaign of 1844, he revisited his boyhood home in Indiana, and in typically romantic fashion was prompted, as he said, to "feelings . . . which were certainly poetry; though whether my expression of those feelings is poetry is quite another question." These powerful feelings, apparently "recollected in tranquillity," resulted in a group of poems beginning with the nostalgic "My Childhood Home I See Again," and including "The Bear Hunt" and perhaps others that have been lost. A literary friendship which he formed with Andrew Johnston, a lawyer of Quincy, Illinois, occasioned Lincoln's inclosing parts of the first, and perhaps all of the second of these poems in letters written to this friend. The manuscript of a third section of the first poem seems to have been lost.

Another piece of writing doubtless the result of his friendship with Johnston is the narrative of a "Remarkable Case," a murder trial with an unusual denouement, which appeared in the *Quincy Whig*, April 15, 1846. Lincoln had told the story earlier, shortly after defending the accused, in his "Letter to Joshua Speed," June 19, 1841. As he wrote it for publication in the *Quincy Whig*, it is a well-told mystery story, worthy of careful study as one of his few ventures in narrative.

Without danger of exaggerating their importance, it is safe to say that Lincoln's poems are superior to the average run of verse published in America before 1850, and that the first and best of them reveals a quality which wears better than Lincoln's biographers have supposed. One cannot read "My Childhood Home I See Again" without sensing faintly the manner and mood of minor English poetry in the late eighteenth century, a typical example of which, William Knox's "Mortality," was Lincoln's favorite poem at this time. Although these verses suffer much when placed beside the "Farewell Address" or the "Second Inaugural Address," they are by no means the pure doggerel that many of Lincoln's biographers have termed them. As literary critics, Lincoln's biographers have displayed, with few exceptions, a lack of literary perspective exceeded only by their preoccupation with political facts. Again, however, the student must find these poems interesting as an art form which Lincoln abandoned along with the realistic satire of the "Rebecca" letter. They are most significant as literary experimentation, which showed promise of growth but was frustrated by the environment and the events of the milieu in which it occurred. In Lincoln we have a literary artist, constrained by social and economic circumstances and a dominant political tradition to deal with facts as facts, yet always motivated by his love of words and symbols and his eternal craving to entertain people and to create beauty. It is this love of words, never completely subservient, which finally flowers in the unique art of his "Gettysburg Address," "Farewell Address," "Second Inaugural Address," and even earlier in his "Concluding Speech" in the campaign of 1858. Lincoln spoke as an artist because he was first of all an artist at heart. Had he otherwise developed these talents, it is not difficult to imagine for him an important place among American poets or writers of fiction.

Of special interest to the student of Lincoln's literary growth is the partnership in law practice which he formed in December, 1844, with William H. Herndon, who earlier had clerked in the store of Lincoln's friend, Speed, and had been a student in the law office of Logan & Lincoln. The partnership continued until 1861, and up to the time of Lincoln's departure for Washington perhaps no other person contributed more to his intellectual development, directly or indirectly, than Herndon did through his perpetual reading and discussion of books. The general impression abetted by Herndon's testimony that Lincoln came to books chiefly through his partner's library is, however, not compatible with the fact that Lincoln's own library was of considerable extent and that he had convenient access to the State Library. The student must gauge carefully Herndon's statement that Lincoln "comparatively speaking had no knowledge of literature. . . . He never in his life sat down and read a book through," as the statement of an omnivorous reader who was more impressed by Lincoln's intellect than by the breadth of his literary culture.

Lincoln's growing prestige in local Whig politics culminated in his election to Congress from the Seventh Congressional District of Illinois in 1846. During the campaign he met strong opposition in the candidacy of Peter Cartwright, the famous Methodist circuit-rider, not on the national issues of the day so much as on personal, moral, and religious issues. Cartwright and his supporters resorted to the "grape-vine telegraph" in spreading reports of Lincoln's infidelity, and the charges thus made clung to Lincoln's name, in spite of his forthright denial, until long after his death. The most significant piece of writing which resulted was the "Letter to the Editor of the *Illinois Gazette*," August 11, 1846, and a political handbill in which Lincoln expressed his religious views. Both of these items were rediscovered in 1941 by Mr. Harry E. Pratt. They contain perhaps the most complete statement of personal religious philosophy which Lincoln wrote during his early career. The nub of his statement, a part of which has already been cited, is as follows:

> That I am not a member of any Christian Church, is true; but I have never denied the truth of the Scriptures; and I have never spoken with intentional disrespect of religion in general, or of any denomination of Christians in particular. It is true that in early life I was inclined to believe in what I understand is called the "Doctrine of Necessity"—that is, that the human mind is impelled to action, or held in rest by some power, over which the mind itself has no control; and I have sometimes (with one, two or three, but never publicly) tried to maintain this opinion in argument—The habit of arguing thus however, I have entirely left off for more than five years—And I add here, I have always understood this same opinion to be held by several of the Christian denominations. The foregoing, is the whole truth, briefly stated, in relation to myself, upon this subject.

Lincoln was elected by an unprecedented majority of 1511 votes, and went to Congress with prospects as bright as any first term congressman could have wished. His experiences in Washington were doubtless important to his growth in many ways. Although politically adept in the Illinois Legislature, he was new to the larger activities of Congress and proceeded to work diligently, attending to routine duties and "learning the ropes." Contacts with congressmen from other parts of the nation gave him an understanding of political currents outside Illinois. Particularly, he was acquainted with the rising importance of slavery as a national issue, not only through the sometimes heated arguments of fellow congressmen who stayed at Mrs. Spriggs's boarding house and through the serious discussions in Congress of various bills and resolutions for abolishing slavery in the District of Columbia and limiting its spread into new territories, but also through his speech-making tour of New England states during the presidential campaign in the summer of 1848. Most of the political animus engendered in Congress by the issues of the Mexican War was concerned directly or indirectly with the question of the extension of slavery, and conservative though he was on the question of abolition, Lincoln took his stand with his party against a war denounced by Henry Clay as being "for the purpose of propagating slavery." In the "Spot Resolutions," which Lincoln introduced on December 22, 1847, shortly after the session opened, and in the speech which he delivered on January 12, 1848, he was sticking close to the tactics of Henry Clay, whom he had heard to declare only a few weeks earlier in Lexington, Kentucky: "This is no war of defence, but one of unnecessary and offensive aggression."

This important Mexican War speech was essentially an apologia for himself and for all those Whig members of Congress who had voted what amounted to a general censure of President Polk for starting an unnecessary war. As exposition it is one of the ablest speeches Lincoln ever delivered and deserves to rank with the best of his later expository writing, though the unpopularity of its theme may make it as difficult of appreciation for some students of his works as it was for his contemporaries. In spite of the vigorous diction and strong figures in which he condemned Polk's action and defended the Whig position, many of his constituents saw in the speech only a betrayal of the national destiny, and as a consequence, his political future became overcast. His letters to Herndon and Linder, written a few weeks later, in spite of their merit as further statements of his case, apparently did little to change the rapidly forming opinion among even his closest friends that his political career was finished.

Of the other speeches delivered before the House, one in particular deserves notice as perhaps the best example of his popular, rough-and-tumble style as a stump speaker. It was delivered on July 27, 1848, shortly after the Whig Convention in Philadelphia had nominated General Taylor, "Old Rough and Ready." The purpose of the speech was entertainment at the political expense of the Democrats, who had nominated General Lewis Cass, and in ridiculing Cass, Lincoln gave satire, sarcasm, and rough humor a free rein. Although it scarcely adds to his stature as a statesman, it has real significance in his development as an artist. His inclination to entertain his audience had been both a strength and a weakness throughout his political career up to this time, getting votes from the people on the one hand and arousing suspicion of demagoguery on the other. The *Illinois Register*, in commenting on one of his political debates in 1839, had noted: "Lincoln's argument was truly ingenious. He has, however, a sort of *assumed clownishness* in his manner which does not become him. . . . Mr. Lincoln will sometimes make his language correspond with this clownish manner, and he can thus frequently raise a loud laugh among his Whig hearers. . . . We seriously advise Mr. Lincoln to correct this clownish fault before it grows upon him." Like the "Rebecca" letter, however, this speech is interesting as a good example of a variety of expression that Lincoln gradually abandoned in his later speeches, except for an occasional recrudescence during the great debates with Douglas in 1858.

At this point perhaps it may be well to comment briefly on Lincoln's use of humor and satire, and in particular on his use of anecdotes, since this speech is one of the few among the selections in this volume in which Lincoln displays his forte as a humorist and a story-teller. In the first place, the stories for which he was famed were generally confined to his impromptu speeches and personal conversations, and became as a result largely a matter of oral tradition. Secondly, by all accounts they depended as much on grimace and mimicry as they did on inherent humor or point in producing their effect, and hence many of them have become but poor reading as told second or third hand. Evidently, however, Lincoln was a master of the art of telling the incident and at the same time withholding the point until it served with an immediate snap at the conclusion to clarify and give meaning to the whole story. This is the fundamental pattern of all good anecdotes, but added to this is Lincoln's practice of withholding not only the point of the story, but also his particular application of it, until the end.

Although in many of the stories credited to Lincoln with a fair degree of authenticity he seems to have been working with didactic purpose, certain apologists have erred in the assumption that he told them only for serious purposes. His love for the writings of Artemus Ward, Petroleum V. Nasby, and other humorists indicates a respect for humor in its own right, and his indulgence in stories as well as his general clowning on the platform was doubtless an expression of a genuine and deep-seated comic urge, not necessarily incompatible with high sincerity when blended in the genius of an artist. Today one can lament only that so few of Lincoln's stories have been preserved in the actual manner of telling which he gave them. Even the most authentic often show less of Lincoln than they do of the person who is authority for the tale.

Flashes of humor repeatedly occur in his letters. In these flashes the humor is less satirical than in his political speeches, and it grows mellower through the years. Nothing in his later writings equals the biting satire of the second "Rebecca" letter, but even in the letters written during his presidency his humor is sharp. He once wrote Secretary Stanton that he wanted Jacob R. Freese appointed colonel of a colored regiment "regardless of whether he can tell the exact shade of Julius Caesar's hair," and another time asked Cuthbert Bullitt, who had written a letter criticizing Army policy at New Orleans, if he would carry on war "with elder-stalk squirts charged with rose-water." But he was as ready to see humor at his own expense and to satirize his own situation. In the "Letter to R. P. Morgan," he returned an expired railroad pass and requested a new one thus: "Says Tom to John 'Here's your old rotten wheelbarrow. I've broke it, usin' on it. I wish you would mend it, case I shall want to borrow it this arternoon.'" In these instances, as in nearly all of Lincoln's humor, the general allusions and the association of ideas for humorous effect are drawn from common experiences of everyday life. In substance it is the common humor of his time, but in the skill with which it is used it is Lincoln's.

In the study of Lincoln's writings it would seem unnecessary to emphasize the necessity of a sense of humor and an appreciation of irony, but, as H. B. Van Hoesen has pointed out in a brochure entitled *The Humor of Lincoln and the Seriousness of His Biographers*, Lincoln's humor has not always been perceived by his readers, though the audiences to which he spoke could scarcely miss the point. This circumstance is the result, in part at least, of the fact that Lincoln's humor is so often ironical, and that the point emphasized by vocal inflection is not always so obvious on the printed page. Even his most serious speeches, such as the "Address at Cooper Institute," contain humor which a reader may miss unless he reads with awareness, but which Lincoln's audience fully appreciated, if one may judge from contemporary newspaper accounts of the occasion. An interesting example of humor missed by Lincoln's editors occurs in the "Speech at Peoria." After a lengthy analysis of Douglas's arguments extolling the virtues of the Nebraska Bill, Lincoln sarcastically continued, "If Nebraska Bill is the real author of these benevolent works, it is rather deplorable, that he has, for so long a time, ceased working altogether." In three separate instances in the same paragraph Lincoln made use of the personification for humorous effect, and in each his editors humorlessly revised the phraseology to read "the Nebraska Bill," and in the sentence quoted emended the pronoun *he* to *it*.

The political eclipse which followed Lincoln's term in Congress was paralleled by an eclipse in his writing and speaking. Until 1854 he devoted himself almost entirely to his law practice, and in consequence achieved a considerable legal reputation and a comfortable income. Aside from the personal letters written during these years, his only work of much literary significance is the "Eulogy on Henry Clay Delivered in the State House at Springfield," July 6, 1852. This was a labor of love and genuine admiration to which Lincoln carried a sympathetic understanding of Clay's personality and a fine assessment of his political worth. It shows what was perhaps unconsciously running through Lincoln's mind, the indebtedness of Lincoln to Clay both politically and intellectually, and the remarkable degree to which their personalities and genius held similar and contrasting qualities. One can hardly read any paragraph in it without feeling that Lincoln was, unconsciously or consciously, inviting comparison and contrast of himself with his "beau ideal of a statesman."

The presidential campaign of 1852 in which Pierce and Scott were opponents produced another speech, worthy of mention only because of its perfunctory mediocrity and because Nicolay and Hay either ignored or conveniently overlooked it when compiling the *Complete Works*. It is entitled "Address before the Springfield Scott Club, in Reply to Judge Douglas's Richmond Speech." Its very mediocrity and futile sarcasm are indicative of the senility of Whig politics at the time. Apparently Lincoln could not, even by choice, find anything worth saying in support of a party which was dying because it strove only to avoid the great issues of the day and could do no better than lift the slavery plank of an opposition platform. Even the satire and humor of the speech are far below Lincoln's average.

IV

Lincoln's political inactivity ended in 1854 with the passage of the Kansas-Nebraska Bill. The next five years saw his steady rise from comparative political oblivion to a position of national importance as the leading opponent of Douglas's doctrine of Popular Sovereignty, and as one of the leading national figures in the new Republican party. The contrast between Lincoln in 1852 and 1854 is remarkable. From a sarcastic politician with a party allegiance but no issue, he emerged a serious statesman with a great issue but as yet no party to lead. From the futile mediocrity of his "Address before the Springfield Scott Club" he rose to the impassioned seriousness of the "Speech at Peoria." The contrast is immense but not mysterious. Lincoln had simply found a theme worthy of his best, and the high level of literary merit in his speeches and other writings is a record of his emotional conviction. Although he did not reach his peak as a literary artist until an even greater theme—preservation of the Union—began to dominate his thinking, during the next six years he composed a body of speeches and letters which in power and distinction of style is second to none other in American political literature.

Careful study of Lincoln's works of this middle period (1854-1861) emphasizes the fact that his later beauty of expression was not an accident of inspiration, as thought by many of his biographers, which simply happened to a man who had no particular care for finely wrought sentences. Indeed, the "Speech at Peoria" (1854), "A House Divided: Speech Delivered at Springfield, Illinois" (1858), and the "Address at Cooper Institute" (1860), to mention only three of the many, have in a large measure the technical distinction of style that is generally credited only to his later masterpieces. It is not so much in technical command of style as it is in power of feeling and imagination that his later works surpass those of his middle period.

A critical examination of Lincoln's more important works of this period reveals the supremacy that has always existed in the works of an indisputable master of language. With vital imagination he infused into the political matter of the pre-Civil War epoch great poetic significance: "If we could first know *where* we are, and *whither* we are tending, we could better judge *what* to do, and *how* to do it. . . . 'A house divided against itself cannot stand.' I believe this government cannot endure, permanently half *slave* and half *free*. I do not expect the Union to be *dissolved*—I do not expect the house to *fall*—but I *do* expect it will cease to be divided. It will become *all* one thing or *all* the other." In language seemingly effortless and yet grandly beautiful he phrased the emotional convictions upon which he believed human political progress to be founded: "Repeal the Missouri Compromise—repeal all compromises—repeal the Declaration of Independence—repeal all past history, you still cannot repeal human nature. It will be the abundance of man's heart, that slavery extension is wrong; and out of the abundance of his heart, his mouth will continue to speak." He took, and made his own, the thought and spirit of those phases of the epoch which he has since come to symbolize, in such a manner that, though others spoke before him and others have spoken since, today one can scarcely think of the common matter of his argument except as matter that is particularly and peculiarly his. From the "Speech at Peoria" to the "Address at Cooper Institute" Lincoln displayed again and again his power to synthesize without recourse to illusive transcendental generalities, and to stamp with unity without narrowing to personal bias, political matter covering nearly a century.

The "Speech at Peoria" was one of many that Lincoln made during the campaign of 1854, most of the others probably expressing the same anti-Nebraska Bill sentiments, and in fact one of them delivered at Springfield on October 4 being the same speech later delivered at Peoria. On one occasion at Bloomington when Stephen A. Douglas was the principal Democratic speaker and Lincoln's friend Jesse W. Fell attempted to arrange a debate, Douglas declined. The "Speech at Peoria" was Lincoln's fourfold answer to Douglas's sponsorship of the Kansas-Nebraska Bill: first, the bill was a reversal of all historical precedents established for limiting the extension of slavery; second, there was no necessity or public demand for repealing the Missouri Compromise; third, the repeal was morally wrong in that it violated a compact agreed upon by two parties and denied that the Negro had any human rights; last, only the restoration of the Missouri Compromise could prevent ultimate political disintegration.

When the election was over, it was clear that anti-Nebraska sentiment had prevailed. In the Illinois Legislature anti-Nebraska men held a majority of five. Since Lincoln had led the fight, it was only natural that he be the choice for United States Senator, although there is no indication in his writings that he entertained any such ambition before the election. What happened afterward is told by Lincoln in his "Letter to E. B. Washburne," February 9, 1855. In short, to insure an anti-Nebraska senator, Lincoln threw his support to Lyman Trumbull, an anti-Nebraska Democrat.

Although the year 1855 was one of political inactivity for Lincoln and apparently no speeches were written, his letters show constant evolution of ideas. The "Letter to George Robertson," August 15, 1855, concludes with a paragraph adumbrating the famous opening of the "House Divided Speech," still three years away: "Our political problem now is, 'Can we as a nation continue together permanently—forever—half slave and half free?' The problem is too mighty for me—may God, in his mercy, superintend the solution." The "Letter to Joshua F. Speed," August 24, 1855, shows his resolution to continue the fight for restoration of the Missouri Compromise, and likewise his insistence that he was still a Whig and certainly not a member of the American party:

> I am not a Know-Nothing. That is certain. How could I be? How can any one who abhors the oppression of negroes, be in favor of degrading classes of white people? Our progress in degeneracy appears to me to be pretty rapid. As a nation, we began by declaring that "*all men are created equal.*" We now practically read it "all men are created equal, except negroes." When the Know-Nothings get control, it will read "all men are created equal, except negroes, *and foreigners, and Catholics.*" When it comes to this I shall prefer emigrating to some country where they make no pretence of loving liberty—to Russia, for instance, where despotism can be taken pure, and without the base alloy of hypocrisy.

In the next year, 1856, Lincoln definitely lined up with the new Republican party and took active lead in organizing the state convention at Bloomington in May. It was here that he delivered the famous so-called "Lost Speech," which according to the local tradition was the supreme effort that fused discordant elements into a unified party. The tradition has it that even hard-boiled newspapermen were so overpowered by his eloquence that they forgot pencil and pad to sit enraptured. A report of the speech, reconstructed by Henry C. Whitney from notes taken at the time, and published in 1896, probably follows the general argument very well, but it hardly reproduces the rhetorical effect claimed for the utterance. In any event, however, the speech did inspire the convention with unity of purpose. Within a month

Lincoln's national importance was recognized by delegates to the Republican National Convention, when 110 of them cast their votes for him on a nomination for Vice-President.

Although Lincoln made many speeches in the campaign that followed, none has been preserved in entirety except the "Speech Delivered at Kalamazoo, Michigan," August 27, 1856. In it Lincoln insisted that the issue of the campaign was, "Shall the Government of the United States prohibit slavery in the United States?" and that it was "very nearly the sole question." He pointed out the political power and position of white men in slave states whose representation in Congress was enhanced by the slave population to the point that a white man's vote in the South was worth two in the North. He stressed the importance of free labor as an essential to the future development of democracy. He claimed that Buchanan, the Democratic candidate, was committed to the extension of slavery into the territories. Finally, he scouted the idea that the election of the Republican candidate, Frémont, would bring disunion. In all it was perhaps his frankest anti-slavery utterance up to this time.

Of two fragments of other speeches made during this campaign, one is preserved in a manuscript entitled "Sectionalism," apparently a portion of a speech which he delivered a number of times. It holds the distinction of being the only considerable speech manuscript known to be in existence from this period. In it Lincoln tried to show that Republicanism was not inherently sectional, and that if it appeared so, such appearance was not its own making but that of the Southerners who refused to take anything but a sectional attitude toward it. This argument he would recur to in later years, but with particular effect in the "Address at Cooper Institute."

In 1857, an off-year in politics, came the Dred Scott decision, handed down by the Supreme Court on March 11. In his one important speech of the year, delivered in Springfield, June 26, after paying his respects to the dilemma of popular sovereignty in Utah and to the election in Kansas, Lincoln attacked the Dred Scott decision and Douglas's speech of two weeks earlier upholding it, and indicated the line of future Republican action: "We know the court that made it has often overruled its own decisions, and we shall do what we can to have it overrule this." Ignoring—as Douglas had done—the merits of the decision, Lincoln nevertheless cut deeply into the ground that Douglas had taken in maintaining that the decision was acceptable and should be respected and upheld. He cited the action of Andrew Jackson in ignoring a court decision—and incidentally Douglas's approval of Jackson—as precedent for Republican endeavor to have the decision reversed. The Republican attitude was particularly justified in that the decision was not unanimous, was not "in accordance with steady practice of [government] departments," and was "based on assumed historical facts which are not really true." Although the speech contains some of the most memorable passages in his writings, it lacks the unity of effect which marks his best. The truth is that Lincoln had no solution to the problem of slavery except the colonization idea which he had inherited from Henry Clay, and when he spoke beyond his points of limiting the extension of slavery, of preserving the essential central idea of human equality, and of respecting the Negro as a human being, his words lacked effectiveness.

V

From June to November, 1858, Lincoln delivered more than sixty speeches which, though they failed in their immediate purpose of defeating Douglas in the campaign for the United States senatorship, made Lincoln's national reputation and eventually led to the Presidency. He began on June 16 with his famous "House Divided Speech" in Springfield, accepting the unanimous nomination of the Republican State Convention as its "first and only choice" for the Senate. A greater speech had never before been delivered to an American political party gathering, and yet, although Lincoln said in it the essential things that he would repeat over and over during the next months, he found so many new ways, some of them memorable, of modifying and clarifying and emphasizing these essentials, that it is exceedingly difficult to eliminate any single speech of the campaign from analysis and comment. He closed his campaign on October 30 in Springfield with a speech which marked yet another peak in political oratory. The striking contrast between the "House Divided Speech" and the "Last Speech in the Campaign of 1858" is in mood rather than in power of expression. The former is an electrifying challenge to conflict; the latter, an avowal of faith and resignation, phrased with lyric calm and cadenced beauty of expression which Lincoln had never before equaled, and would afterward excel only in the three or four passages that are graven in the mind of humanity more permanently than in the granite of all the monuments to his greatness. The summer of 1858 was the literary, as well as the political, climax of his middle period.

His theme in the "House Divided Speech" was that political acts and events had for years been building a trap which would, unless avoided, catch and forever imprison the essential ideal of human liberty. Under the guise of allaying controversy and establishing national unity, the Democratic party had constantly pushed slavery into new territory and had thwarted all efforts aimed at control and ultimate extinction of the evil. The crisis was at hand and the issue clear: either national politics would have to control slavery, or slavery would control national politics. The speech concluded with a plea for party harmony and support of Republican principles.

In a fine though homely figure of speech Lincoln pictured the political "machinery" built for the extension of slavery by the Nebraska Bill and the Dred Scott decision, which would work with the "don't care" policy of Douglas's popular sovereignty not to permit local determination of the issue in the territories, but to guarantee extension of slavery in spite of local opposition. The figure of the "house or mill," constructed by the Democrats for the perpetuation of slavery, constantly reappeared in his other speeches of the campaign and was the spearhead of his attack upon Douglas, implying as it did that Douglas had been consciously or unconsciously working for the extension of slavery. The idea was not new with Lincoln: Republican leaders everywhere had attacked the Supreme Court for complicity in a scheme to spread slavery. It remained for Lincoln to make the charge vivid and persuasive in a figure of speech and to so involve Douglas by implication that the entire effect would weigh heavily not only in the immediate contest, but in any future contest as well.

> We can not absolutely *know* that all these exact adaptations are the result of preconcert. But when we see a lot of framed timbers, different portions of which we know have been gotten out at different times and places and by different workmen—Stephen, Franklin, Roger and James, for instance—and when we see these timbers joined together, and see they exactly make the frame of a house or a mill, all the tenons and mortices exactly fitting, and all the lengths and proportions of the different pieces exactly adapted to their respective places, and not a piece too many or too few—not omitting even scaffolding—or, if a single piece be lacking, we can see the place in the frame exactly fitted and prepared to yet bring such piece in—in *such* a case, we find it impossible to not *believe* that Stephen and Franklin and Roger and James all understood one another from the beginning, and all worked upon a common *plan* or *draft* drawn up before the first lick was struck.

There has prevailed among students of American letters a notion that Lincoln was as a writer and speaker "plain homespun," and that his usual style was unadorned with figures of speech and other rhetorical devices. It would be difficult to find a plainer misstatement of Lincoln's style than the comment of V. L. Parrington in *Main Currents in American Thought*: "His usual style was plain homespun, clear and convincing, but bare of imagery and lacking distinction of phrase. . . . Few men who have risen to enduring eloquence have been so little indebted to rhetoric." Study of Lincoln's works must find otherwise.

Lincoln's use of figures of speech is one of his most distinctive stylistic traits. He is consistently and naturally figurative. His pithy quips, his almost legendary stories, and his most serious analyses as well as his poetic passages constantly reveal this trait. In many instances his figure provides the texture of his thought so unobtrusively that a casual reader may not even be aware of metaphor. Although Lincoln tends to use figures more rather than less than most orators of the time, in his later works he employs them, if not less often, at least less obviously than in his early works, and during his middle period they become more effective and dramatic, though they remain consistently natural, even homely, in quality. Even his finest figures in his later writings are couched in terms that will appeal to the common man. Metaphor in the grand manner of Webster's famous peroration to the "Reply to Hayne" Lincoln seldom uses, and in early speeches where he does employ something of the sort, he seems merely to be experimenting with a technique not compatible with his own style.

Yet one can scarcely agree with Daniel Kilham Dodge's summary opinion expressed in his monograph, *Abraham Lincoln: The Evolution of His Literary Style*, that "Lincoln's figures almost always serve a useful purpose in making an obscure thought clear and a clear thought clearer." The implication of a purely utilitarian motive hardly does justice to Lincoln's imaginative quality of mind. Herndon insisted, and others have agreed, that Lincoln had "no sense of the beautiful except in a moral world." Such a limitation means nothing in an experimental or scientific sense, but even if we grant it we need not presume that Lincoln was oblivious to all but the utilitarian advantage in analogy and metaphor. All of Lincoln's contemporaries did not agree with Herndon. Stephen A. Douglas, as we shall see, thought Lincoln loved figurative language for its own sake.

Lincoln's figures are of two kinds: those which he uses as a method of explanation or a basis for drawing inference, and those which he uses as rhetorical assertions for purposes of persuasion. Only the first type are primarily utilitarian, and then seldom in the sense that Dodge supposes. If Lincoln had been writing scientific treatises, such an employment of analogy might have been very useful, though its usefulness would have diminished as the inferences drawn tended to escape from the realm of unquestioned fact. But, since Lincoln was making political speeches, this type of figure often became more effective in discomfiting his opponent, as the inferences drawn from it tended farther from the unquestioned facts. In Lincoln's speeches the inferential values of such figures nearly always seem to outweigh their explanatory values, and as this is more or less evident in any particular figure, Dodge's comment seems less or more true.

If we examine Lincoln's figure in the "House Divided Speech" as he carries it through the various stages of inference, we shall very likely understand why Douglas sarcastically charged in the "Ottawa Debate": "He studied that out—prepared that one sentence with the greatest care, committed it to memory . . . to show how pretty it is. His vanity is wounded because I will not go into that beautiful figure of his about the building of a house. . . ." Douglas replied in the only way one could reply—with sarcasm—to an effective figure of speech which carried in careful phrases an unforgettable image with implications of something more than rational analysis could maintain. If this figure works toward "making a clear thought clearer," that clearness is like the glass near the edge of a lens, capable of distorting vision rather than improving it. Lincoln's analogy, we may admit, was effective in explaining to his hearers how the Dred Scott decision and the Nebraska Bill were working together for the extension of slavery, but its further and more important immediate implication that Douglas was deliberately working for the extension of slavery seemed to Douglas a distortion of truth. Yet it was true, as Lincoln saw it, that Douglas's political activity did in fact facilitate the extension of slavery, and as Lincoln had observed of another figure of speech with political consequences, "the point—the power to hurt—of all figures, consists in the *truthfulness* of their application."*

Lincoln's repeated use of the figure in later speeches leaves no doubt as to his reason for making it. The pressure which this figure brought upon Douglas, through constant repetition, set the scene for the "Freeport Heresy." Douglas had no rhetorical technique other than sarcasm with which to combat the implication, and sarcasm was insufficient. Then came Lincoln's question: "Can the people of a United States Territory . . . exclude slavery from its limits . . . ?" Asked and answered earlier without the preparation, it could never have produced the impact that it did at Freeport. Lincoln knew Douglas's answer before

* See "The Presidential Question: Speech in the United States House of Representatives," July 27, 1848.

he asked the question. Douglas had said over and over that slavery could not exist without favorable local legislation. So did nearly everyone else know it. The only purpose Lincoln could have had in asking it was to destroy forever any possibility of Douglas's effecting a *rapprochement* with Southern Democrats. Under the implications of Lincoln's figure, constantly pressed, Douglas was constrained to make a statement of opinion that, although it immediately cleared his way in the senatorial contest, eventually cost him the Presidency.

It would be difficult to find in all history a precise instance in which rhetoric played a more important role in human destiny than it did in Lincoln's speeches of 1858.

In Chicago on July 10, after listening to Douglas's speech on the night before, Lincoln delivered his second important speech of the campaign. And again in Springfield on July 17, he covered much the same ground. In these two speeches he explained his declaration of belief that the country would become either all slave or all free. It was not, as Douglas had charged, a statement of wish for or purpose toward disunion, but rather an unpleasant prediction that arose from his interpretation of the direction of political events. He argued again that Douglas's "popular sovereignty" had been emasculated by the Dred Scott decision. He continued his attack on the moral indifference of Douglas's "don't care" attitude toward the extension of slavery. He admitted that, of course, the Declaration of Independence was not meant as a statement of fact that all men were "equal in all respects." The statement was rather an ideal principle to be worked toward: "I say in relation to the principle that all men are created equal, let it be as nearly reached as we can." In his discussion of this principle in the latter part of the "Chicago Speech" he reached high points of persuasion and beauty of language. He concluded the second "Springfield Speech" by renewing his charges of conspiracy, which Douglas had up to this time ignored. Then came the challenge to debate and Douglas's acceptance.

The debates are on the whole inferior to Lincoln's preceding speeches, but for the purpose of comparing and contrasting the rhetorical effectiveness of the two men they offer the student perhaps a better opportunity than the earlier speeches, and for that reason the first debate at Ottawa has been included in the selections in this volume as representative of the lot. This debate was in a sense the climax of the campaign viewed from Lincoln's side. In it, as we have already noted, he finally forced Douglas to take notice of the charge of conspiracy and particularly of the "beautiful figure." In the next debate at Freeport came the denouement in the form of a list of questions, and among them the one that Douglas answered to his eventual undoing.

After the seventh and last debate at Alton on October 15, Lincoln continued making speeches up to the end, and on October 30 concluded in Springfield before "a giant Republican rally." This speech, in style and emotional context, is a foretaste of the later lyric mood of the "Farewell Address," "Gettysburg Address," and the conclusions of the two "Inaugural" addresses. The sentences flow easily with a subtle cadence, unobtrusive but poetic. The diction is simple, but the words play a rich pattern of assonance and alliteration.

> My friends, to-day closes the discussions of this canvass. The planting and the culture are over; and there remains but the preparation, and the harvest.
>
> I stand here surrounded by friends—some *political, all personal* friends, I trust. May I be indulged, in this closing scene, to say a few words of myself. I have borne a laborious, and, in some respects to myself, a painful part in the contest. Through all, I have neither assailed, nor wrestled with any part of the Constitution. The legal right of the Southern people to reclaim their fugitives I have constantly admitted. The legal right of Congress to interfere with their institution in the states, I have constantly denied. In resisting the spread of slavery to new territory, and with that, what appears to me to be a tendency to subvert the first principle of free government itself my whole effort has consisted. To the best of my judgment I have labored *for*, and not *against* the Union. As I have not felt, so I have not expressed any harsh sentiment towards our Southern brethren. I have constantly declared, as I really believed, the only difference between them and us, is the difference of circumstances.

I have meant to assail the motives of no party, or individual; and if I have, in any instance (of which I am not conscious) departed from my purpose, I regret it.

I have said that in some respects the contest has been painful to me. Myself, and those with whom I act have been constantly accused of a purpose to destroy the Union; and bespattered with every imaginable odious epithet; and some who were friends, as it were but yesterday have made themselves most active in this. I have cultivated patience, and made no attempt at a retort.

Ambition has been ascribed to me. God knows how sincerely I prayed from the first that this field of ambition might not be opened. I claim no insensibility to political honors; but today could the Missouri restriction be restored, and the whole slavery question replaced on the old ground of "toleration" by *necessity* where it exists, with unyielding hostility to the spread of it, on principle, I would, in consideration, gladly agree, that Judge Douglas should never be *out*, and I never *in*, an office, so long as we both or either, live.

VI

Although Lincoln lost the ensuing election, the national publicity given the debates and his other speeches placed him among the few top leaders of the Republican party. As shown by his letters during the next few months, he was not immediately aware that he had become important among the various prospective Republican candidates for the next presidential election, but he worked consistently for party harmony and neglected few opportunities to keep himself before the public, filling political speaking engagements during 1859 in Ohio, Indiana, Wisconsin, Iowa, Missouri, and Kansas. These speeches repeated most of the arguments he had used in the campaign of 1858.

He was also in demand for popular lectures and even prepared a somewhat colorless disquisition on the growth of American civilization under the title, "Discoveries, Inventions and Improvements." Although he delivered it a number of times, he never thought much of it, and in truth it did not measure up to his other nonpolitical address delivered before the Wisconsin State Agricultural Fair on September 30, 1859. Lincoln was not at his best in making speeches for their own sake, but on this occasion he had in the general theme of agricultural improvement and the dignity of labor something about which he knew well from his own experience and felt deeply from his own nature. The passages on labor are perhaps the most significant utterances made on that subject by any important political figure of the era:

> The world is agreed that *labor* is the source from which human wants are mainly supplied. There is no dispute upon this point. From this point, however, men immediately diverge. Much disputation is maintained as to the best way of applying and controlling the labor element. By some it is assumed that labor is available only in connection with capital—that nobody labors, unless somebody else, owning capital, somehow, by use of that capital induces him to do it . . .
>
> But another class of reasoners hold the opinion that there is no *such* relation between capital and labor as assumed; and that there is no such thing as a freeman being fatally fixed for life in the condition of a hired laborer; that both these assumptions are false, and all inferences from them groundless. They hold that labor is prior to, and independent of, capital; that in fact, capital is the fruit of labor, and could never have existed if labor had not *first* existed; that labor can exist without capital, but that capital could never have existence without labor. Hence, they hold that labor is the superior—greatly the superior—of capital.
>
> They do not deny that there is, and probably always will be, *a* relation between labor and capital. The error, as they hold, is in assuming that the *whole* labor of the world exists within that relation . . .
>
> . . . As each man has one mouth to be fed, and one pair of hands to furnish food, it was probably intended that that particular pair of hands should feed that particular mouth—that each head is the natural guardian, director and pro-

> tector of the hands and mouth inseparably connected with it; and that being so, every head should be cultivated and improved, by whatever will add to its capacity for performing its charge. In one word, free labor insists on universal education.

His growing popularity as a speaker brought him an invitation to speak in New York before the Young Men's Central Republican Union. The place was Cooper Institute. Evidently Lincoln prepared the address for this occasion with more care than he had given to any speech prior to this except the "House Divided Speech" of two years earlier. In architecture it is if anything the more carefully balanced of the two, and in dignity and precision of expression it is fully the equal of the other, but it lacks perhaps something of the dramatic fire with which the earlier speech burns. The earlier speech is superior as a whole in imagination and feeling, and the later is more consistently polished and perfect in all its paragraphs and sentences. In no prior address, speech, or letter are Lincoln's stylistic effects more carefully calculated. His handling of the sentence taken as a text from Douglas's "Speech at Columbus, Ohio" is for repetitive effect one of his most skillful and adroit rhetorical successes. His straight exposition of the attitude taken toward slavery-extension by the founding fathers is excellent historical analysis based on painstaking factual research. His tempered statement of Republican principles, although a repetition of what he had said often in 1858, is in succinctness and force perhaps his best statement up to this time. His employment of balanced structure in the paragraph which clinches the political point of this analysis and concludes the first part of the address is rhetorically the high-water mark of the piece:

> If any man at this day sincerely believes that a proper division of local from federal authority, or any part of the Constitution, forbids the Federal Government to control as to slavery in the federal territories, he is right to say so, and to enforce his position by all truthful evidence and fair argument which he can. But he has no right to mislead others, who have less access to history, and less leisure to study it,

> into the false belief that "our fathers who framed the Government under which we live" were of the same opinion—thus substituting falsehood and deception for truthful evidence and fair argument. If any man at this day sincerely believes "our fathers who framed the Government under which we live," used and applied principles, in other cases, which ought to have led them to understand that a proper division of local from federal authority or some part of the Constitution, forbids the Federal Government to control as to slavery in the federal territories, he is right to say so. But he should, at the same time, brave the responsibility of declaring that, in his opinion, he understands their principles better than they did themselves; and especially should he not shirk that responsibility by asserting that they "understood the question just as well, and even better, than we do now."

The dramatic analogy of the highwayman, with which he exposed the irrationality of the more intemperate secessionists, is one of his most successful figures:

> Under all these circumstances, do you really feel yourselves justified to break up this Government unless such a court decision as yours is, shall be at once submitted to as a conclusive and final rule of political action? But you will not abide the election of a Republican president! In that supposed event, you say, you will destroy the Union; and then, you say, the great crime of having destroyed it will be upon us! That is cool. A highwayman holds a pistol to my ear, and mutters through his teeth, "Stand and deliver, or I shall kill you, and then you will be a murderer!"

His peroration is one of his most effective and memorable conclusions:

> Neither let us be slandered from our duty by false accusations against us, nor frightened from it by menaces of destruction to the Government nor of dungeons to ourselves. Let us have faith that right makes might, and in that faith, let us, to the end, dare to do our duty as we understand it.

VII

To survey the body of Lincoln's writings during the years of his Presidency, commenting on each significant letter, message, proclamation, or address in chronological order, is perhaps less desirable at this point than a discussion of Lincoln's style in these respective types, with some observations on significant examples of each; for, in fact, one could otherwise hardly decide which pieces to omit from consideration on principle of merit or interest. Among students with a newly acquired interest in Lincoln's writings as well as among inveterate admirers, there is so much diversity of taste and individual preference for one piece over another that one with a catholic taste may well be amazed at the bias with which students of Lincoln privately claim top honor for their favorite passages. The wide range of choice afforded by the writings of the years 1861-1865 has not tended to discourage this diversity of preference.

Particularly difficult is the problem of selecting the best of Lincoln's letters. The most famous of all his letters of condolence, the "Letter to Mrs. Bixby," although it is undoubtedly a gem, can nearly be matched in artistic effect with the "Letter to Colonel Ellsworth's Parents," May 25, 1861, or the "Letter to Fanny McCullough," December 23, 1862.

The differences between these three masterpieces are not differences in literary success and felicity of phrasing so much as differences in purpose and effect. The "Letter to Mrs. Bixby," is a public letter, written, as were many of Lincoln's letters, with the probability of publication in mind, to a woman whom Lincoln knew only through War Department records as a bereaved mother, and about whose sons he knew only the supposed facts stated in the letter. His phraseology, though felicitous in place, might have seemed pompously insincere in the "Letter to Fanny McCullough." Likewise, the personal, fatherly tone and the pleading simplicity of phrase in the "Letter to Fanny McCullough" would have been intolerable in the "Letter to Mrs. Bixby." The eulogy of Colonel Ellsworth to his parents is as fine in its way as either of the other two, and in purpose and effect holds a middle ground between them. Lincoln had known Colonel Ellsworth well as a student in his own law office, had admired and loved him, and in this letter wrote his noblest tribute to a friend.

But when all is said, the "Letter to Mrs. Bixby" is not likely to give way to either of the others in popular appeal, for like the "Gettysburg Address" it so links the private theme of sorrow with the public theme of preservation of freedom, that the letter is in itself an emblem of a national ideal. As Carl Sandburg has poetically phrased it, "Here was a piece of the American Bible. 'The cherished memory of the loved and lost'—these were the blood-colored syllables of a sacred music."

The distinction between Lincoln's public and private style must be kept in mind likewise in reading his letters and telegrams to government officials, army officers, and various public figures. On the one hand Lincoln could write a public masterpiece like the "Letter to Horace Greeley," August 22, 1862, and on the other hand a private masterpiece like the "Letter to General Joseph Hooker," January 23, 1863. The one he expected to be published, the other he expected only Hooker to read. Lincoln found an inimitable manner of writing for each specific occasion that arose.

The degree to which his letters are informal and personal varies considerably with the occasion. The sequence of letters and telegrams to General McClellan runs from strictly formal to informal and personal, and the variations in tone from one occasion to the next make the sequence the most interesting group of letters written by Lincoln to one man. Lincoln used every manner and device he knew in his attempt to handle McClellan, and all failed. His letters are a fascinating literary triumph in the midst of executive failure. Certain of his letters, such as the "Letter to James C. Conkling," August 26, 1863, are in effect public addresses and as such display qualities of argument and style which are typical of Lincoln's addresses of this period rather than of his letters either formal or informal. In logic and in rhetorical effectiveness they are in no way inferior to the best of the addresses.

It may be said that during his Presidency, although he often wrote hurriedly and without revising, Lincoln never wrote a bad letter. A study of every letter included in this volume, its purpose, and its adaptation of language to that purpose, will reveal even in the less known pieces as high a degree of felicity in phrasing, and as remarkable an adaptation of tone to theme, as can be found in the more famous letters. Two days before he wrote the famous "Letter to Mrs. Bixby," he composed a short "Letter to General Rosecrans," November 19, 1864, which in its limited sphere is as succinct, as delicately worded, and as definitive an achievement of language as Lincoln ever composed. Similarly, two days after the excellent public "Letter to Erastus Corning and Others," June 12, 1863, he penned a short "Telegram to General Hooker" which in its small way is no less an artistic triumph: "If the head of Lee's army is at Martinsburg, and the tail of it on the Plank road between Fredericksburg & Chancellorsville, the animal must be very slim somewhere—Could you not break him?" In short, even Lincoln's most casual pieces bear the inimitable marks of literary excellence.

VIII

In his official proclamations and executive orders Lincoln presents a peculiar problem to the biographer and critic. Many of them are of little or no literary significance, being legal documents in precise legal phrase properly utilitarian and without stylistic individuality. Even the "Emancipation Proclamation" has in it little that is distinctly Lincolnian. There is, however, in the proclamations of thanksgiving and fast days, a style of expression which has become the subject of some discussion because it is peculiar to these pieces and is not generally found in any of Lincoln's other writings. Since these proclamations are jointly signed by Seward as Secretary of State and by Lincoln as President, and since the facts concerning their composition are not fully known, the conjecture has been made that Seward wrote them. Joseph H. Barrett, an early biographer of Lincoln, first made the conjecture, but Nicolay and Hay took no notice of it and included the proclamations without question in the *Complete Works*. Daniel Kilham Dodge in his admirable little book, *Abraham Lincoln: Master of Words*, comments on the conjecture but arrives at no definite conclusion, though he seems to assume Lincoln's authorship, while recognizing the possible influence of *The Book of Common Prayer* on the style of the proclamations, and the fact that Seward was an Episcopalian. The chief stylistic trait which sets these pieces apart from Lincoln's other writings is the use of words and phrases in pairs, as for example in the following passage from the "Proclamation of a National Fast Day," August 12, 1861:

> And whereas it is fit and becoming in all people, at all times, to acknowledge and revere the Supreme Government of God; to bow in humble submission to his chastisements; to confess and deplore their sins and transgressions in the full conviction that the fear of the Lord is the beginning of wisdom; and to pray, with all fervency and contrition, for the pardon of their past offences, and for a blessing upon their present and prospective action:

This is a general characteristic of phraseology in legal documents as well as in *The Book of Common Prayer*, but in legal documents the effect is, according to legal tradition at least, to make every statement incontestably clear, whereas in *The Book of Common Prayer* the effect is primarily one of incantation. Obviously, the effect in Lincoln's proclamations is nearer to that of *The Book of Common Prayer*, but it does not therefore necessarily follow that *The Book of Common Prayer* is the source of the device. The fact that the proclamations as official pronouncements are in their nature legal documents may well account for Lincoln's use of a device with which he was thoroughly familiar as a lawyer, and his use of it for rhetorical ends is only natural, in view of the solemnity of the theme and the occasion.

The fact that none of the manuscripts of proclamations included in this volume is entirely in Lincoln's hand neither adds nor subtracts evidence, since it was customary for the official copy to which signatures and seal were to be affixed to be engrossed by an official scribe.

In these proclamations, then, it may be supposed that we have examples of a formal style which Lincoln adopted for the specific purpose, and which for sonorous effect and solemn rhythm is not less interesting than, though different from, the style of his addresses. In his early writings, as we have seen,

Lincoln experimented with various forms of writing and several styles, and it is only logical to assume that in this later period, when confronted with the necessity of composing an expression which required something distinct from his usual style of public address, Lincoln adroitly made use of a device long familiar to him.

IX

Presidential Messages to Congress have rarely ever been noted for literary significance. Their very purpose and nature limit their content to summary of national progress and recommendations for congressional action. And of all Lincoln's writings aside from legal papers and executive orders, his messages are the most strictly utilitarian and necessarily prosaic. In spite of these considerations, several of Lincoln's messages so transcend the limitations of the occasion as to be worthy of inclusion among his best writings. With one exception they suffer generally in comparison with his great addresses, but in certain passages such as the conclusion to the "Annual Message" of December 1, 1862, they reach peaks of eloquence unsurpassed in the annals of history.

Above all, the messages to Congress demonstrate again the rhetorical care and precision with which Lincoln composed even his most factual statements, and his feeling for exact coloring of phrase and choice of word. The well-known incident concerning his use of the term "sugar-coated" in the "Message to Congress in Special Session," July 4, 1861, exemplifies the care with which he chose his words. The public printer John D. Defrees objected to the lack of dignity in the term as used in the sentence, "With rebellion thus sugar-coated they have been drugging the public mind of their section for more than thirty years . . ." To this Lincoln is reported to have replied, "Well, Defrees, if you think the time will ever come when people will not understand what 'sugar-coated' means, I'll alter it; otherwise I think I'll let it go." Like his many homely but effective figures of speech this one demanded simple and idiomatic language, and it was Defrees, rather than Lincoln, whose feeling for diction was awry.

In this first "Message to Congress" Lincoln gave a new statement of his philosophy of government as contained in the "First Inaugural Address," but without the pleading and palliation of that address and with a vigorous statement of courage and conviction in the task of preserving the authority of the national government. On the whole the message is nearer in purpose and effect to his speeches and addresses than are his later messages. This is in part, perhaps, the result of the fact that it was delivered on July 4, and was an address to the nation as well as to Congress. In all his major messages, however, Lincoln tends to keep a tone of public speech, though they were not delivered in person, and in fact generally preserves the architecture of the oration, especially in the peroration. The conclusion of this message, though not so memorable as the peroration of the "Annual Message," December 1, 1862, is effective and somewhat reminiscent of the short peroration of the "Address at Cooper Institute."

The "Annual Message to Congress," December 3, 1861, aside from discussion of specific problems of government, has as its central theme the importance of free labor in a democracy. The student may well compare Lincoln's discussion of labor and capital, as well as his recommendations in regard to a department of agriculture, with the ideas propounded in the "Address before the Wisconsin Agricultural Society" in 1859. In spite of its factuality, the second half of this message contains several inspired passages, and is consistently of high literary merit, though its opening and its close are rhetorically less striking than those of the next "Annual Message."

The "Annual Message to Congress," December 1, 1862, is Lincoln's finest composition of this type. In many respects it is his masterpiece, approximating both of the "Inaugural" addresses in depth of conviction and even surpassing them in breadth of conception and height of imagination. Perhaps no American living at the time save Walt Whitman ever expressed so large a vision of the future of American democracy, the magnitude of its geographic and economic potentialities, and the infinitude of its social destiny in the quest for human liberty. In this huge scope Lincoln saw the immediate problems underlying the Civil War—Union and Emancipation—in their true perspective as subordinate to the necessity of preserving not merely the words of the Declaration of Independence, but its prophetic truth. In the largest sense Lincoln sought not simply to preserve the Union or to free the slaves, but rather to keep open the way to future amelioration in the lot of all humanity and to the progressive achievement of democracy in all human society.

The message reveals how truly Lincoln appreciated the dramatic course of human events. Of all his prior speeches, only the "House Divided Speech" of 1858 approaches it in the clairvoyance with which Lincoln states the meaning of his era as a turning point in the long quest for human dignity. From the opening paragraph to the splendid peroration, the message is charged with an electric feeling for the drama of a crisis in which the citizens of the United States "shall nobly save, or meanly lose, the last best hope of earth."

In spite of its formidable array of facts and figures and the gray steel of its logical armor, the whole message is alive with the dignity of the inspired word. If one thinks only of the "Gettysburg Address" and a few other short, lyrical passages, it is hard to estimate the man's literary stature in comparison with the great orators of other times; for these lyric speeches are scarcely comparable, being unique. But in judging this message the student may with reason bring as a touchstone the best of Edmund Burke, or Cicero, or Demosthenes, and yet find Lincoln's metal too pure to assay by such a test. If one would try, let him select his touchstone and then assay the concluding paragraph of this message:

> Fellow-citizens, *we* cannot escape history. We of this Congress and this administration, will be remembered in spite of ourselves. No personal significance, or insignificance, can spare one or another of us. The fiery trial through which we pass, will light us down, in honor or dishonor, to the latest generation. We *say* we are for the Union. The world will not forget that we say this. We know how to save the Union. The world knows we do know how to save it. We—even *we here*—hold the power, and bear the responsibility. In *giving* freedom to the *slave*, we *assure* freedom to the *free*

—honorable alike in what we give, and what we preserve. We shall nobly save, or meanly lose, the last best hope of earth. Other means may succeed; this could not fail. The way is plain, peaceful, generous, just—a way which, if followed, the world will forever applaud, and God must forever bless.

X

Lincoln's numerous addresses, beginning with the "Farewell Address" and continuing through the "Second Inaugural Address," display little in the way of stylistic traits which differs essentially from the characteristics of his earlier work, except in beauty. As has already been noted, it is not in technical command of style so much as it is in power of feeling and imagination that the addresses of this last period surpass by all odds those of his middle period.

The new intensity seems to have been more the result of internal experience than of external influence. It was a common observation among Lincoln's friends that he was cold and unemotional. Also it is true that no other orator of his time was more coldly logical, more careful of a self-imposed restraint, than Lincoln was from 1854 to 1861. Upon his departure from Springfield in 1861 a note of fathomless emotion, at once heroic and simple, sounded for the first time in his "Farewell Address." This note was sounded again in the prose poem which he made of Seward's suggested peroration for the "First Inaugural Address"; and thenceforth, restrained but full, it suffused the more important lyric utterances of his years in Washington, but above all the "Gettysburg Address" and the "Second Inaugural Address."

It has been said that Lincoln's art is always applied art, utilitarian in purpose and held strictly to the matter in hand. If this implies that it does not therefore reach the heights of imagination to which we conventionally expect only belletristic art to attain, nothing could be farther from the truth. And yet, perhaps, even in the deep-moving cadence and high imagination of the "Gettysburg Address" and the "Second Inaugural Address," he considered his prose chiefly as a means to an end, recognizing that in an emotional crisis of national scope the truest appeal could not be made to the intellect alone. And because he had early learned to eschew the illusion of emotionalism, he was able in his great hour to plumb depths hitherto rarely fathomed by oratory.

The emergence of this new feeling was significantly coincident with his assumption of what he seemed to consider his supreme task—the preservation of the Union, and with it democracy. His utterances regarding slavery, in fact, his words on all other subjects, fine as many of them are, fall into place near or far from the high words in which he defended and pleaded for democracy as symbolized in the Union. Alexander Stephens once said that the Union with Lincoln rose in sentiment to the "sublimity of a religious mysticism." The "Gettysburg Address" is excellent literary evidence in support of Stephens's opinion, for it reveals Lincoln's worship of the Union as the symbol of an ideal yet to be realized.

Lincoln's problem at Gettysburg was to do two things: to commemorate the past and to prophesy for the future. To do these things he took the theme dearest to his audience, honor for the heroic dead sons and fathers, and combined it with the theme nearest to his own heart, the preservation of democracy. Out of this double theme grew his poetic metaphor of birth, death, and spiritual rebirth, of the life of man and the life of the nation. To it he brought the fervor of devoutly religious belief. Democracy was to Lincoln a religion, and he wanted it to be in a real sense the religion of his audience. Thus he combined an elegiac theme with a patriotic theme, skillfully blending the hope of eternal life with the hope of eternal democracy.

Above all Lincoln believed that "all men are created equal," in the only way that a mind as coldly logical as his could believe in it. Just how he believed it, is indicated by his use of one word, *proposition*. This word has proved a stumbling block for some readers of the "Gettysburg Address." Matthew Arnold is reported, probably inaccurately, to have read as far as "dedicated to the proposition" and stopped. Charles Sumner said that at first he did not like the word, but that he later decided it was satisfactory. Yet the word *proposition* was inevitable for Lincoln. He often tried to use his words as exactly as a mathematician uses his formulae. By his own account he had "studied and nearly mastered" Euclid, and hence we may be sure that he used the word naturally in the logician's sense: a statement to be debated, verified, proved. Thus democracy, as an active, living thing, meant to Lincoln the verification or the proving of the proposition to which its very existence was in the beginning dedicated. Eighty-seven years had gone into the proving, the Civil War had come at a critical stage in the argument, the Union Armies at Gettysburg had won an immediate victory, and the affirmation that "all men are created equal" was still a live rather than a dead issue. It was still a proposition open to argument and inviting proof, but not on any account one that had already been proved. The further proof was for "us the living, to be dedicated here to the unfinished work which they who fought here have thus far so nobly advanced."

It was thus that Lincoln believed in democracy, as a living thing striving toward truth, not as an accomplished fact nor as a meaningless form of words incapable of proof. He had said some years before, "the Declaration of Independence contemplated the progressive improvement in the condition of all men." And again, "I say in relation to the principle that all men are created equal let it be as nearly reached as we can." Down through the years, again and again, there had appeared in his speeches and letters this central concept of progressive improvement in the condition of mankind. And at Gettysburg he took the occasion to reaffirm his belief in the necessity of striving on.

So it was no accident that, as he thought on the past life of American democracy, his words and allusions began, in his very first sentence, calling to mind a haunting phrase out of the Old Testament: "the days of our years are three score and ten," and with it the symbolic act of consecration traditionally observed of old by Hebrew and Christian, dedicating their children to the service of God. And thus he wrote, "Fourscore and seven years ago our fathers brought forth on this continent a new nation, conceived in liberty, and dedicated to the proposition that all men are created equal."

But the "new nation" had in eighty-four years grown old. It was already thinking too much in terms of the past. The proposition to which the founding fathers had dedicated it must not mean anything new. Although the proposition had specifically stated *all men*, the laws of the nation had insisted that it had not meant ALL men; it had meant only white men; it must not mean ALL men. The war had come, and with it the death of that old nation, and the birth of a new. Its death was at Gettysburg, symbolized in the graves of those "who here gave their lives that that nation might live." Its life, too, was at Gettysburg, symbolized in Lincoln's audience: "It is for us the living, rather, to be dedicated here . . ."

The key words of the "Gettysburg Address" are three simple ones, two pronouns and an adverb: *they, we, here.* With his usual practice Lincoln repeats them, emphasizing again and again what he wanted his audience to carry away. "It is for us the living to be dedicated here to the unfinished work which they who fought here have thus far so nobly advanced."

Repetition of sounds, as well as of words, is a marked characteristic of Lincoln's style throughout his works. He often employs in poetic flashes alliteration, assonance, and even rhyme sounds. But in the "Gettysburg Address" these several varieties of repetition provide an effect unique in Lincoln's prose. With these devices indicated by italics, the oral peculiarities of the first sentence of the address become apparent: "*Four score* and *seven* years ago our *fathers* brought *forth* on this *continent* a *new nation, conceived* in liberty and dedicated to the *proposition* that all men are *created* equal." The reader may, if he is interested, verify for himself the remarkable extent to which Lincoln employs these devices with fine effect in the remainder of the "Gettysburg Address" as well as in many other passages.

Another variety of repetition, grammatical parallelism, is equally characteristic of Lincoln's general style. He uses this device with such frequency and variety that it seems to have been a consistent habit of his mind to seek repetitive sequences in both diction and sentence structure for the alignment of his thought. That this was the result of his deliberate seeking for an emphasis and simplicity which would prove effective with the common man is implied in the often repeated testimony given by Herndon: "He used to bore me terribly by his methods, processes, manners, etc., etc. Mr. Lincoln would doubly explain things to me that needed no explanation. . . . Lincoln's ambition in this line was this: he wanted to be distinctly understood by the common people . . ." Herndon might have added that Lincoln's favorite ideas—those which appear again and again in his works, and which he turned over and over in his mind through months and even years—and his most memorable phrases almost invariably betray this repetitive pattern.

On this basic pattern of parallelism in thought, Lincoln often elaborates a distinctly poetical cadence, suggesting comparison with the cadenced prose of the seventeenth century. Although balanced rhythms with caesuras are indigenous to English poetry and perhaps to English prose, Hebrew literature through the King James Bible probably provided the literary examples which Lincoln knew best; and from his fondness for Biblical phraseology he may have derived his mastery of the technique.

In his lyrical passages balance becomes most striking, as it enriches his melancholy reflections or his fervent appeals to the hearts of his audience. Within single sentences it occurs in two forms: in a balanced sentence of two parts with a caesura approximately midway; and in a series of phrases or clauses separated by caesuras and grouped in balanced staves of two or more phrase units. Within an individual phrase or clause internal balance and parallelism often occur. A fine example of the first type, with a pointed use of antithesis, is the following sentence from the "Letter to J. H. Hackett," November 2, 1863: "I have endured a great deal of ridicule without much malice; and have received a great deal of kindness, not quite free from ridicule." An example of the second type is the concluding sentence of the "Second Inaugural Address":

> With malice toward none; with charity for all; with firmness in the right, as God gives us to see the right, let us strive on to finish the work we are in; to bind up the nation's wounds; to care for him who shall have borne the battle, and for his widow, and his orphan—to do all which may achieve

> and cherish a just and lasting peace, among ourselves, and with all nations.

Sometimes this rhythm pattern extends over an entire group of sentences, or even the whole of a short address: the "Farewell Address" for example. In this address there are two parallel patterns, of thought and of rhythm. Within and between some sentences they become identical. In others they merely coincide. Between others there is a compensating balance of phrases and pauses, although the sentence movement is reversed from periodic to loose structure, and the rhythm pattern is varied. The only sentence which appears without a compensating rhythm is the first, standing alone as a topic statement. Within this general pattern of close parallels there is enough variety in individual sentences to avoid monotony but sufficient regularity of rhythm to produce distinct cadence, in some phrases approximating loose metrical effect:

> My Friends: No one, not in my situation, can appreciate my feeling of sadness at this parting. To this place, and the kindness of these people, I owe everything. Here I have lived a quarter of a century, and have passed from a young to an old man. Here my children have been born, and one is buried. I now leave, not knowing when or whether ever I may return, with a task before me greater than that which rested upon Washington. Without the assistance of that Divine Being who ever attended him, I cannot succeed. With that assistance, I cannot fail. Trusting in Him who can go with me, and remain with you, and be everywhere for good, let us confidently hope that all will yet be well. To His care commending you, as I hope in your prayers you will commend me, I bid you an affectionate farewell.

As these balanced rhythms sometimes approach meter in their regularity, Lincoln tends to heighten their effect with an occasional metrical phrase or sentence. Such phrases occur most frequently in perorations or passages of high emotional content: as for example, in a phrase of the "Second Inaugural Address": ". . . to do all which may achieve and cherish a just and lasting peace among ourselves . . ."; or in a phrase of the "Gettysburg Address": "The world will little note nor long remember what we say . . ."

Although Lincoln was without doubt consciously deliberate in attention to sound, his choice of words seems to have been guided primarily by other values: meaning more than sound or connotation, concrete words more than abstract words, current idiom more than authoritarian nicety. So much has been written on the qualities of exactness, clarity, and simplicity in his style that it seems unnecessary to stress them further. They are, however, the qualities of prose excellence wherever it is met with, and as such hardly set Lincoln's style apart from that of Edmund Burke, though they do, in their degree, set his style apart from that of Stephen A. Douglas or that of William H. Seward. Important and obvious as these qualities are, one may wonder if Lincoln's memorable passages are not remembered today for their unique effects of arrangement, rhythm, and sound as well as for the intrinsic value of their thought. What Lincoln's own answer might have been we may infer from the following comment in one of Herndon's letters to Jesse W. Weik:

> Mr. Lincoln's habits, methods of reading law, politics, poetry, etc., etc., were to come into the office, pick up book, newspaper, etc., and to sprawl himself out on the sofa, chairs, etc., and read aloud, much to my annoyance. I have asked him often why he did so and his invariable reply was: "I catch the idea by two senses, for when I read aloud I hear what is read and I see it; and hence two senses get it and I remember it better, if I do not understand it better."

There is an old Arabian proverb which holds that "that is the best description which makes the ear an eye." In his use of figures of speech, sound, and rhythm, Lincoln illustrates again and again the truth of the old saying, which he probably had never heard.

Lincoln's composition has so much the stamp of these peculiarities even in the first draft of such a piece as the "Gettysburg Address" that his revisions do little more than accent them. In his revision of Secretary Seward's suggested peroration for the "First Inaugural Address," however, he demonstrates the deliberate artistry of his style, bringing his own peculiar pattern of thought and rhythm to another man's ideas, substituting his own exact and concrete words for orotund and vague terms, removing redundant and useless words, bringing closer together words that will enhance through assonance and alliteration the sound effect of the whole, and finally, changing a vague, transcendental metaphor into a homely but poetic figure which will be understood by every man who hears or reads it.

To label one of the following as Lincoln's is superfluous. Every sentence declares its creator:

I close.	I am loth to close.
We are not, we must not be, aliens or enemies, but fellow-countrymen and brethren.	We are not enemies, but friends. We must not be enemies.
Although passion has strained our bonds of affection too hardly, they must not, I am sure they will not, be broken.	Though passion may have strained, it must not break our bonds of affection.
The mystic chords which, proceeding from so many battle-fields and so many patriot graves, pass through all the hearts and all the hearths in this broad continent of ours, will yet again harmonize in their ancient music when breathed upon by the guardian angel of the nation.	The mystic chords of memory, stretching from every battle-field, and patriot grave, to every living heart and hearth-stone, all over this broad land, will yet swell the chorus of the Union, when again touched, as surely they will be, by the better angels of our nature.

The study of Lincoln's works reveals the dignity of a great mind and heart that seeks for rightness in principle, fairness in act, and beauty in utterance. He is a creative consciousness in whom the reality of nineteenth century America yet lives and breathes. As this reality is in Lincoln intrinsic, and his communication of it inimitable, so his words endure, representative and symbolic with singular completeness of the epoch which nurtured him. And so it is that he becomes as we study him, like the classic literary figures of the past, something more than a man. Time may dissipate the factual significance of his deeds, both as private citizen and as President, but we must always know and acknowledge the shining spirit that illumines his words.

SELECTIONS, WITH NOTES

TO THE PEOPLE OF SANGAMO COUNTY: POLITICAL ANNOUNCEMENT. MARCH 9, 1832

Fellow Citizens:

Having become a candidate for the honorable office of one of your representatives in the next General Assembly of this state, in accordance with an established custom, and the principles of true republicanism, it becomes my duty to make known to you—the people whom I propose to represent—my sentiments with regard to local affairs.

Time and experience have verified to a demonstration, the public utility of internal improvements. That the poorest and most thinly populated countries would be greatly benefitted by the opening of good roads, and in the clearing of navigable streams within their limits, is what no person will deny. But yet it is folly to undertake works of this or any other kind, without first knowing that we are able to finish them—as half finished work generally proves to be labor lost. There cannot justly be any objection to having rail roads and canals, any more than to other good things, provided they cost nothing. The only objection is to paying for them; and the objection to paying arises from the want of ability to pay.

With respect to the County of Sangamo, some more easy means of communication than we now possess, for the purpose of facilitating the task of exporting the surplus products of its fertile soil, and importing necessary articles from abroad, are indispensably necessary. A meeting has been held of the citizens of Jacksonville, and the adjacent country, for the purpose of deliberating and enquiring into the expediency of constructing a railroad from some eligible point on the Illinois river, through the town of Jacksonville, in Morgan county, to the town of Springfield, in Sangamo county. This is, indeed, a very desirable object. No other improvement that reason will justify us in hoping for, can equal in utility the rail road. It is a never failing source of communication, between places of business remotely situated from each other. Upon the rail road the regular progress of commercial intercourse is not interrupted by either high or low water, or freezing weather, which are the principal difficulties that render our future hopes of water communication precarious and uncertain. Yet, however desirable an object the construction of a rail road through our country may be; however high our imaginations may be heated at thoughts of it—there is always a heart appalling shock accompanying the account of its cost, which forces us to shrink from our pleasing anticipations. The probable cost of this contemplated rail road is estimated at $290,000;—the bare statement of which, in my opinion, is sufficient to justify the belief, that the improvement of the Sangamo river is an object much better suited to our infant resources.

Respecting this view, I think I may say, without the fear of being contradicted, that its navigation may be rendered completely practicable, as high as the mouth of the South Fork, or probably higher, to vessels of from 25 to 30 tons burthen, for at least one half of all common years, and to vessels of much greater burthen a part of that time. From my peculiar circumstances, it is probable that for the last twelve months I have given as particular attention to the stage of the water in this river as any other person in the country. In the month of March, 1831, in company with others, I commenced the building of a flat boat on the Sangamo, and finished and took her out in the course of the spring. Since that time, I have been concerned in the mill at New Salem. These circumstances are sufficient evidence, that I have not been very inattentive to the stages of the water.—The time at which we crossed the mill dam, being in the last days of April, the water was lower than it had been since the breaking of winter in February, or than it was for several weeks after. The principal difficulties we encountered in descending the river, were from the drifted timber, which obstructions all know is not difficult to be removed. Knowing almost precisely the height of water at that time, I believe I am safe in saying that it has as often been higher as lower since.

From this view of the subject, it appears that my calculations with regard to the navigation of the Sangamo cannot be unfounded in reason; but whatever may be its natural advantages, certain it is, that it never can be practically useful to any great extent, without being greatly improved by art. The drifted timber, as I have before mentioned, is the most formidable barrier to this object. Of all parts of this river, none will require so much labor in proportion, to make it navigable, as the last thirty or thirty-five miles; and going with the meanderings of the channel, when we are this distance above its mouth, we are only between twelve and eighteen miles above Beardstown, in something near a straight direction; and this route is upon such low ground as to retain water in many places during the season, and in all parts such as to draw two-thirds or three-fourths of the river water at all high stages.

This route is upon prairie land the whole distance;—so that it appears to me, by removing the turf, a sufficient width and damming up the old channel, the whole river in a short time would wash its way through, thereby curtailing the distance, and increasing the velocity of the current very considerably, while there would be no timber upon the banks to obstruct its navigation in future; and being nearly straight, the timber which might float in at the head, would be apt to go clear through. There are also many places above this where the river, in its zig zag course, forms such complete peninsulas, as to be easier cut through at the necks than to remove the obstructions from the bends—which, if done, would also lessen the distance.

What the cost of this work would be, I am unable to say. It is probable, however, it would not be greater than is common to streams of the same length. Finally, I believe the improvement of the Sangamo river, to be vastly important and highly desirable to the people of this county; and if elected, any measure in the legislature having this for its object, which may appear judicious, will meet my approbation, and shall receive my support.

It appears that the practice of loaning money at exorbitant rates of interest, has already been opened as a field for discussion; so I suppose I may enter upon it without claiming the honor, or risking the danger, which may await its first explorer. It seems as though we are never to have an end to this baneful and corroding system, acting almost as prejudicial to the general interests of the community as a direct tax of several thousand dollars annually laid on each county, for the benefit of a few individuals only, unless there be a law made setting a limit to the rates of usury. A law for this purpose, I am of opinion, may be made without materially injuring any class of people. In cases of extreme necessity there could always be means found to cheat the law, while in all other cases it would have its intended effect. I would not favor the passage of a law upon this subject, which might be very easily evaded. Let it be such that the labor and difficulty of evading it, could only be justified in cases of the greatest necessity.

Upon the subject of education, not presuming to dictate any plan or system respecting it, I can only say that I view it as the most important subject which we as a people can be engaged in. That every man may receive at least, a moderate education, and thereby be enabled to read the histories of his own and other countries, by which he may duly appreciate the value of our free institutions, appears to be an object of vital importance, even on this account alone, to say nothing of the advantages and satisfaction to be derived from all being able to read the scriptures and other works, both of a religious and moral nature, for themselves. For my part, I desire to see the time when education, and by its means, morality, sobriety, enterprise and industry, shall become much more general than at present, and should be gratified to have it in my power to contribute something to the advancement of any measure which might have a tendency to accelerate the happy period.

With regard to existing laws, some alterations are thought to be necessary. Many respectable men have suggested that our estray laws—the law respecting the issuing of executions, the road law, and some others, are deficient in their present form, and require alterations. But considering the great probability that the framers of those laws were wiser than myself, I should prefer [not?] meddling with them, unless they were first attacked by others, in which case I should feel it both a privilege and a duty to take that stand, which in my view, might tend most to the advancement of justice.

But, Fellow-Citizens, I shall conclude.—Considering the great degree of modesty which should always attend youth, it is probable I have already been more presuming than becomes me. However, upon the subjects of which I have treated, I have spoken as I thought. I may be wrong in regard to any or all of them; but holding it a sound maxim, that it is better to be only sometimes right, than at all times wrong, so soon as I discover my opinions to be erroneous, I shall be ready to renounce them.

Every man is said to have his peculiar ambition. Whether it be true or not, I can say for one that I have no other so great as that of being truly esteemed of my fellow men, by rendering myself worthy of their esteem. How far I shall succeed in gratifying this ambition, is yet to be developed. I am young and unknown to many of you. I was born and have ever remained in the most humble walks of life. I have no wealthy or popular relations to recommend me. My case is thrown exclusively upon the independent voters of this county, and if elected they will have conferred a favor upon me, for which I shall be unremitting in my labors to compensate. But if the good people in their wisdom shall see fit to keep me in the back ground, I have been too familiar with disappointments to be very much chagrined.

Your friend and fellow-citizen,

A. Lincoln

New Salem, March 9, 1832.

Nicolay and Hay state that this piece was also printed as a political handbill. Although this may quite probably be true, the present editor has not been able to locate any other source than the Sangamo Journal. *It seems likely that Nicolay and Hay also used this* Journal *text, for the deviations in their text from that of the* Journal *are generally in the nature of debatable "improvements" of diction such as they habitually undertook.*

Lincoln's discussion of laws governing usury (paragraph 8) has long been a matter for comment. A very sensible suggestion made by H. B. Van Hoesen in The

Humor of Lincoln and the Seriousness of His Biographers *is that Lincoln's comments on "cases of extreme necessity" is ironical humor of the sort common in Lincoln's speeches, but which is often missed in the printed word, where inflections of voice made it obvious to an audience. Recognizing the difficulty of controlling usury when individuals are resolved to exploit the needs of the borrower to the fullest extent, Lincoln indulges his sardonic realism by making ironical reference to the practical limitations which operate against legislating morality. Certainly Lincoln is not engaging in what is today known as "double-talk." His final sentence in the paragraph makes clear his position, as well as his recognition that in some circumstances the law will be evaded.*

ANNOUNCEMENT OF POLITICAL VIEWS IN *SANGAMO JOURNAL*. JUNE 13, 1836

New Salem, June 13, 1836.

To the Editor of the Journal:

In your paper of last Saturday, I see a communication, over the signature of "Many Voters," in which the candidates who are announced in the Journal, are called upon to "show their hands." Agreed. Here's mine!

I go for all sharing the privileges of the government, who assist in bearing its burthens. Consequently I go for admitting all whites to the right of suffrage, who pay taxes or bear arms, (by no means excluding females.)

If elected, I shall consider the whole people of Sangamon my constituents, as well those that oppose, as those that support me.

While acting as their representative, I shall be governed by their will, on all subjects upon which I have the means of knowing what their will is; and upon all others, I shall do what my own judgment teaches me will best advance their interests. Whether elected or not, I go for distributing the proceeds of the sales of the public lands to the several states, to enable our state, in common with others, to dig canals and construct rail roads, without borrowing money and paying interest on it.

If alive on the first Monday in November, I shall vote for Hugh L. White for President.

Very respectfully,
A. Lincoln

LETTER TO COLONEL ROBERT ALLEN
JUNE 21, 1836

New Salem, June 21, 1836.

Dear Col.

I am told that during my absence last week, you passed through this place, and stated publicly, that you were in possession of a fact or facts, which, if known to the public, would entirely destroy the prospects of N. W. Edwards and myself at the ensuing election; but that, through favour to us, you should forbear to divulge them.

No one has needed favours more than I, and generally, few have been less unwilling to accept them; but in this case, favour to me would be injustice to the public, and therefore I must beg your pardon for declining it. That I once had the confidence of the people of Sangamon, is sufficiently evident, and if I have since done any thing, either by design or misadventure, which if known, would subject me to a forfeiture of that confidence, he that knows of that thing, and conceals it, is a traitor to his country's interest.

I find myself wholly unable to form any conjecture of what

fact or facts, real or supposed, you spoke; but my opinion of your veracity, will not permit me, for a moment, to doubt, that you at least believed what you said.

I am flattered with the personal regard you manifested for me, but I do hope that, on more mature reflection, you will view the public interest as a paramount consideration, and, therefore, determine to let the worst come.

I here assure you, that the candid statement of facts, on your part, however low it may sink me, shall never break the tie of personal friendship between us.

I wish an answer to this, and you are at liberty to publish both if you choose

Verry [*sic*] Respectfully,
A. Lincoln.

This letter was written from New Salem. Allen, a Democrat, lived in Springfield. His gossip was apparently never revealed in print, for there seems to be no record of it. Although Lincoln's allusions to friendship are probably ironical at this time, their later relationship seems to have been neither more nor less than casual and friendly. A number of references to Allen in later letters indicate business dealings.

LETTER TO MISS MARY OWENS DECEMBER 13, 1836

Vandalia, Decr. 13, 1836

Mary

I have been sick ever since my arrival here, or I should have written sooner. It is but little difference, however, as I have very little even yet to write. And more, the longer I can avoid the mortification of looking in the Post Office for your letter and not finding it, the better. You see I am mad about that *old letter* yet. I dont like very well to risk you again. I'll try you once more, any how.

The new State House is not yet finished, and consequently the legislature is doing little or nothing. The Governor delivered an inflamitory [*sic*] political message, and it is expected there will be some sparring between the parties about it as soon as the two Houses get to business. Taylor delivered up his petition for the New County to one of our members this morning. I am told he dispairs [*sic*] of it's success, on account of all the members from Morgan County opposing it. There are names enough on the petition, I think, to justify the members from our county in going for it; but if the members from Morgan oppose it, which they say they will, the chance will be bad.

Our chance to take the seat of Government to Springfield is better than I expected. An Internal Improvement Convention was held here since we met, which recommended a loan of several millions of dollars on the faith of the State to construct Rail Roads. Some of the legislature are for it and some against it: which has the majority I can not tell. There is great strife and struggling for the office of the U. S. Senator here at this time. It is probable we shall ease their pains in a few days The opposition men have no candidate of their own, and consequently they smile as complacently at the angry snarls of the contending Van Buren candidates and their respective friends, as the Christain [*sic*] does at Satan's rage. You recollect I mentioned in the outset of this letter that I had been unwell. That is the fact, though I believe I am about well now; but that, with other things I can not account for, have conspired and have gotten my spirits so low, that I feel that I would rather be any place in the world than here I really can not endure the thought of staying here ten weeks. Write back as soon as you get this, and if possible [say] something that will please me, for really I have n[ot been p]leased since I left you. This letter is so dry an[d stupid that] I am ashamed to send it, but with my p[resent feeli]ngs I can not do any better. Give my best respects to [Mr. and M]rs. Abell [Able?] and family.

Your friend
Lincoln

Miss Mary S. Owens

The story of Lincoln's courtship of Mary Owens as revealed in his letters is so curiously obscure and yet so suggestive of his emotional complexities that it has long been a prime object of speculation among biographers. The few letters themselves were obtained by Herndon, along with some scanty comment and reserved admissions on the part of Mary Owens, after Lincoln's death thirty years later. Because of the obvious lack of romantic sentiment in the letters, the episode has been treated as the antithetical aftermath of the more or less legendary Ann Rutledge romance. Lincoln's desire for feminine companionship and friendship, his chariness of sentiment, and his actual fear of emotional involvement, are apparent and have given both amateur and professional psychoanalysts sufficient, if incomplete, data to diagnose a powerful repressive force in Lincoln's personality which was apparently further complicated by physiological and emotional factors too numerous to mention here. Lincoln's own allusions to the moods of depression which occasionally but often violently afflicted him are numerous, but usually, as in the last paragraph of this letter, too obscure for more than general diagnosis. Three works of genuine but uneven worth may be mentioned for their attempt to solve the personality of Lincoln: Milton Henry Shutes, Lincoln and the Doctors; *Leon Pierce Clark,* Lincoln; a Psychobiography; *William F. Petersen,* Lincoln-Douglas: The Weather as Destiny.

Clark's study indicates the elementary psychological motivations in Lincoln's life to have been a mother fixation and a fear of the father, with narcissism underlying a depressive temperament which is characteristic of Lincoln but not sufficient to be diagnosed as melancholia. Lincoln's development of an unusually powerful super-ego (conscience) is traced to its Freudian source in father-fear. One fault which many students of Lincoln find with Clark's study is the author's lack of discrimination in evaluating his sources of evidence; anything which fits Freudian interpretation is grist to his mill, and much that he credits is either questionable or definitely known to be incorrect. This does not entirely vitiate his analysis, however, which in broad outline is plausible enough. It must be recognized that no practicing analyst would find in the data which Clark uses, sufficient evidence for formulating a complete diagnosis of an actual patient, and it is to be noted that Clark is of little help to the reader in analyzing the situation indicated in the Mary Owens incident as a whole.

SPEECH IN THE ILLINOIS LEGISLATURE JANUARY 11, 1837

Mr. Chairman:

Lest I should fall into the too common error, of being mistaken in regard to which side I design to be upon, I shall make it my first care to remove all doubt on that point, by declaring that I am opposed to the resolution under consideration, in toto. Before I proceed to the body of the subject, I will further remark, that it is not without a considerable degree of apprehension, that I venture to cross the track of the gentleman from Coles (Mr. Linder). Indeed, I do not believe I could muster a sufficiency of courage to come in contact with that gentleman, were it not for the fact, that he, some days since, most graciously condescended to assure us that he would never be found wasting ammunition on *small game.* On the same fortunate occasion, he further gave us to understand, that he regarded *himself* as being decidedly the *superior* of our common friend from Randolph (Mr. Shields); and feeling, as I really do, that I, to say the most of myself, am nothing more than the peer of our friend from Randolph, I shall regard the gentleman from Coles as decidedly my superior also, and consequently, in the course of what I shall have to say, whenever I shall have occasion to allude to that gentleman, I shall endeavor to adopt that kind of court language which I understand to be due to *decided superiority.* In one faculty, at least, there can be no dispute of the gentleman's superiority over me, and most other men; and that is, the faculty of entangling a subject, so that neither himself, or any other man, can find head or tail to it. Here he has introduced a resolution, embracing ninety-nine printed lines across common writing paper, and yet more than one half of his opening speech has been made upon subjects about which there is not one word said in his resolution.

Though his resolution embraces nothing in regard to the constitutionality of the Bank, much of what he has said has been with a view to make the impression that it was unconstitutional in its inception. Now, although I am satisfied that an ample field may be found within the pale of the resolution, at least for small game, yet as the gentleman has travelled out of it, I feel that I may, with all due humility, venture to follow him. The gentleman has discovered that some gentleman at Washington city has been upon the very eve of deciding our Bank unconstitutional, and that he would probably have completed his very authentic decision, had not some one of the Bank officers placed his hand upon his mouth, and begged him to withhold it. The fact that the individuals composing our Supreme Court have, in an official capacity, decided in favor of the constitutionality of the Bank, would, in my mind, seem a sufficient answer to this. It is a fact known to all, that the members of the Supreme Court, together with the Governor, form a Council of Revision, and that this Council approved this Bank Charter. I ask, then, if the extra-judicial decision—not quite, but only almost made, by the gentleman at Washington, before whom, by the way, the question of the constitutionality of our Bank never has, nor never can come—is to be taken as paramount to a decision officially made by that tribunal, by which and which alone, the constitutionality of the Bank can ever be settled? But, aside from this view of the subject, I would ask, if the committee which this resolution proposes to appoint, are to examine into the constitutionality of the Bank? Are they to be clothed with power to send for persons and papers, for this object? And after they have found the bank to be unconstitutional, and decided it so, how are they to enforce their decision? What will their decision amount to? They cannot compel the Bank to cease operations, or to change the course of its operations. What good, then, can their labors result in? Certainly none.

The gentleman asks, if we, without an examination, shall, by giving the State deposits to the Bank, and by taking the stock reserved for the State, legalize its former misconduct. Now I do not pretend to possess sufficient legal knowledge to decide, whether a legislative enactment, proposing to, and accepting from, the Bank, certain terms, would have the effect to legalize or wipe out its former errors, or not; but I can assure the gentleman, if such should be the effect, he has already got behind the settlement of accounts; for it is well known to all, that the Legislature, at its last session, passed a supplemental Bank charter, which the Bank has since accepted, and which, according to his doctrine, has legalized all the alleged violations of its original charter in the distribution of its stock.

I now proceed to the resolution. By examination it will be found that the first thirty-three lines, being precisely one third of the whole, relate exclusively to the distribution of the stock by the commissioners appointed by the State. Now, Sir, it is clear that no question can arise on this portion of the resolution, except a question between capitalists in regard to the ownership of stock. Some gentlemen have the stock in their hands, while others, who have more money than they know what to do with, want it; and this, and this alone, is the question, to settle which we are called on to squander thousands of the people's money. What interest, let me ask, have the people in the settlement of this question? What difference is it to them whether the stock is owned by Judge Smith, or Sam. Wiggins? If any gentleman be entitled to stock in the Bank, which he is kept out of possession of by others, let him assert his right in the Supreme Court, and let him or his antagonist, whichever may be found in the wrong, pay the costs of suit. It is an old maxim, and a very sound one, that he that dances should always pay the fiddler. Now, sir, in the present case, if any gentlemen, whose money is a burden to them, choose to lead off a dance, I am decidedly opposed to the people's money being used to pay the fiddler. No one can doubt that the examination proposed by this resolution must cost the State some ten or twelve thousand dollars; and all this to settle a question in which the people have no interest, and about which they care nothing. These capitalists generally act harmoniously and in concert, to fleece the people, and now, that they have got into a quarrel with themselves, we are called upon to appropriate the people's money to settle the quarrel.

I leave this part of the resolution, and proceed to the remainder. It will be found that no charge in the remaining part of the resolution, if true, amounts to the violation of the Bank charter, except one, which I will notice in due time. It might seem quite sufficient, to say no more upon any of these charges or insinuations, than enough to show they are not violations of the charter; yet, as they are ingeniously framed and handled, with a view to deceive and mislead, I will notice in their order, all the most prominent of them. The first of these, is in relation to a connexion between our Bank and several Banking institutions in other States. Admitting this connection to exist, I should like to see the gentleman from Coles, or any other gentleman, undertake to show that there is any harm in it.—What can there be in such a connexion, that the people of Illinois are willing to pay their money to get a peep into? By a reference to the tenth section of the Bank charter, any gentleman can see that the framers of the act contemplated the holding of stock in the institutions of other corporations. Why, then, is it, when neither law nor justice forbids it, that we are asked to spend our time and money, in inquiring into its truth?

The next charge, in the order of time, is, that some officer, director, clerk or servant of the Bank, has been required to take an oath of secrecy in relation to the affairs of said Bank. Now, I do not know whether this be true or false—neither do I believe any honest man cares. I know that the seventh section of the charter expressly guarantees to the Bank the right of making, under certain restrictions, such by-laws as it may think fit; and I further know that the requiring an oath of secrecy would not transcend those restrictions. What, then, if the Bank has chosen to exercise this right? Who can it injure? Does not every merchant have his secret mark? and who is ever silly enough to complain of it? I presume if the Bank does require any such oath of secrecy, it is done through a motive of delicacy to those individuals who deal with it.—Why, sir, not many days since, one gentleman upon this floor, who, by the way, I have no doubt is now ready to join this hue and cry against the Bank, indulged in a philippic against one of the Bank officers, because, as he said, he had *divulged a secret.*

Immediately following this last charge, there are several insinuations in the resolution, which are too silly to require any sort of notice, were it not for the fact, that they conclude by saying, "*to the great injury of the people at large.*" In answer to this I would say, that it is strange enough, that the people are suffering these "great injuries," and yet are not sensible of it! Singular indeed that the people should be writhing under oppression and injury, and yet not one among them to be found to raise the voice of complaint. If the Bank be inflicting injury upon the people, why is it, that not a single petition is presented to this body on the subject? If the Bank really be a grievance, why is it, that no one of the real people is found to ask redress of it? The truth is, no such oppression exists. If it did, our table would groan with memorials and petitions, and we would not be permitted to rest day or night, till we had put it down. The people know their rights; and they are never slow to assert and maintain them, when they are invaded. Let them call for an investigation, and I shall ever stand ready to respond to the call. But they have made no such call. I make the assertion boldly, and without fear of contradiction, that no man, who does not hold an office, or does not aspire to one, has ever found any fault of the Bank. It has doubled the prices of the products of their farms, and filled their pockets with a sound circulating medium, and they are all well pleased with its operations. No, Sir, it is the *politician* who is the first to sound the alarm, (which, by the way, is a false one.) It is he, who, by these unholy means, is endeavoring to blow up a storm that he may ride upon and direct. It is he, and he alone, that here proposes to spend thousands of the people's public treasure, for no other advantage to them, than to make valueless in their pockets the reward of their industry. Mr. Chairman, this work is exclusively the work of politicians; a set of men who have interests aside from the interests of the people, and who, to say the most of them, are, taken as a mass, at least one long step removed from honest men. I say this with the greater freedom, because, being a politician myself, none can regard it as personal.

Again, it is charged, or rather insinuated, that officers of the Bank have loaned money at usurious rates of interest. Suppose this to be true, are we to send a committee of this House to enquire into it? Suppose the committee should find it true can they redress the injured individuals? Assuredly not. If any individual had been injured in this way, is there not an ample remedy, to be found in the laws of the land? Does the gentleman from Coles know, that there is a statute standing in full force, making it highly penal, for an individual to loan money at a higher rate of interest than twelve per cent? If he does not he is too ignorant to be placed at the head of the committee which his resolution proposes; and if he does, his neglect to mention it, shows him to be too uncandid to merit the respect or confidence of any one.

But besides all this, if the Bank were struck from existence, could not the owners of the capital still loan it usuriously, as well as now? Whatever the Bank, or its officers, may have done, I know that usurious transactions were much more frequent and enormous before the commencement of its operations, than they have ever been since.

The next insinuation is, that the Bank has refused specie payments. This, if true, is a violation of the charter. But there is not the least probability of its truth; because, if such had been the fact, the individual to whom payment was refused, would have had an interest in making it public, by suing for the damages to which the charter entitles him. Yet no such thing has been done; and the strong presumption is, that the insinuation is false and groundless.

From this to the end of the resolution, there is nothing that merits attention—I therefore drop the particular examination of it.

By a general view of the resolution, it will be seen that a

principal object of the committee is, to examine into, and ferret out, a mass of corruption, supposed to have been committed by the commissioners who apportioned the stock of the Bank. I believe it is universally understood and acknowledged, that all men will ever act correctly, unless they have a motive to do otherwise. If this be true, we can only suppose that the commissioners acted corruptly, by also supposing that they were bribed to do so. Taking this view of the subject, I would ask if the Bank is likely to find it more difficult to bribe the committee of seven, which we are about to appoint, than it may have found it to bribe the commissioners?

(Here Mr. Linder called to order. The Chair decided that Mr. Lincoln was not out of order. Mr. Linder appealed to the House;—but, before the question was put, withdrew his appeal, saying, he preferred to let the gentleman go on; he thought he would break his own neck. Mr. Lincoln proceeded:)—

Another *gracious condescension.* I acknowledge it with gratitude. I know I was not out of order; and I know every sensible man in the House knows it. I was not saying that the gentleman from Coles could be bribed, nor, on the other hand, will I say he could not. In that particular, I leave him where I found him. I was only endeavoring to show that there was at least as great a probability of *any* seven members that could be selected from this House, being bribed to act corruptly, as there was, that the twenty-four commissioners had been so bribed. By a reference to the ninth section of the Bank charter, it will be seen that those commissioners were John Tilson, Robert K. McLaughlin, Daniel Wann, A. G. S. Wight, John C. Riley, W. H. Davidson, Edward M. Wilson, Edward L. Pierson, Robert R. Green, Ezra Baker, Aquilla Wren, John Taylor, Samuel C. Christy, Edmund Roberts, Benjamin Godfrey, Thomas Mather, A. M. Jenkins, W. Linn, W. S. Gilman, Charles Prentice, Richard I. Hamilton, A. H. Buckner, W. F. Thornton, and Edmund D. Taylor.

These are twenty-four of the most respectable men in the State. Probably no twenty-four men could be selected in the State, with whom the people are better acquainted, or in whose honor and integrity, they would more readily place confidence. And I now repeat, that there is less probability that those men have been bribed and corrupted, than that *any* seven men, or rather any *six* men, that could be selected from the members of this House, might be so bribed and corrupted; even though they were headed and led on by "decided superiority" himself.

In all seriousness, I ask every reasonable man, if an issue be joined by these twenty-four commissioners, on the one part, and *any* other seven men, on the other part, and the whole depend upon the honor and integrity of the contending parties, to which party would the greatest degree of credit be due? Again: Another consideration is, that we have no right to make the examination. What I shall say upon this head I design exclusively for the law-loving and law-abiding part of the House. To those who claim omnipotence for the Legislature, and who in the plenitude of their assumed powers, are disposed to disregard the Constitution, law, good faith, moral right, and every thing else, I have not a word to say. But to the law-abiding part I say, examine the Bank charter, go examine the Constitution; go examine the acts that the General Assembly of this State has passed, and you will find just as much authority given in each and every of them, to compel the Bank to bring its coffers to this hall, and to pour their contents upon this floor, as to compel it to submit to this examination which this resolution proposes. Why, sir, the gentleman from Coles, the mover of this resolution, very lately denied on this floor, that the Legislature had any right to repeal, or otherwise meddle with its own acts, when those acts were made in the nature of contracts, and had been accepted and acted on by other parties. Now I ask, if this resolution does not propose, for this House alone, to do, what he, but the other day, denied the right of the whole Legislature to do? He must either abandon the position he then took, or he must now vote against his own resolution. It is no difference to me, and I presume but little to any one else, which he does.

I am by no means the special advocate of the Bank. I have long thought that it would be well for it to report its condition to the General Assembly, and that cases might occur, when it might be proper to make an examination of its affairs by a committee. Accordingly, during the last session, while a bill supplemental to the Bank charter, was pending before the House, I offered an amendment to the same, in these words: "The said corporation shall, at the next session of the General Assembly, and at each subsequent General Session, during the existence of its charter, report to the same the amount of debts due *from* said corporation; the amount of debts due *to* the same; the amount of specie in its vaults, and an account of all lands then owned by the same, and the amount for which such lands have been taken; and moreover, if said corporation shall at any time neglect or refuse to submit its books, papers, and all and everything necessary for a full and fair examination of its affairs, to any person or persons appointed by the General Assembly, for the purpose of making such examination, the said corporation shall forfeit its charter."

This amendment was negatived by a vote of 34 to 15. Eleven of the 34 who voted against it, are now members of this House; and though it would be out of order to call their names, I hope they will all recollect themselves, and not vote for this examination to be made without authority, inasmuch as they refused to reserve the authority when it was in their power to do so.

I have said that cases might occur, when an examination might be proper; but I do not believe any such case has now occurred; and if it has, I should still be opposed to making an examination without legal authority. I am opposed to encouraging that lawless and mobocratic spirit, whether in relation to the Bank or any thing else, which is already abroad in the land; and is spreading with rapid and fearful impetuosity, to the ultimate overthrow of every institution, or even moral principle, in which persons and property have hitherto found security.

But supposing we had the authority, I would ask what good can result from the examination? Can we declare the Bank unconstitutional, and compel it to cease operations? Can we compel it to desist from the abuses of its power, provided we find such abuses to exist? Can we repair the injuries which it may have done to individuals? Most certainly we can do none of these things. Why then shall we spend the public money in such employment? O, say the examiners, we can injure the credit of the Bank, if nothing else.—Please tell me, gentlemen, who will suffer most by that? You cannot injure, to any extent, the stockholders. They are men of wealth—of large capital; and consequently, beyond the power of fortune, or even the shafts of malice. But by injuring the credit of the Bank, you will depreciate the value of its paper in the hands of the honest and unsuspecting farmer and mechanic, and that is all you can do. But suppose you could effect your whole purpose; suppose you could wipe the Bank from existence, which is the grand *ultimatum* of the project, what would be the consequence? Why, sir, we should spend several thousand dollars of the public treasure in the operation, annihilate the currency of the State, render valueless in the hands of our people that reward of their former labors, and finally, be once more under the comfortable obligation of paying the Wiggins' loan, principal and interest.

If the student is interested in the political background of this speech, he should consult Albert J. Beveridge, Abraham Lincoln: 1809-1858, *Vol. I, chs. iv-v. Lincoln's speech was made in opposition to a resolution offered by Usher F. Linder, to institute an inquiry into the management of the State Bank. Lincoln's philosophy of law as developed from the particular issue under discussion and stated in the last five paragraphs should be compared with the theme of the Address, "The Perpetuation of Our Political Institutions." The "Shields from Randolph" alluded to in the speech, in friendly if somewhat ironical vein, is the same James Shields, Democratic politician, with whom Lincoln became involved during the summer of 1842 in a farcical challenge to a duel. (See "A Letter from the Lost Townships," August 27, 1842, et seq.)*

LETTER TO MISS MARY OWENS MAY 7, 1837

Springfield May 7 1837

Friend Mary

I have commenced two letters to send you before this, both of which displeased me before I got half done, and so I tore them up. The first I thought was'nt serious enough, and the second was on the other extreme. I shall send this, turn out as it may.

This thing of living in Springfield is rather a dull business after all, at least it is so to me. I am quite as lonesome here as [I?] ever was anywhere in my life. I have been spoken to by but one woman since I've been here, and should not have been by her, if she could have avoided it. I've never been to church yet, nor probably shall not be soon. I stay away because I am conscious I should not know how to behave myself.

I am often thinking about what we said of your coming to live at Springfield. I am afraid you would not be satisfied. There is a great deal of flourishing about in carriages here, which it would be your doom to see without shareing [*sic*] in it. You would have to be poor without the means of hiding your poverty. Do you believe you could bear that patiently? Whatever woman may cast her lot with mine, should any ever do so, it is my intention to do all in my power to make her happy and contented; and there is nothing I can immagine [*sic*], that would make me more unhappy than to fail in the effort. I know I should be much happier with you than the way I am, provided I saw no signs of discontent in you. What you have said to me may have been in jest, or I may have misunderstood it. If so, then let it be forgotten; if otherwise, I much wish you would think seriously before you decide. For my part I have already decided. What I have said I will most positively abide by, provided you wish it. My opinion is that you had better not do it. You have not been accustomed to hardship, and it may be more severe than you now immagine [*sic*]. I know you are capable of thinking correctly on any subject, and if you deliberate maturely upon this, before you decide, then I am willing to abide your decision.

You must write me a good long letter after you get this. You have nothing else to do, and though it might not seem interesting to you, after you had written it, it would be a good deal of company to me in this "busy wilderness". Tell your sister I dont want to hear any more about selling out and moving. That gives me the hypo whenever I think of it.

Yours &c—
Lincoln

Lincoln's vacillation, which has been perhaps too simply interpreted by some biographers as an effort to wriggle out of a compromising situation, is probably a quite sincere attempt to state his indecision. He wanted, and he did not want, Mary Owens. He admired certain qualities in her and wanted her companionship, but he could not contemplate the intimacy of marriage without misgivings. Lincoln's frankness illustrates his lack of taste, perhaps, but scarcely proves his intent to injure, and reveals a condition of mind hardly so abnormal as to require a psychiatric diagnosis of sexual inhibitions such as sometimes has been attempted. In the next letter immediately following, Lincoln's situation becomes as comical as it is serious. He did not know where he stood and was afraid that he would regret whatever developed. To find in this letter, as well as in the other letters to Mary, evidence that Lincoln was trifling with her affections requires a degree of animosity or naïveté which but few students of Lincoln have possessed.

LETTER TO MISS MARY OWENS AUGUST 16, 1837

Springfield Aug. 16th 1837

Friend Mary.

You will, no doubt, think it rather strange, that I should write you a letter on the same day on which we parted; and I can only account for it by supposing, that seeing you lately makes me think of you more than usual, while at our late meeting we had but few expressions of thoughts. You must know that I can not see you, or think of you, with entire indifference; and yet it may be, that you, are mistaken in regard to what my real feelings toward you are. If I knew you were not, I should not trouble you with this letter. Perhaps any other man would know enough without further information; but I consider it *my* peculiar right to plead ignorance, and your bounden duty to allow the plea. I want in all cases to do right; and most particularly so, in all cases with women. I want, at this particular time, more than anything else, to do right with you, and if I *knew* it would be doing right, as I rather suspect it would, to let you alone, I would do it. And for the purpose of making the matter as plain as possible, I now say, that you can now drop the subject, dismiss your thoughts (if you ever had any) from me forever, and leave this letter unanswered, without calling forth one accusing murmer [*sic*] from me. And I will even go further, and say, that if it will add any thing to your comfort, or peace of mind, to do so, it is my sincere wish that you should. Do not understand by this, that I wish to cut your acquaintance. I mean no such thing. What I do wish is, that our further acquaintance shall depend upon yourself. If such further acquaintance would contribute nothing to your happiness, I am sure it would not to mine. If you feel in any degree bound to me, I am now willing to release you, provided you wish it; while, on the other hand, I am willing, and even anxious to bind you faster, if I can be convinced that it will, in any considerable degree, add to your happiness. This, indeed, is the whole question with me. Nothing would make me more miserable than to believe you miserable—nothing more happy, than to know you were so.

In what I have now said, I think I can not be misunderstood; and to make myself understood, is the only object of this letter.

If it suits you best to not answer this—farewell—a long life and a merry one attend you. But if you conclude to write back, speak as plainly as I do. There can be neither harm nor danger, in saying, to me, anything you think, just in the manner you think it.

My respects to your sister.

Your friend
Lincoln

THE PERPETUATION OF OUR POLITICAL INSTITUTIONS: ADDRESS BEFORE THE YOUNG MEN'S LYCEUM OF SPRINGFIELD, ILLINOIS JANUARY 27, 1838

As a subject for the remarks of the evening, *the perpetuation of our political institutions*, is selected.

In the great journal of things happening under the sun, we, the American People, find our account running, under date of the nineteenth century of the Christian era.—We find ourselves in the peaceful possession, of the fairest portion of the earth, as regards extent of territory, fertility of soil, and salubrity of climate. We find ourselves under the government of a system of political institutions, conducing more essentially to the ends of civil and religious liberty, than any of which the history of former times tells us. We, when mounting the stage of existence, found ourselves the legal inheritors of these fundamental blessings. We toiled not in the acquirement or establishment of them—they are a legacy bequeathed us, by a *once* hardy, brave, and patriotic, but *now* lamented and departed race of ancestors. Their's was the task (and nobly they performed it) to possess themselves, and through themselves, us, of this goodly land; and to uprear upon its hills and its valleys, a political edifice of liberty and equal rights; 'tis ours only, to transmit these, the former, unprofaned by the foot of an invader; the latter, undecayed by the lapse of time and untorn by usurpation, to the latest generation that fate shall permit the world to know. This task gratitude to our fathers, justice to ourselves, duty to posterity, and love for our species in general, all imperatively require us faithfully to perform.

How then shall we perform it?—At what point shall we expect the approach of danger? By what means shall we fortify against it?—Shall we expect some transatlantic military giant, to step the Ocean, and crush us at a blow? Never!—All the armies of Europe, Asia and Africa combined, with all the treasure of the earth (our own excepted) in their military chest; with a Buonaparte for a commander, could not by force, take a drink from the Ohio, or make a track on the Blue Ridge, in a trial of a thousand years.

At what point then is the approach of danger to be expected? I answer, if it ever reach us, it must spring up amongst us. It cannot come from abroad. If destruction be our lot, we must ourselves be its author and finisher. As a nation of freemen, we must live through all time, or die by suicide.

I hope I am over wary; but if I am not, there is, even now, something of ill-omen, amongst us. I mean the increasing disregard for law which pervades the country; the growing disposition to substitute the wild and furious passions, in lieu of the sober judgment of Courts; and the worse than savage mobs, for the executive ministers of justice. This disposition is awfully fearful in any community; and that it now exists in ours, though grating to our feelings to admit, it would be a violation of truth, and an insult to our intelligence, to deny. Accounts of outrages committed by mobs, form the every-day news of the times. They have pervaded the country, from New England to Louisiana;—they are neither peculiar to the eternal snows of the former, nor the burning suns of the latter;—they are not the creature of climate—neither are they confined to the slave-holding, or the non-slave-holding States. Alike, they spring up among the pleasure hunting masters of Southern slaves, and the order loving citizens of the land of steady habits.—Whatever, then, their cause may be, it is common to the whole country.

It would be tedious, as well as useless, to recount the horrors of all of them. Those happening in the State of Mississippi, and at St. Louis, are, perhaps, the most dangerous in example and revolting to humanity. In the Mississippi case, they first commenced by hanging the regular gamblers; a set of men, certainly not following for a livelihood, a very useful, or very honest occupation; but one which, so far from being forbidden by the laws, was actually licensed by an act of the Legislature, passed but a single year before. Next, negroes, suspected of conspiring to raise an insurrection, were caught up and hanged in all parts of the State: then, white men, supposed to be leagued with the negroes; and finally, strangers, from neighboring States, going thither on business, were, in many instances subjected to the same fate. Thus went on this process of hanging, from gamblers to negroes, from negroes to white citizens, and from these to strangers; till, dead men were seen literally dangling from the boughs of trees upon every road side; and in numbers almost sufficient, to rival the native Spanish moss of the country, as a drapery of the forest.

Turn, then, to that horror-striking scene at St. Louis. A single victim was only sacrificed there. His story is very short; and is, perhaps, the most highly tragic, of anything of its length, that has ever been witnessed in real life. A mulatto man, by the name of McIntosh, was seized in the street, dragged to the suburbs of the city, chained to a tree, and actually burned to death; and all within a single hour from the time he had been a freeman, attending to his own business, and at peace with the world.

Such are the effects of mob law; and such are the scenes, becoming more and more frequent in this land so lately famed for love of law and order; and the stories of which, have even now grown too familiar, to attract any thing more, than an idle remark.

But you are, perhaps, ready to ask, "What has this to do with the perpetuation of our political institutions?" I answer, it has much to do with it. Its direct consequences are, comparatively speaking, but a small evil; and much of its danger consists, in the proneness of our minds, to regard its direct, as its only consequences. Abstractly considered, the hanging of the gamblers at Vicksburg, was of but little consequence. They constitute a portion of population, that is worse than useless in any community; and their death, if no pernicious example be set by it, is never matter of reasonable regret with any one. If they were annually swept, from the stage of existence, by the plague or small pox, honest men would, perhaps, be much profited, by the operation.—Similar too, is the correct reasoning, in regard to the burning of the negro at St. Louis. He had forfeited his life, by the perpetration of an outrageous murder, upon one of the most worthy and respectable citizens of the city; and had he not died as he did, he must have died by the sentence of the law, in a very short time afterwards. As to him alone, it was as well the way it was, as it could otherwise have been.—But the example in either case, was fearful.—When men take it in their heads to day, to hang gamblers, or burn murderers, they should recollect, that, in the confusion usually attending such transactions, they will be as likely to hang or burn some one who is neither a gambler nor a murderer as one who is; and that, acting upon the example they set, the mob of to-morrow, may, and probably will, hang or burn some of them by the very same mistake. And not only so; the innocent, those who have ever set their faces against violations of law in every shape, alike with the guilty, fall victims to the ravages of mob law; and thus it goes on, step by step, till all the walls erected for the defence of the persons and property of individuals, are trodden down, and disregarded. But all this even, is not the full extent of the evil.—By such examples, by instances of the perpetrators of such acts going unpunished, the lawless in spirit, are encouraged to become lawless in practice; and having been used to no restraint, but dread of punishment, they thus become, absolutely unrestrained.—Having ever regarded Government as their deadliest bane, they make a jubilee of the suspension of its operations; and pray for nothing so much, as its total annihilation. While, on the other hand, good men, men who love tranquility, who desire to abide by the laws, and enjoy their benefits, who would gladly spill their blood in the defence of their country; seeing their property destroyed; their families insulted, and their lives endangered; their persons injured; and seeing nothing in prospect that forebodes a change for the better; become tired of, and disgusted with, a Government that offers them no protection; and are not much averse to a change in which they imagine they have nothing to lose. Thus, then, by the operation of this mobocratic spirit, which all must admit, is now abroad in the land, the strongest bulwark of any Government, and particularly of those constituted like ours, may effectually be broken down and destroyed—I mean the *attachment* of the People. Whenever this effect shall be produced among us; whenever the vicious portion of population shall be permitted to gather in bands of hundreds and thousands, and burn churches, ravage and rob provision-stores, throw printing presses into rivers, shoot editors, and hang and burn obnoxious persons at pleasure, and with impunity; depend on it, this Government cannot last. By such things, the feelings of the best citizens will become more or less alienated from it; and thus it will be left without friends, or with too few, and those few too weak, to make their friendship effectual. At such a time and under such circumstances, men of sufficient talent and ambition will not be wanting to seize the opportunity, strike the blow, and overturn that fair fabric, which for the last half century, has been the fondest hope, of the lovers of freedom, throughout the world.

I know the American People are *much* attached to their Government;—I know they would suffer *much* for its sake;—I know they would endure evils long and patiently, before they would ever think of exchanging it for another. Yet, notwithstanding all this, if the laws be continually despised and disregarded, if their rights to be secure in their persons and property, are held by no better tenure than the caprice of a mob, the alienation of their affections from the Government is the natural consequence; and to that, sooner or later, it must come.

Here then, is one point at which danger may be expected.

The question recurs, "how shall we fortify against it?" The answer is simple. Let every American, every lover of liberty, every well wisher to his posterity, swear by the blood of the Revolution, never to violate in the least particular, the laws of the country;

and never to tolerate their violation by others. As the patriots of seventy-six did to the support of the Declaration of Independence, so to the support of the Constitution and Laws, let every American pledge his life, his property, and his sacred honor;—let every man remember that to violate the law, is to trample on the blood of his father, and to tear the character of his own, and his children's liberty. Let reverence for the laws, be breathed by every American mother, to the lisping babe, that prattles on her lap—let it be taught in schools, in seminaries, and in colleges; let it be written in Primers, spelling books, and in Almanacs;—let it be preached from the pulpit, proclaimed in legislative halls, and enforced in courts of justice. And, in short, let it become the *political religion* of the nation; and let the old and the young, the rich and the poor, the grave and the gay, of all sexes and tongues, and colors and conditions, sacrifice unceasingly upon its altars.

While ever a state of feeling, such as this, shall universally, or even, very generally prevail throughout the nation, vain will be every effort, and fruitless every attempt, to subvert our national freedom.

When I so pressingly urge a strict observance of all the laws, let me not be understood as saying there are no bad laws, nor that grievances may not arise, for the redress of which, no legal provisions have been made.—I mean to say no such thing. But I do mean to say, that, although bad laws, if they exist, should be repealed as soon as possible, still while they continue in force, for the sake of example, they should be religiously observed. So also in unprovided cases. If such arise, let proper legal provisions be made for them with the least possible delay; but, till then, let them, if not too intolerable, be borne with.

There is no grievance that is a fit object of redress by mob law. In any case that arises, as for instance, the promulgation of abolitionism, one of two positions is necessarily true; that is, the thing is right within itself, and therefore deserves the protection of all law and all good citizens; or, it is wrong, and therefore proper to be prohibited by legal enactments; and in neither case, is the interposition of mob law, either necessary, justifiable, or excusable.

But, it may be asked, why suppose danger to our political institutions? Have we not preserved them for more than fifty years? And why may we not for fifty times as long?

We hope there is *no sufficient* reason. We hope all dangers may be overcome; but to conclude that no danger may ever arise, would itself be extremely dangerous. There are now, and will hereafter be, many causes, dangerous in their tendency, which have not existed heretofore; and which are not too insignificant to merit attention. That our government should have been maintained in its original form from its establishment until now, is not much to be wondered at. It had many props to support it through that period, which now are decayed, and crumbled away. Through that period, it was felt by all, to be an undecided experiment; now, it is understood to be a successful one.—Then, all that sought celebrity and fame, and distinction, expected to find them in the success of that experiment. Their *all* was staked upon it:—their destiny was *inseparably* linked with it. Their ambition aspired to display before an admiring world, a practical demonstration of the truth of a proposition, which had hitherto been considered, at best no better, than problematical; namely, *the capability of a people to govern themselves*. If they succeeded, they were to be immortalized; their names were to be transferred to counties and cities, and rivers and mountains; and to be revered and sung, and toasted through all time. If they failed, they were to be called knaves and fools, and fanatics for a fleeting hour; then to sink and be forgotten. They succeeded. The experiment is successful; and thousands have won their deathless names in making it so. But the game is caught; and I believe it is true, that with the catching, end the pleasures of the chase. This field of glory is harvested, and the crop is already appropriated. But new reapers will arise, and *they*, too, will seek a field. It is to deny, what the history of the world tells us is true, to suppose that men of ambition and talents will not continue to spring up amongst us. And, when they do, they will as naturally seek the gratification of their ruling passion, as others have so done before them. The question then, is, can that gratification be found in supporting and maintaining an edifice that has been erected by others? Most certainly it cannot. Many great and good men sufficiently qualified for any task they should undertake, may ever be found, whose ambition would aspire to nothing beyond a seat in Congress, a gubernatorial or a presidential chair; *but such belong not to the family of the lion, or the tribe of the eagle.* What! think you these places would satisfy an Alexander, a Caesar, or a Napoleon?—Never! Towering genius disdains a beaten path. It seeks regions hitherto unexplored.—It sees *no distinction* in adding story to story, upon the monuments of fame, erected to the memory of others. It *denies* that it is glory enough to serve under any chief. It *scorns* to tread in the footsteps of *any* predecessor, however illustrious. It thirsts and burns for distinction; and, if possible, it will have it, whether at the expense of emancipating slaves, or enslaving freemen. Is it unreasonable then to expect, that some man possessed of the loftiest genius, coupled with ambition sufficient to push it to its utmost stretch, will at some time, spring up among us? And when such a one does, it will require the people to be united with each other, attached to the government and laws, and generally intelligent, to successfully frustrate his designs.

Distinction will be his paramount object, and although he would as willingly, perhaps more so, acquire it by doing good as harm; yet, that opportunity being past, and nothing left to be done in the way of building up, he would set boldly to the task of pulling down.

Here then, is a probable case, highly dangerous, and such a one as could not have well existed heretofore.

Another reason which *once was*; but which, to the same extent, is *now no more*, has done much in maintaining our institutions thus far. I mean the powerful influence which the interesting scenes of the revolution had upon the *passions* of the people as distinguished from their judgment. By this influence, the jealousy, envy, and avarice, incident to our nature, and so common to a state of peace, prosperity, and conscious strength, were, for the time, in a great measure smothered and rendered inactive; while the deep-rooted principles of *hate*, and the powerful motive of *revenge*, instead of being turned against each other, were directed exclusively against the British nation. And thus, from the force of circumstances, the basest principles of our nature, were either made to lie dormant, or to become the active agents in the advancement of the noblest of cause—that of establishing and maintaining civil and religious liberty.

But this state of feeling *must fade, is fading, has faded,* with the circumstances that produced it.

I do not mean to say, that the scenes of the revolution *are now* or *ever will* be entirely forgotten; but that like every thing else, they must fade upon the memory of the world, and grow more and more dim by the lapse of time. In history, we hope, they will be read of, and recounted, so long as the bible shall be read;—but even granting that they will, their influence *cannot be* what it heretofore has been. Even then, they *cannot be* so universally known, nor so vividly felt, as they were by the generation just gone to rest. At the close of that struggle, nearly every adult male had been a participator in some of its scenes. The consequence was, that of those scenes, in the form of a husband, a father, a son or a brother, *a living history* was to be found in every family—a history bearing the indubitable testimonies of its own authenticity, in the limbs mangled, in the scars of wounds received, in the midst of the very scenes related—a history, too, that could be read and understood alike by all, the wise and the ignorant, the learned and the unlearned.—But *those* histories are gone. They *can* be read no more forever. They *were* a fortress of strength; but, what invading foeman could *never do,* the silent artillery of time *has done*; the leveling of its walls. They are gone.—They *were* a forest of giant oaks; but the all-resistless hurricane has swept over them, and left only, here and there, a lonely trunk, despoiled of its verdure, shorn of its foliage; unshading and unshaded, to murmur in a few more gentle breezes, and to combat with its mutilated limbs, a few more ruder storms, then to sink, and be no more.

They *were* the pillars of the temple of liberty; and now, that they have crumbled away, that temple must fall, unless we, their descendants, supply their places with other pillars, hewn from the solid quarry of sober reason. Passion has helped us; but can do so no more. It will in future be our enemy. Reason, cold, calculating, unimpassioned reason, must furnish all the materials for our future support and defence.—Let those materials be moulded into *general intelligence, sound morality,* and, in particular, *a reverence for the constitution and laws*: and, that we improved to the last; that we remained free to the last; that we revered his name to the last; that, during his long sleep, we permitted no hostile foot to pass over or desecrate his resting place; shall be that which to learn the last trump shall awaken our WASHINGTON.

Upon these let the proud fabric of freedom rest, as the rock of its basis; and as truly as has been said of the only greater institution, "*the gates of hell shall not prevail against it.*"

Critical estimates of this address have varied considerably. Herndon terms it "highly sophomoric"; Beveridge concludes that it was "the most notable of his life thus far and, in fact, for many years thereafter"; James Weber Linn, in "Such Were His Words" (Abraham Lincoln Association Papers), *claims that the third paragraph from the last was never surpassed by anything Lincoln ever wrote. Perhaps the central paragraphs are most significant, if not for rhetoric, certainly for philosophy of government, for in them the student may trace Lincoln's reasoning in regard to how American political institutions may be preserved and yet modified by the people to rectify errors in the structure of justice. This central philosophy Lincoln held consistently, as his later writings testify.*

LETTER TO MRS. O. H. BROWNING
APRIL 1, 1838

Springfield, April 1. 1838—

Dear Madam:

Without appologising [*sic*] for being egotistical, I shall make the history of so much of my own life, as has elapsed since I saw you, the subject of this letter. And by the way I now discover, that in order to give a full and inteligible [*sic*] account of the things I have done and suffered *since* I saw you, I shall necessarily have to relate some that happened *before.*

It was, then, in the autumn of 1836, that a married lady of my acquaintance, and who was a great friend of mine, being about to pay a visit to her father and other relatives residing in Kentucky, proposed to me, that on her return she would bring a sister of hers with her, upon condition that I would engage to become her brother-in-law with all convenient dispach [*sic*]. I, of course, accepted the proposal; for you know I could not have done otherwise, had I really been averse to it; but privately, between you and me, I was most confoundedly well pleased with the project. I had seen the said sister some three years before, thought her inteligent [*sic*] and agreeable, and saw no good objection to plodding life through hand in hand with her. Time passed on, the lady took her journey, and in due time returned, sister in company sure enough. This stomached me a little; for it appeared to me, that her coming so readily showed that she was a trifle too willing; but on reflection it occured [*sic*] to me, that she might have been prevailed on by her married sister to come, without any thing concerning me ever having been mentioned to her; and so I concluded that if no other objection presented itself, I would consent to waive this. All this occurred to me upon my *hearing* of her arrival in the neighborhood; for, be it remembered, I had not yet *seen* her, except about three years previous, as before mentioned.

In a few days we had an interview, and although I had seen her before, she did not look as my immagination [*sic*] had pictured her. I knew she was over-size, but she now appeared a fair match for Falstaff; I knew she was called an "old maid," and I felt no doubt of the truth of at least half of the appelation [*sic*]; but now, when I beheld her, I could not for my life avoid thinking of my mother; and this, not from withered features, for her skin was too full of fat to permit of its contracting in to wrinkles; but from her want of teeth, weather-beaten appearance in general, and from a kind of notion that ran in my head, that *nothing* could have commenced at the size of infancy, and reached her present bulk in less than thirty-five or forty years; and, in short, I was not all pleased with her. But what could I do?—I had told her sister that I would take her for better or for worse; and I made a point of honor and conscience in all things, to stick to my word, especially if others had been induced to act on it, which in this case, I doubted not they had, for I was now fairly convinced, that no other man on earth would have her, and hence the conclusion that they were bent on holding me to my bargain. Well, thought I, I have said it, and, be consequences what they may, it shall not be my fault if I fail to do it. At once I determined to consider her my wife; and this done, all my powers of discovery were put to the rack, in search of perfections in her, which might be fairly set-off against her defects. I tried to immagine [*sic*] she was handsome, which, but for her unfortunate corpulency, was actually true. Exclusive of this, no woman that I have ever seen, has a finer face. I also tried to convince myself, that the mind was much more to be valued than the person; and in this, she was not inferior, as I could discover, to any with whom I had been acquainted.

Shortly after this, without attempting to come to any positive understanding with her, I set out for Vandalia, where and when you first saw me. During my stay there, I had letters from her, which did not change my opinion of either her intellect or intention; but on the contrary, confirmed it in both.

All this while, although I was fixed "firm as the surge repelling rock" in my resolution, I found I was continually repenting the rashness which had led me to make it. Through life I have been in no bondage, either real or imaginary, from the thraldom of which I so much desired to be free. After my return home, I saw nothing to change my opinion of her in any particular. She was the same and so was I. I now spent my time between planing [*sic*] how I might get along through life after my contemplated change of circumstances should have taken place; and how I might procrastinate the evil day for a time, which I really dreaded as much—perhaps more, than an irishman [*sic*] does the halter.

After all my suffering upon this deeply interesting subject, here I am, wholly unexpectedly, completely out of the "scrape"; and I now want to know, if you can guess how I got out of it. Out clear in every sense of the term; no violation of word, honor or conscience. I dont believe you can guess, and so I might as well tell you at once. As the lawyers say, it was done in the manner following, towit. After I had delayed the matter as long as I thought I could in honor do, which by the way had brought me round into the last fall, I concluded I might as well bring it to a consumation [*sic*] without further delay; and so I mustered my resolution, and made the proposal to her direct; but, shocking to relate, she answered, No. At first I supposed she did it through an affectation of modesty, which I thought but ill-became her, under the peculiar circumstances of her case; but on my renewal of the charge, I found she repeled [*sic*] it with greater firmness than before. I tried it again and again, but with the same success, or rather with the same want of success.

I finally was forced to give it up, at which I very unexpectedly found myself mortified almost beyond endurance. I was mortified, it seemed to me, in a hundred different ways. My vanity was deeply wounded by the reflections, that I had so long been too stupid to discover her intentions, and at the same time never doubting that I understood them perfectly; and also, that she whom I had taught myself to believe nobody else would have, had actually rejected me with all my fancied greatness; and to cap the whole, I then, for the first time, began to suspect that I was really a little in love with her. But let it all go. I'll try and out live it. Others have been made fools of by the girls; but this can never with truth be said of me. I most emphatically, in this instance, made a fool of myself. I have now come to the conclusion never again to think of marrying, and for this reason; I can never be satisfied with any one who would be block-head enough to have me.

When you receive this, write me a long yarn about something to amuse me. Give my respects to Mr. Browning.

Your sincere friend

A. Lincoln

Mrs. O. H. Browning—

Lincoln's sense of the ridiculous and his ability to recognize the grotesque humor in his own actions—from a distance of several months—are not sufficient to account for this letter. That he enjoyed writing it is obvious from its gusto, but why he wrote to Mrs. Browning is difficult to conjecture. If there was any other correspondence between them, there is no record of it. That she was Lincoln's confidante is a conclusion hardly justified by any other evidence of this period, though there is evidence that from early to late Lincoln always enjoyed her company. Some have assumed that he merely had a story to tell and had to get it off his chest. One needs to confess one's vanity, stupidity, and emotional vagaries occasionally perhaps. But to whom? Although the actual record shows very little, it is difficult to escape the inference from this manuscript that Lincoln and Mrs. Browning enjoyed a mutual retailing of small talk, in conversation at least, if not in letters, during the considerable period of years in which Lincoln and Browning were more or less continually associated in common political activities. Like the letter to Mary Speed it suggests, as do the letters to Mary Owens, a desire for feminine associations which are definitely social rather than romantic.

THE SUB-TREASURY: SPEECH AT A POLITICAL DISCUSSION IN THE HALL OF THE HOUSE OF REPRESENTATIVES AT SPRINGFIELD, ILLINOIS DECEMBER [26], 1839

Fellow-Citizens:

It is peculiarly embarrassing to me to attempt a continuance of the discussion, on this evening, which has been conducted in this Hall on several preceding ones. It is so, because on each of those evenings, there was a much fuller attendance than now, without any reason for its being so, except the greater *interest* the community feel in the *Speakers* who addressed them *then*, than they do in *him* who is to do so *now*. I am, indeed, apprehensive, that the few who have attended, have done so, more to spare me of mortification, than in the hope of being interested in any thing I may be able to say.—This circumstance casts a damp upon my spirits, which I am sure I shall be unable to overcome during the evening. But enough of preface.

The subject heretofore, and now to be discussed, is the Sub-Treasury scheme of the present Administration, as a means of collecting, safe-keeping, transferring, and disbursing the revenues of the Nation, as contrasted with a National Bank for the same purposes. Mr. Douglas has said that we (the Whigs) have not dared to meet them, (the Locos.) in argument on this question. I protest against this assertion. I say that we have again and again, during this discussion, urged facts and arguments against the Sub-Treasury, which they have neither dared to deny nor attempted to answer. But lest some may be led to believe that we really wish to avoid the question, I now propose, in my humble way, to urge those arguments again; at the same time, begging the audience to mark well the positions I shall take, and the proof I shall offer to sustain them, and that they will not again permit Mr. Douglas or his friends, to escape the force of them, by a round and groundless assertion, that we "dare not meet them in argument."

Of the Sub-Treasury then, as contrasted with a National Bank, for the before enumerated purposes, I lay down the following propositions, to wit:

1st. It will injuriously affect the community by its operation on the circulating medium.

2d. It will be a more expensive fiscal agent.

3d. It will be a less secure depository for the public money.

To show the truth of the first proposition, let us take a short review of our condition under the operation of a National Bank. It was the depository of the public revenues.—Between the collection of those revenues and the disbursements of them by the government, the Bank was permitted to, and did actually loan them out to individuals, and hence the large amount of money annually collected for revenue purposes, which by any other plan would have been idle, a great portion of time, was kept almost constantly in circulation. Any person who will reflect, that money is only valuable while in circulation, will readily perceive, that any device which will keep the government revenues, in constant circulation, instead of being locked up in idleness, is no inconsiderable advantage.

By the Sub-Treasury, the revenue is to be collected, and kept in iron boxes until the government wants it for disbursement; thus robbing the people of the use of it, while the government does not itself need it, and while the money is performing no nobler office than that of rusting in iron boxes. The natural effect of this change of policy, every one will see, is to reduce the quantity of money in circulation.

But again, by the Sub-Treasury scheme the revenue is to be collected in specie. I anticipate that this will be disputed. I expect to hear it said, that it is not the policy of the Administration to collect the revenue in specie. If it shall, I reply, that Mr. Van Buren, in his message recommended the Sub-Treasury, expended nearly a column of that document in an attempt to persuade Congress to provide for the collection of the revenue in specie exclusively; and he concluded with these words. "It may be safely assumed, that no motive of *convenience* to the *citizen*, requires the reception of Bank paper." In addition to this, Mr. Silas Wright, Senator from New York, and the political, personal and confidential friend of Mr. Van Buren, drafted and introduced into the Senate the first Sub-Treasury Bill, and that bill provided for ultimately collecting the revenue in specie. It is true, I know, that that clause was stricken from the bill, but it was done by the votes of the Whigs, aided by a portion only of the Van Buren Senators.—No Sub-Treasury bill has yet become a law, though two or three have been considered by Congress, some with and some without the specie clause; so that I admit there is room for quibbling upon the question of whether the Administration favor the exclusive specie doctrine or not; but I take it, that the fact that the President at first urged the specie doctrine, and that under his recommendation the first bill introduced embraced it, warrants us in charging it as the policy of the party until their head as publicly recants it, as he at first espoused it.—I repeat then, that by the Sub-Treasury, the revenue is to be collected in *specie*. Now mark what the effect of this must be. By all estimates ever made, there are but between 60 and 80 millions of specie in the United States. The expenditures of the Government for the year 1838, the last for which we have had the report, were 40 millions. Thus it is seen, that if the whole revenue be collected in specie, it will take more than half of all the specie in the nation to do it. By this means, more than half of all the specie belonging to the fifteen million of souls, who compose the whole population of the country, is thrown into the hands of the public office-holders, and other public creditors, composing in number perhaps not more than one quarter of a million; leaving the other fourteen millions and three quarters to get along as they best can, with less than one half of the specie of the country, and whatever rags, and shin-plasters they may be able to put, and keep, in circulation. By this means, every office-holder, and other public creditor may, and most likely will, set up shaver; and a most glorious harvest will the specie men have of it; each specie man, upon a fair division, having to his share, the fleecing of about 59 rag-men.*—In all candor, let me ask, was such a system for bene-

* On January 4, 1839, the Senate of the United States passed the following resolution, to wit:

fiting the few at the expense of the many, ever before devised? And was the sacred name of Democracy, ever before made to endorse such an enormity against the rights of the people?

I have already said that the Sub-Treasury will reduce the quantity of money in circulation. This position is strengthened by the recollection that the revenue is to be collected in specie, so that the mere amount of revenue is not all that is withdrawn, but the amount of paper circulation that the 40 millions would serve to as a basis, is withdrawn; which would be in a sound state at least

---

"*Resolved*, That the Secretary of the Treasury be directed to communicate to the Senate any information he may recently have received in respect to the mode of collecting, keeping, and disbursing public moneys in foreign countries."

Under this resolution, the Secretary communicated to the Senate a letter, the following extract from which clearly shows that the collection of the revenue in *specie* will establish a sound currency for the office-holders, and a depreciated one for the people; and that the office-holders and other public creditors will turn shavers upon all the rest of the community. Here is the extract from the letter, being all of it that relates to the question:

"Hague, October 12, 1838.

"The financial system of Hamburg is, as far as is known, very simple, as may be supposed from so small a territory. The whole amount of Hamburg coined money is about four and a half millions of marks current, or one million two hundred and eighty-two thousand five hundred dollars; and, except under very extraordinary circumstances, *not more than one half that amount is in circulation*, and all duties, taxes, and excise must be paid in Hamburg currency. *The consequence is that it invariably commands a premium of one to three per centum.* Every year one senator and ten citizens are appointed to transact the whole of the financial concern, both as to receipt and disbursement of the funds, *which is always in cash*, and is every day deposited in the bank, to the credit of the chancery; and, on being paid out, the citizen to whose department the payment belongs must appear personally with the check or order, stating the amount and to whom to be paid. The person receiving very seldom keeps the money, *preferring to dispose of it to a money-changer at a premium*, and taking other coin at a discount, of which there is a great variety and a large amount constantly in circulation, and on which in his daily payment *he loses nothing*; and those who have payments to make to the government apply to the *money-changers again for Hamburg currency*, which keeps it in constant motion, and I believe it frequently occurs that the bags, which are sealed and labeled with the amount, are returned again to the bank without being opened.

"With great respect, your obedient servant,

"John Cuthbert."

"To the Hon. Levi Woodbury,
"Secretary of the Treasury,
Washington, D.C."

This letter is found in Senate documents, p. 113 of the session of 1838-9 [Lincoln's note].

100 millions.—When 100 millions, or more, of the circulation we now have, shall be withdrawn, who can contemplate, without terror, the distress, ruin, bankruptcy and beggary, that must follow?

The man who has purchased any article, say a horse, on credit, at 100 dollars, when there are 200 millions circulating in the country, if the quantity be reduced to 100 millions by the arrival of pay-day, will find the horse but sufficient to pay half the debt; and the other half must either be paid out of his other means, and thereby become a clear loss to him, or go unpaid, and thereby become a clear loss to his creditor. What I have here said of a single case of the purchase of a horse, will hold good in every case of a debt existing at the time a reduction in the quantity of money occurs, by whomsoever, and for whatsoever it may have been contracted. It may be said that what the debtor loses, the creditor gains by this operation—but on examination this will be found true only to a very limited extent. It is more generally true, that *all* lose by it.—The *creditor*, by losing more of his debts, than he gains by the increased value of those he collects; the *debtor* by either parting with more of his property to pay his debts, than he received in contracting them; or, by entirely breaking up in his business, and thereby being thrown upon the world in idleness.

The general distress thus created, will, to be sure, be *temporary*; because whatever change may occur in the quantity of money in any community, *time* will adjust the derangement produced; but while that adjustment is progressing, all suffer more or less, and very many lose everything that renders life desirable. Why then, shall we suffer a severe difficulty, even though it be ***but temporary***, unless we receive some equivalent for it?

What I have been saying as to the effect produced by a reduction of the quantity of money, relates to the *whole* country. I now propose to show, that it would produce a *peculiar* and *permanent* hardship upon the citizens of those States and Territories in which the public lands lie. The Land Officers in those States and Territories, as all know, form the great gulf by which all, or nearly all the money in them, is swallowed up. When the quantity of money shall be reduced, and consequently every thing under individual control brought down in proportion, the price of those lands, being fixed by law, will remain as now. Of necessity it will follow, that the *produce* or *labor* that *now* raises money sufficient to purchase 80 acres, will *then* raise but sufficient to purchase 40, or perhaps not that much.—And this difficulty and hardship, will last as long, in some degree, as any portion of these lands shall remain undisposed of. Knowing, as I well do, the difficulty that poor people *now* encounter in procuring homes, I hesitate not to say, that when the price of the public lands shall be doubled or trebled; or, which is the same thing, produce and labor cut down to one half, or one third of their present prices, it will be little less than impossible for them to procure those homes at all.

In answer to what I have said as to the effect the Sub-Treasury would have upon the currency, it is often urged that the money collected for revenue purposes will *not lie idle* in the vaults of the Treasury; and, farther, that a National Bank produces greater derangement in the currency, by a system of contractions and expansions, than the Sub-Treasury would produce in any way. In reply, I need only show, that experience proves the contrary of both these propositions. It is an undisputed fact, that the late Bank of the United States paid the government $75,000 annually, for the *privilege* of using the public money between the times of its collection and disbursement. Can any man suppose, that the Bank would have paid this sum, annually for twenty years, and then offered to renew its obligations to do so, if in reality there was no *time* intervening between the collection and disbursement of the revenue, and consequently no privilege of *using* the money extended to it?

Again, as to the contractions and expansions of a National Bank, I need only point to the period intervening between the time that the late Bank got into successful operation and that at which the Government commenced war upon it, to show that during that period, no such contractions or expansions took place. If before, or after that period, derangement occurred in the currency, it proves nothing. The Bank could not be expected to regulate the currency, either *before* it got into successful operation or *after* it was crippled and thrown into death convulsions, by the removal of the deposits from it, and other hostile measures of the Government, against it. We do not pretend that a National Bank can establish and maintain a sound and uniform state of currency in the country in *spite* of the National Government; but we do say, that it has established and maintained such a currency, and can do so again, by the *aid* of that Government; and we further say, that no duty is more imperative on that Government, than the duty it owes the people, of furnishing them a sound and uniform currency.

I now leave the proposition as to the effect of the Sub-Treasury upon the currency of the country, and pass to that relative to the additional *expense* which must be incurred by it over that incurred by a National Bank, as a fiscal agent of the Government. By the late National Bank, we had the public revenue received, safely kept, transferred and disbursed, not only without expense, but we actually received of the Bank $75,000 annually for its privileges, while rendering us those services. By the Sub-Treasury, according to the estimate of the Secretary of the Treasury, who is the warm advocate of the system and which estimate is the lowest made by any one, the same services are to cost $60,000. Mr. Rives, who, to say the least, is equally talented and honest, estimates that these services, under the Sub-Treasury system, cannot cost less than $600,000. For the sake of liberality, let us suppose that the estimates of the Secretary and Mr. Rives, are the two extremes, and that their mean is about the true estimate, and we shall then find, that when to that sum is added the $75,000 which the Bank paid us, the difference between the two systems, in favor of the Bank and against the Sub-Treasury, is $405,000 a year. This sum, though small when compared to the many millions annually expended by the General Government, is when viewed by itself, very large; and much too large, when viewed in any light, to be thrown away once a year for nothing. It is sufficient to pay the pensions of more than 4,000 Revolutionary Soldiers, or to purchase a 40 acre tract of Government land, for each one of more than 8,000 poor families.

To the argument against the Sub-Treasury, on the score of additional expense, its friends, so far as I know, attempt no answer. They choose, so far as I can learn, to treat the throwing away $405,000 once a year as a matter entirely too small to merit their democratic notice.

I now come to the proposition, that it would be less secure than a National Bank, as a depository of the public money. The experience of the past, I think, proves the truth of this. And here, inasmuch as I rely chiefly upon experience to establish it, let me ask, how is it that we know any thing—that any event will occur, that any combination of circumstances will produce a certain result—except by the analogies of past experience? What has once happened, will invariably happen again, when the same circumstances, which combined to produce it shall again combine in the same way. We all feel that we know that a blast of wind would extinguish the flame of the candle that stands by me. How do we know it? We have never seen this flame thus extinguished. We know it, because we have seen through all our lives, that a blast of wind extinguishes the flame of a candle whenever it is thrown fully upon it. Again, we all feel to *know* that we have to die.—How? We have never died yet. We know it, because we know, or at least think we know, that of all the beings, just like ourselves, who have been coming into the world for six thousand years, not one is now living who was here two hundred years ago.

I repeat, then, that we know nothing of what will happen in future, but by the analogy of experience, and that the fair analogy of past experience fully proves that the Sub-Treasury would be a less safe depository of the public money than a National Bank. Examine it.—By the Sub-Treasury scheme, the public money is to be kept, between the times of its collection and disbursement, by Treasurers of the Mint, Custom-house officers, Land officers, and some new officers to be appointed in the same way that those first enumerated are. Has a year passed, since the organization of the Government, that numerous defalcations have not occurred among this class of officers? Look at Swartwout with his $1,200,000, Price with his $75,000, Harris with his $109,000, Hawkins with his $100,000, Linn with his $55,000, together with some twenty-five hundred lesser lights. Place the public money again in these same hands, and will it not again go the same way? Most assuredly it will. But turn to the history of the National Bank in this country, and we shall there see, that those Banks performed the fiscal operations of the Government thro' a period of 40 years, received, safely kept, transferred, disbursed, an aggregate of nearly five hundred millions of dollars; and that, in all that time, and with all that money, not one dollar, nor one cent, did the Government lose by them. Place the public money again in a similar depository, and will it not again be safe?

But, conclusive as the experience of fifty years is, that individuals are unsafe depositories of the public money, and of forty years that National Banks are safe depositories, we are not left to rely solely upon that experience for the truth of those propositions.—If experience were silent upon the subject, conclusive reasons could be shown for the truth of them.

It is often urged that to say the public money will be more secure in a National Bank, than in the hands of individuals, as proposed in the Sub-Treasury, is to say, that Bank directors and Bank officers are more honest than sworn officers of the Government. Not so. We insist on no such thing. We say that public officers, selected with reference to their capacity and honesty, (which by the way, we deny is the practice in these days,) stand an equal chance, precisely, of being capable and honest, with Bank officers selected by the same rule.—We further say, that with however much care selections may be made, there will be some unfaithful and dishonest in both classes. The experience of the whole world, in all by-gone times, proves this true. The Saviour of the world chose twelve disciples, and even one of that small number, selected by super-human wisdom, turned out a traitor and a devil. And, it may not be improper here to add, that Judas carried the bag—was the Sub-Treasurer of the Saviour and his disciples.

We, then, do not say, nor need we say, to maintain our proposition, that Bank officers are more honest than Government officers, selected by the same rule. What we do say, is, that the *interest* of the Sub-Treasurer is *against his duty*—while the *interest* of the Bank is *on the side of its duty*.—Take instances—a Sub-Treasurer has in his hands one hundred thousand dollars of public money; his *duty* says,—"You ought to pay this money over"—but his *interest* says, "You ought to run away with this sum, and be a nabob the balance of your life." And who that knows any thing of human nature, doubts that, in many instances, interest will prevail over duty, and that the Sub-Treasurer will prefer opulent knavery in a foreign land, to honest poverty at home? But how different is it with a Bank. Besides the Government money deposited with it, it is doing business upon a large capital of its own. If it proves faithful to the Government, it continues its business, if unfaithful it forfeits its charter, breaks up its business, and thereby loses more than all it can make by seizing upon the Government funds in its possession. Its *interest*, therefore, is on the side of its duty—is to be faithful to the Government, and consequently, even the dishonest amongst its managers, have no temptation to be faithless to it. Even if robberies happen in the Bank, the losses are borne by the Bank, and the Government loses nothing. It is for this reason then, that we say a Bank is the more secure. It is because of that admirable feature in the Bank system, which places the *interest* and the *duty* of the depository both on one side; whereas that feature can never enter into the Sub-Treasury system. By the latter, the *interest* of the individuals keeping the public money, will wage an eternal war with their *duty*, and in very many instances must be victorious. In answer to the argument drawn from the fact that individual depositories of public money, have always proved unsafe, it is urged that, even if we had a National Bank, the money has to *pass through* the same individual hands, that it will under the Sub-Treasury. This is only partially true in fact, and wholly fallacious in argument.

It is only partially true, in fact, because by the Sub-Treasury bill, four Receivers-General are to be appointed by the President and Senate. These are new officers, and consequently, it cannot be true that the money, or any portion of it, has heretofore passed thro' their hands. These four new officers are to be located at New York, Boston, Charleston, and St. Louis, and consequently are to be depositories of all the money collected at or near those points; so that more than three-fourths of the public money will fall into the keeping of these four new officers, which did not exist as officers under the National Bank system. It is only partially true, then, that the money passes through the same hands, under a National Bank, as it would do under the Sub-Treasury.

It is true that under either system, individuals must be employed as Collectors of the Customs, Receivers at the Land Offices, &c. &c., but the difference is, that under the Bank system, the Receivers of all sorts, receive the money and pay it over to the Bank once a week when the collections are large, and once a month when they are small, whereas, by the Sub-Treasury system, individuals are not only to collect the money, but they are to *keep* it also, or pay it over to other individuals equally as unsafe as themselves, to be by them kept, until wanted for disbursement. It is during the time that it is thus lying idle in their hands, that opportunity is afforded, and temptation held out to them to embezzle and escape with it. By the Bank system, each Collector or Receiver, is to deposit in Bank all the money in his hands at the end of each month at most, and to send the Bank certificates of deposit, to the Secretary of the Treasury. Whenever that certificate of deposit fails to arrive at the proper time, the Secretary *knows* that the officer thus failing, is acting the knave; and if he is himself disposed to do his duty, he has him immediately removed from office, and thereby cuts him off from the possibility of embezzling but little more than the receipts of a single month. But by the Sub-Treasury System, the money is to lie month after month in the hands of individuals; larger amounts are to accumulate in the hands of the Receivers General, and some others, by perhaps ten to one, than ever accumulated in the hands of individuals before; yet during all this time, in relation to this great stake, the Secretary of the Treasury can comparatively know nothing. Reports, to be sure, he will have; but reports are often false, and always false when made by a knave to cloak his knavery. Long experience has shown, that nothing short of an actual demand of the money will expose an adroit peculator. Ask him for reports and he will give them to your heart's content, send agents to examine and count the money in his hands, and he will borrow of a friend, merely to be counted and then returned, a sufficient sum to make the sum square. Try what you will, it will all fail till you demand the money—then, and not till then, the truth will come.

The sum of the whole matter, I take to be this: Under the Bank system, while sums of money, by the law, were permitted to lie in the hands of individuals, *for very short periods only*, many and very large defalcations occurred by those individuals. Under the Sub-Treasury system, *much larger sums* are to lie in the hands of individuals *for much longer periods*, thereby multiplying *temptation* in proportion as the sums *are larger*; and multiplying *opportunity* in proportion as the periods *are longer* to, and for, those individuals to embezzle and escape with the public treasure; and therefore, just in the proportion, that the *temptation* and the *opportunity* are greater under the Sub-Treasury than the Bank system, will the peculations and defalcations be greater under the former than they have been under the latter. The truth of this, independent of actual experience, is but little less than self-evident. I, therefore, leave it.

But it is said, and truly too, that there is to be a *Penitentiary Department* to the Sub-Treasury. This, the advocates of the system will have it, will be a "king-cure-all." Before I go further, may I not ask if the Penitentiary Department, is not itself an admission that they expect the public money to be stolen? Why build a cage if they expect to catch no birds? But to the question how effectual the Penitentiary will be in preventing defalcations. How effectual have Penitentiaries heretofore been in preventing the crimes they were established to suppress? Has not confinement in them long been the legal penalty of larceny, forgery, robbery, and many other crimes, in almost all the States? And yet, are not those crimes committed weekly, daily, nay, and even hourly, in every one of those States? Again, the gallows has long been the penalty of murder, and yet we scarcely open a newspaper, that does not relate a new case of crime. If then, the Penitentiary has *heretofore* failed to prevent larceny, forgery and robbery, and the gallows and halter have likewise failed to prevent murder, by what process of reasoning, I ask, is it that we are to conclude the Penitentiary will hereafter prevent the stealing of the public money? But our opponents seem to think they answer the charge, that the money will be stolen, fully, if they can show that they will bring the offenders to punishment. Not so. Will the punishment of the thief bring back the stolen money? No more so than the hanging of a murderer restores his victim to life. What is the object desired? Certainly not the greatest number of thieves we can catch, but that the money may not be stolen. If, then, any plan can be devised for depositing the public treasure where it will be never stolen, never embezzled, is not that the plan to be adopted? Turn, then, to a National Bank, and you have that plan, fully and completely successful, as tested by the experience of forty years.

I have now done with the three propositions that the Sub-Treasury would injuriously affect the currency, and would be more *expensive* and *less secure* as a depository of the public money than a National Bank. How far I have succeeded in establishing their truth is for others to judge.

Omitting, for want of time, what I had intended to say as to the effect of the Sub-Treasury, to bring the public money under the more immediate control of the President, than it has ever heretofore been, I now only ask the audience, when Mr. Calhoun shall answer me, *to hold him to the questions*. Permit him not to escape them. Require him *either* to show that the Sub-Treasury *would not* injuriously affect the *currency*, or that we should in some way receive an equivalent for that injurious effect. Require him *either* to show that the Sub-Treasury *would not be more expensive* as a fiscal agent, than a Bank, or that we should, in some way, be compensated for that additional expense. And particularly require him to show that the public money *would be as secure* in the Sub-Treasury as in a National Bank, or that the additional *insecurity* would be overbalanced by some good result of the proposed change.

No one of them, in my humble judgment, will he be able to do; and I venture the prediction, and ask that it may be especially noted, *that he will not attempt to answer the proposition, that the Sub-Treasury would be more expensive than a National Bank, as a fiscal agent of the Government.*

As a sweeping objection to a National Bank, and consequently an argument in favor of the Sub-Treasury as a substitute for it, it often has been urged, and doubtless will be again, that such a bank is unconstitutional. We have often heretofore shown, and therefore, need not in detail, do so again, that a majority of the Revolutionary patriarchs, whoever acted officially upon the question, commencing with Gen. Washington, and embracing Gen. Jackson, the larger number of the signers of the Declaration, and of the framers of the Constitution, who were in the Congress of 1791, have decided upon their oaths that such a Bank is constitutional. We have also shown that the votes of Congress have more often been in favor of, than against its constitutionality. In addition to all this, we have shown that the Supreme Court—that tribunal which the Constitution has itself established to decide Constitutional questions—has solemnly decided that such a Bank is constitutional. Protesting that these authorities ought to settle the question and ought to be conclusive, I will not urge them further now. I now propose to take a view of the question, which I have not known to be taken by any one before. It is that whatever objection ever has, or ever can be made to the constitutionality of a Bank, will apply with equal force in its whole length, breadth and proportions, to the Sub-Treasury. Our opponents say, there is no *express* authority in the Constitution to establish a *Bank* and therefore a Bank is unconstitutional; but we, with equal truth, may say, there is no *express* authority in the Constitution to establish a *Sub-Treasury*, and therefore a Sub-Treasury is unconstitutional. Who, then, has the advantage of this "*express authority*" argument? Does it not cut equally both ways? Does it not wound them as deeply and as deadly as it does us?

Our position is that both are constitutional. The Constitution enumerates expressly several powers which Congress may exercise, super-added to which is a general authority, "to make all laws necessary and proper," for carrying into effect "all the powers vested by the Constitution of the Government of the United States." One of the express powers given Congress is, "to lay and collect taxes; duties, imposts, and excises; to pay the debts, and provide for the common defence and general welfare of the United States."—Now, Congress is expressly authorized to make all laws necessary and proper for carrying this power into execution. To carry it into execution, it is indispensably necessary to collect, safely keep, transfer, and disburse a revenue.

To do this, a Bank is "necessary and proper." But, say our opponents, to authorize the making of a Bank, the *necessity* must be so great, that the power just recited, would be nugatory without it; and that that *necessity* is expressly negatived by the fact, that they have got along *ten* whole years without such a *Bank.* Immediately we turn on them, and say, that that sort of *necessity* for a *Sub-Treasury* does not exist, because we have got along *forty* whole years without one. And this time, it may be observed, that we are not merely equal with them in the argument, but we beat them *forty* to *ten*, or which is the same thing, *four* to *one*. On examination, it will be found, that the absurd rule, which prescribes that before we can constitutionally adopt a National Bank as a fiscal agent, we must show an *indispensable necessity* for it, will exclude every sort of fiscal agent that the mind of man can conceive. A *Bank* is not *indispensable*, because we can take the *Sub-Treasury*; the *Sub-Treasury* is not *indispensable* because we can take the *Bank.*

The rule is too absurd to need further comment. Upon the phrase "*necessary and proper*" in the Constitution, it seems to me more reasonable to say that *some* fiscal agent is *indispensably necessary*; but, inasmuch as no *particular sort* of agent is thus *indispensable*, because some *other* sort might be adopted, we are left to choose that sort of agent, which may be most "*proper*" on grounds of expediency.

But it is said the Constitution gives no power to Congress to pass acts of incorporation. Indeed!—What is the passing an act of incorporation, but the *making of a law*? Is any one wise enough to tell? The Constitution expressly gives Congress power "*to pass all laws necessary and proper,*" &c. If, then, the passing of a Bank charter, be the "*making a law necessary and proper,*" is it not clearly within the constitutional power of Congress to do so?

I now leave the Bank and the Sub-Treasury to try to answer, in a brief way, some of the arguments which, on previous evenings here, have been urged by Messrs. Lamborn and Douglas. Mr. Lamborn admits, that "*errors,*" as he charitably calls them have occurred under the present and late administrations; but he insists that as great "*errors*" have occurred under all administrations. This, we respectfully deny. We admit that errors may have occurred under all administrations: but we insist that there is *no parallel* between them and those of the two last. If they can show that their errors are no greater in number and magnitude, than those of former times, we call off the dogs.

But they can do no such thing. To be brief, I will now attempt a contrast of the "errors" of the two latter, with those of former administrations, in relation to the public expenditures only. What I am now about to say, as to the expenditures, will be, in all cases exclusive of payments on the National debt. By an examination of authentic public documents, consisting of the regular series of annual reports, made by all the Secretaries of the Treasury from the establishment of the Government down to the close of the year 1838, the following contrasts will be presented.

1st. The last *ten* years under Gen. Jackson and Mr. Van Buren, cost more money than the first *twenty-seven* did, (including the heavy expenses of the late British war,) under Washington, Adams, Jefferson, and Madison.

2d. The last year of J. Q. Adams' Adminstration cost, in round numbers, *thirteen* millions, being about *one* dollar to each soul in the nation; the last (1838) of Mr. Van Buren's cost *forty* millions, being about *two dollars and fifty cents* to each soul; and being larger than the expenditures of Mr. Adams in the proportion of *five* to *two*.

3d. The highest annual expenditure during the late British war, being in 1814, and while he had in actual service rising 188,000 militia, together with the whole regular army, swelling the number to greatly over 200,000, and they to be clad, fed, and transported from point to point, with great rapidity and corresponding expense, and to be furnished with arms and ammunition, and they to be transported in like manner, and at like expense, was no more in round numbers than *thirty* millions; whereas the annual expenditure of 1838, under Mr. Van Buren, and while we were at peace with every government in the world, was *forty* millions; being over the highest year of the late and very expensive war, in the proportion of *four* to *three*.

4th. Gen. Washington administered the government *eight*

years for *sixteen* millions; Mr. Van Buren administered it *one* year (1838) for *forty* millions; so that Mr. Van Buren expended *twice and a half* as much in *one* year, as Gen. Washington did in *eight*, and being in the proportion of *twenty* to *one*—or, in other words, had Gen. Washington administered the Government *twenty* years, at the same average expense that he did for *eight*, he would have carried us through the whole *twenty* for no more money than Mr. Van Buren has expended in getting us through the single *one* of 1838.

Other facts, equally astounding, might be presented from the same authentic document; but I deem the foregoing abundantly sufficient to establish the proposition, that there is no parallel between the "*errors*" of the present and late administrations, and those of former times, and that Mr. Van Buren is wholly out of the line of all precedents.

But, Mr. Douglas, seeing that the enormous expenditure of 1838, has no parallel in the olden times, comes in with a long list of excuses for it. This list of excuses, I will rapidly examine, and show, as I think, that the few of them which are true, prove nothing; and that the majority of them are wholly untrue in fact. He first says, that the expenditures of that year were made under the appropriations of Congress—*one branch of which was a Whig body*. It is true that those expenditures were made under the appropriations of Congress; but it is *untrue* that either branch of Congress was a *Whig* body. The Senate had fallen into the hands of the administration, more than a year before, as proven by the passage of the Expunging Resolution; and at the time those appropriations were made, there were too few Whigs in that body, to make a respectable struggle, in point of numbers, upon any question.—This is notorious to all. The House of Representatives that voted those appropriations, was the same that first assembled at the called session of September, 1838. Although it refused to pass the Sub-Treasury Bill, a majority of its members were elected as friends of the administration, and proved their adherence to it, by the election of a Van Buren Speaker, and two Van Buren clerks. It is clear then, that both branches of the Congress that passed those appropriations were in the hands of Mr. Van Buren's friends, so that the Whigs had no power to arrest them, as Mr. Douglas would insist. And is not the charge of extravagant expenditures, equally well sustained, if shown to have been made by a Van Buren Congress, as if shown to have been made in any other way? A Van Buren Congress passed the bills, and Mr. Van Buren himself approved them, and consequently the party are wholly responsible for them.

Mr. Douglas next says, that a portion of the expenditures of that year, was made for the purchase of Public Lands from the Indians. Now it happens that no such purchase was made during that year. It is true, that some money was paid that year in pursuance of Indian treaties; but no more, or rather not as much, as had been paid on the same account in each of several preceding years.

Next, he says, that the Florida war created many millions of this year's expenditure. This is true, and it is also true, that during that and every other year, that that war has existed, it has cost three or four times as much as it would have done under an honest and judicious administration of the Government. The large sums foolishly, not to say corruptly, thrown away in that war, constitute one of the just causes of complaint against the administration. Take a single instance. The agents of the Government in connexion with that war, needed a certain Steam boat; the owner proposed to sell it for ten thousand dollars; the agents refused to give that sum, but hired the boat at one hundred dollars per day, and kept it at hire till it amounted to ninety-two thousand dollars. This fact is not found in the public reports, but depends with me on the verbal statement of an officer of the navy, who said he knew it to be true.

That the administration ought to be credited for the *reasonable* expenses of the Florida war, we have never denied. Those *reasonable* charges, we say, could not exceed one or two millions a year. Deduct such a sum from the forty million expenditure of 1838, and the remainder will still be without a parallel as an annual expenditure.

Again, Mr. Douglas says, that the removal of the Indians to the country west of the Mississippi created much of the expenditure of 1838. I have examined the public documents in relation to this matter, and find that less was paid for the removal of Indians in that, than in some former years. The whole sum expended on that account in that year, did not much exceed one quarter of a million. For this small sum, altho' we do not think the administration entitled to credit, because large sums have been expended in the same way in former years, we consent it may take one and make the most of it.

Next, Mr. Douglas says, that five millions of the expenditures of 1838, consisted of the payment of the French indemnity money to its individual claimants. I have carefully examined the public documents, and thereby find this statement to be wholly untrue. Of the forty millions of dollars expended in 1838, I am enabled to say positively, that not one dollar consisted of payments on the French indemnities. So much for that excuse.

Next comes the Post Office.—He says that five millions were expended during that year to sustain that Department. By a like examination of public documents, I find this also, wholly untrue. Of the so often mentioned forty millions, not one dollar went to the Post Office. I am glad, however, that the Post Office has been referred to, because it warrants me in digressing a little, to enquire how it is, that that department of the Government has become a *charge* upon the Treasury, whereas under Mr. Adams and the Presidents before him, it not only, to use a homely phrase, cut its own fodder, but actually threw a surplus into the Treasury. —Although nothing of the forty millions was paid on that account, in 1838; it is true that five millions are appropriated *to be so expended* in 1839; showing clearly that the department has become a *charge* upon the Treasury.—How has this happened?

I account for it in this way—the chief expense of the Post Office Department consists of the payments of Contractors for carrying the mails—contracts for carrying the mails, are, by law, let to the lowest bidders, after advertisement. This plan introduces competition, and insures the transportation of the mails at fair prices, so long as it is faithfully adhered to. It has ever been adhered to until Mr. Barry was made Post Master General. When he came into office, he formed the purpose of throwing the mail contracts into the hands of his friends to the exclusion of his opponents. To effect this, the plan of letting to the lowest bidder must be evaded, and it must be done in this way—The favorite bid less by perhaps three, or four hundred per cent, than the contract could be performed for, and consequently, shutting out all honest competition, became the contractor. The Post Master General would immediately add some slight additional duty to the contract, and under the pretence of extra allowance for extra services, run the contract to double, triple, and often quadruple what honest and fair bidders had proposed to take it at. In 1834 the finances of the department had become so deranged, that total concealment was no longer possible, and consequently a committee of the Senate were directed to make a thorough investigation of its affairs. Their report is found in the Senate Documents of 1833—'34—vol. 5, Doc. 422—which Documents may be seen at the Secretary's office, and I presume elsewhere in the State. The report shows numerous cases, of similar import, of one of which I give the substance—The contract for carrying the mail upon a certain route, had expired, and of course was to be let again. The old contractor offered to take it for $300 a year, the mail to be transported thereon three times a week, or for $600 transported daily. One James Reeside, bid $40 for three times a week; or $99 daily, and of course received the contract. On the examination of the committee, it was discovered that Reeside had received for the service on this route, which he had contracted to render for less than $100, the enormous sum of $1,999! This is but a single case.—Many similar ones, covering some ten or twenty pages of a large volume, are given in that report. The department was found to be insolvent to the amount of half a million; and to have been so grossly mismanaged, or rather so corruptly managed, in almost every particular, that the best friends of the Post Master General made no defence of his administration of it. They admitted that he was wholly unqualified for that office; but still he was retained in it by the President, until he resigned it voluntarily about a year afterwards. And when he resigned it what do you think became of him? Why, he sunk into obscurity and disgrace, to be sure, you will say. No such thing. Well, then, what did become of him? Why the President immediately expressed his high disapprobation of his almost unequalled incapability and corruption, by appointing him to a foreign mission, with a salary and outfit of $18,000 a year.—The party now attempt to throw *Barry* off and to avoid the responsibility of his sins.—Did not the President endorse those sins, when on the very heel of their commission, he appointed their author to the very highest and most honorable office in his gift, and which is but a single step behind the very *goal* of American political ambition?

I return to another of Mr. Douglas's excuses for the expenditures of 1838, at the same time announcing the pleasing intelligence, that this is the last one. He says that ten millions of that year's expenditures, was a contingent appropriation, to prosecute an anticipated war with Great Britain, on the Maine boundary question. Few words will settle this. First: that the ten millions appropriated was not *made* till 1839, and consequently could not have been expended in 1838, and, second; although it was appropriated, it has never been expended at all.—Those who heard Mr. Douglas, recollect that he indulged himself in a contemptuous expression of pity for me. "Now he's got me," thought I.—But when he went on to say that five millions of the expenditure of 1838, were payments of the French indemnities, *which I knew to be untrue*; that five millions had been for the Post Office, *which I knew to be untrue,* that ten millions had been for the Maine boundary war, *which I not only knew to be untrue but supremely ridiculous also;* and when I saw that he was stupid enough to hope, that I would permit such groundless and audacious assertions to go unexposed, I readily consented, that on the score of both veracity and sagacity, the audience should judge whether he or I were the more deserving of the world's contempt.

Mr. Lamborn insists that the difference between the Van Buren Party, and the Whigs is, that although the former sometimes err in *practice,* they are always correct in *principle*—whereas the latter are wrong in *principle*—and the better to impress this proposition, he uses a figurative expression in these words: "*The Democrats are vulnerable in the heel, but they are sound in the head and the heart.*" The first branch of the figure, that is that the Democrats are vulnerable in the heel, I admit is not merely figuratively, but literally true. Who that looks but for a moment at their Swartwouts, their Prices, their Harringtons, and their hundreds of others, scampering away with the public money to Texas, to Europe, and to every spot of the earth where a villain may hope to find refuge from justice, can at all doubt that they are most distressingly affected in their *heels* with a species of *"running itch."* It seems that this malady of their heels, operates on these *sound-headed* and *honest-hearted* creatures, very much like the cork-leg, in the comic song, did on its owner, which, when he had once got started on it, the more he tried to stop it, the more it would run away. At the hazard of wearing this point thread bare, I will relate an anecdote, which seems too strikingly in point to be omitted. A witty Irish soldier, who was always boasting of his bravery, when no danger was near, but who invariably retreated without orders at the first charge of an engagement, being asked by his Captain why he did so, replied: "Captain, I have as brave a *heart* as Julius Caesar ever had; but somehow or other, whenever danger approaches, my *cowardly* legs will run away with it." So with Mr. Lamborn's party. They take the public money *into* their hand for the most laudable purpose, that *wise heads* and *honest hearts* can dictate; but before they can possibly get it *out* again, their rascally *"vulnerable heels"* will run away with them.

Seriously: this proposition of Mr. Lamborn is nothing more or less, than a request that his party may be tried by their *professions* instead of their *practices*. Perhaps no position that the party assumes is more liable to, or more deserving of exposure, than this very modest request; and nothing but the unwarrantable length to which I have already extended these remarks, forbids me now attempting to expose it. For the reason given, I pass it by.

I shall advert to but one more point.

Mr. Lamborn refers to the late elections in the States, and from their results, confidently predicts, that every State in the Union will vote for Mr. Van Buren at the next Presidential election. Address *that* argument to *cowards* and to *knaves*; with the *free* and the *brave* it will affect nothing. It *may* be true, if it *must*, let it. Many free countries have lost their liberty, and *ours may* lose hers; but if she shall, be it my proudest plume, not that I was the *last* to desert, but that I *never* deserted her.—I know that the great volcano at Washington, aroused and directed by the evil spirit that reigns there, is belching forth the lava of political corruption, in a current broad and deep, which is sweeping with frightful velocity over the whole length and breadth of the land, bidding fair to leave unscathed no green spot or living thing, while on its bosom are riding like demons on the waves of Hell, the imps of that evil spirit, and fiendishly taunting all those who dare resist its destroying course, with the hopelessness of their effort; and knowing this, I cannot deny that all may be swept away. Broken by it, I too, may be; bow to it, I never will. The *probability* that we may fall in the struggle *ought not* to deter us from the support of a cause we believe to be just; it *shall not* deter me. If ever I feel the soul within me elevate and expand to those dimensions not wholly unworthy of its Almighty Architect, it is when I contemplate the cause of my country, deserted by all the world beside, and I standing up boldly alone, and hurling defiance at her victorious oppressors. Here, without contemplating consequences, before High Heaven, and in the face of the world, I swear eternal fidelity to the just cause, as I deem it, of the land of my life, my liberty and my love.—And who, that thinks with me, will not fearlessly adopt the oath that I take. Let none falter, who thinks he is right, and we may succeed. But, if after all, we shall fail, be it so.—We still shall have the proud consolation of saying to our consciences, and to the departed shade of our country's freedom, that the cause approved of our judgment, and adored of our hearts, in disaster, in chains, in torture, in death, we never faltered in defending.

The text of this speech is that of the pamphlet (Fish 518) printed in January or February, 1840, for circulation in the presidential campaign, with some emendations and corrections taken from the text printed in the Sangamo Journal, *March 6, 1840. Comparison of these two texts suggests that Lincoln corrected and revised a copy of the pamphlet for publication in the newspaper, for corrections and changes in diction are numerous. The* Journal *text is, however, marred by typographical errors and omissions.*

The Sub-Treasury has been regarded by many historians as a sound experiment. Theodore Calvin Pease (The Frontier State) *terms it "the boldest and most states-*

manlike measure of his [Van Buren's] career," and calls attention to the fact that the Whigs "ignored the nature of the institution" in their attacks upon it. That Lincoln's argument was effective, if occasionally specious, is attested by the detailed and equally political defense published in the Illinois State Register, *February 8, 14, 1840. Since this editorial refers specifically to the footnote which Lincoln added, it may be inferred that the pamphlet was in circulation before February 8, 1840.*

The date on which the speech was delivered has been determined with fair certainty. Although Nicolay and Hay give December 20, 1839, investigations conducted by Harry E. Pratt indicate that December 26, 1839, is the actual date.

LETTER TO JOHN T. STUART
JANUARY 20, 1841

Springfield, Jany. 20th. 1841

Dear Stuart:

I have had no letter from you since you left. No matter for that. What I wish now is to speak of our Post-Office. You know I desired Dr. Henry to have that place when you left; I now desire it more than ever. I have within the last few days, been making a most discreditable exhibition of myself in the way of hypochondriasm and thereby got an impression that Dr. Henry is necessary to my existence. Unless he gets that place he leaves Springfield. You therefore see how much I am interested in the matter.

We shall shortly forward you a petition in his favour signed by all or nearly all the Whig members of the Legislature as well as other whigs.

This, together with what you know of the Dr.'s position and merits I sincerely hope will secure him the appointment. My heart is very much set upon it.

Pardon me for not writing more; I have not sufficient composure to write a long letter.

As ever yours
A. Lincoln

*Lincoln's mental and physical condition—as referred to here and described in the last paragraph of the next letter, and as numerous references in later letters written in 1841 recur to it—all revolves around the "fatal 1st of January" when apparently he broke his engagement to Mary Todd. Precisely what happened is not known, but Lincoln's close friends were well aware that his psychological unbalance was the result of his misfortune as a lover, and in March his friend Stuart tried, presumably at Lincoln's request, to get him an appointment as Chargé d'Affaires at Bogotá, on the ancient theory, perhaps, that a change in climate might remedy his condition. Psychoanalysts have indicated repression and complexes; William F. Petersen (*Lincoln-Douglas: The Weather as Destiny*) has expounded a theory that inclement weather aggravated Lincoln's psychoneurotic affliction; and students of Lincoln in general are agreed that here again, as in his affair with Mary Owens, Lincoln just could not make up his mind.*

LETTER TO JOHN T. STUART JANUARY 23, 1841

Jany. 23rd. 1841—Springfield, Ills.

Dear Stuart:

Yours of the 3rd. Inst. is recd. & I proceed to answer it as well as I can, tho, from the deplorable state of my mind at this time, I fear I shall give you but little satisfaction About the matter of the congressional election, I can only tell you, that there is a bill now before the Senate adopting the General Ticket system; but whether the party have fully determined on it's adoption is yet uncertain. There is no sign of opposition to you among our friends, and none that I can learn among our enemies; tho, of course, there will be, if the Genl. Ticket be adopted. The Chicago American, Peoria Register, & Sangamo Journal, have already hoisted your flag upon their own responsibility, & the other whig papers of the District are expected to follow immediately. On last evening there was a meeting of our friends at Butler's; and I submitted the question to them & found them unanamously [*sic*] in favor of having you announced as a candidate. A few of us this morning, however, concluded, that as you were already being announced in the papers, we would delay announcing you, *as by your own authority* for a week or two. We thought that to appear too keen about it might spur our opponents on about their Genl. Ticket project. Upon the whole, I think I may say with certainty, that your reelection is sure, if it be in the power of the whigs to make it so.

For not giving you a general summary of news, you *must* pardon me; it is not in my power to do so. I am now the most miserable man living. If what I feel were equally distributed to the whole human family, there would not be one cheerful face on the earth. Whether I shall ever be better, I cannot tell; I awfully forebode I shall not. To remain as I am is impossible; I must die or be better, it appears to me. The matter you speak of on my account, you may attend to as you say, unless you shall hear of my condition forbidding it. I say this, because I fear I shall be unable to attend to any bussiness [*sic*] here, and a change of scene might help me. If I could be myself, I would rather remain at home with Judge Logan. I can write no more.

Your friend, as ever
A. Lincoln

Lincoln's reference to a bill before the Senate "adopting the General Ticket system" recalls the fact that the Whigs were still debating the adoption of the convention system—already made a party procedure by the Democrats—and that the "General Ticket project" was intended to draw strict party lines and issues, to eliminate the multiplicity of candidates, and to tie the candidate more tightly to the party program. Lincoln apparently felt Stuart's position to be strong, but that opposition to him would crystallize around some other candidate if the General Ticket bill passed. In any event Stuart won his re-election to Congress in June by a small majority.

LETTER TO JOSHUA F. SPEED
JUNE 19, 1841

Springfield, June 19th. 1841

Dear Speed:

We have had the highest state of excitement here for a week past that our community has ever witnessed; and although the public feeling is somewhat allayed, the curious affair which aroused it, is very far from being even yet, cleared of mystery. It would take a quire of paper to give you anything like a full account of it, and I therefore only propose a brief outline. The chief personages in the drama, are Archibald Fisher, supposed to be murdered; and Archibald Trailor, Henry Trailor, and William Trailor, supposed to have murdered him. The three Trailors are brothers: the first, Arch., as you know, lives in town; the second, Henry, in Clary's Grove; and the third, Wm., in Warren County; and Fisher, the supposed murderee, being without a family had made his home with William. On Saturday evening, being the 29th May, Fisher and William came to Henry's in a one horse dearborn, and there stayed over sunday, and on monday all three came to Springfield, Henry on horseback, and joined Archibald at Myers', the Dutch carpenter. That evening at supper Fisher was missing, and so next morning. Some ineffectual search was made for him; and on tuesday, at 1 o'clock P.M., Wm. & Henry started home without him. In a day or so Henry and one or two of his Clary Grove neighbors came back and searched for him again, and advertised his disappearance in the paper. The knowledge of the matter thus far had not been general; and here it dropped entirely till about the 10th. Inst., when Keys received a letter from the Post Master in Warren, stating that Wm. had arrived at home, and was telling a very mysterious and improbable story about the disappearance of Fisher, which induced the community there to suppose he had been disposed of unfairly. Keys made this letter public, which immediately set the whole town and adjoining county agog; and so it has continued until yesterday. The mass of the People commenced a systematic search for the dead body, while Wickersham was dispatched to arrest Henry Trailor at the Grove, and Jim Maxcy to Warren to arrest William. On Monday last Henry was brought in, and showed an evident inclination to insinuate that he knew Fisher to be dead, and that Arch. and Wm. had killed him. He said he guessed the body could be found in Spring Creek between the Beardstown road and Hickoxes mill. Away the people swept like a herd of buffaloes, and cut down Hickoxes mill-dam *nolens volens*, to draw the water out of the pond; and then went up and down, and down and up the creek, fishing and raking, and ducking, and diving for two days, and after all no dead body found. In the mean time a sort of scuffling ground had been found in the brush in the angle, or point where the road leading into the woods past the brewery, and the one leading in past the brick-yard join. From the scuffle ground, was the sign of something about the size of a man having been dragged to the edge of the thicket, where it joined the track of some small wheeled carriage which was drawn by one horse, as shown by the horse tracks. The carriage-track led off toward Spring Creek. Near this drag-trail, Dr. Merryman found *two hairs*, which, after a long scientific examination, he pronounced to be triangular human hairs, which term, he says, includes within it, the whiskers, the hair growing under the arms and on other parts of the body; and he judged that these two were of the whiskers, because the ends were cut, showing that they had flourished in the neighborhood of the razor's operations. On thursday last Jim Maxcy brought in William Trailor from Warren. On the same day Arch. was arrested and put in jail. Yesterday (friday) William was put upon his examining trial before May and Lavely. Archibald and Henry were both present. Lamborn prosecuted, and Logan, Baker, and your humble servant defended. A great many witnesses were introduced and examined; but I shall only mention those whose testimony seemed to be the most important. The first of these was Capt. Ransdell. He swore that when William and Henry left Springfield for home on tuesday before mentioned, they did not take the direct route, which, you know, leads by the butcher shop, but that they followed the street North until they got opposite, or nearly opposite May's new house, after which he could not see them from where he stood; and it was afterward proven that in about an hour after they started, they came into the street by the butcher's shop from towards the brick-yard. Dr. Merryman and others swore to what is stated about the scuffle-ground, drag-trail, whiskers, and carriage-tracks. Henry was then introduced by the prosecution. He swore that when they started for home, they went out North, as Ransdell stated, and turned down West by the brick-yard into the woods, and there met Archibald; that they proceeded a small distance farther, where he was placed as a sentinel to watch for, and announce the approach of any one that might happen that way; that William and Arch. took the dearborn out of the road a small distance to the edge of the thicket, where they stopped, and he saw them lift the body of a man into it; that they then moved off with the carriage in the direction of Hickoxes mill, and he loitered about for something like an hour, when William returned with the carriage, but without Arch: and said they had put *him* in a safe place; that they went some how, he did not know exactly how, into the road close to the brewery, and proceeded on to Clary's Grove. He also stated that sometime during the day William told him, that he and Arch. had killed Fisher the evening before; that the way they did it was by him (William) knocking him down with a club, and Arch. then choking him to death. An old man from Warren, called Dr. Gilmore, was then introduced on the part of the defence. He swore that he had known Fisher for several years; that Fisher had resided at his house a long time at each of two different spells; once while he built a barn for him, and once while he was doctored for some chronic disease; that two or three years ago, Fisher had a serious hurt in his head by the bursting of a gun, since which he had been subject to continued bad health, and occasional aberrations of mind. He also stated that on last tuesday, being the same day that Maxcy arrested William Trailor, he (the Dr.) was from home in the early part of the day, and on his return, about 11 o'clock, found Fisher at his house, in bed, and apparently very unwell; that he asked him how he came from Springfield; that Fisher said he had come by Peoria, and also told several other places he had been at not in the direction of Peoria, which showed that he, at the time of speaking, did not know where he had been, or that he had been wandering about in a state of derangement. He further stated that in about two hours he received a note from one of William Trailor's friends, advising him of his arrest, and requesting him to go on to Springfield as a witness, to testify to the state of Fisher's health in former times; that he immediately set off, calling up two of his neighbors, as company, and, riding all evening and all night, overtook Maxcy and William at Lewiston in Fulton County; that Maxcy refusing to discharge Trailor upon his statement, his two neighbors returned and he came on to Springfield. Some question being made whether the doctor's story was not a fabrication, several acquaintances of his among whom was the same Post Master who wrote Keys, as before mentioned, were introduced as sort of compurgators, who all swore, that they knew the doctor to be of good character for truth and veracity, and generally of good character in every way. Here the testimony ended and the Trailors were discharged, Arch. and William expressing, both in word and manner, their entire confidence that Fisher would be found alive at the doctor's by Galloway, Mallory, and Myers, who a day before had been despatched for that purpose; while Henry still protested that no power on earth could ever show Fisher alive. Thus stands this curious affair now. When the doctor's story was first made public, it was amusing to scan and contemplate the countenances, and hear the remarks of those who had been actively engaged in the search for the dead body. Some looked quizzical, some melancholly [*sic*], and some furiously angry. Porter, who had been very active, swore he always knew the man was not dead, and that *he* had not stirred an inch to hunt for him; Langford, who had taken the lead in cutting down Hickoxes mill dam, and wanted to hang Hickox for objecting, looked most awfully wobegone [*sic*]: he seemed the "*wictim of hunrequited haffections,*" as represented in the comic almanic [*sic*] we used to laugh over; and Hart, the little drayman that hauled Molly home once, said it was too *damned* bad, to have so much trouble, and no hanging after all.

I commenced this letter on yesterday, since which I received yours of the 13th. I stick to my promise to come to Louisville. Nothing new here except what I have written. I have not seen Sarah since my long trip, and I am going out there as soon as I mail this letter.

Yours forever,
Lincoln.

For a discussion of the Trailor Case, see the note on "Remarkable Case of Arrest for Murder," April 15, 1846.

Lincoln's reference to "Sarah" designates Sarah Rickard whom Speed had apparently been courting and from whom he had broken off about the same time as Lincoln's break with Mary Todd. Further references to "Sarah" in Lincoln's letters to Speed are to the same person. For a full account of Speed's, as well as Lincoln's difficulties in courtship, see Carl Sandburg and Paul M. Angle, Mary Lincoln: Wife and Widow.

That Speed was undoubtedly the closest friend Lincoln ever had is attested by the several letters included in this volume. It began, according to the story, the day when Lincoln came to Springfield to live and was invited by Speed to share his room, and lasted until Lincoln's death, although in later years they saw less of each other and corresponded infrequently. Robert L. Kincaid's Joshua Fry Speed: Lincoln's Most Intimate Friend *is the best recent account of their long friendship.*

LETTER TO MISS MARY SPEED SEPTEMBER 27, 1841

Bloomington, Illinois. Sept. 27th. 1841

Miss Mary Speed
Louisville, Ky.
My Friend:

Having resolved to write to some of your mother's family, and not having the express permission of any one of them [to?] do so, I have had some little difficulty in determining on which to inflict the task of reading what I now feel must be a most dull and silly letter; but when I remembered that you and I were something of cronies while I was at Farmington, and that while there, I was under the necessity of shutting you up in a room to prevent your committing an assault and battery upon me, I instantly decided that you should be the devoted one.

I assume that you have not heard from Joshua & myself since we left, because I think it doubtful whether he has written.

You remember there was some uneasiness about Joshua's health when we left. That little indisposition of his turned out to be nothing serious; and it was pretty nearly forgotten when we reached Springfield. We got on board the Steam Boat Lebanon, in the locks of the Canal about 12 o'clock M. of the day we left, and reached St. Louis the next Monday at 8 P. M. Nothing of interest happened during the passage, except the vexatious delays occasioned by the sand bars he thought interesting. By the way, a fine example was presented on board the boat for contemplating the effect of *condition* upon human happiness. A gentleman had purchased twelve negroes in different parts of Kentucky, and was taking them to a farm in the South. They were chained six and six together. A small iron clevis was around the left wrist of each, and this fastened to the main chain by a shorter one at a convenient distance from the others; so that the negroes were strung together precisely like so many fish upon a trot-line. In this condition they were being separated forever from the scenes of their childhood, their friends, their fathers and mothers, and brothers and sisters, and many of them, from their wives and children, and going into perpetual slavery where the lash of the master is proverbially more ruthless and unrelenting than any other where; and yet amid all these distressing circumstances, as we would think them, they were the most cheerful and apparently happy creatures on board. One whose offence for which he had been sold was an over-fondness for his wife, played the fiddle almost continually; and the others danced, sung, cracked jokes, and played various games with cards from day to day. How true it is that "God tempers the wind to the shorn lamb," or in other words, that he renders the worst of human conditions tolerable, while he permits the best, to be nothing better than tolerable.

To return to the narative [*sic*]. When we reached Springfield, I staid [*sic*] but one day when I started on this tedious Circuit where I now am. Do you remember my going to the city, while I was in Kentucky, to have a tooth extracted, and making a failure of it? Well, that same old tooth got to paining me so much, that about a week since I had it torn out, bringing with it a bit of the jawbone; the consequence of which is that my mouth is now so sore that I can neither talk nor eat. I am litterally [*sic*] "subsisting on savoury remembrances"—that is, being unable to eat, I am living upon the remembrance of the delicious dishes of peaches and cream we used to have at your house.

When we left, Miss Fanny Henning was owing you a visit, as I understood. Has she paid it yet? If she has are you not convinced that she is one of the sweetest girls in the world? There is but one thing about her, so far as I could perceive, that I would have otherwise than as it is. That is something of a tendency to melancholly [*sic*]. This, let it be observed, is a misfortune not a fault. Give her an assurance of my very highest regard when you see her.

Is little Siss Eliza Davis at your house yet? If she is kiss her "o'er and o'er again" for me.

Tell your mother that I have not got her "present" with me; but that I intend to read it regularly when I return home. I doubt not that it is really, as she says, the best cure for the "Blues" could one but take it according to the truth.

Give my respects to all your sisters (including "Aunt Emma") and brothers. Tell Mrs. Peay, of whose happy face I shall long retain a pleasant remembrance, that I have been trying to think of a name for her homestead, but as yet, can not satisfy myself with one. I shall be very happy to receive a line from you, soon after you receive this; and, in case you choose to favour me with one, address it to Charleston, Coles County, Ills as I shall be there about the time to receive it.

Your sincere friend
A. Lincoln.

This letter to Joshua Speed's sister was written on Lincoln's return trip from Louisville, Kentucky, to St. Louis. He had made an extended visit in the Speed home near Louisville and had formed a strong attachment for his friend's mother and sister. The "present" referred to was an Oxford Bible. The indelible impression which the sight of the manacled slaves made on Lincoln was recalled nearly fourteen years later when he wrote to Speed, who had returned to his home in

Kentucky to live, explaining his stand on the extension of slavery. (See the letter dated August 24, 1855.)

LETTER TO JOSHUA F. SPEED
JANUARY 3, 1842

My dear Speed:

Feeling, as you know I do, the deepest solicitude for the success of the enterprise you are engaged in, I adopt this as the last method I can invent to aid you, in case (which God forbid) you shall need any aid. I do not place what I am going to say on paper, because I can say it any better in that way than I could by word of mouth; but because, were I to say it orrally [*sic*], before we part, most likely you would forget it at the very time when it might do you some good. As I think it reasonable that you will feel very badly some time between this and the final consummation of your purpose, it is intended that you shall read this just at such a time.

Why I say it is reasonable that you will feel very badly yet, is, because of *three special causes,* added to the *general one* which I shall mention.

The general cause is, that you are *naturally of a nervous temperament*; and this I say from what I have seen of you personally, and what you have told me concerning your mother at various times, and concerning your brother William at the time his wife died.

The first special cause is, *your exposure to bad weather* on your journey, which my experience clearly proves to be very severe on defective nerves. The second is, *the absence of all business and conversation of friends,* which might divert your mind, and give it occasional rest from the *intensity* of thought, which will sometimes wear the sweetest idea threadbare and turn it to the bitterness of death.

The third is, *the rapid and near approach of that crisis on which all your thoughts and feelings concentrate.*

If from all these causes you shall escape and go through triumphantly, without another "twinge of the soul" I shall be most happily, but most egregiously deceived.

If, on the contrary, you shall, as I expect you will at some time, be agonized and distressed, let me, who have some reason to speak with judgment on such a subject, beseech you, to ascribe it to the causes I have mentioned; and not to some false and ruinous suggestion of the Devil.

"But" you will say "do not your causes apply to every one engaged in a like undertaking?"

By no means. *The particular causes*, to a greater or less extent, perhaps do apply in all cases; but the *general one*,—nervous debility, which is the key and conductor of all the particular ones, and without which *they* would be utterly harmless, though it *does* pertain to you, *does not* pertain to one in a thousand. It is out of this, that the painful difference between you and the mass of the world springs.

I know what the painful point with you is, at all times when you are unhappy. It is an apprehension that you do not love her as you should. What nonsense!—How came you to court her? Was it because you thought she desired it, and that you had given her reason to expect it? If it was for that, why did not the same reason make you court Ann Todd, and at least twenty others of whom you can think, to whom it would apply with greater force than to *her*? Did you court her for her wealth? Why, you know she had none. But you say you reasoned yourself *into* it. What do you mean by that? Was it not, that you found yourself unable to *reason* yourself *out of it*? Did you not think, and partly form the purpose, of courting her the first time you ever saw or heard of her? What had reason to do with it, at that early stage? There was nothing *at that time* for reason to work upon. Whether she was moral, amiable, sensible, or even of good character, you did not, nor could then know; except, perhaps you might infer the last from the company you found her in. All you then did or could know of her, was her personal *appearance and deport-*

ment; and these, if they impress at all, impress the *heart*, and not the head.

Say candidly, were not those heavenly *black eyes*, the whole basis of all your early *reasoning* on the subject?

After you and I had once been at her residence, did you not go and take me all the way to Lexington and back, for no other purpose but to get to see her again, on our return, in that seeming to take a trip for that express object?

What earthly consideration would you take to find her scouting and despising you, and giving herself up to another? But of this you have no apprehension; and therefore you can not bring it home to your feelings.

I shall be so anxious about you, that I want you to write every mail.

Your friend
Lincoln

The confidence with which Lincoln diagnoses Speed's emotional state leads one to suspect not only that his own unhappy experience has assumed in retrospect a less formidable aspect, but also that he still loves Mary and that he has reason to believe Mary still loves him. How soon prearranged meetings were resumed by Lincoln and Mary, under the matchmaking guidance of Mrs. Simeon Francis, is not certain. They were seeing each other certainly by the summer of 1842, and one is tempted to suspect that perhaps a few "accidental" meetings had taken place by January, 1842. Lincoln's letters to Speed suggest something more than a return to a "rational view"; they suggest an emotional readjustment that can hardly be accounted for unless he has made up his mind, to some extent, about Mary. There is, however, no additional evidence in support of this supposition.

Meserve No. 20. A photograph by Mathew B. Brady made in New York on February 27, 1860. It is known as the Cooper Institute portrait, having been made on the day Lincoln delivered his speech under the auspices of the Young Men's Central Republican Union. This and two other portraits made the same day are the first of Lincoln made by Brady.

LETTER TO JOSHUA F. SPEED FEBRUARY 3, 1842

Springfield, Ills. Feby. 3—1842—

Dear Speed:

Your letter of the 25th. Jany. came to hand to-day. You well know that I do not feel my own sorrows much more keenly than I do yours, when I know of them; and yet I assure you I was not much hurt by what you wrote me of your excessively bad feeling at the time you wrote. Not that I am less capable of sympathising with you now than ever; not that I am less your friend than ever; but because I hope and believe, that your present anxiety and distress about *her* health and *her* life, must and will forever banish those horid [*sic*] doubts, which I know you sometimes felt, as to the truth of your affection for her. If they can be once and forever removed, (and I almost feel a presentiment that the Almighty has sent your present affliction expressly for that object) surely, nothing can come in their stead, to fill their immeasurable measure of misery. The death scenes of those we love, are surely painful enough; but these we are prepared to, and expect to see. They happen to all, and all know they must happen. Painful as they are, they are not an unlooked-for-sorrow. Should she, as you fear, be destined to an early grave, it is indeed a great consolation to know that she is so well prepared to meet it. Her religion, which you once disliked so much, I will venture you now prize most highly.

But I hope your melancholly [*sic*] bodings as to her early death, are not well founded. I even hope, that ere this reaches you, she will have returned with improved and still improving health; and that you will have met her, and forgotten the sorrows of the past, in the enjoyment of the present.

I would say more if I could, but it seems I have said enough. It really appears to me that you yourself ought to rejoice, and not sorrow, at this indubitable evidence of your undying affection for her. Why Speed, if you did not love her, although you might not wish her death, you would most calmly be resigned to it. Perhaps this point is no longer a question with you, and my pertinacious dwelling upon it, is a rude intrusion upon your feelings. If so, you must pardon me. You know the Hell I have suffered on that point, and how tender I am upon it. You know I do not mean wrong.

I have been quite clear of hypo since you left—even better than I was along in the fall.

I have seen Sarah but once. She seemed verry [*sic*] cheerful, and so, I said nothing to her about what we spoke of.

Old Uncle Billy Herndon is dead; and it is said this evening that Uncle Ben Ferguson will not live. This I believe is all the news, and enough at that unless it were better.

Write me immediately on the receipt of this.

Your friend as ever
Lincoln

EULOGY ON BENJAMIN FERGUSON
FEBRUARY 8, 1842

Mr. President:—

The solemn duty has been assigned to me, of announcing to this Society, the sudden and melancholy death of its much respected member, BENJAMIN FERGUSON.

After an illness of only six days, he closed his mortal existence, at a quarter past seven on the evening of the 3d inst., in the bosom of his family at his residence in this city.

Mr. Ferguson was one who became a member of this society without any prospect of advantage to himself. He was, though not totally abstinent, strictly temperate before; and he espoused the cause solely with the hope and benevolent design of being able, by his efforts and example, to benefit others. Would to God, he had been longer spared to the humane work upon which he had so disinterestedly entered.

In his intercourse with his fellow men, he possessed that rare uprightness of character, which was evidenced by his having no disputes or bickerings of his own, while he was ever the chosen arbiter to settle those of his neighbors.

In very truth he was, the noblest work of God—an honest man.

The grateful task commonly vouchsafed to the mournful living, of casting the mantle of charitable forgetfulness over the faults of the lamented dead, is denied to us: for although it is much to say, for any of the erring family of man, we believe we may say, that he whom we deplore was faultless.

To Almighty God we commend him; and, in his name, implore the aid and protection, of his omnipotent right arm, for his bereaved and disconsolate family.

The "Eulogy" and the "Temperance Address" given two weeks later were both delivered before the Washington Temperance Society. It may be noted that although the members were often referred to as "the Washingtonians," the name of the Society was not "Washingtonian" as has generally been supposed. It is not certain that Lincoln was ever a member of the organization.

LETTER TO JOSHUA F. SPEED
FEBRUARY 13, 1842

Springfield, Ills. February 13. 1842—

Dear Speed:

Yours of the 1st. Inst. came to hand three or four days ago. When this shall reach you, you will have been Fanny's husband several days. You know my desire to befriend you is everlasting —that I will never cease, while I know how to do anything.

But you will always hereafter, be on ground that I have never occupied, and consequently, if advice were needed, I might advise wrong. I do fondly hope, however, that you will never again need any comfort from abroad. But should I be mistaken in this—should excessive pleasure still be accompanied with a painful counterpart at times, still let me urge you, as I have ever done, to remember, in the depth and even the agony of despondency, that very shortly you are to feel well again. I am now fully convinced that you love her as ardently as you are capable of loving. Your ever being happy in her presence, and your intense anxiety about her health, if there were nothing else, would place this beyond all dispute in my mind. I incline to think it probable, that your nerves will fail you occasionally for a while; but once you get them fairly graded now, that trouble is over forever. I think, if I were you, in case my mind were not exactly right, I would avoid being *idle*; I would immediately engage in some business, or go to making preparations for it, which would be the same thing.

If you went through the ceremony *calmly*, or even with sufficient composure not to excite alarm in any present, you are safe, beyond question, and in two or three months, to say the most, will be the happiest of men.

I would desire you to give my particular respects to Fanny, but perhaps you will not wish her to know you have received this, lest she should desire to see it. Make her write me an answer to my last letter to her at any rate. I would set great value upon another letter from her.

Write me whenever you have leisure.

Yours forever
A. Lincoln

P. S. I have been quite a man since you left.

Lincoln's chirography is open to question in the phrase "fairly graded," although it seems clear enough. Nicolay and Hay give "firmly guarded," which fits neither chirography nor sense of the sentence so well as "fairly graded." The editor understands Lincoln to be speaking figuratively of smoothing or leveling a state of ragged nerves.

The cryptic postscript is open to anyone's guess. The editor's is that Lincoln had met Mary, at least socially, and had managed to "be himself."

TEMPERANCE ADDRESS DELIVERED BEFORE THE SPRINGFIELD WASHINGTON TEMPERANCE SOCIETY. FEBRUARY 22, 1842

Although the Temperance cause has been in progress for near twenty years, it is apparent to all, that it is, *just now*, being crowned with a degree of success, hitherto unparalleled.

The list of its friends is daily swelled by the additions of fifties, of hundreds, and of thousands. The cause itself seems suddenly transformed from a cold abstract theory, to a living, breathing, active, and powerful chieftain, going forth "conquering and to conquer." The citadels of his great adversary are daily being stormed and dismantled; his temples and his altars, where the rites of his idolatrous worship have long been performed, and where human sacrifices have long been wont to be made, are daily desecrated and deserted. The trump of the conqueror's fame is sounding from hill to hill, from sea to sea, and from land to land, and calling millions to his standard at a blast.

For this new and splendid success, we heartily rejoice. That that success is so much greater *now* than *heretofore*, is doubtless owing to rational causes; and if we would have it to continue, we shall do well to enquire what those causes are. The warfare heretofore waged against the demon of Intemperance, has, some how or other, been erroneous. Either the champions engaged, or the tactics they adopted, have not been the most proper. These champions for the most part, have been Preachers, Lawyers, and hired agents.—Between these and the mass of mankind, there is a want of *approachability*, if the term be admissible, partially at least, fatal to their success. They are supposed to have no sympathy of feeling or interest, with those very persons whom it is their object to convince and persuade.

And again, it is so easy and so common to ascribe motives to men of these classes, other than those they profess to act upon. The *preacher*, it is said, advocates temperance because he is a fanatic, and desires a union of the Church and State; the *lawyer*, from his pride and vanity of hearing himself speak; and the *hired agent*, for his salary. But when one, who has long been known as a victim of intemperance, bursts the fetters that have bound him, and appears before his neighbors "clothed, and in his right mind," a redeemed specimen of long lost humanity, and stands up with tears of joy trembling in eyes, to tell of the miseries *once* endured, *now* to be endured no more forever; of his once naked and starving children, now clad and fed comfortably; of a wife, long weighed down with woe, weeping, and a broken heart, now restored to health, happiness and renewed affection; and how easily it all is done, once it is resolved to be done; however simple his language, there is a logic, and an eloquence in it, that few, with human feelings, can resist. They cannot say that *he* desires a union of church and state, for he is not a church member; they can not say *he* is vain of hearing himself speak, for his whole demeanor shows, he would gladly avoid speaking at all; they cannot say *he* speaks for pay for he receives none, and asks for none. Nor can his sincerity in any way be doubted; or his sympathy for those he would persuade to imitate his example, be denied.

In my judgment, it is to the battles of this new class of champions that our late success is greatly, perhaps chiefly, owing. —But, had the old school champions themselves, been of the most wise selecting, was their *system* of tactics, the most judicious? It seems to me, it was not. Too much denunciation against dram sellers and dram drinkers was indulged in. This, I think, was both impolitic and unjust. It was *impolitic*, because, it is not much in the nature of man to be driven to any thing; still less to be driven about that which is exclusively his own business; and least of all, where such driving is to be submitted to, at the expense of pecuniary interest, or burning appetite. When the dram-seller and drinker, were incessantly told, not in the accents of entreaty and persuasion, diffidently addressed by erring man to an erring brother, but in the thundering tones of anathema and denunciation, with which the lordly Judge often groups together all the crimes of the felon's life, and thrusts them in his face just ere he passes sentence of death upon him, that *they* were the authors of all the vice and misery and crime in the land; that *they* were the manufacturers and material of all the thieves and robbers and murderers that infested the earth; that *their* houses were the workshops of the devil; and that *their persons* should be shunned by all the good and virtuous, as moral pestilences—I say, when they were told all this, and in this way, it is not wonderful that they were slow, *very slow,* to acknowledge the truth of such denunciations, and to join the ranks of their denouncers, in a hue and cry against themselves.

To have expected them to do otherwise than as they did—to have expected them not to meet denunciation with denunciation, crimination with crimination, and anathema with anathema, was to expect a reversal of human nature, which is God's decree, and never can be reversed. When the conduct of men is designed to be influenced, *persuasion*, kind, unassuming persuasion, should ever be adopted. It is an old and a true maxim "that a drop of honey catches more flies than a gallon of gall."—So with men. If you would win a man to your cause, *first* convince him that you are his sincere friend. Therein is a drop of honey that catches his heart, which, say what he will, is the great high road to his reason, and which, when once gained, you will find but little trouble in convincing his judgment of the justice of your cause, if indeed that cause really be a just one. On the contrary, assume to dictate to his judgment, or to command his action, or to mark him as one to be shunned and despised, and he will retreat within himself, close all the avenues to his head and his heart; and though your cause be naked truth itself, transformed to the heaviest lance, harder than steel, and sharper than steel can be made, and tho' you throw it with more than Herculean force and precision, you shall be no more able to pierce him, than to penetrate the hard shell of a tortoise with a rye straw.

Such is man, and so *must* he be understood by those who would lead him, even to his own best interest.

On this point, the Washingtonians greatly excel the temperance advocates of former times. Those whom *they* desire to convince and persuade, are their old friends and companions. They know they are not demons, nor even the worst of men. *They* know that generally, they are kind, generous, and charitable, even beyond the example of their more staid and sober neighbors. *They* are practical philanthropists; and *they* glow with a generous and brotherly zeal, that mere theorizers are incapable of feeling. —Benevolence and charity possess *their* hearts entirely; and out of the abundance of their hearts, their tongues give utterance. "Love through all their actions runs, and all their words are mild." In this spirit they speak and act, and in the same, they are heard and regarded. And when such is the temper of the advocate, and such of the audience, no good cause can be unsuccessful.

But I have said that denunciations against dram-sellers and dram-drinkers are *unjust*, as well as impolitic. Let us see.

I have not enquired at what period of time the use of intoxicating drinks commenced; nor is it important to know. It is sufficient that to all of us who now inhabit the world, the practice of drinking them, is just as old as the world itself,—that is, we have seen the one, just as long as we have seen the other. When all such of us, as have now reached the years of maturity, first opened our eyes upon the stage of existence, we found intoxicating liquor, recognized by every body, used by every body, and repudiated by nobody. It commonly entered into the first draught of the infant, and the last draught of the dying man. From the sideboard of the parson, down to the ragged pocket of the houseless loafer, it was constantly found. Physicians prescribed it in this, that, and the other disease. Government provided it for its soldiers and sailors; And to have a rolling or raising, a husking or hoe-down, any where without it was *positively insufferable.*

So too, it was every where a respectable article of manufacture and of merchandize. The making of it was regarded as an honorable livelihood; and he who could make most, was the most enterprising and respectable. Large and small manufactories of it were every where erected, in which all the earthly goods of their owners were invested. Wagons drew it from town to town—boats bore it from clime to clime, and the winds wafted it from nation to nation; and merchants bought and sold it, by wholesale and by retail, with precisely the same feelings, on the part of the seller, buyer, and by-stander as are felt at the selling and buying of flour, beef, bacon, or any other of the real necessaries of life. Universal public opinion not only tolerated, but recognized and adopted its use.

It is true, that even *then*, it was known and acknowledged, that many were greatly injured by it; but none seemed to think the injury arose from the *use* of a *bad thing*, but from the *abuse* of a *very good thing.*—The victims to it were pitied, and compassionated, just as now are, the heirs of consumptions, and other hereditary diseases. Their failing was treated as a *misfortune*, and not as a *crime*, or even as a *disgrace.*

If, then, what I have been saying be true, is it wonderful that *some* should think and act *now*, as *all* thought and acted *twenty years ago*? And is it *just* to assail, contemn, or despise them, for doing so? The universal *sense* of mankind, on any subject, is an argument, or at least an *influence*, not easily overcome. The success of the argument in favor of the existence of an overruling Providence, mainly depends upon that sense; and men ought not, in justice, to be denounced for yielding to it in any case, or for giving it up slowly, *especially*, where they are backed by interest, fixed habits, or burning appetites.

Another error, as it seems to me, into which the old reformers fell, was, the position that all habitual drunkards were utterly incorrigible, and therefore, must be turned adrift, and damned without remedy, in order that the grace of temperance might abound to the temperate *then*, and to all mankind some hundred years *thereafter*.—There is in this something so repugnant to humanity, so uncharitable, so cold-blooded and feelingless, that it never did, nor ever can enlist the enthusiasm of a popular cause. We could not love the man who taught it—we could not hear him with patience. The heart could not throw open its portals to it. The generous man could not adopt it. It could not mix with his blood. It looked so fiendishly selfish, so like throwing fathers and brothers overboard, to lighten the boat for our security—that the noble minded shrank from the manifest meanness of the thing.

And besides this, the benefits of a reformation to be effected by such a system, were too remote in point of time, to warmly engage many in its behalf. Few can be induced to labor exclusively for posterity; and none will do it enthusiastically. Posterity has done nothing for us; and theorise on it as we may, practically we shall do very little for it, unless we are made to think, we are, at the same time, doing something for ourselves. What an ignorance of human nature does it exhibit, to ask or expect a whole community to rise up and labor for the *temporal* happiness of *others*, after *themselves* shall be consigned to the dust, a majority of which community take no pains whatever to secure their own eternal welfare, at no greater distant day? Great distance, in either time or space, has wonderful power to lull and render quiescent the human mind. Pleasures to be enjoyed, or pains to be endured, *after* we shall be dead and gone, are but little regarded, even in our *own* cases, and much less in the cases of others.

Still, in addition to this, there is something so ludicrous in *promises* of good, or *threats* of evil, a great way off, as to render the whole subject with which they are connected, easily turned into ridicule. "Better lay down that spade you're stealing, Paddy,

—if you don't you'll pay for it at the day of judgment." "By the powers, if ye'll credit me so long, I'll take another, jist."

By the Washingtonians, this system of consigning the habitual drunkard to hopeless ruin, is repudiated. *They* adopt a more enlarged philanthropy. *They* go for present as well as future good. *They* labor for all *now* living, as well as all *hereafter* to live.—*They* teach *hope* to all—*despair* to none. As applying to *their* cause, *they* deny the doctrine of unpardonable sin. As in Christianity it is taught, so in this *they* teach, that

"While the lamp holds out to burn,
The vilest sinner may return."

And, what is a matter of the most profound gratulation, they, by experiment upon experiment, and example upon example, prove the maxim to be no less true in the one case than in the other. On every hand we behold those, who but yesterday, were the chief of sinners, now the chief apostles of the cause. Drunken devils are cast out by ones, by sevens, and by legions; and their unfortunate victims, like the poor possessed, who was redeemed from his long and lonely wanderings in the tombs, are publishing to the ends of the earth how great things have been done for them.

To these *new champions*, and this *new* system of tactics, our late success is mainly owing; and to *them* we must chiefly look for the final consummation. The ball is now rolling gloriously on, and none are so able as *they* to increase its speed and its bulk—to add to its momentum, and its magnitude.—Even though unlearned in letters, for this task, none others are so well educated. To fit them for this work, they have been taught in the true school. *They* have been in *that* gulf, from which they would teach others the means of escape. *They* have passed that prison wall, which others have long declared impassable; and who that has not, shall dare to weigh opinions with *them*, as to the mode of passing?

But if it be true, as I have insisted, that those who have suffered by intemperance *personally*, and have reformed, are the most powerful and efficient instruments to push the reformation to ultimate success, it does not follow, that those who have not suffered, have no part left them to perform. Whether or not the world would be vastly benefitted by a total and final banishment from it of all intoxicating drinks, seems to me not *now* to be an open question. Three-fourths of mankind confess the affirmative with their *tongues*, and, I believe, all the rest acknowledge it in their *hearts*.

Ought *any*, then, to refuse their aid in doing what the good of the *whole* demands?—Shall he, who cannot do *much*, be for that reason, excused if he do *nothing*? "But," says one, "what good can I do by signing the pledge? I never drink even without signing." This question has already been asked and answered more than millions of times. Let it be answered once more. For the man to suddenly, or in any other way, to break off from the use of drams, who has indulged in them for a long course of years, and until his appetite for them has become ten or a hundred fold stronger, and more craving, than any natural appetite can be, requires a most powerful moral effort. In such an undertaking, he needs every moral support and influence, that can possibly be brought to his aid, and thrown around him. And not only so; but every moral prop, should be taken *from* whatever argument might rise in his mind to lure him to his backsliding. When he casts his eyes around him, he should be able to see, all that he respects, all that he admires, and all that [he?] loves, kindly and anxiously pointing him onward; and none beckoning him back, to his former miserable "wallowing in the mire."

But it is said by some, that men will *think* and *act* for themselves; that none will disuse spirits or anything else, merely because his neighbors do; and that *moral influence* is not that powerful engine contended for. Let us examine this. Let me ask the man who would maintain this position most stiffly, what compensation he will accept to go to church some Sunday and sit during the sermon with his wife's bonnet upon his head? Not a trifle, I'll venture. And why not? There would be nothing irreligious in it: nothing immoral, nothing uncomfortable.—Then why not? Is it not because there would be something egregiously unfashionable in it? Then it is the influence of *fashion*; and what is the influence of fashion, but the influence that *other* people's actions have on our actions, the strong inclination each of us feels to do as we see all our neighbors do? Nor is the influence of fashion confined to any particular thing or class of things. It is just as strong on one subject as another. Let us make it as unfashionable to withhold our names from the temperance pledge as for husbands to wear their wives' bonnets to church, and instances will be just as rare in the one case as the other.

"But," say some, "we are no drunkards; and we shall not acknowledge ourselves such by joining a reformed drunkards' society, whatever our influence might be." Surely no Christian will adhere to this objection.—If they believe, as they profess, that Omnipotence condescended to take on himself the form of sinful man, and as such, to die an ignominious death for their sakes, surely they will not refuse submission to the infinitely lesser condescension, for the temporal, and perhaps eternal salvation, of a large, erring, and unfortunate class of their own fellow creatures. Nor is the condescension very great.

In my judgment, such of us as have never fallen victims, have been spared more from the absence of appetite, than from any mental or moral superiority over those who have. Indeed, I believe, if we take habitual drunkards as a class, their heads and their hearts will bear an advantageous comparison with those of any other class. There seems ever to have been a proneness in the brilliant, and the warm-blooded, to fall into this vice—the demon of intemperance ever seems to have delighted in sucking the blood of genius and of generosity. What one of us but can call to mind some dear relative, more promising in youth than all his fellows, who has fallen a sacrifice to his rapacity? He ever seems to have gone forth, like the Egyptian angel of death, commissioned to slay if not the first, the fairest born of every family. Shall he now be arrested in his desolating career? In that arrest, all can give aid that will; and who shall be excused that *can* and will not? Far around as human breath has ever blown, he keeps our fathers, our brothers, our sons, and our friends prostrate in the chains of moral death. To all the living every where, we cry, "come sound the moral resurrection trump, that these may rise and stand up, an exceeding great army"— "Come from the four winds, O breath! and breathe upon these slain, that they may live."

If the relative grandeur of revolutions shall be estimated

by the great amount of human misery they alleviate, and the small amount they inflict, then indeed, will this be the grandest the world shall ever have seen.—Of our political revolution of '76 we all are justly proud. It has given us a degree of political freedom, far exceeding that of any other of the nations of the earth. In it the world has found a solution of the long mooted problem, as to the capability of man to govern himself. In it was the germ which has vegetated, and still is to grow and expand into the universal liberty of mankind.

But with all these glorious results, past, present, and to come, it had its evils too.—It breathed forth famine, swam in blood and rode on fire; and long, long after, the orphan's cry, and the widow's wail, continued to break the sad silence that ensued. These were the price, the inevitable price, paid for the blessings it bought.

Turn now, to the temperance revolution. In *it* we shall find a stronger bondage broken; a viler slavery manumitted; a greater tyrant deposed. In *it*, more of want supplied, more disease healed, more sorrow assuaged. By *it* no orphans starving, no widows weeping. By *it*, none wounded in feeling, none injured in interest. Even the dram maker and dram seller, will have glided into other occupations *so* gradually, as never to have felt the shock of change; and will stand ready to join all others in the universal song of gladness.

And what a noble ally this, to the cause of political freedom. With such an aid, its march cannot fail to be on and on, till every son of earth shall drink in rich fruition, the sorrow quenching draughts of perfect liberty. Happy day, when, all appetites controlled, all passions subdued, all matters subjected, *mind*, all conquering *mind*, shall live and move the monarch of the world. Glorious consummation! Hail, fall of Fury! Reign of Reason, all hail!

And when the victory shall be complete—when there shall be neither a slave nor a drunkard on the earth—how proud the title of that *Land*, which may truly claim to be the birthplace and the cradle of both those revolutions, that shall have ended in that victory. How nobly distinguished that People, who shall have planted, and nurtured to maturity, both the political and moral freedom of their species.

This is the one hundred and tenth anniversary of the birthday of Washington.—We are met to celebrate this day. Washington is the mightiest name of earth—*long since* mightiest in the cause of civil liberty; *still* mightiest in moral reformation. On that name an eulogy is expected. It cannot be. To add brightness to the sun, or glory to the name of Washington, is alike impossible. Let none attempt it. In solemn awe pronounce the name, and in its naked deathless splendor, leave it shining on.

LETTER TO JOSHUA F. SPEED FEBRUARY 25, 1842

Springfield, Feby. 25 1842—

Dear Speed:

Yours of the 16th. Inst., announcing that Miss Fanny and you are "no more twain, but one flesh," reached me this morning. I have no way of telling you how much happiness I wish you both; tho I believe you both can conceive it. I feel somewhat jealous of both of you now; you will be so exclusively concerned for one another, that I shall be forgotten entirely. My acquaintance with Miss Fanny (I call her this, lest you should think I am speaking of your mother) was too short for me to reasonably hope to long be remembered by her; and still, I am sure I shall not forget her soon. Try if you can not remind her of that debt she owes me; and be sure you do not interfere to prevent her paying it.

I regret to learn that you have resolved to not return to Illinois. I shall be very lonesome without you. How miserably things seem to be arranged in this world. If we have no friends, we have no pleasure; and if we have them, we are sure to lose them, and be doubly pained by the loss. I did hope she and you would make your home here; but I own I have no right to insist. You owe obligations to her, ten thousand times more sacred than any you can owe to others; and in that light, let them be respected and observed. It is natural that she should desire to remain with her relatives and friends. As to friends, however, she could not need them any where; she would have them in abundance here.

Give my kind rememberance [*sic*] to Mr. Williamson and his family, particularly Miss Elizabeth. Also to your Mother, brothers, and sisters. Ask little Eliza Davis if she will ride to town with me if I come there again. And finally, give Fanny a double reciprocation of all the love she sent me. Write me often, and believe me

Yours forever,
Lincoln.

P. S. Poor Eastham is gone at last. He died awhile before day this morning. They say he was very loth to die.

No clerk is appointed yet.

L

As indicated by the context of the second of the two letters bearing this date, both were sent together and the second was for Speed's eyes only. Lincoln's analysis of his friend is indubitably as much self-analysis as it is analysis of Speed, and, although it lacks a good deal of penetrating the unconscious for the spectres which psychoanalysis reveals, it is an adequate job of rationalizing the inevitable.

The postscript to the first letter refers to the Clerk of Sangamon County Court.

LETTER TO JOSHUA F. SPEED FEBRUARY 25, 1842

Springfield, Feb: 25—1842—

Dear Speed:

I received yours of the 12th. written the day you went down to William's place, some days since; but delayed answering it, till I should receive the promised one, of the 16th., which came last night. I opened the latter, with intense anxiety and trepidation—so much, that although it turned out better than I expected, I have hardly yet, at the distance of ten hours, become calm.

I tell you, Speed, our *forebodings*, for which you and I are rather peculiar, are all the worst sort of nonsense. I fancied, from the time I received your letter of saturday, that the one of wednesday was never to come; and yet it *did* come, and what is more, it is perfectly clear, both from its *tone* and *handwriting*, that you were much *happier*, or, if you think the term preferable, less miserable, when you wrote *it* than when you wrote the last one before. You had so obviously improved, at the very time I so much feared, you would have grown worse. You say that "something indescribably horrible and alarming still haunts you. You will not say *that* three months from now, I will venture. When your nerves once get steady now, the whole trouble will be over forever. Nor should you become impatient at their being even very slow in becoming steady. Again; you say you much fear that that Elysium of which you have dreamed so much is never to be realized. Well, if it shall not, I dare swear it will not be the fault of her who is now your wife. I now have no doubt that it is the peculiar misfortune of both you and me, to dream dreams of Elysium far exceeding all that anything earthly can realize. Far short of your dreams as you may be, no woman could do more to realize them, than that same black eyed Fanny. If you could but contemplate her through my imagination, it would appear ridiculous to you that any one should for a moment think of being unhappy with her.

My old Father used to have a saying that "If you make a bad bargain, *hug* it all the tighter", and it occurs to me, that if the bargain you have just closed can possibly be called a bad one, it is certainly the most *pleasant one* for applying that maxim to, which my fancy can, by any effort, picture.

I write another letter enclosing this, which you can show her, if she desires it. I do this because, she would think strangely perhaps, should you tell her that you received no letters from me; or, telling her you do, should refuse to let her see them.

I close this, entertaining the confident hope, that every successive letter I shall have from you, (which I here pray may not be few, nor far between,) may show you possessing a more steady hand, and cheerful heart than the last preceding it.

As ever, your friend
Lincoln

LETTER TO JOSHUA F. SPEED
MARCH 27, 1842

Springfield, March 27th., 1842

Dear Speed:

Yours of the 10th. Inst. was received three or four days since. You know I am sincere, when I tell you, the pleasure it's contents gave me was and is inexpressible. As to your farm matter, I have no sympathy with you. *I* have no farm, nor ever expect to have; and, consequently, have not studied the subject enough to be much interested with it. I can only say that I am glad *you* are satisfied and pleased with it.

But on that other subject, to me of the most intense interest, whether in joy or sorrow, I never had the power to withhold my sympathy from you. It can not be told, how it now thrills me with joy, to hear you say you are "*far happier than you ever expected to be.*" That much I know is enough. I know you too well to suppose your expectations were not, at least sometimes, extravagant; and if the reality exceeds them all, I say, enough dear Lord. I am not going beyond the truth, when I tell you, that the short space it took me to read your last letter, gave me more pleasure, than the total sum of all I have enjoyed since that fatal first Jany. '41. Since then, it seems to me, I should have been entirely happy, but for the never-absent idea, that there is *one* still unhappy whom I have contributed to make so. That still kills my soul. I can not but reproach myself, for ever wishing to be happy while she is otherwise. She accompanied a large party on the Rail Road cars, to Jacksonville last Monday; and on her return, spoke, so that I heard of it, of having enjoyed the trip exceedingly. God be praised for that.

You know with what sleepless vigilance I have watched you, ever since the commencement of your affair; and altho I am now almost confident it is useless, I can not forbear once more to say that I think it is even yet possible for your spirits to flag down and leave you miserable. If they should, don't fail to remember that they can not long remain so.

One thing I can tell you which I know you will be glad to hear; and that is, that I have seen Sarah, and scrutinized her feelings as well as I could, and am fully convinced, she is far happier now, than she has been for the last fifteen months past.

You will see by the last Sangamo Journal that I made a Temperance speech on the 22—of Feb. which I claim Fanny and you shall read as an act of charity to me; for I can not learn that any body else has read it, or is likely to. Fortunately, it is not very long; and I shall deem it a sufficient compliance with my request, if one of you listens while the other reads it. As to your Lockridge matter, it is only necessary to say that there has been no court since you left, and that the next commences to-morrow morning, during which I suppose we can not fail to get a judgement.

I wish you would learn of Everett what he will take, over and above a discharge for all trouble we have been at, to take his business out of our hands and give it to some body else. It is impossible to collect money on that or any other claim here now;

and altho you know I am not a very petulant man, I declare I am almost out of patience with Mr. Everett's endless importunity. It seems like he not only writes all the letters he can himself; but gets every body else in Louisville and vicinity to be constantly writing to us about his claim. I have always said that Mr. Everett is a very clever fellow, and I am very sorry he can not be obliged; but it does seem to me he ought to know we are interested to collect his money, and therefore *would* do it if we could. I am neither joking nor in a pet when I say we would thank him to transfer his business to some other, without any compensation for what we have done, provided he will see the court cost paid, for which we are security.

The sweet violet you enclosed, came safely to hand, but it was so dry, and mashed so flat, that it crumbled to dust at the first attempt to handle it. The juice that mashed out of it, stained a place on the letter, which I mean to preserve and cherish for the sake of her who procured it to be sent. My renewed good wishes to her in particular, and generally to all such of your relatives as know me.

As ever
Lincoln

LETTER TO JOSHUA F. SPEED
JULY 4, 1842

Springfield, Ills—July 4th. 1842—

Dear Speed:

Yours of the 16th. June was received only a day or two since. It was not mailed at Louisville till the 25th. You speak of the great time that has elapsed since I wrote you. Let me explain that. Your letter reached here a day or two after I started on the circuit; I was gone five or six weeks, so that I got the letter only a few weeks before Butler started to your country. I thought it scarcely worth while to write you the news, which he could and would tell you more in detail. On his return, he told me you would write me soon; and so I waited for your letter. As to my having been displeased with your advice, surely you know better than that. I know you do; and therefore I will not labor to convince you. True, that subject is painful to me; but it is not your silence, or the silence of all the world that can make me forget it. I acknowledge the correctness of your advice too; but before I resolve to do the one thing or the other, I must regain my confidence in my own ability to keep my resolves when they are made. In that ability, you know, I once prided myself as the only, or at least the chief, gem of my character; that gem I lost—how, and where, you too well know. I have not yet regained it; and until I do, I can not trust myself in any matter of much importance. I believe now that had you understood my case at the time, as well as I understood yours afterwards, by the aid you would have given me, I should have sailed through clear; but that does not now afford me sufficient confidence, to begin that, or the like of that, again.

You make a kind acknowledgment of your obligations to me for your present happiness. I am pleased with that acknowledgment; but a thousand times more am I pleased to know, that you enjoy a degree of happiness, worthy of an acknowledgment. The truth is, I am not sure that there was any merit, with me, in the part I took in your difficulty; I was drawn to it as by fate; if I would, I could not have done less than I did. I always was superstitious; and as part of my superstition, I believe God made me one of the instruments of bringing your Fanny and you together, which union, I have no doubt He had fore-ordained. Whatever he designs, he will do for *me* yet. "Stand *still*, and see the salvation of the Lord" is my text just now. If, as you say, you have told Fanny *all*, I should have no objection to her seeing this letter, but for its reference to our friend here. Let her seeing it, depend upon whether she has ever known anything of my affair; and if she has not, do not let her.

I do not think I can come to Kentucky this season. I am so poor, and make so little headway in the world, that I drop back in a month of idleness, as much as I gain in a year's rowing. I should like to visit you again. I should like to see that "Sis" of yours, that was absent when I was there; tho I suppose she would run away again, if she were to hear I was coming.

About your collecting business. We have sued Branson; and will sue the others to the next court, unless they give deeds of trust as you require. Col Allen happened in the office since I commenced this letter, and promises to give a deed of trust. He says he had made the arrangement to pay you, and would have done it, but for the going down of the Shawnee money. We did not get the note in time to sue Hall at the last Tazewell court. Lockridge's property is levied on for you. John Irwin has done nothing with that Baker & Van Bergen matter. We will not fail to bring the suits for your use, where they are in the name of James Bell & Co. I have made you a suscriber to the Journal; and also sent the number containing the temperance speech. My respect and esteem to all your friends there; and, by your permission, my love to your Fanny.

Ever yours—
Lincoln

A LETTER FROM THE LOST TOWNSHIPS
AUGUST 27, 1842

Lost Townships, August 27, 1842.

Dear Mr. Printer:

I see you printed that long letter I sent you a spell ago. I'm quite encouraged by it, and can't keep from writing again. I think the printing of my letters will be a good thing all round,—it will give me the benefit of being known by the world, and give the world the advantage of knowing what's going on in the Lost Townships, and give your paper respectability besides. So here comes another.—Yesterday afternoon I hurried through cleaning up the dinner dishes, and stepped over to neighbor S—— to see if his wife Peggy was as well as mought be expected, and hear what they called the baby. Well, when I got there, and just turned round the corner of his log cabin, there he was, setting on the door-step reading a newspaper.

'How are you, Jeff?' says I. He sorter started when he heard me, for he hadn't seen me before. 'Why,' says he, 'I'm mad as the devil, aunt Becca!'

'What about?' says I; 'ain't its hair the right color? None of that nonsense, Jeff—there ain't an honester woman in the Lost Township than—'

'Than who?' says he; 'what the mischief are you about?'

I began to see I was running the wrong trail, and so says I, 'O! nothing, I guess I was mistaken a little, that's all. But what is it you're mad about?'

'Why,' says he, 'I've been tugging ever since harvest getting out wheat and hauling it to the river to raise State Bank paper enough to pay my tax this year, and a little school debt I owe; and now just as I've got it, here I open this infernal Extra Register, expecting to find it full of "glorious democratic victories," and "High Comb'd Cocks," when, lo and behold! I find a set of fellows, calling themselves *officers of State*, have forbidden the tax collectors and school commissioners to receive State paper at all; and so here it is, dead on my hands. I don't now believe all the plunder I've got will fetch ready cash enough to pay my taxes and that school debt.'

I was a good deal thunderstruck myself; for that was the first I had heard of the proclamation, and my old man was pretty much in the same fix with Jeff. We both stood a moment, staring at one another without knowing what to say. At last says I, 'Mr. S—— let me look at that paper.' He handed it to me, when I read the proclamation over.

'There now,' says he, 'did you ever see such a piece of impudence and imposition as that?' I saw Jeff was in a good tune for saying some ill-natured things, and so I tho't I would just argue a little on the contrary side, and make him rant a spell if I could.

'Why,' says I, looking as dignified and thoughtful as I could, 'it seems pretty tough to be sure, to have to raise silver where there's none to be raised; but then, you see, "*there will be danger of loss*" if it ain't done.'

'Loss, damnation!' says he. 'I defy Daniel Webster, I defy King Solomon, I defy the world,—I defy—I defy—yes, I defy even you, aunt Becca, to show how the people can lose any thing by paying their taxes in State paper.' 'Well,' says I, 'you see what the *officers of State* say about it, and they are a desarnin set of men.' 'But,' says I, 'I guess you're mistaken about what the proclamation says; it don't say *the people* will lose any thing by the paper money being taken for taxes. It only says *"there will be danger of loss,"* and though it is tolerable plain that the people can't lose by paying their taxes in something they can get easier than silver, instead of having to pay silver; and though it is just as plain, that the State can't lose by taking State Bank paper, however low it may be, while she owes the Bank more than the whole revenue, and can pay that paper over on her debt, dollar for dollar; still *there is danger of loss* to the *"officers of State"*; and you know, Jeff, we can't get along without *officers of State.*'

'Damn officers of State,' says he; 'that's what you whigs are always hurraing for.' 'Now don't swear so, Jeff,' says I, 'you know I belong to the meetin, and swearin hurts my feelins.' 'Beg pardon, aunt Becca,' says he, 'but I do say it's enough to make Dr. Goddard swear, to have tax to pay in silver, for nothing only that Ford may get his two thousand a year, and Shields his twenty four hundred a year, and Carpenter his sixteen hundred a year, and all without "danger of loss" by taking it in State paper. Yes, yes, it's plain enough now what these *officers of State* mean by "danger of loss." Wash, I 'spose, actually lost fifteen hundred dollars out of the three thousand that two of these "officers of State" let him steal from the Treasury, by being compelled to take it in State paper.—Wonder if we don't have a proclamation before long, commanding us to make up this loss to Wash in silver.'

And so he went on, till his breath run out, and he had to stop. I couldn't think of anything to say just then: and so I begun to look over the paper again. 'Aye! here's another proclamation, or something like it.' 'Another!' says Jeff, 'and whose egg is it, pray?' I looked to the bottom of it, and read aloud,

'Your obedient servant,
'Jas. Shields, Auditor.'

'Aha!' says Jeff, 'one of them same three fellows again. Well, read it, and let's hear what of it.' I read on till I came to where it says, *'The object of this measure is to suspend the collection of the revenue for the current year.'* 'Now stop, now stop,' says he, 'that's a lie aready, and I don't want to hear of it.' 'O, may be not,' says I.

'I say *it—is—a—lie.*—Suspend the collection, indeed! Will the collectors that have taken their oaths to make the collection, DARE to suspend it? Is there any thing in the law requiring them to perjure themselves at the bidding of Jas. Shields? Will the greedy gullet of the penitentiary be satisfied with swallowing *him* instead of all *them* if they should venture to obey him? And would he not discover some "danger of loss," and be off, about the time it came to taking their places?'

'And suppose the people attempt to suspend by refusing to pay, what then? The collectors would just jerk up their horses, and cows, and the like, and sell them to the highest bidder for silver in hand, without valuation or redemption. Why, Shields didn't believe that story himself—it was never meant for the truth. If it was true, why was it not writ till five days after the proclamation? Why didn't Carlin and Carpenter sign it as well as Shields? Answer me that, aunt Becca. I say it's a lie, and not a well told one at that. It grins out like a copper dollar. Shields is a fool as well as a liar. With him truth is out of the question, and as for getting a good bright passable lie out of him, you might as well try to strike fire from a cake of tallow. I stick to it, it's all an infernal whig lie.'

'A *whig* lie,—Highty! Tighty!!'

'Yes, a *whig* lie; and it's just like every thing the cursed British whigs do. First they'll do some divilment, and then they'll tell a lie to hide it. And they don't care how plain a lie it is; they think they can cram any sort of a one down the throats of the ignorant loco focos, as they call the democrats.'

'Why, Jeff, you're crazy—you don't mean to say Shields is a whig.'

'Yes, I do.'

'Why, look here, the proclamation is in your own democratic paper as you call it.'

'I know it, and what of that? They only printed it to let us democrats see the deviltry the whigs are at.'

'Well, but Shields is the Auditor of this loco—I mean this democratic State.'

'So he is, and Tyler appointed him to office.'

'Tyler appointed him?'

'Yes (if you must chaw it over) Tyler appointed him, or if it wasn't him it was old granny Harrison, and that's all one. I tell you, aunt Becca, there's no mistake about his being a whig—why, his very looks shows it—every thing about him shows it—if I was deaf and blind I could tell him by the smell. I seed him when I was down in Springfield last winter. They had a sort of a gatherin there one night, among the grandees, they called a fair. All the galls about town was there, and all the handsome widows, and married women, finickin about, trying to look like galls, tied as tight in the middle, and puffed out at both ends like bundles of fodder that hadn't been stacked yet, but wanted stackin pretty bad. And then they had tables all round the house kivered over with baby caps, and pin-cushions, and ten thousand such little nick-nacks, tryin to sell 'em to the fellows that were bowin, and scrapin and kungeerin about 'em. They wouldn't let no democrats in, for fear they'd disgust the ladies, or scare the little galls, or dirty the floor. I looked in at the window, and there was this same fellow Shields floatin about on the air, without heft or earthly substance, just like a lock of cat-fur where cats had been fightin.

'He was paying his money to this one and that one, and tother one, and sufferin great loss because it wasn't silver instead of State paper; and the sweet distress he seemed to be in,—his very features, in the exstatic agony of his soul, spoke audibly and distinctly—'Dear girls, *it is distressing*, but I cannot marry you all. Too well I know how much you suffer; but do, *do* remember, it is not my fault that I am *so* handsome and *so* interesting.'

'As this last was expressed by a most exquisite contortion of his face, he seized hold of one of their hands and squeezed, and held on to it about a quarter of an hour. O, my good fellow, says I to myself, if that was one of our democratic galls in the Lost Township, the way you'd get a brass pin let into you, would be about up to the head. He a democrat! Fiddle-sticks! I tell you, aunt

Becca, he's a whig, and no mistake: nobody but a whig could make such a conceity dunce of himself.'

'Well, says I, may be he is, but if he is, I'm mistaken the worst sort.'

'May be so; may be so; but, if I am, I'll suffer by it; I'll be a democrat if it turns out that Shields is a whig; considerin you shall be a whig if he turns out a democrat.'

'A bargain, by jingoes,' says he; 'but how will we find out.'

'Why,' says I, 'we'll just write and ax the printer.' 'Agreed again,' says he, 'and by thunder if it does turn out that Shields is a democrat, I never will——'

'Jefferson,—Jefferson—'

'What do you want, Peggy?'

'Do get through your everlasting clatter some time, and bring me a gourd of water; the child's been crying for a drink this livelong hour.'

'Let it die, then, it may as well die for water as to be taxed to death to fatten *officers of State.*'

Jeff run off to get the water though, just like he hadn't been sayin any thing spiteful; for he's a raal good-hearted fellow, after all, once you get at the foundation of him.

I walked into the house, and, 'why, Peggy,' says I, 'I declare, we like to forgot you altogether.' 'Oh, yes,' says she, 'when a body can't help themselves, every body soon forgets 'em; but thank God by day after to-morrow I shall be well enough to milk the cows, and pen the calves, and wring the contrary one's tails for 'em, and no thanks to nobody.' 'Good evening, Peggy,' says I, and so I sloped, for I seed she was mad at me, for making Jeff neglect her so long.

And now, Mr. Printer, will you be sure to let us know in your next paper whether this Shields is a whig or a democrat? I don't care about it for myself, for I know well enough how it is already, but I want to convince Jeff. It may do some good to let him, and others like him, know *who* and *what* these *officers of State* are. It may help to send the present hypocritical set to where they belong, and to fill the places they now disgrace with men who will do more work, for less pay, and take a fewer airs while they are doing it. It ain't sensible to think that the same men who get us into trouble will change their course; and yet it's pretty plain, if some change for the better is not made, it's not long that neither Peggy, or I, or any of us, will have a cow left to milk, or a calf's tail to wring.

Yours truly,
Rebecca——.

The several "Rebecca" letters, Lincoln's unfortunate entanglement with James A. Shields which ensued, and the correspondence leading up to the duel which never came off, have never been adequately studied by any biographer of Lincoln whose work is known to the editor. Beveridge gives perhaps the most adequate treatment, but also contributes considerable confusion and inaccuracy to the facts as well as to the interpretation of this material. The reader who may be interested in a special study of the style of the various letters should see "The Authorship of the 'Rebecca' Letters," The Abraham Lincoln Quarterly, *June, 1942.*

To summarize the essential facts of the whole affair, the first of these letters, dated August 10, 1842, purporting to come from "Lost Township" and signed "Rebecca," was published in the Sangamo Journal *of August 19, 1842. It was largely a lament for the sad predicament in which the people of Illinois found themselves following the failure of the State Bank in February, 1842. Several allusions to the financial tangle which involved all business appear in Lincoln's letters to Speed. The worthless State Bank currency had driven good money out of circulation and such transactions as were carried on were largely by barter. Of course, "Rebecca" blamed the Democratic office-holders and commented on the report circulating throughout the state that "the Governor was going to send instructions to collectors, not to take anything but gold and silver for taxes." This was the peak of perfidy—the State refusing to honor the currency of its own institution.*

Such instructions were sent out in a circular letter dated August 20, 1842, and signed by the State Auditor, James A. Shields, which letter was published in the Journal *of August 26, 1842. The furor which ensued was an opportunity that Whig politicians took care not to neglect, and first among them was Lincoln, avid for the political scalp of James A. Shields. Perhaps Lincoln disliked Shields personally, but even if he had not disliked him, the implications of personal corruption and chicanery which he proceeded to heap upon the unfortunate Auditor were more or less to be expected as part of a political technique long practiced by politicians of both parties.*

The second "Rebecca" letter, which Lincoln later admitted writing, dated August 27, 1842 (the day after the publication of Shields's circular letter), was published in the Journal *of September 2, 1842. Unlike the first letter, which contained only a mild condemnation of Democratic office-holders in general, the second letter made Shields as State Auditor the butt of ridicule and contumely.*

A third brief letter from "Rebecca" dated August 29, 1842, inclosing a letter purporting to come from her sister, appeared in the Journal *of September 9, 1842. The two communications were mild in nature and apparently of the same vintage as the first letter, but in the same issue of the* Journal *appeared a fourth letter dated September 8, 1842, also signed "Rebecca," which in attacking Shields's personal courage exceeded the second in contumely but was childishly amateurish in execution. Then, in the* Journal *of September 16, 1842, appeared some doggerel signed "Cathleen," again ridiculing the "Irish" blarney of Shields.*

Upon learning from Simeon Francis, the editor of the Journal, *that Lincoln was responsible for these anonymous screeds directed against himself, Shields wrote Lincoln a letter that assumed Lincoln to be the sole author, demanded a retraction of "all offensive allusions" in all the letters, and concluded with the following sentence: "This may prevent consequences which no one will regret more than myself." To this letter Lincoln replied in a note which took particular notice of the threat implied in the concluding sentence, and pointed out that there was in Shields's letter "so much assumption of facts, and so much menace as to consequences," that he could not "submit to answer that note any further . . ."*

From this point onward the whole affair was so "honorably" mismanaged by Shields's friend, Whiteside, and Lincoln's friend, Merryman, that a duel seemed imminent. Fortunately, however, Lincoln finally made, and Shields accepted, the admission: "I did write the 'Lost Township' letter which appeared in the Journal *of the 2d inst., but had no participation in any form, in any other article alluding to you."*

CORRESPONDENCE ABOUT THE LINCOLN-SHIELDS DUEL. SEPTEMBER 17, 1842

Tremont, Sept. 17th, 1842.

A. Lincoln, Esq.

I regret that my absence on public business compelled me to postpone a matter of private consideration a little longer than I could have desired. It will only be necessary, however, to account for it by informing you that I have been to Quincy on business that would not admit of delay. I will now state briefly the reasons of my troubling you with this communication, the disagreeable nature of which I regret—as I had hoped to avoid any difficulty with any one in Springfield, while residing there, by endeavoring to conduct myself in such a way amongst both my political friends and opponents, as to escape the necessity of any. Whilst thus abstaining from giving provocation, I have become the object of slander, vituperation and personal abuse, which were I capable of submitting to, I would prove myself worthy of the whole of it.

In two or three of the last numbers of The Sangamo Journal, articles of the most personal nature and calculated to degrade me, have made their appearance. On enquiring I was informed by the editor of that paper, through the medium of my friend, Gen. Whiteside, that you are the author of those articles. This information satisfies me that I have become by some means or other, the object of your secret hostility. I will not take the trouble of enquiring into the reason of all this, but I will take the liberty of requiring a full, positive and absolute retraction of all offensive allusions used by you in these communications, in relation to my private character and standing as a man, as an apology for the insults conveyed in them.

This may prevent consequences which no one will regret more than myself.

Your ob't serv't,
Jas. Shields.

Tremont, Sept. 17, 1842.

Jas. Shields, Esq.

Your note of to-day was handed me by Gen. Whiteside. In that note you say you have been informed, through the medium of the editor of the Journal, that I am the author of certain articles in that paper which you deem personally abusive of you: and without stopping to inquire whether I really am the author, or to point out what is offensive in them, you demand an unqualified retraction of all that is offensive; and then proceed to hint at consequences.

Now, sir, there is in this so much assumption of facts, and so much of menace as to consequences, that I cannot submit to answer that note any farther than I have, and to add, that the consequence to which I suppose you allude, would be matter of as great regret to me as it possibly could to you.

Respectfully,
A. Lincoln.

Tremont, Sept. 17, 1842.

A. Lincoln, Esq.

In reply to my note of this date, you intimate that I assume facts and menace consequences, and that you cannot submit to answer it further. As now, sir, you desire it, I will be a little more particular. The editor of the Sangamo Journal gave me to understand that you are the author of an article which appeared I think in that paper of the 2d Sept. inst, headed the Lost Townships, and signed Rebecca or Becca. I would therefore take the liberty of asking whether you are the author of said article or any other over the same signature, which has appeared in any of the late numbers of that paper. If so, I repeat my request of an absolute retraction of all offensive allusion contained therein in relation to my private character and standing. If you are not the author of any of the articles, your denial will be sufficient. I will say further, it is not my intention to menace, but to do myself justice.

Your obd't serv't,

Jas. Shields.

These letters were printed in the Sangamo Journal, *October 14, 1842, by E. H. Merryman, Lincoln's second, in reply to a version of the affair which had been published by General Whiteside, Shields's second, and which had presented Lincoln's position and actions with considerable bias. Merryman's account relates that, after reading Shields's second note, Lincoln returned it to Whiteside "telling him verbally, that he did not think it consistent with his honor to negociate for peace with Mr. Shields, unless Mr. Shields would withdraw his former offensive letter." The letter which Lincoln thus refused, as may be seen, did in effect in the last sentence, withdraw the threat. The statement which Lincoln finally made, and which Shields finally accepted, would have been equally acceptable at this earlier point, it would seem. Why Lincoln did not at this time make a frank statement is not quite clear, even if one assumes that Lincoln was standing rather stiffly on what he considered "consistent with his honor." Mary Todd's involvement as author of the fourth "Rebecca" letter, in which there were implications of Shields's femininity, may have caused Lincoln hesitation in admitting that he had not written all the letters. Whiteside's personality may have irritated Lincoln, and Lincoln's friend Merryman may have "backed him up" a little too strenuously. In any event, Lincoln seems here to have missed an excellent opportunity to avoid an unpleasant episode which he was to regret for the rest of his life.*

MEMORANDUM OF INSTRUCTIONS TO E. H. MERRYMAN, LINCOLN'S SECOND SEPTEMBER 19, 1842

In case Whiteside shall signify a wish to adjust this affair without further difficulty, let him know that if the present papers be withdrawn, and a note from Mr. Shields asking to know if I am the author of the articles of which he complains, and asking that I shall make him gentlemanly satisfaction, if I am the author, and this without menace, or dictation as to what that satisfaction shall be, a pledge is made that the following answer shall be given:

"I did write the 'Lost Townships' letter which appeared in the Journal of the 2d inst., but had no participation in any form, in any other article alluding to you. I wrote that, wholly for political effect. I had no intention of injuring your personal or private character or standing as a man or a gentleman; and I did not then think, and do not now think that that article could produce or has produced that effect against you; and had I anticipated such an effect would have forborne to write it. And I will add that your conduct toward me, so far as I knew, had always been gentlemanly; and that I had no personal pique against you, and no cause for any."

If this should be done, I leave it with you to manage what shall and what shall not be published.

If nothing like this is done, the preliminaries of the fight are to be—

1st. WEAPONS—Cavalry broad swords of the largest size precisely equal in all respects—and such as now used by the cavalry company at Jacksonville.

2d. POSITION—A plank ten feet long, and from nine to twelve inches broad, to be firmly fixed on edge, on the ground, as the line between us, which neither is to pass his foot over upon forfeit of his life. Next a line drawn on the ground on either side of said plank and parallel with it, each at the distance of the whole length of the sword and three feet additional from the plank; and the passing of his own such line by either party during the fight, shall be deemed a surrender of the contest.

3d. TIME—On Thursday evening at 5 o'clock if you can get it so; but in no case to be at a greater distance of time than Friday evening, at 5 o'clock.

4th. PLACE—Within three miles of Alton, on the opposite side of the river, the particular spot to be agreed on by you.

Any preliminary details coming within the above rules, you are at liberty to make at your discretion, but you are in no case to swerve from these rules or to pass beyond their limits.

While Lincoln's biographers differ in their rendering of the account of the duel chiefly in the degree to which they seem ashamed of, or actually condemn, Lincoln's part in it, all seem to overlook the possibility that Lincoln's sense of the ridiculous may have motivated his actions no less than a possible sense of chivalry (Mary Todd was involved as author of the fourth letter), and a personal pique at Shields's punctilio. The instructions for the duel, when carefully studied, are hard to reconcile with a serious purpose, inasmuch as, because of disparity in the stature of the two men, Lincoln could stand back far enough to prevent Shields's getting at him very effectively, while Shields could not possibly retreat far enough to avoid a blow without stepping behind his line. Although one is suspicious of travesty, the respective accounts given by General Whiteside and Dr. Merryman in the Journal, *October 7, 1842, seem unaware of it. There is no hint of physical cowardice in Lincoln's life elsewhere, and to suppose that he drew up these rules purely as a matter of taking advantage of a smaller man who had a shorter reach, is certainly incompatible with everything else that we know of Lincoln. The supposition that Merryman, rather than Lincoln, drew up the instructions is another possibility, which, however, does not seem too plausible to the editor.*

LETTER TO JOSHUA F. SPEED
OCTOBER 5, 1842

Springfield, Oct. 5 1842—

Dear Speed:

You have heard of my duel with Shields, and I have now to inform you that the duelling business still rages in this city. Day before yesterday Shields challenged Butler, who accepted, and proposed fighting next morning at sunrising in Bob Allen's meadow, one hundred yards distance with rifles. To this, Whitesides [*sic*], Shields's second, said "No" because of the law. Thus ended, duel No. 2. Yesterday, Whitesides [*sic*] chose to consider himself insulted by Dr. Merryman, and so, sent him a kind of *quasi* challenge, inviting him to meet him at the planter's House in St. Louis on the next friday to settle their difficulty. Merryman made me his friend, and sent W. a note enquiring to know if he meant his note as a challenge, and if so, that he would, according to the law in such case made and provided, prescribe the terms of the meeting. W.

returned for answer, that if M. would meet him at the Planter's House as desired, he would challenge him. M. replied in a note, that he denied W's right to dictate time and place; but that he M. would waive the question of *time*, and meet him at Louisiana Missouri. Upon my presenting this note to W. and stating, verbally, its contents, he declined receiving it, saying he had business at St. Louis, and it was as near as Louisiana. Merryman then directed me to notify Whitesides, that he should publish the correspondence between them with such comments as he thought fit. This I did. Thus it stood at bed time last night. This morning Whitesides, by his friend Shields, is praying for a new-trial, on the ground that he was mistaken in Merrymans proposition to meet him at Louisiana Missouri thinking it was the State of Louisiana. This Merryman hoots at, and is preparing his publication—while the town is in a ferment and a street fight somewhat anticipated.

But I began this letter not for what I have been writing; but to say something on that subject which you know to be of such infinite solicitude to me. The immense suffering you endured from the first days of September till the middle of February you never tried to conceal from me, and I well understood. You have now been the husband of a lovely woman nearly eight months. That you are happier now than you were the day you married her I well know; for without, you would not be living. But I have your word for it too; and the returning elasticity of spirits which is manifested in your letters. But I want to ask a closer question. "Are you now in *feeling* as well as *judgement*, glad that you are married as you are?" From anybody but me, this would be an impudent question not to be tolerated; but I know you will pardon it in me. Please answer it quickly as I feel impatient to know.

I have sent my love to your Fanny so often I fear she is getting tired of it; however, I venture to tender it again.

Yours forever,

Lincoln

William Butler, who apparently caught the duelling contagion from acting as friend of Lincoln, was a close friend of Speed's. He married Elizabeth Rickard, sister of the "Sarah" mentioned in Lincoln's letters of June 19, 1841, and February 3, 1842, whom Speed had courted and broken off with at about the same time as Lincoln's "fatal 1st of January." Butler later named a son "Speed" in honor of his friend.

LETTER TO JAMES S. IRWIN
NOVEMBER 2, 1842

Springfield, Nov. 2 1842.

Jas. S. Irwin Esq.

Owing to my absence, yours of the 22nd. ult. was not received till this moment.

Judge Logan & myself are willing to attend to any business in the Supreme Court you may send us. As to fees, it is impossible to establish a rule that will apply in all, or even a great many cases. We believe we are never accused of being very unreasonable in this particular; and we would always be easily satisfied, provided we could see the money—but whatever fees we earn at a distance, if not paid *before*, we have noticed we never hear of after the work is done. We therefore, are growing a little sensitive on that point.

Yours &c
A. Lincoln

According to information furnished by Mr. Oliver R. Barrett, owner of the original of this letter, James S. Irwin was a native of Woodford County, Kentucky, a graduate of Center College, and a classmate of John C. Breckinridge. Upon removing to Jacksonville, Illinois, Irwin studied law in the office of Brown & McClure and received his license to practice January 1, 1842. He moved to Mt. Sterling in Brown County the same year, and, if one may draw inferences from Lincoln's letter, entertained highly optimistic hopes for his future in arguing cases before the Illinois Supreme Court. Perhaps Lincoln's jocular caution in specifying payment in advance may be attributed to his suspicion of the young lawyer's overoptimism and willingness to take cases which promised little in the way of fees.

LETTER TO SAMUEL D. MARSHALL
NOVEMBER 11, 1842

Springfield, Nov. 11th. 1842—

Dear Sam

Yours of the 10th. Oct. enclosing five dollars was taken from the office in my absence by Judge Logan who neglected to hand it to me till about a week ago, and just an hour before I took a wife. Your other of the 3rd. Inst. is also received. The Forbes & Hill case, of which you speak has not been brought up as yet.

I have looked into the Dorman & Lane case, till I believe I understand the facts of it; and I also believe we can reverse it. In the last I may be mistaken, but I think the case, at least worth the experiment; and if Dorman will risk the cost, I will do my best for the "biggest kind of a fee" as you say, if we succeed, and nothing if we fail. I have not had a chance to consult Logan since I read your letters, but if the case comes up, I can have the use of him if I need him.

I would advise you to procure the Record and send it up

immediately. Attend to the making out of the Record yourself, or most likely, the clerk will not get it all together right.

Nothing new here, except my marrying, which to me, is matter of profound wonder.

Yours forever
A. Lincoln

Marshall was a Shawneetown lawyer handling the case, which involved the attempt of Mrs. Dorman to recover property that her guardian John Lane had obtained during her minority (Carl Sandburg, in The Prairie Years, *uses the phrase "cheated out of"). Lincoln did win the case in the Supreme Court and finally settled his fee more than ten years later, on April 8, 1853, for one hundred dollars (Harry E. Pratt,* Personal Finances of Abraham Lincoln, *p. 31).*

LETTER TO JOSHUA F. SPEED
MARCH 24, 1843

Springfield, March 24. 1843—

Dear Speed:

Hurst tells me that Lockridge has redeemed the land in your case, & paid him the money; and that he has written you about it. I now have the pleasure of informing you that Walters has paid me $703.25 (in gold) for you. There is something still due you from him,—I think near a hundred dollars, for which I promised him a little additional time. The gold, (except the toll) we hold subject to your order.

We had a meeting of the whigs of the county here on last Monday to appoint delegates to a district convention, and Baker beat me & got the delegation instructed to go for him. The meeting, in spite of my attempt to decline it, appointed me one of the delegates; so that in getting Baker the nomination, I shall be "fixed" a good deal like a fellow who is made groomsman to the man what has cut him out, and is marrying his own dear "gal". About the prospect of your having a namesake at our house cant say, exactly yet.

[No signature]

Lincoln's "can't say exactly yet" concerning his prospects for becoming a father, and his seeming resentment toward his friend Butler for spreading the news to Speed, as expressed in the next letter, May 18, may seem strange in view of the fact that the child was born on August 1. Lincoln certainly knew, and his intimacy with Speed certainly justified Speed's solicitous inquiries. Can the supposed reticence of the Victorian era account for this, or was Lincoln a bit touchy on the question?

The child was born within a scant nine months after the marriage, and it may have been that Lincoln's acute awareness of local tongue-wagging over his erratic courtship and marriage made him unusually sensitive concerning the "coming event." On the other hand, one may suppose, but with less satisfaction, that Lincoln merely kept his fingers crossed in the next letter when he claimed that he "had not heard one word," and that he is merely joking with Speed throughout.

LETTER TO JOSHUA F. SPEED
MAY 18, 1843

Springfield, May 18th. 1843—

Dear Speed:

Yours of the 9th. Inst. is duly received, which I do not meet as a "bore," but as a most welcome visiter [*sic*]. I will answer the business part of it first. The note you enclosed on Cannan & Harlan, I have placed in Moffett's hands according to your directions. Harvey is the Constable to have it. I have called three times to get the note, you mention, on B. C. Webster & Co; but did not find Hurst. I will yet get it, and do with it, as you bid. At the April court at Tazewell, I saw Hall; and he then gave me an order on Jewett to draw of him, all rent which may fall due, after the 12th. day of Jany. last, till your debt shall be paid. The rent is for the house Ranson did live in just above the Globe; and is $222 per year payable quarterly, so that one quarter fell due the 12th. April. I presented the order to Jewett, since the 12th. and he said it was right, and he would accept it, which, however, was not done in writing for want of pen & ink at the time & place. He acknowledged that the quarter's rent was due, and said he would pay it in a short time but could not at the moment. He also said that he thought, by some former arrangement, a portion of that quarter would have to be paid to the Irwins. Thus stands the Hall matter. I think we will get the money on it, in the course of this year. You ask for the amount of interest on your Van Bergen note of $572.32, and also upon the judgement against Van assigned by Baker. The note drew 12 per cent from date, and bore date Oct. 1st. 1841. I suppose the 12 per cent ceased, at the time we bought in Walter's house which was on the 23rd. Decr. 1842. If I count right, the interest up to that time, was $78.69 cents, which added to the principal makes $651.01. On this aggregate sum you are entitled to interest at 6 per cent only, from the said 23rd. Decr. 1842 until paid. What that will amount to, you can calculate for yourself. The judgement assigned by Baker to you for $219.80, was so assigned on the 2nd. of April 1841, and of course draws 6 per cent from that time until paid. This too you can calculate for yourself. About the 25th. of March 1843 (the precise date I dont now remember) Walters paid $703.25. This, of course must be remembered on counting interest. According to my count, there was due you of principal & interest on both claims on the 25th. of March 1843—$906.70. Walters then paid $703.25—which leaves still due you, $203.45, drawing 6 per cent from that date. Walters is promising to pay the ballance [*sic*] every day, but still has not done it. I think he will do it soon. Allen has gone to nothing, as Butler tells you. There are 200 acres of the tract I took the deed of trust on. The improvements I should suppose you remember as well as I. It is the stage stand on the Shelbyville road, where you always said I wouldn't pay Baker's tavern bill. It seems to me it must be worth much more than the debt; but whether any body will redeem it in these hard times, I can not say.

In relation to our Congress matter here, you were right in supposing I would support the nominee. Neither Baker or I, however is the man; but *Hardin.* So far as I can judge from present appearances, we shall have no split or trouble about the matter; all will be harmony. In relation to the "coming events" about which Butler wrote you, I had not *heard* one word before I got your letter; but I have so much confidence in the judgment of a Butler on such a subject, that I incline to think there may be some reality in it. What *day* does Butler appoint? By the way, how do "events" of the same sort come on in your family? Are you possessing houses and lands, and oxen and asses, and men-servants and maid-servants, and begetting sons and daughters? We are not keeping house; but boarding at the Globe Tavern, which is very well kept now by a widow lady of the name of Beck. Our room (the same Dr. Wallace occupied there) and boarding only costs four dollars a week. Ann Todd was married something more than a year since to a fellow by the name of Campbell, and who Mary says, is pretty much of a "dunce" though he has a little money & property. They live in Boonville, Mo. and have not been heard from lately enough to enable me to say anything about her health. I reckon it will scarcely be in our power to visit Kentucky this year. Besides poverty, and the necessity of attending to business, those "coming events" I suspect would be somewhat in the way. I most heartily wish you and your Fanny would not fail to come. Just let us know the time a week in advance, and we will have a room provided for you at our house, and all be merry together for a while. Be sure to give my respects to your mother and family. Assure her, that if I ever come near her I will not fail to call and see her. Mary joins in sending love to your Fanny and you.

Yours as ever,
A. Lincoln

P. S. Since I wrote the above I saw Hurst and discovered that the note on B. C. Webster & Co. does not fall due till the 9th. June. Hurst says it will be paid when due.

LETTER TO WILLIAMSON DURLEY
OCTOBER 3, 1845

Springfield, Oct. 3. 1845

Friend Durley:

When I saw you at home, it was agreed that I should write to you and your brother Madison. Until I then saw you, I was not aware of your being what is generally called an abolitionist, or, as you call yourself, a Liberty man; though I well knew there were many such in your county. I was glad to hear you say that you intend to attempt to bring about, at the next election in Putnam, a union of the whigs proper, and such of the liberty men, as are whigs in principle on all questions save only that of slavery. So far as I can perceive, by such union, neither party need yield any thing on *the* point in difference between them. If the whig abolitionists of New York had voted with us last fall, Mr. Clay would now be president, whig principles in the ascendent, and Texas not annexed; whereas by the division, all that either had at stake in the contest, was lost. And, indeed, it was extremely probable, beforehand, that such would be the result. As I always understood, the Liberty-men deprecated the annexation of Texas extremely; and, this being so, why they should refuse to so cast their votes as to prevent it, even to me seemed wonderful. What was their process of reasoning, I can only judge from what a single one of them told me. It was this:

"We are not to do *evil* that good may come." This general proposition is doubtless correct; but did it apply? If by your votes you could have prevented the *extention* [*sic*], &c., of slavery, would it not have been *good* and not *evil* so to have used your votes, even though it involved the casting of them for a slaveholder? By the *fruit* the tree is to be known. An *evil* tree can not bring forth *good* fruit. If the fruit of electing Mr. Clay would have been to prevent the extension of slavery, could the act of electing have been *evil*?

But I will not argue farther. I perhaps ought to say that individually I never was much interested in the Texas question. I never could see much good to come of annexation; inasmuch, as they were already a free republican people on our own model; on the other hand, I never could very clearly see how the annexation would augment the evil of slavery. It always seemed to me that slaves would be taken there in about equal numbers, with or without annexation. And if more *were* taken because of annexation, still there would be just so many the fewer left, where they were taken from. It is possibly true, to some extent, that with annexation, some slaves may be sent to Texas and continued in slavery, that otherwise might have been liberated. To whatever extent this may be true, I think annexation an evil. I hold it to be a paramount duty of us in the free states, due to the Union of the States, and perhaps to liberty itself (paradox though it may seem) to let the slavery of the other states alone; while, on the other hand, I hold it to be equally clear, that we should never knowingly lend ourselves directly or indirectly, to prevent that slavery from dying a natural death—to find new places for it to live in, when it can no longer exist in the old. Of course I am not now considering what would be our duty, in cases of insurrection among the slaves.

To recur to the Texas question, I understand the Liberty men to have viewed annexation as a much greater evil than I ever did; and I would like to convince you if I could, that they could have prevented it, without violation of principle if they had chosen.

I intend this letter for you and Madison together; and if you and he or either shall think fit to drop me a line, I shall be pleased.

Yours with respect
A Lincoln

This letter is significant for its exposition of Lincoln's position on the extension of slavery. The resolutions which he drew up with Dan Stone and placed before the Legislature in 1837 anticipate, but do not define, the position taken here, which Lincoln was to maintain until elected President.

Durley, a Whig of Hennepin, Putnam County, was an ardent supporter of Lincoln's candidacy for Congress the following year.

LETTER TO HENRY E. DUMMER
NOVEMBER 18, 1845

Springfield, Nov: 18th. 1845

Friend Dummer:

Before Baker left, he said to me, in accordance with what had long been an understanding between him and me, that the track for the next congressional race was clear to me, so far as he was concerned; and that he would say so publicly in any manner and at any time I might desire. I said, in reply, that as to the manner and time, I would consider a while and write him. I understand friend Delahay to have already informed you of the substance of the above.

I now wish to say to you that if it be consistent with your feelings, you would set a few stakes for me. I do not certainly know, but I strongly suspect, that Genl. Hardin wishes to run again. I know of no argument to give me a preference over him, unless it be "Turn about is fair play."

The Pekin paper has lately nominated or suggested Hardin's name for Governor, and the Alton paper, noticing that, indirectly nominates him for Congress. I wish you would, if you can, see that, while these things are bandied about among the papers, the Beardstown paper takes no stand that may injure my chance, unless the conductor really prefers Genl. Hardin, in which case, I suppose it would be fair.

Let this be confidential, and please write me in a few days.

Yours as ever

A. Lincoln

Henry E. Dummer was the law partner of Lincoln's friend, John T. Stuart, from 1833 to 1837, when he moved to Beardstown, Illinois, and Lincoln became Stuart's partner. For an account of Lincoln's long friendship with Dummer, see Paul M. Angle, "The Record of a Friendship," in the Journal of the Illinois State Historical Society.

LETTER TO B. F. JAMES
FEBRUARY 9, 1846

Springfield, Feb. 9. 1846

Dear James:

You have seen, or will see what I am inclined to think you will regard as rather an extraordinary communication in the Morgan Journal. The "excessive modesty" of it's tone is certainly admirable. As an excuse for getting before the public, the writer sets out with a pretence of answering an article which I believe appeared in the Lacon paper some time since; taking the ground that the Pekin convention had settled the rotation principle. Now whether the Pekin convention did or did not settle that principle, I care not. If I am not, in what I *have done*, and am *able to do*, for the party, near enough the equal of Genl. Hardin, to entitle me to the nomination, now that he has one, I scorn it on *any* and *all* other grounds.

So far then, as this Morgan Journal communation [*sic*] may relate to the Pekin convention, I rather prefer that your paper shall let it "stink and die" unnoticed.

There is, however, as you will see, another thing in the communication which is, an attempt to injure me because of my declining to reccommend [*sic*] the adoption of a *new plan*, for the selecting a candidate. The attempt is to make it appear that I am unwilling to have a *fair* expression of the whigs of the District upon our respective claims. Now, nothing can be more false in fact; and if Genl. Hardin, had chosen, to furnish his friend with my *written reason* for declining that part of his plan; and that friend had chosen to publish that *reason*, instead of his own construction of the act, the falsehood of his insinuation would have been most apparent. That written reason was as follows, to wit:

"As to your proposals that a poll shall be opened in *every* precinct, and that the whole shall take place on the *same* day, I do not personally object. They seem to me to not be unfair; and

I forbear to join in proposing them, only because I rather choose to leave the decision in each county, to the whigs of the county, to be made as their own judgment and convenience may dictate."

I send you this as a weapon with which to demolish, what I can not but regard as a mean insinuation against me. You may use it as you please; I prefer however that you should show it to some of our friends, and not publish it, unless in your judgement it becomes rather urgently necessary.

The reason I want to keep all points of controversy out of the papers, so far as possible, is, that it will be *just all we can do*, to keep out of a quarrel—and I am resolved to do my part to keep peace.

Yours truly
A. Lincoln

This is one of the most interesting letters written by Lincoln during his maneuvering for the Whig nomination for Congress. An earlier agreement between Lincoln and Edward D. Baker that Baker would not seek re-election had been arrived at, and Lincoln sought to have General John J. Hardin, another chief contender, stand aside. Hardin sought the nomination but withdrew in Lincoln's favor in a letter written February 16.

James, who was editor of the Tazewell Whig *at Tremont, had been actively supporting Lincoln. He published Hardin's letter of withdrawal on February 21, and editorialized in behalf of Lincoln's "worth, energy and patriotic exertions."*

REMARKABLE CASE OF ARREST FOR MURDER APRIL 15, 1846

(The following narrative has been handed us for publication by a member of the Bar. There is no doubt of the truth of every fact stated; and the whole affair is of so extraordinary a character as to entitle it to publication, and commend it to the attention of those at present engaged in discussing reforms in criminal jurisprudence, and the abolition of capital punishment.) ED. WHIG.

In the year 1841, there resided, at different points in the State of Illinois, three brothers by the name of Trailor. Their christian names were William, Henry and Archibald. Archibald resided at Springfield, then as now the Seat of Government of the State. He was a sober, retiring and industrious man, of about thirty years of age; a carpenter by trade, and a bachelor, boarding with his partner in business—a Mr. Myers. Henry, a year or two older, was a man of like retiring and industrious habits; had a family and resided with it on a farm at Clary's Grove, about twenty miles distant from Springfield in a Northwesterly direction.—William, still older, and with similar habits, resided on a farm in Warren county, distant from Springfield something more than a hundred miles in the same North-westerly direction. He was a widower, with several children. In the neighborhood of William's residence, there was, and had been for several years, a man by the name of Fisher, who was somewhat above the age of fifty; had no family, and no settled home; but who boarded and lodged a while here, and a while there, with the persons for whom he did little jobs of work. His habits were remarkably economical, so that an impression got about that he had accumulated a considerable amount of money. In the latter part of May in the year mentioned, William formed the purpose of visiting his brothers at Clary's Grove, and Springfield; and Fisher, at the time having his temporary residence at his house, resolved to accompany him. They set out together in a buggy with a single horse. On Sunday evening they reached Henry's residence, and staid [*sic*] over night. On Monday Morning, being the first Monday of June, they started on to Springfield, Henry accompanying them on horseback. They reached town about noon, met Archibald, went with him to his boarding house, and there took up their lodgings for the time they should remain. After dinner, the three Trailors and Fisher left the boarding house in company, for the avowed purpose of spending the evening together in looking about the town. At supper, the Trailors had all returned, but Fisher was missing, and some inquiry was made about him. After supper, the Trailors went out professedly in search of him. One by one they returned, the last coming in after late tea time, and each stating that he had been unable to discover anything of Fisher. The next day, both before and after breakfast, they went professedly in search again, and returned at noon, still unsuccessful. Dinner again being had, William and Henry expressed a determination to give up the search and start for their homes. This was remonstrated against by some of the boarders about the house, on the ground that Fisher was somewhere in the vicinity, and would be left without any conveyance, as he and William had come in the same buggy. The remonstrance was disregarded, and they departed for their homes respectively. Up to this time, the knowledge of Fisher's mysterious disappearance, had spread very little beyond the few boarders at Myers', and excited no considerable interest. After the lapse of three or four days, Henry returned to Springfield, for the ostensible purpose of making further search for Fisher. Procuring some of the boarders, he, together with them and Archibald, spent another day in ineffectual search, when it was again abandoned, and he returned home. No general interest was yet excited. On the Friday, week after Fisher's disappearance, the Postmaster at Springfield received a letter from the Postmaster nearest William's residence in Warren county, stating that William had returned home without Fisher, and was saying, rather boastfully, that Fisher was dead, and had willed him his money, and that he had got about fifteen hundred dollars by it. The letter further stated that William's story and conduct seemed strange; and desired the Postmaster at Springfield to ascertain and write what was the truth in the matter. The Postmaster at

Springfield made the letter public, and at once, excitement became universal and intense. Springfield, at that time had a population of about 3500, with a city organization. The Attorney General of the State resided there. A purpose was forthwith formed to ferret out the mystery, in putting which into execution, the Mayor of the city, and the Attorney General took the lead. To make search for, and, if possible, find the body of the man supposed to be murdered, was resolved on as the first step. In pursuance of this, men were formed into large parties, and marched abreast, in all directions, so as to let no inch of ground in the vicinity, remain unsearched. Examinations were made of cellars, wells, and pits of all descriptions, where it was thought possible the body might be concealed. All the fresh, or tolerably fresh graves in the grave-yard, were pried into, and dead horses and dead dogs were disinterred, where, in some instances, they had been buried by their partial masters. This search, as has appeared, commenced on Friday. It continued until Saturday afternoon without success, when it was determined to despatch officers to arrest William and Henry at their residences respectively. The officers started on Sunday morning, meanwhile, the search for the body was continued, and rumors got afloat of the Trailors having passed, at different times and places, several gold pieces, which were readily supposed to have belonged to Fisher. On Monday, the officers sent for Henry, having arrested him, arrived with him. The Mayor and Attorney Gen'l took charge of him, and set their wits to work to elicit a discovery from him. He denied, and denied, and persisted in denying. They still plied him in every conceivable way, till Wednesday, when, protesting his own innocence, he stated that his brothers, William and Archibald had murdered Fisher; that they had killed him, without his (Henry's) knowledge at the time, and made a temporary concealment of his body; that immediately preceding his and William's departure from Springfield for home, on Tuesday, the day after Fisher's disappearance, William and Archibald communicated the fact to him, and engaged his assistance in making a permanent concealment of the body; that at the time he and William left professedly for home, they did not take the road directly, but meandering their way through the streets, entered the woods at the North West of the city, two or three hundred yards to the right of where the road where they should have travelled entered them; that penetrating the woods some few hundred yards, they halted and Archibald came a somewhat different route, on foot, and joined them; that William and Archibald then stationed him (Henry) on an old and disused road that ran near by, as a sentinel, to give warning of the approach of any intruder; that William and Archibald then removed the buggy to the edge of a dense brush thicket, about forty yards distant from his (Henry's) position, where, leaving the buggy, they entered the thicket, and in a few minutes returned with the body and placed it in the buggy; that from his station, he could and did distinctly see that the object placed in the buggy was a dead man, of the general appearance and size of Fisher; that William and Archibald then moved off with the buggy in the direction of Hickox's mill pond, and after an absence of half an hour returned, saying they had put him in a safe place; that Archibald then left for town, and he and William found their way to the road, and made for their homes. At this disclosure, all lingering credulity was broken down, and excitement rose to an almost inconceivable height. Up to this time, the well known character of Archibald had repelled and put down all suspicions as to him. Till then, those who were ready to swear that a murder had been committed, were almost as confident that Archibald had had no part in it. But now, he was seized and thrown into jail; and, indeed, his personal security rendered it by no means objectionable to him. And now came the search for the brush thicket, and the search of the mill pond. The thicket was found, and the buggy tracks at the point indicated. At a point within the thicket the signs of a struggle were discovered, and a trail from thence to the buggy track was traced. In attempting to follow the track of the buggy from the thicket, it was found to proceed in the direction of the mill pond, but could not be traced all the way. At the pond, however, it was found that a buggy had been backed down to, and partially into the water's edge. Search was now to be made in the pond; and it was made in every imaginable way. Hundreds and hundreds were engaged in raking, fishing, and draining. After much fruitless effort in this way, on Thursday

Morning, the mill dam was cut down, and the water of the pond partially drawn off, and the same processes of search again gone through with. About noon of this day, the officer sent for William, returned having him in custody; and a man calling himself Dr. Gilmore, came in company with them. It seems that the officer arrested William at his own house early in the day on Tuesday, and started to Springfield with him; that after dark awhile, they reached Lewiston in Fulton county, where they stopped for the night; that late in the night this Dr. Gilmore arrived, stating that Fisher was alive at his house; and that he had followed on to give the information, so that William might be released without further trouble; that the officer, distrusting Dr. Gilmore, refused to release William, but brought him on to Springfield, and the Dr. accompanied them. On reaching Springfield, the Dr. re-asserted that Fisher was alive, and at his house. At this the multitude for a time, were utterly confounded. Gilmore's story was communicated to Henry Trailor, who, without faltering, re-affirmed his own story about Fisher's murder. Henry's adherence to his own story was communicated to the crowd, and at once the idea started, and became nearly, if not quite universal that Gilmore was a confederate of the Trailors, and had invented the tale he was telling, to secure their release and escape. Excitement was again at its zenith. About 3 o'clock the same evening, Myers, Archibald's partner, started with a two horse carriage, for the purpose of ascertaining whether Fisher was alive, as stated by Gilmore, and if so, of bringing him back to Springfield with him. On Friday a legal examination was gone into before two Justices, on the charge of murder against William and Archibald. Henry was introduced as a witness by the prosecution, and on oath, re-affirmed his statements, as heretofore detailed; and, at the end of which, he bore a thorough and rigid cross-examination without faltering or exposure. The prosecution also proved by a respectable lady, that on the Monday evening of Fisher's disappearance, she saw Archibald whom she well knew, and another man whom she did not then know, but whom she believed at the time of testifying to be William, (then present,) and still another, answering the description of Fisher, all enter the timber at the North West of town, (the point indicated by Henry,) and after one or two hours, saw William and Archibald return without Fisher. Several other witnesses testified, that on Tuesday, at the time William and Henry professedly gave up the search for Fisher's body and started for home, they did not take the road directly, but did go into the woods, as stated by Henry. By others also, it was proved, that since Fisher's disappearance, William and Archibald had passed rather an unusual number of gold pieces. The statements heretofore made about the thicket, the signs of a struggle, the buggy tracks, &c., were fully proven by numerous witnesses. At this the prosecution rested. Dr. Gilmore was then introduced by the defendants. He stated that he resided in Warren county about seven miles distant from William's residence; that on the morning of William's arrest, he was out from home and heard of the arrest, and of its being on a charge of the murder of Fisher; that on returning to his own house, he found Fisher there; that Fisher was in very feeble health, and could give no rational account as to where he had been during his absence; that he (Gilmore) then started in pursuit of the officer as before stated, and that he should have taken Fisher with him only that the state of his health did not permit. Gilmore also stated that he had known Fisher for several years, and that he had understood he was subject to temporary derangement of mind, owing to an injury about his head received in early life. There was about Dr. Gilmore so much of the air and manner of truth, that his statement prevailed in the minds of the audience and of the court, and the Trailors were discharged, although they attempted no explanation of the circumstances proven by the other witnesses. On the next Monday, Myers arrived in Springfield, bringing with him the now famed Fisher, in full life and proper person. Thus ended this strange affair; and while it is readily conceived that a writer of novels could bring a story to a more perfect climax, it may well be doubted, whether a stranger affair ever really occurred. Much of the matter remains in mystery to this day. The going into the woods with Fisher, and returning without him, by the Trailors; their going into the woods at the same place the next day, after they professed to have given up the search; the signs of a struggle in the thicket, the buggy tracks at the edge of it; and the location of the thicket and the signs about it, corresponding precisely with Henry's story, are circumstances that have never been explained.

William and Archibald have both died since—William in less than a year, and Archibald in about two years after the supposed murder. Henry is still living, but never speaks of the subject.

It is not the object of the writer of this, to enter into the many curious speculations that might be indulged upon the facts of this narrative; yet he can scarcely forbear a remark upon what would, almost certainly have been the fate of William and Archibald, had Fisher not been found alive. It seems he had wandered away in mental derangement, and, had he died in this condition, and his body been found in the vicinity, it is difficult to conceive what could have saved the Trailors from the consequence of having murdered him. Or, if he had died, and his body never found, the case against them, would have been quite as bad, for, although it is a principle of law that a conviction for murder shall not be had, unless the body of the deceased be discovered, it is to be remembered, that Henry testified he saw Fisher's dead body.

Andrew Johnston was a lawyer who served as Clerk of the Illinois Senate in 1839, when Lincoln probably made his acquaintance, and was editor of the Quincy Whig. *He may have solicited the narrative from Lincoln's pen as a result of having heard Lincoln recount the story orally. Their "literary" friendship and correspondence had been of some duration prior to the writing of the article, as is indicated in the letter to Johnston, April 18, 1846. That Lincoln is the "member of the bar" mentioned as author by the editor of the* Whig *in the prefatory note seems obvious from the circumstances of the exchange between Lincoln and Johnston of other "literary" compositions and from the fact that the story was reprinted in the* Sangamo Journal, *April 23, 1846. The readers should compare the general narrative with Lincoln's "Letter to Joshua F. Speed," June 19, 1841, which was written the day following the "examining trial" held in a justice of peace court, at which Lincoln was one of the attorneys representing William Trailor. A plausible solution to the mystery has been worked out by Mr. Roger W. Barrett, who edited the piece in a brochure entitled* A Strange Affair *(1933). With Mr. Barrett's permission the following paragraphs, including in the first paragraph part of an earlier solution proposed by Alexander Shields, who had attended Archibald Trailor's last illness, are reproduced herewith:*

*" 'The result was that Archibald Trayler's [*sic*] usefulness was destroyed, and he wandered about like a person in a dream. About two years after, a messenger came for me at twelve o'clock at night, to see Trayler, who was very sick; when I saw him he was exhausted, and in a few hours departed this life. The plain, natural and just solution of this mysterious affair appears to be simply this. Wm. Trayler had a great fancy for Capt. Ransdell's niece, and she had a fancy for him, and the Captain was intensely opposed to it. Trayler was determined to steal the girl, and she was willing to be stolen, and in order to be prepared for the theft, the three men went down into the timber to find if there were any byroads that would lead into the Beardstown road; then Fisher is sent home on foot, and arrangements made with the girl to meet him in the timber. When he departed from home he took that direction, and the girl being unable to escape the vigilance of the Captain and his spies, did not appear; after waiting a reasonable time, he then went to the Beardstown road on his way home.'*

"The statement of Dr. Shields, instead of solving, seems only to cast the shadow of a new mystery. It is improbable that Henry Trailor would charge his brothers with an atrocious murder merely to avoid the mention of a girl in whom one of his brothers was interested.

"The real mystery of the case is why Archibald and William Trailor would never reveal what occurred, nor the circumstances under which they parted from Fisher, nor tell why, after leaving the searching party on the

following day ostensibly to go to their homes, they again returned to the thicket and remained there for an hour or so while Henry stood guard. In the silence of the three brothers, these questions have remained unanswered for almost a century and there is no voice that can 'provoke the silent dust' to reveal their secret.

"But, subject to information that may yet be discovered, and to any more plausible explanation which may be suggested, the following is offered as a solution which is consistent with all the facts and circumstances of the case as now known.

"Lincoln, in his letter to Speed, relates that 'Fisher had a serious hurt in his head by the bursting of a gun, since which he had been subject to continued bad health and occasional aberration of mind.' Such an injury may cause mental aberration or epileptic fit, followed by catalepsy, leaving the sufferer in a state closely resembling, and occasionally mistaken for death.

"Entering the thicket—either to meet the young lady or with a premonition of the impending attack—Fisher, seized with a fit, or mental aberration, may have struggled with the brothers, or, if he went in alone, may in falling, have sustained some visible mark of injury before the Trailors followed him into the thicket. The brothers, mistaking the unconscious or cataleptic state of Fisher for the sign of death, and fearing that because of the evidence of the struggle, or the possession of his money, they would be suspected of foul play, concealed the body in order to gain time to determine what course to pursue. Fisher may have turned his money over to them, or they may have taken it from his person to safeguard it.

"Returning the following day and finding the body as they had left it, they apparently determined to dispose of it in the mill pond, so that when found it would be supposed that Fisher had accidentally drowned. Presumably the Trailors drove hastily away and Fisher, regaining consciousness through the effect of his sudden

immersion, escaped drowning to wander in a daze over the prairies.

"The Trailors must have been puzzled when the pond was drained and no body found, and bewildered when Fisher turned up alive. After their acquittal and vindication at the town meeting, it is not to be wondered that Archibald and William would never reveal their part in this strange affair."

LETTER TO ANDREW JOHNSTON
APRIL 18, 1846

Tremont, April 18, 1846.

Friend Johnston:

Your letter, written some six weeks since, was received in due course, and also the paper with the parody. It is true, as suggested it might be, that I have never seen Poe's "Raven"; and I very well know that a parody is almost entirely dependent for its interest upon the reader's acquaintance with the original. Still there is enough in the polecat, self-considered, to afford one several hearty laughs. I think four or five of the last stanzas are decidedly funny, particularly where Jeremiah "scrubbed and washed, and prayed and fasted."

I have not your letter now before me; but, from memory, I think you ask me who is the author of the piece I sent you, and that you do so ask as to indicate a slight suspicion that I myself am the author. Beyond all question, I am not the author. I would give all I am worth, and go in debt, to be able to write so fine a piece as I think that is. Neither do I know who is the author. I met it in a straggling form in a newspaper last summer, and I remember to have seen it once before, about fifteen years ago, and this is all I know about it. The piece of poetry of my own which I alluded to, I was led to write under the following circumstances. In the fall of 1844, thinking I might aid some to carry the State of Indiana for Mr. Clay, I went into the neighborhood in that State in which I was raised, where my mother and only sister were buried, and from which I had been absent about fifteen years. That part of the country is, within itself, as unpoetical as any spot of the earth; but still, seeing it and its objects and inhabitants aroused feelings in me which were certainly poetry; though whether my expression of those feelings is poetry is quite another question. When I got to writing, the change of subject divided the thing into four little divisions or cantos, the first only of which I send you now, and may send the others hereafter.

Yours truly,
A. Lincoln.

The poem to which Lincoln refers in the second paragraph was William Knox's "Mortality," Lincoln's favorite poem at this time.

The first ten stanzas of "My Childhood Home I See Again" were apparently inclosed with this letter. The rest of this poem, which Lincoln calls "the second canto," was included in his next "Letter to Andrew Johnston," September 6, 1846. The manuscript of this poem which is in the Library of Congress contains two stanzas (the two last as printed in this volume) not included in either letter, and the manuscript of the letter of September 6 contains one stanza which is not in the Library of Congress manuscript (the third from the last stanza as printed in this volume). The other "cantos," if there ever were any, have apparently been lost. Although the name "Johnston" is correct, Lincoln spells it "Johnson" in the letter of September 6.

Lincoln's admission that he had not read Poe's "The Raven" is not surprising, since it had appeared for the first time in N. P. Willis's Evening Mirror *in January, 1845. Later, possibly as a result of Johnston's parody, "The Raven" seems to have been read and memorized by Lincoln, as indicated by Albert J. Beveridge (*Abraham Lincoln: 1809-1858, *Vol. II, p. 228).*

RELIGIOUS VIEWS: LETTER TO THE EDITOR OF THE *ILLINOIS GAZETTE*. AUGUST 11, 1846

Springfield, August 11th, 1846.

Mr. Ford:—

I see in your paper of the 8th inst. a communication in relation to myself, of which it is perhaps expected of me to take some notice.

Shortly before starting on my tour through yours, and the other Northern counties of the District, I was informed by letter from Jacksonville that Mr. Cartwright was whispering the charge of infidelity against me in that quarter.—I at once wrote a contradiction of it, and sent it to my friends there, with the request that they should publish it or not, as in their discretion they might think proper, having in view the extent of the circulation of the charge, as also the extent of credence it might be receiving. They did not publish it. After my return from your part of the District, I was informed that he had been putting the same charge in circulation against me in some of the neighborhoods in our own, and one or two of the adjoining counties.—I believe nine persons out of ten had not heard the charge at all; and, in a word, its extent of circulation was just such as to make a public notice of it appear uncalled for; while it was not entirely safe to leave it unnoticed. After some reflection, I published the little hand-bill, herewith enclosed, and sent it to the neighborhoods above referred to.

I have little doubt now, that to make the same charge—to slyly sow the seed in select spots—was the chief object of his mission through your part of the District, at a time when he knew I could not contradict him, either in person or by letter before the election. And, from the election returns in your county, being so different from what they are in parts where Mr. Cartwright and I are both well known, I incline to the belief that he has succeeded in deceiving some honest men there.

As to Mr. Woodward, "our worthy commissioner from Henry," spoken of by your correspondent, I must say it is a little singular that he should know so much about me, while, if I ever saw *him*, or heard of him, save in the communication in your paper, I have forgotten it. If Mr. Woodward has given such assurance of my character as your correspondent asserts, I can still suppose him to be a worthy man; he may have believed what he said; but there is, even in that charitable view of his case, one lesson in morals which he might, not without profit, learn of even me—and that is, never to add the weight of his character to a charge against his fellow man, without *knowing* it to be true.—I believe it is an established maxim in morals that he who makes an assertion without knowing whether it is true or false, is guilty of falsehood; and the accidental truth of the assertion, does not justify or excuse him. This maxim ought to be particularly held in view, when we contemplate an attack upon the reputation of our neighbor. I suspect it will turn out that Mr. Woodward got his information in relation to me, from Mr. Cartwright; and I here aver, that he, Cartwright, never heard me utter a word in any way indicating my opinions on religious matters, in his life.

It is my wish that you give this letter, together with the accompanying hand-bill, a place in your paper.

Yours truly,
A. Lincoln

TO THE VOTERS OF THE SEVENTH CONGRESSIONAL DISTRICT.

Fellow Citizens:

A charge having got into circulation in some of the neighborhoods of this District, in substance that I am an open scoffer at *Christianity*, I have by the advice of some friends concluded to notice the subject in this form. That I am not a member of any Christian Church, is true; but I have never denied the truth of the Scriptures; and I have never spoken with intentional disrespect of religion in general, or of any denomination of Christians in particular. It is true that in early life I was inclined to believe in what I understand is called the "Doctrine of Necessity" —that is, that the human mind is impelled to action, or held in rest by some power, over which the mind itself has no control; and I have sometimes (with one, two or three, but never publicly) tried to maintain this opinion in argument—the habit of arguing thus however, I have, entirely left off for more than five years—And I add here, I have always understood this same opinion to be held by several of the Christian denominations. The foregoing, is the whole truth, briefly stated, in relation to myself, upon this subject.

I do not think I could myself, be brought to support a man for office, whom I knew to be an open enemy of, and scoffer at, religion.—Leaving the higher matter of eternal consequences, between him and his Maker, I still do not think any man has the right thus to insult the feelings, and injure the morals, of the community in which he may live.—If, then, I was guilty of such conduct, I should blame no man who should condemn me for it; but I do blame those, whoever they may be, who falsely put such a charge in circulation against me.

A Lincoln.

July 31, 1846.

Allen N. Ford, editor of the Illinois Gazette, *had written Lincoln of the charges being circulated against him by the Reverend Peter Cartwright and followers. Lincoln's answer came too late to influence the election results in Marshall County, but was published afterwards. Cartwright came off a poor second in the controversy as well as in the election. In the same issue of the* Gazette *Ford editorialized that it was "quite bad enough" for a minister "to meddle with politics at all; but when in the canvass he descends from the arena of honorable warfare to revel in the filth of defamation and falsehood, what shall we say of his character as a man, and what the world of religion he professes?"*

Another letter appears following Lincoln's, signed "D.," which calls attention to the fact that Lincoln's supposed infidelity "has been well endorsed by probably 1000 of a majority," and undertakes to show that "it was owing to Atheists, and Deists in the convention that formed our Constitution that Religious liberty was secured to the citizens of the Union . . . and I do know that religious sects denounced the Constitution, because 'it did not begin with and made no provision for religion.'"

As a curious footnote to the tactics of Cartwright in this election, there came a time when Lincoln defended Cartwright's grandson, Quinn Harrison, for murder and gained his acquittal after one of his bitterest legal battles. (See Emanuel Hertz, editor, The Hidden Lincoln, *pp. 106-108).*

LETTER TO ANDREW JOHNSTON SEPTEMBER 6, 1846

Springfield, Sept. 6th. 1846

Friend Johnson [*sic*]:

You remember when I wrote you from Tremont last spring, sending you a little canto of what I called poetry, I promised to bore you with another some time. I now fulfil the promise. The subject of the present one is an insane man. His name is Matthew Gentry. He is three years older than I, and when we were boys we went to school together. He was rather a bright lad, and the son of *the* rich man of our very poor neighbourhood. At the age of nineteen he unaccountably became furiously mad, from which condition he gradually settled down into harmless insanity. When, as I told you in my other letter I visited my old home in the fall of 1844, I found him still lingering in this wretched condition. In my poetizing mood I could not forget the impressions his case made upon me. Here is the result.

[Here follows the second half, excepting the last two stanzas, of the poem which is printed next in order.]

If I should ever send another, the subject will be a "Bear-hunt."

Yours as ever
A. Lincoln

MY CHILDHOOD HOME I SEE AGAIN. 1846

[I]

My childhood-home I see again,
  And gladden with the view;
And still as mem'ries crowd my brain,
  There's sadness in it too.

O memory! thou mid-way world
  'Twixt Earth and Paradise,
Where things decayed, and loved ones lost
  In dreamy shadows rise.

And freed from all that's gross or vile,
  Seem hallowed, pure, and bright,
Like scenes in some enchanted isle,
  All bathed in liquid light.

As distant mountains please the eye,
  When twilight chases day—
As bugle-tones, that, passing by,
  In distance die away—

As leaving some grand water-fall
  We ling'ring, list it's roar,
So memory will hallow all
  We've known, but know no more.

Now twenty years have passed away,
  Since here I bid farewell
To woods, and fields, and scenes of play
  And school-mates loved so well.

Where many were, how few remain
  Of old familiar things!
But seeing these to mind again
  The lost and absent brings.

The friends I left that parting day—
  How changed, as time has sped!
Young childhood grown, strong manhood gray,
  And half of all are dead.

I hear the lone survivors tell
  How nought from death could save,
Till every sound appears a knell,
  And every spot a grave.

I range the fields with pensive tread,
  And pace the hollow rooms;
And feel (companions of the dead)
  I'm living in the tombs.

[II]

A[nd] here's an object more of dread,
  Than aught the grave contains—
A human-form, with reason fled,
  While wretched life remains.

Poor Matthew! Once of genius bright,—
  A fortune-favored child—
Now locked for aye, in mental night,
  A haggard mad-man wild.

Poor Matthew! I have ne'er forgot
  When first with maddened will,
Yourself you maimed, your father fought,
  And mother strove to kill;

And terror spread, and neighbors ran,
  Your dang'rous strength to bind;
And soon a howling crazy man,
  Your limbs were fast confined.

How then you writhed and shrieked aloud,
  Your bones and sinews bared;
And fiendish on the gaping crowd,
  With burning eye-balls glared.

And begged, and swore, and wept, and prayed,
  With maniac laughter joined—
How fearful are the signs displayed,
  By pangs that kill the mind!

And when at length, the drear and long
  Time soothed your fiercer woes—
How plaintively your mournful song,
  Upon the still night rose.

I've heard it oft, as if I dreamed,
  Far-distant, sweet, and lone;
The funeral dirge it ever seemed
  Of reason dead and gone.

To drink its strains, I've stole away,
  All silently and still,
Ere yet the rising god of day
  Had streaked the Eastern hill.

Air held his breath; the trees all still
  Seemed sorr'wing angels round.
Their swelling tears in dew-drops fell
  Upon the list'ning ground.

But this is past, and naught remains
  That raised you o'er the brute.
Your mad'ning shrieks, and soothing strains
  Are like forever mute.

Now fare thee well: more thou the cause
  Than subject now of woe.
All mental pangs, by time's kind laws,
  Hast lost the power to know.

O death! thou awe-inspiring prince,
  That keepst the world in fear;
Why dost thou tear more blest ones hence,
  And leave him ling'ring here?—

And now away to seek some scene
  Less painful than the last—
With less of horror mingled in
  The present and the past.

The very spot where grew the bread
  That formed my bones, I see.
How strange, old field, on thee to tread
  And feel I'm part of thee!

The stanza third from the last does not appear in the manuscript in the Library of Congress, but is included in the text as it appears in the manuscript enclosed by Lincoln with the "Letter to Andrew Johnston," September 6, 1846.

THE BEAR HUNT. [1846]

A wild-bear chace, didst never see?
  Then hast thou lived in vain.
Thy richest bump of glorious glee,
  Lies desert in thy brain.

When first my father settled here,
  'Twas then the frontier line:
The panther's scream, filled night with fear
  And bears preyed on the swine.

But wo for Bruin's short lived fun,
When rose the squealing cry;
Now man and horse, with dog and gun,
For vengeance, at him fly.

A sound of danger strikes his ear;
He gives the breeze a snuff:
Away he bounds, with little fear,
And seeks the tangled *rough.*

On press his foes, and reach the ground,
Where's left his half munched meal;
The dogs, in circles, scent around,
And find his fresh made trail.

With instant cry, away they dash,
And men as fast pursue;
O'er logs they leap, through water splash,
And shout the brisk halloo.

Now to elude the eager pack,
Bear shuns the open ground;
Though [*sic*] matted vines, he shapes his track
And runs it, round and round.

The tall fleet cur, with deep-mouthed voice,
Now speeds him, as the wind;
While half-grown pup, and short-legged fice,
Are yelping far behind.

And fresh recruits are dropping in
To join the merry *corps*:
With yelp and yell,—a mingled din—
The woods are in a roar.

And round, and round the chace now goes,
The world's alive with fun;

Nick Carter's horse, his rider throws,
  And more, Hill drops his gun.

Now sorely pressed, bear glances back,
  And lolls his tired tongue;
When is, to force him from his track,
  An ambush on him sprung.

Across the glade he sweeps for flight,
  And fully is in view.
The dogs, new-fired, by the sight,
  Their cry, and speed, renew.

The foremost ones, now reach his rear,
  He turns, they dash away;
And circling now, the wrathful bear,
  They have him full at bay.

At top of speed, the horse-men come,
  All screaming in a row.
"Whoop! Take him Tiger—Seize him Drum"—
  Bang,—Bang—the rifles go.

And furious now, the dogs he tears,
  And crushes in his ire—
Wheels right and left, and upward rears,
  With eyes of burning fire.

But leaden death is at his heart,
  Vain all the strength he plies—
And, spouting blood from every part,
  He reels, and sinks, and dies.

And now a dinsome clamor rose,
  'Bout who should have his skin;
Who first draws blood, each hunter knows,
  This prize must always win.

But who did this, and how to trace
  What's true from what's a lie,
Like lawyers, in a murder case
  They stoutly *argufy*.

Aforesaid fice, of blustering mood,
  Behind, and quite forgot,
Just now emerging from the wood,
  Arrives upon the spot.

With grinning teeth, and up-turned hair—
  Brim full of spunk and wrath,
He growls, and seizes on dead bear,
  And shakes for life and death.

And swells as if his skin would tear,
  And growls and shakes again;
And swears, as plain as dog can swear,
  That he has won the skin.

Conceited whelp! we laugh at thee—
  Nor mind, that not a few
Of pompous, two-legged dogs there be,
  Conceited quite as you.

LETTER TO JOSHUA F. SPEED
OCTOBER 22, 1846

Springfield, Octr. 22nd 1846

Dear Speed:

Owing to my absence, yours of the 10th. Inst. was not received until yesterday. Since then I have been devoting myself to arive [*sic*] at a correct conclusion upon your matter of business.

It may be that you do not precisely understand the nature and result of the suit against you and Bell's estate. It is a chancery suit, and has been brought to a final decree, in which, you are treated as a nominal party only. The decree is, that Bell's administration pay the Nelson Fry debt out of the proceeds of Bell's half of the store. So far, you are not injured; because you are released from the debt, without having paid any thing, and Hurst is in no way left liable to you, because the debt he and Bell undertook to pay, is, or will be, paid without your paying it, or any part of it. The question then, is, "How are you injured?"—By diverting so much of the assets of Bell's estate, to the payment of the Fry debt, the general assets are lessened, and so, will pay a smaller dividend to general creditors; one of which creditors I suppose you are, in effect, as assignor of the note to W. P. Speed. It incidentally enlarges your liability to W. P. Speed; and to that extent, you are injured. How much will this be? I think, $100—or $120—being the dividend of 25 or 30 per cent, that Hurst's half of the Fry debt, would pay on the W. P. S. debt. Hurst's undertaking was, in effect, that he would pay the *whole* of the Fry debt, if Bell did not pay any part of it; but it was not his undertaking, that if Bell should pay the whole of it, he would refund the whole, so that Bell should be the better able to pay his other debts. You are not losing on the Fry debt, because that is, or will be paid; but your loss will be on the W. P. S. debt,—a debt that Hurst is under no obligation to indemnify you against. Hurst is bound to account to Bell's estate, for one half of the Fry debt; because he owed half, and Bell's estate pays all; and if, upon such accounting any thing is due the estate from Hurst, it will swell the estate, and so far enlarge the dividend to the W. P. S. debt. But when Bell's estate shall call Hurst to account, he will I am informed show that the estate, after paying the whole of the Fry debt is still indebted to him. If so, not much, if any thing can come from that quarter—nothing, unless it can be turned, as to compel him [to?] pay *all* he owes the estate, and take a *dividend* only, upon what the estate owes him. If you had paid the Fry debt yourself, you could then turn on Hurst and make him refund you; but this would only bring [you?] where you started from, excepting it would leave Bell's estate able to pay a larger dividend; and Hurst would then turn upon the estate to contribute one half, which would enlarge the indebtedness of the estate in the same proportion, and so reduce the dividend again. I believe the only thing that can be done for your advantage in the matter, is for Bell's administrator to call Hurst to account for one half the Fry debt, and then fight off, the best he can, Hurst's claim of indebtedness against the estate.

I should be much pleased to see [you?] here again; but I must, in candour, say I do not perceive how your personal presence would do any good in the business matter.

You, no doubt, assign the suspension of our correspondence to the true philosophical cause, though it must be confessed, by both of us, that this is rather a cold reason for allowing a friendship, such as ours, to die out by degrees. I propose now, that, upon receipt of this, you shall be considered in my debt, and under obligation to pay soon, and that neither shall remain long in arrears hereafter. Are you agreed?

Being elected to Congress, though I am very grateful to our friends, for having done it, has not pleased me as much as I expected.

We have another boy, born the 10th of March last. He is very much such a child as Bob was at his age—rather of a longer order. Bob is "short and low," and, I expect, always will be. He talks very plainly—almost as plainly as any body. He is quite smart enough. I sometimes fear he is one of the little rare-ripe sort, that are smarter at about five than ever after. He has a great deal of that sort of mischief that is the offspring of such animal spirits. Since I began this letter, a messenger came to tell me, Bob was lost; but by the time I reached the house, his mother had found him, and had him whipped—and, by now, very likely he is run away again.

Mary has read your letter, and wishes to be remembered to Mrs. S. and you, in which I most sincerely join her.

As ever yours

A. Lincoln

LETTER TO WILLIAM H. HERNDON DECEMBER 12, 1847

Washington, Dec. 12. 1847

Dear William:

As soon as the Congressional Globe and Appendix begins to issue, I shall send you a copy of it regularly. I wish you to read it, or as much of it as you please, and be careful to preserve all the numbers, so that we can have a complete file of it

There is nothing new here, but what you see in the papers.

Yours as ever—

A. Lincoln

RESOLUTIONS IN THE UNITED STATES HOUSE OF REPRESENTATIVES. DECEMBER 22, 1847

WHEREAS the President of the United States, in his message of May 11, 1846, has declared that "the Mexican Government not only refused to receive him, [the envoy of the United States,] or listen to his propositions, but, after a long-continued series of menaces, has at last invaded *our territory* and shed the blood of our fellow-citizens on our *own soil*:"

And again, in his message of December 8, 1846, that "we had ample cause of war against Mexico long before the breaking out of hostilities; but even then we forbore to take redress into our own hands until Mexico herself became the aggressor, by invading *our soil* in hostile array, and shedding the blood of our citizens:"

And yet again, in his message of December 7, 1847, that "the

Mexican Government refused even to hear the terms of adjustment which he [our minister of peace] was authorized to propose, and finally, under wholly unjustifiable pretexts, involved the two countries in war, by invading the territory of the State of Texas, striking the first blow, and shedding the blood of our citizens on *our own soil.*"

And whereas this House is desirous to obtain a full knowledge of all the facts which go to establish whether the particular spot on which the blood of our citizens was so shed was or was not at that time *our own soil*: Therefore,

Resolved By the House of Representatives, That the President of the United States be respectfully requested to inform this House—

1*st.* Whether the spot on which the blood of our citizens was shed, as in his messages declared, was or was not within the territory of Spain, at least after the treaty of 1819, until the Mexican revolution.

2*d.* Whether that spot is or is not within the territory which was wrested from Spain by the revolutionary Government of Mexico.

3*d.* Whether that spot is or is not within a settlement of people, which settlement has existed ever since long before the Texas revolution, and until its inhabitants fled before the approach of the United States army.

4*th.* Whether that settlement is or is not isolated from any and all other settlements by the Gulf and the Rio Grande on the south and west, and by wide uninhabited regions on the north and east.

5*th.* Whether the people of that settlement, or a majority of them, or any of them, have ever submitted themselves to the government or laws of Texas or of the United States, by consent or by compulsion, either by accepting office, or voting at elections, or paying tax, or serving on juries, or having process served upon them, or in any other way.

6*th.* Whether the people of that settlement did or did not flee from the approach of the United States army, leaving unprotected their homes and their growing crops, *before* the blood was shed, as in the messages stated; and whether the first blood, so shed, was or was not shed within the enclosure of one of the people who had thus fled from it.

7th. Whether our *citizens,* whose blood was shed, as in his message declared, were or were not, at that time, armed officers and soldiers, sent into that settlement by the military order of the President, through the Secretary of War.

8th. Whether the military force of the United States was or was not so sent into that settlement after General Taylor had more than once intimated to the War Department that, in his opinion, no such movement was necessary to the defence or protection of Texas.

Although the work of modern historians has in general sustained President Polk's course in the events leading up to the War with Mexico, the position taken by the Whigs in Congress was not without its justification. For the anti-slavery men, the whole situation was regarded as the direct result of Democratic efforts to extend the bounds of the slave-holding portion of the United States through the annexation of Texas. But with the fact of annexation accomplished, many others, South as well as North, felt that Polk's action in sending United States troops into an area which was still open to dispute as to sovereignty was provocative of war. The question of boundary had not been settled to the satisfaction of both countries and was open to settlement by treaty at the time the first blood was shed on a "spot" in the disputed territory. Polk's assumption that the "spot" was American territory is the occasion of Lincoln's "Resolutions."

The interesting thing about Lincoln's "Resolutions" is that they were introduced by a new Congressman who had taken his seat only a few weeks earlier. As Beveridge observes, "few new members of Congress, during a first term, have been so active as Lincoln was; but he made practically no impression on anybody, and such impression as he did make was not favorable." Although the second half of the comment is a bit overstated, it is true that the chief result of Lincoln's activities was the alienation of the electorate back home. The "Resolutions" raised no new points which had not been reiterated time and again by Polk's opponents in Congress for months past, and Lincoln's object in submitting them seems to have been little more than his means of going on record with his party.

The brackets appearing in the "Resolutions" and in both speeches delivered in the United States House of Representatives—January 12, 1848, and July 27, 1848—are not the editor's, but the text's.

THE WAR WITH MEXICO: SPEECH IN THE UNITED STATES HOUSE OF REPRESENTATIVES. JANUARY 12, 1848

Mr. Chairman:

Some, if not all, the gentlemen on the other side of the House, who have addressed the committee within the last two days, have spoken rather complainingly, if I have rightly understood them, of the vote given a week or ten days ago, declaring that the war with Mexico was unnecessarily and unconstitutionally commenced by the President. I admit that such a vote should not be given in mere party wantonness, and that the one given is justly censurable, if it have no other or better foundation. I am one of those who joined in that vote; and I did so under my best impression of the *truth* of the case. How I got this impression, and how it may possibly be removed, I will now try to show. When the war began, it was my opinion that all those who, because of knowing too *little*, or because of knowing too *much*, could not conscientiously approve the conduct of the President, (in the beginning of it,) should, nevertheless, as good citizens and patriots, remain silent on that point, at least till the war should be ended. Some leading Democrats, including ex-President Van Buren, have taken this same view, as I understand them; and I adhered to it and acted upon it, until since I took my seat here; and I think I should still adhere to it, were it not that the President and his friends will not allow it to be so. Besides, the continual effort of the President to argue every silent vote given for supplies into an endorsement of the justice and wisdom of his conduct; besides that singularly candid paragraph in his late message, in which he tells us that Congress, with great unanimity, (only two in the Senate and fourteen in the House dissenting,) had declared that "by the act of the Republic of Mexico a state of war exists between that Government and the United States;" when the same journals that informed him of this, also informed him that, when that declaration stood disconnected from the question of supplies, sixty-seven in the House, and not fourteen, merely, voted against it; besides this open attempt to prove by telling the *truth*, what he could not prove by telling the *whole truth*, demanding of all who will not submit to be misrepresented, in justice to themselves, to speak out; besides all this, one of my colleagues, [MR. RICHARDSON,] at a very early day in the session, brought in a set of resolutions, expressly indorsing the original justice of the war on the part of the President. Upon these resolutions, when they shall be put on their passage, I shall be *compelled* to vote; so that I cannot be silent if I would. Seeing this, I went about preparing myself to give the vote understandingly, when it should come. I carefully examined the President's messages, to ascertain what he himself had said and proved upon the point. The result of this examination was to make the impression, that, taking for true all the President states as facts, he falls far short of proving his justification; and that the President would have gone further with his proof, if it had not been for the small matter that the *truth* would not permit him. Under the impression thus made, I gave the vote before mentioned. I propose now to give, concisely, the process of the examination I made, and how I reached the conclusion I did.

The President, in his first message of May, 1846, declares that the soil was *ours* on which hostilities were commenced by Mexico;

and he repeats that declaration, almost in the same language, in each successive annual message—thus showing that he esteems that point a highly essential one. In the importance of that point, I entirely agree with the President. To my judgment, it is the *very point* upon which he should be justified or condemned. In his message of December, 1846, it seems to have occurred to him, as is certainly true, that title, ownership to soil or anything else, is not a simple fact, but is a conclusion following one or more simple facts; and that it was incumbent upon him to present the facts from which he concluded the soil was ours on which the first blood of the war was shed.

Accordingly, a little below the middle of page twelve, in the message last referred to, he enters upon that task; forming an issue and introducing testimony, extending the whole to a little below the middle of page fourteen. Now, I propose to try to show that the whole of this—issue and evidence—is, from beginning to end, the sheerest deception. The issue, as he presents it, is in these words: "But there are those who, conceding all this to be true, assume the ground that the true western boundary of Texas is the Nueces, instead of the Rio Grande; and that, therefore, in marching our army to the east bank of the latter river, we passed the Texan line, and invaded the territory of Mexico." Now, this issue is made up of two affirmatives and no negative. The main deception of it is, that it assumes as true that *one* river or the *other* is necessarily the boundary, and cheats the superficial thinker entirely out of the idea that *possibly* the boundary is somewhere *between* the two, and not actually at either. A further deception is, that it will let in *evidence* which a true issue would exclude. A true issue made by the President would be about as follows: "I say the soil *was ours* on which the first blood was shed; there are those who say it was not."

I now proceed to examine the President's evidence, as applicable to such an issue. When that evidence is analyzed, it is all included in the following propositions:

1. That the Rio Grande was the western boundary of Louisiana, as we purchased it of France in 1803.

2. That the Republic of Texas always *claimed* the Rio Grande as her western boundary.

3. That, by various acts, she had claimed it *on paper.*

4. That Santa Anna, in his treaty with Texas, recognized the Rio Grande as her boundary.

5. That Texas *before*, and the United States *after* annexation, had *exercised* jurisdiction *beyond* the Nueces, *between* the two rivers.

6. That our Congress *understood* the boundary of Texas to extend beyond the Nueces.

Now for each of these in its turn:

His first item is, that the Rio Grande was the western boundary of Louisiana, as we purchased it of France in 1803; and, seeming to expect this to be disputed, he argues over the amount of nearly a page to prove it true; at the end of which, he lets us know that, by the treaty of 1819, we sold to Spain the whole country, from the Rio Grande eastward to the Sabine. Now, admitting, for the present, that the Rio Grande was the boundary of Louisiana, what, under heaven, had that to do with the *present* boundary between us and Mexico? How, Mr. Chairman, the line that once divided your land from mine can *still* be the boundary between us *after* I have sold my land to you, is, to me, beyond all comprehension. And how any man, with an honest purpose only of proving the truth, could ever have *thought* of introducing such a fact to prove such an issue, is equally incomprehensible. The outrage upon common *right*, of seizing as our own what we have once sold, merely because it *was* ours *before* we sold it, is only equalled by the outrage on common *sense* of any attempt to justify it.

The President's next piece of evidence is, that "the Republic of Texas always *claimed* this river (Rio Grande) as her western boundary." That is not true, in fact. Texas *has* claimed it, but she has not *always* claimed it. There is, at least, one distinguished exception. Her State constitution—the Republic's most solemn and well-considered act; that which may, without impropriety, be called her last will and testament, revoking all others—makes no such claim. But suppose she had always claimed it. Has not Mexico always claimed the contrary? So that there is but *claim* against *claim*, leaving nothing proved until we get back of the claims, and find which has the better *foundation.*

Though not in the order in which the President presents his evidence, I now consider that class of his statements, which are, in substance, nothing more than that Texas has, by various acts of her Convention and Congress, claimed the Rio Grande as her boundary—*on paper*. I mean here what he says about the fixing of the Rio Grande as her boundary, in her old constitution, (not her State constitution,) about forming congressional districts, counties, &c. Now, all of this is but naked *claim*; and what I have already said about claims is strictly applicable to this. If I should claim your land by word of mouth, that certainly would not make it mine; and if I were to claim it by a deed which I had made myself, and with which you had had nothing to do, the claim would be quite the same in substance, or rather in utter nothingness.

I next consider the President's statement that Santa Anna, in his *treaty* with Texas, recognized the Rio Grande as the western boundary of Texas. Besides the position so often taken that Santa Anna, while a prisoner of war—a captive—*could* not bind Mexico by a treaty, which I deem conclusive; besides this, I wish to say something in relation to this treaty,* so called by the President, with Santa Anna. If any man would like to be amused by a sight at that *little* thing, which the President calls by that *big* name, he can have it by turning to Niles's Register, volume 50, page 336. And if any one should suppose that Niles's Register is a curious repository of so mighty a document as a solemn treaty between nations, I can only say that I learned, to a tolerable degree of certainty, by inquiry at the State Department, that the President himself never saw it anywhere else. By the way, I believe I should not err if I were to declare, that during the first ten years of the existence of that document, it was never by anybody *called* a treaty; that it was never so called till the President, in his extremity, attempted, by so calling it, to wring something from it in justification of himself in connection with the Mexican war. It has none of the distinguishing features of a treaty. It does not call itself a treaty. Santa Anna does not therein assume to bind Mexico; he assumes only to act as the President, Commander-in-chief of the Mexican army and navy; stipulates that the then present hostilities should

* For the text of this "treaty" see note following this speech.

cease, and that he would not *himself* take up arms, nor *influence* the Mexican people to take up arms, against Texas, during the existence of the war of independence. He did not recognize the independence of Texas; he did not assume to put an end to the war, but clearly indicated his expectation of its continuance; he did not say one word about boundary, and most probably never thought of it. It *is* stipulated therein that the Mexican forces should evacuate the territory of Texas, *passing to the other side of the Rio Grande*; and in another article it is stipulated, that to prevent collisions between the armies, the Texan army should not approach nearer than within five leagues—of *what* is not said—but clearly, from the object stated, it is of the Rio Grande. Now, if this is a treaty recognizing the Rio Grande as the boundary of Texas, it contains the singular feature of stipulating that Texas shall not go within five leagues of *her own* boundary.

Next comes the evidence of Texas before annexation, and the United States afterwards, *exercising* jurisdiction *beyond* the Nueces, and *between* the two rivers. This actual *exercise* of jurisdiction is the very class or quality of evidence we want. It is excellent so far as it goes; but does it go far enough? He tells us it went *beyond* the Nueces, but he does not tell us it went *to* the Rio Grande. He tells us jurisdiction was exercised *between* the two rivers, but he does not tell us it was exercised over *all* the territory between them. Some simple-minded people think it *possible* to cross one river and go *beyond* it, without going *all the way* to the next; that jurisdiction may be exercised *between* two rivers without covering *all* the country between them. I know a man, not very unlike myself, who exercises jurisdiction over a piece of land between the Wabash and the Mississippi; and yet so far is this from being *all* there is between those rivers, that it is just one hundred and fifty-two feet long by fifty wide, and no part of it much within a hundred miles of either. He has a neighbor between him and the Mississippi—that is, just across the street, in that direction—whom, I am sure, he could neither *persuade* nor *force* to give up his habitation; but which, nevertheless, he could certainly annex, if it were to be done, by merely standing on his own side of the street and *claiming* it, or even sitting down and writing a *deed* for it.

But next, the President tells us, the Congress of the United States *understood* the State of Texas they admitted into the Union to extend *beyond* the Nueces. Well, I suppose they did—I certainly so understand it—but how *far* beyond? That Congress did *not* understand it to extend clear to the Rio Grande, is quite certain by the fact of their joint resolutions for admission expressly leaving all questions of boundary to future adjustment. And, it may be added, that Texas herself is proved to have had the same understanding of it that our Congress had, by the fact of the exact conformity of her new constitution to those resolutions.

I am now through the whole of the President's evidence; and it is a singular fact, that if any one should declare the President sent the army into the midst of a settlement of Mexican people, who had never submitted, by consent or by force to the authority of Texas or of the United States, and that *there*, and *thereby*, the first blood of the war was shed, there is not one word in all the President has said which would either admit or deny the declaration. In this strange omission chiefly consists the deception of the President's evidence—an omission which, it does seem to me, could scarcely have occurred but by design. My way of living leads me to be about the courts of justice; and there I have sometimes seen a good lawyer, struggling for his client's neck, in a desperate case, employing every artifice to work round, befog, and cover up with many words some position pressed upon him by the prosecution, which he *dared* not admit, and yet *could* not deny. Party bias may help to make it appear so; but, with all the allowance I can make for such bias, it still does appear to me that just such, and from just such necessity, is the President's struggles in this case.

Some time after my colleague [MR. RICHARDSON] introduced the resolutions I have mentioned, I introduced a preamble, resolution, and interrogatories, intended to draw the President out, if possible, on this hitherto untrodden ground. To show their relevancy, I propose to state my understanding of the true rule for ascertaining the boundary between Texas and Mexico. It is, that *wherever* Texas was *exercising* jurisdiction was hers; and *wherever Mexico* was exercising jurisdiction was hers; and that *whatever* separated the actual exercise of jurisdiction of the one from that of the other, was the true boundary between them. If, as is probably true, Texas was exercising jurisdiction along the western bank of the Nueces, and Mexico was exercising it along the eastern bank of the Rio Grande, then *neither* river was the boundary, but the uninhabited country between the two was. The extent of our territory in that region depended, not on any *treaty-fixed* boundary, (for no treaty had attempted it,) but on revolution. Any people anywhere, being inclined and having the power, have the *right* to rise up and shake off the existing government, and form a new one that suits them better. This is a most valuable, a most sacred right—a right which, we hope and believe, is to liberate the world. Nor is this right confined to cases in which the whole people of an existing government may choose to exercise it. Any portion of such people that *can may* revolutionize, and make their *own* of so much of the territory as they inhabit. More than this, a *majority* of any portion of such people may revolutionize, putting down a *minority*, intermingled with, or near about them, who may oppose their movements. Such minority was precisely the case of the Tories of our own Revolution. It is a quality of revolutions not to go by *old* lines, or *old* laws; but to break up both, and make new ones. As to the country now in question, we bought it of France in 1803, and sold it to Spain in 1819, according to the President's statement. After this, all Mexico, including Texas, revolutionized against Spain; and still later, Texas revolutionized against Mexico. In my view, just so far as she carried her revolution, by obtaining the *actual*, willing or unwilling, submission of the people, *so far* the country was hers, and no farther.

Now, sir, for the purpose of obtaining the very best evidence as to whether Texas had actually carried her revolution to the place where the hostilities of the present war commenced, let the President answer the interrogatories I proposed, as before mentioned, or some other similar ones. Let him answer fully, fairly, and candidly. Let him answer with *facts*, and not with arguments. Let him remember he sits where Washington sat; and, so remembering, let him answer as Washington would answer. As a nation *should* not, and the Almighty *will* not, be evaded, so let him attempt no evasion, no equivocation. And if, so answering, he can show that the soil was ours where the first blood of the war was shed—that it was not within an inhabited country, or, if within such, that the inhabitants had submitted themselves to the civil authority of Texas, or of the United States, and that the same is true of the site of Fort Brown—then I am with him for his justification. In that case, I shall be most happy to reverse the vote I gave the other day. I have a selfish motive for desiring that the President may do this; I expect to give some votes, in connection with the war, which, without his so doing, will be of doubtful propriety, in my own judgment, but which will be free from the doubt, if he does so. But if he *cannot* or *will not* do this—if, on any pretence, or no pretence, he shall refuse or omit it—then I shall be fully convinced, of what I more than suspect already, that he is deeply conscious of being in the wrong; that he feels the blood of this war, like the blood of Abel, is crying to Heaven against him; that he ordered General Taylor into the midst of a peaceful Mexican settlement, purposely to bring on a war; that originally having some strong motive—what I will not stop now to give my opinion concerning—to involve the two countries in a war, and trusting to escape scrutiny by fixing the public gaze upon the exceeding brightness of military glory—that attractive rainbow that rises in showers of blood—that serpent's eye that charms to destroy—he plunged into it, and has swept *on* and *on*, till, disappointed in his calculation of the ease with which Mexico might be subdued, he now finds himself he knows not where. How like the half-insane mumbling of a fever dream is the whole war part of the late message! At one time telling us that Mexico has nothing whatever that we can get but territory; at another, showing us how we can support the war by levying contributions on Mexico. At one time urging the national honor, the security of the future, the prevention of foreign interference, and even the good of Mexico herself, as among the objects of the war; at another, telling us that, "to reject indemnity, by refusing to accept a cession of territory, would be to abandon all our just demands, and to wage the war, bearing all its expenses, *without a purpose or definite object.*" So, then, the national honor, security of the future, and everything but territorial indemnity, may be considered the *no-purposes* and *indefinite* objects of the war! But, having it now settled that territorial indemnity is the only object, we are urged to seize, by legislation here, all that he was content to take a few months ago, and the whole province of Lower California to boot, and to still carry on the war—to take *all* we are fighting for, and *still* fight on. Again, the President is resolved, under all circumstances, to have full territorial indemnity for the expenses of the war; but he forgets to tell us how we are to get the *excess* after those expenses shall have surpassed the value of the *whole* of the Mexican territory. So, again, he insists that the separate national existence of Mexico shall be maintained; but he does not tell us *how* this can be done after we shall have taken *all* her territory. Lest the questions I here suggest be considered speculative merely, let me be indulged a moment in trying to show they are not.

The war has gone on some twenty months; for the expenses of which, together with an inconsiderable old score, the President now claims about one half of the Mexican territory, and that by far the better half, so far as concerns our ability to make anything out of it. *It* is comparatively uninhabited; so that we could establish land offices in it, and raise some money in that way. But the other half is already inhabited, as I understand it, tolerably densely for the nature of the country; and all its lands, or all that are valuable, already appropriated as private property. How, then, are we to make anything out of these lands with this encumbrance on them, or how remove the encumbrance? I suppose no one will say we should kill the people, or drive them out, or make slaves of them, or even confiscate their property? How, then, can we make much out of this part of the territory? If the prosecution of the war has, in expenses, already equaled the *better* half of the country, how long its future prosecution will be in equaling the less valuable half is not a *speculative*, but a *practical* question, pressing closely upon us; and yet it is a question which the President seems never to have thought of.

As to the mode of terminating the war and securing peace, the President is equally wandering and indefinite. First, it is to be done by a more vigorous prosecution of the war in the vital parts of the enemy's country; and, after apparently talking himself tired on this point, the President drops down into a half despairing tone, and tells us, that "with a people distracted and divided by contending factions, and a Government subject to constant changes, by successive revolutions, *the continued success of our arms may fail to obtain a satisfactory peace*." Then he suggests the propriety of wheedling the Mexican people to desert the counsels of their own leaders, and, trusting in our protection, to set up a Government from which we can secure a satisfactory peace, telling us that "*this may become the only mode of obtaining such a peace*." But soon he falls into doubt of this too, and then drops back on to the already half-abandoned ground of "more vigorous prosecution." All this shows that the President is in no wise satisfied with his own positions. First, he takes up one, and, in attempting to argue us *into* it, he argues himself *out* of it; then seizes another, and goes through the same process; and then, confused at being able to think of nothing new, he snatches up the old one again, which he has some time before cast off. His mind, tasked beyond its power, is running hither and thither, like some tortured creature on a burning surface, finding no position on which it can settle down and be at ease.

Again, it is a singular omission in this message, that it nowhere intimates *when* the President expects the war to terminate. At its beginning, General Scott was, by this same President, driven into disfavor, if not disgrace, for intimating that peace could not be conquered in less than three or four months. But now, at the end of about twenty months, during which time our arms have given us the most splendid successes—every department, and every part, land and water, officers and privates, regulars and volunteers, doing all that men *could* do, and hundreds of things which it had ever before been thought men could *not* do; after all this, this same President gives us a long message without showing us that, *as to the end*, he has himself even an imaginary conception. As I have before said, he knows not where he is. He is a bewildered, confounded, and miserably-perplexed man. God grant he may be able to show there is not something about his conscience more painful than all his mental perplexity!

The so-called "Treaty" referred to in this speech, as printed in the Congressional Globe, *is as follows:*

ARTICLES OF AGREEMENT ENTERED INTO BETWEEN HIS EXCELLENCY DAVID G. BURNET, PRESIDENT OF THE REPUBLIC OF TEXAS, OF THE ONE PART, AND HIS EXCELLENCY GENERAL SANTA ANNA, PRESIDENT-GENERAL-IN-CHIEF OF THE MEXICAN ARMY, OF THE OTHER PART.

ARTICLE 1. *General Antonio Lopez de Santa Anna agrees that he will not take up arms, nor will he exercise his influence to cause them to be taken up, against the people of Texas, during the present war of independence.*

ART. 2. *All hostilities between the Mexican and Texan troops will cease immediately, both by land and water.*

ART. 3. *The Mexican troops will evacuate the territory of Texas, passing to the other side of the Rio Grande Del Norte.*

ART. 4. *The Mexican army, in its retreat, shall not take the property of any person without his consent and just indemnification, using only such articles as may be necessary for its subsistence, in cases when the owner may not be present, and remitting to the commander of the army of Texas, or to the Commissioners to be appointed for the adjustment of such matters, an account of the value of the property consumed, the place where taken, and the name of the owner, if it can be ascertained.*

ART. 5. *That all private property, including cattle, horses, negro slaves, or indentured persons, of whatever denomination, that may have been captured by any portion of the Mexican army, or may have taken refuge in the said army, since the commencement of the late invasion, shall be restored to the commander of the Texan army, or to such other persons as may be appointed by the Government of Texas to receive them.*

ART. 6. *The troops of both armies will refrain*

from coming into contact with each other; and to this end, the commander of the army of Texas will be careful not to approach within a shorter distance than five leagues.

ART. 7. *The Mexican army shall not make any other delay, on its march, than that which is necessary to take up their hospitals, baggage, etc., and to cross the rivers; and delay not necessary to these purposes to be considered an infraction of this agreement.*

ART. 8. *By an express, to be immediately despatched, this agreement shall be sent to General Vincente Filisola, and to General T. J. Rusk, commander of the Texan army, in order that they may be apprized of its stipulations; and to this end, they will exchange engagements to comply with the same.*

ART. 9. *That all Texan prisoners now in the possession of the Mexican army, or its authorities, be forthwith released, and furnished with free passports to return to their homes; in consideration of which, a corresponding number of Mexican prisoners, rank and file, now in possession of the Government of Texas, shall be immediately released—the remainder of the Mexican prisoners, that continue in the possession of the Government of Texas to be treated with due humanity; any extraordinary comforts that may be furnished them to be at the charge of the Government of Mexico.*

ART. 10. *General Antonio Lopez de Santa Anna will be sent to Vera Cruz as soon as it shall be deemed proper.*

The contracting parties sign this instrument for the above mentioned purposes, in duplicate, at the port of Velasco, this fourteenth day of May, 1836.

DAVID G. BURNET, *President,*
JAS. COLLINGSWORTH, *Secretary of State,*
ANTONIO LOPEZ DE SANTA ANNA,
B. HARDIMAN, *Secretary of the Treasury,*
P. W. GRAYSON, *Attorney-General.*

The excerpt printed below is from a speech made before the House on February 2, 1848, by Alexander Stephens of Georgia, later Vice-President of the Confederacy. It is reproduced here chiefly for the purpose of illustrating the similarity of views and emotional convictions held by the two men on the Mexican War. It is Stephens at his rhetorical best during this period. For Lincoln's testimony concerning the effectiveness of the speech as a whole see his "Letter to William H. Herndon," February 2, 1848. The paragraph is as follows:

"The honor of this country does not and cannot require us to force and compel the people of any other to sell theirs. I have, I trust, as high a regard for national honor as any man. It is the brightest gem in the chaplet of a nation's glory; and there is nothing of which I am prouder than the high character for honor this country has acquired throughout the civilized world—that code of honor which was established by Washington and the men of the Revolution and which rests upon truth, justice, and honesty, which is the offspring of virtue and integrity, and which is seen in the length and breadth of our land, in all the evidences of art, and civilization, and moral advancement, and everything that tends to elevate, dignify, and ennoble man. This is the honor of my admiration, and it is made of 'sterner,' purer, nobler 'stuff' than that aggressive and degrading, yea, odious principle now avowed of waging a war against a neighboring people to compel them to sell their country. Who is here so base as to be willing, under any circumstances, to sell his country? For myself, I can only say, if the last funeral pile of liberty were lighted, I would mount it and expire in its flames before I would be coerced by any power however great and strong, to sell or surrender the land of my home, the place of my nativity, and the graves of my sires! Sir, the principle is not only dishonorable, but infamous. As the Representative upon this floor of

a high-minded and honorable constituency, I repeat, that the principle of waging war against a neighboring people to compel them to sell their country, is not only dishonorable, but disgraceful and infamous. What! shall it be said that American honor aims at nothing higher than land—than the ground on which we tread? Do we look no higher, in our aspirations for honor, than do the soulless brutes? Shall we disavow the similitude of our Maker, and disgrace the very name of man? Tell it not to the world. Let not such an aspersion and reproach rest upon our name. I have heard of nations whose honor could be satisfied with gold—that glittering dust which is so precious in the eyes of some—but never did I expect to live to see the day when the Executive of this country should announce that our honor was such a loathsome, beastly thing, that it could not be satisfied with any achievements in arms, however brilliant and glorious, but must feed on earth—gross, vile dirt!—and require even a prostrate foe to be robbed of mountain rocks and desert plains!"

Stephens and Lincoln were closely associated in a group of young Whigs who called themselves the Young Indians. Stephens's colleague from Georgia, Robert Toombs, three Virginia Congressmen—Preston, Flournoy, and Pendleton—and Smith of Connecticut formed the original group. The mutual respect of Lincoln and Stephens in particular continued until and during the Civil War.

LETTER TO WILLIAM H. HERNDON FEBRUARY 1, 1848

Washington, February 1, 1848.

Dear William:

Your letter of the 19th ultimo was received last night, and for which I am much obliged. The only thing in it that I wish to talk to you at once about is that because of my vote for Ashmun's amendment you fear that you and I disagree about the war. I regret this, not because of any fear we shall remain disagreed after you have read this letter, but because if you misunderstand I fear other good friends may also. That vote affirms that the war was unnecessarily and unconstitutionally commenced by the President; and I will stake my life that if you had been in my place you would have voted just as I did. Would you have voted what you felt and knew to be a lie? I know you would not. Would you have gone out of the House—skulked the vote? I expect not. If you had skulked one vote, you would have had to skulk many more before the end of the session. Richardson's resolutions, introduced before I made any move or gave any vote upon the subject, make the direct question of the justice of the war; so that no man can be silent if he would. You are compelled to speak; and your only alternative is to tell the truth or a lie. I cannot doubt which you would do.

This vote has nothing to do in determining my votes on the questions of supplies. I have always intended, and still intend, to vote supplies; perhaps not in the precise form recommended by the President, but in a better form for all purposes, except Locofoco party purposes. It is in this particular you seem mistaken. The Locos are untiring in their efforts to make the impression that all who vote supplies or take part in the war do of necessity approve the President's conduct in the beginning of it; but the Whigs have from the beginning made and kept the distinction between the two. In the very first act nearly all the Whigs voted against the preamble declaring that war existed by the act of Mexico; and yet nearly all of them voted for the supplies. As to the Whig men who have participated in the war, so far as they have spoken in my hearing they do not hesitate to denounce as unjust the President's conduct in the beginning of the war. They do not suppose that such denunciation is directed by undying hatred to him, as "The Register" would have it believed. There are two such Whigs on this floor (Colonel Haskell and Major James). The former fought as a colonel by the side of Colonel Baker at Cerro Gordo, and stands side by side with me in the vote that you seem dissatisfied with. The latter, the history of whose capture with Cassius Clay you well know, had not arrived here when that vote was given; but, as I understand, he stands ready to give just such a vote whenever an occasion shall present. Baker, too, who is now here, says the truth is undoubtedly that way; and whenever he shall speak out, he will say so. Colonel Doniphan, too, the favorite Whig of Missouri, and who overran all Northern Mexico, on his return home in a public speech at St. Louis condemned the administration in relation to the war, if I remember. G.T.M. Davis, who has been through almost the whole war, declares in favor of Mr. Clay; from which I infer that he adopts the sentiments of Mr. Clay, generally at least. On the other hand, I have heard of but one Whig who has been to the war attempting to justify the President's conduct. That one was Captain Bishop, editor of the "Charleston Courier," and a very clever fellow. I do not mean this letter for the public, but for you. Before it reaches you, you will have seen and read my pamphlet speech, and perhaps been scared anew by it. After you get over your scare, read it over again, sentence by sentence, and tell me honestly what you think of it. I condensed all I could for fear of being cut off by the hour rule, and when I got through I had spoken but forty-five minutes.

Yours forever,

A. Lincoln.

This and the three succeeding letters indicate the ardor with which Lincoln personally felt the views he and other Whigs were expressing. Herndon's letters were an accurate sounding board of sentiment back home even among Lincoln's closest associates. All were disturbed, many plainly antagonized, by Lincoln's stand. The Locofocos referred to were, of course, the Democrats. For its derisive import, see Webster's Dictionary.

LETTER TO WILLIAM H. HERNDON
FEBRUARY 2, 1848

Washington, Feb. 2. 1848

Dear William

I just take up my pen to say, that Mr. Stephens of Georgia, a little slim, pale-faced, consumptive man, with a voice like Logan's has just concluded the very best speech, of an hours length, I ever heard.

My old, withered, dry eyes, are full of tears yet.

If he writes it out any thing like he delivered it, our people shall see a good many copies of it.

Yours truly
A. Lincoln

To W H Herndon

LETTER TO WILLIAM H. HERNDON
FEBRUARY 15, 1848

Washington, Feb. 15. 1848

Dear William:

Your letter of the 29th. Jany. was receved [*sic*] last night. Being exclusively a constitutional argument, I wish to submit some reflections upon it in the same spirit of kindness that I know actuates you. Let me first state what I understand to be your position. It is, that if it shall become *necessary, to repel invasion*, the President may, without violation of the Constitution, cross the line, and *invade* the teritory [*sic*] of another country; and that whether such *necessity* exists in any given case, the President is to be the *sole* judge.

Before going further, consider well whether this is, or is not your position. If it is, it is a position that neither the President himself, nor any friend of his, so far as I know, has ever taken. Their only positions are first, that the soil was *ours* where hostilities commenced, and second, that whether it was rightfully *ours* or not, *Congress had annexed it*, and the President, for that reason was bound to defend it, both of which are as clearly proved to be false in fact, as you can prove that your house is not mine. That soil was not ours; and Congress did not annex or attempt to annex it. But to return to your position: Allow the President to invade a neighboring nation, whenever *he* shall deem it necessary to repel an invasion, and you allow him to do so, *whenever he may choose to say* he deems it necessary for such purpose—and you allow him to make war at pleasure. Study to see if you can fix *any limit* to his power in this respect, after you have given him so much as you propose. If, to-day, he should choose to say he thinks it necessary to invade Canada, to prevent the British from invading us, how could you stop him? You may say to him, "I see no probability of the British invading us" but he will say to you "be silent; I see it, if you dont".

The provision of the Constitution giving the war-making power to Congress, was dictated, as I understand it, by the following reasons. Kings had always been involving and impoverishing their people in wars, pretending generally, if not always, that the good of the people was the object. This, our convention understood to be the most oppressive of all Kingly oppressions; and they resolved to so frame the Constitution that *no one man* should hold the power of bringing this oppression upon us. But your view destroys the whole matter, and places our President where Kings have always stood. Write soon again.

Yours truly,
A Lincoln

LETTER TO USHER F. LINDER
MARCH 22, 1848

Washington, March 22—1848—

Friend Linder:

Yours of the 15th. is just received, as was a day or two ago, one from Dunbar on the same subject. Although I address this to you alone, I intend it for you, Dunbar, and Bishop, and wish you to show it to them. In Dunbar's letter, and in Bishop's paper, it is assumed that Mr. Crittenden's position on the war is correct. Well, so I think. Please wherein is my position different from his? Has *he* ever approved the President's conduct in the beginning of the war, or his mode or objects in prossecuting [*sic*] it? Never. He condemns both. True, he votes supplies, and so do I. What, then, is the difference, except that he is a great man and I am a small one?

Towards the close of your letter you ask three questions, the first of which is "Would it not have been just as easy to have elected Genl. Taylor without opposing the war as by opposing it?" I answer, I suppose it would, if we could do *neither*—could be *silent* on the question; but the Locofocos here will not let the whigs be *silent*. Their very first act in Congress was to present a preamble declaring that war existed by the act of Mexico, and the whigs were obliged to vote on it—and this policy is followed up by them, so that they are compelled to *speak* and their only option is whether they will, when they do speak, tell the *truth*, or tell a foul, villanous [*sic*], and bloody falsehood. But, while on this point, I protest against your calling the condemnation of Polk "opposing the war." In thus assuming that all must be opposed to the war, even though they vote supplies, who do not not [*sic*] endorse Polk, with due deference I say I think you fall into one of the artfully set traps of Locofocoism.

Your next question is "And suppose we could succeed in proving it a wicked and unconstitutional war, do we not thereby strip Taylor and Scott of more than half their laurels?" Whether it would so strip them is not matter of demonstration, but of *opinion* only; and my opinion is that it would not; but as your opinion seems to be different, let us call in some others as umpire. There are in this H. R. some more than forty members who support Genl. Taylor for the Presidency, every one of whom has voted that the war was "unnecessarily and unconstitutionally commenced by the President" every one of whom has spoken to the same effect, who has spoken at all, and not one of whom supposes he thereby strips Genl. of any laurels. More than this; two of these, Col. Haskell and Major Gaines, themselves fought in Mexico; and yet they vote and speak just as the rest of us do, without ever dreaming that they "strip" themselves of any laurels. There may be others, but Capt. Bishop is the only intelligent whig who has been to Mexico, that I have heard of taking different ground.

Your third question is "And have we as a party, ever gained any thing by falling in company with abolitionists?" Yes. We gained our only national victory by falling in company with them in the election of Genl. Harrison. Not that we fell into abolition doctrines; but that we took up a man whose position induced them to join us in his election. But this question is not so significant as a *question*, as it is as a charge of abolitionism against those who have chosen to speak their minds against the President. As you and I perhaps would again differ as to the justice of this charge, let us once more call in our umpire. There are in this H. R. whigs from the slave states as follows: one from Louisiana, one from Mississippi, one from Florida, two from Alabama, four from Georgia, five from Tennessee, six from Kentucky, six from North Carolina, six from Virginia, four from Maryland, and one from Delaware, making thirtyseven in all, and all slave-holders, every one of whom votes the commencement of the war "unnecessary and unconstitutional" and so falls subject to your charge of abolitionism!—

"*En passant*" these are all *Taylor* men, except one in Tenn—two in Ky, one in N. C. and one in Va. Besides which we have one in Ills—two in Ia, three in Ohio, five in Penn—four in N. J. and one in Conn. While this is less than half the whigs of the H. R. it is three times as great as the strength of any other one candidate.

You are mistaken in your impression that any one has communicated expressions of yours and Bishop's to me. In my letter to Dunbar, I only spoke from the impression made by seeing in the paper that you and he were, "in the degree, though not in the extreme" on the same tack with Latshaw.

Yours as ever
A. Lincoln

Linder was a Democrat who had turned Whig in 1838 and who returned to the Democratic party when "the Whigs were merged in the Abolitionists." Lincoln had verbally crossed swords with him in the Legislature in 1837, in an exchange of sarcasm and ridicule, one side of which is recorded in Lincoln's opening observations in the "Speech in the Illinois Legislature," January 11, 1837. Linder's protests, like those of Herndon, were representative of the reception Lincoln's congressional activities were receiving in the home district.

LETTER TO DAVID LINCOLN
MARCH 24, 1848

Washington, March 24th. 1848.

Mr. David Lincoln
Dear Sir:

Your very worthy representative, Gov. McDowell has given me your name and address, and, as my father was born in Rockingham, from whence his father, Abraham Lincoln, emigrated to Kentucky about the year 1782, I have concluded to address you to ascertain whether we are not of the same family. I shall be much obliged, if you will write me, telling me, whether you, in any way, know any thing of my grandfather, what relation you are to him, and so on. Also, if you know, where your family came from, when they settled in Virginia, tracing them back as far as your knowledge extends.

Very respectfully
A. Lincoln

LETTER TO DAVID LINCOLN
APRIL 2, 1848

Washington, April 2nd. 1848

Dear Sir,

Last evening I was much gratified by receiving and reading your letter of the 30th. of March. There is no longer any doubt that your uncle Abraham, and my grandfather was the same man. His family did reside in Washington County, Kentucky, just as you say you found them in 1801 or 2. The oldest son, Uncle Mordecai, near twenty years ago, removed from Kentucky to Hancock County, Illinois, where within a year or two afterwards, he died, and where his surviving children now live. His two sons there now are Abraham & Mordecai; and their Post-office is "La Harp" Uncle Josiah, farther back than my recollection, went from Kentucky to Blue River in Indiana. I have not heard from him in a great many years, and whether he is still living I can not say. My recollection of what I have heard is, that he has several daughters & only one son, Thomas. Their Post-office is "Corydon, Harrisson [*sic*] County, Indiana.

My father, Thomas, is still living, in Coles County Illinois, being in the 71st. year of his age. His Post-office is Charleston, Coles Co. Ills. I am his only child. I am now in my 40th. year; and I live in Springfield, Sangamon County, Illinois. This is the outline of my grandfather's family in the West.

I think my father has told me that grandfather had four brothers, Isaac, Jacob, John and Thomas. Is that correct? and which of them was your father? Are any of them alive? I am quite sure that Isaac resided on Wataga [*sic*], near a point where Virginia and Tennessee join; and that he has been dead more than twenty, perhaps thirty, years,—Also, that Thomas removed to Kentucky, near Lexington, where he died a good while ago.

What was your grandfather's Christian name? Was he or not, a Quaker? About what *time* did he emigrate from Berks County, Pa. to Virginia?—Do you know anything of your family (or rather I may now say, *our* family) farther back than your grandfather?

If it be not too much trouble to you, I shall be much pleased to hear from you again. Be assured I will call on you, should any thing ever bring me near you. I shall give your respects to Gov. McDowell, as you desire.

Very truly yours—
A. Lincoln—

LETTER TO MARY TODD LINCOLN
APRIL 16, 1848

Washington, April 16—1848.

Dear Mary:

In this troublesome world we are never quite satisfied. When you were here, I thought you hindered me some in attending to business; but now, having nothing but business—no variety—it has grown exceedingly tasteless to me. I hate to sit down and direct documents, and I hate to stay in this old room by myself. You know I told you in last Sunday's letter, I was going to make a little speech during the week; but the week has passed away without my getting a chance to do so; and now my interest in the subject has passed away too. Your second and third letters have been received since I wrote before. Dear Eddy thinks father is "gone tapila." Has any further discovery been made as to the breaking into your grand-mother's house? If I were she, I would not remain there alone. You mention that your Uncle John Parker is likely to be at Lexington. Dont forget to present him my very kindest regards.

I went yesterday to hunt the little plaid stockings as you wished; but found that McKnight has quit business and Allen had not a single pair of the description you give and only one plaid pair of any sort that I thought would fit "Eddy's dear little feet." I have a notion to make another trial to-morrow morning. If I could get them, I have an excellent chance of sending them. Mr. Warrich Tunstall, of St. Louis is here. He is to leave early this week and to go by Lexington. He says he knows you and will call to see you; and he voluntarily asked if I had not some package to send to you.

I wish you to enjoy yourself in every possible way, but is there no danger of wounding the feelings of your good father, by being so openly intimate with the Wickliffe family?

Mrs. Broome has not removed yet; but she thinks of doing so

to-morrow. All the house—or rather, all with whom you were on decided good terms—send their love to you. The others say nothing.

Very soon after you went away I got what I think a very pretty set of shirt-bosom studs—modest little ones, jet set in gold, only costing 50 cents a piece or 1.50 for the whole.

Suppose you do not prefix the "Hon" to the address on your letters to me any more. I like the letters very much but I would rather they should not have that upon them. It is not necessary, as I suppose you have thought, to have them to come free.

And you are entirely free from headache? That is good—good considering it is the first spring you have been free from it since we were acquainted. I am afraid you will get so well, and fat, and young, as to be wanting to marry again. Tell Louisa I want her to watch you a little for me. Get weighed and write me how much you weigh.

I did not get rid of the impression of that foolish dream about dear Bobby till I got your letter written the same day. What did he and Eddy think of the little letters father sent them? Dont let the blessed fellows forget father.

A day or two ago Mr. Strong, here in Congress, said to me that Matilda would visit here within two or three weeks. Suppose you write her a letter, and enclose it in one of mine, and if she comes I will deliver it to her, and if she does not, I will send it to her.

Most affectionately
A. Lincoln

This letter and the two succeeding ones are Lincoln's most interesting letters of family concern. That the separation was due to more than Mary's wish to visit her family is obvious from the second letter, in which Lincoln's question, "Will you be a good girl in all things," speaks so explicitly of marital difficulties that even Herndon indicated his wish to suppress its publication. The reference to Mary's headaches perhaps indicates migraine and may have had some connection with the mental and emotional disorder which plagued her life and finally destroyed her reason. For discussion of Mary's illness the reader may consult the works referred to in the note following Lincoln's "Letter to Mary Owens," December 13, 1836. For the best treatment of Mary's life see Carl Sandburg and Paul M. Angle, Mary Lincoln: Wife and Widow.

LETTER TO MARY TODD LINCOLN
JUNE 12, 1848

Washington, June 12. 1848—

My dear wife:

On my return from Philadelphia, yesterday, where, in my anxiety I had been led to attend the whig convention, I found your last letter. I was so tired and sleepy, having ridden all night, that I could not answer it till to-day; and now I have to do so in the H. R. The leading matter in your letter, is your wish to return to the side of the mountains. Will you be a *good girl* in all things, if I consent? Then come along, and that as *soon* as possible. Having got the idea in my head, I shall be impatient till I see you. You will not have money enough to bring you; but I presume your uncle will supply you, and I will refund him here. By the way you do not mention whether you have received the fifty dollars I sent you. I do not much fear but that you got it; because the want of it would have induced you [to?] say something in relation to it. If your uncle is already at Lexington, you might induce him to start on earlier than the first of July; he could stay in Kentucky longer on his return, and so make up for lost time. Since I began this letter, the H. R. has passed a resolution for adjourning on the 17th. July, which probably will pass the Senate. I hope this letter will not be disagreeable to you; which, together with the circumstances under which I write, I hope will excuse me from not writing a longer one. Come on just as soon as you can. I want to see you, and our dear—*dear* boys very much. Every body here wants to see our dear Bobby.

Affectionately
A Lincoln

LETTER TO MARY TODD LINCOLN
JULY 2, 1848

Washington, July 2. 1848

My dear wife:

Your letter of last sunday came last night. On that day (sunday) I wrote the principal part of a letter to you, but did not finish it, or send it till tuesday, when I had provided a draft for $100 which I sent in it. It is now probable that on that day (tuesday) you started to Shelbyville; so that when the money reaches Lexington, you will not be there. Before leaving, did you make any provision about letters that might come to Lexington for you? Write me whether you got the draft, if you shall not have already done so, when this reaches you. Give my kindest regards to your uncle John, and all the family. Thinking of them reminds me that I saw your acquaintance, Newton, of Arkansas, at the Philadelphia Convention. We had but a single interview, and that was so brief, and in so great a multitude of strange faces, that I am quite sure I should not recognize him, if I were to meet him again. He was a sort of Trinity, three in one, having the right, in his own person, to cast the three votes of Arkansas. Two or three days ago I sent your uncle John, and a few of our other friends each a copy of the speech I mentioned in my last letter; but I did not send any to you, thinking you would be on the road here, before it would reach you. I send you one now. Last wednesday, P. H. Hood & Co, dunned me for a little bill of $5.38 cents, and Walter Harper & Co, another for $8.50 cents, for goods which they say you bought. I hesitated to pay them, because my recollection is that you told me when you went away, there was nothing left unpaid. Mention in your next letter whether they are right. Mrs. Richardson is still here; and what is more, has a baby—so Richardson says, and he ought to know. I believe Mary Hewett has left here and gone to Boston. I met her on the street about fifteen or twenty days ago, and she told me she was going soon. I have seen nothing of her since. The music in the Capitol grounds on saturdays, or, rather, the interest in it, is dwindling down to nothing. Yesterday evening the attendance was rather thin. Our two girls, whom you remember seeing first at Carusis, at the exhibition of the Ethiopian Serenaders, and whose peculiarities were the wearing of black fur bonnets, and never being seen in close company with other ladies, were at the music yesterday. One of them was attended by their brother, and the other had a member of Congress in tow. He went home with her; and if I were to guess, I would say, he went away a somewhat altered man—most likely in his pockets, and in some other particular. The fellow looked conscious of guilt, although I believe he was unconscious that every body around knew who it was that had caught him.

I have had no letter from home, since I wrote you before, except short business letters, which have no interest for you.

By the way, you do not intend to do without a girl, because the one you had has left you? Get another as soon as you can to take charge of the dear codgers. Father expected to see you all sooner; but let it pass; stay as long as you please, and come when you please. Kiss and love the dear rascals.

Affectionately
A. Lincoln

The reading of the name "Carusis" requires more than the manuscript for verification, since to all appearances the writing seems to read "Canisis" (as given in Paul M. Angle, editor, New Letters and Papers of Lincoln*). Search in contemporary sources, however, reveals no corroboration for "Canisis," while "Carusis" seems certain. Lincoln's* r *and* n, *as well as his* i *and* u *are often indistinguishable. The following advertisement appears in the* Daily National Intelligencer, *January 5, 1848:*

CARUSI'S SALOON

For Nine Nights, commencing Thursday, January 6th, 1848

FIRST APPEARANCE *of the celebrated* ETHIOPIAN SERENADERS, *Messrs. Germon, Stanwood, Harrington, Pell, White, and Howard, since their return from Europe, where they had the distinguished honor of appearing before Her Majesty, Queen Victoria, H.R.H. Prince Albert, the Royal Family, the Nobility and Gentry of England, &c.*

Under the direction of Mr. J. A. Dumbolton.

Admission 25 cents. Doors open at 7; Concert to commence at 7½ o'clock.

Carusi's Saloon (i.e., *salon) was in fact the old Washington Theater, built by public subscription and opened in 1805, which was partially destroyed by fire fifteen years later and was remodeled and opened in 1822 by Louis Carusi as a dancing academy under the name of Carusi's Assembly Rooms. For a third of a century thereafter this was the smartest of the Capital's public social resorts. Most of the inaugural balls from John Quincy Adams's in 1825 to James Buchanan's in 1857 were given there (Federal Writers' Project,* Washington, City and Capital).

LETTER TO WILLIAM H. HERNDON JULY 11, 1848

Washington, July 11—1848

Dear William:

Yours of the 3rd. is this moment received; and I hardly need say, it gives unalloyed pleasure. I now almost regret writing the serious, long faced letter, I wrote yesterday; but let the past as nothing be. Go it while you're young! I write this in the confusion of the H. R, and with several other things to attend to. I will send you about eight different speeches this evening; and as to kissing a pretty girl, I know one very pretty one, but I guess she wont let me kiss her.

Yours forever
A Lincoln

Lincoln's letter of July 10—in answer to a letter in which Herndon had apparently voiced disappointment with his advancement, a feeling of self-pity, and an inclination to throw everything overboard—had given fatherly advice and expressed the wish "to save you from a fatal error." On the following day Lincoln received a letter of different tenor and hastened to reply in kind. The "go it while you're young" and the allusion to a pretty girl are open to anyone's guess, but in view of Lincoln's marital status may sound somewhat regretful of opportunities missed in his own youth, too much pre-occupied with getting on in the world.

THE PRESIDENTIAL QUESTION: SPEECH IN THE UNITED STATES HOUSE OF REPRESENTATIVES JULY 27, 1848

THE MESSAGE OF THE PRESIDENT IN RELATION TO THE BOUNDARIES OF THE TERRITORIES CEDED BY MEXICO TO THE UNITED STATES, BEING UNDER CONSIDERATION—

Mr. Speaker:

Our Democratic friends seem to be in great distress because they think our candidate for the Presidency don't suit *us*. Most of them cannot find out that General Taylor has any principles at all; some, however, have discovered that he has *one*, but that that one is entirely wrong. This one principle is his position on the veto power. The gentleman from Tennessee [MR. STANTON,] who has just taken his seat, indeed, has said there is very little if any difference on this question between General Taylor and all the Presidents; and he seems to think it sufficient detraction from General Taylor's position on it, that it has nothing new in it. But all others, whom I have heard speak, assail it furiously. A new member from Kentucky, [MR. CLARK] of very considerable ability, was in particular concern about it. He thought it altogether novel and unprecedented for a President, or a Presidential candidate, to think of approving bills whose constitutionality may not be entirely clear to his own mind. He thinks the ark of our safety is gone, unless Presidents shall always veto such bills as, in their judgment, may be of *doubtful* constitutionality. However clear Congress may be of their authority to pass any particular act, the gentleman from Kentucky thinks the President must veto it if *he* has *doubts* about it. Now I have neither time nor inclination to argue with the gentleman on the veto power as an original question; but I wish to show that General Taylor, and not he, agrees with the earlier statesmen on this question. When the bill chartering the first Bank of the United States passed Congress, its constitutionality was questioned; Mr. Madison, then in the House of Representatives, as well as others, had opposed it on that ground. General Washington, as President, was called on to approve or reject it. He sought and obtained, on the constitutional question, the separate written opinion of Jefferson, Hamilton, and Edmund Randolph, they then being respectively Secretary of State, Secretary of the Treasury, and Attorney-General. Hamilton's opinion was for the power; while Randolph's and Jefferson's were both against it. Mr. Jefferson, after giving his opinion decidedly against the constitutionality of that bill, closes his letter with the paragraph which I now read:

"It must be admitted, however, that unless the President's mind, on a view of everything which is urged for and against this bill, is tolerably clear that it is unauthorized by the Constitution; if the pro and the con hang so even as to balance his judgment, a just respect for the wisdom of the legislature would naturally decide the balance in favor of their opinion; it is chiefly for cases where they are clearly misled by error, ambition, or interest, that the Constitution has placed a check in the negative of the President.

"Thomas Jefferson

"February 15, 1791."

General Taylor's opinion, as expressed in his Allison letter, is as I now read:

"The power given by the veto is a high conservative power; but, in my opinion, should never be exercised, except in cases of clear violation of the Constitution, or manifest haste and want of consideration by Congress."

It is here seen that, in Mr. Jefferson's opinion, if, on the constitutionality of any given bill, the President *doubts*, he is not to veto it, as the gentleman from Kentucky would have him do, but is to defer to Congress and approve it. And if we compare the opinions of Jefferson and Taylor, as expressed in these paragraphs, we shall find them more exactly alike than we can often find any two expressions having any literal difference. None but interested fault-finders, I think, can discover any substantial variation.

But gentlemen on the other side are unanimously agreed that General Taylor has no other principles. They are in utter darkness as to his opinions on any of the questions of policy which occupy the public attention. But is there any doubt as to what he will *do* on the prominent questions, if elected? Not the least. It is not possible to know what he will or would do in every imaginable case; because many questions have passed away, and others doubtless will arise which none of us have yet thought of; but on the prominent questions of currency, tariff, internal improvements, and Wilmot proviso, General Taylor's course is at least as well defined as is General Cass's. Why, in their eagerness to get at General Taylor, several Democratic members here have desired to know whether, in case of his election, a bankrupt law is to be established. Can they tell us General Cass's opinion on this question? [Some member answered, "He is against it."] Aye, how do you know he is? There is nothing about it in the platform, nor elsewhere, that I have seen. If the gentleman knows anything which I do not, he can show it. But to return: General Taylor, in his Allison letter, says:

"Upon the subject of the tariff, the currency, the improvement of our great highways, rivers, lakes, and harbors, the will of the people, as expressed through their Representatives in Congress, ought to be respected and carried out by the Executive."

Now, this is the whole matter—in substance, it is this: The people say to General Taylor, "If you are elected, shall we have a national bank?" He answers, "*Your* will, gentlemen, not *mine*." "What about the tariff?" "Say yourselves." "Shall our rivers and harbors be improved?" "Just as you please." "If you desire a bank, an alteration of the tariff, internal improvements, any or all, I will not hinder you; if you do not desire them, I will not attempt to force them on you." "Send up your members of Congress from the various districts, with opinions according to your own, and if they are for these measures, or any of them, I shall have nothing to oppose; if they are not for them, I shall not, by any appliances whatever, attempt to dragoon them into their adoption." Now, can there be any difficulty in understanding this? To you, Democrats, it may not seem like principle; but surely you cannot fail to perceive the position plainly enough. The distinction between it and the position of your candidate is broad and obvious, and I admit you have a clear right to show it is wrong, if you can; but you have no right to pretend you cannot see it at all. We see it, and to us it appears like principle, and the best sort of principle at that—the principle of allowing the people to do as they please with their own business. My friend from Indiana [MR. C. B. SMITH] has aptly asked, "Are you willing to trust the people?" Some of you answered, substantially, "We are willing to trust the people; but the President is as much the representative of the people as Congress." In a certain sense, and to a certain extent, he is the representative of the people. He is elected by them, as well as Congress is. But can he, in the nature of things, know the wants of the people as well as three hundred other men coming from all the various localities of the nation? If so, where is the propriety of having a Congress? That the Constitution gives the President a negative on legislation, all know; but that this negative should be so combined with platforms and other appliances as to enable him, and, in fact, almost compel him, to take the whole of legislation into his own hands, is what we object to—is what General Taylor objects to—and is what constitutes the broad distinction between you and us. To thus transfer legislation is clearly to take it from those who understand with minuteness the interest of the people, and give it to one who does not and cannot so well understand it. I understand your idea, that if a Presidential candidate avow his opinion upon a given question, or rather upon all questions, and the people, with full knowledge of this, elect him, they thereby distinctly approve all those opinions. This, though plausible, is a most pernicious deception. By means of it measures are adopted or rejected, contrary to the wishes of the whole of one party, and often nearly half of the other. The process is this: Three, four, or half a dozen questions are prominent at a given time; the party selects its candidate, and he takes his position on each of these questions. On all but one his positions have already been endorsed at former elections, and his party fully committed to them; but that one is new, and a large portion of them are against it. But what are they to do? The whole are strung together, and they must take all or reject all. They cannot take what they like and leave the rest. What they are already committed to, being the majority, they shut their eyes and gulp the whole. Next election, still another is introduced in the same way. If we run our eyes along the line of the past, we shall see that almost, if not quite, all the articles of the present Democratic creed have been at first forced upon the party in this very way. And just now, and just so, opposition to internal improvements is to be established if General Cass shall be elected. Almost half the Democrats here are for improvements, but they will vote for Cass, and if he succeeds, their votes will have aided in closing the doors against improvements. Now, this is a process which we think is wrong. We prefer a candidate who, like General Taylor, will allow the people to have their own way regardless of his private opinion; and I should think the internal-improvement Democrats at least, ought to prefer such a candidate. He would force nothing on them which they don't want, and he would allow them to have improvements, which their own candidate, if elected, will not.

Mr. Speaker, I have said General Taylor's position is as well defined as is that of General Cass. In saying this, I admit I do not certainly know what he would do on the Wilmot proviso. I am a northern man, or, rather, a western free State man, with a constituency I believe to be, and with personal feelings I know to be, against the extension of slavery. As such, and with what information I have, I hope, and *believe*, General Taylor, if elected, would not veto the proviso; but I do not *know* it. Yet, if I knew he would, I still would vote for him. I should do so, because, in my judgment, his election alone can defeat General Cass; and because, *should* slavery thereby go into the territory we now have, just so much will certainly happen by the election of Cass; and, in addition, a course of policy leading to new wars, new acquisitions of territory, and still further extensions of slavery. One of the two is to be President: which is preferable?

But there is as much doubt of Cass on improvements as there is of Taylor on the proviso. I have no doubt myself of General Cass on this question, but I know the Democrats differ among themselves as to his position. My internal-improvement colleague [MR. WENTWORTH] stated on this floor the other day, that he was satisfied Cass was for improvements, because he had voted all the bills that he [Mr. W.] had. So far so good. But Mr. Polk vetoed some of these very bills; the Baltimore Convention passed a set of resolutions, among other things, approving these vetoes, and Cass declares, in his letter accepting the nomination, that he has carefully read these resolutions, and that he adheres to them as firmly as he approves them cordially. In other words, General Cass voted for the bills, and thinks the President did right to veto them; and his friends here are amiable enough to consider him as being on one side or the other, just as one or the other may correspond with their own respective inclinations. My colleague admits that the platform declares against the constitutionality of a general system of improvements, and that General Cass endorses the platform; but he still thinks General Cass is in favor of some sort of improvements. Well, what are they? As he is against *general* objects, those he is *for*, must be *particular* and *local*. Now, this is taking the subject precisely by the wrong end. *Particularity*—expending the money of the *whole* people for an object which will benefit only a *portion* of them, is the greatest real objection to improvements, and has been so held by General Jackson, Mr. Polk, and all others, I believe, till now. But now, behold, the objects most general, nearest free from this objection, are to be rejected, while those most liable to it are to be embraced. To return: I cannot help believing that General Cass, when he wrote his letter of acceptance, well understood he was to be claimed by the advocates of both sides of this question, and that he then closed the door against all further expressions of opinion, purposely to retain the benefits of that double position. His subsequent equivocation at Cleveland, to my mind, proves such to have been the case.

One word more, and I shall have done with this branch of the subject. You Democrats, and your candidate, in the main, are in favor of laying down, in advance, a platform—a set of party positions, as a unit; and then of enforcing the people, by every sort of appliance, to ratify them, however unpalatable some of them may be. We, and our candidate, are in favor of making Presidential elections and the legislation of the country distinct matters; so that the people can elect whom they please, and afterwards, legislate just *as* they please, without any hindrance, save only so much as may guard against infractions of the Constitution, undue haste, and want of consideration. The difference between us is clear as noon-day. That we are right we cannot doubt. We hold the true Republican position. In leaving the people's business in their hands, we cannot be wrong. We are willing, and even anxious, to go to the people on this issue.

But I suppose I cannot reasonably hope to convince you that we have any principles. The most I can expect is, to assure you that we think we have, and are quite contented with them. The other day, one of the gentlemen from Georgia [MR. IVERSON], an eloquent man, and a man of learning, so far as I can judge, not being learned myself, came down upon us astonishingly. He spoke in what the Baltimore American calls the "scathing and withering style." At the end of his second severe flash I was struck blind, and found myself feeling with my fingers for an assurance of my continued physical existence. A little of the bone was left, and I gradually revived. He eulogized Mr. Clay in high and beautiful terms, and then declared that we had deserted all our principles, and had turned Henry Clay out, like an old horse, to root. This is terribly severe. It cannot be answered by argument; at least, I cannot so answer it. I merely wish to ask the gentleman if the Whigs are the only party he can think of, who sometimes turn old horses out to root. Is not a certain Martin Van Buren an old horse, which your own party have turned out to root? and is he not rooting a little to your discomfort about now? But in not nominating Mr. Clay, we deserted our principles, you say. Ah! in what? Tell us, ye men of principles, what principle we violated? We say you did violate principle in discarding Van Buren, and we can tell you how. You violated the primary, the cardinal, the one great living principle of all Democratic representative government—the principle that the representative is bound to carry out the known will of his constituents. A large majority of the Baltimore Convention of 1844 were, by their constituents, instructed to procure Van Buren's nomination if they could. In violation, in utter, glaring contempt of this, you rejected him—rejected him, as the gentleman from New York, [MR. BIRDSALL], the other day expressly admitted, for *availability*—that same "general availability" which you charge upon us, and daily chew over here, as something exceedingly odious and unprincipled. But the gentleman from Georgia [MR. IVERSON,] gave us a second speech yesterday, all well considered and put down in writing, in which Van Buren was scathed and withered a "few" for his present position and movements. I cannot remember the gentleman's precise language, but I do remember he put Van Buren down, down, till he got him where he was finally to "stink" and "rot."

Mr. Speaker, it is no business or inclination of mine to defend Martin Van Buren. In the war of extermination now waging between him and his old admirers, I say, devil take the hindmost—and the foremost. But there is no mistaking the origin of the breach; and if the curse of "stinking" and "rotting" is to fall on the first and greatest violators of principle in the matter, I disinterestedly suggest, that the gentleman from Georgia and his present co-workers are bound to take it upon themselves.

But the gentleman from Georgia further says, we have deserted all our principles, and taken shelter under General Taylor's military coat tail; and he seems to think this is exceedingly degrading. Well, as his faith is, so be it unto him. But can he remember no other military coat tail under which a certain other party have been sheltering for near a quarter of a century? Has he no acquaintance with the ample military coat tail of General Jackson? Does he not know that his own party have run the last five Presidential races under that coat tail, and that they are now running the sixth under that same cover? Yes, sir, that coat tail was used, not only for General Jackson himself, but has been clung to with the grip of death by every Democratic candidate since. You have never ventured, and dare not now venture, from under it. Your campaign papers have constantly been "Old Hickories," with rude likenesses of the old General upon them; hickory poles and hickory brooms your never-ending emblems; Mr. Polk, himself, was "Young Hickory," "Little Hickory," or something so; and even now your campaign paper here is proclaiming that Cass and Butler are of the true "Hickory stripe." No, sir; you dare not give it up. Like a horde of hungry ticks, you have stuck to the tail of the Hermitage lion to the end of his life, and you are still sticking to it, and drawing a loathsome sustenance from it after he is dead. A fellow once advertised that he had made a discovery, by which he could make a new man out of an old one, and have enough of the stuff left to make a little yellow dog. Just such a discovery has General Jackson's popularity been to you. You not only twice made President of him out of it, but you have had enough of the stuff left to make Presidents of several comparatively small men since; and it is your chief reliance now to make still another.

Mr. Speaker, old horses and military coat tails, or tails of any sort, are not figures of speech such as I would be the first to introduce into discussions here; but as the gentleman from Georgia has thought fit to introduce them, he and you are welcome to all you have made, or can make, by them. If you have any more old horses, trot them out; any more tails, just cock them, and come at us.

I repeat, I would not introduce this mode of discussion here; but I wish gentlemen on the other side to understand, that the use of degrading figures is a game at which they may not find themselves able to take all the winnings. [We give it up.] Aye, you give it up, and well you may, but from a very different reason from that which you would have us understand. The point—the power to hurt—of all figures, consists in the *truthfulness* of their application; and understanding this, you may well give it up. They are weapons which hit you, but miss us.

But, in my hurry, I was very near closing on the subject of military tails, before I was done with it. There is one entire article of the sort I have not discussed yet; I mean the military tail you Democrats are now engaged in dovetailing on to the great Michigander. Yes, sir, all his biographers (and they are legion) have him in hand, tying him to a military tail, like so many mischievous boys tying a dog to a bladder of beans. True, the material they have is very limited; but they drive at it, might and main. He *in*vaded Canada without resistance, and he *out*vaded it without pursuit. As he did both under orders, I suppose there was, to him, neither credit nor discredit in them; but they are made to constitute a large part of the tail. He was not at Hull's surrender, but he was close by. He was volunteer aid to General Harrison on the day of the battle of the Thames; and, as you said in 1840, Harrison was picking whortleberries two miles off, while the battle was fought, I suppose it is a just conclusion, with you, to say Cass was aiding Harrison to pick whortleberries. This is about all, except the mooted question of the broken sword. Some authors say he broke it; some say he threw it away; and some others, who ought to know, say nothing about it. Perhaps it would be a fair historical compromise to say, if he did not break it, he did not do anything else with it.

By the way, Mr. Speaker, did you know I am a military hero? Yes, sir, in the days of the Black Hawk war, I fought, bled, and came away. Speaking of General Cass's career, reminds me of my own. I was not at Stillman's defeat, but I was about as near it as Cass was to Hull's surrender; and, like him, I saw the place very soon afterwards. It is quite certain I did not break my sword, for I had none to break; but I bent a musket pretty badly on one occasion. If Cass broke his sword, the idea is, he broke it in desperation; I bent the musket by accident. If General Cass went in advance of me in picking whortleberries, I guess I surpassed him in charges upon the wild onions. If he saw any live fighting Indians, it was more than I did, but I had a good many bloody struggles with the mosquitoes; and although I never fainted from loss of blood, I can truly say I was often very hungry.

Mr. Speaker, if I should ever conclude to doff whatever our Democratic friends may suppose there is of black-cockade Federalism about me, and, thereupon, they shall take me up as their candidate for the Presidency, I protest they shall not make fun of me, as they have of General Cass, by attempting to write me into a military hero.

While I have General Cass in hand, I wish to say a word about his political principles. As a specimen, I take the record of his progress on the Wilmot proviso. In the Washington Union, of March 2, 1847, there is a report of a speech of General Cass, made the day before in the Senate, on the Wilmot proviso, during the delivery of which Mr. Miller, of New Jersey, is reported to have interrupted him as follows, to wit:

"MR. MILLER expressed his great surprise at the change in the sentiments of the Senator from Michigan, who had been regarded as the great champion of freedom in the northwest, of which he was a distinguished ornament. Last year the Senator from Michigan was understood to be decidedly in favor of the Wilmot proviso; and, as no reason had been stated for the change, he (Mr. M.) could not refrain from the expression of his extreme surprise."

To this General Cass is reported to have replied as follows, to wit:

"Mr. Cass said, that the course of the Senator from New Jersey was most extraordinary. Last year he (Mr. C.) should have voted for the proposition had it come up. But circumstances had altogether changed. The honorable Senator then read several passages from the remarks as given above, which he had committed to writing, in order to refute such a charge as that of the Senator from New Jersey."

In the "remarks above committed to writing," is one numbered 4, as follows, to wit:

"4th. Legislation would now be wholly inoperative, because no territory hereafter to be acquired can be governed without an act of Congress providing for its government. And such an act, on its passage, would open the whole subject, and leave the Congress, called on to pass it, free to exercise its own discretion, entirely uncontrolled by any declaration found in the statute book."

In Niles's Register, vol. 73, page 293, there is a letter of General Cass to A. O. P. Nicholson, of Nashville, Tennessee, dated December 24, 1847, from which the following are correct extracts:

"The Wilmot proviso has been before the country some time. It has been repeatedly discussed in Congress, and by the public press. I am strongly impressed with the opinion that a great change has been going on in the public mind upon this subject—in my own as well as others; and that doubts are resolving themselves into convictions, that the principle it involves should be kept out of the National Legislature, and left to the people of the Confederacy in their respective local Governments . . ."

"Briefly, then, I am opposed to the exercise of any jurisdiction by Congress over this matter; and I am in favor of leaving the people of any territory which may be hereafter acquired the right to regulate it themselves, under the general principles of the Constitution. Because,

"1. I do not see in the Constitution any grant of the requisite power to Congress; and I am not disposed to extend a doubtful precedent beyond its necessity—the establishment of territorial governments when needed—leaving to the inhabitants all the rights compatible with the relations they bear to the Confederation."

These extracts show that, in 1846, General Cass was for the proviso *at once*; that in March, 1847, he was still for it, *but not just then*; and that, in December, 1847, he was *against* it altogether. This is a true index to the whole man. When the question was raised in 1846, he was in a blustering hurry to take ground for it. He sought to be in advance, and to avoid the uninteresting position of a mere follower; but soon he began to see glimpses of the great Democratic ox-gad waving in his face, and to hear, indistinctly, a voice saying, "Back," "back, sir," "Back a little." He shakes his head; and bats his eyes, and blunders back to his position of March, 1847; but still the gad waves, and the voice grows more distinct, and sharper still—"Back, sir!" "Back, I say!" "Further back!" and back he goes to the position of December, 1847; at which the gad is still, and the voice soothingly says—"So!" "Stand at that."

Have no fears, gentlemen, of your candidate; he exactly suits you, and we congratulate you upon it. However much you may be distressed about *our* candidate, you have all cause to be contented and happy with your own. If elected, he may not maintain all, or even any, of his positions previously taken; but he will be sure to do whatever the party exigency, for the time being, may require; and that is precisely what you want. He and Van Buren are the same "manner of men;" and, like Van Buren, he will never desert *you* till you first desert *him*.

Mr. Speaker, I adopt the suggestion of a friend, that General Cass is a general of splendidly successful *charges*—charges, to be sure, not upon the public enemy, but upon the public treasury.

He was Governor of Michigan Territory, and, *ex-officio*, superintendent of Indian affairs, from the 9th of October, 1813, till the 31st of July, 1831—a period of seventeen years, nine months, and twenty-two days. During this period, he received from the United States treasury, for personal services and personal expenses, the aggregate sum of $96,028—being an average sum of $14.79 per day for every day of the time. This large sum was reached by assuming that he was doing service and incurring expenses at several different *places*, and in several different *capacities* in the *same* place, all at the same *time*. By a correct analysis of his accounts during that period, the following propositions may be deduced:

First. He was paid in *three* different capacities during the *whole* of the time—that is to say:

1. As Governor's salary, at the rate, per year, of $2,000.

2. As estimated for office rent, clerk hire, fuel, &c., in superintendence of Indian affairs *in* Michigan, at the rate, per year, of $1,500.

3. As compensation and expenses, for various miscellaneous items of Indian service *out* of Michigan, an average, per year, of $625.

Second. During *part* of the time, that is, from the 9th of October, 1813, to the 29th of May, 1822, he was paid in *four* different capacities—that is to say:

The three as above, and in addition thereto the commutation of ten rations per day, amounting per year, to $730.

Third. During *another* part of the time, that is, from the beginning of 1822 to the 31st of July, 1831, he was also paid in *four* different capacities—that is to say:

The *first* three, as above, (the rations being dropped after the 29th of May, 1822,) and, in addition thereto, for superintending Indian agencies at Piqua, Ohio, Fort Wayne, Indiana, and Chicago, Illinois, at the rate, per year, of $1,500. It should be observed here, that the last item, commencing at the beginning of 1822, and the item of rations, ending on the 29th of May, 1822, lap on each other during so much of the time as lies between those two dates.

Fourth. Still another part of the time, that is, from the 31st of October, 1821, to the 29th of May, 1822, he was paid in *six* different capacities—that is to say:

The three first, as above; the item of rations, as above; and, in addition thereto, another item of ten rations per day while at Washington, settling his accounts; being at the rate, per year, of $730.

And, also, an allowance for expenses travelling to and from Washington, and while there, of $1,022; being at the rate, per year, of $1,793.

Fifth. And yet, during the little portion of time which lies between the 1st of January, 1822, and the 29th of May, 1822, he was paid in *seven* different capacities; that is to say:

The six last mentioned, and also at the rate of $1,500 per year for the Piqua, Fort Wayne, and Chicago service, as mentioned above.

These accounts have already been discussed some here; but when we are amongst them, as when we are in the Patent Office, we must peep about a good while before we can see all the curiosities. I shall not be tedious with them. As to the large item of $1,500 per year, amounting in the aggregate to $26,715, for office rent, clerk hire, fuel, &c., I barely wish to remark that, so far as I can discover in the public documents, there is no evidence, by word or inference, either from any disinterested witness, or of General Cass himself, that he ever rented or kept a separate office, ever hired or kept a clerk, or ever used any extra amount of fuel, &c., in consequence of his Indian services. Indeed, General Cass's entire silence in regard to these items in his two long letters, urging his claims upon the Government, is, to my mind, almost conclusive that no such items had any real existence.

But I have introduced General Cass's accounts here, chiefly to show the wonderful physical capacities of the man. They show that he not only did the labor of several men at the same *time*, but that he often did it at several *places* many hundred miles apart, *at the same time.* And at eating, too, his capacities are shown to be quite as wonderful. From October, 1821, to May, 1822, he ate ten rations a day in Michigan, ten rations a day here in Washington, and near five dollars' worth a day besides, partly on the road between the two places. And then there is an important discovery in his example—the art of being paid for what one eats, instead of having to pay for it. Hereafter, if any nice young man shall owe a bill which he cannot pay in any other way, he can just board it out. Mr. Speaker, we have all heard of the animal standing in doubt between two stacks of hay, and starving to death; the like of that would never happen to General Cass. Place the stacks a thousand miles apart, he would stand stock-still midway between them, and eat them both at once; and the green grass along the line would be apt to suffer some too, at the same time. By all means, make him President, gentlemen. He will feed you bounteously—if—if there is any left after he shall have helped himself.

But as General Taylor is, par excellence, the hero of the Mexican War; and, as you Democrats say we Whigs have always opposed the war, you think it must be very awkward and embarrassing for us to go for General Taylor. The declaration that we have always opposed the war is true or false, accordingly as one may understand the term "opposing the war." If to say "the war was unnecessarily and unconstitutionally commenced by the President," be opposing the war, then the Whigs have very generally opposed it. Whenever they have spoken at all, they have said this; and they have said it on what has appeared good reason to them. The marching an army into the midst of a peaceful Mexican settlement, frightening the inhabitants away, leaving their growing crops, and other property to destruction, to *you* may appear a perfectly amiable, peaceful, unprovoking procedure; but it does not appear so to *us*. So to call such an act, to us appears no other than a naked, impudent absurdity, and we speak of it accordingly. But if, when the war had begun, and had become the cause of the country, the giving of our money and our blood, in common with yours, was support of the war, then it is not true that we have always opposed the war. With few individual exceptions, you have constantly had our votes here for all the necessary supplies. And, more than this, you have had the services, the blood, and the lives of our political brethren in every trial, and on every field. The beardless boy, and the mature man—the humble and the distinguished, you have had them. Through suffering and death, by disease, and in battle, they have endured, and fought, and fell with you. Clay and Webster each gave a son, never to be returned. From the State of my own residence, besides other worthy but less known Whig names, we sent Marshall, Morrison, Baker, and Hardin; they all fought, and one fell, and in the fall of that one, we lost our best Whig man. Nor were the Whigs few in number, or laggard in the day of danger. In that fearful, bloody, breathless struggle at Buena Vista, where each man's hard task was to beat back five foes or die himself, of the five high officers who perished, four were Whigs.

In speaking of this, I mean no odious comparison between the lion-hearted Whigs and Democrats who fought there. On other occasions, and among the lower officers and privates on *that* occasion, I doubt not the proportion was different. I wish to do justice to all. I think of all those brave men as Americans, in whose proud fame, as an American, I too have a share. Many of them, Whigs and Democrats, are my constituents and personal friends; and I thank them—more than thank them—one and all, for the high imperishable honor they have conferred on our common State.

But the distinction between the cause of the *President* in beginning the war, and the cause of the *country* after it was begun, is a distinction which you cannot perceive. To *you*, the President, and the country, seem to be all one. You are interested to see no distinction between them; and I venture to suggest that *possibly* your interest blinds you a little. We see the distinction, as we think, clearly enough; and our friends who have fought in the war have no difficulty in seeing it also. What those who have fallen would say, were they alive and here, of course we can never know; but with those who have returned there is no difficulty. Colonel Haskell and Major Gaines, members here, both fought in the war; and one of them underwent extraordinary perils and hardships; still they, like all other Whigs here, vote on the record that the war was unnecessarily and unconstitutionally commenced by the President. And even General Taylor himself, the noblest Roman of them all, has declared that, as a citizen, and particularly as a soldier, it is sufficient for him to know that his country is at war with a foreign nation, to do all in his power to bring it to a speedy and honorable termination, by the most vigorous and energetic operations, without inquiring about its justice, or anything else connected with it.

Mr. Speaker, let our Democratic friends be comforted with the assurance, that we are content with our position, content with our company, and content with our candidate; and that, although they, in their generous sympathy, think we ought to be miserable, we really are not, and that they may dismiss the great anxiety they have on *our* account.

Mr. Speaker, I see I have but three minutes left, and this forces me to throw out one whole branch of my subject. A single word on still another. The Democrats are kind enough to frequently remind us that we have some dissensions in our ranks. Our good friend from Baltimore, immediately before me [MR. MC LANE,] expressed some doubt the other day as to which branch of our party General Taylor would ultimately fall into the hands of. That was a new idea to me. I knew we had dissenters, but I did not know they were trying to get our candidate away from us. I would like to say a word to our dissenters, but I have not the time. Some such *we* certainly have; have *you* none, gentlemen Democrats? Is it all union and harmony in *your* ranks? No bickerings? No divisions? If there be doubt as to which of our divisions will get our candidate, is there no doubt as to which of your candidates will get your party? I have heard some things from New York; and if they are true, we might well say of your party there, as a drunken fellow once said when he heard the reading of an indictment for hog-stealing. The clerk read on till he got to, and through the words "did steal, take, and carry away, ten boars, ten sows, ten shoats, and ten pigs," at which he exclaimed—"Well, by golly, that is the most equally divided gang of hogs I ever did hear of." If there is any gang of hogs more equally divided than the Democrats of New York are about this time, I have not heard of it.

The campaign pamphlet printing of this speech carrying the title, "Speech of Mr. A. Lincoln of Illinois, on the Presidential Question," contains no major alterations except subtitles distributed throughout, marking it into sections. Lincoln's numerous allusions to incidents in the military record of General Cass were aimed at the campaign efforts of the Democrats to make General Cass into a military hero comparable to the Whig candidate, General Taylor. The sarcastic reference to a broken sword is an allusion to the story that Cass broke his sword in anger and disgust upon learning of the surrender of Detroit by General Hull in the War of 1812.

LETTERS TO THOMAS LINCOLN AND JOHN D. JOHNSTON. DECEMBER 24, 1848

Washington, Decr. 24th. 1848.

My dear father:

Your letter of the 7th. was received night before last. I very cheerfully send you the twenty dollars, which sum you say is necessary to save your land from sale. It is singular that you should have forgotten a judgment against you; and it is more singular that the plaintiff should have let you forget it so long, particularly as I suppose you have always had property enough to satisfy a judgment of that amount. Before you pay it, it would be well to be sure you have not paid it, or at least, that you can not prove you have paid it. Give my love to Mother, and all the connections.

Affectionately your Son
A. Lincoln

Dear Johnston:

Your request for eighty dollars I do not think it best to comply with now. At the various times when I have helped you a little, you have said to me, "We can get along very well now" but in a very short time I find you in the same difficulty again.

Now this can only happen by some defect in your *conduct*. What that defect is, I think I know. You are not *lazy*, and still you *are* an *idler*. I doubt whether since I saw you, you have done a good whole day's work, in any one day. You do not very much dislike to work; and still you do not work much, merely because it does not seem to you that you could get much for it. This habit of uselessly wasting time, is the whole difficulty; and it is vastly important to you, and still more so to your children that you should break this habit. It is more important to them, because they have longer to live, and can keep out of an idle habit before they are in it, easier than they can get out after they are in.

You are now in need of some [ready?] money; and what I propose is, that you shall go to work, "tooth and nails" for somebody who will give you money for it. Let father and your boys take charge of things at home—prepare for a crop, and make the crop; and you go to work for the best money wages, or in discharge of any debt you owe, that you can get. And to secure you a fair reward for your labor, I now promise you that for every dollar you will, between this and the first of next May, get for your own labor, either in money, or on your own indebtedness, I will then give you one other dollar. By this, if you hire yourself at ten dolla[rs] a month, from me you will get ten more, making twenty dollars a month for your work. In this, I do not mean you shall go off to St. Louis, or the lead mines, or the gold mines in Calif[ornia,] but I [mean for you to go at it for the best wages you] can get close to home in Coles county. Now if you will do this, you will be soon out of debt, and what is better, you will have a habit that will keep you from getting in debt again. But if I should now clear you out, next year you would be just as deep in as ever. You say you would almost give your place in Heaven for $70 or $80. Then you value your place in Heaven very cheapl[y] for I am sure you can with the offer I make you get the seventy or eighty dollars for four or five months work. You say if I furnish you the money you will deed me the land, and, if you dont pay the money back, you will deliver possession. Nonsense! If you cant now live *with* the land, how will you then live without it? You have always been [kind] to me, and I do not now mean to be unkind to you. On the contrary, if you will but follow my advice, you will find it worth more than eight times eighty dollars to you.

Affectionately
Your brother
A. Lincoln

The manuscript of these letters is one and the same. The letter to Johnston, which Nicolay and Hay erroneously give under the date of January (2?), 1851, begins on the bottom of the same page following the letter to Lincoln's father. The circumstance arose from the fact that Johnston, Lincoln's stepbrother, had penned for Thomas Lincoln the letter requesting twenty dollars, and had added a request of his own on the same sheet. The financial difficulties of Thomas Lincoln, and in particular of Lincoln's stepbrother Johnston, caused Lincoln some embarrassment. He was willing to help, but not to encourage importunity. Lincoln's letters to his father show no disrespect, but neither do they even suggest any filial attachment comparable to that shown for his stepmother, Sarah Bush Johnston Lincoln.

LETTER TO WILLIAM H. HERNDON
JANUARY 5, 1849

Washington, Jan. 5. 1849

Dear William

Your two letters were received last night. I have a great many letters to write, and so can not write very long ones. There must be some mistake about Walter Davis saying I promised him the Post-Office; I did not so promise him. I did tell him, that if the distribution of the offices should fall into my hands, he should have *something*; and if I shall be convinced he has said any more than this, I shall be disappointed. I said this much to him, because, as I understand, he is of *good character*, is one of the *young* men, is of the *mechanics*, an always *faithful*, and never *troublesome* whig, and is *poor*, with the support of a widow mother thrown almost exclusively on him by the death of his brother. If these are wrong reasons, then I have been wrong; but I have certainly not been selfish in it; because in my greatest need of friends he was against me and for Baker.

Yours as ever
A. Lincoln

P. S. Let the above be confidential
To W H Herndon

Lincoln's reference to the fact that Davis "is of the mechanics" *may require comment. Many of the young radical Whigs were mechanics by trade who were organizing for political reasons in "mechanics associations" hardly comparable to our modern labor unions, but which nevertheless were efforts to protect labor and exert political pressure as a group. The Know-Nothings were in large part made up from this portion of the electorate. One of the chief grievances of the "mechanics" was the immigrant labor rapidly flowing into the country. Hence the anti-alien and anti-Catholic bias of the Know-Nothing party.*

LETTER TO C. U. SCHLATER
JANUARY 5, 1849

Washington, Jan: 5. 1849

Mr. C. U. Schlater:
Dear Sir:

Your note, requesting my "signature with a sentiment" was received, and should have been answered long since, but that it was mislaid. I am not a very sentimental man; and the best sentiment I can think of is, that if you collect the signatures of all persons who are no less distinguished than I, you will have a very undistinguishing mass of names.

Very respectfully
A. Lincoln

LETTER TO C. R. WELLES
FEBRUARY 20, 1849

Washington, Feb. 20. 1849

C. R. Welles, Esq.
Dear Sir:

This is tuesday evening, and your letter enclosing the one of Young & Brothers to you, saying the money you sent by me to them had not been received, came to hand last saturday night. The facts, which are perfectly fresh in my recollection, are these: You gave me the money in a letter (open I believe) directed to Young & Brothers. To make it more secure than it would be in my hat, where I carry most all my packages, I put it in my trunk. I had a great many jobs to do in St. Louis; and by the very extra care I had taken of yours, overlooked it. On the Steam Boat near the mouth of the Ohio, I opened the trunk, and discovered the letter. I then began to cast about for some safe hand to send it back by. Mr. Yeatman, Judge Pope's son-in-law, and step-son of Mr. Bell of Tennessee, was on board, and was to return immediately to St. Louis from the Mouth of Cumberland. At my request, he took the letter and promised to deliver it—and I heard no more about it till I received your letter on saturday. It so happens that Mr. Yeatman is now in this city; I called on him last night about it; he said he remembered my giving him the letter, and he could remember nothing more of it. He told me he would try to refresh his memory, and see me again concerning it to-day—which however he has not done. I will try to see him tomorrow and write you again. He is a young man, as I understand, of unquestioned, and unquestionable character; and this makes me fear some pick-pocket on the boat may have seen me give him the letter, and slipped it from him. In this way, never seeing the letter again, he would, naturally enough, never think of it again.

Yours truly
A. Lincoln

Charles Roger Welles was a resident of Springfield, lawyer and land agent, who represented John Grigg of Philadelphia, a capitalist and investor in western lands. The incident of the lost letter recalls the fact that the older custom of having travelers carry important letters —particularly those containing money—survived well into the nineteenth century in spite of the development of an efficient Post Office Department.

LETTER TO JOSHUA F. SPEED
FEBRUARY 20, 1849

Washington, Feb: 20. 1849.

Dear Speed:

Your letter of the 13th. was received yesterday. I showed it to Baker. I did this because he knew I had written you, and was expecting an answer; and he still enquired what I had received; so that I could not well keep it a secret. Besides this, I knew the contents of the letter would not affect him as you seemed to think it would. He knows he did not make a favorable impression while in Congress, and he and I had talked it over frequently. He tells me to write you that he has too much self-esteem to be put out of humor with himself by the opinion of any man who does not know him better than Mr. Crittenden does; and that he thinks you ought to have known it. The letter will not affect him the least in regard to either Mr. Crittenden or you. He understands you to have acted the part of a discreet friend; and he intends to make Mr. Crittenden think better of him hereafter. I am flattered to learn that Mr. Crittenden has any recollection of me which is not unfavorable; and for the manifestation of your kindness towards me, I sincerely thank you. Still there is nothing about me which would authorize me to think of a first class office; and a second class one would not compensate me for being snarled at by others who want it for themselves. I believe that, so far as the whigs in Congress, are concerned, I could have the Genl. Land Office almost by common consent; but then Sweet, and Don: Morrison, and Browning, and Cyrus Edwards all want it. And what is worse, while I think I could easily take it myself, I fear I shall have trouble to get it for any other man in Illinois. The reason is, that McGaughey, an Indiana ex-member of Congress is here after it; and being personally known, he will be hard to beat by any one who is not.

Baker showed me your letter, in which you make a passing

allusion to the Louisville Post-Office. I have told Garnett Duncan I am for you. I like to open a letter of yours, and I therefore hope you will write me again on the receipt of this.

Give my love, to Mrs. Speed.

Yours as ever.
A. Lincoln

P. S. I have not read the Frankfort papers this winter; and consequently do not know whether you have made a speech. If you have, and it has been printed send me a copy.

A. L.

Lincoln's reference to the Land Office appointment recalls that it was one of the notable disappointments of his political career up to this time. At first he wanted his friend Cyrus Edwards to get the appointment, but when he decided that this was an impossibility he went after the job strenuously. In the end he lost out to Justin Butterfield who was appointed June 21, 1849, to Lincoln's complete chagrin.

McGaughey was Edward Wilson McGaughey, Representative from Indiana in the 29th and 31st Congresses. Don Morrison was James Lowery Donaldson Morrison, a Belleville lawyer and member of the Illinois Senate in 1848. M. P. Sweet, O. H. Browning, and Cyrus Edwards were all prominent Whig politicians, Browning becoming United States Senator in 1861. Edward Dickinson Baker was Lincoln's predecessor in Congress. Crittenden, of course, refers to John Jordan Crittenden, Senator from Kentucky.

LETTER TO ABRAM BALE
FEBRUARY 22, 1850

Springfield, Feb. 22. 1850

Mr. Abraham [*sic*] Bale.
Dear Sir:

I understand Mr. Hickox will go, or send to Petersburg to-morrow, for the purpose of meeting you to settle the difficulty about the wheat. I sincerely hope you will settle it. I think you *can* if you *will*, for I have always found Mr. Hickox a fair man in his dealings. If you settle, I will charge nothing for what I have done, and thank you to boot. By settling, you will most likely get your money sooner, and with much less trouble & expense.

Yours truly
A. Lincoln—

"Abram" was the man's name, although Lincoln spelled it like his own. He was a Baptist preacher who settled in the deserted village of New Salem, which by this time had become "Old Salem." Hickox "was probably Virgil Hickox, a prominent Springfield merchant" (Paul M. Angle, editor, News Letters and Papers of Lincoln*).*

LETTER TO JOHN D. JOHNSTON JANUARY 12, 1851

Springfield, Jany. 12. 1851—

Dear Brother:

On the day before yesterday I received a letter from Harriett, written at Greenup. She says she has just returned from your house; and that Father is very low and will hardly recover. She also say[s you] have written me two letters; and that [although] you do not expect me to come now, you [wonder] that I do not write. I received both your [letters, and] although I have not answered them, it is no[t because] I have forgotten them, or been uninterested about them—but because it appeared to me I could write nothing which could do any good. You already know I desire that neither Father or Mother shall be in want of any comfort either in health or sickness while they live; and I feel sure you have not failed to use my name, if necessary, to procure a doctor, or any thing else for Father in his present sickness. My business is such that I could hardly leave home now, if it were not, as it is, that my own wife is sick-abed. (It is a case of baby sickness, and I suppose is not dangerous.) I sincerely hope Father may yet recover his health; but at all events tell him to remember to call upon, and confide in, our great, and good, and merciful Maker, who will not turn away from him in any extremity. He notes the fall of a sparrow, and numbers the hairs of our heads; and He will not forget the dying man who puts his trust in Him. Say to him that if we could meet now, it is doubtful whether it would not be more painful than pleasant; but that if it be his lot to go now, he will soon have a joyous [meeting] with many loved ones gone before; and where [the rest] of us, through the help of God, hope ere long [to join] them.

Write to me again when you receive this.

Affectionately

A. Lincoln

Lincoln's father died a few days after this letter was written. Much has been made, by some of Lincoln's detractors, of his neglect of his father. Actually, Lincoln seems to have had little sentiment for his father, but the circumstances in his own home at this time fully account for his inability to leave and the tone of the letter gives little cause for supposing that Lincoln was wholly indifferent to his father's illness and death, although father and son had apparently never been genuinely compatible.

LETTER TO ANDREW McCALLEN
JULY 4, 1851

Springfield, Ills. July. 4. 1851.

Andrew McCallen.
Dear Sir:

I have news from Ottawa, that we *win* our Galatin [*sic*] & Salem county case. As the dutch Justice said, when he married folks "Now, vere ish my hundred tollars"

Yours truly
A. Lincoln

The spelling of McCallen's name has been a matter of some uncertainty. The manuscript appears plainly to read McCallan, *but Lincoln's* a *and* e *are often indistinguishable. Illinois State Bar records have him listed as* Andrew McCallen, *admitted to the Bar in 1847. John M. Palmer, editor of* The Bench and Bar of Illinois, *gives his name as* McCallon. The History of Gallatin, Saline, Hamilton, Franklin, and Williamson Counties, Illinois *gives his name as* Andrew McCallen.

In any event, he was a Shawneetown merchant and, later, lawyer who "devoted nearly his entire time to the criminal practice" (John M. Palmer, editor, The Bench and Bar of Illinois, *Vol. II, p. 857). The editor has not been able to identify the case about which Lincoln writes.*

LETTER TO JOHN D. JOHNSTON NOVEMBER 4, 1851

Shelbyville, November 4, 1851.

Dear Brother:

When I came into Charleston day before yesterday, I learned that you are anxious to sell the land where you live and move to Missouri. I have been thinking of this ever since, and cannot but think such a notion is utterly foolish. What can you do in Missouri better than here? Is the land any richer? Can you there, any more than here, raise corn and wheat and oats without work? Will anybody there, any more than here, do your work for you? If you intend to go to work, there is no better place than right where you are; if you do not intend to go to work, you cannot get along anywhere. Squirming and crawling about from place to place can do no good. You have raised no crop this year; and what you really want is to sell the land, get the money, and spend it. Part with the land you have, and, my life upon it, you will never after own a spot big enough to bury you in. Half you will get for the land you will spend in moving to Missouri, and the other half you will eat, drink, and wear out, and no foot of land will be bought. Now, I feel it my duty to have no hand in such a piece of foolery. I feel that it is so even on your own account, and particularly on mother's account. The eastern forty acres I intend to keep for mother while she lives; if you will not cultivate it, it will rent for enough to support her—at least, it will rent for something. Her dower in the other two forties she can let you have, and no thanks to me. Now, do not misunderstand this letter; I do not write it in any unkindness. I write it in order, if possible, to get you to face the truth, which truth is, you are destitute because you have idled away all your time. Your thousand pretenses for not getting along better are all nonsense; they deceive nobody but yourself. Go to work is the only cure for your case.

A word to mother. Chapman tells me he wants you to go and live with him. If I were you I would try it awhile. If you get tired of it (as I think you will not), you can return to your own home. Chapman feels very kindly to you, and I have no doubt he will make your situation very pleasant.

Sincerely your son,
A. Lincoln.

The last paragraph of this letter in effect is advising Johnston's mother (Lincoln's stepmother) to leave her home and live with relatives. Chapman was the husband of a granddaughter of Lincoln's stepmother—a child of Dennis Hanks and Elizabeth Johnston. This letter and the two succeeding ones indicate clearly the scale on which the family lived as well as the uselessness of Lincoln's advice to the shiftless Johnston. Lincoln's expression of willingness to help Johnston's son Abram, in the following letter of November 9, is interesting for its carefulness of statement.

LETTER TO JOHN D. JOHNSTON NOVEMBER 9, 1851

Shelbyville, Novr. 9. 1851

Dear Brother:

When I wrote you before I had not received your letter. I still think as I did; but if the land can be sold so that I get three hundred dollars to put to interest for mother, I will not object if she does not. But before I will make a deed, the money must be had, or secured, beyond all doubt, at ten per cent.

As to Abram, I do not want him *on my own account*; but I understand he wants to live with me so that he can go to school, and get a fair start in the world, which I very much wish him to have. When I reach home, if I can make it convenient to take, I will take him provided there is no mistake between us as to the object and terms of my taking him.

In haste
As ever
A. Lincoln

LETTER TO JOHN D. JOHNSTON NOVEMBER 25, 1851

Springfield, Novr. 25. 1851.

Dear Brother

Your letter of the 22nd. is just received. Your proposal about selling the East forty acres of land is all that I want or could claim for *myself*; but I am not satisfied with it on *Mother's* account. I want her to have her living, and I feel that it is my duty, to some extent, to see that she is not wronged. She had a right of Dower (that is, the use of one third for life) in the other two forties; but, it seems, she has already let you take that, hook and line. She now has the use of the whole of the East forty, as long as she lives; and if it be sold, of course, she is entitled to the interest on *all* the money it brings, as long as she lives; but you propose to sell it for three hundred dollars, take one hundred away with you, and leave her two hundred, at 8 per cent, making her the *enormous* sum of 16 dollars a year. Now, if you are satisfied with treating her in that way, I am not. It is true, that you are to have that forty for two hundred dollars, *at* Mother's death; but you are not to have it *before*. I am confident that land can be made to produce for Mother, at least $30 a year, and I can not, to oblige any living person, consent that she shall be put on an allowance of sixteen dollars a year.

Yours &c
A. Lincoln

EULOGY ON HENRY CLAY DELIVERED IN THE STATE HOUSE AT SPRINGFIELD, ILLINOIS. JULY 6, 1852

On the fourth day of July, 1776, the people of a few feeble and oppressed colonies of Great Britain, inhabiting a portion of the Atlantic coast of North America, publicly declared their national independence, and made their appeal to the justice of their cause, and to the God of battles, for the maintainance of that declaration. That people were few in numbers, and without resources, save only their own wise heads and stout hearts. Within the first year of that declared independence, and while its maintainance was yet problematical—while the bloody struggle between those resolute rebels, and their haughty would-be-masters, was still waging, of undistinguished parents, and in an obscure district of one of those colonies, Henry Clay was born.

The infant nation, and the infant child began the race of life together. For three quarters of a century they have travelled hand in hand. They have been companions ever. The nation has passed its perils, and is free, prosperous, and powerful. The child has reached his manhood, his middle age, his old age, and is dead. In all that has concerned the nation the man ever sympathised; and now the nation mourns for the man.

The day after his death, one of the public Journals, opposed to him politically, held the following pathetic and beautiful language, which I adopt, partly because such high and exclusive eulogy, originating with a political friend, might offend good taste, but chiefly, because I could not, in any language of my own, so well express my thoughts—

"Alas! who can realize that Henry Clay is dead! Who can realize that never again that majestic form shall rise in the council-chambers of his country to beat back the storms of anarchy which may threaten, or pour the oil of peace upon the troubled billows as they rage and menace around? Who can realize, that the workings of that mighty mind have ceased—that the throbbings of that gallant heart are stilled—that the mighty sweep of that graceful arm will be felt no more, and the magic of that eloquent tongue, which spake as spake no other tongue besides, is hushed—hushed forever! Who can realize that freedom's champion—the champion of a civilized world, and of all tongues and kindreds and people, has indeed fallen! Alas, in those dark hours, which, as they come in the history of all nations, must come in ours—those hours of peril and dread which our land has experienced, and which she may be called to experience again—to whom now may her people look up for that counsel and advice, which only wisdom and experience and patriotism can give, and which only the undoubting confidence of a nation will receive? Perchance, in the whole circle of the great and gifted of our land, there remains but one on whose shoulders the mighty mantle of the departed statesman may fall—one, while we now write, is doubtless pouring his tears over the bier of his brother and his friend—brother, friend ever, yet in political sentiment, as far apart as party could make them. Ah, it is at times like these, that the petty distinctions of mere party disappear. We see only the great, the grand, the noble features of the departed statesman; and we do not even beg permission to bow at his feet and mingle our tears with those who have ever been his political adherents—we do [not?] beg this permission—we claim it as a right, though we feel it as a privilege. Henry Clay belonged to his country—to the world, mere party cannot claim men like him. His career has been national—his fame has filled the earth—his memory will endure to "the last syllable of recorded time."

"Henry Clay is dead!—He breathed his last on yesterday at twenty minutes after eleven, in his chamber at Washington. To those who followed his lead in public affairs, it more appropriately belongs to pronounce his eulogy, and pay specific honors to the memory of the illustrious dead—but all Americans may show the grief which his death inspires, for, his character and fame are national property. As on a question of liberty, he knew no North, no South, no East, no West, but only the Union, which held them all in its sacred circle, so now his countrymen will know no grief, that is not as wide-spread as the bounds of the confederacy. The career of Henry Clay was a public career. From his youth he has been devoted to the public service, at a period too, in the world's history justly regarded as a remarkable era in human affairs. He witnessed in the beginning the throes of the French Revolution. He saw the rise and fall of Napoleon. He was called upon to legislate for America, and direct her policy when all Europe was the battle-field of contending dynasties, and when the struggle for supremacy imperilled the rights of all neutral nations. His voice spoke war and peace in the contest with Great Britain.

"When Greece rose against the Turks and struck for liberty, his name was mingled with the battle-cry of freedom. When South America threw off the thraldom of Spain, his speeches were read at the head of her armies by Bolivar. His name has been, and will continue to be, hallowed in two hemispheres, for it is—

"One of the few the immortal names
That were not born to die,"

"To the ardent patriot and profound statesman, he added a quality possessed by few of the gifted on earth. His eloquence has not been surpassed. In the effective power to move the heart of man, Clay was without an equal, and the heaven born endowment, in the spirit of its origin, has been most conspicuously exhibited against intestine feud. On at least three important occasions, he has quelled our civil commotions, by a power and influence, which belonged to no other statesman of his age and times. And in our last internal discord, when this Union trembled to its center—in old age, he left the shades of private life and gave the death blow to fraternal strife, with the vigor of his earlier years in a series of Senatorial efforts, which in themselves would bring immortality, by challenging comparison with the efforts of any statesman in any age. He exorcised the demon which possessed the body politic, and gave peace to a distracted land. Alas! the achievement cost him his life! He sank day by day to the tomb—his pale, but noble brow, bound with a triple wreath, put there by a grateful country. May his ashes rest in peace, while his spirit goes to take its station among the great and good men who preceded him!"

While it is customary, and proper, upon occasions like the present, to give a brief sketch of the life of the deceased, in the case of Mr. Clay, it is less necessary than most others; for his biography has been written and re-written, and read and re-read, for the last twenty-five years; so that, with the exception of a few of the latest incidents of his life, all is as well known, as it can be. The short sketch which I give is, therefore, merely to maintain the connection of this discourse.

Henry Clay was born on the twelfth of April 1777, in Hanover County, Virginia. Of his father, who died in the fourth or fifth year of Henry's age, little seems to be known, except that he was a respectable man, and a preacher of the Baptist persuasion. Mr. Clay's education, to the end of life, was comparatively limited. I say "*to the end of life,*" because I have understood that, from time to time, he added something to his education during the greater part of his whole life. Mr. Clay's lack of a more perfect early education, however it may be regretted generally, teaches at least one profitable lesson: it teaches that in this country, one can scarcely be so poor, but that, if he *will*, he *can* acquire sufficient education to get through the world respectably. In his twenty-third year Mr. Clay was licensed to practise law, and emigrated to Lexington, Kentucky. Here he commenced and continued the practice till the year 1803, when he was first elected to the Kentucky legislature. By successive elections he was continued in the Legislature till the latter part of 1806, when he was elected to fill a vacancy, of a single session, in the United States Senate. In 1807 he was again elected to the Kentucky House of Representatives, and by that body, chosen its Speaker. In 1808 he was re-elected to the same body. In 1809 he was again chosen to fill a vacancy of two years in the United States Senate. In 1811 he was elected to the United States House of Representatives, and on the first day of taking his seat in that body, he was chosen its Speaker. In 1813 he was again elected Speaker. Early in 1814, being the period of our last British war, Mr. Clay was sent as commissioner, with others, to negotiate a treaty of peace, which treaty was concluded in the latter part of the same year. On his return from Europe he was again elected to the lower branch of Congress, and on taking his seat in December 1815, was called to his old post—the Speaker's chair, a position in which he was retained by successive elections, with one brief intermission, till the inauguration of John Q. Adams, in March, 1825. He was then appointed Secretary of State, and occupied that important station till the inauguration of Gen. Jackson in March 1829. After this he returned to Kentucky, resumed the practice of the law, and continued it till the autumn of 1831, when he was by the legislature of Kentucky, again placed in the United States Senate. By a re-election he continued in the Senate till he resigned his seat, and retired, in March 1848. In December 1849 he again took his seat in the Senate, which he again resigned only a few months before his death.

By the foregoing it is perceived that the period from the beginning of Mr. Clay's official life, in 1803, to the end of it in 1852, is but one year short of half a century; and that the sum of all the intervals in it, will not amount to ten years. But mere duration of time in office, constitutes the smallest part of Mr. Clay's history. Throughout that long period, he has constantly been the most loved, and most implicitly followed by friends, and the most dreaded by opponents, of all living American politicians.

In all the great questions which have agitated the country, and particularly in those fearful crises, the Missouri question—the Nullification question, and the late slavery question, as connected with the newly acquired territory, involving and endangering the stability of the Union, his has been the leading and most conspicuous part. In 1824 he was first a candidate for the Presidency, and was defeated; and although he was successively defeated for the same office in 1832 and in 1844, there has never been a moment since 1824 till after 1848 when a very large portion of the American people did not cling to him with an enthusiastic hope and purpose of still elevating him to the Presidency. With other men, to be defeated, was to be forgotten; but to him, defeat was but a trifling incident, neither changing him, or the world's estimate of him. Even those of both political parties who have been preferred to him for the highest office, have run far briefer courses than he, and left him, still shining high in the heavens of the political world. Jackson, Van Buren, Harrison, Polk, and Taylor, all rose *after*, and set long before him. The spell—the long-enduring spell—with which the souls of men were bound to him, is a miracle. Who can compass it? It is probably true he owed his pre-eminence to no one quality, but to a fortunate combination of several. He was surpassingly eloquent; but many eloquent men fail utterly; and they are not, as a class, generally successful. His judgment was excellent; but many men of good judgment, live and die unnoticed.—His will was indomitable; but this quality often secures to its owner nothing better than a character for useless obstinacy. These then were Mr. Clay's leading qualities. No one of them is very uncommon; but all together are rarely combined in a single individual; and this is probably the reason why such men as Henry Clay are so rare in the world.

Mr. Clay's eloquence did not consist, as many fine specimens of eloquence do, of types and figures—of antithesis, and elegant arrangement of words and sentences; but rather of that deeply earnest and impassioned tone, and manner, which can proceed only from great sincerity, and thorough conviction, in the speaker of the justice and importance of his cause. This it is, that truly touches the chords of sympathy; and those who heard Mr. Clay never failed to be moved by it, or ever afterwards, forgot the impression. All his efforts were made for practical effect. He never spoke merely to be heard. He never delivered a Fourth of July oration, or an eulogy on an occasion like this. As a politician or statesman, no one was so habitually careful to avoid all sectional ground. Whatever he did, he did for the whole country. In the construction of his measures he ever carefully surveyed every part of the field, and duly weighed every conflicting interest. Feeling as he did, and as the truth surely is, that the world's best hope depended on the continued Union of these States, he was ever jealous of, and watchful for, whatever might have the slightest tendency to separate them.

Mr. Clay's predominant sentiment, from first to last, was a deep devotion to the cause of human liberty—a strong sympathy with the oppressed everywhere, and an ardent wish for their elevation. With him, this was a primary and all controlling passion. Subsidiary to this was the conduct of his whole life. He loved his country partly because it was his own country, but mostly because it was a free country; and he burned with a zeal for its advancement, prosperity and glory, because he saw in such, the advancement, prosperity, and glory, of human liberty, human right and human nature. He desired the prosperity of his countrymen partly because they were his countrymen, but chiefly to show to the world that freemen could be prosperous.

That his views and measures were always the wisest, needs not to be affirmed; nor should it be, on this occasion, where so many, thinking differently, join in doing honor to his memory. A free people, in times of peace and quiet—when pressed by no common danger—naturally divide into parties. At such times the man who is of neither party, is not—cannot be, of any consequence. Mr. Clay, therefore, was of a party. Taking a prominent part, as he did, in all the great political questions of his country for the last half century, the wisdom of his course on many, is doubted and denied by a large portion of his countrymen; and of such it is not now proper to speak particularly.—But there are many others, about his course upon which, there is little or no disagreement amongst intelligent and patriotic Americans. Of these last are the war of 1812, the Missouri question, Nullification, and the now recent compromise measures. In 1812 Mr. Clay, though not unknown, was still a young man. Whether we should go to war with Great Britain, being the question of the day, a minority opposed the declaration of war by Congress, while the majority, though apparently inclining to war, had for years, wavered, and hesitated to act decisively. Meanwhile British aggressions multiplied, and grew more daring and aggravated. By Mr. Clay, more than any other man, the struggle was brought to a decision in Congress. The question, being now fully before congress, came up in a variety of ways, in rapid succession, on most of which occasions Mr. Clay spoke. Adding to all the logic, of which the subject was susceptible, that noble inspiration, which came to him as it came to no other, he aroused, and nerved, and inspired his friends, and confounded and bore down all opposition. Several of his speeches, on these occasions, were reported, and are still extant, but the best of these all never was. During its delivery the reporters forgot their vocations, dropped their pens, and sat enchanted from near the beginning to quite the close. The speech now lives only in the memory of a few old men; and the enthusiasm with which they cherish their recollection of it is absolutely astonishing. The precise language of this speech we shall never know; but we do know—we cannot help knowing—that, with deep pathos, it pleaded the cause of the injured sailor—that it invoked the genius of the revolution—that it apostrophized the names of Otis, of Henry and of Washington—that it appealed to the interest, the pride, the honor and the glory of the nation—that it shamed and taunted the timidity of friends—that it scorned, and scouted, and withered the temerity of domestic foes—that it bearded and defied the British Lion—and rising, and swelling, and maddening in its course, it sounded the onset, till the charge, the shock, the steady struggle, and the glorious victory, all passed in vivid review before the entranced hearers.

Important and exciting as was the war question, of 1812, it never so alarmed the sagacious statesmen of the country for the safety of the republic, as afterward did the Missouri question. This sprang from that unfortunate source of discord—negro slavery. When our Federal Constitution was adopted, we owned no territory beyond the limits or ownership of the States, except the territory North-West of the River Ohio, and east of the Mississippi.—What has since been formed into the States of Maine, Kentucky, and Tennessee, was, I believe, within the limits of or owned by Massachusetts, Virginia, and North Carolina. As to the North Western Territory, provision had been made, even before the adoption of the Constitution, that slavery should never go there. On the admission of the States into the Union carved from the territory we owned before the constitution, no question—or at most, no considerable question—arose about slavery—those which were within the limits of or owned by the old states, following respectively, the condition of the parent state, and those within the North West territory, following the previously made provision. But in 1803 we purchased Louisiana of the French; and it included with much more, what has since been formed into the State of Missouri. With regard to it, nothing had been done to forestall the question of slavery. When, therefore, in 1819, Missouri, having formed a State constitution, without excluding slavery, and with slavery already actually existing within its limits, knocked at the door of the Union for admission, almost the entire representation of the non-slaveholding states, objected. A fearful and angry struggle instantly followed. This alarmed thinking men, more than any previous question, because, unlike all the former, it divided the country by geographical lines. Other questions had their opposing partizans in all localities of the country and in almost every family; so that no division of the Union could follow such, without a separation of friends, to quite as great an extent, as that of opponents.—Not so with the Missouri question. On this a geographical line could be traced which, in the main, would separate opponents only. This was the danger. Mr. Jefferson, then in retirement, wrote:

"I had for a long time ceased to read newspapers, or to pay any attention to public affairs, confident they were in good hands, and content to be a passenger in our bark to the shore from which I am not distant. But this momentous question, like a fire bell in the night, awakened, and filled me with terror. I considered it at once as the knell of the Union. It is hushed, indeed, for the moment. But this is a reprieve only, not a final sentence. A geographical line, co-inciding with a marked principle, moral and political, once conceived and held up to the angry passions of men, will never be obliterated, and every irritation will mark it deeper and deeper. I can say with conscious truth, that there is not a man on earth who would sacrifice more than I would to relieve us from this heavy reproach, in any *practicable* way. The cession of that kind of property, for so it is misnamed, is a bagatelle which would not cost me a second thought, if, in that way, a general emancipation, and *expatriation* could be effected; and, gradually, and with due sacrifices I think it might be. But as it is, we have the wolf by the ears, and we can neither hold him, nor safely let him go. Justice is in one scale, and self-preservation in the other."

Mr. Clay was in congress, and, perceiving the danger, at once engaged his whole energies to avert it. It began, as I have said, in 1819; and it did not terminate till 1821. Missouri would not yield the point; and congress—that is, a majority in congress—by repeated votes, showed a determination to not admit the State unless it should yield. After several failures, and great labor on the part of Mr. Clay to so present the question that a majority could consent to the admission, it was by a vote, rejected, and as all seemed to think, finally. A sullen gloom hung over the nation. All felt that the rejection of Missouri, was equivalent to a dissolution of the Union, because those states which already had, what Missouri was rejected for refusing to relinquish, would go with Missouri. All deprecated and deplored this, but none saw how to avert it. For the judgment of members to be convinced of the necessity of yielding, was not the whole difficulty; each had a constituency to meet, and to answer to. Mr. Clay, though worn down, and exhausted, was appealed to by members, to renew his efforts at compromise.—He did so, and by some judicious modifications of his plan, coupled with laborious efforts with individual members, and his own over-mastering eloquence upon the floor, he finally secured the admission of the State. Brightly, and captivating as it had previously shown, it was now perceived that his great eloquence, was a mere embellishment, or at most, but a helping hand to his inventive genius, and his devotion to his country in the day of her extreme peril.

After the settlement of the Missouri question, although a portion of the American people have differed with Mr. Clay, and a majority even, appear generally to have been opposed to him on questions of ordinary administration, he seems constantly to have been regarded by all, as *the* man for a crisis. Accordingly, in the days of Nullification, and more recently in the re-appearance of the slavery question, connected with our territory newly acquired of Mexico, the task of devising a mode of adjustment, seems to have been cast upon Mr. Clay, by common consent—and his performance of the task, in each case, was little else than, a literal fulfilment of the public expectation.

Mr. Clay's efforts in behalf of the South Americans, and afterwards, in behalf of the Greeks, in the times of their respective struggles for civil liberty are among the finest on record, upon the noblest of all themes, and bear ample corroboration of what I have said was his ruling passion—a love of liberty and right, unselfishly, and for their own sakes.

Having been led to allude to domestic slavery so frequently already, I am unwilling to close without referring more particularly to Mr. Clay's views and conduct in regard to it. He ever was on principle and in feeling, opposed to slavery. The very earliest, and one of the latest public efforts of his life, separated by a period of more than fifty years;—were both made in favor of gradual emancipation of the slave in Kentucky. He did not perceive, that on a question of human right, the negroes were to be excepted from the human race. And yet Mr. Clay was the owner of slaves. Cast into life where slavery was already widely spread and deeply seated, he did not perceive, as I think no wise man has perceived, how it could be at *once* eradicated, without producing a greater evil, even to the cause of human liberty itself. His feeling and his judgment, therefore, ever led him to oppose both extremes of opinion on the subject. Those who would shiver into fragments the Union of these States; tear to tatters its now venerated constitution; and even burn the last copy of the Bible, rather than slavery should continue a single hour, together with all their more halting sympathisers, have received, and are receiving their just execration; and the name, and opinions, and influence of Mr. Clay, are fully, and, as I trust, effectually and enduringly, arrayed against them. But I would also, if I could, array his name, opinions, and influence against the opposite extreme—against a few, but an increasing number of men, who, for the sake of perpetuating slavery, are beginning to assail and to ridicule the white man's charter of freedom—the declaration that "all men are created free and equal." So far as I have learned, the first American, of any note, to do or attempt this, was the late John C. Calhoun; and if I mistake not, it soon after found its way into some of the messages of the Governors of South Carolina. We, however, look for and are not much shocked by, political eccentricities and heresies in South Carolina. But, only last year, I saw with astonishment, what purported to be a letter of a very distinguished and influential clergyman of Virginia, copied, with apparent approbation, into a St. Louis news-paper, containing the following, to me, very unsatisfactory language—

"I am fully aware that there is a text in some Bibles that is not in mine. Professional abolitionists have made more use of it, than of any passage in the Bible. It came, however, as I trace it, from Saint Voltaire, and was baptized by Thomas Jefferson, and since almost universally regarded as canonical authority, *'All men are born free and equal.'*

"This is a genuine coin in the political currency of our generation. I am sorry to say that I have never seen two men of whom it is true. But I must admit I never saw the Siamese Twins, and therefore will not dogmatically say that no man ever saw a proof of this sage aphorism."

This sounds strangely in republican America.—The like was not heard in the fresher days of the Republic. Let us contrast with it the language of that truly national man, whose life and death we now commemorate and lament. I quote from a speech of Mr. Clay delivered before the American Colonization Society in 1827:

"We are reproached with doing mischief by the agitation of this question. The society goes into no household to disturb its domestic tranquillity; it addresses itself to no slaves to weaken their obligations of obedience. It seeks to affect no man's property. It neither has the power nor the will to affect the property of any one contrary to his consent.—The execution of its scheme would augment instead of diminishing the value of the property left behind. The society, composed of free men, concerns itself only with the free. Collateral consequences we are not responsible for. It is not this society which has produced the great moral revolution which the age exhibits. What would they, who thus reproach us, have done? If they would repress all tendencies towards liberty, and ultimate emancipation, they must do more than put down the benevolent efforts of this society. They must go back to the era of our liberty and independence, and muzzle the cannon which thunders its annual joyous return. They must renew the slave trade with all its train of atrocities. They must suppress the workings of British philanthropy, seeking to meliorate the condition of the unfortunate West Indian slave. They must arrest the career of South American deliverance from thraldom. They must blow out the moral lights around us, and extinguish that greatest torch of all which America presents to a benighted world—pointing the way to their rights, their liberties, and their happiness. And when thcy have achieved those purposes their work will be yet incomplete. They must penetrate the human soul, and eradicate the light of reason and the love of liberty. Then, and not till then, when universal darkness and despair prevail, can you perpetuate slavery, and repress all sympathy, and all humane, and benevolent efforts among free men, in behalf of the unhappy portion of our race doomed to bondage."

The American Colonization Society was organized in 1816. Mr. Clay, though not its projector, was one of its earliest members; and he died, as for the many preceding years he had been, its President.—It was one of the most cherished objects of his direct care and consideration; and the association of his name with it has probably been its very greatest collateral support. He considered it no demerit in the society, that it tended to relieve slave-holders from the troublesome presence of the free negroes; but this was far from being its whole merit in his estimation. In the same speech from which I have quoted he says:

"There is a moral fitness in the idea of returning to Africa her children, whose ancestors have been torn from her by the ruthless hand of fraud and violence. Transplanted in a foreign land, they will carry back to their native soil the rich fruits of religion, civilization, law and liberty. May it not be one of the great designs of the Ruler of the universe, (whose ways are often inscrutable by short-sighted mortals,) thus to transform an original crime, into a signal blessing to that most unfortunate portion of the globe?"

This suggestion of the possible ultimate redemption of the African race and African continent, was made twenty-five years ago. Every succeeding year has added strength to the hope of its realization.—May it indeed be realized! Pharaoh's country was cursed with plagues, and his hosts were drowned in the Red Sea for striving to retain a captive people who had already served them more than four hundred years. May like disasters never befall us! If as the friends of colonization hope, the present and coming generations of our countrymen shall by any means, succeed in freeing our land from the dangerous presence of slavery; and, at the same time, in restoring a captive people to their long-lost father-land, with bright prospects for the future; and this too, so gradually, that neither races nor individuals shall have suffered by the change, it will indeed be a glorious consummation. And if, to such a consummation, the efforts of Mr. Clay shall have contributed, it will be what he most ardently wished, and none of his labors will have been more valuable to his country and his kind.

But Henry Clay is dead. His long and eventful life is closed. Our country is prosperous and powerful; but could it have been quite all it has been, and is, and is to be, without Henry Clay? Such a man the times have demanded, and such, in the providence of God was given us. But he is gone. Let us strive to deserve, as far as mortals may, the continued care of Divine Providence, trusting that in future national emergencies, He will not fail to provide us the instruments of safety and security.

Although this speech has been dated July 16 in the Complete Works, *Beveridge's* Abraham Lincoln, *and other works, apparently it was delivered ten days earlier on July 6. An account of the memorial service commemorating Henry Clay, which was held in the State House at Springfield on July 6, appears in the* Illinois State Journal, *July 9. The "Eulogy" was printed in full in the* Journal *on July 21.*

FRAGMENTS: ON SLAVERY

[JULY 1, 1854?]

If A. can prove, however conclusively, that he may, of right, enslave B.—why may not B. snatch the same argument, and prove equally, that he may enslave A?—

You say A. is white, and B. is black. It is *color*, then; the lighter, having the right to enslave the darker? Take care. By this rule, you are to be slave to the first man you meet, with a fairer skin than your own.

You do not mean *color* exactly? You mean the whites are *intellectually* the superiors of the blacks; and, therefore have the right to enslave them? Take care again. By this rule, you are to be slave to the first man you meet, with an intellect superior to your own.

But, say you, it is a question of *interest*; and, if you can make it your *interest*, you have the right to enslave another. Very well. And if he can make it his interest, he has the right to enslave you.

* * * * * *

dent truth. Made so plain by our good Father in Heaven, that all *feel* and understand it, even down to brutes and creeping insects. The ant who has toiled and dragged a crumb to his nest, will furiously defend the fruit of his labor, against whatever robber assails him. So plain, that the most dumb and stupid slave that ever toiled for a master, does constantly *know* that he is wronged. So plain that no one, high or low, ever does mistake it, except in a plainly *selfish* way; for although volume upon volume is written to prove slavery a very good thing, we never hear of the man who wishes to take the good of it *by being a slave himself.*

Most governments have been based, practically, on the denial of the equal rights of men, as I have, in part, stated them; *ours* began by *affirming* those rights. *They* said, some men are too *ignorant,* and *vicious* to share in government. Possibly so, said we; and, by your system, you would always keep them ignorant, and vicious. We proposed to give *all* a chance; and we expected the weak to grow stronger, the ignorant, wiser; and all better, and happier together.

We made the experiment; and the fruit is before us. Look at it—think of it. Look at it in its aggregate grandeur, of extent of country, and numbers of population—of ship, and steamboat, and rail-

LETTER TO J. M. PALMER
SEPTEMBER 7, 1854

(Confidential)

Springfield, Sept. 7, 1854

Hon. J. M. Palmer
Dear Sir.

You know how anxious I am that this Nebraska measure shall be rebuked and condemned every where. Of course I hope something from your position; yet I do not expect you to do any thing which may be wrong in your own judgment; nor would I have you do anything personally injurious to yourself. You are, and always have been, *honestly,* and *sincerely* a democrat; and I know how painful it must be to an honest sincere man to be urged by his party to the support of a measure, which on his conscience he believes to be wrong. You have had a severe struggle with yourself, and you have determined *not* to swallow the *wrong.* Is it not just to yourself that you should, in a few public speeches, state your reasons, and thus justify yourself? I wish you would; and yet I say "dont do it, if you think it will injure you." You may have given your word to vote for Major Harris, and if so, of course you will stick to it. But allow me to suggest that you should avoid speaking of this; for it probably would induce some of your friends, in like manner, to cast their votes. You understand. And now let me beg your pardon for obtruding this letter upon you, to whom I have ever been opposed in politics. Had your party omitted to make Nebraska a test of party fidelity; you probably would have been the Democratic candidate for Congress in the district. You deserved it, and I believe it would have been given you. In that case I should have been quit, happy that Nebraska was to be rebuked at all events. I still should have voted for the Whig candidate; but I should have made no speeches, written no letters; and you would have been elected by at least a thousand majority.

Yours truly
A. Lincoln—

Palmer went over to the anti-Nebraska forces as a Democratic member of the Legislature, but did not vote for Lincoln for United States senator. He stuck to Trumbull, also an anti-Nebraska Democrat, until Lincoln threw his votes to Trumbull. (See "Letter to E. B. Washburne," February 9, 1855.) Palmer became a Republican in 1856 and ran for Congress (an unexpired term) in 1859. It was he who offered the resolution in the Decatur convention, 1860, making Lincoln Illinois' "favorite son."

THE 14th SECTION: AN EDITORIAL IN THE *ILLINOIS JOURNAL*. SEPTEMBER 11, 1854

The following is the 14th section of the Kansas-Nebraska law. It repeals the Missouri Compromise; and then puts in a declaration that it is not intended by this repeal to legislate slavery in or exclude it therefrom, the territory.

Sec. 14. That the constitution, and all the laws of the United States which are not locally inapplicable, shall have the same force and effect within said territory of Nebraska as elsewhere in the United States, except the 8th section of the act preparatory to the admission of Missouri into the Union, approved March sixth, eighteen hundred and twenty, which being inconsistent with the principles of non-intervention by congress with slavery in the States and Territories as recognized by the legislation of eighteen hundred and fifty, commonly called the compromise measures, is hereby declared inoperative and void; it being the true intent and meaning of this act not to legislate slavery into any territory or State, nor to exclude it therefrom, but to leave the people thereof perfectly free to form and regulate their domestic institutions in their own way, subject only to the constitution of the United States: Provided, that nothing herein contained shall be construed to revive or put in force any law or regulation which may have existed prior to the act of sixth of March, eighteen hundred and twenty, either protecting, establishing, prohibiting, or abolishing slavery.

The state of the case in a few words, is this: The Missouri Compromise excluded slavery from the Kansas-Nebraska territory. The repeal opened the territories to slavery. If there is any meaning to the declaration in the 14th section, that it does not mean to legislate slavery into the territories, [it?] is this: that it does not require slaves to be sent there. The Kansas and Nebraska territories are now as open to slavery as Mississippi or Arkansas were when they were territories.

To illustrate the case—Abraham Lincoln has a fine meadow, containing beautiful springs of water, and well fenced, which John Calhoun had agreed with Abraham (originally owning the land in common) should be his, and the agreement had been consummated in the most solemn manner, regarded by both as sacred. John Calhoun, however, in the course of time, had become owner of an extensive herd of cattle—the prairie grass had become dried up and there was no convenient water to be had. John Calhoun then looks with a longing eye on Lincoln's meadow, and goes to it and throws down the fences, and exposes it to the ravages of his starving and famishing cattle. "You rascal," says Lincoln, "what have you done? What do you do this for?"—"Oh," replies Calhoun, "everything is right. I have taken down your fence; but nothing more. It is my true intent and meaning not to drive my cattle into your meadow, nor to exclude them therefrom, but to leave them perfectly free to form their own notions of the feed, and to direct their movements in their own way!"

Now would not the man who committed this outrage be deemed both a knave and a fool,—a knave in removing the restrictive fence, which he had solemnly pledged himself to sustain; —and a fool in supposing that there could be one man found in the country to believe that he had not pulled down the fence for the purpose of opening the meadow for his cattle?

This unsigned editorial, discovered in the Illinois State Journal *by Paul M. Angle, was undoubtedly written by Lincoln. Probably other editorials which appeared in the* Journal *were also written by Lincoln, but as Mr. Angle has pointed out "it is generally dangerous to designate such unsigned articles as indisputably Lincoln's." The "illustration" is an excellent example of Lincoln's employment of homely analogy to make brief and clear a complex political issue—here the fundamental concept which Lincoln presents at great length in the "Speech at Peoria."*

THE REPEAL OF THE MISSOURI COMPROMISE AND THE PROPRIETY OF ITS RESTORATION: SPEECH AT PEORIA, ILLINOIS, IN REPLY TO SENATOR DOUGLAS OCTOBER 16, 1854

The repeal of the Missouri Compromise, and the propriety of its restoration, constitute the subject of what I am about to say.

As I desire to present my own connected view of this subject, my remarks will not be, specifically, an answer to Judge Douglas; yet, as I proceed, the main points he has presented will arise, and will receive such respectful attention as I may be able to give them.

I wish further to say, that I do not propose to question the patriotism, or to assail the motives of any man, or class of men; but rather to strictly confine myself to the naked merits of the question.

I also wish to be no less than National in all the positions I may take; and whenever I take ground which others have thought, or may think, narrow, sectional, and dangerous to the Union, I hope to give a reason, which will appear sufficient, at least to some, why I think differently.

And, as this subject is no other, than part and parcel of the larger general question of domestic slavery, I wish to MAKE and to KEEP the distinction between the EXISTING institution, and the EXTENSION of it, so broad, and so clear, that no honest man can misunderstand me, and no dishonest one, successfully misrepresent me.

In order to [get?] a clear understanding of what the Missouri Compromise is, a short history of the preceding kindred subjects will perhaps be proper. When we established our independence, we did not own, or claim, the country to which this compromise applies. Indeed, strictly speaking, the confederacy then owned no country at all; the States respectively owned the country within their limits; and some of them owned territory beyond their strict State limits. Virginia thus owned the North-Western territory—the country out of which the principal part of Ohio, all Indiana, all Illinois, all Michigan and all Wisconsin, have since been formed. She also owned (perhaps within her then limits) what has since been formed into the State of Kentucky. North Carolina thus owned what is now the State of Tennessee; and South Carolina and Georgia, in separate parts, owned what are now Mississippi and Alabama. Connecticut, I think, owned the little remaining part of Ohio—being the same where they now send Giddings to Congress, and beat all creation at making cheese. These territories, together with the States themselves, constituted all the country over which the confederacy then claimed any sort of jurisdiction. We were then living under the Articles of Confederation, which were superseded by the Constitution several years afterwards. The question of ceding these territories to the general government was set on foot. Mr. Jefferson, the author of the Declaration of Independence, and otherwise a chief actor in the Revolution; then a delegate in Congress; afterwards twice President; who was, is, and perhaps will continue to be, the most distinguished politician of our history; a Virginian by birth and continued residence, and withal, a slave-holder; conceived the idea of taking that occasion, to prevent slavery ever going into the north-western territory. He prevailed on the Virginia legislature to adopt his views, and to cede the territory, making the prohibition of slavery therein, a condition of the deed.* Congress accepted the cession, with the condition; and in the first Ordinance (which the acts of Congress were then called) for the government of the territory, provided that slavery should never be permitted therein. This is the famed ordinance of '87 so often spoken of. Thenceforward, for sixty-one years, and until in 1848, the last scrap of this territory came into the Union as the State of Wisconsin, all parties acted in quiet obedience to this ordinance. It is now what Jefferson foresaw and intended—the happy

* "'Mr. Lincoln afterward authorized the correction of the error into which the report here falls, with regard to the prohibition being made a condition of the deed. It was not a condition.'"—Nicolay and Hay, *Complete Works of Abraham Lincoln*, Vol. II, p. 194.

home of teeming millions of free, white, prosperous people, and no slave amongst them.

Thus, with the author of the declaration of Independence, the policy of prohibiting slavery in new territory originated. Thus, away back of the Constitution, in the pure, fresh, free breath of the revolution, the State of Virginia, and the National Congress put that policy in practice.—Thus, through sixty odd of the best years of the republic did that policy steadily work to its great and beneficent end. And thus, in those five states, and five millions of free, enterprising people, we have before us the rich fruits of this policy. But *now* new light breaks upon us.—Now Congress declares this ought never to have been; and the like of it, must never be again.—The sacred right of self-government is grossly violated by it! We even find some men, who drew their first breath, and every other breath of their lives, under this very restriction, now live in dread of absolute suffocation, if they should be restricted in the "sacred right" of taking slaves to Nebraska. That *perfect* liberty they sigh for—the liberty of making slaves of other people—Jefferson never thought of; their own father never thought of, they never thought of themselves, a year ago. How fortunate for them, they did not sooner become sensible of their great misery! Oh, how difficult it is to treat with respect such assaults upon all we have ever really held sacred!

But to return to history. In 1803 we purchased what was then called Louisiana, of France. It included the now States of Louisiana, Arkansas, Missouri, and Iowa; also the territory of Minnesota, and the present bone of contention, Kansas and Nebraska. Slavery already existed among the French at New Orleans; and to some extent at St. Louis. In 1812 Louisiana came into the Union as a slave state, without controversy. In 1818 or '19, Missouri showed signs of a wish to come in with slavery. This was resisted by Northern members of Congress; and thus began the first great slavery agitation in the nation. This controversy lasted several months, and became very angry and exciting; the House of Representatives voting steadily for the prohibition of slavery in Missouri, and the Senate voting as steadily against it. Threats of breaking up the Union were freely made; and the ablest public men of the day became seriously alarmed. At length a compromise was made, in which, like all compromises, both sides yielded something. It was a law passed on the 6th day of March, 1820, providing that Missouri might come into the Union *with* slavery, but that in all the remaining part of the territory purchased of France, which lies north of 36 degrees and 30 minutes north latitude, slavery should never be permitted. This provision of law, *is the Missouri Compromise.* In excluding slavery north of the line, the same language is employed as in the ordinance of '87. It directly applied to Iowa, Minnesota, and to the present bone of contention, Kansas and Nebraska. Whether there should or should not, be slavery south of that line, nothing was said in the law; but Arkansas constituted the principal remaining part, south of the line; and it has since been admitted as a slave state, without serious controversy. More recently, Iowa, north of the line, came in as a free state without controversy. Still later, Minnesota, north of the line, had a territorial organization without controversy. Texas principally south of the line, and west of Arkansas; though originally within the purchase from France, had, in 1819, been traded off to Spain, in our treaty for the acquisition of Florida. It had thus become a part of Mexico. Mexico revolutionized and became independent of Spain. American citizens began settling rapidly, with their slaves, in the southern part of Texas. Soon they revolutionized against Mexico, and established an independent government of their own, adopting a constitution, with slavery, strongly resembling the constitutions of our slave states. By still another rapid move, Texas, claiming a boundary much further West, than when we parted with her in 1819, was brought back to the United States, and admitted into the Union as a slave state. There then was little or no settlement in the northern part of Texas, a considerable portion of which lay north of the Missouri line; and in the resolutions admitting her into the Union, the Missouri restriction was expressly extended westward across her territory. This was in 1845, only nine years ago.

Thus originated the Missouri Compromise; and thus has it been respected down to 1845.—And even four years later, in 1849, our distinguished Senator, in a public address, held the following language in relation to it:

"The Missouri Compromise had been in practical operation for about a quarter of a century, and had received the sanction and approbation of men of all parties in every section of the Union. It had allayed all sectional jealousies and irritations growing out of this vexed question, and harmonized and tranquilized the whole country. It has given to Henry Clay, as its prominent champion, the proud sobriquet of the "*Great Pacificator*," and by that title and for that service, his political friends had repeatedly appealed to the people to rally under his standard, as a presidential candidate, as the man who had exhibited the patriotism and the power to suppress, an unholy and treasonable agitation, and preserve the Union. He was not aware that any man or any party from any section of the Union, had ever urged as an objection to Mr. Clay, that he was the great champion of the Missouri Compromise. On the contrary, the effort was made by the opponents of Mr. Clay, to prove that he was not entitled to the exclusive merit of that great patriotic measure, and that the honor was equally due to others as well as to him, for securing its adoption—that it had its origin in the hearts of all patriotic men, who desired to preserve and perpetuate the blessings of our glorious Union—an origin akin that of the Constitution of the United States, conceived in the same spirit of fraternal affection, and calculated to remove forever, the only danger, which seemed to threaten, at some distant day, to sever the social bond of union. All the evidences of public opinion at that day, seemed to indicate that this Compromise had been canonized in the hearts of the American people, as a sacred thing which no ruthless hand would ever be reckless enough to disturb."

I do not read this extract to involve Judge Douglas in an inconsistency—If he afterwards thought he had been wrong, it was right for him to change—I bring this forward merely to show the high estimate placed on the Missouri Compromise by all parties up to so late as the year 1849.

But, going back a little, in point of time, our war with Mexico broke out in 1846. When Congress was about adjourning that session, President Polk asked them to place two millions of dollars under his control, to be used by him in the recess, if found practicable and expedient, in negotiating a treaty of peace with Mexico, and acquiring some part of her territory.—A bill was duly got up, for the purpose, and was progressing swimmingly, in the House of Representatives, when a member by the name of David Wilmot, a democrat from Pennsylvania, moved as an amendment "Provided that in any territory thus acquired, there shall never be slavery."

This is the origin of the far-famed "Wilmot Proviso." It created a great flutter; but it stuck like wax, was voted into the bill, and the bill passed with it through the House. The Senate, however, adjourned without final action on it and so both appropriation and proviso were lost, for the time.—The war continued, and at the next session, the President renewed his request for the appropriation, enlarging the amount, I think, to three million. Again came the proviso; and defeated the measure.—Congress adjourned again, and the war went on. In Dec. 1847, the new congress assembled.—I was in the lower House that term.—The "Wilmot Proviso" or the principle of it, was constantly coming up in some shape or other, and I think I may venture to say I voted for it at least forty times; during the short term I was there. The Senate, however, held it in check, and it never became a law. In the spring of 1848 a treaty of peace was made with Mexico; by which we obtained that portion of her country which now constitutes the territories of New Mexico and Utah, and the now state of California. By this treaty the Wilmot Proviso was defeated, as so far as it was intended to be a condition of the acquisition of territory. Its friends, however, were still determined to find some way to restrain slavery from getting into the new country. This new acquisition lay directly west of our old purchase from France, and extended west to the Pacific Ocean—and was so situated that if the Missouri line should be extended straight west, the new country would be divided by such extended line, leaving some north and some south of it. On Judge Douglas' motion a bill, or provision of a bill, passed the Senate to so extend the Missouri line. The Proviso men in the House, including myself, voted it down, because by implication, it gave up the southern part to slavery, while we were bent on having it *all* free.

In the fall of 1848 the gold mines were discovered in California. This attracted people to it with unprecedented rapidity, so that on, or soon after, the meeting of the new congress in Dec., 1849, she already had a population of nearly a hundred thousand, had called a convention, formed a state constitution, excluding slavery, and was knocking for admission into the Union.—The Proviso men, of course, were for letting her in, but the Senate, always true to the other side, would not consent to her admission. And there California stood, kept *out* of the Union, because she would not let slavery *into* her borders. Under all the circumstances perhaps this was not wrong. There were other points of dispute, connected with the general question of slavery, which equally needed adjustment. The South clamored for a more efficient fugitive slave law. The North clamored for the abolition of a peculiar species of slave trade in the District of Columbia, in connection with which, in view from the windows of the capitol, a sort of negro-livery stable, where droves of negroes were collected, temporarily kept, and finally taken to Southern markets, precisely like droves of horses, had been openly maintained for fifty years. Utah and New Mexico needed territorial governments; and whether slavery should or should not be prohibited within them, was another question. The indefinite western boundary of Texas was to be settled. She was received a slave state; and consequently the farther west the slavery men could push her boundary, the more slave country they secured. And the farther east the slavery opponents could thrust the boundary back, the less slave ground was secured. Thus this was just as clearly a slavery question as any of the others.

These points all needed adjustment; and they were held up, perhaps wisely, to make them help to adjust one another. The Union, now, as in 1820, was thought to be in danger; and devotion to the Union rightfully inclined men to yield somewhat, in points where nothing else could have so inclined them. A compromise was finally effected. The South got their new fugitive-slave law; and the North got California, (the far best part of our acquisition from Mexico,) as a free State. The South got a provision that New Mexico and Utah, *when admitted as States*, may come in *with* or *without* slavery as they may then choose; and the North got the slave-trade abolished in the District of Columbia. The North got the western boundary of Texas, thence further back eastward than the South desired; but, in turn, they gave Texas ten millions of dollars, with which to pay her old debts. This is the compromise of 1850.

Preceding the presidential election of 1852, each of the great political parties, democrats and whigs, met in convention and adopted resolutions endorsing the compromise of '50, as a "finality," a final settlement, so far as these parties could make it so, of all slavery agitation. Previous to this, in 1851, the Illinois Legislature had indorsed it.

During this long period of time Nebraska had remained, substantially an uninhabited country, but now emigration to, and settlement within it began to take place. It is about one third as large as the present United States, and its importance so long overlooked, begins to come into view. The restriction of slavery by the Missouri Compromise directly applies to it; in fact, was first made, and has since been maintained, expressly for it. In 1853, a bill to give it a territorial government passed the House of Representatives, and, in the hands of Judge Douglas, failed of passing the Senate only for want of time. This bill contained no repeal of the Missouri Compromise. Indeed, when it was assailed because it did not contain such repeal, Judge Douglas defended it in its existing form. On January 4th, 1854, Judge Douglas introduces a new bill to give Nebraska territorial government. He accompanies this bill with a report, in which last, he expressly recommends that the Missouri Compromise shall neither be affirmed nor repealed.

Before long the bill is so modified as to make two territories instead of one; calling the southern one Kansas.

Also, about a month after the introduction of the bill, on the judge's own motion, it is so amended as to declare the Missouri Compromise inoperative and void; and, substantially, that the people who go and settle there may establish slavery, or exclude it, as they may see fit. In this shape the bill passed both branches of congress, and became a law.

This is the *repeal* of the Missouri Compromise. The foregoing history may not be precisely accurate in every particular; but

I am sure it is sufficiently so, for all the uses I shall attempt to make of it, and in it, we have before us, the chief material enabling us to correctly judge whether the repeal of the Missouri Compromise is right or wrong.

I think, and shall try to show, that it is wrong; wrong in its direct effect, letting slavery into Kansas and Nebraska—and wrong in its prospective principle, allowing it to spread to every other part of the wide world, where men can be found inclined to take it.

This *declared* indifference, but, as I must think, covert *real zeal* for the spread of slavery, I can not but hate. I hate it because of the monstrous injustice of slavery itself. I hate it because it deprives our republican example of its just influence in the world —enables the enemies of free institutions, with plausibility, to taunt us as hypocrites—causes the real friends of freedom to doubt our sincerity, and especially because it forces so many really good men amongst ourselves into an open war with the very fundamental principles of civil liberty—criticizing the Declaration of Independence, and insisting that there is no right principle of action but *self-interest.*

Before proceeding, let me say that I think I have no prejudice against the Southern people. They are just what we would be in their situation. If slavery did not now exist amongst them, they would not introduce it. If it did now exist amongst us, we should not instantly give it up.—This I believe of the masses north and south.—Doubtless there are individuals on both sides, who would not hold slaves under any circumstances; and others who would gladly introduce slavery anew, if it were out of existence. We know that some southern men do free their slaves, go north, and become tip-top abolitionists; while some northern ones go south, and become most cruel slave-masters.

When southern people tell us they are no more responsible for the origin of slavery, than we; I acknowledge the fact. When it is said that the institution exists, and that it is very difficult to get rid of it, in any satisfactory way, I can understand and appreciate the saying. I surely will not blame them for not doing what I should not know how to do myself. If all earthly power were given me, I should not know what to do, as to the existing institution. My first impulse would be to free all the slaves, and send them to Liberia,—to their own native land. But a moment's reflection would convince me, that whatever of high hope, (as I think there is) there may be in this, in the long run, its sudden execution is impossible. If they were all landed there in a day, they would all perish in the next ten days; and there are not surplus shipping and surplus money enough in the world to carry them there in many times ten days. What then? Free them all, and keep them among us as underlings? Is it quite certain that this betters their condition? I think I would not hold one in slavery, at any rate; yet the point is not clear enough to me to denounce people upon. What next?—Free them, and make them politically and socially, our equals? My own feelings will not admit of this; and if mine would, we well know that those of the great mass of white people will not. Whether this feeling accords with justice and sound judgment, is not the solė question, if indeed, it is any part of it. A universal feeling, whether well or ill-founded, can not be safely disregarded. We can not, then, make them equals. It does seem to me that systems of gradual emancipation might be adopted; but for their tardiness in this, I will not undertake to judge our brethren of the south.

When they remind us of their constitutional rights, I acknowledge them, not grudgingly, but fully, and fairly; and I would give them any legislation for the reclaiming of their fugitives, which should not, in its stringency, be more likely to carry a free man into slavery, than our ordinary criminal laws are to hang an innocent one.

But all this, to my judgment, furnishes no more excuse for permitting slavery to go into our own free territory, than it would for reviving the African slave trade by law. The law which forbids the bringing of slaves *from* Africa; and that which has so long forbid the taking them *to* Nebraska, can hardly be distinguished on any moral principle; and the repeal of the former could find quite as plausible excuses as that of the latter.

The arguments by which the repeal of the Missouri Compromise is sought to be justified, are these:

First, that the Nebraska country needed a territorial government.

Second, that in various ways, the public had repudiated it, and demanded the repeal; and therefore should not now complain of it.

And lastly, that the repeal establishes a principle, which is intrinsically right.

I will attempt an answer to each of them in its turn.

First, then, if that country was in need of a territorial organization, could it not have had it as well without as with the repeal? Iowa and Minnesota, to both of which the Missouri restriction applied, had, without its repeal, each in succession, territorial organizations. And even, the year before, a bill for Nebraska itself, was within an ace of passing, without the repealing clause; and this in the hands of the same men who are now the champions of repeal. Why no necessity then for the repeal? But still later, when this very bill was first brought in, it contained no repeal. But, say they, because the public had demanded, or rather commanded the repeal, the repeal was to accompany the organization, whenever that should occur.

Now, I deny that the public ever demanded any such thing —ever repudiated the Missouri Compromise—ever commanded its repeal. I deny it, and call for the proof. It is not contended, I believe, that any such command has ever been given in express terms. It is only said that it was done *in principle*. The support of the Wilmot Proviso, is the first fact mentioned, to prove that the Missouri restriction was repudiated in *principle*, and the second is, the refusal to extend the Missouri line over the country acquired from Mexico. These are near enough alike to be treated together. The one was to exclude the chances of slavery from the *whole* new acquisition by the lump; and the other was to reject a division of it, by which one *half* was to be given up to those chances. Now whether this was a repudiation of the Missouri line, in *principle*, depends upon whether the Missouri law contained any *principle* requiring the line to be extended over the country acquired from Mexico. I contend it did not. I insist that it contained no general principle, but that it was, in every sense, specific. That its terms limit it to the country purchased from France, is undenied and undeniable. It could have no principle beyond the intention of those who made it. They did not intend to extend the line to country which they did not own. If they intended to extend it, in the event of acquiring additional territory, why did they not say so? It was just as easy to say, that "in all the country west of the Mississippi, which we now own, *or may hereafter acquire* there shall never be slavery," as to say what they did say; and they would have said it if they had meant it. An intention to extend the law is not only not mentioned in the law, but is not mentioned in any contemporaneous history. Both the law itself, and the history of the times are a blank as to any *principle* of extension; and by neither the known rules of construing statutes and contracts, nor by common sense, can any such *principle* be inferred.

Another fact showing the *specific* character of the Missouri law—showing that it intended no more than it expressed—showing that the line was not intended as a universal dividing line between free and slave territory, present and prospective—north of which slavery could never go—is the fact that by that very law, Missouri came in as a slave State, *north* of the line. If that law contained any prospective *principle*, the whole law must be looked to in order to ascertain what the *principle* was. And by this rule, the South could fairly contend that inasmuch as they got one slave state north of the line at the inception of the law, they have the right to have another given them *north* of it occasionally—now and then in the indefinite westward extension of the line. This demonstrates the absurdity of attempting to deduce a prospective *principle* from the Missouri Compromise line.

When we voted for the Wilmot Proviso, we were voting to keep slavery *out* of the whole Missouri [Mexican?] acquisition; and little did we think we were thereby voting, to let it *into* Nebraska, laying several hundred miles distant. When we voted against extending the Missouri line, little did we think we were voting to destroy the old line, then of near thirty years standing. To argue that we thus repudiated the Missouri Compromise is no less absurd than it would be to argue that because we have, so far, forborne to acquire Cuba, we have thereby, *in principle*, repudiated our former acquisitions, and determined to throw them out of the Union! No less absurd than it would be to say that because I may have refused to build an addition to my house, I thereby have decided to destroy the existing house! And if I catch you setting fire to my house, you will turn upon me and say I INSTRUCTED you to do it! The most conclusive argument, however, that, while voting for the Wilmot Proviso, and while voting against the EXTENSION of the Missouri line, we never thought of disturbing the original Missouri Compromise, is found in the fact that there was then, and still is, an unorganized tract of fine country, nearly as large as the State of Missouri, lying immediately west of Arkansas, and south of the Missouri Compromise line; and that we never attempted to prohibit slavery as to it. I wish particular attention to this. It adjoins the original Missouri Compromise line, by its northern boundary; and consequently is part of the country, into which, by implication, slavery was permitted to go, by that compromise. There it has lain open ever since, and there it still lies. And yet no effort has been made at any time to wrest it from the South. In all our struggles to prohibit slavery within our Mexican acquisitions, we never so much as lifted a finger to prohibit it, as to this tract. Is not this entirely conclusive that at all times, we have held the Missouri Compromise as a sacred thing; even when against ourselves, as well as when for us?

Senator Douglas sometimes says the Missouri line itself was, *in principle*, only an extension of the line of the ordinance of '87—that is to say, an extension of the Ohio River. I think this is weak enough on its face. I will remark, however, that, as a glance at the map will show, the Missouri line is a long way farther south than the Ohio; and that if our Senator, in proposing his extension, had stuck to the *principle* of jogging southward, perhaps it might not have been voted down so readily.

But next it is said that the compromises of '50 and the ratification of them by both political parties, in '52, established a *new principle*, which required the repeal of the Missouri Compromise. This again I deny. I deny it, and demand the proof. I have already stated fully what the compromises of '50 are. The particular part of those measures, for which the virtual repeal of the Missouri Compromise is sought to be inferred (for it is admitted they contain nothing about it, in express terms) is the provision in the Utah and New Mexico laws, which permits them when they seek admission into the Union as States, to come in with or without slavery as they shall then see fit. Now I insist this provision was made for Utah and New Mexico, and for no other place whatever. It had no more direct reference to Nebraska than it had to the territories of the moon. But, say they, it had reference to Nebraska, *in principle*. Let us see. The North consented to this provision, not because they considered it right in itself; but because they were compensated—paid for it.—They, at the same time, got California into the Union as a free State. This was far the best part of all they had struggled for by the Wilmot Proviso. They also got the area of slavery somewhat narrowed in the settlement of the boundary of Texas. Also, they got the slave trade abolished in the District of Columbia. For all these desirable objects the North could afford to yield something; and they did yield to the South the Utah and New Mexico provision. I do not mean that the whole North, or even a majority, yielded, when the law passed; but enough yielded, when added to the vote of the South, to carry the measure. Now can it be pretended that the *principle* of this arrangement requires us to permit the same provision to be applied to Nebraska, *without any equivalent at all?* Give us another free State; press the boundary of Texas still further back; give us another step toward the destruction of slavery in the District, and you present us a similar case. But ask us not to repeat, for nothing, what you paid for in the first instance. If you wish the thing again, pay again. That is the *principle* of the compromises of '50, if indeed they had any principles beyond their specific terms—it was the system of equivalents.

Again, if Congress, at that time, intended that all future territories should, when admitted as States, come in with or without slavery, at their own option, why did it not say so? With such an universal provision, all know the bills could not have passed. Did they, then—could they—establish a *principle* contrary to their own intention? Still further, if they intended to establish the principle that wherever Congress had control, it should be left to the people to do as they thought fit with slavery, why did they not authorize the people of the District of Columbia at their adoption to abolish slavery within these limits? I personally know that this has not been left undone, because it was unthought of.

It was frequently spoken of by members of Congress and by citizens of Washington six years ago; and I heard no one express a doubt that a system of gradual emancipation, with compensation to owners, would meet the approbation of a large majority of the white people of the District. But without the action of Congress they could say nothing; and Congress said "no." In the measures of 1850, Congress had the subject of slavery in the District expressly on hand. If they were then establishing the *principle* of allowing the people to do as they please with slavery, why did they not apply the *principle* to that people?

Again, it is claimed that by the Resolutions of the Illinois Legislature, passed in 1851, the repeal of the Missouri Compromise was demanded. This I deny also. Whatever may be worked out by a criticism of the language of those resolutions, the people have never understood them as being any more than an endorsement of the compromises of 1850, and a release of our Senators from voting for the Wilmot Proviso. The whole people are living witnesses, that this only, was their view. Finally, it is asked "If we did not mean to apply the Utah and New Mexico provision, to all future territories, what did we mean, when we, in 1852, endorsed the compromise of '50?"

For myself, I can answer this question most easily. I meant not to ask a repeal, or modification of the fugitive slave law. I meant not to ask for the abolition of slavery in the District of Columbia. I meant not to resist the admission of Utah and New Mexico, even should they ask to come in as slave States. I meant nothing about additional territories, because, as I understood, we then had no territory whose character as to slavery was not already settled. As to Nebraska, I regarded its character as being fixed, by the Missouri Compromise, for thirty years—as unalterably fixed as that of my own home in Illinois. As to new acquisitions I said "sufficient unto the day is the evil thereof."—When we make new acquaintances [acquisitions?], we will, as heretofore, try to manage them somehow. That is my answer. That is what I meant and said; and I appeal to the people to say, each for himself, whether that was not also the universal meaning of the free States.

And now, in turn, let me ask a few questions. If by any, or all these matters, the repeal of the Missouri Compromise was commanded, why was not the command sooner obeyed? Why was the repeal omitted in the Nebraska bill of 1853?—Why was it omitted in the original bill of 1854? Why, in the accompanying report, was such a repeal characterized as a *departure* from the course pursued in 1850? and its continued omission recommended?

I am aware Judge Douglas now argues that the subsequent express repeal is no substantial alteration of the bill. This argument seems wonderful to me. It is as if one should argue that white and black are not different. He admits, however, that there is a literal change in the bill; and that he made the change in deference to other Senators, who would not support the bill without. This proves that those other Senators thought the change a substantial one; and that the Judge thought their opinions worth deferring to. His own opinions, therefore, seem not to rest on a very firm basis even in his own mind—and I suppose the world believes, and will continue to believe, that precisely on the substance of that change this whole agitation has arisen.

I conclude then, that the public never demanded the repeal of the Missouri Compromise.

I now come to consider whether the repeal, with its avowed principle, is intrinsically right. I insist that it is not. Take the particular case. A controversy had arisen between the advocates and opponents of slavery, in relation to its establishment within the country we had purchased of France. The southern, and then best part of the purchase, was already in as a slave State.—The controversy was settled by also letting Missouri in as a slave State; but with the agreement that within all the remaining part of the purchase, north of a certain line, there should never be slavery. As to what was to be done with the remaining part south of the line, nothing was said; but perhaps the fair implication was, that it should come in with slavery if it should so choose. The southern part, except a portion heretofore mentioned, afterwards did come in with slavery, as the State of Arkansas. All these many years since 1820, the Northern part had remained a wilderness. At length settlements began in it also. In due course, Iowa, came in as a free State, and Minnesota was given a territorial government, without removing the slavery restriction. Finally the sole remaining part, north of the line, Kansas and Nebraska, was to be organized; and it is proposed, and carried, to blot out the old dividing line of thirty-four years standing, and to open the whole of that country to the introduction of slavery. Now, this, to my mind, is manifestly unjust. After an angry and dangerous controversy, the parties made friends by dividing the bone of contention. The one party first appropriates her own share, beyond all power to be disturbed in the possession of it; and then seizes the share of the other party. It is as if two starving men had divided their only loaf; the one had hastily swallowed his half, and then grabbed the other half just as he was putting it to his mouth.

Let me here drop the main argument, to notice what I consider rather an inferior matter. It is argued that slavery will not go to Kansas and Nebraska, *in any event*. This is a *palliation*—a *lullaby*. I have some hope that it will not; but let us not be too confident. As to climate, a glance at the map shows that there are five slave States—Delaware, Maryland, Virginia, Kentucky, and Missouri—and also the District of Columbia, all north of the Missouri Compromise line. The census returns of 1850 show that, within these, there are 867,276 slaves—being more than one-fourth of all the slaves in the nation.

It is not climate, then, that will keep slavery out of these territories. Is there any thing in the peculiar nature of the country? Missouri adjoins these territories, by her entire western boundary, and slavery is already within every one of her western counties. I have even heard it said that there are more slaves, in proportion to whites, in the north western county of Missouri, than within any county of the State. Slavery pressed entirely up to the old western boundary of the State, and when, rather recently, a part of that boundary, at the north-west was moved out a little farther west, slavery followed on quite up to the new line. Now, when the restriction is removed, what is to prevent it from going still further? Climate will not.—No peculiarity of the country will—nothing in *nature* will. Will the disposition of the people prevent it? Those nearest the scene, are all in favor of the extension. The yankees, who are opposed to it, may be more numerous; but, in military phrase, the battle-field is too far from *their* base of operations.

But it is said, there now is *no* law in Nebraska on the subject of slavery; and that, in such case, taking a slave there, operates his freedom. That is good book-law; but is not the rule of actual practice. Wherever slavery is, it has been first introduced without law. The oldest laws we find concerning it, are not laws introducing it; but *regulating* it, as an already existing thing. A white man takes his slave to Nebraska now; who will inform the negro that he is free?—Who will take him before court to test the question of his freedom? In ignorance of his legal emancipation, he is kept chopping, splitting and plowing. Others are brought, and move on in the same track. At last, if ever the time for voting comes, on the question of slavery, the institution already in fact exists in the country, and cannot well be removed. The facts of its presence, and the difficulty of its removal, will carry the vote in its favor. Keep it out until a vote is taken, and a vote in favor of it, can not be got in any population of forty thousand, on earth, who have been drawn together by the ordinary motives of emigration and settlement. To get slaves into the country simultaneously with the whites, in the incipient stages of settlement, is the precise stake played for, and won in this Nebraska measure.

The question is asked us, "If slaves will go in, notwithstanding the general principle of law liberates them, why would they not equally go in against positive statute law?—go in, even if the Missouri restriction were maintained?" I answer, because it takes a much bolder man to venture in, with his property, in the latter case, than in the former—because the positive congressional enactment is known to, and respected by all, or nearly all; whereas the negative principle that *no* law is free law, is not much known except among lawyers. We have some experience of this practical difference. In spite of the Ordinance of '87, a few negroes were brought into Illinois, and held in a state of quasi slavery; not enough, however, to carry a vote of the people in favor of the institution when they came to form a constitution. But in the adjoining Missouri country, where there was no ordinance of '87—was no restriction—they were carried ten times, nay a hundred times, as fast, and actually made a slave State. This is fact —naked fact.

Another LULLABY argument is, that taking slaves to new countries does not increase their number, does not make any one slave who otherwise would be free. There is some truth in this, and I am glad of it, but it is not WHOLLY true. The African slave trade is not yet effectually suppressed; and if we make a reasonable deduction for the white people amongst us, who are foreigners, and the descendants of foreigners, arriving here since 1808, we shall find the increase of the black population outrunning that of the white, to an extent unaccountable, except by supposing that some of them too, have been coming from Africa. If this be so, the opening of new countries to the institution, increases the demand for, and augments the price of slaves, and so does, in fact, make slaves of freemen by causing them to be brought from Africa, and sold into bondage.

But, however this may be, we know the opening of new countries to slavery, tends to the perpetuation of the institution, and so does KEEP men in slavery who otherwise would be free. This result we do not FEEL like favoring, and we are under no legal obligation to suppress our feelings in this respect.

Equal justice to the South, it is said, requires us to consent to the extending of slavery to new countries. That is to say, inasmuch as you do not object to my taking my hog to Nebraska, therefore I must not object to you taking your slave. Now, I admit this is perfectly logical, if there is no difference between hogs and negroes. But while you thus require me to deny the humanity of the negro, I wish to ask whether you of the south yourselves, have ever been willing to do as much? It is kindly provided that of all those who come into the world, only a small percentage are natural tyrants. That percentage is no larger in the slave States than in the free. The great majority, south as well as north, have human sympathies, of which they can no more divest themselves than they can of their sensibility to physical pain. These sympathies in the bosoms of the southern people, manifest in many ways, their sense of the wrong of slavery, and their consciousness that, after all, there is humanity in the negro. If they deny this, let me address them a few plain questions. In

1820 you joined the north, almost unanimously, in declaring the African slave trade piracy, and in annexing to it the punishment of death. Why did you do this? If you did not feel that it was wrong, why did you join in providing that men should be hung for it? The practice was no more than bringing wild negroes from Africa, to sell to such as would buy them. But you never thought of hanging men for catching and selling wild horses, wild buffaloes or wild bears.

Again, you have amongst you, a sneaking individual, of the class of native tyrants, known as the "SLAVE-DEALER." He watches your necessities, and crawls up to buy your slave, at a speculating price. If you cannot help it, you sell to him; but if you can help it, you drive him from your door. You despise him utterly. You do not recognize him as a friend, or even as an honest man. Your children must not play with his; they may rollick freely with the little negroes, but not with the "slave-dealer's" children. If you are obliged to deal with him, you try to get through the job without so much as touching him. It is common with you to join hands with the men you meet; but with the slave-dealer you avoid the ceremony—instinctively shrinking from the snaky contact. If he grows rich and retires from business, you still remember him, and still keep up the ban of non-intercourse upon him and his family. Now why is this? You do not so treat the man who deals in corn, cattle or tobacco.

And yet again, there are in the United States and territories, including the District of Columbia, 433,643 free blacks. At $500 per head they are worth over two hundred millions of dollars. How comes this vast amount of property to be running about without owners? We do not see free horses or free cattle running at large. How is this? All these free blacks are the descendants of slaves, or have been slaves themselves, and they would be slaves now, but for SOMETHING which has operated on their white owners, inducing them, at vast pecuniary sacrifices, to liberate them. What is that SOMETHING? Is there any mistaking it? In all these cases it is your sense of justice, and human sympathy, continually telling you, that the poor negro has some natural right to himself—that those who deny it, and make mere merchandise of him, deserve kickings, contempt and death.

And now, why will you ask us to deny the humanity of the slave? and estimate him only as the equal of the hog? Why ask us to do what you will not do yourselves? Why ask us to do for *nothing*, what two hundred million of dollars could not induce you to do?

But one great argument in the support of the repeal of the Missouri Compromise, is still to come. That argument is "the sacred right of self government." It seems our distinguished Senator has found great difficulty in getting his antagonists, even in the Senate, to meet him fairly on this argument. Some poet has said:

"Fools rush in where angels fear to tread."

At the hazzard [*sic*] of being thought one of the fools of this quotation, I meet that argument—I rush in, I take that bull by the horns.

I trust I understand, and truly estimate the right of self-government. My faith in the proposition that each man should do precisely as he pleases with all which is exclusively his own, lies at the foundation of the sense of justice there is in me. I extend the principles to communities of men, as well as to individuals. I so extend it, because it is politically wise, as well as naturally just; politically wise in saving us from broils about matters which do not concern us.—Here or at Washington, I would not trouble myself with the oyster laws of Virginia, or the cranberry laws of Indiana.

The doctrine of self-government is right—absolutely and eternally right—but it has no just application, as here attempted. Or perhaps I should rather say that whether it has such application depends upon whether a negro is *not* or *is* a man. If he is *not* a man, why in that case, he who *is* a man may, as a matter of self-government, do just as he pleases with him. But if the negro *is* a man, is it not to that extent a total destruction of self-government, to say that he too shall not govern *himself*? When the white man governs himself that is self-government; but when he governs himself, and also governs *another* man, that is *more* than self-government—that is despotism. If the negro is a *man*, why then my ancient faith teaches me that "all men are created equal;" and that there can be no moral right in connection with one man's making a slave of another.

Judge Douglas frequently, with bitter irony and sarcasm, paraphrases our argument by saying: "The white people of Nebraska are good enough to govern themselves, *but they are not good enough to govern a few miserable negroes!!*"

Well I doubt not that the people of Nebraska are, and will continue to be as good as the average of people elsewhere. I do not say the contrary. What I do say is, that no man is good enough to govern another man, *without that other's consent.* I say this is the leading principle—the sheet anchor of American republicanism. Our Declaration of Independence says:

"We hold these truths to be self evident: That all men are created equal; that they are endowed by their Creator with certain inalienable rights; that among these are life, liberty and the pursuit of happiness. That to secure these rights, governments are instituted among men, DERIVING THEIR JUST POWERS FROM THE CONSENT OF THE GOVERNED."

I have quoted so much at this time merely to show that according to our ancient faith, the just powers of governments are derived from the consent of the governed. Now the relation of masters and slaves is PROTANTO, a total violation of this principle. That master not only governs the slave without his consent; but he governs him by a set of rules altogether different from those which he prescribes for himself. Allow ALL the governed an equal voice in the government, and that, and that only, is self-government.

Let it not be said I am contending for the establishment of political and social equality between the whites and blacks. I have already said the contrary. I am not now combating the argument of NECESSITY, arising from the fact that the blacks are already amongst us; but I am combating what is set up as MORAL argument for allowing them to be taken where they have never yet been—arguing against the EXTENSION of a bad thing, which where it already exists we must of necessity, manage as we best can.

In support of his application of the doctrine of self-government, Senator Douglas has sought to bring to his aid the opinions and examples of our revolutionary fathers. I am glad he has done this. I love the sentiments of those old-time men; and shall be most happy to abide by their opinions. He shows us that when it was in contemplation for the colonies to break off from Great Britain, and set up a new government for themselves, several of the states instructed their delegates to go for the measure, PROVIDED EACH STATE SHOULD BE ALLOWED TO REGULATE ITS DOMESTIC CONCERNS IN ITS OWN WAY. I do not quote; but this in substance. This was right. I see nothing objectionable in it. I also think it probable that it had some reference to the existence of slavery amongst them. I will not deny that it had. But had it, in any reference, to the carrying of slavery into NEW COUNTRIES? That is the question; and we will let the fathers themselves answer it.

This same generation of men, and mostly the same individuals of the generation, who declared this principle—who declared independence—who fought the war of the revolution through—who afterwards made the constitution under which we still live—these same men passed the ordinance of '87, declaring that slavery should never go to the north-west territory. I have no doubt Judge Douglas thinks they were very inconsistent in this. It is a question of discrimination between them and him. But there is not an inch of ground left for his claiming that their opinions—their example—their authority—are on his side in this controversy.

Again, is not Nebraska, while a territory, a part of us? Do we not own the country? And if we surrender the control of it, do we not surrender the right of self-government? It is part of ourselves. If you say we shall not control it because it is ONLY part, the same is true of every other part; and when all the parts are gone, what has become of the whole? What is then left of us? What use for the General Government, when there is nothing left for it [to?] govern?

But you say this question should be left to the people of Nebraska, because they are more particularly interested. If this be the rule, you must leave it to each individual to say for himself whether he will have slaves. What better moral right have thirty-one citizens of Nebraska to say, that the thirty-second shall not hold slaves, than the people of the thirty-one States have to say that slavery shall not go into the thirty-second State at all?

But if it is a sacred right for the people of Nebraska to take and hold slaves there, it is equally their sacred right to buy them where they can buy them cheapest; and that undoubtedly will be on the coast of Africa; provided you will consent to not hang them for going there to buy them. You must remove this restriction too, from the sacred right of self-government. I am aware you say that taking slaves from the States to Nebraska, does not make slaves of freemen; but the African slave-trader can say just as much. He does not catch free negroes and bring them here. He finds them already slaves in the hands of their black captors, and he honestly buys them at the rate of about a red cotton handkerchief a head. This is very cheap, and it is a great abridgment of the sacred right of self-government to hang men for engaging in this profitable trade!

Another important objection to this application of the right of self-government, is that it enables the first FEW, to deprive the succeeding MANY, of a free exercise of the right of self-government. The first few may get slavery IN, and the subsequent many cannot easily get it OUT. How common is the remark now in the slave States—"If we were only clear of our slaves, how much better it would be for us." They are actually deprived of the privilege of governing themselves as they would, by the action of a very few, in the beginning. The same thing was true of the whole nation at the time our constitution was formed.

Whether slavery shall go into Nebraska, or other new territories, is not a matter of exclusive concern to the people who may go there. The whole nation is interested that the best use shall be made of these territories. We want them for the homes of free white people. This they cannot be, to any considerable extent, if slavery shall be planted within them. Slave States are places for poor white people to remove FROM; not to remove TO. New free States are the places for poor people to go to and better their condition. For this use, the nation needs these territories.

Still further; there are constitutional relations between the slave and free States, which are degrading to the latter. We are under legal obligations to catch and return their runaway slaves to them—a sort of dirty, disagreeable job which I believe, as a general rule, the slave-holders will not perform for one another. Then again, in the control of the government—the management of the partnership affairs—they have greatly the advantage of us. By the constitution, each State has two Senators, each has a number of Representatives, in proportion to the number of its people—and each has a number of presidential electors, equal to the whole number of its Senators and Representatives together. But in ascertaining the number of the people, for this purpose, five slaves are counted as being equal to three whites. The slaves do not vote; they are only counted and so used as to swell the influence of the white people's votes. The practical effect of this is more aptly shown by a comparison of the States of South Carolina and Maine. South Carolina has six representatives, and so has Maine; South Carolina has eight presidential electors, and so has Maine. This is precise equality so far; and, of course they are equal in Senators, each having two. Thus in the control of the government, the two States are equals precisely. But how are they in the number of their white people? Maine has 581,813—while South Carolina has 274,567. Maine has twice as many as South Carolina, and 32,679 over.—Thus each white man in South Carolina is more than the double of any man in Maine. This is all because South Carolina, besides her free people, has 384,984 slaves. The South Carolinian has precisely the same advantage over the white man in every other free State, as well as in Maine. He is more than the double of any one of us in this crowd. The same advantage, but not to the same extent, is held by all the citizens of the slave States, over those of the free; and it is an absolute truth, without an exception, that there is no voter in any slave State, but who has more legal power in the government, than any voter in any free State. There is no instance of exact equality; and the disadvantage is against us the whole chapter through. This principle, in the aggregate, gives the slave States in the present Congress, twenty additional representatives—being seven more than the whole majority by which they passed the Nebraska bill.

Now all this is manifestly unfair; yet I do not mention it to complain of it, in so far as it is already settled. It is in the constitution; and I do not, for that cause, or any other cause, propose to destroy, or alter, or disregard the constitution. I stand to it, fairly, fully, and firmly.

But when I am told I must leave it altogether to OTHER PEOPLE to say whether new partners are to be bred up and brought into the firm, on the same degrading terms against me, I respectfully demur. I insist, that whether I shall be a whole man, or only the half of one, in comparison with others, is a question in which I am somewhat concerned; and one which no other man can have a sacred right of deciding for me. If I am wrong in this—if it really be a sacred right of self-government, in the man who shall go to Nebraska, to decide whether he will be the EQUAL of me or the DOUBLE of me, then, after he shall have exercised that right, and thereby shall have reduced me to a still smaller fraction of a man than I already am, I should like for some gentleman, deeply skilled in the mysteries of sacred rights, to provide himself with a microscope, and peep about, and find out, if he can, what has become of my sacred rights!—They will surely be too small for detection with the naked eye.

Finally, I insist that if there is ANY THING which it is the duty of the WHOLE PEOPLE to never entrust to any hands but their own, that thing is the preservation and perpetuity, of their own liberties, and institutions. And if they shall think, as I do, that the extension of slavery endangers them, more than any, or all other causes, how recreant to themselves, if they submit the question, and with it, the fate of their country, to a mere hand-full of men, bent only on temporary self-interest. If this question of slavery extension were an insignificant one—one having no power to do harm—it might be shuffled aside in this way. But being, as it is, the great Behemoth of danger, shall the strong gripe of the nation be loosened upon him, to entrust him to the hands of such feeble keepers?

I have done with this mighty argument, of self-government. Go, sacred thing! Go in peace.

But Nebraska is urged as a great Union-saving measure. Well, I too, go for saving the Union. Much as I hate slavery, I would consent to the extension of it rather than see the Union dissolved, just as I would consent to any GREAT evil, to avoid a GREATER one. But when I go to Union saving, I must believe, at least, that the means I employ have some adaptation to the end. To my mind, Nebraska has no such adaptation.

"It hath no relish of salvation in it."

It is an aggravation, rather, of the only one thing which ever endangers the Union. When it came upon us, all was peace and quiet. The nation was looking to the forming of new bonds of Union; and a long course of peace and prosperity seemed to lie before us. In the whole range of possibility, there scarcely appears to me to have been any thing, out of which the slavery agitation could have been revived, except the very project of repealing the Missouri Compromise.—Every inch of territory we owned, already had a definite settlement of the slavery question, and by which all parties were pledged to abide. Indeed, there was no uninhabited country on the continent, which we could acquire; if we except some extreme northern regions, which are wholly out of the question. In this state of case, the genius of Discord himself, could scarcely have invented a way of again setting us by the ears, but by turning back and destroying the peace measures of the past. The councils of that genius seem to have prevailed, the Missouri Compromise was repealed; and here we are, in the midst of a new slavery agitation, such, I think, as we have never seen before. Who is responsible for this? Is it those who resist the measure; or those who, causelessly, brought it forward, and pressed it through, having reason to know, and, in fact, knowing it must and would be so resisted? It could not but be expected by its author, that it would be looked upon as a measure for the extension of slavery, aggravated by a gross breach of faith. Argue as you will, and long as you will, this is the naked FRONT and ASPECT, of the measure. And in this aspect, it could not but produce agitation. Slavery is founded in the selfishness of man's nature—opposition to it, is [*sic*] his love of justice. These principles are an eternal antagonism; and when brought into collision so fiercely, as slavery extension brings them, shocks, and throes, and convulsions must ceaselessly follow. Repeal the Missouri compromise—repeal all compromises—repeal the declaration of independence—repeal all past history, you still can not repeal human nature. It still will be the abundance of man's heart, that slavery extension is wrong; and out of the abundance of his heart, his mouth will continue to speak.

The structure, too, of the Nebraska bill is very peculiar. The people are to decide the question of slavery for themselves; but WHEN they are to decide, or HOW they are to decide; or whether, when the question is once decided, it is to remain so, or is to be subject to an indefinite succession of new trials, the law does not say. Is it to be decided by the first dozen settlers who arrive there? or is it to await the arrival of a hundred? Is it to be decided by a vote of the people? or a vote of the legislature? or, indeed, by a vote of any sort? To these questions, the law gives no answer. There is a mystery about this; for when a member proposed to give the legislature express authority to exclude slavery, it was hooted down by the friends of the bill. This fact is worth remembering. Some Yankees, in the east, are sending emigrants to Nebraska to exclude slavery from it; and, so far as I can judge, they expect the question to be decided by voting, in some way or other. But the Missourians are awake too. They are within a stone's throw of the contested ground. They hold meetings, and pass resolutions, in which not the slightest allusion to voting is made. They resolve that slavery already exists in the territory; that more shall go there; that they, remaining in Missouri, will protect it; and that abolitionists shall be hung, or driven away. Through all this, bowie-knives and six-shooters are seen plainly enough; but never a glimpse of the ballot-box. And, really, what is to be the result of this? Each party WITHIN, having numerous and determined backers WITHOUT, is it not probable that the contest will come to blows, and bloodshed? Could there be a more apt invention to bring about collision and violence, on the slavery question, than this Nebraska project is? I do not charge, or believe, that such was intended by Congress; but if they had literally formed a ring, and placed champions within it to fight out the controversy, the fight could be no more likely to come off, than it is. And if this fight should begin, is it likely to take a very peaceful, Union-saving turn? Will not the first drop of blood so shed, be the real knell of the Union?

The Missouri Compromise ought to be restored. For the sake of the Union, it ought to be restored. We ought to elect a House of Representatives which will vote its restoration. If by any means, we omit to do this, what follows!—Slavery may or may not be established in Nebraska. But whether it be or not, we shall have repudiated—discarded from the councils of the Nation—the SPIRIT OF COMPROMISE; for who after this will ever trust in a national compromise? The spirit of mutual concession—that spirit which first gave us the constitution, and which has thrice saved the Union—we shall have strangled and cast from us forever. And what shall we have in lieu of it? The South flushed with triumph and tempted to excesses; the North, betrayed, as they believe, brooding on wrong and burning for revenge. One side will provoke; the other resent. The one will taunt, the other defy; one agrees [aggresses?], the other retaliates. Already a few in the North, defy all constitutional restraints, resist the execution of the fugitive slave law, and even menace the institution of slavery in the states where it exists.

Already a few in the South, claim the constitutional right to take and to hold slaves in the free states—demand the revival of the slave trade: and demand a treaty with Great Britain by which fugitive slaves may be reclaimed from Canada. As yet they are but few on either side. It is a grave question for the lovers of the Union, whether the final destruction of the Missouri Compromise, and with it the spirit of all compromise will or will not embolden and embitter each of these, and fatally increase the numbers of both.

But restore the compromise, and what then? We thereby restore the national faith, the national confidence, the national feeling of brotherhood. We thereby reinstate the spirit of concession and compromise—that spirit which has never failed us in past perils, and which may be safely trusted for all the future. The south ought to join in doing this. The peace of the nation is as dear to them as to us. In memories of the past and hopes of the future, they share as largely as we. It would be on their part a great act—great in its spirit, and great in its effect. It would be worth to the nation a hundred years purchase of peace and prosperity. And what of sacrifice would they make? They only surrender to us, what they gave us for a consideration long, long ago; what they have not now, asked for, struggled or cared for; what has been thrust upon them, not less to their own astonishment than to ours.

But it is said we cannot restore it; that though we elect every member of the lower house, the Senate is still against us. It is quite true, that of the Senators who passed the Nebraska bill, a majority of the whole Senate will retain their seats in spite of the elections of this and the next year. But if at these elections, their several constituencies shall clearly express their will against Nebraska, will these Senators disregard their will? Will they neither obey, nor make room for those who will?

But even if we fail to technically restore the compromise, it is still a great point to carry a popular vote in favor of the restoration. The moral weight of such a vote can not be estimated too highly. The authors of Nebraska are not at all satisfied with the destruction of the compromise—an endorsement of this PRINCIPLE they proclaim to be the great object. With them, Nebraska alone is a small matter—to establish a principle, for FUTURE USE, is what they particularly desire.

That future use is to be the planting of slavery wherever in the wide world, local and unorganized opposition can not prevent it. Now if you wish to give them this endorsement—if you wish to establish this principle—do so. I shall regret it; but it is your right. On the contrary if you are opposed to the principle—intend to give it no such endorsement—let no wheedling, no sophistry, divert you from throwing a direct vote against it.

Some men, mostly whigs, who condemn the repeal of the Missouri Compromise, nevertheless hesitate to go for its restoration, lest they be thrown in company with the abolitionists. Will they allow me as an old whig to tell them good humoredly, that I think this is very silly? Stand with anybody that stands RIGHT. Stand with him while he is right and PART with him when he goes wrong. Stand WITH the abolitionist in restoring the Missouri Compromise; and stand AGAINST him when he attempts the repeal of the fugitive slave law. In the latter case you stand with the southern disunionist. What of that? you are still right. In both cases you are right. In both cases you expose the dangerous extremes. In both you stand on middle ground and hold the ship level and steady. In both you are national and nothing less than national. This is the good old whig ground. To desert such ground, because of any company, is to be less than a whig—less than a man—less than an American.

I particularly object to the NEW position which the avowed principle of this Nebraska law gives to slavery in the body politic. I object to it because it assumes that there can be MORAL RIGHT in the enslaving of one man by another. I object to it as a dangerous dalliance for a few people—a sad evidence that, feeling prosperity, we forget right—that liberty, as a principle, we have ceased to revere. I object to it because the fathers of the republic eschewed, and rejected it. The argument of "Necessity" was the only argument they ever admitted in favor of slavery; and so far, and so far only as it carried them, did they ever go. They found the institution existing among us, which they could not help; and they cast blame upon the British King for having permitted its introduction. BEFORE the constitution, they prohibited its introduction into the northwestern Territory—the only country we owned, then free from it. AT the framing and adoption of the constitution, they forbore to so much as mention the word "slave" or "slavery" in the whole instrument. In the provision for the recovery of fugitives, the slave is spoken of as a "PERSON HELD TO SERVICE OR LABOR." In that prohibiting the abolition of the African slave trade for twenty years, that trade is spoken of as "The migration or importation of such persons as any of the States NOW EXISTING, shall think proper to admit," &c. These are the only provisions alluding to slavery. Thus, the thing is hid away, in the constitution, just as an afflicted man hides away a wen or a cancer, which he dares not cut out at once, lest he bleed to death; with the promise, nevertheless, that the cutting may begin at the end of a given time.—Less than this our fathers COULD not do; and NOW they WOULD not do. Necessity drove them so far, and further, they would not go. But this is not all. The earlier Congress, under the constitution, took the same view of slavery. They hedged and hemmed it in to the narrowest limits of necessity.

In 1794, they prohibited an out-going slave trade—that is, the taking of slaves FROM the United States to sell.

In 1798, they prohibited the bringing of slaves from Africa

INTO the Mississippi Territory, this territory then comprising what are now the States of Mississippi and Alabama. This was TEN YEARS before they had the authority to do the same thing as to the States existing at the adoption of the constitution.

In 1800 they prohibited AMERICAN CITIZENS from trading in slaves between foreign countries—as, for instance, from Africa to Brazil.

In 1803 they passed a law in aid of one or two State laws, in restraint of the internal slave trade.

In 1807, in apparent hot haste, they passed the law, nearly a year in advance, to take effect the first day of 1808—the very first day the constitution would permit—prohibiting the African slave trade by heavy pecuniary and corporal penalties.

In 1820, finding these provisions ineffectual, they declared the trade piracy, and annexed to it, the extreme penalty of death. While all this was passing in the general government, five or six of the original slave States had adopted systems of gradual emancipation; by which the institution was rapidly becoming extinct within these limits.

Thus we see, the plain unmistakable spirit of that age, towards slavery, was hostility to the PRINCIPLE, and toleration, ONLY BY NECESSITY.

But NOW it is to be transformed into a "sacred right." Nebraska brings it forth, places it on the high road to extension and perpetuity; and, with a pat on its back, says to it, "Go, and God speed you." Henceforth it is to be the chief jewel of the nation—the very figurehead of the ship of State. Little by little, but steadily as man's march to the grave, we have been giving up the OLD for the NEW faith. Near eighty years ago we began by declaring that all men are created equal; but now from that beginning we have run down to the other declaration, that for SOME men to enslave OTHERS is a "sacred right of self-government." These principles can not stand together. They are as opposite as God and mammon; and whoever holds to the one, must despise the other. When Pettit, in connection with his support of the Nebraska bill, called the Declaration of Independence "a self-evident lie," he only did what consistency and candor require all other Nebraska men to do. Of the forty odd Nebraska

Senators who sat present and heard him, no one rebuked him. Nor am I apprized that any Nebraska newspaper, or any Nebraska orator, in the whole nation, has ever yet rebuked him. If this had been said among Marion's men, Southerners though they were, what would have become of the man who said it? If this had been said to the men who captured Andre, the man who said it, would probably have been hung sooner than Andre was. If it had been said in old Independence Hall, seventy-eight years ago, the very door-keeper would have throttled the man, and thrust him into the street.

Let no one be deceived. The spirit of seventy-six and the spirit of Nebraska, are utter antagonisms; and the former is being rapidly displaced by the latter.

Fellow-countrymen—Americans south, as well as north, shall we make no effort to arrest this? Already the liberal party throughout the world, express the apprehension "that the one retrograde institution in America, is undermining the principles of progress, and fatally violating the noblest political system the world ever saw." This is not the taunt of enemies, but the warning of friends. Is it quite safe to disregard it—to despise it? Is there no danger to liberty itself, in discarding the earliest practice, and first precept of our ancient faith? In our greedy chase to make profit of the negro, let us beware, lest we "cancel and tear to pieces" even the white man's charter of freedom.

Our republican robe is soiled, and trailed in the dust. Let us re-purify it. Let us turn and wash it white, in the spirit, if not the blood, of the Revolution. Let us turn slavery from its claims of "moral right" back upon its existing legal rights, and its arguments of "necessity."—Let us return it to the position our fathers gave it; and there let it rest in peace. Let us re-adopt the Declaration of Independence, and with it, the practices, and policy, which harmonize with it. Let north and south—let all Americans—let all lovers of liberty everywhere—join in the great and good work. If we do this, we shall not only have saved the Union; but we shall have so saved it, as to make, and to keep it, forever worthy of the saving. We shall have so saved it, that the succeeding millions of free happy people, the world over, shall rise up, and call us blessed, to the latest generations.

At Springfield, twelve days ago, where I had spoken substantially as I have here, Judge Douglas replied to me—and as he is to reply to me here, I shall attempt to anticipate him, by noticing some of the points he made there.

He commenced by stating I had assumed all the way through, that the principle of the Nebraska bill, would have the effect of extending slavery. He denied that this was INTENDED, or that this EFFECT would follow.

I will not re-open the argument upon this point. That such WAS the intention, the world believed at the start, and will continue to believe. This was the COUNTENANCE of the thing; and, both friends and enemies, instantly recognized it as such. That countenance can not now be changed by argument. You can as easily argue the color out of the negro's skin. Like the "bloody hand" you may wash it, and wash it, the red witness of guilt still sticks, and stares horribly at you.

Next he says, congressional intervention never prevented slavery any where—that it did not prevent it in the north west territory, now in Illinois—that in fact, Illinois came into the Union as a slave State—that the principle of the Nebraska bill expelled it from Illinois, from several old States, from every where.

Now this is mere quibbling all the way through. If the ordinance of '87 did not keep slavery out of the north west territory, how happens it that the north west shore of the Ohio River is entirely free from it; while the south east shore, less than a mile distant, along nearly the whole length of the river, is entirely covered with it?

If that ordinance did not keep it out of Illinois, what was it that made the difference between Illinois and Missouri? They lie side by side, the Mississippi river only dividing them; while their early settlements were within the same latitude. Between 1810 and 1820 the number of slaves in Missouri INCREASED 7,211; while in Illinois, in the same ten years, they DECREASED 51.—This appears by the census returns. During nearly all of that ten years, both were territories—not States. During this time the ordinance forbid slavery to go into Illinois; and NOTHING forbid it to go into Missouri. It DID go into Missouri, and did NOT go into Illinois.—That is the fact. Can any one doubt as to the reason of it?

But, he says, Illinois came into the Union as a slave State. Silence, perhaps, would be the best answer to this flat contradiction of the known history of the country. What are the facts upon which this bold assertion is based? When we first acquired the country, as far back as 1787, there were some slaves within it, held by the French inhabitants at Kaskaskia. The territorial legislation, admitted a few negroes, from the slave States, as indentured servants. One year after the adoption of the first State constitution the whole number of them was—what do you think? just 117—while the aggregate free population was 55,094—about 470 to one. Upon this state of facts, the people framed their constitution prohibiting the further introduction of slavery, with a sort of guaranty to the owners of the few indentured servants, giving freedom to their children to be born thereafter, and making no mention whatever, of any supposed slave for life. Out of this small matter, the Judge manufactures his argument that Illinois came into the Union as a slave State. Let the facts be the answer to the argument.

The principles of the Nebraska bill, he says, expelled slavery from Illinois. The principle of that bill first planted it here—that is, it first came, because there was no law to prevent it—first came before we owned the country; and finding it here, and having the ordinance of '87 to prevent its increasing, our people struggled along, and finally got rid of it as best they could.

But the principle of the Nebraska bill abolished slavery in several of the old States.—Well, it is true that several of the old States, in the last quarter of the last century, did adopt systems of gradual emancipation, by which the institution has finally become extinct within their limits; but it MAY OR MAY NOT be true that the principle of the Nebraska bill was the cause that led to the adoption of these measures. It is now more than fifty years, since the last of these States adopted its system of emancipation. If Nebraska Bill is the real author of these benevolent works, it is rather deplorable, that he has, for so long a time, ceased working altogether. Is there not some reason to suspect that it was the principle of the REVOLUTION, and not the principle of Nebraska Bill, that led to emancipation in these old States? Leave it to the people of these old emancipating States, and I am quite sure they will decide, that neither that, nor any other good thing, ever did, or ever will come of Nebraska Bill.

In the course of my main argument, Judge Douglas interrupted me to say, that the principle of the Nebraska bill was very old; that it originated when God made man and placed good and evil before him, allowing him to choose for himself, being responsible for the choice he should make. At the time I thought this was merely playful; and I answered it accordingly. But in his reply to me he renewed it, as a serious argument. In seriousness then, the facts of this proposition are not true as stated. God did not place good and evil before man, telling him to make his choice. On the contrary, he did tell him there was one tree, of the fruit of which, he should not eat, upon pain of certain death. I should scarcely wish so strong a prohibition against slavery in Nebraska.

But this argument strikes me as not a little remarkable in another particular—in its strong resemblance to the old argument for the 'Divine right of Kings.' By the latter, the King is to do just as he pleases with his white subjects, being responsible to God alone. By the former, the white man is to do just as he pleases with his black slaves, being responsible to God alone. The two things are precisely alike, and it is but natural that they should find similar arguments to sustain them.

I had argued, that the application of the principle of self-government, as contended for, would require the revival of the African slave trade—that no argument could be made in favor of a man's right to take slaves to Nebraska, which could not be equally well made in favor of his right to bring them from the coast of Africa.—The judge replied that the Constitution requires the suppression of the foreign slave-trade; but does not require the prohibition of slavery in the territories. That is a mistake, in point of fact. The Constitution does NOT require the action of Congress in either case; and it does AUTHORIZE it in both. And so, there is still no difference between the cases.

In regard to what I had said, the advantage the slave States have over the free, in the matter of representation, the Judge replied that we, in the free States, count five free negroes as five white people, while in the slave States, they count five slaves as three whites only; and that the advantage, at last, was on the side of the free States.

Now, in the slave States, they count free negroes just as we do; and it so happens that besides their slaves, they have as many free negroes as we have, and thirty-three thousand over.—Thus their free negroes more than balance ours; and their advantage over us, in consequence of their slaves, still remains as I stated it.

In reply to my argument, that the compromise measures of 1850, were a system of equivalents; and that the provisions of no one of them could fairly be carried to other subjects, without its corresponding equivalent being carried with it, the judge denied out-right, that these measures had any connection with, or dependence upon, each other. This is mere desperation. If they have no connection, why are they always spoken of in connection? Why has he so spoken of them, a thousand times? Why has he constantly called them a SERIES of measures? Why does everybody call them a compromise? Why was California kept out of the Union, six or seven months, if it was not because of its connection with the other measures? Webster's leading definition of the verb "to compromise" is "to adjust and settle a difference, by mutual agreement, with concessions of claims by the parties." This conveys precisely the popular understanding of the word "compromise." We knew, before the judge told us, that these measures passed separately, and in distinct bills; and that no two of them were passed by the votes of precisely the same members. But we also know, and so does he know, that no one of them could have passed both branches of Congress but for the understanding that the others were to pass also. Upon this understanding each got votes, which it could have got in no other way. It is this fact, which gives to the measures their true character; and it is the universal knowledge of this fact, that has given them the name of "compromise," so expressive of that true character.

I had asked "If in carrying the provisions of the Utah and New Mexico laws to Nebraska, you could clear away other objection, how can you leave Nebraska "perfectly free" to introduce slavery BEFORE she forms a constitution—during her territorial government?—while the Utah and New Mexico laws only authorize it WHEN they form constitutions, and are admitted into the Union?" To this Judge Douglas answered that the Utah and New Mexico laws, also authorized it BEFORE; and to prove this, he read from one of their laws, as follows: "That the legislative power of said territory shall extend to all rightful subjects of legislation consistent with the constitution of the United States and the provisions of this act."

Now it is perceived from the reading of this, that there is nothing express upon the subject; but that the authority is sought to be implied merely, for the general provision of "all rightful subjects of legislation." In reply to this, I insist, as a legal rule of construction, as well as the plain popular view of the matter, that the EXPRESS provision for Utah and New Mexico coming in with slavery if they choose, when they shall form constitutions, is an EXCLUSION of all implied authority on the same subject—that Congress, having the subject distinctly in their minds, when they made the express provision, they therein expressed their WHOLE meaning on that subject.

The judge rather insinuated that I had found it convenient to forget the Washington territorial law passed in 1853. This was a division of Oregon, organizing the northern part, as the territory of Washington. He asserted that, by this act, the ordinance of '87 theretofore existing in Oregon, was repealed; that nearly all the members of Congress voted for it, beginning in the H. R., with Charles Allen of Massachusetts, and ending with Richard Yates, of Illinois; and that he could not understand how those who now oppose the Nebraska bill, so voted then, unless it was because it was then too soon after both the great political parties had ratified. the compromises of 1850, and the ratification therefore too fresh, to be then repudiated.

Now I had seen the Washington act before; and I have carefully examined it since; and I aver that there is no repeal of the ordinance of '87, or of any prohibition of slavery, in it. In express terms, there is absolutely nothing in the whole law upon the subject—in fact, nothing to lead a reader to THINK of the subject. To my judgment, it is equally free from every thing from which such repeal can be legally implied; but however this may be, are men now to be entrapped by a legal implication, extracted from covert language, introduced perhaps, for the very purpose of entrapping them? I sincerely wish every man could read this law quite through, carefully watching every sentence, and every line, for a repeal of the ordinance of '87 or any thing equivalent to it.

Another point on the Washington act. If it was intended to be modelled after the Utah and New Mexico acts, as Judge Douglas insists, why was it not inserted in it, as in them, that Washington was to come in with or without slavery as she may choose at the adoption of her constitution? It has no such provision in it; and I defy the ingenuity of man to give a reason for the omission, other than that it was not intended to follow the Utah and New Mexico laws in regard to the question of slavery.

The Washington act not only differs vitally from the Utah and New Mexico acts; but the Nebraska act differs vitally from both. —By the latter act the people are left "perfectly free" to regulate their own domestic concerns, &c.; but in all the former, all their laws are to be submitted to Congress, and if disapproved are to be null. The Washington act goes even further; it absolutely prohibits the territorial legislation, by very strong and guarded language, from establishing banks, or borrowing money on the faith of the territory. Is this the sacred right of self-government we hear vaunted so much? No sir, the Nebraska bill finds no model in the acts of '50 or the Washington act. It finds no model in any law from Adam till to-day. As Phillips says of Napoleon, the Nebraska act is grand, gloomy, and peculiar; wrapped in the solitude of its own originality; without a model, and without a shadow upon the earth.

In the course of his reply, Senator Douglas remarked, in substance, that he had always considered this government was made for the white people and not for the negroes. Why, in point of mere fact, I think so too. But in this remark of the Judge, there is a significance, which I think is the key to the great mistake (if there is any such mistake) which he has made in this Nebraska measure. It shows that the Judge has no very vivid impression that the negro is a human; and consequently has no idea that there can be any moral question in legislating about him. In his view, the question of whether a new country shall be slave or free, is a matter of as utter indifference, as it is whether his neighbor shall plant his farm with tobacco, or stock it with horned cattle. Now, whether this view is right or wrong, it is very certain that the great mass of mankind take a totally different view.—They consider slavery a great moral wrong; and their feeling against it, is not evanescent, but eternal. It lies at the very foundation of their sense of justice; and it cannot be trifled with.—It is a great and durable element of popular action, and I think, no statesman can safely disregard it.

Our Senator also objects that those who oppose him in this measure do not entirely agree with one another. He reminds me that in my firm adherence to the constitutional rights of the slave States, I differ widely from others who are co-operating with me in opposing the Nebraska bill; and he says it is not quite fair to oppose him in this variety of ways. He should remember that he took us by surprise—astounded us—by this measure. We were thunderstruck and stunned; and we reeled and fell in utter confusion. But we rose each fighting, grasping whatever he could first reach—a scythe—a pitchfork—a chopping axe, or a butcher's cleaver. We struck in the direction of the sound, and we are rapidly closing in upon him. He must not think to divert us from our purpose, by showing us that our drill, our dress, and our weapons, are not entirely perfect and uniform. When the storm shall be past, he shall find us still Americans; no less devoted to the continued Union and prosperity of the country than heretofore.

Finally, the Judge invokes against me, the memory of Clay and of Webster. They were great men, and men of great deeds. But where have I assailed them? For what is it, that their life-long enemy, shall now make profit, by assuming to defend them against me, their life-long friend? I go against the repeal of the Missouri Compromise; did they ever go for it? They went for the compromise of 1850; did I ever go against them? They were greatly devoted to the Union; to the small measure of my ability, was I ever less so? Clay and Webster were dead before this question arose; by what authority shall our Senator say they would espouse his side of it, if alive? Mr. Clay was the leading spirit in making the Missouri Compromise; is it very credible that if now alive, he would take the lead in the breaking of it? The truth is that some support from whigs is now a necessity with the Judge, and for this it is, that the names of Clay and Webster are now invoked. His old friends have deserted him in such numbers as to leave too few to live by. He came to his own, and his own received him not, and Lo! he turns unto the Gentiles.

A word now as to the Judge's desperate assumption that the compromises of '50 had no connection with one another; that Illinois came into the Union as a slave State, and some other similar ones. This is no other than a bold denial of the history of the country. If we do not know that the compromises of '50 were dependent on each other; if we do not know that Illinois came into the Union as a free State—we do not know any thing. If we do not know these things, we do not know that we ever had a revolutionary war, or such a chief as Washington. To deny these things is to deny our national axioms, or dogmas, at least; and it puts an end to all argument. If a man will stand up and assert, and repeat, and re-assert, that two and two do not make four, I know nothing in the power of argument that can stop him. I think I can answer the Judge so long as he sticks to the premises; but when he flies from them, I cannot work an argument into the consistency of a maternal gag, and actually close his mouth with it. In such a case I can only commend him to the seventy thousand answers just in from Pennsylvania, Ohio and Indiana.

Lincoln's seriousness in this speech has so often impressed his readers that they have missed the humor and sarcasm which no audience could possibly have failed to enjoy. To follow Lincoln as he drags Douglas over the coals, exposing his inconsistency and lack of historical perspective not merely by counter arguments but by trenchant irony and sarcasm, one must disillusion oneself of the somewhat pale image of the martyred saint and savior of the nation, and recognize the hard-hitting, dangerous opponent in political debate whom Douglas learned to respect long before the nation ever awakened to Lincoln's power with words.

A case in point is Lincoln's sarcastic figure of speech

in the last paragraph. That the identity of "a maternal gag" bothered even Nicolay and Hay is indicated by the fact that they emended the word maternal *to* mental, *leaving to the reader the even more difficult problem of deciding what "the consistency of a* mental *gag" could possibly be, and how it could close the mouth of an incoherent babbler. Lincoln was alluding to the perhaps now archaic maternal practice of stopping the mouth of a yelling infant with something—sugar-tit or other variety of pacifier—in order that adults in the vicinity might be heard. What the figure lacks in dignity is more than made up in effectiveness.*

The text of this speech is from the Illinois State Journal. *So far as the editor is aware, this is the only complete and authorized version of the speech published at the time. The first installment in the* Journal *of October 21, 1854, is preceded by the following prefatory remarks:*

"On Monday, October 16, Senator Douglas, by appointment, addressed a large audience at Peoria. When he closed he was greeted with six hearty cheers; and the band in attendance played a stirring air. The crowd then began to call for LINCOLN, *who, as Judge Douglas had announced was, by agreement, to answer him. Mr. Lincoln took the stand and said—*

"'I do not arise to speak now, if I can stipulate with the audience to meet me here at half past 6 or 7 o'clock. It is now several minutes past five, and Judge Douglas has spoken over three hours. If you hear me at all, I wish you to hear me thro'. It will take me as long as it has taken him. That will carry us beyond eight o'clock at night. Now every one of you who can remain that long can just as well get his supper, meet me at seven, and remain one hour or two later. The judge has already informed you that he is to have an hour to reply to me. I doubt not but you have been a little surprised to learn that I have consented to give one of his high reputation and known ability, this advantage of me. Indeed, my

consenting to it, though reluctant, was not wholly unselfish, for I suspected if it were understood, that the judge was entirely done, you democrats would leave and not hear me; but by giving him the close, I felt confident you would stay for the fun of hearing him skin me.'

"The audience signified their assent to the arrangement, and adjourned to 7 o'clock P.M., at which time they reassembled, and MR. LINCOLN *spoke substantially as follows . . ."*

LETTER TO E. B. WASHBURNE DECEMBER 14, 1854

Springfield, Dec: 14. 1854

Hon: E. B. Washburne
My dear Sir:

So far as I am concerned, there must be something wrong about U. S. Senator, at Chicago. My most intimate friends there do not answer my letters; and I can not get a word from them. Wentworth has a knack of knowing things better than most men. I wish you would pump him, and write me what you get from him. Please do this as soon as you can, as the time is growing short. Dont let *any one* know I have written you this; for there may be those opposed to me, nearer about you than you think.

Very truly Yours &c
A. Lincoln

Lincoln wrote numerous "political" letters during his first race for the United States Senate. Many of them are shrewd, deft, and political in the best sense, but few are of as much interest to the general reader as the series written to Washburne of Galena, Whig Congressman,

1853-59. Of these, this and the succeeding letter, in which Lincoln recounts the story of his defeat, are the most interesting. John Wentworth, "Long John" as he was known, was editor of the Chicago Democrat, *Congressman, 1844-58, an old anti-slavery man and one of the founders of the Republican party.*

LETTER TO E. B. WASHBURNE
FEBRUARY 9, 1855

Springfield, Feby. 9 1855—

Hon: E. B. Washburne.
My dear Sir:

The agony is over at last; and the result you doubtless know. I write this only to give you some particulars to explain what might appear difficult of understanding. I began with 44 votes, Shields 41, and Trumbull 5—yet Trumbull was elected. In fact 47 different members voted for me—getting three new ones on the second ballot, and losing four old ones. How came my 47 to yield to T's 5? It was Govr. Matteson's work. He has been secretly a candidate every [*sic*] since (before, even) the fall election. All the members round about the canal were Anti-Nebraska, but were, nevertheless nearly all democrats, and old personal friends of his. His plan was to privately impress them with the belief that he was as good Anti-Nebraska as any one else—at least could be secured to be so by instructions, which could be easily passed. In this way he got from four to six of that sort of men to really prefer his election to that of any other man—all "sub rosa" of course. One notable instance of this sort was with Mr. Strunk of Kankakee. At the beginning of the session he came a volunteer to tell me he was for me and would walk a hundred miles to elect me; but lo, it was not long before he leaked it out that he was going for me the first few ballots and then for Govr. Matteson.

The Nebraska men, of course, were not for Matteson; but when they found they could elect no avowed Nebraska man they tardily determined, to let him get whomever of our men he could by whatever means he could and ask him no questions. In the mean time Osgood, Don Morrison & Trapp of St. Clair had openly gone over from us. With the united Nebraska force, and their recruits, open & covert, it gave Matteson more than enough to elect him. We saw into it plainly ten days ago; but with every possible effort, could not head it off. All that remained of the Anti-Nebraska force, excepting Judd, Cook, Palmer Baker & Allen of Madison, & two or three of the secret Matteson men, would go into caucus, & I could get the nomination of that caucus. But the three Senators & one of the two representatives above named "could never vote for a whig" and this incensed some twenty whigs to "think" they would never vote for the man of the five. So we stood, and so we went into the fight yesterday; the Nebraska men very confident of the election of Matteson, though denying that he was a candidate; and we very much believing also, that they would elect him. But they wanted first to make a show of good faith to Shields by voting for him a few times, and our secret Matteson men also wanted to make a show of good faith by voting with us a few times. So we led off. On the seventh ballot, I think, the signal was given to the Neb. men, to turn on to Matteson, which they acted on to a man, with one exception; my old friend Strunk going with them giving him 44 votes. Next ballot the remaining Neb. man, & one pretended Anti. went on to him, giving him 46. The next still another giving him 47, wanting only three of an election. In the mean time, our friends with a view of detaining our expected bolters had been turning from me to Trumbull till he he [*sic*] had risen to 35 & I had been reduced to 15. These would never desert me except by my direction; but I became satisfied that if we could prevent Matteson's election one or two ballots more, we could not possibly do so a single ballot after my friends should begin to return to me from Trumbull. So I determined to strike at once; and accordingly advised my remaining friends to go for him, which they did & elected him on that the 10th. ballot.

Such is the way the thing was done. I think you would have

done the same under the circumstances; though Judge Davis, who came down this morning, declares he never would have consented to the 47 men being controlled by the 5. I regret my defeat moderately, but I am not nervous about it. I could have headed off every combination and been elected, had it not been for Matteson's double game—and his defeat now gives me more pleasure than my own gives me pain. On the whole, it is perhaps as well for our general cause that Trumbull is elected. The Neb. men confess that they hate it worse than any thing that could have happened. It is a great consolation to see them worse whipped than I am. I tell them it is their own fault—that they had abundant opertunity [*sic*] to choose between him & me, which they declined, and in stead forced it on me to decide between him & Matteson.

With my grateful acknowledgments for the kind, active, and continued interest you have taken for me in this matter, allow me to subscribe myself

Yours forever
A. Lincoln—

LETTER TO OWEN LOVEJOY
AUGUST 11, 1855

Springfield, August 11—1855

Hon: Owen Lovejoy:
My dear Sir:

Yours of the 7th. was received the day before yesterday. Not even *you* are more anxious to prevent the extension of slavery than I; and yet the political atmosphere is such, just now, that I fear to do any thing, lest I do wrong. Knownothingism has not yet entirely tumbled to pieces—nay, it is even a little encouraged by the late elections in Tennessee, Kentucky & Alabama. Until we can get the elements of this organization, there is not sufficient materials to successfully combat the Nebraska democracy with.

We can not get them so long as they cling to a hope of success under their own organization; and I fear an open push by us now, may offend them, and tend to prevent our ever getting them. About us here, they are mostly my old political and personal friends; and I have hoped their organization would die out without the painful necessity of my taking an open stand against them. Of their principles I think little better than I do of those of the slavery extentionists [*sic*]. Indeed I do not perceive how any one professing to be sensitive to the wrongs of the negroes, can join in a league to degrade a class of white men.

I have no objection to "fuse" with any body provided I can fuse on ground which I think is right; and I believe the opponents of slavery extension could now do this, if it were not for the K. N.ism. In many speeches last summer I advised those who did me the honor of a hearing to "stand with any body who stands right" —and I am still quite willing to follow my own advice. I lately saw, in the Quincy Whig, the report of a preamble and resolutions, made by Mr. Williams, as chairman of a Committee, to a public meeting and adopted by the meeting. I saw them but once, and have them not now at command; but so far as I can remember them, they occupy about the ground I should be willing to "fuse" upon.

As to my personal movements this summer, and fall, I am quite busy trying to pick up my lost crumbs of last year. I shall be here till September; then to the circuit till the 20th. then to Cincinnati, awhile, after a Patent right case; and back to the circuit to the end of November. I can be seen here any time this month; and at Bloomington at any time from the 10th. to the 17th. of September. As to an extra session of the Legislature, I should know no better how to bring that about, than to lift myself over a fence by the straps of my boots.

Yours truly
A. Lincoln—

Lovejoy was a radical anti-slavery man and an organizer of the Republican party in Illinois who had been trying for more than a year to get Lincoln lined up with the new party. This letter, together with the immediately following ones to Robertson and Speed, illustrates Lincoln's indecision in the summer of 1855 as to his party allegiance. Whigism was dead, but Lincoln clung to it. He was slow to accept "fusion" as Republicanism was called, though not entirely opposed to it. In contrast with this indecision, his personal position in regard to principle is wholly clear to his own mind. Not until he became convinced that the new party could be restrained in its more radical elements was he ready to "fuse."

LETTER TO GEORGE ROBERTSON AUGUST 15, 1855

Springfield, Ills. Aug: 15. 1855

Hon: Geo. Robertson
Lexington, Ky.
My dear Sir:

The volume you left for me has been received. I am really grateful for the honor of your kind remembrance, as well as for the book. The partial reading I have already given it, has afforded me much of both pleasure and instruction. It was new to me that the exact question which led to the Missouri Compromise, has arisen before it arose in regard to Missouri; and that you had taken so prominent a part in it. Your short, but able and patriotic speech upon that occasion, has not been improved upon since, by those holding the same views; and, with all the lights you then had, the views you took appear to me as very reasonable.

You are not a friend to slavery in the abstract. In that speech you spoke of "*the peaceful extinction of slavery*" and used other expressions indicating your belief that the thing was, at some time, to have an end Since then we have had thirty six years of experience; and this experience has demonstrated, I think, that there is no peaceful extinction of slavery in prospect for us. The signal failure of Henry Clay, and other good and great men, in 1849, to effect anything in favor of gradual emancipation in Kentucky, together with a thousand other signs, extinguishes that hope utterly. On the question of liberty, as a principle, we are not what we have been.

When we were the political slaves of King George, and wanted to be free, we called the maxim that "all men are created equal" a self evident truth; but now when we have grown fat, and have lost all dread of being slaves ourselves, we have become so greedy to be *masters* that we call the same maxim "a self-evident lie" The fourth of July has not quite dwindled away; it is still a great day—*for burning fire-crackers!!!*

That spirit which desired the peaceful extinction of slavery, has itself become extinct, with the *occasion*, and the *men* of the Revolution. Under the impulse of that occasion, nearly half the states adopted systems of emancipation at once; and it is a significant fact, that not a single state has done the like since. So far as peaceful, voluntary emancipation is concerned, the condition of the negro slave in America, scarcely less terrible to the contemplation of a free mind, is now so fixed, and hopeless of change for the better, as that of the lost souls of the finally impenitent. The Autocrat of all the Russias will resign his crown, and proclaim his subjects free republicans, sooner than will our American masters voluntarily give up their slaves.

Our political problem now is "Can we, as a nation, continue together *permanently—forever*—half slave, and half free?" The problem is too mighty for me. May God, in his mercy, superintend the solution.

Your much obliged friend,
and humble servant
A. Lincoln—

Judge George Robertson of Lexington, Kentucky, counsel for Lincoln and the other Illinois heirs in their suit against Robert Wickliffe, was Professor of Law in

Transylvania College, and a member of the Sixteenth Congress which had adopted the Missouri Compromise. He had published a collection of his speeches on slavery and other topics of public interest, entitled Scrap Book on Law and Politics, Men and Times, *a copy of which he had left in Lincoln's office on a visit which found Lincoln away. Lincoln had claimed in his "Speech at Peoria" that Congress had not acted upon the question of the extension of slavery into the Territories before the Missouri Compromise of 1820, but learned from Robertson's book that the question had been acted upon in regard to the Arkansas Territory in 1819. The last paragraph of the letter should be noted as the earliest suggestion in Lincoln's writings of the phraseology which electrified the campaign against Douglas in the "House Divided Speech," June 16, 1858.*

LETTER TO JOSHUA F. SPEED
AUGUST 24, 1855

Springfield, Aug: 24. 1855

Dear Speed:

You know what a poor correspondent I am. Ever since I received your very agreeable letter of the 22nd. of May I have been intending to write you in answer to it. You suggest that in political action now, you and I would differ. I suppose we would; not quite as much, however, as you may think. You know I dislike slavery; and you fully admit the abstract wrong of it. So far there is no cause of difference. But you say that sooner than yield your legal right to the slave—especially at the bidding of those who are not themselves interested, you would see the Union dissolved. I am not aware that *any one* is bidding you to yield that right; very certainly *I* am not. I leave that matter entirely to yourself. I also acknowledge *your* rights and *my* obligations, under the constitution, in regard to your slaves. I confess I hate to see the poor creatures hunted down, and caught, and carried back to their stripes, and unrewarded toils; but I bite my lip and keep quiet. In 1841 you and I had together a tedious low-water trip, on a Steam Boat from Louisville to St. Louis. You may remember, as I well do, that from Louisville to the mouth of the Ohio, there were, on board, ten or a dozen slaves, shackled together with irons. That sight was a continued torment to me; and I see something like it every time I touch the Ohio, or any other slave-border. It is hardly fair for you to assume, that I have no interest in a thing which has, and continually exercises, the power of making me miserable. You ought rather to appreciate how much the great body of the Northern people do crucify their feelings, in order to maintain their loyalty to the Constitution and the Union.

I do oppose the extension of slavery, because my judgment and feelings so prompt me; and I am under no obligation to the contrary. If for this you and I must differ, differ we must. You say if you were President, you would send an army and hang the leaders of the Missouri outrages upon the Kansas elections; still, if Kansas fairly votes herself a slave state, she must be admitted, or the Union must be dissolved. But how if she votes herself a slave State *unfairly*—that is, by the very means for which you say you would hang men? Must she still be admitted, or the Union be dissolved? That will be the phase of the question when it first becomes a practical one. In your assumption that there may be a *fair* decision of the slavery question in Kansas, I plainly see you and I would differ about the Nebraska-law. I look upon that enactment not as a *law*, but as *violence* from the beginning. It was conceived in violence, passed in violence, is maintained in violence, and is being executed in violence. I say it was *conceived* in violence, because the destruction of the Missouri Compromise, under the circumstances, was nothing less than violence. It was *passed* in violence, because it could not have passed at all but for the votes of many members in violence of the known will of their constituents. It is *maintained* in violence because the elections since, clearly demand it's repeal, and this demand is openly disregarded. *You* say men ought to be hung for the way they are executing that law; and *I* say the way it is being executed is quite as good as any of its antecedents. It is being executed in the precise way which was intended from the first; else why does no Nebraska man express astonishment or condemnation? Poor Reeder is the only public man who has been silly enough to believe that any thing like fairness was ever intended; and he has been bravely undeceived.

That Kansas will form a Slave Constitution, and, with it, will ask to be admitted into the Union, I take to be an already settled question; and so settled by the very means you so pointedly condemn. By every principle of law, ever held by any court, North or South, every negro taken to Kansas is free; yet, in utter disregard of this—in the spirit of violence merely—that beautiful Legislature gravely passes a law to hang men who shall venture to inform a negro of his legal rights. This is the substance, and real object of the law. If, like Haman, they should hang upon the gallows of their own building, I shall not be among the mourners for their fate.

In my humble sphere, I shall advocate the restoration of the Missouri Compromise, so long as Kansas remains a territory; and when, by all these foul means, it seeks to come into the Union as a Slave-state, I shall oppose it. I am very loth, in any case, to withhold my assent to the enjoyment of property *acquired*, or *located*, in good faith; but I do not admit that *good faith*, in taking a negro to Kansas, to be held in slavery, is a *possibility* with any man. Any man who has sense enough to be the controller of his own property, has too much sense to misunderstand the outrageous character of this whole Nebraska business. But I digress. In my opposition to the admission of Kansas I shall have some company; but we may be beaten. If we are, I shall not, on that account, attempt to dissolve the Union. On the contrary, if we succeed, there will be enough of us to take care of the Union. I think it probable, however, we shall be beaten. Standing as a unit among yourselves, you can, directly, and indirectly, bribe enough of our men to carry the day—as you could on an open proposition to establish monarchy. Get hold of some man in the North, whose position and ability is such, that he can make the support of your measure—whatever it may be—*a democratic party necessity*, and the thing is done. *Appropos* [*sic*] of this, let me tell you an anecdote. Douglas introduced the Nebraska bill in January. In February afterwards, there was a call session of the Illinois Legislature. Of the one hundred members composing the two branches of that body, about seventy were democrats. These latter held a caucus, in which the Nebraska bill was talked of, if not formally discussed. It was thereby discovered that just three, and no more, were in favor of the measure. In a day or two Dougla's [*sic*] orders came on to have resolutions passed approving the bill; and they were passed by large majorities!!! The truth of this is vouched for by a bolting democratic member. The masses too, democratic as well as whig, were even, nearer unanamous [*sic*] against it; but as soon as the party necessity of supporting it, became apparent, the way the democracy began to see the *wisdom* and *justice* of it, was perfectly astonishing.

You say if Kansas fairly votes herself a free state, as a Christian you will rather rejoice at it. All decent slaveholders *talk* that way; and I do not doubt their candor. But they never *vote* that way. Although in a private letter, or conversation, you will express your preference that Kansas shall be free, you would vote for no man for Congress who would say the same thing publicly. No such man could be elected from any district in a slave-state. You think Stringfellow & Co ought to be hung; and yet, at the next presidential election you will vote for the exact type and representative of Stringfellow. The slave-breeders and slave-traders, are a small, odious and detested class, among you; and yet in politics, they dictate the course of all of you, and are as completely your masters, as you are the master of your own negroes. You inquire where I now stand. That is a disputed point—I think I am a whig; but others say there are no whigs, and that I am an abolitionist. When I was at Washington I voted for the Wilmot Proviso as good as forty times, and I never heard of any one attempting to unwhig me for that. I now do no more than oppose the *extension* of slavery.

I am not a Know-Nothing. That is certain. How could I be? How can any one who abhors the oppression of negroes, be in favor of degrading classes of white people? Our progress in degeneracy appears to me to be pretty rapid. As a nation, we began by declaring that "*all men are created equal.*" We now practically read it "all men are created equal, *except negroes*" When the Know-Nothings get control, it will read "all men are created equal, except negroes, *and foreigners, and Catholics.*" When it comes to this I should prefer emigrating to some country where they make no pretence of loving liberty—to Russia, for instance, where despotism can be taken pure, and without the base alloy of hypocracy [*sic*].

Mary will probably pass a day to two in Louisville in October. My kindest regards to Mrs. Speed. On the leading subject of this letter, I have more of her sympathy than I have of yours. And yet let me say I am

Your friend forever
A. Lincoln.

Presumably this is the last significant letter Lincoln wrote to his friend Speed and the first one written since 1849. Two short notes, one in 1860 and the other in 1862, concluded the correspondence, but the friendship continued until Lincoln's death. Speed called to see Lincoln last about two weeks before the assassination. The story of that last visit between the two friends, as well as numerous other episodes in their lives, is told in Speed's Reminiscences of Abraham Lincoln. *The trip by steamboat which Lincoln recalls so vividly in this letter is the same which he describes in his fine "Letter to Miss Mary Speed," September 27, 1841.*

LETTER TO ISHAM REAVIS
NOVEMBER 5, 1855

Springfield, Novr. 5. 1855

Isham Reavis, Esq.
My Dear Sir:

I have just reached home, and found your letter of the 23rd. ult. I am from home too much of my time, for a young man to read law with me advantageously. If you are resolutely determined to make a lawyer of yourself, the thing is more than half done already. It is but a small matter whether you read *with* any body or not. I did not read with any one. Get the books, and read and study them till, you understand them in their principal features; and that is the main thing. It is of no consequence to be in a large town while you are reading. I read at New Salem, which never had three hundred people living in it. The *books*, and your *capacity* for understanding them, are just the same in all places. Mr. Dummer is a very clever man and an excellent lawyer (much better than I, in law-learning); and I have no doubt he will cheerfully tell you what books to read, and also loan you the books.

Always bear in mind that your own resolution to succeed, is more important than any other one thing.

Very truly your friend
A. Lincoln.

Apparently Isham Reavis lived in Beardstown, Cass County, Illinois, for the Illinois Supreme Court file records that he was admitted to the Bar from Cass County, July 30, 1857. That he followed Lincoln's advice and studied with Lincoln's old friend Henry Dummer, a Beardstown lawyer, seems probable. The advice given Reavis is much the same that Lincoln gave another hopeful student in the "Letter to James T. Thornton," December 2, 1858.

LETTER TO R. P. MORGAN
FEBRUARY 13, 1856

Springfield, Feby 13 1856

R. P. Morgan, Esq
Dear Sir:

Says Tom to John "Heres your old rotten wheelbarrow" "Ive broke it, usin on it" "I wish you would mend it, case I shall want to borrow it this arternoon."

Acting on this as a precedent, I say "Heres your old "chalked hat" "I wish you would take it, and send me a new one, case I shall want to use it the first of March"

Yours truly
A. Lincoln—

Morgan is listed in the Bloomington City Directory for 1855 as "Superintendent of the Chicago, Alton & St. Louis R.R." According to his own recollection years later, he was Superintendent of the "Chicago & M. Rd." (Ida M. Tarbell, In the Footsteps of the Lincolns, *p. 314). At any rate, Lincoln was returning an expired railroad pass and requesting a new one.*

FRÉMONT, BUCHANAN, AND THE EXTENSION OF SLAVERY: SPEECH DELIVERED AT KALAMAZOO, MICHIGAN. AUGUST 27, 1856

Fellow countrymen:—

Under the Constitution of the U. S. another Presidential contest approaches us. All over this land—that portion at least, of which I know much—the people are assembling to consider the proper course to be adopted by them. One of the first considerations is to learn what the people differ about. If we ascertain what we differ about, we shall be better able to decide. The question of slavery, at the present day, should be not only the greatest question, but very nearly the sole question. Our opponents, however, prefer that this should not be the case. To get at this question, I will occupy your attention but a single moment. The question is simply this:—Shall slavery be spread into the new Territories, or not? This is the naked question. If we should support Fremont successfully in this, it may be charged that we will not be content with restricting slavery in the new territories. If we should charge that James Buchanan, by his platform, is bound to extend slavery into the territories, and that he is in favor of its being thus spread, we should be puzzled to prove it. We believe it, nevertheless. By taking the issue as I present it, whether it shall be permitted as an issue, is made up between the parties. Each takes his own stand. This is the question: Shall the Government of the United States prohibit slavery in the United States.

We have been in the habit of deploring the fact that slavery exists amongst us. We have ever deplored it. Our forefathers did, and they declared, as we have done in later years, the blame rested on the mother Government of Great Britain. We constantly condemn Great Britain for not preventing slavery from coming amongst us. She would not interfere to prevent it, and so individuals were enabled to introduce the institution without opposition. I have alluded to this, to ask you if this is not exactly the policy of Buchanan and his friends, to place this government in the attitude then occupied by the government of Great Britain —placing the nation in the position to authorize the territories to reproach it, for refusing to allow them to hold slaves. I would like to ask your attention, any gentleman to tell me when the people of Kansas are going to decide. When are they to do it, How are they to do it? I asked that question two years ago—when, and how are [we?] to do it? Not many weeks ago, our new Senator from Illinois, (Mr. Trumbull) asked Douglas how it could be done. Douglas is a great man—at keeping from answering questions he don't want to answer. He would not answer. He said it was a question for the Supreme Court to decide. In the North, his friends argue that the people can decide it at any time. The Southerners say there is no power in the people, whatever. We know that from the time that white people have been allowed in the territory, they have brought slaves with them. Suppose the people come up to vote as freely, and with as perfect protection as we could do it here. Will they be at liberty to vote their sentiments? If they can, then all that has ever been said about our provincial ancestors is untrue, and they could have done so, also. We know our Southern friends say that the General Government cannot interfere. The people, say they, have no right to interfere. They could as truly say,—"It is amongst us—we cannot get rid of it."

But I am afraid I waste too much time on this point. I take it as an illustration of the principle, that slaves are admitted into the territories. And, while I am speaking of Kansas, how will that operate? Can men vote truly? We will suppose that there are ten men who go into Kansas to settle. Nine of these are opposed to slavery. One has ten slaves. The slaveholder is a good man in other respects; he is a good neighbor, and being a wealthy man, he is enabled to do the others many neighborly kindnesses. They like the man, though they don't like the system by which he holds his fellow-men in bondage. And here let me say, that in intellectual and physical structure, our Southern brethren do not differ from us. They are, like us, subject to passions, and it is only their odious institution of slavery, that makes the breach between us. These ten men of whom I was speaking, live together three or four years; they intermarry; their family ties are strengthened. And who wonders that in time, the people learn to look upon slavery with complacency? This is the way in which slavery is planted, and gains so firm a foothold. I think this is a strong card that the Nebraska party have played, and won upon, in this game.

I suppose that this crowd are opposed to the admission of slavery into Kansas, yet it is true that in all crowds there are some who differ from the majority. I want to ask the Buchanan men, who are against the spread of slavery, if there be any present, why not vote for the man who is against it? I understand that Mr. Fillmore's position is precisely like Buchanan's. I understand that, by the Nebraska bill, a door has been opened for the spread of slavery in the Territories. Examine, if you please, and see if they have ever done any such thing as try to shut the door. It is true that Fillmore tickles a few of his friends with the notion that he is not the cause of the door being opened. Well; it brings him into this position: he tries to get both sides, one by denouncing those who opened the door, and the other by hinting that he doesn't care a fig for its being open. If he were President, he would have one side or the other—he would either restrict slavery or not. Of course it would be so. There could be no middle way. You who hate slavery and love freedom, why not, as Fillmore and Buchanan are on the same ground, vote for Fremont? Why not vote for the man who takes your side of the question? "Well," says Buchanier [*sic*], "it is none of our business." But is it not *our* business? There are several reasons why I think it is our business. But let us see how it is. Others have urged these reasons before, but they are still of use. By our Constitution we are represented in Congress in proportion to numbers, and in counting the numbers that give us our representatives, three slaves are counted as two people. The State of Maine has six representatives in the lower house of Congress. In strength South Carolina is equal to her. But stop! Maine has *twice as many* white people, and 32,000 to boot! And is that fair? I don't complain of it. This regulation was put in force when the exigencies of the times demanded it, and could not have been avoided. Now, one man in South Carolina is the same as two men here. Maine should have twice as many men in Congress as South Carolina. It is a fact that any man in South

Carolina has more influence and power in Congress to-day than any two now before me. The same thing is true of all slave States, though it may not be in the same proportion. It is a truth that cannot be denied, that in all the free States no white man is the equal of the white man of the slave States. But this is in the Constitution, and we must stand up to it. The question, then is, "Have we no interest as to whether the white man of the North shall be the equal of the white man of the South?" Once when I used this argument in the presence of Douglas, he answered that in the North the black man was counted as a full man, and had an equal vote with the white, while at the South they were counted at but three-fifths. And Douglas, when he made this reply, doubtless thought he had forever silenced the objection.

Have we no interest in the free Territories of the United States—that they should be kept open for the homes of free white people? As our Northern States are growing more and more in wealth and population, we are continually in want of an outlet, through which it may pass out to enrich our country. In this we have an interest—a deep and abiding interest. There is another thing, and that is the mature knowledge we have—the greatest interest of all. It is the doctrine, that the people are to be driven from the maxims of our free Government, that despises the spirit which for eighty years has celebrated the anniversary of our national independence.

We are a great empire. We are eighty years old. We stand at once the wonder and admiration of the whole world, and we must enquire what it is that has given us so much prosperity, and we shall understand that to give up that one thing, would be to give up all future prosperity. This cause is that every man can make himself. It has been said that such a race of prosperity has been run nowhere else. We find a people on the North-east, who have a different government from ours, being ruled by a Queen. Turning to the South, we see a people who, while they boast of being free, keep their fellow beings in bondage. Compare our Free States with either, shall we say here that we have no interest in keeping that principle alive? Shall we say—"Let it be." No—we have an interest in the maintenance of the principles of the Government, and without this interest, it is worth nothing. I have noticed in Southern newspapers, particularly the Richmond *Enquirer*, the Southern view of the Free States. They insist that slavery has a right to spread. They defend it upon principle. They insist that their slaves are far better off than Northern freemen. What a mistaken view do these men have of Northern laborers! They think that men are always to remain laborers here—but there is no such class. The man who labored for another last year, this year labors for himself, and next year he will hire others to labor for him. These men don't understand when they think in this manner of Northern free labor. When these reasons can be introduced, tell me not that we have no interest in keeping the Territories free for the settlement of free laborers.

I pass, then, from this question. I think we have an ever growing interest in maintaining the free institutions of our country.

It is said that our party is a sectional party. It has been said in high quarters that if Fremont and Dayton were elected the Union would be dissolved. The South do not think so. I believe it! I believe it! It is a shameful thing that the subject is talked of so much. Did we not have a Southern President and Vice-President at one time? And yet the Union has not yet been dissolved. Why, at this very moment, there is a Northern President and Vice-President. Pierce and King were elected, and King died without ever taking his seat. The Senate elected a Northern man from their own numbers, to perform the duties of the Vice-President. He resigned his seat, however, as soon as he got the job of making a slave State out of Kansas. Was not that a great mistake?

(A voice.—"He didn't mean that!")

Then why didn't he speak what he did mean? Why did not he speak what he ought to have spoken? That was the very thing. He should have spoken manly, and we should then have known where to have found him. It is said we expect to elect Fremont by Northern votes. Certainly we do not think the South will elect him. But let us ask the question differently. Does not Buchanan expect to be elected by Southern votes? Fillmore, however, will go out of this contest the most national man we have. He has no prospect of having a single vote on either side of Mason and Dixon's line, to trouble his poor soul about.

We believe that it is right that slavery should not be tolerated in the new territories, yet we cannot get support for this doctrine, except in one part of the country. Slavery is looked upon by men in the light of dollars and cents. The estimated worth of the slaves at the South is $1,000,000,000, and in a very few years, if the institution shall be admitted into the territories, they will have increased fifty per cent in value.

Our adversaries charge Fremont with being an abolitionist. When pressed to show proof, they frankly confess that they can show no such thing. They then run off upon the assertion that his supporters are abolitionists. But this they have never attempted to prove. I know of no word in the language that has been used so much as that one "abolitionist," having no definition. It has no meaning unless taken as designating a person who is abolishing something. If that be its signification, the supporters of Fremont are not abolitionists. In Kansas all who come there are perfectly free to regulate their own social relations. There has never been a man there who was an abolitionist—for what was there to be abolished? People there had perfect freedom to express what they wished on the subject, when the Nebraska bill was first passed. Our friends in the South, who support Buchanan, have five disunion men to one at the North. This disunion is a sectional question. Who is to blame for it? Are we? I don't care how you express it. This government is sought to be put on a new track. Slavery is to be made a ruling element in our government. The question can be avoided in but two ways. By the one, we must submit, and allow slavery to triumph, or, by the other, we must triumph over the black demon. We have chosen the latter manner. If you of the North wish to get rid of this question, you must decide between these two ways—submit and vote for Buchanan, submit and vote that slavery is a just and good thing and immediately get rid of the question; or unite with us, and help us to triumph. We would all like to have the question done away with, but we cannot submit.

They tell us that we are in company with men who have long been known as abolitionists. What care we how many may feel disposed to labor for our cause? Why do not you, Buchanan men, come in and use your influence to make our party respectable? How is the dissolution of the Union to be consummated? They tell us that the Union is in danger. Who will divide it? Is it those who make the charge? Are they themselves the persons who wish to see this result? A majority will never dissolve the Union. Can a minority do it? When this Nebraska bill was first introduced into Congress, the sense of the Democratic party was outraged. That party has ever prided itself, that it was the friend of individual, universal freedom. It was that principle upon which they carried their measures. When the Kansas scheme was conceived, it was natural that this respect and sense should have been outraged. Now I make this appeal to the Democratic citizens here. Don't you find yourself making arguments in support of these measures, which you never would have made before? Did you ever do it before this Nebraska bill compelled you to do it? If you answer this in the affirmative, see how a whole party have been turned away from their love of liberty! And now, my Democratic friends, come forward. Throw off these things, and come to the rescue of this great principle of equality. Don't interfere with anything in the Constitution.—That must be maintained, for it is the only safeguard of our liberties. And not to Democrats alone do I make this appeal, but to all who love these great and true principles. Come, and keep coming! Strike, and strike again! So sure as God lives, the victory shall be yours.

The discovery of this important speech in the files of the Detroit Daily Advertiser *only a few years ago raises the question whether there may not be other important speeches undiscovered in the files of newspapers of the time. Although Lincoln campaigned strenuously for Frémont and made numerous speeches, this and "Sectionalism" are the only notable pieces we have. Earlier, in May, at the Bloomington Convention, Lincoln had delivered the legendary "Lost Speech" which has been supposed by some biographers to have been his greatest piece of oratory. However that may be, the year 1856 is notable in Lincoln's writings chiefly for the speech at*

Kalamazoo, which is hardly the equal of any one of several speeches delivered in 1858, or the "Dred Scott Speech" of 1857.

LETTER TO JULIAN M. STURTEVANT SEPTEMBER 27, 1856

Springfield, Sept. 27. 1856

Rev. J. M. Sturtevant
Jacksonville, Ills
My dear Sir:

Owing to absence yours of the 16th. was not received till the day-before yesterday. I thank you for your good opinion of me personally, and still more for the deep interest you take in the cause of our common country. It pains me a little that you have deemed it necessary to point out to me how I may be compensated for throwing myself in the breach now. This assumes that I am merely calculating the chances of personal advancement. Let me assure you that I decline to be a candidate for congress, on my clear conviction, that my running would *hurt*, & not *help* the cause. I am willing to make any personal sacrifice; but I am not willing to do, what in my own judgment, is a sacrifice of the cause itself.

Very truly Yours
A. Lincoln.

Julian M. Sturtevant was President of Illinois College at Jacksonville and a well-known anti-slavery man.

SECTIONALISM
[OCTOBER 1?], 1856

SECTIONALISM

It is constantly objected to Fremont & Dayton, that they are supported by a *sectional* party, who, by their *sectionalism*, endanger the National Union. This objection, more than all other, causes men, really opposed to slavery extension, to hesitate. Practically, it is the most difficult objection we have to meet.

For this reason, I now propose to examine it, a little more carefully than I have heretofore done, or seen it done by others.

First, then, what is the question between the parties, respectively represented by Buchanan and Fremomont [*sic*]?

Simply this: "*Shall slavery be allowed to extend into U. S. terrtories [*sic*], now legally free?*" Buchanan says it *shall*; and Fremont says it shall *not*.

That is the *naked* issue, and the *whole* of it. Lay the respective platforms side by side; and the difference between them, will be found to amount to precisely that.

True, each party charges upon the other, *designs* much beyond what is involved in the issue, as stated; but as these charges can not be fully proved either way, it is probably better to reject them on both sides, and stick to the naked issue, as it is clearly made up on the record.

And now, to restate the question "*Shall slavery be allowed to extend into U. S. terrtories [*sic*], now legally free?* I beg to know *how one* side of that question is more sectional than the other? Of course I expect to effect nothing with the man who makes this charge of sectionalism, without caring whether it is just or not. But of the *candid*, *fair*, man who has been puzzled with this charge, I do ask how is *one* side of this question, more *sectional*, than the other? I beg of him to consider well, and answer calmly.

If one side be as sectional as the other, nothing is gained, as to sectionalism, by changing sides; so that each must choose sides of the question on some other ground. As I should think, according, as the one side or the other, shall appear nearest right. If he shall really think slavery *ought* to be extended, let him go to Buchanan; if he think it ought *not* let [him?] go to Fremont.

But, Fremont and Dayton, are both residents of the free-states; and this fact has been vaunted, in high places, as excessive *sectionalism.*

While interested individuals become *indignant* and *excited,* against this manifestation of *sectionalism,* I am very happy to know, that the Constitution remains calm—keeps cool—upon the subject. It does say that President and Vice President shall be resident of different states; but it does not say one must live in a *slave,* and the other in a *free* state.

It has been a *custom* to take one from a slave, and the other from a free state; but the custom has not, at all been uniform. In 1828 Gen. Jackson and Mr. Calhoun, both from slave states, were placed on the same ticket; and Mr. Adams and Dr. Rush both from the free-states, were pitted against them. Gen. Jackson and Mr. Calhoun were elected; and qualified and served under the election; yet the whole thing never suggested the idea of sectionalism.

In 1841, the president, Gen. Harrison, died, by which Mr. Tyler, the Vice-President & a slave state man, became president. Mr. Mangum, another slave-state man, was placed in the Vice Presidential chair, served out the term, and no fuss about it—no sectionalism thought of.

In 1853 the present president came into office. He is a free-state man. Mr. King, the new Vice President elect, was a slave state man; but he died without entering on the duties of his office. At first, his vacancy was filled by Atchison, another slave-state man; but he soon resigned, and the place was supplied by Bright, a free-state man. So that right now, and for the year and a half last past, our president and vice-president are both actually free-state men.

But, it is said, the friends of Fremont, avow the purpose of electing him exclusively by free-state votes, and that this is unendurable sectionalism.

This statement of fact, is not exactly true. With the friends of Fremont, it is an *expected necessity*, but it is not an "*avowed purpose*," to elect him, if at all, principally, by free state votes; but it is, with equal intensity, true that Buchanan's friends expect to elect him, if at all, chiefly by slave-state votes.

Here, agan [*sic*], the sectionalism, is just as much on one side as the other.

The thing which gives most color to the charge of Sectionalism, made against those who oppose the spread of slavery into free terrtory [*sic*], is the fact that *they* can get no votes in the slave-states, while their opponents get all, or nearly so, in the slave-states, and also, a large number in the free States. To state it in another way, the Extensionists, can get votes all over the Nation, while the Restrictionists can get them only in the free states.

This being the fact, *why* is it so? It is not because one *side* of the question dividing them, is more sectional than the *other*; nor because of any difference in the mental or moral structure of the people North and South. It is because, in that question, the people of the South have an immediate palpable and immenesly [*sic*] great pecuniary interest; while, with the people of the North, it is merely an abstract question of moral right, with only *slight*, and *remote* pecuniary interest added.

The slaves of the South, at a moderate estimate, are worth a thousand millions of dollars. Let it be permanently settled that this property may extend to new teritory [*sic*], without restraint, and it greatly *enhances*, perhaps quite *doubles*, its value at once. This immense, palpable pecuniary interest, on the question of extending slavery, unites the Southern people, as one man. But it can not be demonstrated that the *North* will gain a dollar by restricting it.

Moral principle is all, or nearly all, that unites us of the North. Pity 'tis, it is so, but this is a looser bond than pecuniary interest. Right here is the plain cause of *their perfect* union and *our want of it*. And see how *it* works. If a Southern man aspires to be president, they choke him down instantly, in order that the glittering prize of the presidency, may be held up, on Southern terms, to the greedy eyes of Northern ambition. With this they tempt us, and break in upon us.

The democratic party, in 1844, elected a Southern president. Since then, they have neither had a Southern candidate for *election*, or *nomination*. Their conventions of 1848-1852 and 1856, have been struggles exclusively among *Northern* men, each vieing [*sic*] to outbid the other for the Southern vote—the South standing calmly by to finally cry going, going, gone, to the highest bidder; and, at the same time, to make its power more distinctly seen, and thereby to secure a still higher bid at the next succeeding struggle.

"Actions speak louder than words" is the maxim; and, if true, the South now distinctly says to the North "Give us the *measures*, and you take the *men*"

The total withdrawal of Southern aspirants, for the presidency, multiplies the number of Northern ones. These last, in competing with each other, commit themselves to the utmost verge that, through their own greediness, they have the least hope their Northern supporters will bear. Having got committed, in a race of competition, necessity drives them into union to sustain themselves. Each, at first secures all he can, on personal attachments to him, and through *hopes* resting on him personally. Next, they unite with one another, and with the perfectly banded South, to make the offensive position they have got into, "a party measure." This done, large additional members are secured. When the repeal of the Missouri Compromise was first proposed, at the North there was litterally [*sic*] "*nobody*" in favor of it. In February 1854 our Legislature met in call, or extra, session. From them Douglas sought an indorsement of his then pending measure of Repeal. In our Legislature were about 70 democrats to 30 whigs. The former held a caucus, in which it was resolved to give Douglas the desired indorsement. Some of the members of that caucus bolted—would not stand it—and they now divulge the secrets. They say that the caucus fairly confessed that the Repeal was wrong; and they placed their determination to indorse it, solely on the ground that it was *necessary* to sustain Douglas. Here we have the direct evidence of how the Nebraska-bill obtained its strength in Illinois. It was given, not in a sense of right, but in the teeth of a sense of wrong, to *sustain Douglas.* So Illinois was divided. So New England, for Pierce; Michigan for Cass, Pensylvania [*sic*] for Buchan [*sic*], and all for the Democratic party.

And when, by such means, they have got a large portion of the Northern people into a position contrary to their own honest impulses, and sense of right; they have the impudence to turn upon those who do stand firm, and call them *sectional.*

Were it not too serious a matter, this cool impudence would be laughable, to say the least.

Recurring to the question "*Shall slavery be allowed to extend into U. S. terrtory* [sic] *now legal* [sic] *free?*

This *is* a sectional question—that is to say, it is a question, in its nature calculated to divide the American people geographically. Who is to *blame* for that? *Who* can help it? Either side *can* help it; but how? Simply by yielding to the other side. There is no other way. In the whole range of possibility, there is no other way. Then, which side shall yield? To this again, there can be but one answer—the side which is in the *wrong.* True, we differ, as to which side *is* wrong; and we boldly say, let all who really think slavery ought to spread into free terrtory [*sic*], openly go over against us. There is where they rightfully belong.

But why should any go, who really think slavery ought not to spread? Do they really think the *right* ought to yield to the wrong? Are they afraid to stand by the *right*? Do they fear that the constitution is too weak to sustain them in the right? Do they really think that by right surrendering to wrong, the hopes of our Constitution, our Union, and our liberties, can possibly be bettered?

The date of this speech or portion of a speech is given as above by Nicolay and Hay. Earlier at Galena, on July 23, Lincoln had spoken much to the same effect, as indicated by the report in the Galena Advertiser *and copied by the* Illinois State Journal, *August 8, 1856. Also, on September 2, a speech on sectionalism was delivered at Lincoln, Illinois, as reported in the* Journal, *September*

4, 1856. Perhaps the substance of the manuscript was thus used several times. In any event the date October 1 is not very well supported by evidence, as Lincoln was most probably traveling to Alton, where he spoke the next day during the State Fair, perhaps using the general contents if not the actual manuscript of "Sectionalism" as part of the speech.

THE DRED SCOTT DECISION:
SPEECH AT SPRINGFIELD, ILLINOIS. JUNE 26, 1857

Fellow-citizens:—

I am here to-night, partly by the invitation of some of you, and partly by my own inclination. Two weeks ago Judge Douglas spoke here on the several subjects of Kansas, the Dred Scott decision, and Utah. I listened to the speech at the time, and have read the report of it since. It was intended to controvert opinions which I think just, and to assail (politically, not personally,) those men who, in common with me, entertain those opinions. For this reason I wished then, and still wish, to make some answer to it, which I now take the opportunity of doing.

I begin with Utah. If it prove to be true, as is probable, that the people of Utah are in open rebellion to the United States, then Judge Douglas is in favor of repealing their territorial organization, and attaching them to the adjoining States for judicial purposes. I say, too, if they are in rebellion, they ought to be somehow coerced to obedience; and I am not now prepared to admit or deny that the Judge's mode of coercing them is not as good as any. The Republicans can fall in with it without taking back anything they have ever said. To be sure, it would be a considerable backing down by Judge Douglas from his much-vaunted doctrine of self-government for the territories; but this is only additional proof of what was very plain from the beginning, that that doctrine was a mere deceitful pretense for the benefit of slavery. Those who could not see that much in the Nebraska act itself, which forced Governors, and Secretaries, and Judges on the people of the territories, without their choice or consent, could not be made to see, though one should rise from the dead to testify.

But in all this, it is very plain the Judge evades the only question the Republicans have ever pressed upon the Democracy in regard to Utah. That question the Judge well knows to be this: "If the people of Utah shall peacefully form a State Constitution tolerating polygamy, will the Democracy admit them into the Union?" There is nothing in the United States Constitution or law against polygamy; and why is it not a part of the Judge's "sacred right of self-government" for that people to have it, or rather to *keep* it, if they choose? These questions, so far as I know, the Judge never answers. It might involve the Democracy to answer them either way, and they go unanswered.

As to Kansas. The substance of the Judge's speech on Kansas is an effort to put the free State men in the wrong for not voting at the election of delegates to the Constitutional Convention. He says: *"There is every reason to hope and believe that the law will be fairly interpreted and impartially executed, so as to insure to every bona fide inhabitant the free and quiet exercise of the elective franchise."*

It appears extraordinary that Judge Douglas should make such a statement. He knows that, by the law, no one can vote who has not been registered; and he knows that the free State men place their refusal to vote on the ground that but few of them have been registered. It is *possible* this is not true, but Judge Douglas knows it is asserted to be true in letters, newspapers, and public speeches, and borne by every mail, and blown by every breeze to the eyes and ears of the world. He knows it is boldly declared that the people of many whole counties, and many whole neighborhoods in others, are left unregistered; yet, he does not venture to contradict the declaration, nor to point out how they *can* vote without being registered; but he just slips along, not seeming to know there is any such question of fact, and complacently declares: "There is every reason to hope and believe that the law will be fairly and impartially executed, so as to insure to every *bona fide* inhabitant the free and quiet exercise of the elective franchise."

I readily agree that if all had a chance to vote, they ought to have voted. If, on the contrary, as they allege, and Judge Douglas ventures not to particularly contradict, few only of the free State men had a chance to vote, they were perfectly right in staying from the polls in a body.

By the way since the Judge spoke, the Kansas election has come off. The Judge expressed his confidence that all the Democrats in Kansas would do their duty—including "free state Democrats" of course. The returns received here as yet are very incomplete; but so far as they go, they indicate that only about one sixth of the registered voters, have really voted; and this too, when not more, perhaps, than one half of the rightful voters have been registered, thus showing the thing to have been altogether the most exquisite farce ever enacted. I am watching with considerable interest, to ascertain what figure "the free-state Democrats" cut in the concern. Of course they voted—all democrats do their duty—and of course they did not vote for slave-state candidates. We soon shall know how many delegates *they* elected, how many candidates they had, pledged for a free state; and how many votes were cast for them.

Allow me to barely whisper my suspicion that there were no such things in Kansas as "free state Democrats"—that they were altogether mythical, good only to figure in newspapers and speeches in the free states. If there should prove to be one real living free state Democrat in Kansas, I suggest that it might be well to catch him, and stuff and preserve his skin, as an interesting specimen of that soon-to-be-extinct variety of the genus, Democrat.

And now as to the Dred Scott decision. That decision declares two propositions—first, that a negro cannot sue in the U. S. Courts; and secondly, that Congress cannot prohibit slavery in the Territories. It was made by a divided court—dividing differently on the different points. Judge Douglas does not discuss the merits of the decision; and, in that respect, I shall follow his example, believing I could no more improve on McLean and Curtis, than he could on Taney.

He denounces all who question the correctness of that decision, as offering violent resistance to it. But who resists it? Who has, in spite of the decision, declared Dred Scott free, and resisted the authority of his master over him?

Judicial decisions have two uses—first, to absolutely determine the case decided; and secondly, to indicate to the public how other similar cases will be decided when they arise. For the latter use, they are called "precedents" and "authorities."

We believe, as much as Judge Douglas, (perhaps more) in obedience to, and respect for, the judicial department of government. We think its decisions on Constitutional questions, when fully settled, should control, not only the particular cases decided, but the general policy of the country, subject to be disturbed only by amendments of the Constitution as provided in that instrument itself. More than this would be revolution. But we think the Dred Scott decision is erroneous. We know the court that made it, has often overruled its own decisions, and we shall do what we can to have it to over rule this. We offer no *resistance* to it.

Judicial decisions are of greater or less authority as precedents, according to circumstances. That this should be so, accords both with common sense, and the customary understanding of the legal profession.

If this important decision had been made by the unanimous concurrence of the judges, and without any apparent partisan bias, and in accordance with legal public expectation, and with the steady practice of the departments throughout our history, and had been in no part, based on assumed historical facts which are not really true; or, if wanting in some of these, it had been before the court more than once, and had there been affirmed and re-affirmed through a course of years, it then might be, perhaps would be, factious, nay, even revolutionary, not to acquiesce in it as a precedent.

But when, as it is true we find it wanting in all these claims to the public confidence, it is not resistance, it is not factious, it is not even disrespectful, to treat it as not having yet quite established a settled doctrine for the country. But Judge Douglas considers this view awful. Hear him:

"The courts are the tribunals prescribed by the Constitution and created by the authority of the people to determine, expound and enforce the law. Hence, whoever resists the final decision of the highest judicial tribunal, aims a deadly blow to our whole Republican system of government—a blow, which if successful would place all our rights and liberties at the mercy of passion, anarchy and violence. I repeat, therefore, that if resistance to the decisions of the Supreme Court of the United States, in a matter like the points decided in the Dred Scott case, clearly within their jurisdiction as defined by the Constitution, shall be forced upon the country as a political issue, it will become a distinct and naked issue between the friends and enemies of the Constitution —the friends and the enemies of the supremacy of the laws."

Why, this same Supreme court once decided a national bank to be constitutional; but Gen. Jackson, as President of the United States, disregarded the decision, and voted a bill for a re-charter, partly on constitutional ground, declaring that each public functionary must support the Constitution, *"as he understands it."* But hear the General's own words. Here they are, taken from his veto message:

"It is maintained by the advocates of the bank, that its constitutionality, in all its features, ought to be considered as settled by precedent, and by the decision of the Supreme Court. To this conclusion I cannot assent. Mere precedent is a dangerous source of authority, and should not be regarded as deciding questions of constitutional power, except where the acquiescence of the people and the States can be considered as well settled. So far from this being the case on this subject, an argument against the bank might be based on precedent. One Congress in 1791, decided in favor of a bank; another in 1811, decided against it. One Congress in 1815 decided against a bank; another in 1816 decided in its favor. Prior to the present Congress, therefore, the precedents drawn from that source were equal. If we resort to the States, the expressions of legislative, judicial and executive opinions against the bank have been probably to those in its favor as four to one. There is nothing in precedent, therefore, which if its authority were admitted, ought to weigh in favor of the act before me."

I drop the quotations merely to remark that all there ever was, in the way of precedent up to the Dred Scott decision, on the points therein decided, had been against that decision. But hear Gen. Jackson further—

"If the opinion of the Supreme Court covered the whole ground of this act, it ought not to control the co-ordinate authorities of this Government. The Congress, the executive and the court must each for itself be guided by its own opinion of the Constitution. Each public officer, who takes an oath to support the Constitution, swears that he will support it as he understands it, and not as it is understood by others."

Again and again have I heard Judge Douglas denounce that bank decision, and applaud Gen. Jackson for disregarding it. It would be interesting for him to look over his recent speech, and see how exactly his fierce philippics against us for resisting Supreme Court decisions, fall upon his own head. It will call to his mind a long and fierce political war in this country, upon an issue which, in his own language, and, of course, in his own changeless estimation, was "a distinct and naked issue between the friends and the enemies of the Constitution," and in which war he fought in the ranks of the enemies of the Constitution.

I have said, in substance, that the Dred Scott decision was, in part, based on assumed historical facts which were not really true; and I ought not to leave the subject without giving some reasons for saying this; I therefore give an instance or two, which I think fully sustain me. Chief Justice Taney, in delivering the opinion of the majority of the Court, insists at great length that negroes were no part of the people who made, or for whom was made, the Declaration of Independence, or the Constitution of the United States.

On the contrary, Judge Curtis, in his dissenting opinion, shows that in five of the then thirteen States, to wit, New Hampshire, Massachusetts, New York, New Jersey and North Carolina, free negroes were voters, and, in proportion to their numbers, had the same part in making the Constitution that the white people had. He shows this with so much particularity as to leave no doubt of its truth; and, as a sort of conclusion on that point, holds the following language:

"The Constitution was ordained and established by the people of the United States, through the action, in each State, of those persons who were qualified by its laws to act thereon in behalf of themselves and all other citizens of the State. In some of the States, as we have seen, colored persons were among those qualified by law to act on the subject. These colored persons were not only included in the body of 'the people of the United States,' by whom the Constitution was ordained and established; but in at least five of the States they had the power to act, and, doubtless, did act, by their suffrages, upon the question of its adoption."

Again, Chief Justice Taney says: "It is difficult, at this day, to realize the state of public opinion in relation to that unfortunate race, which prevailed in the civilized and enlightened portions of the world at the time of the Declaration of Independence, and when the Constitution of the United States was framed and adopted." And again, after quoting from the Declaration, he says: "The general words above quoted would seem to include the whole human family, and if they were used in a similar instrument at this day, would be so understood."

In these the Chief Justice does not directly assert, but plainly assumes, as a fact, that the public estimate of the black man is more favorable *now* than it was in the days of the Revolution. This assumption is a mistake. In some trifling particulars, the condition of that race has been ameliorated; but, as a whole, in this country, the change between then and now is decidedly the other way; and their ultimate destiny has never appeared so hopeless as in the last three or four years. In two of the five States—New Jersey and North Carolina—that then gave the free negro the right of voting, the right has since been taken away; and in a third—New York—it has been greatly abridged; while it has not been extended, so far as I know, to a single additional State, though the number of the States has more than doubled. In those days, as I understand, masters could, at their own pleasure, emancipate their slaves; but since then, such legal restraints have been made upon emancipation, as to amount almost to prohibition. In those days, Legislatures held the unquestioned power to abolish slavery in their respective States, but now it is becoming quite fashionable for State Constitutions to withhold that power from the Legislatures. In those days, by common consent, the spread of the black man's bondage to new countries was prohibited; but now, Congress decides that it *will* not continue the prohibition, and the Supreme Court decides that it *could* not if it would. In those days, our Declaration of Independence was held sacred by all, and thought to include all; but now, to aid in making the bondage of the negro universal and eternal, it is assailed, and sneered at, and construed, and hawked at, and torn, till, if its framers could rise from their graves, they could not at all recognize it. All the powers of earth seem rapidly combining against him. Mammon is after him; ambition follows, and philosophy follows, and the Theology of the day is fast joining the cry. They have him in his prison house; they have searched his person, and left no prying instrument with him. One after another they have closed the heavy iron doors upon him, and now they have him, as it were, bolted in with a lock of a hundred keys, which can never be unlocked without the concurrence of every key; the keys in the hands of a hundred different men, and they scattered to a hundred different and distant places; and they stand musing as to what invention, in all the dominions of mind and matter, can be produced to make the impossibility of his escape more complete than it is.

It is grossly incorrect to say or assume, that the public estimate of the negro is more favorable now than it was at the origin of the government.

Three years and a half ago, Judge Douglas brought forward his famous Nebraska bill. The country was at once in a blaze. He scorned all opposition, and carried it through Congress. Since then he has seen himself superseded in a Presidential nomination, by one indorsing the general doctrine of his measure, but at the same time standing clear of the odium of its untimely agitation, and its gross breach of national faith; and he has seen that successful rival Constitutionally elected, not by the strength of friends, but by the division of adversaries, being in a popular minority of nearly four hundred thousand votes. He has seen his chief aids in his own State, Shields and Richardson, politically speaking, successively tried, convicted, and executed, for an offense not their own, but his. And now he sees his own case, standing next on the docket for trial.

There is a natural disgust in the minds of nearly all white people, to the idea of an indiscriminate amalgamation of the white and black races; and Judge Douglas evidently is basing his chief hope upon the chances of his being able to appropriate the benefit of this disgust to himself. If he can, by much drumming and repeating, fasten the odium of that idea upon his adversaries, he thinks he can struggle through the storm. He therefore clings to this hope, as a drowning man to the last plank. He makes an occasion for lugging it in from the opposition to the Dred Scott decision. He finds the Republicans insisting that the Declaration of Independence includes ALL men, black as well as white; and forthwith he boldly denies that it includes negroes at all, and proceeds to argue gravely that all who contend it does, do so only because they want to vote, and eat, and sleep, and marry with negroes! He will have it that they cannot be consistent else. Now I protest against that counterfeit logic which concludes that, because I do not want a black woman for a *slave* I must necessarily want her for a *wife*. I need not have her for either, I can just leave her alone. In some respects she certainly is not my equal; but in her natural right to eat the bread she earns with her own hands without asking leave of any one else, she is my equal, and the equal of all others.

Chief Justice Taney, in his opinion in the Dred Scott case, admits that the language of the Declaration is broad enough to include the whole human family, but he and Judge Douglas argue that the authors of that instrument did not intend to include negroes, by the fact that they did not at once, actually place them on an equality with the whites. Now this grave argument comes to just nothing at all, by the other fact, that they did not at once, *or ever afterwards*, actually place all white people on an equality with one another. And this is the staple argument of both the Chief Justice and the Senator, for doing this obvious violence to the plain, unmistakable language of the Declaration. I think the authors of that notable instrument intended to include *all* men, but they did not intend to declare all men equal *in all respects*. They did not mean to say all were equal in color, size, intellect, moral developments, or social capacity. They defined with tolerable distinctness, in what respects they did consider all men created equal—equal in "certain inalienable rights, among which are life, liberty, and the pursuit of happiness." This they said, and this meant. They did not mean to assert the obvious untruth, that all were then actually enjoying that equality, nor yet, that they were about to confer it immediately upon them. In fact they had no power to confer such a boon. They meant simply to declare the *right*, so that the *enforcement* of it might follow as fast as circumstances should permit. They meant to set up a standard maxim for free society, which could be familiar to all, and revered by all; constantly looked to, constantly labored for, and even though never perfectly attained, constantly approximated, and thereby constantly spreading and deepening its influence, and augmenting the happiness and value of life to all people of all colors everywhere. The assertion that "all men are created equal" was of no practical use in effecting our separation from Great Britain; and it was placed in the Declaration, not for that, but for future use. Its authors meant it to be, thank God, it is now proving itself, a stumbling block to those who in after times might seek to turn a free people back into the hateful paths of despotism. They knew the proneness of prosperity to breed tyrants, and they meant when such should re-appear in this fair land and commence their vocation they should find left for them at least one hard nut to crack.

I have now briefly expressed my view of the *meaning* and *objects* of that part of the Declaration of Independence which declares that "all men are created equal."

Now let us hear Judge Douglas' view of the same subject, as I find it in the printed report of his late speech. Here it is:

"No man can vindicate the character, motives and conduct of the signers of the Declaration of Independence, except upon the hypothesis that they referred to the white race alone, and not to the African, when they declared all men to have been created equal—that they were speaking of British subjects on this continent being equal to British subjects born and residing in Great Britain—that they were entitled to the same inalienable rights, and among them were enumerated life, liberty and the pursuit of happiness. The Declaration was adopted for the purpose of justifying the colonists in the eyes of the civilized world in withdrawing their allegiance from the British crown, and dissolving their connection with the mother country."

My good friends, read that carefully over some leisure hour, and ponder well upon it—see what a mere wreck—mangled ruin—it makes of our once glorious Declaration.

"They were speaking of British subjects on this continent being equal to British subjects born and residing in Great Britain!" Why, according to this, not only negroes but white people outside of Great Britain and America are not spoken of in that instrument. The English, Irish and Scotch, along with white Americans, were included to be sure, but the French, Germans and other white people of the world are all gone to pot along with the Judge's inferior races.

I had thought the Declaration promised something better than the condition of British subjects; but no, it only meant that we should be *equal* to them in their own oppressed and *unequal* condition. According to that, it gave no promise that having kicked off the King and Lords of Great Britain, we should not at once be saddled with a King and Lords of our own.

I had thought the Declaration contemplated the progressive improvement in the condition of all men everywhere; but no, it merely "was adopted for the purpose of justifying the colonists in the eyes of the civilized world in withdrawing their allegiance from the British crown, and dissolving their connection with the mother country." Why, that object having been effected some eighty years ago, the Declaration is of no practical use now—mere rubbish—old wadding left to rot on the battle-field after the victory is won.

I understand you are preparing to celebrate the "Fourth," to-morrow week. What for? The doings of that day had no reference to the present; and quite half of you are not even descendants of those who were referred to at that day. But I suppose you will celebrate; and will even go so far as to read the Declaration. Suppose after you read it once in the old fashioned way, you read it once more with Judge Douglas' version. It will then run thus: "We hold these truths to be self-evident that all British subjects who were on this continent eighty-one years ago, were created equal to all British subjects born and *then* residing in Great Britain."

And now I appeal to all—to Democrats as well as others,—are

you really willing that the Declaration shall be thus frittered away?—thus left no more at most, than an interesting memorial of the dead past? thus shorn of its vitality, and practical value; and left without the *germ* or even the *suggestion* of the individual rights of man in it?

But Judge Douglas is especially horrified at the thought of the mixing of blood by the white and black races: agreed for once—a thousand times agreed. There are white men enough to marry all the white women, and black men enough to marry all the black women; and so let them be married. On this point we fully agree with the Judge; and when he shall show that his policy is better adapted to prevent amalgamation than ours we shall drop ours, and adopt his. Let us see. In 1850 there were in the United States 405,751 mulattoes. Very few of these are the offspring of whites and *free* blacks; nearly all have sprung from black *slaves* and white masters. A separation of the races is the only perfect preventive of amalgamation; but as an immediate separation is impossible the next best thing is to *keep* them apart *where* they are not already together. If white and black people never get together in Kansas, they will never mix blood in Kansas. That is at least one self-evident truth. A few free colored persons may get into the free States, in any event; but their number is too insignificant to amount to much in the way of mixing blood. In 1850 there were in the free States, 56,649 mulattoes; but for the most part they were not born there—they came from the slave States, ready made up. In the same year the slave States had 348,874 mulattoes, all of home production. The proportion of free mulattoes to free blacks—the only colored classes in the free states—is much greater in the slave than in the free states. It is worthy of note too, that among the free states those which make the colored man the nearest to equal the white, have proportionably the fewest mulattoes, the least of amalgamation. In New Hampshire, the State which goes farthest toward equality between the races, there are just 184 mulattoes, while there are in Virginia—how many do you think?—79,775, being 23,126 more than in all the free States together.

These statistics show that slavery is the greatest source of amalgamation; and next to it, not the elevation, but the degradation of the free blacks. Yet Judge Douglas dreads the slightest restraints on the spread of slavery, and the slightest human recognition of the negro, as tending horribly to amalgamation.

The very Dred Scott case affords a strong test as to which party most favors amalgamation, the Republicans or the dear Union-saving Democracy. Dred Scott, his wife and two daughters were all involved in the suit. We desired the court to have held that they were citizens so far at least as to entitle them to a hearing as to whether they were free or not; and then, also, that they were in fact and in law really free. Could we have had our way, the chances of these black girls ever mixing their blood with that of white people, would have been diminished at least to the extent that it could not have been without their consent. But Judge Douglas is delighted to have them decided to be slaves, and not human enough to have a hearing, even if they were free, and thus left subject to the forced concubinage of their masters, and liable to become the mothers of mulattoes in spite of themselves—the very state of case that produces nine tenths of all the mulattoes —all the mixing of blood in the nation.

Of course, I state this case as an illustration only, not meaning to say or intimate that the master of Dred Scott and his family, or any more than a per centage of masters generally, are inclined to exercise this particular power which they hold over their female slaves.

I have said that the separation of the races is the only perfect preventive of amalgamation. I have no right to say all the members of the Republican party are in favor of this, nor to say that as a party they are in favor of it. There is nothing in their platform directly on the subject. But I can say a very large proportion of its members are for it, and that the chief plank in their platform —opposition to the spread of slavery—is most favorable to that separation.

Such separation, if ever effected at all, must be effected by colonization; and no political party, as such, is now doing anything directly for colonization. Party operations at present only favor or retard colonization incidentally. The enterprise is a difficult one; but "where there is a will there is a way," and what colonization needs most is a hearty will. Will springs from the two elements of moral sense and self-interest. Let us be brought to believe it is morally right, and at the same time, favorable to, or, at least, not against, our interest, to transfer the African to his native clime, and we shall find a way to do it, however great the task may be. The children of Israel, to such numbers as to include four hundred thousand fighting men, went out of Egyptian bondage in a body.

How differently the respective courses of the Democratic and Republican parties incidentally bear on the question of forming a will—a public sentiment—for colonization, is easy to see. The Republicans inculcate, with whatever of ability they can, that the negro is a man, that his bondage is cruelly wrong, and that the field of his oppression ought not to be enlarged. The Democrats deny his manhood; deny, or dwarf to insignificance, the wrong of his bondage; so far as possible, crush all sympathy for him, and cultivate and excite hatred and disgust against him; compliment themselves as Union-savers for doing so; and call the indefinite outspreading of his bondage "a sacred right of self-government."

The plainest print cannot be read through a gold eagle; and it will be ever hard to find many men who will send a slave to Liberia, and pay his passage, while they can send him to a new country Kansas, for instance, and sell him for fifteen hundred dollars, and the rise.

The circumstances under which Lincoln delivered this speech are generally indicated by the context. Douglas had spoken on the subject two weeks earlier, arguing as usual that popular sovereignty was the solution to the problem of slavery extension and taking an ultra-conservative position in regard to the sanctity of a Supreme Court decision. The reference to unrest among the Mormons in Utah recalls that twenty years earlier they had fled from their city of Zion at Independence, Missouri, in order to escape the persecutions of the non-Mormon inhabitants and the jurisdiction of federal laws. Many of the Mormons had come originally from New

York to Ohio and while there and en route to Missouri had proselyted in central Illinois. During the thirties numerous references appear in the Journal *to their difficulties and disturbances. The treaty concluded with Mexico in 1847-48 brought them again under federal jurisdiction almost as soon as their advanced guard had settled in Utah. Accordingly, under the leadership of Brigham Young, a convention was called and a constitution adopted for a state to be called "Deseret." Congress, however, refused recognition of the state, and instead organized the Territory of Utah. By 1857, the people of the territory, largely Mormon, were indignant and restless, to say the least, and hence the "rebellion" alluded to in the speech.*

LETTER TO E. B. WASHBURNE
APRIL 26, 1858

Urbana, Ills. April 26. 1858.

Hon. E. B. Washburne.
My dear Sir:

I am rather a poor correspondent, but I think perhaps I ought to write you a letter just now. I am here at this time; but I was at home during the sitting of the two democratic conventions. The day before those conventions I received a letter from Chicago having, among other things, on other subjects, the following in it: "A reliable republican, but an old line whig lawyer, in this city told me to-day that *he himself had seen* a letter from one of our republican congressmen, advising us all to go for the re-election of Judge Douglass [*sic*]. He said he was informed to keep the author a secret & he was going to do so. From him I learnt that he was not an old line democrat, or abolitionist This narrows the contest down to the congressmen from the Galena and Fulton Dists."

The above is a litteral [*sic*] copy of all the letter contained on that subject. The morning of the conventions Mr. Herndon showed me your letter of the 15th. to him, which convinced me that the story in the letter from Chicago was based upon some mistake, misconstruction of language, or the like. Several of our friends were down from Chicago, and they had something of the same story amongst them, some half suspecting that you were inclined to favor Douglas, and others thinking there was an effort to wrong you.

I thought neither was exactly the case; that the whole had originated in some misconstruction, coupled with a high degree of sensitiveness on the point, and that the whole matter was not worth another moment's consideration. Such is my opinion now, and I hope you will have no concern about it. I have written this because Charley Wilson told me he was writing you, and because I expect Dr. Ray, (who was a little excited about the matter) has also written you; and because I think, I perhaps, have taken a calmer view of the thing than they may have done. I am satisfied you have done no wrong, and nobody has intended any wrong to you.

A word about the conventions. The democracy parted in not a very encouraged state of mind.

On the contrary, our friends, a good many of whom were present, parted in high spirits. They think if we do not triumph the fault will be our own, and so I really think.

Your friend as ever

A Lincoln

The Charlie Wilson alluded to was Charles Lush Wilson, editor of the Chicago Journal *and a supporter of Lincoln's candidacy. The letter referred to here and in the two succeeding letters to Washburne, May 15 and May 27, apparently caused Lincoln considerable uneasiness for the reasons indicated in the context.*

LETTER TO E. B. WASHBURNE
MAY 15, 1858

Springfield, May 15. 1858.

Hon. E. B. Washburne
My dear Sir

Yours of the 6th. accompanied by yours of April 12th. to C. L. Wilson was received day-before-yesterday.

There certainly is nothing in the letter to Wilson, which I, in particular, or republicans in general, could complain of. Of that I was quite satisfied before I saw the letter. I believe there has been no malicious intent to misrepresent you; I hope there is no longer any misunderstanding, and that the matter may drop.

Eight or ten days ago I wrote Kellogg from Beardstown. Get him to show you the letter. It gave my view of the *field*, as it appeared then. Nothing has occurred since, except that it grows more and more quiet since the passage of the English contrivance. The State Register, here, is evidently laboring to bring it's old friends into what the doctors call the "*comatose state*"—that is, a sort of drowsy, dreamy condition, in which they may not perceive or remember that there has ever been, or is, any difference between Douglas & the President. This could be done, *if* the Buchanan men would allow it—which, however, the latter seem determined not to do.

I think our prospects gradually, and steadily, grow better; though we are not yet clear out of the woods by a great deal. There is still some effort to make trouble out of "Americanism." If that were out of the way, for all the rest, I believe we should be "out of the woods"

Yours very truly
A. Lincoln

LETTER TO JEDIAH F. ALEXANDER
MAY 15, 1858

Springfield, May 15. 1858

J. F. Alexander, Esq
Greenville, Ills.
My dear Sir

I reached home a week ago and found yours of the 1st. inviting me to name a time to meet and address a political meeting in Bond county. It is too early, considering that when I once begin making political speeches I shall have no respite till November. The *labor* of that I might endure, but I really can not spare the time from my business.

Nearer the time I will try to meet the people of Bond, if they desire.

I will only say now that, as I understand, there remains all the difference there ever was between Judge Douglas & the Republicans—*they* insisting that Congress *shall*, and *he* insisting that congress *shall not*, keep slavery out of the Teritories [*sic*] *before* & *up to the time* they form State constitutions. No republican has ever contended that, *when* a constitution is to be formed, any but the *people* of the teritory [*sic*] shall form it. Republicans have never contended that congress should *dictate* a constitution to any state or teritory [*sic*]; but they have contended that the people should be *perfectly* free to form their constitution in their own way—as *perfectly* free from the *presence* of *slavery* amongst them, as from every other improper influence.

In voting together in opposition to a constitution being forced upon the people of Kansas, neither Judge Douglas nor the Republicans, has conceded anything which was ever in dispute between them.

Yours very truly
A. Lincoln

Alexander was founder and editor of the Greenville Advocate. *Greenville, county seat of Bond County in southern Illinois, was in a region generally strong for Douglas, and the Republican editor was anxious to get Lincoln committed to a speaking engagement even in advance of the campaign, presuming, of course, that Lincoln would be the party candidate even though no formal announcement had yet been made.*

LETTER TO E. B. WASHBURNE
MAY 27, 1858

Springfield, May 27—1858—

Hon. E. B. Washburne
My dear Sir

Yours requesting me to return you the now some what noted "Charley Wilson letter" is received; and I herewith return that letter.

Political matters just now bear a very *mixed* and *incongruous* aspect. For several days the signs have been that Douglas and the President had probably buried the hatchet. Doug's friends at Washington going over to the President's side, and his friends here & South of here, talking as if there never had been any serious difficulty, while the President himself does nothing for his own peculiar friends here. But this morning my partner, Mr. Herndon, receives a letter from Mr. Medill of the Chicago Tribune, showing the writer to be in great alarm at the prospect North of Republicans going over to Douglas, on the idea that Douglas is going to assume steep free-soil ground, and furiously assail the administration on the stump when he comes home.

There certainly is a double game being played some how. Possibly—even *probably*—Douglas is temporarily deceiving the

President in order to crush out the 8th. of June convention here.

Unless he plays his double game more successfully than we have often seen done, he can not carry many republicans North; without at the same time losing a larger number of his old friends South.

Let this be confidential.

Yours as ever
A. Lincoln

LETTER TO SAMUEL WILKINSON
JUNE 10, 1858

Springfield, June 10. 1858

Samuel Wilkinson Esq
My dear Sir

Yours of the 26th. May came to hand *only* last night. I *know* of no effort to unite the Reps. & Buc. men, and *believe* there is none. Of course the Republicans do not try to keep the common enemy from dividing; but, so far as I *know*, or *believe*, they will not unite with either branch of the division. Indeed it is difficult for me to see, on what ground they could unite; but it is useless to spend words, there is simply nothing of it. It is a trick of our enemies to try to excite all sorts of suspicions and jealosies [*sic*] amongst us. We hope that our Convention on the 16th. bringing us together, and letting us hear each other talk will put an end to most of this.

Yours truly
A. Lincoln

"When Douglas refused to support the Lecompton Constitution he precipitated a bitter battle with the

Buchanan administration. . . . In many counties Buchanan candidates for the legislature were put forward with the scarcely hidden purpose of so dividing the Democracy that a Republican victory would be certain. The situation seemed to make a combination between Republicans and Buchanan Democrats almost unavoidable, yet in the following letter to Samuel Wilkinson, an acquaintance who lived at Farmington in Fulton County, Lincoln emphatically denied that one existed" (Paul M. Angle, editor, New Letters and Papers of Lincoln, *pp. 177-8).*

A HOUSE DIVIDED: SPEECH DELIVERED AT SPRINGFIELD, ILLINOIS, AT THE CLOSE OF THE REPUBLICAN STATE CONVENTION. JUNE 16, 1858

If we could first know *where* we are, and *whither* we are tending, we could better judge *what* to do, and *how* to do it.

We are now far into the *fifth* year, since a policy was initiated, with the *avowed* object, and *confident* promise, of putting an end to slavery agitation.

Under the operation of that policy, that agitation has not only, *not ceased*, but has *constantly augmented*.

In my opinion, it *will* not cease, until a *crisis* shall have been reached, and passed—

"A house divided against itself cannot stand."

I believe this government cannot endure, permanently half *slave* and half *free*.

I do not expect the Union to be *dissolved*—I do not expect the house to *fall*—but I *do* expect it will cease to be divided.

It will become *all* one thing, or *all* the other.

Either the *opponents* of slavery, will arrest the further spread of it, and place it where the public mind shall rest in the belief that it is in course of ultimate extinction; or its *advocates* will push it forward, till it shall become alike lawful in *all* the States, *old* as well as *new*—*North* as well as *South.*

Have we no *tendency* to the latter condition?

Let any one who doubts, carefully contemplate that now almost complete legal combination—piece of *machinery* so to speak—compounded of the Nebraska doctrine, and the Dred Scott decision. Let him consider not only *what work* the machinery is adapted to do, and *how well* adapted; but also, let him study the history of its construction, and trace, if he can, or rather *fail,* if he can, to trace the evidences of design, and concert of action, among its chief bosses, from the beginning.

The new year of 1854 found slavery excluded from more than half the States by State Constitutions, and from most of the national territory by congressional prohibition.

Four days later, commenced the struggle, which ended in repealing that congressional prohibition.

This opened all the national territory to slavery; and was the first point gained.

But, so far, *Congress* only, had acted; and an *indorsement* by the people, *real* or *apparent,* was indispensable, to *save* the point already gained, and give chance for more.

This necessity had not been overlooked; but had been provided for, as well as might be, in the notable argument of "squatter sovereignty," otherwise called *"sacred right of self government,"* which latter phrase, though expressive of the only rightful basis of any government, was so perverted in this attempted use of it as to amount to just this: That if any *one* man, choose to enslave *another,* no *third* man shall be allowed to object.

That argument was incorporated into the Nebraska bill itself, in the language which follows: *"It being the true intent and meaning of this act not to legislate slavery into any Territory or State, nor to exclude it therefrom; but to leave the people thereof perfectly free to form and regulate their domestic institutions in their own way, subject only to the Constitution of the United States."*

Then opened the roar of loose declamation in favor of "Squatter Sovereignty," and "Sacred right of self government."

"But," said opposition members, "let us be more *specific*—let us *amend* the bill so as to expressly declare that the people of the Territory *may* exclude slavery." "Not we," said the friends of the measure; and down they voted the amendment.

While the Nebraska bill was passing through congress, a *law case*, involving the question of a negro's freedom, by reason of his owner having voluntarily taken him first into a free State and then a territory covered by the congressional prohibition, and held him as a slave for a long time in each, was passing through the U. S. Circuit Court for the District of Missouri; and both Nebraska bill and law suit were brought to a decision in the same month of May, 1854. The negro's name was "Dred Scott," which name now designates the decision finally made in the case.

Before the *then* next Presidential election, the law case came *to*, and was argued *in* the Supreme Court of the United States; but the *decision* of it was deferred until *after* the election. Still, *before* the election, Senator Trumbull, on the floor of the Senate, requests the leading advocate of the Nebraska bill to state *his opinion* whether the people of a territory can constitutionally exclude slavery from their limits; and the latter answers, "That is a question for the Supreme Court."

The election came. Mr. Buchanan was elected, and the *indorsement*, such as it was, secured. That was the *second* point gained. The indorsement, however, fell short of a clear popular majority by nearly four hundred thousand votes, and so, perhaps, was not over-whelmingly reliable and satisfactory.

The *outgoing* President, in his last annual message, as impressively as possible *echoed back* upon the people the *weight* and *authority* of the indorsement.

The Supreme Court met again; *did not* announce their decision, but ordered a re-argument.

The Presidential inauguration came, and still no decision of the court; but the *incoming* President, in his inaugural address, fervently exhorted the people to abide by the forthcoming decision, *whatever it might be*.

Then, in a few days, came the decision.

The reputed author of the Nebraska bill finds an early occasion to make a speech at this capitol indorsing the Dred Scott Decision, and vehemently denouncing all opposition to it.

The new President, too, seizes the early occasion of the Silliman letter to indorse and strongly *construe* that decision, and to express his *astonishment* that any different view had ever been entertained.

At length a squabble springs up between the President and the author of the Nebraska bill, on the *mere* question of *fact*, whether the Lecompton constitution was or was not, in any just sense, made by the people of Kansas; and in that quarrel the latter declares that all he wants is a fair vote for the people, and that he *cares* not whether slavery be voted *down* or voted *up*. I do not understand his declaration that he cares not whether slavery be voted down or voted up, to be intended by him other than as an *apt definition* of the *policy* he would impress upon the public mind—the *principle* for which he declares he has suffered much, and is ready to suffer to the end.

And well may he cling to that principle. If he has any parental feeling, well may he cling to it. That principle, is the only shred left of his original Nebraska doctrine. Under the Dred Scott decision, "squatter sovereignty" squatted out of existence, tumbled down like temporary scaffolding—like the mold at the foundry served through one blast and fell back into loose sand—helped to carry an election, and then was kicked to the winds. His late *joint* struggle with the Republicans, against the Lecompton Constitution, involves nothing of the original Nebraska doctrine. That struggle was made on a point, the right of a people to make their own constitution, upon which he and the Republicans have never differed.

The several points of the Dred Scott decision, in connection with Senator Douglas' "care not" policy, constitute the piece of machinery, in its *present* state of advancement.

The *working* points of that machinery are:

First, that no negro slave, imported as such from Africa, and no descendant of such slave can ever be a *citizen* of any State, in the sense of that term as used in the Constitution of the United States.

This point is made in order to deprive the negro, in every

possible event, of the benefit of that provision of the United States Constitution, which declares that—

"the citizens of each State shall be entitled to all privileges and immunities of citizens in the several States."

Secondly, that "subject to the Constitution of the United States," neither *Congress* nor a *Territorial Legislature* can exclude slavery from any United States Territory.

This point is made in order that individual men may *fill up* the territories with slaves, without danger of losing them as property, and thus enhance the chances of *permanency* to the institution through all the future.

Thirdly, that whether the holding a negro in actual slavery in a free State, makes him free, as against the holder, the United States courts will not decide, but will leave to be decided by the courts of any slave State the negro may be forced into by the master.

This point is made, not to be pressed *immediately*; but, if acquiesced in for a while, and apparently *indorsed* by the people at an election, *then* to sustain the logical conclusion that what Dred Scott's master might lawfully do with Dred Scott, in the free State of Illinois, every other master may lawfully do with any other *one* or one *thousand* slaves, in Illinois, or in any other free State.

Auxiliary to all this, and working hand in hand with it, the Nebraska doctrine, or what is left of it, is to *educate* and *mould* public opinion, at least *Northern* public opinion, to not *care* whether slavery is voted *down* or voted *up*.

This shows exactly where we now *are*; and *partially* also, whither we are tending.

It will throw additional light on the latter, to go back, and run the mind over the string of historical facts already stated. Several things will *now* appear less *dark* and *mysterious* than they did *when* they were transpiring. The people were to be left "perfectly free" "subject only to the Constitution." What the *Constitution* had to do with it, outsiders could not *then* see. Plainly enough *now*, it was an exactly fitted *nitch* for the Dred Scott decision to afterward come in, and declare that *perfect freedom* of the people, to be just no freedom at all.

Why was the amendment, expressly declaring the right of the people to exclude slavery, voted down? Plainly enough *now*, the adoption of it, would have spoiled the nitch for the Dred Scott decision.

Why was the court decision held up? Why, even a Senator's individual opinion withheld, till *after* the Presidential election? Plainly enough *now*, the speaking out *then* would have damaged the "*perfectly free*" argument upon which the election was to be carried.

Why the *outgoing* President's felicitation on the indorsement? Why the delay of a reargument? Why the incoming President's *advance* exhortation in favor of the decision?

These things *look* like the cautious *patting* and *petting* of a spirited horse, preparatory to mounting him, when it is dreaded that he may give the rider a fall.

And why the hasty after indorsements of the decision by the President and others?

We cannot absolutely *know* that all these exact adaptations are the result of preconcert. But when we see a lot of framed timbers, different portions of which we know have been gotten out at different times and places and by different workmen—Stephen, Franklin, Roger, and James, for instance—and we see these timbers joined together, and see they exactly make the frame of a house or a mill, all the tenons and mortises exactly fitting, and all the lengths and proportions of the different pieces exactly adapted to their respective places, and not a piece too many or too few—not omitting even scaffolding—or, if a single piece be lacking, we see the place in the frame exactly fitted and prepared to yet bring such piece in—in *such* a case, we find it impossible not to *believe* that Stephen and Franklin and Roger and James all understood one another from the beginning, and all worked upon a common *plan* or *draft* drawn up before the first lick was struck.

It should not be overlooked that, by the Nebraska bill, the people of a *State* as well as *Territory*, were to be left "*perfectly free*" "*subject only to the Constitution.*"

Why mention a *State*? They were legislating for *territories*, and not *for* or *about* States. Certainly the people of a *State are* and *ought to be* subject to the Constitution of the United States; but why is mention of this *lugged* into this merely *territorial* law? Why are the people of a *territory* and the people of a *state* therein *lumped* together, and their relation to the Constitution therein treated as being *precisely* the same?

While the opinion of the Court, by Chief Justice Taney, in the Dred Scott case, and the separate opinions of all the concurring Judges, expressly declare that the Constitution of the United States neither permits Congress nor a territorial legislature to exclude slavery from any United States territory, they all *omit* to declare whether or not the same Constitution permits a state, or the people of a State, to exclude it.

Possibly, this is a mere *omission*; but who can be *quite* sure, if McLean or Curtis had sought to get into the opinion a declaration of unlimited power in the people of a state to exclude slavery from their limits, just as Chase and Mace sought to get such declaration, in behalf of the people of a territory, into the Nebraska bill—I ask, who can be quite *sure* that it would not have been voted down, in the one case, as it had been in the other?

The nearest approach to the point of declaring the power of a State over slavery, is made by Judge Nelson. He approaches it more than once, using the precise idea, and *almost* the language too, of the Nebraska act. On one occasion his exact language is, "except in cases where the power is restrained by the Constitution of the United States, the law of the State is supreme over the subject of slavery within its jurisdiction."

In what *cases* the power of the *states* is so restrained by the U. S. Constitution is left an *open* question, precisly [*sic*] as the same question, as to the restraint on the power of the *territories* was left open in the Nebraska act. Put *that* and *that* together, and we have another nice little nitch, which we may, ere long, see filled with another Supreme Court decision, declaring that the Constitution of the United States does not permit a state to exclude slavery from its limits.

And this may especially be expected if the doctrine of "care not whether slavery be voted *down* or voted *up*," shall gain upon the public mind sufficiently to give promise that such a decision can be maintained when made.

Such a decision is all that slavery now lacks of being alike lawful in all the States.

Welcome or unwelcome, such decision *is* probably coming, and will soon be upon us, unless the power of the present political dynasty shall be met and overthrown. We shall *lie down* pleasantly dreaming that the people of *Missouri* are on the verge of making their State *free*; and we shall *awake* to the *reality*, instead, that the *Supreme* Court has made *Illinois* a *slave* State.

To meet and overthrow the power of that dynasty, is the work now before all those who would prevent that consummation.

That is *what* we have to do.

But *how* can we best do it?

There are those who denounce us *openly* to their *own* friends, and yet whisper *us softly*, that *Senator Douglas* is the *aptest* instrument there is, with which to effect that object. *They* do *not* tell us, nor has *he* told us, that he *wishes* any such object to be effected. They wish us to *infer* all, from the facts, that he now has a little quarrel with the present head of the dynasty; and that he has regularly voted with us, on a single point, upon which, he and we, have never differed.

They remind us that *he* is a *great* man, and that the largest of *us* are very small ones. Let this be granted. But "a *living dog* is better than a *dead lion*." Judge Douglas, if not a *dead* lion *for this work*, is at least a *caged* and *toothless* one. How can he oppose the advances of slavery? He don't *care* anything about it. His avowed *mission is impressing* the "public heart" to *care* nothing about it.

A leading Douglas Democratic newspaper thinks Douglas' superior talent will be needed to resist the revival of the African slave trade.

Does Douglas believe an effort to revive that trade is approaching? He has not said so. Does he *really* think so? But if it is, how can he resist it? For years he has labored to prove it a *sacred right* of white men to take negro slaves into the new territories. Can he possibly show that it is *less* a sacred right to *buy* them where they can be bought cheapest? And, unquestionably they can be bought *cheaper* in *Africa* than in *Virginia*.

He has done all in his power to reduce the whole question of slavery to one of a mere *right of property*; and as such, how can *he* oppose the foreign slave trade—how can he refuse that trade in that "property" shall be "perfectly free"—unless he does it as a *protection* to the home production? And as the home *producers* will probably not *ask* the protection, he will be wholly without a ground of opposition.

Senator Douglas holds, we know, that a man may rightfully be *wiser to-day* than he was *yesterday*—that he may rightfully *change* when he finds himself wrong.

But, can we for that reason, run ahead, and *infer* that he *will* make any particular change, of which he, himself, has given no intimation? Can we *safely* base *our* action upon any such *vague* inference?

Now, as ever, I wish to not misrepresent Judge Douglas' *position*, question his *motives*, or do aught that can be personally offensive to him.

Whenever, *if ever*, he and we can come together on *principle* so that *our great cause* may have assistance from *his great ability*, I hope to have interposed no adventitious obstacle.

But clearly, he is not *now* with us—he does not *pretend* to be—he does not *promise* to *ever* be.

Our cause, then, must be intrusted to, and conducted by its own undoubted friends—those whose hands are free, whose hearts are in the work—who *do care* for the result.

Two years ago the Republicans of the nation mustered over thirteen hundred thousand strong.

We did this under the single impulse of resistance to a common danger, with every external circumstance against us.

Of *strange, discordant*, and even, *hostile* elements, we gathered from the four winds, and *formed* and fought the battle through, under the constant hot fire of a disciplined, proud, and pampered enemy.

Did we brave all *then* to *falter* now?—now—when that same enemy is *wavering*, dissevered, and belligerent?

The result is not doubtful. We shall not fail—if we stand firm, we shall not fail.

Wise counsels may *accelerate* or *mistakes delay* it, but sooner or later the victory is *sure* to come.

The text of this speech is basically that of the Illinois State Journal, *but with a few emendations taken from the later printing,* Political Debates *(Columbus: Follet, Foster and Company, 1860). The puctuation of the* Journal *text is so typical of Lincoln's punctuation in speech manuscripts as to leave no doubt that it is generally accurate. Horace White's account of the printing of this version, as given by Herndon, specifies that the* Journal *text was set up from the manuscript and the final proof read by Lincoln himself. The superiority of this version over later printings lies chiefly in the extent to which it reproduces, in so far as can be, the oral emphasis Lincoln gave to each sentence, phrase, and word. This emphasis is well illustrated by the comma (omitted in later versions) which divides the famous sentence, "I believe this government cannot endure, permanently half* slave *and half* free."

In addition, the personal "scrap book" of newspaper clippings of the debates and preceding speeches, which Lincoln prepared and which was used in preparation of the Follett, Foster Debates, *has been checked (through the kindness of Mr. Oliver R. Barrett), particularly for Lincoln's personal emendations, in this and the succeeding speeches of July 10 and July 17, and the debate of August 21.*

In each of these speeches, the numerous interruptions as indicated in newspaper versions—heckling, cheers and applause—have been omitted except when necessary to the context.

LETTER TO JOSEPH MEDILL
JUNE 25, 1858

Springfield, June 25 1858

J Medill, Esq.
My dear Sir

Your note of the 23rd. did not reach me till last evening. The Times article I saw yesterday morning. I will give you a brief history of facts, upon which you may rely with entire confidence, and from which you can frame such articles or paragraphs as you see fit.

I was in Congress but a single term. I was a candidate when the Mexican war broke out—and I then took the ground, which I never varied from, that the Administration had done wrong in getting us into the war, but that the Officers and soldiers who went to the field must be supplied and sustained at all events. I was elected the first Monday of August 1846, but, in regular course, only took my seat December 6, 1847. In the interval all the battles had been fought, and the war was substantially ended, though our army was still in Mexico, and the treaty of peace was not finally concluded till May 30. 1848. Col. E. D. Baker had been elected to congress from the same district, for the regular term next preceding mine; but having gone to Mexico himself, and having resigned his seat in Congress, a man by the name of John Henry, was elected to fill Baker's vacancy, and so came into congress before I did. On the 23rd. day of February 1847 (the very day I believe, Col. John Hardin was killed at Buena Vista, and certainly more than nine months before I took a seat in congress) a bill corresponding with great accuracy to that mentioned by the Times, passed the House of Representatives, and *John Henry* voted against it, as may be seen in the Journal of that session at pages 406-7. The bill became a law; and is found in the U. S. Statutes at Large—Vol. 9. Page 149.

This I suppose is the real origin of the Times' attack upon

me. In its blind rage to assail me, it has seized on a vague recollection of Henry's vote, and appropriated it to me. I scarcely think any one is quite vile enough to make such a charge in such terms, without some slight belief in the truth of it.

Henry was my personal and political friend, and, as I thought, a very good man; and when I first learned of that vote, I well remember how astounded and mortified I was. This very bill, voted against by Henry, passed into a law, and made the appropriations for the year ending June 30. 1848—extending a full month beyond the actual and formal ending of the war. When I came into Congress, money was needed to meet the appropriations made, and to be made; and accordingly on the 17th. day of Feb. 1848, a bill to borrow 18,500 000—passed the House of Representatives, for which I voted, as will appear by the Journal of that session page 426, 427. The act itself, reduced to 16,000 000 (I suppose in the Senate) is found in U. S. Statutes at Large Vol. 9-217.

Again, on the 8th of March 1848, a bill passed the House of Representatives, for which I voted as may be seen by the Journal 520-521 It passed into a law, and is found in U. S. Statutes at Large Page 215 and forward. The last section of the act on page 217—contains an appropriation of 800 000—for clothing the volunteers.

It is impossible to refer to all the votes I gave but the above I think are sufficient as specimens; and you may safely deny that I ever gave any vote for withholding any supplies whatever, from officers or soldiers of the Mexican war. I have examined the Journals a good deal; and hence I can not be mistaken; for I have my eye always upon it. I must close to get this into the mail.

Yours very truly
A. Lincoln

Lincoln's opposition to the Mexican War had cropped up to plague him again during his campaign against Douglas, the Chicago Times, *Douglas's spokesman in Chicago, making false charges that Lincoln had voted against a bill appropriating money for medicines and the employment of nurses for wounded American soldiers. Medill, one of the owners of the* Chicago Daily Press and Tribune, *immediately wrote Lincoln for a refutation, which Lincoln supplied promptly in this letter.*

LETTER TO JAMES W. SOMERS JUNE 25, 1858

Springfield, June 25. 1858.

James W. Somers, Esq
My dear Sir

Yours of the 22nd. enclosing a draft of $200 was duly received. I have paid it on the judgment, and herewith you have the receipt.

I do not wish to say any thing as to who shall be the Republican candidate for the Legislature in your District, further than that I have full confidence in Dr. Hull. Have you ever got in the way of consulting with McKinley, in political matters? He is true as steel, and his judgment is very good. The last I heard from him he rather thought Weldon of DeWitt was our best timber for representative, all things considered. But you there, must settle it among yourselves.

It may well puzzle older heads than yours to understand *how*, as the Dred Scott decision holds, Congress can authorize a terrtorial [*sic*] Legislature to do every thing else, and can *not* authorize them to prohibit slavery. That is one of the things the court can *decide*, but can never give an intelligible reason for.

Yours very truly,
A. Lincoln

James W. Somers was a lawyer of Urbana, Illinois, who after Lincoln's election was appointed to a position in the pension office which he held for more than a quarter of a century. Lincoln's succinct comment at the end of this letter is perhaps his briefest statement of the essential contradiction involved in the Dred Scott decision.

SPEECH IN REPLY TO DOUGLAS AT CHICAGO, ILLINOIS. JULY 10, 1858

My Fellow-Citizens:—

On yesterday evening, upon the occasion of the reception given to Senator Douglas, I was furnished with a seat very convenient for hearing him, and was otherwise very courteously treated by him and by his friends, and for which I thank him and them. During the course of his remarks my name was mentioned in such a way, as I suppose renders it at least not improper that I should make some sort of reply to him. I shall not attempt to follow him in the precise order in which he addressed the assembled multitude upon that occasion, though I shall perhaps do so in the main.

There was one question to which he asked the attention of the crowd, which I deem of somewhat less importance—at least of propriety for me to dwell upon—than the others, which he brought in near the close of his speech, and which I think it would not be entirely proper for me to omit attending to, and yet if I were not to give some attention to it now, I should probably forget it altogether. While I am upon this subject, allow me to say that I do not intend to indulge in that inconvenient mode sometimes adopted in public speaking, of reading from documents; but I shall depart from that rule so far as to read a little scrap from his speech, which notices this first topic of which I shall speak—that is, provided I can find it in the paper:

"I have made up my mind to appeal to the people against the combination that has been made against me:—the Republican leaders having formed an alliance, an unholy and unnatural alliance, with a portion of unscrupulous federal office-holders. I intend to fight that allied army wherever I meet them. I know they deny the alliance, but yet these men who are trying to divide the Democratic party for the purpose of electing a Republican Senator in my place, are just as much the agents and tools of the supporters of Mr. Lincoln. Hence, I shall deal with this allied army just as the Russians dealt with the Allies at Sebastopol—that is, the Russians did not stop to inquire, when they fired a broadside, whether it hit an Englishman, a Frenchman, or a Turk. Nor will I stop to inquire, nor shall I hesitate, whether my blows shall hit these Republican leaders or their allies who are holding the federal offices and yet acting in concert with them."

Well, now, gentlemen, is not that very alarming? Just to think of it! right at the outset of his canvass, I, a poor, kind, amiable, intelligent gentlemen, I am to be slain in this way. Why, my friend, the Judge, is not only, as it turns out, not a dead lion; nor even a living one—he is the rugged Russian Bear!

But if they will have it—for he says that we deny it—that there is any such alliance, as he says there is—and I don't propose hanging very much upon this question of veracity—but if he will have it that there is such an alliance—that the Administration men and we are allied, and we stand in the attitude of English, French, and Turk, and he occupying the position of the Russian, in that case, I beg that he will indulge us while we barely suggest to him, that these allies took Sebastopol.

Gentlemen, only a few more words as to this alliance. For my part, I have to say, that whether there be such an alliance, depends, so far as I know, upon what may be a right definition of the term *alliance.* If for the Republican party to see the other great party to which they are opposed divided among themselves, and not try to stop the division and rather be glad of it—if that is an alliance I confess I am in; but if it is meant to be said that the Republicans had formed an alliance going beyond that, by which there is contribution of money or sacrifice of principle on the one side or the other, so far as the Republican party is concerned, if there be any such thing, I protest that I neither know of it, nor do I believe it. I will however say—as I think this branch of the argument is lugged in—I would, before I leave it, state, for the benefit of those concerned, that one of those same Buchanan men did once tell me of an argument that he made for his opposition to Judge Douglas. He said that a friend of our Senator Douglas has been talking to him, and had among other things said to him: "Why, you don't want to beat Douglas?" "Yes" said he, "I do want to beat him, and I will tell you why. I believe his original Nebraska Bill was right in the abstract, but it was wrong in the time that it was brought forward. It was wrong in the application to a Territory in regard to which the question had been settled; it was brought forward at a time when nobody asked him; it was tendered to the South when the South had not asked for it, but when they could not well refuse it; and for this same reason he forced that question upon our party: it has sunk our best men all over the nation, everywhere; and now when our President, struggling with the difficulties of this man's getting up, has reached the very hardest point to turn in the case, he deserts him, and I *am* for putting him where he will trouble us no more."

Now, gentlemen, that is not my argument—that is not my argument at all. I have only been stating to you an argument of a Buchanan man. You will judge if there is any force in it. Popular Sovereignty! everlasting Popular Sovereignty! Let us for a moment inquire into this vast matter of Popular Sovereignty. What is Popular Sovereignty? We recollect that at an early period in the history of this struggle there was another name for this same thing—*Squatter Sovereignty.* It was not exactly Popular Sovereignty, but Squatter Sovereignty. What do those terms mean? What do they mean when used now? And vast credit is taken by our friend, the Judge, in regard to his support of it, when he declares the last years of his life have been, and all the future years of his life shall be, devoted to this matter of Popular Sovereignty. What is it? Why, it is the sovereignty of the people. What was Squatter Sovereignty? I suppose if it had any significance at all, it was the right of the people to govern themselves, to be sovereign over their own affairs, while they were squatted down in a country not their own, while they had squatted on a territory that did not belong to them, in the sense that a State belongs to the people who inhabit it,—when it belonged to the nation—such right to govern themselves was called "Squatter Sovereignty."

Now, I wish you to mark. What has become of that Squatter Sovereignty? What has become of it? Can you get anybody to tell you now that the people of a Territory have any authority to govern themselves, in regard to this mooted question of slavery, before they form a State Constitution? No such thing at all, although there is a general running fire, and although there has been a hurrah made in every speech on that side, assuming that that policy had given the people of a Territory the right to govern themselves upon this question: yet the point is dodged. To-day it has been decided—no more than a year ago it was decided by the Supreme Court of the United States, and is insisted upon to-day, that the people of a Territory have no right to exclude slavery from a Territory, that if any one man chooses to take slaves into a Territory, all the rest of the people have no right to keep them out. This being so, and this decision being made one of the points that the Judge approved, and one in the approval of which he says he means to keep me down—*put* me down I should not say, for I have never been up. He says he is in favor of it, and sticks to it, and expects to win his battle on that decision, which says that there is no such thing as Squatter Sovereignty, but that any one man may take slaves into a Territory, and all the other men of the Territory may be opposed to it, and yet by reason of the constitution they cannot prohibit it. When that is so, how much is left of this vast matter of Squatter Sovereignty, I should like to know?

When we get back, we get to the point of the right of the people to make a constitution. Kansas was settled, for example, in 1854. It was a Territory yet, without having formed a constitution, in a very regular way, for three years. All this time negro slavery could be taken in by any few individuals, and by that decision of the Supreme Court, which the Judge approves, all the rest of the people cannot keep it out; but when they come to make a constitution, they may say they will not have slavery. But it is there; they are obliged to tolerate it in some way, and all experience shows that it will be so—for they will not take the negro slaves and absolutely deprive the owners of them. All experience shows this to be so. All that space of time that runs from the beginning of the settlement of the Territory until there is a sufficiency of people to make a State Constitution—all that portion of time Popular Sovereignty is given up. The seal is absolutely put down upon it by the Court decision, and Judge Douglas puts his on the top of that; yet he is appealing to the people to give him vast credit for his devotion to Popular Sovereignty.

Again, when we get to the question of the right of the people to form a State Constitution as they please, to form it with slavery or without slavery—if that is anything new, I confess I don't know it. Has there ever been a time when any one said that anybody other than the people of a Territory itself should form their constitution? What is new in it, that Judge Douglas should have fought several years of his life, and pledge himself to fight all the remaining years of his life for? Can Judge Douglas find anybody on earth that said that anybody else should form a constitution for a people? (A voice, "Yes.") Well, I should like you to name him; I should like to know who he was. (Same voice, "John Calhoun.")

Mr. Lincoln—No, Sir, I never heard of even John Calhoun saying such a thing. He insisted on the same principle as Judge Douglas; but his mode of applying it in fact, was wrong. It is enough for my purpose to ask this crowd, when ever a Republican said anything against it? They never said anything against it, but they have constantly spoken for it; and whosoever will undertake to examine the platform, and the speeches of responsible men of the party, and of irresponsible men, too, if you please, will be unable to find one word from anybody in the Republican ranks, opposed to that Popular Sovereignty which Judge Douglas thinks that he has invented. I suppose that Judge Douglas will claim, in a little while, that he is the inventor of the idea that the people should govern themselves; that nobody ever thought of such a thing until he brought it forward. We do remember that in that old Declaration of Independence, it is said that "We hold these truths to be self-evident, that all men are created equal; that they are endowed by their Creator with certain inalienable rights; that among these are life, liberty, and the pursuit of happiness; that to secure these rights, governments are instituted among men, deriving their just powers from the consent of the governed." There is the origin of Popular Sovereignty. Who, then, shall come in at this day and claim that he invented it?

The Lecompton Constitution connects itself with this question, for it is in this matter of the Lecompton Constitution that our friend Judge Douglas claims such vast credit. I agree that in opposing the Lecompton Constitution, so far as I can perceive, he was right. I do not deny that at all; and gentlemen, you will readily see why I could not deny it, even if I wanted to. But I do not wish to; for all the Republicans in the nation opposed it, and they would have opposed it just as much without Judge Douglas' aid, as with it. They had all taken ground against it long before he did. Why, the reason that he urges against that Constitution, I urged against him a year before. I have the printed speech in my hand. The argument that he makes, why that Constitution should not be adopted, that the people were not fairly represented nor allowed to vote, I pointed out in a speech a year ago, which I hold in my hand now, that no fair chance was to be given the people. ("Read it, Read it.") I shall not waste your time by trying to read it. ("Read it, Read it.") Gentlemen, reading from speeches is a very tedious business, particularly for an old man that has to put on spectacles, and the more so if the man be so tall that he has to bend over to the light.

A little more, now, as to this matter of popular sovereignty and the Lecompton Constitution. The Lecompton Constitution, as the Judge tells us, was defeated. The defeat of it was a good thing or it was not. He thinks the defeat of it was a good thing and so do I, and we agree in that. Who defeated it?

A voice—"Judge Douglas."

Mr. Lincoln—Yes, he furnished himself, and if you suppose he controlled the other Democrats that went with him, he furnished *three* votes; while the Republicans furnished *twenty*.

That is what he did to defeat it. In the House of Representatives he and his friends furnished some twenty votes, and the Republicans furnished *ninety odd*. Now who was it that did the work?

A voice—"Douglas."

Mr. Lincoln—Why yes, Douglas did it! To be sure he did.

Let us, however, put that proposition another way. The Republicans could not have done it without Judge Douglas. Could he have done it without them? Which could have come the nearest to doing it without the other?

A voice—"Who killed the bill?"

Another voice—"Douglas."

Mr. Lincoln—Ground was taken against it by the Republicans long before Douglas did it. The proportion of opposition to that measure is about five to one.

A voice—"Why don't they come out on it?"

Mr. Lincoln—You don't know what you are talking about, my friend. I am quite willing to answer any gentleman in the crowd who asks an *intelligent* question.

Now, who in all this country has ever found any of our friends of Judge Douglas' way of thinking, and who have acted upon this main question, that has ever thought of uttering a word in behalf of Judge Trumbull? (A voice—"We have.") I defy you to show a printed resolution passed in a Democratic meeting—I take it upon myself to defy any man to show a printed resolution of a Democratic meeting, large or small, in favor of Judge Trumbull, or any of the five to one Republicans who beat that bill. Everything must be for the Democrats! They did everything, and the five to one that really did the thing, they snub over, and they do not seem to remember that they have an existence upon the face of the earth.

Gentlemen: I fear that I shall become tedious. I leave this branch of the subject to take hold of another. I take up that part of Judge Douglas' speech in which he respectfully attended to me.

Judge Douglas makes two points upon my recent speech at Springfield. He says they are to be the issues of this campaign. The first one of these points he bases upon the language in a speech which I delivered at Springfield, which I believe I can quote correctly from memory. I said there that "we are now far into the fifth year since a policy was instituted for the avowed object and with the confident promise of putting an end to slavery agitation; under the operation of that policy, that agitation had [not?] only not ceased, but has constantly augmented. I believe it will not cease until a crisis shall have been reached and passed. A house divided against itself cannot stand. I believe this government cannot endure permanently half slave and half free. I do not expect the Union to be dissolved,"—I am quoting from my speech—"I do not expect the house to fall, but I do expect it will cease to be divided. It will become all one thing or all the other. Either the opponents of slavery will arrest the spread of it, and place it where the public mind shall rest in the belief that it is in the course of ultimate extinction, or its advocates will push it forward until it shall become alike lawful in all the States North as well as South."

What is the paragraph? In this paragraph which I have quoted in your hearing, and to which I ask the attention of all, Judge Douglas thinks he discovers great political heresy. I want your attention particularly to what he has inferred from it. He says I am in favor of making all the States of this Union uniform in all their internal regulations; that in all their domestic concerns I am in favor of making them entirely uniform. He draws this inference from the language I have quoted to you. He says that I am in favor of making war by the North upon the South for the extinction of slavery; that I am also in favor of inviting, as he expresses it, the South to a war upon the North for the purpose of nationalizing slavery. Now, it is singular enough, if you will carefully read that passage over, that I did not say that I was in favor of anything in it. I only said what I expected would take place. I made a prediction only—it may have been a foolish one perhaps. I did not even say that I desired that slavery should be put in course of ultimate extinction. I do say so now, however, so there need be no longer any difficulty about that. It may be written down in the next speech.

Gentlemen, Judge Douglas informed you that this speech of mine was probably carefully prepared. I admit that it was.

I am not master of language; I have not a fine education; I am not capable of entering into a disquisition upon dialectics, as I believe you call it; but I do not believe the language I employed bears any such construction as Judge Douglas put upon it. But I don't care about a quibble in regard to words. I know what I meant, and I will not leave this crowd in doubt, if I can explain it to them, what I really meant in the use of that paragraph.

I am not, in the first place, unaware that this Government has endured eighty-two years, half slave and half free. I know that. I am tolerably well acquainted with the history of the country, and I know that it has endured eighty-two years, half slave and half free. I *believe*—and that is what I meant to allude to there—I *believe* it has endured because, during all that time, until the introduction of the Nebraska Bill, the public mind did rest, all the time, in the belief that slavery was in course of ultimate extinction. That was what gave us the rest that we had through that period of eighty-two years;—at least, so I believe. I have always hated slavery, I think, as much as any Abolitionist. I have been an Old Line Whig. I have always hated it, but I have always been quiet about it until this new era of the introduction of the Nebraska Bill began. I always believed that everybody was against it, and that it was in course of ultimate extinction. (Pointing to Mr. Browning, who stood near by,) Browning thought so; the great mass of the nation have rested in the belief that slavery was in course of ultimate extinction. They had reason so to believe.

The adoption of the Constitution and its attendant history led the people to believe so; and that such was the belief of the framers of the Constitution itself. Why did those old men, about the time of the adoption of the Constitution, decree that slavery should not go into the new Territory, where it had not already gone? Why declare that within twenty years the African Slave Trade, by which slaves are supplied, might be cut off by Congress? Why were all these acts? I might enumerate more of such acts —but enough. What were they but a clear indication that the framers of the Constitution intended and expected the ultimate extinction of that institution? And now when I say, as I say in this speech, that Judge Douglas has quoted from, when I say that I think the opponents of slavery will resist the farther spread of it, and place it where the public mind shall rest with the belief that it is in course of ultimate extinction, I only mean to say, that they will place it where the founders of this government originally placed it.

I have said a hundred times, and I have now no inclination to take it back, that I believe there is no right, and ought to be no inclination, in the people of the free States to enter into the slave States, and interfere with the question of slavery at all. I have said that always. Judge Douglas has heard me say it—if not quite a hundred times, at least as good as a hundred times; and when it is said that I am in favor of interfering with slavery where it exists, I know it is unwarranted by anything I have ever *intended*, and, as I believe, by anything I have ever *said*. If, by any means, I have ever used language which could fairly be so construed, (as, however, I believe I never have,) I now correct it.

So much, then, for the inference that Judge Douglas draws, that I am in favor of setting the sections at war with one another. I know that I never meant any such thing, and I believe that no fair mind can infer any such thing from anything I have ever said.

Now, in relation to his inference that I am in favor of a general consolidation of all the local institutions of the various States. I will attend to that for a little while, and try to inquire if I can how on earth it could be that any man could draw such an inference from anything I said. I have said, very many times, in Judge Douglas' hearing, that no man believed more than I in the principle of self-government; that it lies at the bottom of all my ideas of just government from beginning to end. I have denied that his use of that term applies properly. But for the thing itself I deny that any man has ever gone ahead of me in his devotion to the principle, whatever he may have done in efficiency in advocating it. I think that I have said it in your hearing—that I believe each individual is naturally entitled to do as he pleases with himself and the fruit of his labor, so far as it in no wise interferes with any other man's rights, that each community, as a State, has a right to do exactly as it pleases with all the concerns within that State that interfere with the rights of no other State, and that the general government, upon principle, has no right to interfere with any thing other than that general class of things that does concern the whole. I have said that at all times. I have said, as illustrations, that I do not believe in the right of Illinois to interfere with the cranberry laws of Indiana, the oyster laws of Virginia, or the Liquor Laws of Maine. I have said these things over and over again and I repeat them here as my sentiments.

How is it, then, that Judge Douglas infers, because I hope to see slavery put where the public mind shall rest in the belief that it is in the course of ultimate extinction, that I am in favor of Illinois going over and interfering with the cranberry laws of Indiana? What can authorize him to draw any such inference? I suppose there might be one thing that at least enabled *him* to draw such an inference that would not be true with me or with many others—that is, because he looks upon all this matter of slavery as an exceedingly little thing—this matter of keeping one sixth of the population of the whole nation in a state of oppression and tyranny unequalled in the world. He looks upon it as being an exceedingly little thing—only equal to the question of the cranberry laws of Indiana—as something having no moral question in it—as something on a par with the question of whether a man shall pasture his land with cattle, or plant it with tobacco—so little and so small a thing, that he concludes if I could desire that anything should be done to bring about the ultimate extinction of that little thing, I must be in favor of bringing about an amalgamation of all the other little things in the Union. Now, it so happens—and there, I presume, is the foundation of this mistake—that the Judge thinks thus; and it so happens that there is a vast portion of the American people that do *not* look upon that matter as being this very little thing. They look upon it as a vast moral evil; they can prove it is such by the writings of those who gave us the blessings of liberty which we enjoy, and that they so looked upon it and not as an evil merely confining itself to the States where it is situated; and while we agree that, by the Constitution we assented to, in the States where it exists we have no right to interfere with it because it is in the Constitution and we are by both duty and inclination to stick by that Constitution in all its letter and spirit from beginning to end.

So much then as to my disposition—my wish—to have all the State legislatures blotted out, and to have one general consolidated government, and a uniformity of domestic regulations in all the States, by which I suppose it is meant if we raise corn here, we must make sugar-cane grow here too, and we must make those which grow North, grow in the South. All this I suppose the Judge understands I am in favor of doing. Now, so much for all this nonsense—for I must call it so. The Judge can have no issue with me on a question of establishing uniformity in the domestic regulations of the States.

A little now on the other point—the Dred Scott Decision. Another one of the issues he says that is to be made with me, is upon his devotion to the Dred Scott Decision, and my opposition to it.

I have expressed heretofore, and I now repeat, my opposition to the Dred Scott Decision, but I should be allowed to state the nature of that opposition, and I ask your indulgence while I do so. What is fairly implied by the term Judge Douglas has used, "resistance to the Decision?" I do not resist it. If I wanted to take Dred Scott from his master, I would be interfering with property, and that terrible difficulty that Judge Douglas speaks of, of interfering with property, would arise. But I am doing no such thing as that, but all that I am doing is refusing to obey it as a political rule. If I were in Congress, and a vote should come up on a question whether slavery should be prohibited in a new Territory, in spite of that Dred Scott Decision, I would vote that it should.

That is what I would do. Judge Douglas said last night, that before the Decision he might advance his opinion, and it might be contrary to the decision when it was made; but *after* it was made he would abide by it until it was reversed. Just so! We let this property abide by the decision, but we will try to reverse that decision. We will try to put it where Judge Douglas would not object, for he says he will obey it until it is reversed. Somebody has to reverse that decision, since it is made, and we mean to reverse it, and we mean to do it peaceably.

What are the uses of decisions of courts? They have two uses.

As rules of property they have two uses. First—they decide upon the question before the court. They decide in this case that Dred Scott is a slave. Nobody resists that. Not only that, but they say to everybody else, that persons standing just as Dred Scott stands, are as he is. That is, they say that when a question comes up upon another person it will be so decided again, unless the court decides another way, unless the court overrules its decision. Well, we mean to do what we can to have the court decide the other way. That is one thing we mean to try to do.

The sacredness that Judge Douglas throws around this decision, is a degree of sacredness that has never been before thrown around any other decision. I have never heard of such a thing. Why, decisions apparently contrary to that decision, or that good lawyers thought were contrary to that decision, have been made by that very court before. It is the first of its kind; it is an *astonisher* in legal history. It is a new wonder of the world. It is based upon falsehood in the main as to the facts—allegations of facts upon which it stands are not facts at all in many instances, and no decision made on any question—the first instance of a decision made under so many unfavorable circumstances—thus placed has ever been held by the profession as law, and it has always needed confirmation before the lawyers regarded it as a settled law. But Judge Douglas will have it that all hands must take this extraordinary decision, made under these extraordinary circumstances, and give their vote in Congress in accordance with it, yield to it and obey it in every possible sense. Circumstances alter cases. Do not gentlemen here remember the case of that same Supreme Court, some twenty-five or thirty years ago, deciding that a National Bank was constitutional? I ask, if somebody does not remember that a National Bank was declared to be constitutional? Such is the truth, whether it be remembered or not. The Bank charter ran out, and a re-charter was granted by Congress. That re-charter was laid before Gen. Jackson. It was urged upon him, when he denied the constitutionality of the bank, that the Supreme Court had decided that it was constitutional; and Gen. Jackson then said that the Supreme Court had no right to lay down a rule to govern a co-ordinate branch of the government, the members of which had sworn to support the Constitution—that each member had sworn to support that Constitution as he understood it. I will venture here to say, that I have heard Judge Douglas say that he approved of Gen. Jackson for that act. What has now become of all his tirade about "resistance to the Supreme Court?"

My fellow-citizens, getting back a little, for I pass from these points, when Judge Douglas makes his threat of annihilation upon the "alliance," he is cautious to say that that warfare of his is to fall upon the leaders of the Republican party. Almost every word he utters and every distinction he makes, has its significance. He means for the Republicans that do not count themselves as leaders, to be his friends; he makes no fuss over them; it is the leaders that he is making war upon. He wants it understood that the mass of the Republican party are really his friends. It is only the leaders that are doing something, that are intolerant, and that require extermination at his hands. As this is clearly and unquestionably the light in which he presents that matter, I want to ask your attention, addressing myself to the Republicans here, that I may ask you some questions, as to where you, as the Republican party, would be placed if you sustained Judge Douglas in his present position by a re-election? I do not claim, gentlemen, to be unselfish; I do not pretend that I would not like to go to the United States Senate, I make no such hypocritical pretense, but I do say to you that in this mighty issue, it is nothing to you—nothing to the mass of the people of the nation, whether or not Judge Douglas or myself shall ever be heard of after this night; it may be a trifle to either of us, but in connection with this mighty question, upon which hang the destinies of the nation, perhaps, it is absolutely nothing; but where will you be placed if you re-endorse Judge Douglas? Don't you know how apt he is —how exceedingly anxious he is at all times to seize upon anything and everything to persuade you that something *he* has done *you* did yourselves? Why, he tried to persuade you last night that our Illinois Legislature instructed him to introduce the Nebraska Bill. There was nobody in that Legislature ever thought of such a thing; and when he first introduced the bill, he never thought of it; but still he fights furiously for the proposition, and that he did it because there was a standing instruction to our Senators to be always introducing Nebraska bills. He tells you he is for the Cincinnati Platform, he tells you he is for the Dred Scott Decision. He tells you, not in his speech last night, but substantially in a former speech, that he cares not if slavery is voted up or down—he tells you the struggle on Lecompton is passed—it may come up again or not and if it does he stands where he stood when in spite of him and his opposition you built up the Republican party. If you endorse him, you tell him you do not care whether slavery be voted up or down, and he will close, or try to close your mouths with his declaration, repeated by the day, the week, the month, and the year. Is that what you mean? (Cries of "no;" one voice "yes.") Yes, I have no doubt you who have always been for him, if you mean that. No doubt of that, soberly I have said, and I repeat it. I think, in the position in which Judge Douglas stood in opposing the Lecompton Constitution he was right; he does not know that it will return, but if it does we may know where to find him, and if it does not we may know where to look for him, and that is on the Cincinnati Platform. Now I could ask the Republican party, after all the hard names that Judge Douglas has called them by—all his repeated charges of their inclination to marry with and hug negroes, all his declarations of Black Republicanism—by the way, we are improving, the black has got rubbed off—but with all that, if he be endorsed by Republican votes, where do you stand? Plainly, you stand ready saddled, bridled and harnessed and waiting to be driven over into the slavery extension camp of the nation,—just ready to be driven over, tied together in a lot—to be driven over, every man with a rope around his neck, that halter being held by Judge Douglas. That is the question. If Republican men have been in earnest in what they have done, I think they had better not do it, but I think that the Republican party is made up of those who, as far as they can peaceably, will oppose the extension of slavery, and who will hope for its ultimate extinction—who will believe, if it ceases to spread, that it is in course of ultimate extinction. If they believe it is wrong in grasping up the new lands of the continent, and keeping them from the settlement of free white laborers, who want the land to bring up their families upon; if they are in earnest, although they may make a mistake, they will grow restless, and the time will come when they will come back again and reorganize, if not by the same name, at least upon the same principles as their party now has. It is better, then, to save the work while it is begun. You have done the labor; maintain it—keep it. If men choose to serve you, go with them; but as you have made up your organization upon principle, stand by it; for, as surely as God reigns over you, and has inspired your mind, and given you a sense of propriety, and continues to give you hope, so surely will you still cling to these ideas, and you will at last come back again after your wanderings, merely to do your work over again.

We were often—more than once, at least—in the course of Judge Douglas' speech last night, reminded that this government was made for white men—that he believed it was made for white men! Well, that is putting it in a shape in which no one wants to deny it; but the Judge then goes into his passion for drawing inferences that are not warranted. I protest, now and forever, against that counterfeit logic which presumes that because I did not want a negro woman for a slave, I do necessarily want her for a wife. My understanding is that I need not have her for either, but, as God made us separate, we can leave one another alone, and do one another much good thereby. There are white men enough to marry all the white women, and enough black men to marry all the black women, and in God's name let them be so married. The Judge regales us with the terrible enormities that take place by the mixture of races; that the inferior race bears the superior down. Why, Judge, if we will not let them get together in the Territories, they won't mix there.

A voice—"Three cheers for Lincoln." (The cheers were given with a hearty good-will.)

Mr. Lincoln—I should say at least that that is a self-evident truth.

Now, it happens that we meet together once every year, sometimes about the 4th of July, for some reason or other. These 4th of July gatherings, I suppose, have their uses. If you will indulge me, I will state what I suppose to be some of them.

We are now a mighty nation, we are thirty—or about thirty millions of people, and we own and inhabit about one-fifteenth part of the dry land of the whole earth. We run our memory back over the pages of history for about eighty-two years, and we discover that we were then a very small people in point of numbers, vastly inferior to what we are now, with a vastly less extent of country,—with vastly less of everything we deem desirable among men,—we look upon the change as exceedingly advantageous to us and to our posterity, and we fix upon something that happened away back, as in some way or other being connected with this rise of prosperity. We find a race of men living in that day whom we claim as our fathers and grandfathers; they were iron men; they fought for the principle that they were contending for; and we understand that by what they then did it has followed that the degree of prosperity that we now enjoy has come to us. We hold this annual celebration to remind ourselves of all the good done in this process of time, of how it was done and who did it, and how we are historically connected with it; and we go from these meetings in better humor with ourselves—we feel more attached the one to the other, and more firmly bound to the country we inhabit. In every way we are better men in the age, and race, and country in which we live, for these celebrations. But after we have done all this we have not yet reached the whole. There is something else connected with it. We have besides these men—descended by blood from our ancestors—among us perhaps half our people who are not descendants at all of these men, they are men who have come from Europe—German, Irish, French and Scandinavian—men that have come from Europe themselves, or whose ancestors have come hither and settled here, finding themselves our equals in all things. If they look back through this history to trace their connection with those days by blood, they find they have none, they cannot carry themselves back into that glorious epoch and make themselves feel that they are part of us, but when they look through that old Declaration of Independence, they find that those old men say that "We hold these truths to be self-evident, that all men are created equal," and then they feel that that moral sentiment taught in that day evidences their relation to those men, that it is the father of all moral principle in them, and that they have a right to claim it as though they were blood of the blood, and flesh of the flesh, of the men who wrote that Declaration, and so they are. That is the electric cord in that Declaration that links the hearts of patriotic and liberty-loving men together, that will link those patriotic hearts as long as the love of freedom exists in the minds of men throughout the world.

Now, sirs, for the purpose of squaring things with this idea of "don't care if slavery is voted up or voted down," for sustaining the Dred Scott Decision, for holding that the Declaration of Independence did not mean anything at all, we have Judge Douglas giving his exposition of what the Declaration of Independence means, and we have him saying that the people of America were equal to the people of England. According to his construction, you Germans are not connected with it. Now, I ask you in all soberness, if all these things, if indulged in, if ratified, if confirmed and endorsed, if taught to our children and repeated to them, do not tend to rub out the sentiment of liberty in the country, and to transform this government into a government of some other form. These arguments that are made, that the inferior race are to be treated with as much allowance as they are capable of enjoying; that as much is to be done for them as their condition will allow. What are these arguments? They are the arguments that kings have made for enslaving the people in all ages of the world. You will find that all the arguments in favor of kingcraft were of this class; they always bestrode the necks of the people, not that they wanted to do it, but because the people were better off for being ridden. That is their argument, and this argument of the Judge is the same old serpent that says, you work, and I eat, you toil, and I will enjoy the fruits of it. Turn it whatever way you will—whether it come from the mouth of a King, an excuse for enslaving the people of his country, or from the mouth of men of one race as a reason for enslaving the men of another race, it is all the same old serpent, and I hold if that course of argumentation that is made for the purpose of convincing the public mind that we should not care about this, should be granted, it does not stop with the negro. I should like to know if taking this old Declaration of Independence, which declares that all men are equal upon principle, and making exceptions to it, where will it stop? If one man says it does not mean a negro, why may not another say it does not mean some other man? If that Declaration is not the truth, let us get the Statute book in which we find it and tear it out! Who is so bold as to do it! If it is not true let us tear it out! (cries of "no, no,") let us stick to it then (cheers). Let us stand firmly by it then (applause).

It may be argued that there are certain conditions that make necessities and impose them upon us, and to the extent that a necessity is imposed upon a man, he must submit to it. I think that was the condition in which we found ourselves when we established this government. We had slavery among us, we could not get our Constitution unless we permitted them to remain in slavery, we could not secure the good we did secure if we grasped for more, and having by necessity submitted to that much, it does not destroy the principle that is the charter of our liberties. Let that charter stand as our standard.

My friend has said to me that I am a poor hand to quote Scripture. I will try it again, however. It is said in one of the admonitions of the Lord, "As your Father in heaven is perfect, be ye also perfect." The Saviour, I suppose, did not expect that any human creature could be perfect as the Father in Heaven; but He said, "As your Father in Heaven is perfect, be ye also perfect." He set that up as a standard, and he who did most towards reaching that standard, attained the highest degree of moral perfection. So I say in relation to the principle that all men are created equal, let it be as nearly reached as we can. If we cannot give freedom to every creature, let us do nothing that will impose slavery upon any other creature. Let us then turn this government back into the channel in which the framers of the Constitution originally placed it. Let us stand firmly by each other. If we do not do so, we are turning in the contrary direction, that our friend Judge Douglas proposes—not intentionally—as working in the traces that tend to make this one universal Slave Nation. He is one that runs in that direction, and as such I resist him.

My friends, I have detained you about as long as I desired to do, and I have only to say, let us discard all this quibbling about this man and the other man—this race and that race and the other race being inferior, and therefore they must be placed in an inferior position—discarding our standard that we have left us. Let us discard all these things, and unite as one people throughout this land, until we shall once more stand up declaring that all men are created equal.

My friends, I could not, without launching off upon some new topic, which would detain you too long, continue to-night. I thank you for this most extensive audience that you have furnished me to-night. I leave you, hoping that the lamp of liberty will burn in your bosoms until there shall no longer be a doubt that all men are created free and equal.

The Lecompton Constitution, which occupies so much of Lincoln's attention in this speech of July 10 and the next speech of July 17, was drawn up by the constitutional convention of the Kansas Territory convened in the town of Lecompton. The principal fault in the document, as free-state men saw it, was its guaranteeing property in slaves already in Kansas. In addition, it contained a special clause that would have prohibited both the possibility of legally emancipating slaves without consent of the owners and the possibility of legally denying further entrance of slaves into the state. This clause was the only part of the document submitted to the voters following the convention in 1857, and hence the opponents of slavery denounced the whole document as a trick, inasmuch as, whether the clause was voted in or out, the constitution would still guarantee property in slaves already in the state. As a result, Kansas free-state voters stayed away from the polls and denounced the election as a fraud. Although Douglas opposed, the Democratic majority in the United States Senate voted to admit Kansas under the Lecompton Constitution. The House of Representatives did not concur, however, and when the Lecompton Constitution was resubmitted to the voters in August, 1858, it was rejected by an overwhelming majority, in spite of the

English Bill, which offered Kansans what was in effect a bribe in the form of public lands, provided that they accept the Lecompton Constitution.

SPEECH IN REPLY TO DOUGLAS AT SPRINGFIELD, ILLINOIS. JULY 17, 1858

Fellow-citizens:

Another election which is deemed an important one is approaching, and, as I suppose, the Republican party will without much difficulty elect their State ticket. But in regard to the Legislature, we, the Republicans, labor under some disadvantages. In the first place, we have a Legislature to elect upon an apportionment of the representation made several years ago, when the proportion of the population was far greater in the south (as compared with the north) than it now is; and in as much as our opponents hold almost entire sway in the south, and we a correspondingly large majority in the north, the fact that we are now to be represented as we were years ago, when the population was different, is to us a very great disadvantage. We had, in the year 1855, according to law, a census or an enumeration of the inhabitants, taken for the purpose of a new apportionment of representation. We know what a fair apportionment of representation upon that census would give us. We know that it could not, if fairly made, fail to give the Republican party from six to ten more members of the Legislature than they can probably get as the law now stands. It so happened at the last session of the Legislature, that our opponents, holding the control of both branches of the Legislature, steadily refused to give us such an apportionment as we were rightfully entitled to have upon the census then taken. The Legislature steadily refused to give us such an apportionment as we were rightfully entitled to have upon the census taken of the population of the State. The Legislature would pass no bill upon that subject, except such as was at least as unfair to us as the old one, and in which, in some instances, two men in the Democratic regions were allowed to go as far toward sending a member to the Legislature as three were in the Republican regions. Comparison was made at the time as to representative and senatorial districts, which completely demonstrated that such was the fact. Such a bill was passed, and tendered to the Republican Governor for his signature; but principally for the reasons I have stated, he withheld his approval, and the bill fell without becoming a law.

Another disadvantage under which we labor, is, that there are one or two Democratic Senators who will be members of the next legislature, and will vote for the election of Senator, who are holding over in districts in which we could, on all reasonable calculation, elect men of our own, if we only had the chance of an election. When we consider that there are but twenty-five Senators in the Senate, taking two from the side where they rightfully belong, and adding them to the other, is to us a disadvantage not to be lightly regarded. Still, so it is. We have this to contend with. Perhaps there is no ground of complaint on our part. In attending to the many things involved in the last general election for President, Governor, Auditor, Treasurer, Superintendent of Public Instruction, Members of Congress, of the Legislature, county officers and so on, we allowed these things to happen by want of sufficient attention, and we have no cause to complain of our adversaries, so far as this matter is concerned. But we have some cause to complain of the refusal to give us a fair apportionment.

There is still another disadvantage under which we labor, and to which I will ask your attention. It arises out of the relative positions of the two persons who stand before the State as candidates for the Senate. Senator Douglas is of world wide renown. All the anxious politicians of his party, or who have been of his party, for years past, have been looking upon him, as certainly, at no very distant day to be the President of the United States. They have seen in his round, jolly, fruitful face, postoffices, land offices, marshalships and cabinet appointments, chargeships and foreign missions, bursting and sprouting out in wonderful exuberance, ready to be laid hold of by their greedy hands. And as they have been gazing upon this attractive picture so long they cannot, in the little distraction that has taken place in the party, bring themselves to quite give up the charming hope; but with greedier anxiety they rush about him, sustain him, and give him marches, triumphal entries, and receptions beyond what even in the days of his highest prosperity they could have brought about in his favor. On the contrary, no body has ever expected me to be President. In my poor, lean, lank face nobody has ever seen that any cabbages were sprouting out. These are disadvantages all taken together that the Republicans labor under. *We* have to fight this battle upon principle, and upon principle alone. I am, in a certain sense made the standard bearer in behalf of the Republicans. I was made so, merely because there had to be some one so placed—I being, in no wise preferable to any other one of the twenty—fifty—perhaps a hundred we have in the Republican ranks. Then I say I wish it to be distinctly understood, and borne in mind, that we have to fight this battle without many—perhaps without any—of the external aids, which are brought to bear against us. So I hope those with whom I am surrounded have principle enough to nerve themselves for the task and leave nothing undone that can be fairly done, to bring about the right result.

After Senator Douglas left Washington, as his movements were made known by the public prints, he tarried a considerable time in the city of New York; and it was heralded that, like another Napoleon, he was lying by, and framing the plan of his campaign. It was telegraphed to Washington City, and published in the *Union*, that he was framing this plan for the purpose of going to Illinois to pounce upon and annihilate the treasonable and disunion speech which Lincoln had made here on the 16th of June. Now, I do suppose that the Judge really spent some time in New York maturing the plan of the campaign, as his friends heralded for him. I have been able, by noting his movements since his arrival in Illinois, to discover evidences confirmatory of that allegation. I think I have been able to see what are the material points of that plan. I will, for a little while, ask your attention to some of them. What I shall point out, though not showing the whole plan, are, nevertheless, the main points, as I suppose.

They are not very numerous. The first is popular sovereignty. The second and third are attacks upon my speech made on the 16th of June. Out of these three points—drawing within the range of popular sovereignty the question of the Lecompton Constitution—he makes his principal assault. Upon these his successive speeches are substantially one and the same. On this matter of popular sovereignty I wish to be a little careful. Auxiliary to these main points, to be sure, are their thunderings of cannon, their marching and music, their fizzle-gigs and fireworks; but I will not waste time with them. They are but the little trappings of the campaign.

Coming to the substance—the first point—"popular sovereignty." It is to be labeled upon the cars in which he travels; put upon the hacks he rides in; to be flaunted upon the arches he passes under, and the banners which wave over him. It is to be dished up in as many varieties as a French cook can produce soups from potatoes. Now, as this is so great a staple of the plan of the campaign, it is worth while to examine it carefully; and if we examine only a very little, and do not allow ourselves to be misled, we shall be able to see that the whole thing is the most arrant Quixotism that was ever enacted before a community. What is this matter of popular sovereignty? The first thing, in order to understand it, is to get a good definition of what it is, and after that to see how it is applied.

I suppose almost every one knows, that in this controversy, whatever has been said, has had reference to the question of negro slavery. We have not been in a controversy about the right of the people to govern themselves in the *ordinary* matters of domestic concern in the States and Territories. Mr. Buchanan in one of his late messages (I think when he sent up the Lecompton Constitution), urged that the main points to which the public attention had been directed, was not in regard to the great variety of small domestic matters, but was directed to the question of negro slavery; and he asserted, that if the people had had a fair chance to vote on that question, there was no reasonable ground of objection in regard to minor questions. Now, while I think that the people had *not* had given, or offered them, a fair chance upon that slavery question; still, if there had been a fair submission to a vote upon that main question, the President's proposition would have been true to the uttermost. Hence, when hereafter, I speak of popular sovereignty, I wish to be understood as applying what I say to the question of slavery only, and not to other minor domestic matters of a territory or a State.

Does Judge Douglas, when he says that several of the past years of his life have been devoted to the question of "popular sovereignty," and that all the remainder of his life shall be devoted to it, does he mean to say that he has been devoting his life to securing to the people of the Territories the right to exclude slavery from the Territories? If he means so to say, he means to deceive; because he, and every one knows that the decision of the Supreme Court, which he approves and makes special ground of attack upon me for disapproving, forbids the people of a Territory to exclude slavery. This covers the whole ground, from the settlement of a Territory till it reaches the degree of maturity entitling it to form a State Constitution. So far as all that ground is concerned, the Judge is not sustaining popular sovereignty, but absolutely opposing it. He sustains the decision which declares that the popular will of the Territories has no constitutional power to exclude slavery during their territorial existence. This being so, the period of time from the first settlement of a Territory, till it reaches the point of forming a State Constitution, is not the thing that the Judge has fought for, or is fighting for, but on the contrary, he has fought for, and is fighting for, the thing that annihilates and crushes out that same popular sovereignty.

Well, so much being disposed of, what is left? Why, he is contending for the right of the people, when they come to make a State Constitution, to make it for themselves, and precisely as best suits themselves. I say again, that is Quixotic. I defy contradiction when I declare that the Judge can find no one to oppose him on that proposition. I repeat, there is no body opposing that proposition on *principle*. Let me not be misunderstood. I know that, with reference to the Lecompton Constitution, I may be misunderstood; but when you understand me correctly, my proposition will be true and accurate. No body is opposing or has opposed the right of the people, when they form a constitution, to form it for themselves. Mr. Buchanan and his friends have not done it; they, too, as well as the Republicans and the anti-Lecompton Democrats, have not done it; but, on the contrary, they together have insisted on the right of the people to form a constitution for themselves. The difference between the Buchanan men on the one hand, and the Douglas men and the Republicans on the other, has not been on a question of principle, but on a question of *fact.*

The dispute was upon the question of fact, whether the Lecompton Constitution had been fairly formed by the people or not. Mr. Buchanan and his friends have not contended for the contrary principle any more than the Douglas men or the Republicans. They have insisted that whatever of small irregularities existed in getting up the Lecompton Constitution, were such as happen in the settlement of all new Territories. The question was, was it a fair emanation of the people? It was a question of fact and not of principle. As to the principle, all were agreed. Judge Douglas voted with the Republicans upon that matter of fact.

He and they, by their voices and votes, denied that it was a fair emanation of the people. The Administration affirmed that it was. With respect to the evidence bearing upon that question of fact, I readily agree that Judge Douglas and the Republicans had the right on their side, and that the Administration was wrong. But I state again that as a matter of principle, there is no dispute upon the right of the people in a Territory merging into a State to form a Constitution for themselves without outside interference from any quarter. This being so, what is Judge Douglas going to spend his life for?—Is he going to spend his life in maintaining a principle that no body on earth opposes?—Does he expect to stand up in majestic dignity, and go through his *apotheosis* and become a God, in the maintaining of a principle which, neither a man nor a mouse in all God's creation is opposing? Now something in regard to the Lecompton Constitution more specifically; for I pass from this other question of popular sovereignty as the most arrant humbug that has ever been attempted on an intelligent community.

As to the Lecompton Constitution I have already said that on the question of fact as to whether it was a fair emanation of the people or not, Judge Douglas with the Republicans and some Americans had greatly the argument against the Administration; and while I repeat this, I wish to know what there is in the opposition of Judge Douglas to the Lecompton Constitution that entitles him to be considered the only opponent to it—as being *par excellence* the very *quintessence* of that opposition. I agree to the rightfulness of his opposition. He in the Senate and his class of men there formed the number *three* and no more. In the House of Representatives his class of men—the anti-Lecompton Democrats—formed a number of about twenty. It took one hundred and twenty to defeat the measure against one hundred and twelve. Of the votes of that one hundred and twenty, Judge Douglas' friends furnished twenty, to add to which there were six Americans and ninety-four Republicans. I do not say that I am precisely accurate in their numbers, but I am sufficiently so for any use I am making of it.

Why is it that twenty shall be entitled to all the credit of doing that work, and the hundred none of it? Why, if, as Judge Douglas says, the honor is to be divided and due credit is to be given to other parties, why, is just so much given as is consonant with the wishes, the interests and advancement of the twenty? My understanding is, when a common job is done, or a common enterprize prosecuted, that if I put in five dollars to your one, I have a right to take out five dollars to your one. But he does not so understand it. He declares the dividend of credit for defeating Lecompton upon a basis which seems unprecedented and incomprehensible.

Let us see. Lecompton, in the run was defeated. It afterwards took a sort of cooked up shape, and was passed in the English bill. It is said by the Judge, that the defeat was a good and proper thing. If it was a good thing, why is he entitled to more credit than others, for the performance of that good act, unless there was something in the antecedents of the Republicans that might induce every one to expect that they would join in that good work, and at the same time, something leading them to doubt that he would? Does he place his superior claim to credit, on the ground that he performed a good, which was never expected of him? He says I have a proneness for quoting scripture. If I should do so now, it occurs, that perhaps he places himself somewhat upon the ground of the parable of the lost sheep which went astray upon the mountains, and when the owner of the hundred sheep found the one that was lost, and threw it upon his shoulders, and came home rejoicing, it was said that there was more rejoicing over the one sheep that was lost and had been found, than over the ninety and nine in the fold. The moral is applied by the Saviour in this parable, thus—"Verily, I say unto you, there is more rejoicing in Heaven, over one sinner that repenteth, than over ninety and nine just persons that need no repentance." And now, if the Judge claims the benefit of this parable, *let him repent.* Let him not come up here and say: "I am the only just person; and you are the ninety-nine sinners!" *Repentance*, before *forgiveness* is a provision of the Christian system, and on that condition alone will the Republicans grant his forgiveness.

How will he prove that we have ever occupied a different position in regard to this Lecompton Constitution or any principle in it? He says he did not make his opposition on the ground as to whether it was a free or slave constitution, and he would have you understand that the Republicans made their opposition, because it ultimately became a slave constitution. To make proof in favor of himself on this point, he reminds us that he opposed Lecompton before the vote was taken declaring whether the State was to be free or slave. But he forgets to say that our Republican Senator, Trumbull, made a speech against Lecompton, even before he did.

Why did he oppose it? Partly, as he declares, because the members of the Convention who framed it were not fairly elected by the people; that the people were not allowed to vote unless they had been registered; and that the people of whole counties, in some instances, were not registered. For these reasons he declares the constitution was not an emanation, in any true sense, from the people. He also has an additional objection as to the mode of submitting the constitution back to the people. But bearing on the question of whether the delegates were fairly elected, a speech of his, made something more than twelve months ago, from this stand, becomes important. It was made a little while before the election of the delegates who made Lecompton. In that speech he declared there was every reason to hope and believe the election would be fair; and if any one failed to vote, it would be his own culpable fault.

I, a few days after, made a sort of answer to that speech. In that answer, I made, substantially, the very argument with which he combatted his Lecompton adversaries in the Senate last winter. I pointed to the facts that the people could not vote without being registered, and that the time for registering had gone by. I commented on it as wonderful that Judge Douglas could be ignorant of these facts, which every one else in the nation so well knew.

I now pass from popular sovereignty and Lecompton. I may have occasion to refer to one or both.

When he was preparing his plan of campaign, Napoleon like, in New York, as appears by two speeches I have heard him deliver since his arrival in Illinois, he gave special attention to a speech of mine, delivered here on the 16th of June last. He says that he carefully read that speech. He told us that at Chicago a week ago last night, and he repeated it at Bloomington last night. Doubtless, he repeated it again to-day, though I did not hear him. In the two first places—Chicago and Bloomington—I heard him; to-day I did not. He said he had carefully examined that speech; *when*, he did not say; but there is no reasonable doubt it was when he was in New York preparing his plan of campaign. I am glad he did read it carefully. He says it was evidently prepared with great care. I freely admit it was prepared with care. I claim not to be more free from errors than others—perhaps scarcely so much; but I was very careful not to put anything in that speech as a matter of fact, or make any inferences which did not appear to me to be true, and fully warrantable. If I had made any mistake, I was willing to be corrected; if I had drawn any inference in regard to Judge Douglas, or any one else, which was not warranted, I was fully prepared to modify it as soon as discovered. I planted myself upon the truth, and the truth only, so far as I knew it, or could be brought to know it.

Having made that speech, with the most kindly feelings towards Judge Douglas, as manifested therein, I was gratified when I found that he had carefully examined it, and had detected no error of fact, nor any inference against him, nor any misrepresentations, of which he thought fit to complain. In neither of the two speeches I have mentioned, did he make any such complaint. I will thank any one who will inform me that he, in his speech to-day, pointed out anything I had stated, respecting him, as being erroneous. I presume there is no such thing. I have reason to be gratified that the care and caution used in that speech, left it so that he, most of all others interested in discovering error, has not been able to point out one thing against him, which he could say was wrong. He seizes upon the doctrines he supposes to be included in that speech, and declares that upon them will turn the issues of this campaign. He then quotes, or attempts to quote from my speech. I will not say that he willfully misquotes, but he does fail to quote accurately. His attempt at quoting is from a passage which I believe I can quote accurately from memory. I shall make the quotation now, with some comments upon it, as I have already said, in order that the Judge shall be left entirely without excuse for misrepresenting me. I do so now, as I hope, for the last time. I do this, in great caution, in order that if he repeats his misrepresentation, it shall be plain to all that he does so willfully. If, after all, he still persists, I shall be compelled to reconsider the course I have marked out for myself, and draw upon such humble resources as I have, for a new course, better suited to the real exigencies of the case. I set out in this campaign, with the intention of conducting it, strictly as a gentleman, in substance at least, if not in the outside polish. The latter, I shall never be, but that which constitutes the inside of a gentleman, I hope I understand, and am not less inclined to practice than others. It was my purpose and expectations that this canvass would be conducted upon principle, and with fairness on both sides; and it shall not be my fault, if this purpose and expectation shall be given up.

He charges, in substance, that I invite a war of sections; that I propose all the local institutions of the different States shall become consolidated and uniform. What is there in the language of that speech which expresses such purpose, or bears such construction? I have again and again said that I would not enter into

Meserve No. 26. A photograph by Alexander Hesler made in Springfield on June 3, 1860. The purchase of this negative by Mr. George B. Ayres doubtless saved it from loss in the Hesler Gallery, which was burned in the Chicago fire of 1871.

any of the States to disturb the institution of slavery. Judge Douglas said, at Bloomington, that I used language most able and ingenious for concealing what I really meant; and that while I had protested against entering into the slave States, I nevertheless did mean to go on the banks of the Ohio and throw missiles into Kentucky, to disturb them in their domestic institutions.

I said in that speech, and I meant no more, that the institution of slavery ought to be placed in the very attitude where the framers of this government placed it, and left it. I do not understand that the framers of our Constitution left the people of the free States in the attitude of firing bombs or shells into the slave States. I was not using that passage for the purpose for which he infers I did use it. I said, "We are now far advanced into the fifth year since a policy was created for the avowed object and with the confident promise of putting an end to slavery agitation. Under the operation of that policy that agitation has not only not ceased, but has constantly augmented. In my opinion it will not cease till a crisis shall have been reached and passed. 'A house divided against itself cannot stand.' I believe that this government cannot endure permanently half slave and half free. It will become all one thing or all the other. Either the opponents of slavery will arrest the further spread of it, and place it where the public mind shall rest in the belief that it is in the course of ultimate extinction, or its advocates will push it forward till it shall become alike lawful in all the States, old as well as new, North as well as South."

Now you all see, from that quotation, I did not express my *wish* on any thing. In that passage I indicated no wish or purpose of my own; I simply expressed my *expectation*. Can not the Judge perceive a distinction between a *purpose* and an *expectation*? I have often expressed an expectation to die, but I have never expressed a *wish* to die. I said at Chicago, and now repeat, that I am quite aware this government has endured, half slave and half free, for eighty two years. I understand that little bit of history. I expressed the opinion I did, because I perceived—or thought I perceived—a new set of causes introduced. I did say, at Chicago, in my speech then, that I do wish to see the spread of slavery arrested, and to see it placed where the public mind shall rest in the belief that it is in the course of ultimate extinction. I said that because I supposed, when the public mind shall rest in that belief, we shall have peace on the slavery question. I have believed—and now believe—the public mind did rest in that belief up to the introduction of the Nebraska bill.

Although I have ever been opposed to slavery, so far I rested in the hope and belief that it was in the course of ultimate extinction. For that reason, it had been a minor question with me. I might have been mistaken; but I had believed, and now believe, that the whole public mind, that is, the mind of the great majority, had rested in that belief up to the repeal of the Missouri Compromise. But, upon that event, I became convinced, that either I had been resting in a delusion, or the institution was being placed on a new basis; a basis for making it perpetual, national, and universal. Subsequent events have greatly confirmed me in that belief. I believe that bill to be the beginning of a conspiracy for that purpose. So believing, I have since then, considered that question a paramount one. So believing, I have thought the public mind will never rest till the power of Congress to restrict the spread of it, shall again be acknowledged and exercised on the one hand; or on the other, all resistance be entirely crushed out. I have expressed that opinion, and I entertain it to-night. It is denied that there is any tendency to the nationalization of slavery in these States.

Mr. Brooks of South Carolina, in one of his speeches, when they were presenting him with canes, silver plate, gold pitchers and the like, for assaulting Senator Sumner, distinctly affirmed his opinion that when this Constitution was formed, it was the belief of no man that slavery would last to the present day.

He said what I think, that the framers of our Constitution placed the institution of slavery where the public mind rested in the hope that it was in course of ultimate extinction. But he went on to say that the men of the present age, by their experience, have become wiser than the framers of the Constitution; and the inventor of the cotton-gin had made the perpetuity of slavery a necessity in this country.

As another piece of evidence tending to the same point, quite recently in Virginia, a man—the owner of slaves—made a will providing that after his death certain of his slaves should have their freedom, if they should so choose, and go to Liberia, rather than remain in slavery. They chose to be liberated. But the persons to whom they would descend as property, claimed them as slaves. A suit was instituted, which finally came to the Supreme Court of Virginia, and was therein decided against the slaves, upon the ground that a negro cannot make a choice—that they had no legal power to choose—could not perform the condition upon which their freedom depended.

I do not mention this with any purpose of criticizing, but to connect it with the arguments as affording additional evidence of the change of sentiment upon this question, of slavery in the direction of making it perpetual and national. I argue now as I did before, that there is such a tendency, and I am backed, not merely, by the facts, but by the open confession in the slave States.

And now as to the Judge's inference, that because I wish to see slavery placed in the course of ultimate extinction—placed where our fathers originally placed it—I wish to annihilate the State Legislatures—to force the cotton to grow upon the tops of the Green Mountains—to freeze ice in Florida—to cut timber on the broad Illinois prairies—that I am in favor of all these ridiculous and impossible things.

It seems to me it is a complete answer to all this, to ask if, when Congress did have the fashion of restricting slavery from free territory, when courts did have the fashion of deciding that taking a slave into a free country made him free, I say it is a sufficient answer, to ask, if any of this ridiculous nonsense about consolidation, and uniformity, did actually follow. Who heard of any such thing, because of the ordinance of '87? because of the Missouri Restriction? because of the numerous court decisions of that character?

Now as to the Dred Scott decision: for upon that he makes his last point upon me. He boldly takes ground in favor of that decision.

This is one half the onslaught, and one third of the entire plan of the campaign. I am opposed to that decision in a certain sense, but not in the sense which he puts on it. I say that in so far as it decided in favor of Dred Scott's master, and against Dred Scott and his family, I do not propose to disturb or resist the decision.

I never have proposed to do any such thing. I think, that in respect for judicial authority, my humble history would not suffer in a comparison with that of Judge Douglas. He would have the citizen conform his vote, to that decision; the member of Congress, his; the President his use of the veto power. He would make it a rule of political action, for the people and all the departments of the government. I would not. By resisting it as a political rule, I disturb no right of property, create no disorder, excite no mobs.

When he spoke at Chicago, on Friday evening of last week, he made this same point upon me. On Saturday evening I replied and reminded him of a Supreme Court decision which he opposed for at least several years. Last night at Bloomington he took some notice of that reply; but entirely forgot to remember that part of it.

He renews his onslaughts upon me, forgetting to remember that I have turned the tables against himself on that very point. I renew the effort to draw his attention to it. I wish to stand erect before the country, as well as before Judge Douglas, on this question of judicial authority, and therefore I add something to the authority in favor of my own position. I wish to show that I am sustained by authority, in addition to that heretofore presented. I do not expect to convince the Judge. It is part of the plan of his campaign, and he will cling to it with a desperate grip. Even, turn it upon him—turn the sharp point against him, and gaff him through—he will still cling to it till he can invent some new dodge to take the place of it.

In public speaking it is tedious reading from documents; but I must beg to indulge the practice to a limited extent. I shall read from a letter written by Mr. Jefferson in 1820, and now to be found in the seventh volume of his correspondence, at page 177. It seems he had been presented by a gentleman of the name of Jarvis with a book, or essay, or periodical, called the "Republican," and he was writing in acknowledgment of the present, and noting some of its contents. After expressing the hope that the work will produce a favorable effect upon the minds of the young, he proceeds to say:

"That it will have this tendency may be expected, and for that reason I feel an urgency to note what I deem an error in it, the more requiring notice as your opinion is strengthened by that of many others. You seem, in pages 84 and 148, to consider the judges as the ultimate arbiters of all constitutional questions—a very dangerous doctrine indeed, and one which would place us under the despotism of an oligarchy. Our judges are as honest as other men, and not more so. They have, with others, the same passions for party, for power, and the privilege for their corps. Their maxim is, 'boni judicis est ampliare jurisdictionem;' and their power the more dangerous as they are in office for life, and not responsible, as the other functionaries are, to the elective control. The Constitution has erected no such single tribunal, knowing that to whatever hands confided, with the corruptions of time and party, its members would become despots. It has more wisely made all the departments co-equal and co-sovereign within themselves."

Thus we see the power claimed for the Supreme Court by Judge Douglas, Mr. Jefferson holds, would reduce us to the despotism of an oligarchy.

Now, I have said no more than this—in fact, never quite so much as this—at least, I am sustained by Mr. Jefferson.

Let us go a little further. You remember we once had a national bank. Some man owed the bank a debt, he was sued and sought to avoid payment, on the ground that the bank was unconstitutional. The case went to the Supreme Court, and then it was decided that the bank was constitutional. The whole Democratic party revolted against that decision. General Jackson himself asserted that he, as President, would not be bound to hold a national bank to be constitutional, even though the court had decided it to be so. He fell in precisely with the view of Mr. Jefferson, and acted upon it under his official oath, in vetoing a charter for a national bank. The declaration that Congress does not possess this constitutional power to charter a bank, has gone into the Democratic platforms, at their national conventions, and was brought forward and reaffirmed in their last convention at Cincinnati. They have contended for that declaration, in the very teeth of the Supreme Court, for more than a quarter of a century. In fact, they have reduced the decision to an absolute nullity. That decision, I repeat, is repudiated in the Cincinnati platform; and still, as if to show that effrontery can go no farther, Judge Douglas vaunts in the very speeches in which he denounces me for opposing the Dred Scott decision, that he stands on the Cincinnati platform.

Now, I wish to know what the Judge can charge upon me, with respect to decisions of the Supreme Court which does not lie in all its length, breadth, and proportions at his own door. The plain truth is simply this: Judge Douglas is *for* Supreme Court decisions when he likes them, and against them when he does not like them. He is for the Dred Scott decision because it tends to nationalize slavery—because it is part of the original combination for that object. It so happens singularly enough, that I never stood opposed to a decision of the Supreme Court till this. On the contrary, I have no recollection that he was ever particularly in favor of one till this. He never was in favor of any, nor I opposed to any, till the present one, which helps to nationalize slavery.

Free men of Sangamon, free men of Illinois—free men everywhere—judge ye between him and me, upon this issue.

He says this Dred Scott case is a very small matter at most—that it has no practical effect; that at best, or rather, I suppose, at worst, it is but an abstraction. I submit that the proposition that the thing which determines whether a man is free or a slave, is rather *concrete* than *abstract*. I think you would conclude that it was, if your liberty depended upon it, and so would Judge Douglas if his liberty depended upon it. But suppose it was on the question of slavery over the new Territories that he considers it as being merely an abstract matter, and one of no practical importance. How has the planting of slavery in new countries always been effected? It has now been decided that slavery cannot be kept out of our new Territories by any legal means. In what do our new Territories now differ in this respect, from the old Colonies when slavery was first planted within them? It was planted, as Mr. Clay once declared, and as history proves true, by industrious men in spite of the wishes of the people; the mother government refusing to prohibit it, and withholding from the people of the Colonies the authority to prohibit it for themselves. Mr. Clay says this was one of the great and just causes of complaint, against Great Britain by the Colonies, and the best apology we can now make for having the institution amongst us. In that precise condition, our Nebraska politicians have at last succeeded in placing our own new Territories: the government will not prohibit slavery within them, nor allow the people to prohibit it.—

I defy any man to find any difference between the policy which originally planted slavery in these Colonies and that policy which now prevails in our new Territories. If it does not go into them, it is only because no individual wishes it to go. The Judge indulged himself, doubtless, to-day, with the question as to what I am going to do with or about the Dred Scott decision. Well, Judge, will you please tell me what you did about the Bank decision? Will you not graciously allow us to do with the Dred Scott decision precisely as you did with the Bank decision? You succeeded in breaking down the moral effect of that decision; did you find it necessary to amend the Constitution? or to set up a court of negroes in order to do it?

There is one other point. Judge Douglas has a very affectionate leaning towards the Americans and old Whigs. Last evening, in a sort of weeping tone, he described to us a death-bed scene. He had been called to the side of Mr. Clay, in his last moments, in order that the genius of "popular sovereignty" might duly descend from the dying man and settle upon him, this loving and most worthy successor. He could do no less than promise that he would devote the remainder of his life to "popular sovereignty;" and then the great statesman departed in peace. By this part of the "plan of the campaign," the Judge has evidently promised himself, that tears shall be drawn down the cheeks of all old Whigs, as large as half-grown apples.

Mr. Webster, too, was mentioned; but it did not quite come to a death-bed scene, as to him. It would be amusing, if it were not disgusting, to see how quick these compromise-breakers administer on the political effects of their dead adversaries, trumping up claims never before heard of, and dividing the assets among themselves. If I should be found dead to-morrow morning, nothing but my insignificance could prevent a speech being made on my authority, before the end of next week. It so happens that in that "popular sovereignty" with which Mr. Clay was identified, the Missouri Compromise was expressly reserved; and it was a little singular if Mr. Clay cast his mantle upon Judge Douglas on purpose to have that compromise repealed.

Again, the Judge did not keep faith with Mr. Clay when he first brought in his Nebraska bill. He left the Missouri Compromise unrepealed, and in his report accompanying the bill, he told the world he did it on purpose. The manes of Mr. Clay must have been in great agony, till thirty days later, when "popular sovereignty" stood forth in all its glory.

One more thing. Last night Judge Douglas tormented himself with horrors about my disposition to make negroes perfectly equal with white men in social and political relations. He did not stop to show that I have said any such things, or that they legitimately follow from anything I have said, but he rushes on with his assertions. I adhere to the Declaration of Independence. If Judge Douglas and his friends are not willing to stand by it, let them come up and amend it. Let them make it read that all men are created equal, except negroes. Let us have it decided, whether the Declaration of Independence, in this blessed year of 1858, shall be thus amended. In his construction of the Declaration last year, he said it only meant that Americans in America, were equal to Englishmen in England. Then, when I pointed out to him that by that rule, he excludes the Germans, the Irish, the Portuguese, and all the other people who have come amongst us since the Revolution, he reconstructs his construction. In his last speech he tells us it meant Europeans.

I press him a little further, and ask if it meant to include the Russians in Asia? or does he mean to exclude that vast population from the principles of our Declaration of Independence? I expect ere long, he will introduce another amendment to his definition. He is not at all particular. He is satisfied with anything which does not endanger the nationalizing of negro slavery. It may draw white men down, but it must not lift negroes up. Who shall say, "I am the superior, and you are the inferior?"

My declarations upon this subject of negro slavery may be misrepresented, but cannot be misunderstood. I have said I do not understand the Declaration to mean that all men were created equal in all respects. They are not our equal in color; but I suppose that it does mean to declare that all men are equal in some respects; they are equal in their right to "life, liberty and the pursuit of happiness." Certainly the negro is not our equal in color—perhaps not in many other respects; still, in the right to put into his mouth the bread that his own hands have earned, he is the equal of every other man, white or black. In pointing out that more has been given you, you can not be justified in taking away the little which has been given him. All I ask for the negro is that if you do not like him, let him alone. If God gave him but little, that little let him enjoy.

When our government was established, we had the institution of slavery among us. We were in a certain sense compelled to tolerate its existence. It was a sort of necessity. We had gone through our struggle and secured our own independence. The framers of the Constitution found the institution of slavery amongst their other institutions at the time. They found that by an effort to eradicate it, they might lose much of what they had already gained. They were obliged to bow to the necessity. They gave power to Congress to abolish the slave trade at the end of twenty years. They also prohibited it in the Territories where it did not exist. They did what they could and yielded to necessity for the rest. I also yield to all which follows from that necessity. What I would most desire would be the separation of the white and black races.

One more point in this Springfield speech which Judge Douglas says he has read so carefully. I had expressed my belief in the existence of a conspiracy to perpetuate and nationalize slavery. I did not profess to know it, nor do I now. I showed the part Judge Douglas had played in the string of facts, constituting to my mind, the proof of that conspiracy. I showed the parts played by others.

I charged that the people had been deceived into carrying the last Presidential election, by the impression that the people of the Territories might exclude slavery if they chose, when it was known in advance by the conspirators, that the court was to decide that neither Congress nor the people could so exclude slavery. These charges are more distinctly made than anything else in the speech.

Judge Douglas has carefully read and re-read that speech. He has not, so far as I know, contradicted those charges. In the two speeches which I heard, he certainly did not. On his own tacit admission I renew that charge. I charge him with having been a party to that conspiracy and to that deception for the sole purpose of nationalizing slavery.

LETTER TO JOHN MATHERS
JULY 20, 1858

Springfield, July 20 1858

Jno. Mathers, Esq.
My dear Sir:

Your kind and interesting letter of the 19th was duly received. Your suggestions as to placing one's self on the offensive, rather than the *defensive*, are certainly correct. That is a point which I shall not disregard. I spoke here on Saturday-night. The speech, not very well reported, appears in the State Journal of this morning. You, doubtless, will see it; and I hope you will perceive in it, that I am already improving. I would mail you a copy now, but I have not one at hand.

I thank you for your letter; and shall be pleased to hear from you again.

Yours very truly
A. Lincoln—

*Mathers was a resident of Jacksonville, Illinois, who upon reading Douglas's opening speech at Chicago on July 9, and Lincoln's reply on the following night, wrote Lincoln advising that he saw in Douglas's tactics the effort to put Lincoln on the defensive by attacking the "House Divided Speech" and the "alliance" referred to in the Chicago speeches. He suggested that Lincoln should "turn the tables" by assailing Douglas "and holding up before the people his (Douglass' [*sic*]) political record." (Mathers' "Letter to Richard Mills," January 11, 1873,* Jacksonville Daily Journal, *February 13, 1909.)*

LETTER TO HENRY ASBURY
JULY 31, 1858

Springfield, July 31, 1858

Henry Asbury, Esq
My dear Sir

Yours of the 28th is received. The points you propose to press upon Douglas, he will be very hard to get up to. But I think you labor under a mistake when you say no one cares how he answers. This implies that it is equal with him whether he is injured here or at the South. That is a mistake. He cares nothing for the South—he knows he is already dead there. He only leans Southward now to keep the Buchanan party from growing in Illinois. You shall have hard work to get him directly to the point whether a territorial Legislature has or has not the power to exclude slavery. But if you succeed in bringing him to it, though he will be compelled to say it possesses no such power; he will instantly take ground that slavery can not actually exist in the territories, unless the people desire it, and so give it protective territorial legislation. If this offends the South he will let it offend them; as at all events he means to hold on to his chances in Illinois. You will soon learn by the papers that both the Judge and myself, are to be in Quincy on the 13th of October, when & where I expect the pleasure of seeing you.

Yours very truly
A. Lincoln

The manuscript of this letter, now owned by Mr. Oliver R. Barrett of Chicago, has on the back an interesting notation by Asbury as follows:

"July 1883—

"The main question I had urged Mr. Lincoln to put to Judge Douglas—as may be perceived from his letter to me was the question 2 at Freeport "Can the people of a United States territory in any lawful way against the wish of any citizen of the United States exclude Slavery from its limits prior to the formation of a state constitution"

"The Judge answered that they could, and went on to state how, but the answer I think lapped over and went further than Mr. Lincoln expected it would, when he answered my letter of the 31 of July. I have always thought that the Judge's answer whilst it probably secured his reelection to the Senate laid the foundation of his defeat for the Presidency. Whilst on the other hand it made a large factor in securing to Mr. Lincoln his own nomination & election in 1860.

"Henry Asbury"

FRAGMENT: ON SLAVERY
[AUGUST 1, 1858?]

As I would not be a *slave*, so I would not be a *master*. This expresses my idea of democracy. Whatever differs from this, to the extent of the difference, is not democracy.

A. Lincoln—

LETTER TO HENRY E. DUMMER
AUGUST 5, 1858

Springfield, Aug: 5. 1858

Friend Dummer

Yours, not dated, just received. No accident preventing, I shall be at Beardstown on the 12th. I thank you for the contents of your letter generally. I have not time now to notice the various points you suggest, but I will say I do not understand the Republican party to be committed to the proposition "No more slave States." I think they are not so committed. Most certainly they prefer there should be no more; but I know there are many of them who think we are under obligation to admit slave states from Texas, if such shall be presented for admission; but I think the party as such is not committed either way.

Your friend as ever
A. Lincoln

FIRST DEBATE, AT OTTAWA, ILLINOIS AUGUST 21, 1858

MR. DOUGLAS'S OPENING SPEECH

Ladies and Gentlemen:

I appear before you to-day for the purpose of discussing the leading political topics which now agitate the public mind. By an arrangement between Mr. Lincoln and myself, we are present here to-day for the purpose of having a joint discussion, as the representatives of the two great political parties of the State and Union, upon the principles in issue between those parties, and this vast concourse of people shows the deep feeling which pervades the public mind in regard to the questions dividing us.

Prior to 1854 this country was divided into two great political parties, known as the Whig and Democratic parties. Both were national and patriotic, advocating principles that were universal in their application. An Old Line Whig could proclaim his principles in Louisiana and Massachusetts alike. Whig principles had no boundary sectional line; they were not limited by the Ohio River, nor by the Potomac, nor by the line of the Free and Slave States, but applied and were proclaimed wherever the Constitution ruled or the American flag waved over the American soil. So it was, and so it is with the great Democratic party, which, from the days of Jefferson until this period, has proven itself to be the historic party of this nation. While the Whig and Democratic parties differed in regard to a bank, the tariff, distribution, the specie circular, and the sub-treasury, they agreed on the great slavery question which now agitates the Union. I say that the Whig party and the Democratic party agreed on this slavery question, while they differed on those matters of expediency to which I have referred. The Whig party and the Democratic party jointly adopted the compromise measures of 1850 as the basis of a proper and just solution of this slavery question in all its forms.

Clay was the great leader, with Webster on his right and Cass on his left, and sustained by the patriots in the Whig and Democratic ranks who had devised and enacted the Compromise measures of 1850.

In 1851 the Whig party and the Democratic party united in Illinois in adopting resolutions indorsing and approving the principles of the Compromise measures of 1850, as the proper adjustment of that question. In 1852, when the Whig party assembled in Convention at Baltimore for the purpose of nominating a candidate for the Presidency, the first thing it did was to declare the Compromise measures of 1850, in substance and in principle, a suitable adjustment of that question. [Here the speaker was interrupted by loud and long continued applause] My friends, silence will be more acceptable to me in the discussion of these questions than applause. I desire to address myself to your judgment, your understanding, and your consciences, and not to your passions or your enthusiasm. When the Democratic convention assembled in Baltimore in the same year, for the purpose of nominating a Democratic candidate for the Presidency, it also adopted the Compromise measures of 1850 as the basis of Democratic action. Thus you see that up to 1853-'54, the Whig party and the Democratic party both stood on the same platform with regard to the slavery question. That platform was the right of the people of each State and each Territory to decide their local and domestic institutions for themselves, subject only to the Federal Constitution.

During the session of Congress of 1853-'54, I introduced into the Senate of the United States a bill to organize the Territories of Kansas and Nebraska on that principle which had been adopted in the Compromise measures of 1850, approved by the Whig party and the Democratic party in Illinois in 1851, and indorsed by the Whig party and the Democratic party in National Convention in 1852. In order that there might be no misunderstanding in relation to the principle involved in the Kansas and Nebraska bill, I put forth the true intent and meaning of the Act in these words: "It is the true intent and meaning of this Act not to legislate slavery into any State or Territory, or to exclude it therefrom, but to leave the people thereof perfectly free to form and regulate their domestic institutions in their own way, subject only to the Federal Constitution." Thus you see that up to 1854, when the Kansas and Nebraska bill was brought into Congress for the purpose of carrying out the principles which both parties had up to that time indorsed and approved, there had been no division in this country in regard to that principle except the opposition of the Abolitionists. In the House of Representatives of the Illinois Legislature, upon a resolution asserting that principle, every Whig and every Democrat in the House voted in the affirmative, and only four men voted against it, and those four were Old Line Abolitionists.

In 1854, Mr. Abraham Lincoln and Mr. Trumbull entered into an arrangement, one with the other, and each with his respective friends, to dissolve the Old Whig party on the one hand, and to dissolve the old Democratic party on the other, and to connect the members of both into an Abolition party, under the name and disguise of a Republican party. The terms of that arrangement between Mr. Lincoln and Mr. Trumbull have been published to the world by Mr. Lincoln's special friend, James H. Matheny, Esq., and they were, that Lincoln should have Shields's place in the United States Senate, which was then about to become vacant, and that Trumbull should have my seat when my term expired. Lincoln went to work to Abolitionize the old Whig party all over the State, pretending that he was then as good a Whig as ever; and Trumbull went to work in his part of the State preaching Abolitionism in its milder and lighter form, and trying to Abolitionize the Democratic party, and bring old Democrats handcuffed and bound hand and foot into the Abolition camp.

In pursuance of the arrangement, the parties met at Springfield in October, 1854, and proclaimed their new platform. Lincoln was to bring into the Abolition camp the Old Line Whigs, and transfer them over to Giddings, Chase, Fred Douglass, and Parson Lovejoy, who were ready to receive them and christen them in their new faith. They laid down on that occasion a platform for their new Republican party, which was to be thus constructed. I have the resolutions of the State Convention then held, which was the first mass State Convention ever held in Illinois by the Black Republican party, and I now hold them in my hands, and will read a part of them, and cause the others to be printed. Here are the most important and material resolutions of this Abolition platform:

"1. *Resolved,* That we believe this truth to be self-evident, that when parties become subversive of the ends for which they are established, or incapable of restoring the government to the true principles of the Constitution, it is the right and duty of the people to dissolve the political bands by which they may have been connected therewith, and to organize new parties, upon such principles and with such views as the circumstances and the exigencies of the nation may demand.

"2. *Resolved,* That the times imperatively demand the reorganization of parties, and, repudiating all previous party attachments, names and predilections, we unite ourselves together in defense of the liberty and Constitution of the country, and will hereafter cooperate as the Republican party, pledged to the accomplishment of the following purposes: To bring the administration of the government back to the control of first principles; to restore Nebraska and Kansas to the position of Free Territories, that, as the Constitution of the United States vests in the States, and not in Congress, the power to legislate for the extradition of fugitives from labor, to repeal and entirely abrogate the Fugitive-Slave law; to restrict slavery to those States in which it exists; to prohibit the admission of any more Slave States into the Union; to abolish slavery in the District of Columbia; to exclude slavery from all the Territories over which the General Government has exclusive jurisdiction; and to resist the acquirement of any more Territories, unless the practice of slavery therein forever shall have been prohibited.

"3. *Resolved,* That in furtherance of these principles we will use such constitutional and lawful means as shall seem best adapted to their accomplishment, and that we will support no man for office, under the General or State government, who is not positively and fully committed to the support of these principles, and whose personal character and conduct is not a guarantee that he is reliable, and who shall not have abjured old party allegiance and ties."

Now, gentlemen, your Black Republicans have cheered every one of those propositions, and yet I venture to say that you cannot get Mr. Lincoln to come out and say that he is now in favor of each one of them. That these propositions, one and all, constitute the platform of the Black Republican party of this day, I have no doubt; and when you were not aware for what purpose I was reading them, your Black Republicans cheered them as good Black Republican doctrines. My object in reading these resolutions was to put the question to Abraham Lincoln this day, whether he now stands and will stand by each article in that creed and carry it out. I desire to know whether Mr. Lincoln to-day stands, as he did in 1854, in favor of the unconditional repeal of the Fugitive-Slave law. I desire him to answer whether he stands pledged to-day, as he did in 1854, against the admission of any more Slave States into the Union, even if the people want them. I want to know whether he stands pledged against the admission of a new State into the Union with such a constitution as the people of that State may see fit to make. I want to know whether he stands to-day pledged to the abolition of slavery in the District of Columbia. I desire him to answer whether he stands pledged to the prohibition of the slave-trade between the different States. I desire to know whether he stands pledged to prohibit slavery in all the Territories of the United States, North as well as South of the Missouri Compromise line. I desire him to answer whether he is opposed to the acquisition of any more territory, unless slavery is prohibited therein.

I want his answer to these questions. Your affirmative cheers in favor of this Abolition platform are not satisfactory. I ask Abraham Lincoln to answer these questions, in order that, when I trot him down to lower Egypt, I may put the same questions to him. My principles are the same everywhere. I can proclaim them alike in the North, the South, the East, and the West. My principles will apply wherever the Constitution prevails, and the American flag waves. I desire to know whether Mr. Lincoln's principles will bear transplanting from Ottawa to Jonesboro? I put these questions to him to-day distinctly, and ask an answer. I have a right to an answer, for I quote from the platform of the Republican party, made by himself and others at the time that party was formed, and the bargain made by Lincoln to dissolve and kill the old Whig party, and transfer its members, bound hand and foot, to the Abolition party, under the direction of Giddings and Fred Douglass.

In the remarks I have made on this platform, and the position of Mr. Lincoln upon it, I mean nothing personally disrespectful or unkind to that gentleman. I have known him for nearly twenty-five years. There were many points of sympathy between us when we first got acquainted. We were both comparatively boys, and both struggling with poverty in a strange land. I was a school-teacher in the town of Winchester, and he a flourishing grocery-keeper in the town of Salem. He was more successful in his occupation than I was in mine, and hence more fortunate in this world's goods. Lincoln is one of those peculiar men who perform with admirable skill everything which they undertake. I made as good a school-teacher as I could, and when a cabinet-maker I made a good bedstead and tables, although my boss said I succeeded better with bureaus and secretaries than with anything else; but I believe that Lincoln was always more successful in business than I, for his business enabled him to get into the Legislature. I met him there, however, and had a sympathy with him, because of the up-hill struggle we both had in life. He was then just as good at telling an anecdote as now. He could beat any of the boys wrestling, or running a foot-race, in pitching quoits or tossing a copper; could ruin more liquor than all the boys of the town together, and the dignity and impartiality with which he presided at a horse-race or fist-fight excited the admiration and won the praise of everybody that was present and participated. I sympathized with him because he was struggling with difficulties, and so was I.

Mr. Lincoln served with me in the Legislature in 1836, when we both retired, and he subsided, or became submerged, and he was lost sight of as a public man for some years. In 1846, when Wilmot introduced his celebrated proviso, and the Abolition tornado swept over the country, Lincoln again turned up as a member of Congress from the Sangamon district. I was then in the Senate of the United States, and was glad to welcome my old friend and companion. Whilst in Congress, he distinguished himself by his opposition to the Mexican war, taking the side of the common enemy against his own country; and when he returned home, he found that the indignation of the people followed him everywhere, and he was again submerged, or obliged to retire into private life, forgotten by his former friends. He came up again in 1854, just in time to make this Abolition or Black Republican platform, in company with Giddings, Lovejoy, Chase, and Fred Douglass, for the Republican party to stand upon.

Trumbull, too, was one of our own contemporaries. He was born and raised in old Connecticut, was bred a Federalist, but removing to Georgia, turned Nullifier when Nullification was popular, and as soon as he disposed of his clocks and wound up his business, migrated to Illinois, turned politician and lawyer here, and made his appearance in 1841 as a member of the Legislature. He became noted as the author of the scheme to repudiate a large portion of the State debt of Illinois, which, if successful, would have brought infamy and disgrace upon the fair escutcheon of our glorious State. The odium attached to that measure consigned him to oblivion for a time. I helped to do it. I walked into a public meeting in the hall of the House of Representatives, and replied to his repudiating speeches, and resolutions were carried over his head denouncing repudiation, and asserting the moral and legal obligation of Illinois to pay every dollar of the debt she owed, and every bond that bore her seal. Trumbull's malignity has followed me since I thus defeated his infamous scheme.

These two men having formed this combination to Abolitionize the Old Whig party and the old Democratic party, and put themselves into the Senate of the United States, in pursuance of their bargain, are now carrying out that arrangement. Matheny states that Trumbull broke faith; that the bargain was that Lincoln should be the senator in Shields's place, and Trumbull was to wait for mine; and the story goes that Trumbull cheated Lincoln, having control of four or five Abolitionized Democrats who were holding over in the Senate; he would not let them vote for Lincoln, which obliged the rest of the Abolitionists to support him in order to secure an Abolition senator. There are a number of authorities for the truth of this besides

Matheny, and I suppose that even Mr. Lincoln will not deny it.

Mr. Lincoln demands that he shall have the place intended for Trumbull, as Trumbull cheated him and got his, and Trumbull is stumping the State traducing me for the purpose of securing the position for Lincoln, in order to quiet him. It was in consequence of this arrangement that the Republican convention was empaneled to instruct for Lincoln and nobody else, and it was on this account that they passed resolutions that he was their first, their last, and their only choice. Archy Williams was nowhere, Browning was nobody, Wentworth was not to be considered; they had no man in the Republican party for the place except Lincoln, for the reason that he demanded that they should carry out the arrangement.

Having formed this new party for the benefit of deserters from Whiggery, and deserters from Democracy, and having laid down the Abolition platform which I have read, Lincoln now takes his stand and proclaims his Abolition doctrines. Let me read a part of them. In his speech at Springfield to the convention which nominated him for the Senate, he said:

"In my opinion it will not cease until a crisis shall have been reached and passed. 'A house divided against itself cannot stand.' I believe this government *cannot endure permanently half Slave and half Free*. I do not expect the Union to be dissolved—I do not expect the house to fall—*but I do expect it will cease to be divided*. It will become all one thing, or all the other. Either the opponents of slavery *will arrest the further spread of it*, and place it where the public mind shall rest, in the belief *that it is in the course of ultimate extinction*, or its advocates *will push it forward till it shall become alike lawful in all the States*—old as well as new, North as well as South." ["Good," "good," and cheers.]

I am delighted to hear you Black Republicans say "good." I have no doubt that doctrine expresses your sentiments, and I will prove to you now, if you will listen to me, that it is revolutionary and destructive of the existence of this government. Mr. Lincoln, in the extract from which I have read, says that this government cannot endure permanently in the same condition in which it was made by its framers,—divided into Free and Slave States. He says that it has existed for about seventy years thus divided, and yet he tells you that it cannot endure permanently on the same principles and in the same relative condition in which our fathers made it. Why can it not exist divided into Free and Slave States? Washington, Jefferson, Franklin, Madison, Hamilton, Jay, and the great men of that day, made this government divided into Free States and Slave States, and left each State perfectly free to do as it pleased on the subject of slavery. Why can it not exist on the same principles on which our fathers made it? They knew when they framed the Constitution that in a country as wide and broad as this, with such a variety of climate, production, and interest, the people necessarily required different laws and institutions in different localities. They knew that the laws and regulations which would suit the granite hills of New Hampshire would be unsuited to the rice plantations of South Carolina, and they therefore provided that each State should retain its own Legislature and its own sovereignty, with the full and complete power to do as it pleased within its own limits, in all that was local and not national.

One of the reserved rights of the States was the right to regulate the relations between master and servant, on the slavery question. At the time the Constitution was framed, there were thirteen States in the Union, twelve of which were slaveholding States and one a free State. Suppose this doctrine of uniformity preached by Mr. Lincoln, that the States should all be free or all be slave, had prevailed, and what would have been the result? Of course, the twelve slaveholding States would have overruled the one Free State, and slavery would have been fastened by a Constitutional provision on every inch of the American republic, instead of being left, as our fathers wisely left it, to each State to decide for itself. Here I assert that uniformity in the local laws and institutions of the different States is neither possible or desirable. If uniformity had been adopted when the government was established, it must inevitably have been the uniformity of slavery everywhere, or else the uniformity of negro citizenship and negro equality everywhere.

We are told by Lincoln that he is utterly opposed to the Dred Scott decision, and will not submit to it, for the reason that he says it deprives the negro of the rights and privileges of citizenship. That is the first and main reason which he assigns for his warfare on the Supreme Court of the United States and its decision. I ask you, are you in favor of conferring upon the negro the rights and privileges of citizenship? Do you desire to strike out of our State Constitution that clause which keeps slaves and free negroes out of the State, and allows the free negroes to flow in, and cover your prairies with black settlements? Do you desire to turn this beautiful State into a free negro colony, in order that when Missouri abolishes slavery she can send one hundred thousand emancipated slaves into Illinois, to become citizens and voters, on an equality with yourselves? If you desire negro citizenship, if you desire to allow them to come into the State and settle with the white man, if you desire them to vote on an equality with yourselves, and to make them eligible to office, to serve on juries, and to adjudge your rights, then support Mr. Lincoln and the Black Republican party, who are in favor of the citizenship of the negro. For one, I am opposed to negro citizenship in any and every form. I believe this Government was made on the white basis. I believe it was made by white men, for the benefit of white men and their posterity forever, and I am in favor of confining citizenship to white men, men of European birth and descent, instead of conferring it upon negroes, Indians, and other inferior races.

Mr. Lincoln, following the example and lead of all the little Abolition orators, who go around and lecture in the basements of schools and churches, reads from the Declaration of Independence that all men were created equal, and then asks, How can you deprive a negro of that equality which God and the Declaration of Independence award to him? He and they maintain that negro equality is guaranteed by the laws of God, and that it is asserted in the Declaration of Independence. If they think so, of course they have a right to say so, and so vote. I do not question Mr. Lincoln's conscientious belief that the negro was made his equal, and hence is his brother; but for my own part, I do not regard the negro as my equal, and positively deny that he is my brother, or any kin to me whatever. Lincoln has evidently learned by heart Parson Lovejoy's catechism. He can repeat it as well as Farnsworth, and he is worthy of a medal from Father Giddings and Fred Douglass for his Abolitionism. He holds that the negro was born his equal and yours, and that he was endowed with equality by the Almighty, and that no human law can deprive him of these rights, which were guaranteed to him by the Supreme Ruler of the universe.

Now, I do not believe that the Almighty ever intended the negro to be the equal of the white man. If he did, he has been a long time demonstrating the fact. For thousands of years the negro has been a race upon the earth, and during all that time, in all latitudes and climates, wherever he has wandered or been taken, he has been inferior to the race which he has there met. He belongs to an inferior race, and must always occupy an inferior position. I do not hold that because the negro is our inferior therefore he ought to be a slave. By no means can such a conclusion be drawn from what I have said. On the contrary, I hold that humanity and Christianity both require that the negro shall have and enjoy every right, every privilege, and every immunity consistent with the safety of the society in which he lives. On that point, I presume, there can be no diversity of opinion. You and I are bound to extend to our inferior and dependent beings every right, every privilege, every facility and immunity consistent with the public good.

The question then arises, What rights and privileges are consistent with the public good? This is a question which each State and each Territory must decide for itself—Illinois has decided it for herself. We have provided that the negro shall not be a slave, and we have also provided that he shall not be a citizen, but protect him in his civil rights, in his life, his person and his property, only depriving him of all political rights whatsoever, and refusing to put him on an equality with the white man. That policy of Illinois is satisfactory to the Democratic party and to me, and if it were to the Republicans, there would then be no question upon the subject. But the Republicans say that he ought to be made a citizen, and when he becomes a citizen he becomes your equal, with all your rights and privileges. They assert the Dred Scott decision to be monstrous because it denies that the negro is or can be a citizen under the Constitution. Now, I hold that Illinois had a right to abolish and prohibit slavery as she did, and I hold that Kentucky has the same right to continue and protect slavery that Illinois had to abolish it. I hold that New York had as much right to abolish slavery as Virginia has to continue it, and that each and every State of this Union is a sovereign power, with the right to do as it pleases upon this question of slavery, and upon all its domestic institutions.

Slavery is not the only question which comes up in this controversy. There is a far more important one to you, and that is, what shall be done with the free negro? We have settled the slavery question as far as we are concerned; we have prohibited it in Illinois forever; and in doing so, I think we have done wisely, and there is no man in the State who would be more strenuous in his opposition to the introduction of slavery than I would. But when we settled it for ourselves, we exhausted all our power over that subject. We have done our whole duty, and can do no more. We must leave each and every other State to decide for itself the same question. In relation to the policy to be pursued toward the free negroes, we have said that they shall not vote; whilst Maine, on the other hand, has said that they shall vote. Maine is a sovereign State, and has the power to regulate the qualifications of voters within her limits. I would never consent to confer the right of voting and of citizenship upon a negro, but still I am not going to quarrel with Maine for differing from me in opinion. Let Maine take care of her own negroes, and fix the qualifications of her own voters to suit herself, without interfering with Illinois, and Illinois will not interfere with Maine. So with the State of New York. She allows the negro to vote, provided he owns two hundred and fifty dollars' worth of property, but not otherwise. While I would not make any distinction whatever between a negro who held property and one who did not; yet if the sovereign State of New York chooses to make that distinction, it is her business and not mine, and I will not quarrel with her for it. She can do as she pleases on this question if she minds her own business, and we will do the same thing.

Now, my friends, if we will only act conscientiously and

rigidly upon this great principle of popular sovereignty, which guarantees to each State and Territory the right to do as it pleases on all things, local and domestic, instead of Congress interfering, we will continue at peace one with another. Why should Illinois be at war with Missouri, or Kentucky with Ohio, or Virginia with New York, merely because their institutions differ? Our fathers intended that our institutions should differ. They knew that the North and the South, having different climates, productions, and interests, required different institutions. This doctrine of Mr. Lincoln, of uniformity among the institutions of the different states, is a new doctrine, never dreamed of by Washington, Madison, or the framers of this government. Mr. Lincoln and the Republican party set themselves up as wiser than these men who made this government, which has flourished for seventy years under the principle of popular sovereignty, recognizing the right of each State to do as it pleased. Under that principle, we have grown from a nation of three or four millions to a nation of about thirty millions of people; we have crossed the Allegheny mountains and filled up the whole Northwest, turning the prairie into a garden, and building up churches and schools, thus spreading civilization and Christianity where before there was nothing but savage barbarism. Under that principle we have become, from a feeble nation, the most powerful on the face of the earth, and if we only adhere to that principle, we can go forward increasing in territory, in power, in strength, and in glory until the Republic of America shall be the North Star that shall guide the friends of freedom throughout the civilized world.

And why can we not adhere to the great principle of self-government, upon which our institutions were originally based? I believe that this new doctrine preached by Mr. Lincoln and his party will dissolve the Union if it succeeds. They are trying to array all the Northern States in one body against the South, to excite a sectional war between the Free States and the Slave States, in order that the one or the other may be driven to the wall.

I am told that my time is out. Mr. Lincoln will now address you for an hour and a half, and I will then occupy an half hour in replying to him.

MR. LINCOLN'S REPLY IN THE OTTAWA DEBATE

My Fellow-citizens:

When a man hears himself somewhat misrepresented, it provokes him—at least, I find it so with myself; but when misrepresentation becomes very gross and palpable, it is more apt to amuse him. The first thing I see fit to notice is the fact that Judge Douglas alleges, after running through the history of the old Democratic and the old Whig parties, that Judge Trumbull and myself made an arrangement in 1854, by which I was to have the place of General Shields in the United States Senate, and Judge Trumbull was to have the place of Judge Douglas. Now all I have to say upon that subject is that I think no man—not even Judge Douglas—can prove it, *because it is not true*. I have no doubt he is "*conscientious*" in saying it.

As to those resolutions that he took such a length of time to read, as being the platform of the Republican party in 1854, I say I never had anything to do with them, and I think Trumbull never had. Judge Douglas cannot show that either of us ever did have anything to do with them. I believe *this* is true about those resolutions. There was a call for a Convention to form a Republican party at Springfield, and I think that my friend Mr. Lovejoy, who is here upon this stand, had a hand in it. I think this is true, and I think if he will remember accurately, he will be able to recollect that he tried to get me into it, and I would not go in. I believe it is also true that I went away from Springfield when the convention was in session, to attend court in Tazewell County. It is true they did place my name, though without authority, upon the committee, and afterward wrote me to attend the meeting of the committee; but I refused to do so, and I never had anything to do with that organization. This is the plain truth about all that matter of the resolutions.

Now, about this story that Judge Douglas tells of Trumbull bargaining to sell out the old Democratic party, and Lincoln agreeing to sell out the old Whig party, I have the means of *knowing* about that: Judge Douglas cannot have; and I know there is no substance to it whatever. Yet I have no doubt he is "*conscientious*" about it. I know that after Mr. Lovejoy got into the Legislature that winter, he complained of me that I had told all the old Whigs of his district that the old Whig party was good enough for them, and some of them voted against him because I told them so. Now, I have no means of totally disproving such charges as this which the judge makes. A man cannot prove a negative, but he has a right to claim that when a man makes an affirmative charge, he must offer some proof to show the truth of what he says. I certainly cannot introduce testimony to show the negative about things, but I have a right to claim that if a man says he *knows* a thing, then he must show *how* he knows it. I always have a right to claim this, and it is not satisfactory to me that he may be "conscientious" on the subject.

Now, gentlemen, I hate to waste my time on such things, but in regard to that general Abolition tilt that Judge Douglas makes, when he says that I was engaged at that time in selling out and Abolitionizing the Old Whig party, I hope you will permit me to read a part of a printed speech that I made then at Peoria, which will show altogether a different view of the position I took in that contest of 1854.

A voice.—"Put on your specs."

Mr. Lincoln.—Yes, sir, I am obliged to do so. I am no longer a young man.

"This is the *repeal* of the Missouri Compromise. The foregoing history may not be precisely accurate in every particular, but I am sure it is sufficiently so for all the uses I shall attempt to make of it, and in it we have before us the chief materials enabling us to correctly judge whether the repeal of the Missouri Compromise is right or wrong.

"I think, and shall try to show, that it is wrong,—wrong in its direct effect, letting slavery into Kansas and Nebraska, and wrong in its prospective principle, allowing it to spread to every other part of the wide world where men can be found inclined to take it.

"This *declared* indifference, but, as I must think, covert *real* zeal for the spread of slavery, I cannot but hate. I hate it because of the monstrous injustice of slavery itself. I hate it because it deprives our republican example of its just influence in the world,—enables the enemies of free institutions, with plausibility, to taunt us as hypocrites; causes the real friends of freedom to doubt our sincerity, and especially because it forces so many really good men amongst ourselves into an open war with the very fundamental principles of civil liberty,—criticizing the Declaration of Independence, and insisting that there is no right principle of action but *self-interest.*

"Before proceeding, let me say I think I have no prejudice against the Southern people. They are just what we would be in their situation. If slavery did not now exist among them, they would not introduce it. If it did now exist among us, we should not instantly give it up. This I believe of the masses North and South. Doubtless there are individuals on both sides who would not hold slaves under any circumstances; and others who would gladly introduce slavery anew, if it were out of existence. We know that some Southern men do free their slaves, go North, and become tip-top Abolitionists; while some Northern ones go South, and become most cruel slave-masters.

"When Southern people tell us they are no more responsible for the origin of slavery than we, I acknowledge the fact. When it is said that the institution exists, and that it is very difficult to get rid of it, in any satisfactory way, I can understand and appreciate the saying. I surely will not blame them for not doing what I should not know how to do myself. If all earthly power were given me, I should not know what to do as to the existing institution. My first impulse would be to free all the slaves, and send them to Liberia,—to their own native land. But a moment's reflection would convince me that whatever of high hope (as I think there is) there may be in this, in the long run, its sudden execution is impossible. If they were all landed there in a day, they would all perish in the next ten days; and there are not surplus shipping and surplus money enough in the world to carry them there in many times ten days. What then? Free them all, and keep them among us as underlings? Is it quite certain that this betters their condition? I think I would not hold one in slavery, at any rate; yet the point is not clear enough to me to denounce people upon. What next? Free them, and make them politically and socially our equals? My own feelings will not admit of this; and if mine would, we well know that those of the great mass of white people will not. Whether this feeling accords with justice and sound judgment is not the sole question, if, indeed, it is any part of it. A universal feeling, whether well or ill-founded, cannot be safely disregarded. We cannot, then, make them equals. It does seem to me that systems of gradual emancipation might be adopted; but for their tardiness in this, I will not undertake to judge our brethren of the South.

"When they remind us of their constitutional rights, I acknowledge them, not grudgingly but fully and fairly; and I would give them any legislation for the reclaiming of their fugitives which should not, in its stringency, be more likely to carry a free man into slavery, than our ordinary criminal laws are to hang an innocent one.

"But all this, to my judgment, furnishes no more excuse for permitting slavery to go into our own Free Territory, than it would for reviving the African slave-trade by law. The law which forbids the bringing of slaves *from* Africa, and that which has so long forbidden the taking of them *to* Nebraska, can hardly be distinguished on any moral principle; and the repeal of the former could find quite as plausible excuses as that of the latter."

I have reason to know that Judge Douglas *knows* that I said this. I think he has the answer here to one of the questions he put to me. I do not mean to allow him to catechize me unless he pays back for it in kind. I will not answer questions one after another, unless he reciprocates; but as he has made this inquiry, and I have answered it before, he has got it without my getting anything in return. He has got my answer on the fugitive-Slave law.

Now, gentlemen, I don't want to read at any greater length, but this is the true complexion of all I have ever said in regard to the institution of slavery and the black race. This is the whole of it, and anything that argues me into his idea of perfect social and political equality with the negro is but a specious and fantastic arrangement of words, by which a man can prove a horse-chestnut to be a chestnut horse.

I will say here, while upon this subject, that I have no purpose, directly or indirectly, to interfere with the institution of slavery in the States where it exists. I believe I have no lawful right to do so, and I have no inclination to do so. I have no purpose to introduce political and social equality between the white and black races. There is a physical difference between the two, which, in my judgment, will probably forever forbid their living together upon the footing of perfect equality; and inasmuch as it becomes a necessity that there must be a difference, I, as well as Judge Douglas, am in favor of the race to which I belong having the superior position. I have never said anything to the contrary, but I hold that, notwithstanding all this, there is no reason in the world why the negro is not entitled to all the natural rights enumerated in the Declaration of Independence—the right to life, liberty, and the pursuit of happiness. I hold that he is as much entitled to these as the white man. I agree with Judge Douglas he is not my equal in many respects—certainly not in color, perhaps not in moral or intellectual endowment. But in the right to eat the bread, without the leave of anybody else, which his own hand earns, he is my equal, and the equal of Judge Douglas, and the equal of every living man.

Now I pass on to consider one or two more of these little follies. The Judge is woefully at fault about his early friend Lincoln being a "grocery-keeper." I don't know that it would be a great sin if I had been; but he is mistaken. Lincoln never kept a grocery anywhere in the world. It is true that Lincoln did work the latter part of one winter in a little still-house up at the head of a hollow.

And so I think my friend, the Judge, is equally at fault when he charges me at the time when I was in Congress of having opposed our soldiers who were fighting in the Mexican war. The Judge did not make his charge very distinctly, but I can tell you what he can prove, by referring to the record. You remember I was an old Whig, and whenever the Democratic party tried to get me to vote that the war had been righteously begun by the President, I would not do it. But whenever they asked for any money, or land-warrants, or anything to pay the soldiers there, during all that time, I gave the same vote that Judge Douglas did. You can think as you please as to whether that was consistent.

Such is the truth; and the Judge has the right to make all he can out of it. But when he, by a general charge, conveys the idea that I withheld supplies from the soldiers who were fighting in the Mexican war, or did anything else to hinder the soldiers, he is, to say the least, grossly and altogether mistaken, as a consultation of the records will prove to him.

As I have not used up so much of my time as I had supposed, I will dwell a little longer upon one or two of these minor topics upon which the Judge has spoken. He has read from my speech in Springfield in which I say "that a house divided against itself can not stand." Does the Judge say it can stand? I don't know whether he does or not. The Judge does not seem to be attending to me just now, but I would like to know if it is his opinion that a house divided against itself can stand. If he does, then there is a question of veracity, not between him and me, but between the Judge and an authority of a somewhat higher character.

Now, my friends, I ask your attention to this matter for the purpose of saying something seriously. I know the Judge may readily enough agree with me that the maxim which was put forth by the Saviour is true, but he may allege that I misapply it; and the Judge has a right to urge that, in my application, I do misapply it and then I have a right to show that I do *not* misapply it. When he undertakes to say that because I think this nation, so far as the question of slavery is concerned, will all become one thing or all the other, I am in favor of bringing about a dead uniformity in the various States in all their institutions, he argues erroneously. The great variety of the local institutions in the States, springing from differences in the soil, differences in the face of the country, and in the climate, are bonds of union. They do not make "a house divided against itself," but they make a house united. If they produce in one section of the country what is called for by the wants of another section, and this other section can supply the wants of the first, they are not matters of discord, but bonds of union, true bonds of union.

But can this question of slavery be considered as among *these* varieties in the institutions of the country? I leave it to you to say whether, in the history of our Government, this institution of slavery has not always failed to be a bond of union, and, on

Meserve No. 68. A photograph by Mathew B. Brady made in Washington on February 23, 1861, the day the President-elect arrived for the inauguration. The original glass negative is in the Meserve Collection.

the contrary, been an apple of discord and an element of division in the house. I ask you to consider whether, so long as the moral constitution of men's minds shall continue to be the same, after this generation and assemblage shall sink into the grave, and another race shall arise, with the same moral and intellectual development we have,—whether, if that institution is standing in the same irritating position in which it now is, it will not continue an element of division? If so, then I have a right to say that, in regard to this question, the Union is a house divided against itself; and when the Judge reminds me that I have often said to him that the institution of slavery has existed for eighty years in some States, and yet it does not exist in some others, I agree to the fact, and I account for it by looking at the position in which our fathers originally placed it,—restricting it from the new Territories where it had not gone, and legislating to cut off its source by the abrogation of the slave-trade, thus putting the seal of legislation *against its spread.*

The public mind *did* rest in the belief that it was in the course of ultimate extinction. But lately, I think—and in this I charge nothing on the Judge's motives—lately, I think, that he, and those acting with him, have placed that institution on a new basis, which looks to the *perpetuity and nationalization of slavery.* And while it is placed upon this new basis, I say, and I have said, that I believe we shall not have peace upon the question until the opponents of slavery arrest the further spread of it, and place it where the public mind shall rest in the belief that it is in the course of ultimate extinction; or, on the other hand, that its advocates will push it forward until it shall become alike lawful in all the States, old as well as new, North as well as South. Now I believe if we could arrest the spread, and place it where Washington and Jefferson and Madison placed it, it would be in the course of ultimate extinction, and the public mind *would,* as for eighty years past, believe that it was in the course of ultimate extinction. The crisis would be past, and the institution might be let alone for a hundred years, if it should live so long, in the States where it exists; yet it would be going out of existence in the way best for both the black and the white races.

A voice.—"Then do you repudiate popular sovereignty?"

Mr. Lincoln.—Well, then, let us talk about popular sovereignty. What is popular sovereignty? Is it the right of the people to have slavery or not have it, as they see fit, in the Territories? I will state—and I have an able man to watch me—my understanding is that Popular Sovereignty, as now applied to the question of slavery, does allow the people of a Territory to have slavery if they want to, but does not allow them *not* to have it if they *do not* want it. I do not mean that if this vast concourse of people were in a Territory of the United States, any one of them would be obliged to have a slave if he did not want one; but I do say that, as I understand the Dred Scott decision, if any one man wants slaves, all the rest have no way of keeping that one man from holding them.

When I made my speech at Springfield, of which the Judge complains, and from which he quotes, I really was not thinking of the things which he ascribes to me at all. I had no thought in the world that I was doing anything to bring about a war between the Free and Slave States. I had no thought in the world that I was doing anything to bring about a political and social equality of the black and white races. It never occurred to me that I was doing anything, or favoring anything to reduce to a dead uniformity all the local institutions of the various States. But I must say, in all fairness to him, if he thinks I am doing something which leads to these bad results, it is none the better that I did not mean it. It is just as fatal to the country, if I have any influence in producing it, whether I intend it or not. But can it be true, that placing this institution upon the original basis—the basis upon which our fathers placed it—can have any tendency to set the Northern and the Southern States at war with one another, or that it can have any tendency to make the people of Vermont raise sugar-cane because they raise it in Louisiana, or that it can compel the people of Illinois to cut pine logs on the Grand Prairie, where they will not grow, because they cut pine logs in Maine, where they do grow?

The Judge says this is a new principle started in regard to this question. Does the Judge claim that he is working on the plan of the founders of the government? I think he says in some of his speeches—indeed, I have one here now—that he saw evidence of a policy to allow slavery to be south of a certain line, while north of it it should be excluded, and he saw an indisposition on the part of the country to stand upon that policy, and therefore he set about studying the subject upon *original principles*, and upon *original principles* he got up the Nebraska bill! I am fighting it upon these "original principles,"—fighting it in the Jeffersonian, Washingtonian, and Madisonian fashion.

Now, my friends, I wish you to attend for a little while to one or two other things in that Springfield speech. My main object was to show, so far as my humble ability was capable of showing, to the people of this country, what I believed was the truth—that there was a tendency, if not a conspiracy, among those who have engineered this slavery question for the last four or five years, to make slavery perpetual and universal in this nation. Having made that speech principally for that object, after arranging the evidences that I thought tended to prove my proposition, I concluded with this bit of comment:

"We cannot absolutely know that these exact adaptations are the result of pre-concert; but when we see a lot of framed timbers, different portions of which we know have been gotten out at different times and places, and by different workmen,—Stephen, Franklin, Roger, and James, for instance,—and when we see these timbers joined together, and see they exactly make the frame of a house or a mill, all the tenons and mortices exactly fitting, and all the lengths and proportions of the different pieces exactly adapted to their respective places, and not a piece too many or too few,—not omitting even the scaffolding,—or if a single piece be lacking, we see the place in the frame exactly fitted and prepared yet to bring such piece in—in such a case we feel it impossible not to believe that Stephen and Franklin, and Roger and James, all understood one another from the beginning, and all worked upon a common plan or draft drawn before the first blow was struck."

When my friend, Judge Douglas came to Chicago on the 9th of July, this speech having been delivered on the 16th of June, he made an harangue there, in which he took hold of this speech of mine, showing that he had carefully read it; and while he paid no attention to *this* matter at all, but complimented me as being a "kind, amiable, and intelligent gentleman," notwithstanding I had said this, he goes on and deduces, or draws out, from my speech this tendency of mine to set the States at war with one another, to make all the institutions uniform, and set the niggers* and white people to marrying together. Then, as the Judge had complimented me with these pleasant titles (I must confess to my weakness), I was a little "taken," for it came from a great man. I was not very much accustomed to flattery, and it came the sweeter to me. I was rather like the Hoosier with the gingerbread, when he said he reckoned he loved it better than any other man, and got less of it. As the Judge had so flattered me, I could not make up my mind that he meant to deal unfairly with me; so I went to work to show him that he misunderstood the whole scope of my speech, and that I really never intended to set the people at war with one another.

As an illustration, the next time I met him, which was at Springfield, I used this expression, that I claimed no right under the Constitution, nor had I any inclination, to enter into the Slave States, and interfere with the institutions of slavery. He says upon that: Lincoln will not enter into the Slave States, but will go to the banks of the Ohio, on this side, and shoot over! He runs on, step by step, in the horse-chestnut style of argument, until in the Springfield speech he says: "Unless he shall be successful in firing his batteries, until he shall have extinguished slavery in all the States, the Union shall be dissolved." Now I don't think that was exactly the way to treat "a kind, amiable, intelligent gentleman." I know if I had asked the Judge to show when or where it was I had said that if I didn't succeed in firing into the Slave States until slavery should be extinguished, the Union should be dissolved, he could not have shown it. I understand what he would do. He would say, "I don't mean to quote

* There has been some difference of opinion as to whether Lincoln ever used the word *nigger*, and the supposition has been made in other instances that the reporter of a speech was responsible for the word (see Paul M. Angle's note, *New Letters and Papers of Lincoln*, p. 188). It seems more likely that, although the word never appears in Lincoln's manuscripts or in speeches printed from manuscript, in extempore speaking Lincoln sometimes used it as the common and quite natural colloquial term.—R.P.B.

from you, but this was the *result* of what you say." But I have the right to ask, and I do ask now, Did you not put it in such a form that an ordinary reader or listener would take it as an expression from me?

In a speech at Springfield, on the night of the 17th, I thought I might as well attend to my own business a little, and I recalled his attention as well as I could to this charge of conspiracy to nationalize slavery. I called his attention to the fact that he had acknowledged, in my hearing twice, that he had carefully read the speech, and, in the language of the lawyers, as he had twice read the speech, and still had put in no plea or answer, I took a default on him. I insisted that I had a right then to renew that charge of conspiracy. Ten days afterward I met the Judge at Clinton,—that is to say, I was on the ground, but not in the discussion,—and heard him make a speech. Then he comes in with his plea to this charge, for the first time; and his plea when put in, as well as I can recollect it, amounted to this: that he never had any talk with Judge Taney or the President of the United States with regard to the Dred Scott decision before it was made. I (Lincoln) ought to know that the man who makes a charge without knowing it to be true, falsifies as much as he who knowingly tells a falsehood; and lastly, that he would pronounce the whole thing a falsehood; but he would make no personal application of the charge of falsehood, not because of any regard for the "kind, amiable, intelligent gentleman," but because of his own personal self-respect!

I have understood since then (but will not hold the Judge to it if he is not willing) that he has broken through the "self-respect," and has got to saying the thing *out*. The Judge nods to me that it is so. It is fortunate for me that I can keep as good-humored as I do, when the Judge acknowledges that he has been trying to make a question of veracity with me. I know the Judge is a great man, while I am only a small man, but *I feel that I have got him*. I demur to that plea. I waive all objections that it was not filed till after default was taken, and demur to it upon the merits. What if Judge Douglas never did talk with Chief Justice Taney and the President before the Dred Scott decision was made; does it follow that he could not have had as perfect an understanding without talking as with it? I am not disposed to stand upon my legal advantage. I am disposed to take his denial as being like an answer in chancery, that he neither had any knowledge, information, or belief in the existence, of such a conspiracy. I am disposed to take his answer as being as broad as though he had put it in these words. And now, I ask, even if he had done so, have not I a right to *prove it on him,* and to offer the evidence of more than two witnesses, by whom to prove it; and if the evidence proves the existence of the conspiracy, does his broad answer, denying all knowledge, information, or belief, disturb the fact? It can only show that he was used by conspirators, and was not a leader of them.

Now, in regard to his reminding me of the moral rule that persons who tell what they do not know to be true, falsify as much as those who knowingly tell falsehoods. I remember the rule, and it must be borne in mind that in what I have read to you, I do not say that I *know* such a conspiracy to exist. To that I reply, I *believe it.* If the Judge says that I do not believe it, then he says what he does not know, and falls within his own rule, that he who asserts a thing which he does not know to be true, falsifies as much as he who knowingly tells a falsehood.

I want to call your attention to a little discussion on that branch of the case, and the evidence which brought my mind to the conclusion which I expressed as my *belief.* If, in arraying that evidence, I had stated anything which was false or erroneous, it needed but that Judge Douglas should point it out, and I would have taken it back, with all the kindness in the world. I do not deal in that way. If I have brought forward anything not a fact, if he will point it out, it will not even ruffle me to take it back. But if he will not point out anything erroneous in the evidence, is it not rather for him to show, by a comparison of the evidence, that I have *reasoned* falsely, than to call the "kind, amiable, intelligent gentleman" a liar? If I have reasoned to a false conclusion, it is the vocation of an able debater to show by argument that I have wandered to an erroneous conclusion.

I want to ask your attention to a portion of the Nebraska bill, which Judge Douglas has quoted: "It being the true intent and meaning of this Act, not to legislate slavery into any Territory or State, nor to exclude it therefrom, but to leave the people thereof perfectly free to form and regulate their domestic institutions in their own way, subject only to the Constitution of the United States." Thereupon Judge Douglas and others began to argue in favor of "Popular Sovereignty,"—the right of the people to have slaves if they wanted them, and to exclude slavery if they did not want them. "But," said, in substance, a senator from Ohio (Mr. Chase, I believe), "we more than suspect that you do not mean to allow the people to exclude slavery if they wish to; and if you do mean it, accept an amendment which I propose, expressly authorizing the people to exclude slavery."

I believe I have the amendment here before me, which was offered, and under which the people of the Territory, through their proper representatives, might, if they saw fit, prohibit the existence of slavery therein. And now I state it as a fact, to be taken back if there is any mistake about it, that Judge Douglas and those acting with him voted that amendment down. I now think that those men who voted it down had a *real reason* for doing so. They know what that reason was. It looks to us, since we have seen the Dred Scott decision pronounced, holding that, "under the Constitution," the people cannot exclude slavery,—I say it looks to outsiders, poor, simple, "amiable, intelligent gentlemen," as though the niche was left as a place to put that Dred Scott decision in,—a niche which would have been spoiled by adopting the amendment. And now, I say again, if *this* was not the reason, it will avail the judge much more to calmly and good-humoredly point out to these people what that *other* reason was for voting the amendment down, than, swelling himself up, to vociferate that he may be provoked to call somebody a liar.

Again: There is in that same quotation from the Nebraska bill this clause: "It being the true intent and meaning of this bill not to legislate slavery into any Territory or *State*." I have always been puzzled to know what business the word "State" had in that connection. Judge Douglas knows. *He put it there.* He knows what he put it there for. We outsiders cannot say what he put it there for. The law they were passing was not about States, and was not making provision for States. What was it placed there for? After seeing the Dred Scott decision, which holds that the people cannot exclude slavery from a *Territory*, if another Dred Scott decision shall come, holding that they cannot exclude it from a State, we shall discover that when the word was originally put there, it was in view of something which was to come in due time, we shall see that it was the other half of something. I now say again, if there is any different reason for putting it there, Judge Douglas, in a good-humored way, without calling anybody a liar, *can tell what the reason was.*

When the Judge spoke at Clinton, he came very near making a charge of falsehood against me. He used, as I found it printed in a newspaper, which, I remember, was very nearly like the real speech, the following language:—

"I did not answer the charge [of conspiracy] before, for the reason that I did not suppose there was a man in America with a heart so corrupt as to believe such a charge could be true. I have too much respect for Mr. Lincoln to suppose he is serious in making the charge."

I confess this is rather a curious view, that out of respect for me he should consider I was making what I deemed rather a grave charge, in fun. I confess it strikes me rather strangely. But I let it pass. As the Judge did not for a moment believe that there was a man in America whose heart was so "corrupt" as to make such a charge, and as he places me among the "men in America," who have hearts base enough to make such a charge, I hope he will excuse me if I hunt out another charge very like this; and if it should turn out that in hunting I should find that other, and it should turn out to be Judge Douglas himself who made it, I hope he will reconsider this question of the deep corruption of heart he has thought fit to ascribe to me. In Judge Douglas's speech of March 22, 1858, which I hold in my hand, he says:—

"In this connection there is another topic to which I desire to allude. I seldom refer to the course of newspapers, or notice the articles which they publish in regard to myself; but the course of the Washington *Union* has been so extraordinary, for the last two or three months, that I think it well enough to make some allusion to it. It has read me out of the Democratic party every other day, at least for two or three months, and keeps reading me out, and, as if it had not succeeded, still continues to read me out, using such terms as 'traitor,' 'renegade,' 'deserter,' and other kind and polite epithets of that nature. Sir, I have no vindication to make of my Democracy against the Washington *Union*, or any other newspaper. I am willing to allow my history and action for the last twenty years to speak for themselves as to my political principles and my fidelity to political obligations. The Washington *Union* has a personal grievance. When the editor was nominated for public printer, I declined to vote for him, and stated that at some time I might give my reasons for doing so. Since I declined to give that vote, this scurrilous abuse, these vindictive and constant attacks have been repeated almost daily on me. Will my friend from Michigan read the article to which I allude?"

This is a part of the speech. You must excuse me from reading the entire article of the Washington *Union*, as Mr. Stuart read it for Mr. Douglas. The Judge goes on and sums up, as I think, correctly:—

"Mr. President, you here find several distinct propositions advanced boldly by the Washington *Union* editorially, and apparently *authoritatively*; and any man who questions any of them is denounced as an Abolitionist, a Free-soiler, a fanatic. The propositions are, first, that the primary object of all government at its original institution is the protection of person and property; second, that the Constitution of the United States declares that the citizens of each State shall be entitled to all the privileges and immunities of citizens in the several States; and that, therefore, thirdly, all State laws, whether organic or otherwise, which prohibit the citizens of one State from settling in another with their slave property, and especially declaring it forfeited, are direct violations of the original intention of the government and Constitution of the United States; and, fourth, that the emancipation of the slaves of the Northern States was a gross outrage on the rights of property, inasmuch as it was involuntarily done on the part of the owner.

"Remember that this article was published in the *Union* on

the 17th of November, and on the 18th appeared the first article giving the adhesion of the *Union* to the Lecompton Constitution. It was in these words:—

"'KANSAS AND HER CONSTITUTION.—The vexed question is settled. The problem is solved. The dead point of danger is passed. All serious trouble to Kansas affairs is over and gone'—

"And a column nearly of the same sort. Then, when you come to look into the Lecompton Constitution, you find the same doctrine incorporated in it which was put forth editorially in the *Union*. What is it?

"'Article 7, *Section* 1. The right of property is before and higher than any constitutional sanction; and the right of the owner of a slave to such slave and its increase is the same and as inviolable as the right of the owner of any property whatever.'

"Then in the schedule is a provision that the Constitution may be amended after 1864 by a two-thirds vote.

"'But no alteration shall be made to affect the right of property in the ownership of slaves.'

"It will be seen by these clauses in the Lecompton Constitution that they are identical in spirit with the *authoritative* article in the Washington *Union* of the day previous to its indorsement of this constitution."

I pass over some portions of the speech, and I hope that any one who feels interested in this matter will read the entire section of the speech, and see whether I do the Judge injustice. He proceeds:—

"When I saw that article in the *Union* of the 17th of November, followed by the glorification of the Lecompton Constitution on the 18th of November, and this clause in the Constitution asserting the doctrine that a State has no right to prohibit slavery within its limits, I saw that there was a *fatal blow* being struck at the sovereignty of the States of this Union."

I stop the quotation there, again requesting that it may all be read. I have read all of the portion I desire to comment upon. What is this charge that the Judge thinks I must have a very corrupt heart to make? It was a purpose on the part of certain high functionaries to make it impossible for the people of one State to prohibit the people of any other State from entering it with their "property," so called, and making it a slave State. In other words it was a charge implying a design to make the institution of slavery national. And now I ask your attention to what Judge Douglas has himself done here. I know he made that part of the speech as a reason why he had refused to vote for a certain man for public printer; but when we get at it, the charge itself is the very one I made against him, that he thinks I am so corrupt for uttering. Now, whom does he make that charge against? Does he make it against that newspaper editor merely? No; he says it is identical in spirit with the Lecompton Constitution, and so the framers of that Constitution are brought in with the editor of the newspaper in that "fatal blow being struck." He did not call it a "conspiracy." In his language, it is a "fatal blow being struck." And if the words carry the meaning better when changed from a "conspiracy" into a "fatal blow being struck," I will change *my* expression and call it "fatal blow being struck." We see the charge made not merely against the editor of the *Union*, but all the framers of the Lecompton Constitution; and not only so, but the article was an *authoritative* article. By whose authority? Is there any question but that he means it was by the authority of the President and his Cabinet,—the Administration?

Is there any sort of question but that he means to make that charge? Then there are the editors of the *Union*, the framers of the Lecompton Constitution, the President of the United States and his Cabinet, and all the supporters of the Lecompton Constitution, in Congress and out of Congress, who are all involved in this "fatal blow being struck." I commend to Judge Douglas's consideration the question of how corrupt a man's heart must be to make such a charge!

Now, my friends, I have but one branch of the subject, in the little time I have left, to which to call your attention; and as I shall come to a close at the end of that branch, it is probable that I shall not occupy quite all the time allotted to me. Although on these questions I would like to talk twice as long as I have, I could not enter upon another head and discuss it properly without running over my time. I ask the attention of the people here assembled and elsewhere, to the course that Judge Douglas is pursuing every day as bearing upon this question of making slavery national. Not going back to the records, but taking the speeches he makes, the speeches he made yesterday and day before, and makes constantly all over the country,—I ask your attention to them. In the first place, what is necessary to make the institution national? Not war. There is no danger that the people of Kentucky will shoulder their muskets, and, with a young nigger stuck on every bayonet, march into Illinois and force them upon us. There is no danger of our going over there and making war upon them. Then what is necessary for the nationalization of slavery? It is simply the next Dred Scott decision. It is merely for the Supreme Court to decide that no State under the Constitution can exclude it, just as they have already decided that under the Constitution neither Congress nor the Territorial Legislature can do it. When that is decided and acquiesced in, the whole thing is done.

This being true, and this being the way, as I think, that slavery is to be made national, let us consider what Judge Douglas is doing every day to that end. In the first place, let us see what influence he is exerting on public sentiment. In this and like communities, public sentiment is everything. With public sentiment, nothing can fail; without it, nothing can succeed. Consequently he who moulds public sentiment goes deeper than he who enacts statutes or pronounces decisions. He makes statutes and decisions possible or impossible to be executed. This must be borne in mind, as also the additional fact that Judge Douglas is a man of vast influence, so great that it is enough for many men to profess to believe anything, when they once find out that Judge Douglas professes to believe it. Consider also the attitude he occupies at the head of a large party,—a party which he claims has a majority of all the voters in the country. This man sticks to a decision which forbids the people of a Territory from excluding slavery, and he does so, not because he says it is right in itself,—he does not give any opinion on that,—but because it has been decided by the court; and being decided by the court, he is, and you are, bound to take it in your political action as law, not that he judges at all of its merits, but because a decision of the court is to him a "Thus saith the Lord." He places it on that ground alone; and you will bear in mind that thus committing himself unreservedly to this decision commits him to the next one just as firmly as to this. He did not commit himself on account of the merit or demerit of the decision, but it is a "Thus saith the Lord." The next decision, as much as this, will be a "Thus saith the Lord."

There is nothing that can divert or turn him away from this decision. It is nothing that I point out to him that his great prototype, General Jackson, did not believe in the binding force of decisions. It is nothing to him that Jefferson did not so believe. I have said that I have often heard him approve of Jackson's course in disregarding the decision of the Supreme Court pronouncing a National Bank constitutional. He says, I did not hear him say so. He denies the accuracy of my recollection. I say he ought to know better than I, but I will make no question about this thing, though it still seems to me that I heard him say it twenty times. I will tell him, though, that he now claims to stand on the Cincinnati platform, which affirms that Congress *cannot* charter a National Bank, in the teeth of that old standing decision that Congress *can* charter a bank.

And I remind him of another piece of history on the question of respect for judicial decisions: and it is a piece of Illinois history, belonging to a time when the large party to which Judge Douglas belonged were displeased with a decision of the Supreme Court of Illinois; because they had decided that a governor could not remove a Secretary of State. You will find the whole story in Ford's History of Illinois, and I know that Judge Douglas will not deny that he was then in favor of overslaughing that decision by the mode of adding five new judges, so as to vote down the four old ones. Not only so, but it ended *in the Judge's sitting down on the very bench as one of the five new judges to break down the four old ones.* It was in this way precisely that he got his title of Judge. Now, when the Judge tells me that men appointed conditionally to sit as members of a court will have to be catechised beforehand upon some subject, I say, "You know, Judge; you have tried it." When he says a court of this kind will lose the confidence of all men, will be prostituted and disgraced by such a proceeding, I say, "You know best, Judge; you have been through the mill."

But I cannot shake Judge Douglas's teeth loose from the Dred Scott decision. Like some obstinate animal (I mean no disrespect) that will hang on when he has once got his teeth fixed, you may cut off a leg, or you may tear away an arm, still he will not relax his hold. And so I may point out to the Judge, and say, that he is bespattered all over, from the beginning of his political life to the present time, with attacks upon judicial decisions; I may cut off limb after limb of his public record, and strive to wrench him from a single dictum of the court,—yet I cannot divert him from it. He hangs, to the last, to the Dred Scott decision. These things show there is a purpose *strong as death and eternity* for which he adheres to this decision, and for which he will adhere to *all other decisions* of the same court.

A Hibernian.—"Give us something besides Dred Scott."

Mr. Lincoln.—Yes; no doubt you want to hear something that don't hurt. Now, having spoken of the Dred Scott decision, one more word, and I am done. Henry Clay, my *beau ideal* of a statesman, the man for whom I fought all my humble life,—Henry Clay once said of a class of men who would repress all tendencies to liberty and ultimate emancipation, that they must, if they would do this, go back to the era of our Independence, and muzzle the cannon which thunders its annual joyous return; they must blow out the moral lights around us; they must penetrate the human soul, and eradicate there the love of liberty; and then, and not till then, could they perpetuate slavery in this country! To my thinking, Judge Douglas is, by his example and vast influence, doing that very thing in this community, when he says that the negro has nothing in the Declaration of Independence. Henry Clay plainly understood the contrary.

Judge Douglas is going back to the era of our Revolution, and to the extent of his ability, muzzling the cannon which thunders its annual joyous return. When he invites any people, willing to have slavery, to establish it, he is blowing out the moral lights around us. When he says he "cares not whether slavery is voted down or voted up,"—that it is a sacred right of self-government,—he is, in my judgment, penetrating the human soul and eradicating the light of reason and the love of liberty in this American people. And now I will only say that when, by all these means and appliances, Judge Douglas shall succeed in bringing public sentiment to an exact accordance with his own views; when these vast assemblages shall echo back all these sentiments; when they shall come to repeat his views and to avow his principles, and to say all that he says on these mighty questions,—then it needs only the formality of the second Dred Scott decision, which he indorses in advance, to make slavery alike lawful in all the States, old as well as new, North as well as South.

My friends, that ends the chapter. The Judge can take his half hour.

MR. DOUGLAS'S REJOINDER

Fellow-Citizens:

I will now occupy the half hour allotted to me in replying to Mr. Lincoln. The first point to which I will call your attention is as to what I said about the organization of the Republican party in 1854, and the platform that was formed on the 5th of October of that year, and I will then put the question to Mr. Lincoln, whether or not he approves of each article in that platform, and ask for a specific answer. I did not charge him with being a member of the committee which reported that platform. I charged that that platform was the platform of the Republican party adopted by them. The fact that it was the platform of the Republican party is not denied; but Mr. Lincoln now says that although his name was on the committee which reported it, he does not think he was there, but thinks he was in Tazewell, holding court. Now, I want to remind Mr. Lincoln that he was at Springfield when that Convention was held and those resolutions were adopted.

The point I am going to remind Mr. Lincoln of is this: that after I had made my speech in 1854, during the Fair, he gave me notice that he was going to reply to me the next day. I was sick at the time, but I stayed over in Springfield to hear his reply, and to reply to him. On that day this very Convention, the resolutions adopted by which I have read, was to meet in the Senate chamber. He spoke in the hall of the House; and when he got through his speech,—my recollection is distinct, and I shall never forget it,—Mr. Codding walked in as I took the stand to reply, and gave notice that the Republican State Convention would meet instantly in the Senate chamber, and called upon the Republicans to retire there and go into this very Convention, instead of remaining and listening to me.

Mr. Lincoln.—Judge, add that I went along with them.

Mr. Douglas.—Gentlemen, Mr. Lincoln tells me to add that he went along with them to the senate chamber. I will not add that, because I do not know whether he did or not.

Mr. Lincoln.—I know he did not.

Mr. Douglas.—I do not know whether he knows it or not, that is not the point and I will yet bring him to the question.

In the first place, Mr. Lincoln was selected by the very men who made the Republican organization on that day, to reply to me. He spoke for them and for that party, and he was the leader of the party; and on the very day he made his speech in reply to me, preaching up this same doctrine of negro equality under the Declaration of Independence, this Republican party met in Convention. Another evidence that he was acting in concert with them is to be found in the fact that that Convention waited an hour after its time of meeting to hear Lincoln's speech, and Codding, one of their leading men, marched in the moment Lincoln got through, and gave notice that they did not want to hear me, and would proceed with the business of the Convention. Still another fact. I have here a newspaper printed at Springfield, Mr. Lincoln's own town, in October, 1854, a few days afterward, publishing these resolutions, charging Mr. Lincoln with entertaining these sentiments, and trying to prove that they were also the sentiments of Mr. Yates, then candidate for Congress. This has been published on Mr. Lincoln over and over again, and never before has he denied it.

But, my friends, this denial of his that he did not act on the committee, is a miserable quibble to avoid this main issue, which is, that this Republican platform declares in favor of the unconditional repeal of the Fugitive-Slave law. Has Lincoln answered whether he indorsed that or not? I called his attention to it when I first addressed you, and asked him for an answer, and I then predicted that he would not answer. How does he answer? Why, that he was not on the committee that wrote the resolutions. I then repeated the next proposition contained in the resolutions, which was to restrict slavery in those States in which it exists, and asked him whether he indorsed it. Does he answer yes, or no? He says in reply, "I was not on the committee at the time; I was up in Tazewell." The next question I put to him was, whether he was in favor of prohibiting the admission of any more Slave States into the Union. I put the question to him distinctly, whether, if the people of the Territory, when they had sufficient population to make a State, should form their Constitution recognizing slavery, he would vote for or against its admission. He is a candidate for the United States Senate, and it is possible, if he should be elected, that he would have to vote directly on that question. I asked him to answer me and you, whether he would vote to admit a State into the Union, with slavery or without it, as its own people might choose. He did not answer that question. He dodges that question also, under the cover that he was not on the committee at the time, that he was not present when the platform was made. I want to know, if he should happen to be in the Senate when a State applied for admission, with a Constitution acceptable to her own people, [whether?] he would vote to admit that State, if slavery was one of its institutions. He avoids the answer.

Mr. Lincoln—No, Judge.

It is true he gives the Abolitionists to understand by a hint that he would not vote to admit such a State. And why? He goes on to say that the man who would talk about giving each State the right to have slavery or not, as it pleased, was akin to the man who would muzzle the guns which thundered forth the annual joyous return of the day of our Independence. He says that that kind of talk is casting a blight on the glory of this country. What is the meaning of that? That he is not in favor of each State to have the right of doing as it pleases on the slavery question? I will put the question to him again and again, and I intend to force it out of him.

Then, again, this platform which was made at Springfield

by his own party when he was its acknowledged head, provides that Republicans will insist on the abolition of slavery in the District of Columbia, and I asked Lincoln specifically whether he agreed with them in that? ["Did you get an answer?"] He is afraid to answer it. He knows I will trot him down to Egypt. I intend to make him answer there, or I will show the people of Illinois that he does not intend to answer these questions. The Convention to which I have been alluding goes a little further, and pledges itself to exclude slavery from all the Territories over which the General Government has exclusive jurisdiction north of 36 deg. 30 min., as well as south. Now I want to know whether he approves that provision. I want him to answer, and when he does, I want to know his opinion on another point, which is, whether he will redeem the pledge of this platform, and resist the acquirement of any more territory unless slavery therein shall be forever prohibited. I want him to answer this last question.

Each of the questions I have put to him are practical questions,—questions based upon the fundamental principles of the Black Republican party; and I want to know whether he is the first, last, and only choice of a party with whom he does not agree in principle. He does not deny but that that principle was unanimously adopted by the Republican party; he does not deny that the whole Republican party is pledged to it; he does not deny that a man who is not faithful to it is faithless to the Republican party; and now I want to know whether that party is unanimously in favor of a man who does not adopt that creed and agree with them in their principles; I want to know whether the man who does not agree with them, and who is afraid to avow his differences, and who dodges the issue, is the first, last, and only choice of the Republican party.

A voice.—"How about the conspiracy?"

Never mind, I will come to that soon enough. But the platform which I have read to you not only lays down these principles, but it adds:—

"*Resolved,* That, in furtherance of these principles, we will use such constitutional and lawful means as shall seem best adapted to their accomplishment, and that we will support no man for office, under the General or State Government, who is not positively and fully committed to the support of these principles, and whose personal character and conduct are not a guarantee that he is reliable, and who shall not have abjured old party allegiance and ties."

The Black Republican party stands pledged that they will never support Lincoln until he has pledged himself to that platform; but he cannot devise his answer. He has not made up his mind whether he will or not. He talked about everything else he could think of to occupy his hour and a half, and when he could not think of anything more to say, without an excuse for refusing to answer these questions, he sat down long before his time was out.

In relation to Mr. Lincoln's charge of conspiracy against me, I have a word to say. In his speech to-day he quotes a playful part of his speech at Springfield, about Stephen, and James, and Franklin, and Roger, and says that I did not take exception to it. I did not answer it, and he repeats it again. I did not take exception to this figure of his. He has a right to be as playful as he pleases in throwing his arguments together, and I will not object; but I did take objection to his second Springfield speech, in which he stated that he intended his first speech as a charge of corruption or conspiracy against the Supreme Court of the United States, President Pierce, President Buchanan, and myself. That gave the offensive character to the charge. He then said that when he made it he did not know whether it was true or not; but inasmuch as Judge Douglas had not denied it, although he had replied to the other parts of his speech three times, he repeated it as a charge of conspiracy against me, thus charging me with moral turpitude. When he put it in that form, I did say, that inasmuch as he repeated the charge simply because I had not denied it, I would deprive him of the opportunity of ever repeating it again, by declaring that it was, in all its bearings, an infamous lie. He says he will repeat it until I answer his folly and nonsense about Stephen, and Franklin, and Roger, and Bob, and James.

He studied that out, prepared that one sentence with the

greatest care, committed it to memory, and put it in his first Springfield speech; and now he carries that speech around, and reads that sentence to show how pretty it is. His vanity is wounded because I will not go into that beautiful figure of his about the building of a house. All I have to say is, that I am not green enough to let him make a charge which he acknowledges he does not know to be true, and then take up my time in answering it, when I know it to be false, and nobody else knows it to be true.

I have not brought a charge of moral turpitude against him. When he, or any other man, brings one against me, instead of disproving it, I will say that it is a lie, and let him prove it if he can.

I have lived twenty-five years in Illinois. I have served you with all the fidelity and ability which I possess, and Mr. Lincoln is at liberty to attack my public action, my votes, and my conduct; but when he dares to attack my moral integrity by a charge of conspiracy between myself, Chief Justice Taney and the Supreme Court, and two Presidents of the United States, I will repel it.

Mr. Lincoln has not character enough for integrity and truth, merely on his own *ipse dixit*, to arraign President Buchanan, President Pierce, and nine Judges of the Supreme Court, not one of whom would be complimented by being put on an equality with him. There is an unpardonable presumption in a man putting himself up before thousands of people, and pretending that his *ipse dixit*, without proof, without fact, and without truth, is enough to bring down and destroy the purest and best of living men.

Fellow-citizens, my time is fast expiring; I must pass on. Mr. Lincoln wants to know why I voted against Mr. Chase's amendment to the Nebraska bill. I will tell him. In the first place, the bill already conferred all the power which Congress had, by giving the people the whole power over the subject. Chase offered a proviso that they might abolish slavery, which by implication would convey the idea that they could prohibit by not introducing that institution. General Cass asked him to modify his amendment so as to provide that the people might either prohibit or introduce slavery, and thus make it fair and equal. Chase refused to so modify his proviso, and then General Cass and all the rest of us voted it down. Those facts appear on the journals and debates of Congress, where Mr. Lincoln found the charge; and if he had told the whole truth, there would have been no necessity for me to occupy your time in explaining the matter.

Mr. Lincoln wants to know why the word "State," as well as "Territory," was put into the Nebraska bill? I will tell him. It was put there to meet just such false arguments as he has been adducing. That first, not only the people of the Territories should do as they pleased, but that when they come to be admitted as States, they should come into the Union with or without slavery, as the people determined. I meant to knock in the head this Abolition doctrine of Mr. Lincoln's, that there shall be no more Slave States, even if the people want them. And it does not do for him to say, or for any other Black Republican to say, that there is nobody in favor of the doctrine of no more Slave States, and that nobody wants to interfere with the right of the people to do as they please. What was the origin of the Missouri difficulty and the Missouri Compromise? The people of Missouri formed a Constitution as a Slave State, and asked admission into the Union, but the Free-soil party of the North, being in a majority, refused to admit her because she had slavery as one of her institutions. Hence this first slavery agitation arose upon a State, and not upon a Territory; and yet Mr. Lincoln does not know why the word "State" was placed in the Kansas-Nebraska bill. The whole Abolition agitation arose on that doctrine of prohibiting a State from coming in with slavery or not, as it pleased, and that same doctrine is here in this Republican platform of 1854; it has never been repealed; and every Black Republican stands pledged by that platform never to vote for any man who is not in favor of it. Yet Mr. Lincoln does not know that there is a man in the world who is in favor of preventing a State from coming in as it pleases, notwithstanding. The Springfield platform says that they, the Republican party, will not allow a State to come in under such circumstances. He is an ignorant man.

Now you see that upon these very points I am as far from bringing Mr. Lincoln up to the line as I ever was before. He does not want to avow his principles. I do want to avow mine, as clear as sunlight in midday. Democracy is founded upon the eternal principle of right. The plainer these principles are avowed before the people, the stronger will be the support which they will receive. I only wish I had the power to make them so clear that they would shine in the heavens for every man, woman, and child to read. The first of those principles that I would proclaim would be in opposition to Mr. Lincoln's doctrine of uniformity between the different States, and I would declare instead the sovereign right of each State to decide the slavery question as well as all other domestic questions for themselves, without interference from any other State or power whatsoever.

When that principle is recognized, you will have peace and harmony and fraternal feeling between all the States of this Union; until you do recognize that doctrine, there will be sectional warfare agitating and distracting the country. What does Mr. Lincoln propose? He says that the Union cannot exist divided into Free and Slave States. If it cannot endure thus divided, then he must strive to make them all Free or all Slave, which will inevitably bring about a dissolution of the Union.

Gentlemen, I am told that my time is out, and I am obliged to stop.

The propriety of including Douglas's portion of this debate in a volume of Lincoln's writings has precedent in the Complete Works of Abraham Lincoln, *but in addition, in the editor's opinion, the inclusion is justified on the ground that Douglas's speech and rebuttal afford an excellent opportunity for gauging the two men. One thing in particular is worth noting—the extent to which Douglas dealt in Lincoln's personal and public history, and the manner of Lincoln's replies to the charges and insinuations, with his ironical, even sarcastic, reference to Douglas's "conscientiousness." This is typical of Lincoln's sarcastic humor as revealed in his political speeches up to this time. It is interesting to observe that Lincoln took no notice of Douglas's charge that Lincoln was a habitual participant in the cruder pastimes of the frontier and could "ruin more liquor than all the boys of the town together," especially in view of the notorious fact that Douglas was a hard drinker and Lincoln a truly temperate man. That Lincoln neglected an opportunity for scathing sarcasm of a very personal nature is significant. Sarcasm was his forte, but there were apparently restrictions upon it, of expediency as well as inclination. Lincoln was shooting for bigger game, in the realm of political philosophy rather than of petty personalities. The reason for Lincoln's notice of the term "grocery-keeper" may not be obvious today when eatables are chiefly inferred from its use. In Lincoln's day it was a euphemism for* barroom. *The value of Douglas's biographical sketch of Lincoln lies in its revelation of Douglas's personality more than in its characterization of Lincoln.*

All queries from the audience and explanatory material inclosed in brackets in the text of the debate are the reporter's, not the editor's.

FRAGMENT: SPEECH AT EDWARDSVILLE, ILLINOIS SEPTEMBER 11, 1858

I have been requested to give a concise statement, as I understand it, of the difference between the Democratic and the Republican parties on the leading issues of this campaign. The question has just been put to me by a gentleman whom I do not know. I do not even know whether he is a friend of mine or a supporter of Judge Douglas in this contest; nor does that make any difference. His question is a pertinent one and, though it has not been asked me anywhere in the State before, I am very glad that my attention has been called to it to-day. Lest I should forget it, I will give you my answer before proceeding with the line of argument I had marked out for this discussion.

The difference between the Republican and the Democratic parties on the leading issue of this contest, as I understand it, is, that the former consider slavery a moral, social and political wrong, while the latter *do not* consider it either a moral, social or political wrong; and the action of each, as respects the growth of the country and the expansion of our population, is squared to meet these views. I will not allege that the Democratic party consider slavery morally, socially and politically *right*, though their tendency to that view has, in my opinion, been constant and unmistakable for the past five years. I prefer to take, as the accepted maxim of the party, the idea put forth by Judge Douglas, that he "don't care whether slavery is voted down or voted up." I am quite willing to believe that many Democrats would prefer that slavery be always voted down, and I am sure that some prefer that it be always "voted up;" but I have a right to insist that their action, especially if it be their *constant and unvarying action*, shall determine their ideas and preferences on the subject. Every measure of the Democratic party of late years, bearing directly or indirectly on the slavery question, has corresponded with this notion of utter indifference whether slavery or freedom shall outrun in the race of empire across the Pacific—every measure, I say, up to the Dred Scott decision, where, it seems to me, the idea is boldly suggested that slavery is *better* than freedom. The Republican party, on the contrary, hold that this government was instituted to secure the blessings of freedom, and that slavery is an unqualified evil to the negro, to the white man, to the soil, and to the State. Regarding it an evil, they will not molest it in the States where it exists; they will not overlook the constitutional guards which our forefathers have placed around it; they will do nothing that can give proper offence to those who hold slaves by legal sanction; but they will use every constitutional method to prevent the evil from becoming larger and involving more negroes, more white men, more soil, and more States in its deplorable consequences. They will, if possible, place it where the public mind shall rest in the belief that it is in course of ultimate peaceable extinction, in God's own good time. And to this end they will, if possible, restore the government to the policy of the fathers—the policy of preserving the new territories from the baneful influence of human bondage, as the Northwestern territories were sought [thought?] to be preserved by the ordinance of 1787 and the compromise act of 1820.

They will oppose, in all its length and breadth, the modern Democratic idea that slavery is as good as freedom, and ought to have room for expansion all over the continent, if people can be found to carry it. All, or very nearly all, of Judge Douglas' arguments about "Popular Sovereignty" as he calls it, are logical if you admit that slavery is as good and as right as freedom; and not one of them is worth a rush if you deny it. This is the difference, as I understand it, between the Republican and the Democratic parties; and I ask the gentleman, and all of you, whether his question is not satisfactorily answered.

In this connection let me read to you the opinions of our old leader Henry Clay, on the question of whether slavery *is* as good as freedom. The extract which I propose to read is contained [in?] a letter written by Mr. Clay in his old age, as late as 1849. The circumstances which called it forth were these. A convention had been called to form a new constitution for the State of Kentucky. The old Constitution had been adopted in the year 1799—half a century before, when Mr. Clay was a young man just rising into public notice. As long ago as the adoption of the old Constitution, Mr. Clay had been the earnest advocate of a system of gradual emancipation and colonization of the [slaves] of Kentucky. And again in his old age, in the maturity of his great mind, we find the same wise project still uppermost in his thoughts. Let me read a few passages from his letter of 1849: "I know there are those who draw an argument in favor of slavery from the alleged intellectual inferiority of the black race. Whether this argument is founded in fact or not, I will not now stop to inquire, but merely say that if it proves anything at all, it proves too much. It proves that among the white races of the world any one might properly be enslaved by any other which had made greater advances in civilization. And, if this rule applies to nations there is no reason why it should not apply to individuals; and it might easily be proved that the wisest man in the world could rightfully reduce all other men and women to bondage," &c., &c.

* * * * * *

Let us inquire, what Douglas really invented, when he introduced, and drove through Congress, the Nebraska bill. He called it "Popular Sovereignty." What does Popular Sovereignty mean? Strictly and literally it means the sovereignty of the people over their own affairs—in other words, the right of the people of every nation and community to govern themselves. Did Mr. Douglas invent this? Not quite. The idea of Popular Sovereignty was floating about the world several ages before the author of the Nebraska bill saw daylight—indeed before Columbus set foot on the American continent. In the year 1776 it took tangible form in the noble words which you are all familiar with: "We hold these truths to be self-evident: That all men are created equal; That they are endowed by their Creator with certain inalienable rights; That among these are life, liberty and the pursuit of happiness; That to secure these rights governments are instituted among men, *deriving their just powers from the consent of the governed.*" Was not this the origin of Popular Sovereignty as applied to the American people? Here we are told that Governments are instituted among men to secure certain rights, and that they derive their just powers *from the consent of the governed.* If that is not Popular Sovereignty, then I have no conception of the meaning of words.

Then, if Mr. Douglas did not invent *this* kind of sovereignty, let us pursue the inquiry and find out what the invention really was. Was it the right of emigrants in Kansas and Nebraska to govern themselves and a gang of niggers too, if they wanted them? Clearly this was no invention of his, because Gen. Cass put forth the same doctrine in 1848, in his so-called Nicholson letter—six whole years before Douglas thought of such a thing. Gen. Cass could have taken out a patent for the idea, if he had chosen to do so, and have prevented his Illinois rival from reaping a particle of benefit from it. Then what was it, I ask again, that this "Little Giant" invented? It never occurred to Gen. Cass to call his discovery by the odd name of "Popular Sovereignty." He had not the *impudence* to say that the *right of people to govern niggers* was the *right of people to govern themselves.* His notions of the fitness of things were not moulded to the brazen degree of calling the right to put a hundred niggers through under the lash in Nebraska, a "*sacred right of self-government.*" And here, I submit to this intelligent audience and the whole world, was Judge

Douglas' discovery, and the whole of it. He invented *a name* for Gen. Cass' old Nicholson letter dogma. He discovered that the right of the white man to breed and flog niggers in Nebraska was POPULAR SOVEREIGNTY!

* * * * * *

My friends, I have endeavored to show you the logical consequences of the Dred Scott decision, which holds that the people of a Territory cannot prevent the establishment of Slavery in their midst. I have stated what cannot be gainsayed—that the grounds upon which this decision is made are equally applicable to the Free States as to the Free Territories, and that the peculiar reasons put forth by Judge Douglas for endorsing this decision, commit him in advance to the next decision, and to all other decisions emanating from the same source. Now, when by all these means, you have succeeded in dehumanizing the negro; when you have put him down and made it forever impossible for him to be but as the beasts of the field; when you have extinguished his soul, and placed him where the ray of hope is blown out in darkness like that which broods over the spirits of the damned; are you quite sure the demon which you have roused *will not turn and rend you*? What constitutes the bulwark of our own liberty and independence? It is not our frowning battlements, our bristling sea coasts, the guns of our war steamers, or the strength of our gallant and disciplined army. These are not our reliance against a resumption of tyranny in our fair land. All of them may be turned against our liberties, without making us stronger or weaker for the struggle. Our reliance is in *the love of liberty* which God has planted in our bosoms. Our defense is in the preservation of the spirit which prizes liberty as the heritage of all men, in all lands, everywhere. Destroy this spirit, and you have planted the seeds of despotism around your own doors. Familiarize yourselves with the chains of bondage, and you are preparing your own limbs to wear them. Accustomed to trample on the rights of those around you, you have lost the genius of your own independence, and become the fit subjects of the first cunning tyrant who rises. And let me tell you, all these things are prepared for you with the logic of history, if the elections shall promise that the next Dred Scott decision and all future decisions will be quietly acquiesced in by the people.

The text of this speech is here more inclusive than in the Complete Works of Abraham Lincoln, *but is evidently a slight part of the whole, as indicated by the accompanying comment in the* Alton Courier, *September 16, 1858:*

"An enthusiastic audience greeted Mr. Lincoln at Edwardsville on Saturday, and we learn from all sources that his speech gave more than satisfaction to his listeners—that it was warmly applauded throughout. We can do nothing better than give a few extracts from his speech (which was something over two hours in length,) for the benefit of those of our readers who were unable to hear the convincing arguments and eloquent appeals pronounced by Mr. Lincoln himself . . ."

Lincoln's definition of the difference between the Republican and the Democratic parties on the issues involved in the senatorial contest, in particular the last paragraph of the text, contains his fundamental philosophy of equality and freedom for all men, as it is grounded in the same theory that is central to Jefferson's philosophy—that the individual's love of liberty is the source of political liberty and that no man can deny liberty to another without endangering his own.

LETTER TO M. P. SWEET
SEPTEMBER 16, 1858

Centralia, Sept. 16 1858

Hon: M. P. Sweet
My dear Sir

Yesterday Douglas and I met at Jonesboro. A very trifling thing occurred which gives me a little uneasiness. I was, at the suggestion of friends, putting in, some resolutions and the like of abolition caste, passed by Douglas friends, some time ago, as a Set-off to his attempts of a like character against me. Among others I put the questions to T. Campbell and his answers to them, in 1850 when you and he ran for Congress. As my attention was divided, half lingering upon that case, and half advancing to the next one, I mentioned your name, as Campbell's opponent, in a confused sentence, which, when I heard it myself, struck me as having something disparaging to you in it. I instantly corrected it, and asked the reporters to suppress it; but my fear now is that those villainous reporters Douglas has with him will try to make something out of it. I do not myself exactly remember what it was, so little connection had it with any distinct thought in my my [*sic*] mind, and I really hope no more may be heard of it; but if there should, I write this to assure you that nothing can be farther from me than to *feel*, much less, intentionally *say* anything disrespectful to you.

I sincerely hope you may hear nothing of it except what I have written.

Yours very truly,
A. Lincoln

Sweet was an old-line Whig who had been associated with Lincoln in politics for many years. In 1850 Thomas Campbell had defeated Sweet in the race for Congress in the Galena District.

VERSES: TO ROSA
SEPTEMBER 28, 1858

TO ROSA—

You are young, and I am older;
  You are hopeful, I am not.
Enjoy life, ere it grow colder.
  Pluck the roses ere they rot.

Teach your beau to heed the lay—
  That sunshine soon is lost in shade—
That *now's* as good as any day—
  To take thee, Rosa, ere she fade.

A. Lincoln—

Winchester, Sep. 28, 1858.

These verses to Rosa Haggard and those written two days later, "To Linnie," were penned by Lincoln in the autograph books of the daughters of the proprietor of the hotel where Lincoln stopped in Winchester, Illinois, while filling a campaign speaking engagement.

VERSES: TO LINNIE
SEPTEMBER 30, 1858

TO LINNIE—

A sweet plaintive song did I hear,
And I fancied that she was the singer.
May emotions as pure as that song set a-stir
Be the worst that the future shall bring her.

A. Lincoln—

Winchester Sep. 30—1858—

FRAGMENT: ON SLAVERY
[OCTOBER 1, 1858?]

Suppose it is true, that the negro is inferior to the white, in the gifts of nature; is it not the exact reverse justice that the white should, for that reason, take from the negro, any part of the little which has been given him? "*Give* to him that is needy" is the Christian rule of charity; but "Take from him that is needy" is the rule of slavery.

PRO-SLAVERY THEOLOGY

The sum of pro-slavery theology seems to be this: "Slavery is not universally *right*, nor yet universally *wrong*; it is better for *some* people to be slaves; and, in such cases, it is the Will of God that they be such."

Certainly there is no contending against the Will of God; but still there is some difficulty in ascertaining, and applying it, to particular cases. For instance we will suppose the Rev. Dr. Ross has a slave named Sambo, and the question is "Is it the Will of God that Sambo shall remain a slave, or be set free?" The Almighty gives no audable [*sic*] answer to the question, and his revelation —the Bible—gives none—or, at most, *none* but such as admits of a squabble, as to it's meaning. No one thinks of asking Sambo's opinion on it. So, at last, it comes to this, that *Dr. Ross* is to decide the question. And while he consider [*sic*] it, he sits in the shade, with gloves on his hands, and subsists on the bread that Sambo is earning in the burning sun. If he decides that God Wills Sambo to continue a slave, he thereby retains his own comfortable position; but if he decides that God wills Sambo to be free, he thereby has to walk out of the shade, throw off his gloves, and delve for his own bread. Will Dr. Ross be actuated by that perfect impartiality, which has ever been considered most favorable to correct decisions?

But, slavery is good for some people!!! As a *good* thing, slavery is strikingly perculiar [*sic*], in this, that it is the only good thing which no man ever seeks the good of, *for himself*.

Nonsense! Wolves devouring lambs, not because it is good for their own greedy maws, but because it is good for the lambs!!!

LETTER TO J. N. BROWN
OCTOBER 18, 1858

Springfield, Oct. 18. 1858

Hon. J. N. Brown
My dear Sir

I do not perceive how I can express myself, more plainly, than I have done in the foregoing extracts. In four of them I have expressly disclaimed all intention to bring about social and political equality between the white and black races, and, in all the rest, I have done the same thing by clear implication

I have made it equally plain that I think the negro is included in the word "men" used in the Declaration of Independence.

I believe the declara-[*sic*] that "all men are created equal" is the great fundamental principle upon which our free institutions rest; that negro slavery is violative of that principle; but that, by our frame of government, that principle has not been made one of legal obligation; that by our frame of government, the states which have slavery are to retain it, or surrender it at their own pleasure; and that all others—individuals, free-states and national government—are constitutionally bound to leave them alone about it.

I believe our government was thus framed because of the *necessity* springing from the actual presence of slavery, when it was framed.

That such necessity does not exist in the teritories [*sic*], when slavery is not present.

In his Mendenhall speech Mr. Clay says

"Now, as an abstract principle, there is no doubt of the truth of that declaration (all men created equal) and it is desireable [*sic*], in the original construction of society, and in organized societies, to keep it in view, as a great fundamental principle"

Again, in the same speech Mr. Clay says:

"If a state of nature existed, and we were about to lay the foundations of society, no man would be more strongly opposed than I should to incorporate the institution of slavery among it's elements"

Exactly so. In our new free teritories [*sic*], a state of nature *does* exist. In them Congress lays the foundations of society; and, in laying those foundations, I say, with Mr. Clay, it is desireable [*sic*] that the declaration of the equality of all men shall be kept in view, as a great fundamental principle; and that Congress, which lays the foundations of society, should, like Mr. Clay, be strongly opposed to the incorporation of slavery among it's elements.

But it does not follow that social and political equality between whites and blacks, *must* be incorporated, because slavery must *not*. The declaration does not so require.

Yours as ever

A. Lincoln

The extracts referred to in this letter were newspaper clippings of the passages on slavery from Lincoln's speeches at Peoria (1854), at Springfield (1857), at Chicago (1858), at Ottawa (1858), and at Charleston (1858). The clippings were put together and sent to Brown in a little notebook, on the first pages of which Lincoln penned the letter. Brown, an old Whig, had served in the Illinois Legislature several terms and was associated with Lincoln in Whig politics. From the tone of Lincoln's letter and his sending extracts from his speeches dealing with his position on slavery in particular, one gathers that Brown like many old Whigs was having a hard time swallowing the more radical Republicanism. Lincoln's emphasis on the fact that he is a disciple of Henry Clay is significant.

LAST SPEECH IN SPRINGFIELD, ILLINOIS, IN THE CAMPAIGN OF 1858. [OCTOBER 30, 1858]

My friends, to-day closes the discussions of this canvass. The planting and the culture are over; and there remains but the preparation, and the harvest.

I stand here surrounded by friends—some *political, all personal* friends, I trust. May I be indulged, in this closing scene, to say a few words of myself. I have borne a laborious, and, in some respects to myself, a painful part in the contest. Through all, I have neither assailed, nor wrestled with any part of the Constitution. The legal right of the Southern people to reclaim their fugitives I have constantly admitted. The legal right of Congress to interfere with their institution in the states, I have constantly denied. In resisting the spread of slavery to new teritory [*sic*], and with that, what appears to me to be a tendency to subvert the first principle of free government itself my whole effort has consisted. To the best of my judgment I have labored *for*, and not *against* the Union. As I have not felt, so I have not expressed any harsh sentiment towards our Southern bretheren [*sic*]. I have constantly declared, as I really believed, the only difference between them and us, is the difference of circumstances.

I have meant to assail the motives of no party, or individual; and if I have, in any instance (of which I am not conscious) departed from my purpose, I regret it.

I have said that in some respects the contest has been painful to me. Myself, and those with whom I act have been constantly accused of a purpose to destroy the Union; and bespattered with every immaginable [*sic*] odious epithet; and some who were friends, as it were but yesterday have made themselves most active in this. I have cultivated patience, and made no attempt at a retort.

Ambition has been ascribed to me. God knows how sincerely I prayed from the first that this field of ambition might not be opened. I claim no insensibility to political honors; but today could the Missouri restriction be restored, and the whole slavery question replaced on the old ground of "toleration" by *necessity* where it exists, with unyielding hostility to the spread of it, on principle, I would, in consideration, gladly agree, that Judge Douglas should never be *out*, and I never *in*, an office, so long as we both or either, live.

There is evidence in the account of the day's events published in the Illinois State Journal *that Lincoln made a long speech, and a particular reference to the conclusion as "one of the most eloquent appeals ever addressed to the American people" seems appropriate to this selection. However, the rhetorical structure of this composition suggests that it might have served equally well as a formal opening to be followed by further extempore remarks, or as a short speech complete in itself.*

LETTER TO HENRY ASBURY
NOVEMBER 19, 1858

Springfield, Novr. 19 1858

Henry Asbury, Esq
My dear Sir

Yours of the 13th. was received some days ago. The fight must go on. The cause of civil liberty must not be surrendered at the end of *one* or even, one *hundred* defeats. Douglas had the ingenuity to be supported in the late contest both as the best means to *break down*, and to *uphold* the Slave interest. No ingenuity can keep those antagonistic elements in harmony long. Another explosion will soon come.

Yours truly
A. Lincoln—

LETTER TO DOCTOR C. H. RAY
NOVEMBER 20, 1858

Springfield, Nov. 20, 1858

Dr. C. H. Ray
My dear Sir

I wish to preserve a Set of the late debates (if they may be called so) between Douglas and myself. To enable me to do so, please get two copies of each number of your paper containing the whole, and send them to me by Express; and I will pay you for the papers & for your trouble. I wish the two sets, in order to lay one away in the room, and to put the other in a Scrap-book. Remember, if part of any debate is on *both* sides of one sheet, it will take two sets to make one scrap-book. I believe, according to a letter of yours to Hatch you are "feeling like h-ll yet". Quit that. You will soon feel better. Another "blow-up" is coming; and we shall have fun again. Douglas managed to be supported both as the best instrument to *put down* and to *uphold* the slave power; but no ingenuity can long keep these antagonisms in harmony.

Yours as ever

A. Lincoln

Ray was editor of the Chicago Daily Press and Tribune. *The "scrap book" was duly prepared and the text emended in some passages by Lincoln himself. It was used as the basis for the official Follett, Foster* Debates. *Ray had at an earlier date practiced medicine in Muscatine, Iowa, and Tazewell County, Illinois. His journalism began with writing for a temperance paper in Springfield. In 1847 he removed to Galena and soon after became editor of the* Galena Jeffersonian. *With Joseph Medill and John C. Vaughn he became associated in purchasing the* Chicago Tribune, *of which he was editor-in-chief, 1855-63.*

NOTES OF AN ARGUMENT
[DECEMBER ?], 1858

Legislation and *adjudication* must follow, and conform to, the progress of society.

The progress of society now begins to produce cases of the transfer, for debts, of the entire property of Railroad corporations; and to enable transferees to use, and enjoy, the transferred property, *legislation,* and *adjudication,* begins to be necessary.

Shall this class of legislation, just now beginning with us, be *general* or *special*?

Section Ten, of our Constitution, requires that it should be general, if possible. (Read the section)

Special legislation always trenches upon the judicial department; and in so far violates Section Two of the Constitution. (Read it.)

Just reasoning—policy—is in favor of general legislation—else the legislature will be *loaded down* with the investigation of special cases—a work which the courts *ought* to perform, and can perform much more perfectly. How can the Legislature rightly decide the facts between P. & B. & S. C. & Co.

It is said that, under a general law, whenever a R. R. Co. gets tired of its debts, it may transfer *fraudulently*, to get rid of them.

So they may—so may individuals; and which—the *legislature* or the *courts* is best suited to try the question of fraud in either case?

It is said, if a purchaser have acquired legal rights, let him not be robbed of them; but if he needs *legislation*, let him submit to just terms to obtain it.

Let him, say we, have general law in advance (guarded in every possible way against fraud) so that when he acquires a legal right, he will have no occasion to wait for additional legislation—and if he has practiced fraud, let the courts so decide.

LETTER TO JAMES T. THORNTON DECEMBER 2, 1858

Springfield, Decr. 2. 1858

James T. Thornton, Esq
Dear Sir

Yours of the 29th. written in behalf of Mr. John H. Widmer, is received. I am absent altogether too much to be a suitable instructer [*sic*] for a law student. When a man has reached the age that Mr. Widner [*sic*] has, and has already been doing for himself, my judgment is, that he reads the books for himself without an instructer [*sic*]. That is precisely the way I came to the law. Let Mr. Widner [*sic*] read Blackstone's Commentaries, Chitty's Pleadings—Greenleaf's Evidence, Story's Equity, and Story's Equity Pleadings, get a license, and go to the practice, and still keep reading. That is my judgment of the cheapest, quickest, and best way for Mr. Widner [*sic*] to make a lawyer of himself.

Yours truly
A. Lincoln.

The editor has been able to find little identifying Thornton or the prospective lawyer Widmer (Widner) beyond the comment which appeared with the facsimile of the letter in the Oregon Historical Society Quarterly, *Vol. 23, 1922: "Following autograph letter was brought to Oregon from Urbana, Champaign Co., Ill., by J. W. Thornton, in Feb., 1906—given him by his father, the gentleman to whom it was written. Widmer began the study of law . . . enlisted in first call for volunteers in Civil War . . . became a Colonel. . . . After the war he resumed his law studies and in a few years became eminent in his profession and now lives in Urbana, Ill."*

On the other hand, the only Widmer of record as

admitted to the Illinois Bar was John H. Widmer, admitted from LaSalle in 1860. He became a Major rather than a Colonel, and was until the time of his death in 1923 a resident of Ottawa, rather than Urbana. That he is the person about whom Lincoln wrote this letter seems probable.

The name which Lincoln spells both Widmer *and* Widner *is likewise confusing, appearing in Paul M. Angle,* Lincoln: 1854-1861, *as* Widner *and* Widener, *and in Carl Sandburg,* Abraham Lincoln: The Prairie Years *as* Widener. *Michael C. O'Byrne,* History of LaSalle County, Illinois, *lists the man as* John H. Widmer.

James T. Thornton was a native of Kentucky who moved to Sangamon County, Illinois, in 1833, and later became a farmer in Putnam County. He is listed in David Lyman Phillips, Biographies of the State Officers, *as "a Republican, as old as the party itself, and no less vigorous."*

LETTER TO LYMAN TRUMBULL DECEMBER 11, 1858

Springfield, Decr. 11. 1858

Hon. L. Trumbull:
My dear Sir

Your letter of the 7th. enclosing one from Mr. Underwood, is received. I have not the slightest thought of being a candidate for Congress in this District. I am not spoken of in that connection; and I can scarcely conceive what has misled Mr. Underwood in regard to the matter.

As to what we shall do, the Republicans are a little divided. The Danites say if we will stand out of the way, they will run a man, and divide the democratic forces with the Douglasites; and some of our friends are in favor of this course. Others think such a course would demoralize us, and hurt us in the future; and they, of course, are in favor of running a man of our own at all events. This latter view will probably prevail.

Since you left, Douglas has gone South, making characteristic speeches, and seeking to re-instate himself in that section. The majority of the democratic politicians of the nation mean to kill him; but I doubt whether they will adopt the aptest way to do it. Their true way is to present him with no new test, let him into the Charleston convention, and then outvote him, and nominate another. In that case, he will have no pretext for bolting the nomination, and will be as powerless as they can wish. On the other hand, if they push a Slave Code upon him, as a test, he will bolt at once, turn upon us, as in the case of Lecompton, and claim that all Northern men shall make common cause in electing him President as the best means of breaking down this Slave power. In that case, the democratic party go into a minority inevitably; and the struggle in the whole North will be, as it was in Illinois last summer and fall, whether the Republican party can maintain it's identity, or be broken up to form the tail of Dougla's [*sic*] new kite. Some of our great Republican doctors will then have a splendid chance to swallow the pills they so eagerly prescribed for us last Spring. Still I hope they will not swallow them; and although I do not feel that I owe the said doctors much, I will help them, to the best of my ability, to reject the said pills. The truth is, the Republican principle can, in no wise live with Douglas; and it is arrant folly now, as it was last Spring, to waste time, and scatter labor already performed, in dallying with him.

Your friend as ever

A. Lincoln—

The "Danites" alluded to were anti-Douglas Democrats who resented Douglas's split with the Buchanan forces over the Lecompton Constitution, so called from the town in Kansas where the Constitutional Convention met.

LETTER TO H. L. PIERCE AND OTHERS
APRIL 6, 1859

Springfield, Ills, April 6, 1859

Messrs. Henry L. Pierce, & others.

Gentlemen

Your kind note inviting me to attend a Festival in Boston, on the 13th. Inst. in honor of the birth-day of Thomas Jefferson, was duly received. My engagements are such that I can not attend.

Bearing in mind that about seventy years ago, two great political parties were first formed in this country, that Thomas Jefferson was the head of one of them, and Boston the head-quarters of the other, it is both curious and interesting that those supposed to descend politically from the party opposed to Jefferson should now be celebrating his birthday in their own original seat of empire, while those claiming political descent from him have nearly ceased to breathe his name everywhere.

Remembering too, that the Jefferson party were formed upon its supposed superior devotion to the *personal* rights of men, holding the rights of *property* to be secondary only, and greatly inferior, and then assuming that the so-called democracy of to-day, are the Jefferson, and their opponents, the anti-Jefferson parties, it will be equally interesting to note how completely the two have changed hands as to the principle upon which they were originally supposed to be divided.

The democracy of to-day hold the *liberty* of one man to be absolutely nothing, when in conflict with another man's right of *property*. Republicans, on the contrary, are for both the *man* and the *dollar*; but in cases of conflict, the man *before* the dollar.

I remember once being much amused at seeing two partially intoxicated men engage in a fight with their great-coats on, which fight, after a long, and rather harmless contest, ended in each having fought himself *out* of his own coat, and *into* that of the other. If the two leading parties of this day are really identical with the two in the days of Jefferson and Adams, they have performed the same feat as the two drunken men.

But soberly, it is now no child's play to save the principles of Jefferson from total overthrow in this nation.

One would start with great confidence that he could convince any sane child that the simpler propositions of Euclid are true; but, nevertheless, he would fail, utterly, with one who should deny the definitions and axioms. The principles of Jefferson are the definitions and axioms of free society.

And yet they are denied and evaded, with no small show of success.

One dashingly calls them "glittering generalities"; another bluntly calls them "self evident lies"; and still others insidiously argue that they apply only to "superior races."

These expressions, differing in form, are identical in object and effect—the supplanting the principles of free government, and restoring those of classification, caste, and legitimacy. They would delight a convocation of crowned heads, plotting against the people. They are the van-guard—the miners, and sappers—of returning despotism.

We must repulse them, or they will subjugate us.

This is a world of compensations; and he who would *be* no slave, must consent to *have* no slave. Those who deny freedom to others, deserve it not for themselves; and, under a just God, can not long retain it.

All honor to Jefferson—to the man who, in the concrete pressure of a struggle for national independence by a single people, had the coolness, forecast, and capacity to introduce into a merely revolutionary document, an abstract truth, applicable to all men and all times, and so to embalm it there, that to-day, and in all coming days, it shall be a rebuke and a stumbling-block to the very harbingers of re-appearing tyranny and oppression.

Your obedient Servant

A. Lincoln—

As a result of his growing reputation, Lincoln was receiving numerous invitations to speak, and although he accepted a number he had to refuse a good many. In this instance, however, he did the next best thing by writing a letter which, apparently, he intended to be read to the meeting. That he relished the possibilities of speaking in honor of Jefferson is obvious, and what he has to say about the Republican party being the true heir of Jeffersonian principles is in keeping with numerous similar references in his speeches of 1858.

The second half of the letter, beginning with the reference to Euclid, is of particular interest as an early use of the analogy linking Euclid's propositions and the Jeffersonian proposition in the Declaration of Independence, which Lincoln turned into the memorable phrase in the "Gettysburg Address."

LETTER TO T. J. PICKETT
APRIL 16, 1859

Springfield, April 16. 1859.

T. J. Pickett, Esq
My dear Sir:

Yours of the 13th. is just received. My engagements are such that I can not, at any very early day, visit Rock Island, to deliver a lecture, or for any other object.

As to the other matter you kindly mention, I must, in candor say, I do not think myself fit for the Presidency. I certainly am flattered and gratified, that some partial friends think of me in that connection; but I really think it best for our cause that no concerted effort, such as you suggest, should be made.

Let this be considered confidential.

Yours very truly
A. Lincoln

Pickett was a newspaper editor of Rock Island, Illinois. The lecture referred to was the one on "Discoveries, Inventions and Improvements" which Lincoln had delivered a number of times, but which he thought little of. (See "Letter to F. C. Herburger," April 7, 1860.) Lincoln's categorical statement concerning his unfitness for the Presidency was made, in the editor's opinion, not because he thought lightly of the possibility that he might be a candidate, but because he was acutely aware of it. He knew that his name was being discussed widely, and was beginning to feel qualms at the possibility.

LETTER TO SALMON PORTLAND CHASE
JUNE 9, 1859

Springfield, Ills. June 9. 1859

Hon: S. P. Chase:
Dear Sir

Please pardon the liberty I take in addressing you, as I now do. It appears by the papers that the late Republican State Convention of Ohio adopted a Platform, of which the following is one plank, "A repeal of the atrocious Fugitive Slave Law."

This is already damaging us here. I have no doubt that if that plank be even *introduced* into the next Republican National Convention, it will explode it. Once introduced, its supporters and it's opponents will quarrel irreconcilably. The latter believe the U. S. constitution declares a fugitive slave "*shall be delivered up*"; and they look upon the above plank as dictated by the spirit which declares a fugitive slave "*shall not be delivered up.*"

I enter upon no argument one way or the other; but I assure you the cause of Republicanism is hopeless in Illinois, if it be in any way made responsible for that plank. I hope you can, and will, contribute something to relieve us from it.

Your Obt. Servt.
A. Lincoln

LETTER TO SALMON PORTLAND CHASE
JUNE 20, 1859

Springfield, Ills. June 20. 1859

Hon. S. P. Chase
My dear Sir

Yours of the 13th. Inst. is received. You say you would be glad to have my views. Although I think Congress has Constitutional authority to enact a Fugitive Slave law, I have never elaborated an opinion upon the subject. My view has been, and is, simply this: The U. S. Constitution says the fugitive slave "*shall be delivered up*" but it does not expressly say *who* shall deliver him up. Whatever the Constitution says "*shall be done*" and has omitted saying who shall do it, the government established by that Constitution, *ex vi termini*, is vested with the power of doing; and Congress is, by the Constitution, expressly empowered to make all laws which shall be necessary and proper for carrying into execution all powers vested by the constitution in the government of the United States. This would be my view, on a simple reading of the Constitution; and it is greatly strengthened by the historical fact that the constitution was adopted, in great part, in order to get a government which could execute it's own behests, in contradistinction to that under the Articles of Confederation, which depended, in many respects, upon the States, for it's execution; and the other fact that one of the earliest congresses, under the constitution, did enact a Fugitive Slave law.

But I did not write you on this subject, with any view of discussing the constitutional question. My only object was to impress you with what I believe is true, that the introduction of a proposition for repeal of the Fugitive Slave law, into the next Republican National convention, will explode the Convention and the party. Having turned your attention to the point, I wish to do no more.

Yours very truly
A. Lincoln.

AGRICULTURE: ANNUAL ADDRESS BEFORE THE WISCONSIN STATE AGRICULTURAL SOCIETY, AT MILWAUKEE, WISCONSIN. SEPTEMBER 30, 1859

Members of the Agricultural Society and Citizens of Wisconsin:

Agricultural fairs are becoming an institution of the country. They are useful in more ways than one. They bring us together, and thereby make us better acquainted, and better friends than we otherwise should be. From the first appearance of man upon the earth, down to very recent times, the words "*stranger*" and "*enemy*" were *quite* or *almost* synonymous. Long after civilized nations had defined robbery and murder as high crimes, and had affixed severe punishments to them, when practiced among and upon their own people respectively, it was deemed no offence, but even meritorious, to rob, and murder, and enslave *strangers*, whether as nations or as individuals. Even yet, this has not totally disappeared. The man of the highest moral cultivation, in spite of all that abstract principle can do, likes him whom he *does* know, much better than him whom he does *not* know. To correct the evils, great and small, which spring from want of sympathy and from positive enmity, among *strangers*, as nations or as individuals, is one of the highest functions of civilization. To this end, our agricultural fairs contribute in no small degree. They make more pleasant, and more strong, and more durable, the bond of social and political union among us.

Again, if, as Pope declares, "happiness is our being's end and aim," our fairs contribute much to that end and aim, as occasions of recreation—as holidays. Constituted as man is, he has positive need of occasional recreation, and whatever can give him this, associated with virtue and advantage, and free from vice and disadvantage, is a positive good. Such recreation our fairs afford. They are a present pleasure, to be followed by no pain as a consequence. They are a present pleasure, making the future more pleasant.

But the chief use of agricultural Fairs is to aid in improving the great calling of *Agriculture*, in all its departments and minute divisions; to make mutual exchange of agricultural discovery, information and knowledge, so that, at the end, *all* may know everything which may have been known to but *one* or to but *few*, at the beginning—to bring together especially all which is supposed to not be generally known, because of recent discovery or invention.

And not only to bring together, and to impart, all that has been accidentally discovered or invented upon ordinary motive; but by exciting emulation, for premiums, and for the pride and honor of success—of triumph, in some sort—to stimulate discovery and invention into extraordinary activity. In this, these fairs are kindred to the patent clause in the Constitution of the United States; and to the department and practical system based upon that clause.

One feature I believe of every fair, is a regular *address*. The Agricultural Society of the young, prosperous, and soon to be great State of Wisconsin, has done me the high honor of selecting me to make that address on this occasion—an honor for which I make my profound and grateful acknowledgment.

I presume I am not expected to employ the time assigned me in the mere flattery of farmers, as a class. My opinion of them is that, in proportion to numbers, they are neither better nor worse than other people. In the nature of things they are more numerous than any other class; and I believe there really are more attempts at flattering them than any other; the reason of which I cannot perceive, unless it be that they can cast more votes than any other. On reflection, I am not quite sure there is not cause of suspicion against you in selecting me, in some sort a politician and in no sort a farmer, to address you.

But farmers being the most numerous class, it follows that their interest is the largest interest. It also follows that that interest is most worthy of all to be cherished and cultivated—that if there be inevitable conflict between that interest and any other, that other should yield.

Again, I suppose it is not expected of me to impart to you much specific information on Agriculture. You have no reason to believe, and do not believe, that I possess it. If that were what you seek in this address, any one of your own number, or class, would be more able to furnish it.

You, perhaps, do expect me to give some general interest to the occasion; and to make some general suggestions, on practical matters. I shall attempt nothing more. And in such suggestions by me, quite likely very little will be new to you, and a large part of the rest possibly already known to be erroneous.

My first suggestion is an inquiry as to the effect of greater *thoroughness* in all the departments of agriculture than now prevails in the Northwest—perhaps I might say, in America. To speak entirely within bounds, it is known that fifty bushels of wheat, or one hundred bushels of Indian corn, can be produced from an acre. Less than a year ago I saw it stated that a man, by extraordinary care and labor, had produced of wheat, what was equal to two hundred bushels from an acre. But take fifty of wheat, and one hundred of corn, to be the *probability*, and compare it with the actual crops of the country. Many years ago I saw it stated in a Patent Office Report that eighteen bushels to the acre was the average crop throughout the wheat growing region of the United States; and this year, an intelligent farmer of Illinois assured me that he did not believe the land harvested in that State this season, had yielded more than an average of eight bushels to the acre. The brag crop I heard of in our vicinity was two thousand bushels from ninety acres; many crops were threshed, producing no more than three bushels to the acre; much was cut, and then abandoned as not worth threshing; and much was abandoned without cutting. As to Indian corn, and indeed, most other crops, the case has not been much better. For the last four years I do not believe the ground planted with corn in Illinois has produced an average of twenty bushels to the acre. It is true that heretofore we have had better crops with no better cultivation; but I believe it is also true that the soil has never been pushed up to one-half of its capacity.

What would be the effect upon the farming interest to push the soil up to something near its full capacity? Unquestionably it will take more labor to produce *fifty* bushels from an acre, than it will to produce *ten* bushels from the same acre. But will it take more labor to produce fifty bushels from *one* acre than from *five*? Unquestionably, thorough cultivation will require more labor to the *acre*; but will it require more to the *bushel*? If it should require just as *much* to the bushel, there are some *probable*, and several *certain* advantages in favor of the thorough practice. It is probable it would develope those unknown causes, or develope unknown cures for those causes, which of late years have cut down our crops below their former average. It is almost certain, I think, that in the deeper plowing, analysis of soils, experiments with manures and varieties of seeds, observance of seasons, and the like, these cures would be found.

It is certain that thorough cultivation would spare half, or more than half, the cost of land, simply because the same product would be got from half, or from less than half, the quantity of land. This proposition is self-evident; and can be made no plainer by repetitions or illustrations. The cost of land is a great item, even in new countries, and constantly grows greater and greater, in comparison with other items, as the country grows older.

It also would spare a large proportion of the making and maintaining of inclosures—the same, whether these inclosures should be hedges, ditches or fences. This, again, is a heavy item—heavy at first, and heavy in its continual demand for repairs. I remember once being greatly astonished by an apparently authentic exhibition of the proportion the cost of inclosures bears to all the other expenses of the farmer, though I cannot remember, exactly, what that proportion was. Any farmer, if he will, can ascertain, it in his own case, for himself.

Again, a great amount of "locomotion" is spared by thorough cultivation. Take fifty bushels of wheat, ready for harvest, standing upon a *single* acre; and it can be harvested, in any of the known ways, with less than half the labor which would be required if it were spread over *five* acres. This would be true, if cut by the old hand sickle; true, to a greater extent, if by the scythe and cradle; and to a still greater extent, if by the machinery now in use. These machines are chiefly valuable, as a means of substituting animal power for the power of men in this branch of farm-work. In the highest degree of perfection yet reached, in applying the horse power to harvesting, fully nine-tenths of the power is expended by the animal in carrying himself and dragging the machine over the field; leaving certainly not more than one-tenth to be applied directly to the only end of the whole operation—the gathering in the grain, and clipping of the straw. When grain is very thin on the ground, it is always more or less intermingled with weeds, chess and the like; and a large part of the power is expended in cutting these. It is plain that when the crop is very thick upon the ground, a larger proportion of the power is directly applied to gathering in and cutting it, and the smaller to that which is totally useless as an end. And what I have said of harvesting is true, in a greater or less degree, of mowing, plowing, gathering in of crops generally; and, indeed, of almost all farm work.

The effect of thorough cultivation upon the farmer's own mind, and, in reaction through his mind, back upon his business, is perhaps quite equal to any other of its effects. Every man is proud of what he does *well*, and no man is proud of what he does *not* do well. With the former, his heart is in his work; and he will do twice as much of it with less fatigue. The latter he performs a little imperfectly, looks at it in disgust, turns from it, and imagines himself exceedingly tired. The little he does comes to nothing, for want of finishing.

The man who produces a good full crop will scarcely ever let any part of it go to waste. He will keep up the inclosures about it, and allow neither man nor beast to trespass upon it. He will gather it in due season, and store it in perfect security. Thus he labors with satisfaction, and saves to himself the whole fruit of his labor.

The other, starting with no purpose for a full crop, labors

less, and with less satisfaction; allows his fences to fall, and cattle to trespass; gathers not in due season, or not at all; and stores insecurely, or not at all. Thus the labor he has performed is wasted away, little by little, till, in the end, he derives scarcely anything from it.

The ambition for broad acres leads to poor farming, even with men of energy. I scarcely ever knew a mammoth farm to sustain itself, much less, to return a profit upon the outlay. I have more than once known a man to spend a respectable fortune upon one, fail, and leave it, and then some man of more moderate aims, get a small fraction of the ground and make a good living upon it. Mammoth farms are like tools, or weapons, which are too heavy to be handled. Erelong they are thrown aside at a great loss.

The successful application of *steam power* to farm work is a *desideratum*—especially a steam-plow. It is not enough that a machine operated by steam will really plow. To be successful, it must, all things considered, plow *better* than can be done with animal power. It must do all the work as well, and *cheaper* or more *rapidly*, so as to get through more perfectly *in season*; or in some way afford an advantage over plowing with animals, else it is no success. I have never seen a machine intended for a steam-plow. Much praise and admiration are bestowed upon some of them; and they may be, for aught I know, already successful; but I have not perceived the demonstration of it. I have thought a good deal, in an abstract way, about a steam-plow. That one which shall be so contrived as to apply the larger proportion of its power to the cutting and turning of the soil, and the smallest to the moving itself over the field, will be the best one. A very small stationary engine would draw a large gang of plows through the ground from a short distance to itself; but when it is not stationary, but has to move along like a horse, dragging the plows after it, it must have additional power to carry itself; and the difficulty grows by what is intended to overcome it; for what adds power, also adds size and weight to the machine, thus increasing again the demand for power. Suppose you should construct the machine so as to cut a succession of short furrows, say a rod in length, transversely to the course the machine is locomoting, something like the shuttle in weaving. In such case the whole machine would move north only the width of a furrow, while in length the furrow would be a rod from east to west. In such case a very large proportion of the power would be applied to the actual plowing. But in this, too, there would be a difficulty, which would be, the getting of the plow *into* and *out* of the ground at the ends of all these short furrows.

I believe, however, ingenious men will, if they have not already, overcome the difficulties I have suggested. But there is still another, about which I am less sanguine. It is the supply of *fuel*, and especially of *water*, to make steam. Such supply is clearly practicable, but can the expense of it be borne? Steamboats live upon the water, and find their fuel at stated places. Steam-mills and other stationary steam-machinery, have their stationary supplies of fuel and water. Railroad-locomotives have their regular wood and water stations. But the steam-plow is less fortunate. It does not live upon the water; even if it be once at a water station, it will work away from it, and when it gets dry cannot return without leaving its work, at a great expense of its time and strength. It will occur that a wagon and horse team might be employed to supply it with fuel and water; but this, too, is expensive; and the question recurs, "Can the expense be borne?" When this is added to all other expenses, will not the plowing cost more than in the old way?

It is to be hoped that the steam plow will finally be successful; and if it shall be, "*thorough cultivation*"—putting the soil to the top of its capacity—producing the largest crop possible from a given quantity of ground will be most favorable to it. Doing a large amount of work upon a small quantity of ground, it will be, as nearly as possible, stationary while working, and as free as possible from locomotion; thus expending its strength, as much as possible, upon its work, and as little as possible in traveling. Our thanks, and something more substantial than thanks, are due to every man engaged in the effort to produce a successful steam plow. Even the unsuccessful, will bring something to light, which in the hands of others will contribute to the final success. I have not pointed out difficulties in order to discourage, but in order that being seen, they may be the more readily overcome.

The world is agreed that *labor* is the source from which human wants are mainly supplied. There is no dispute upon this point. From this point, however, men immediately diverge. Much disputation is maintained as to the best way of applying and controlling the labor element. By some it is assumed that labor is available only in connection with capital—that nobody labors, unless somebody else, owning capital, somehow, by the use of that capital, induces him to do it. Having assumed this, they proceed to consider whether it is best that capital shall *hire* laborers, and thus induce them to work by their own consent; or *buy* them, and drive them to it without their consent. Having proceeded so far, they naturally conclude that all laborers are necessarily either *hired* laborers or *slaves*. They further assume that whoever is once a *hired* laborer, is fatally fixed in that condition for life; and thence, again, that his condition is as bad as, or worse than, that of a slave. This is the "*mud-sill*" theory.

But another class of reasoners hold the opinion that there is no *such* relation between capital and labor as assumed; and that there is no such thing as a freeman being fatally fixed for life in the condition of a hired laborer; that both these assumptions are false, and all inferences from them groundless. They hold that labor is prior to, and independent of, capital; that, in fact, capital is the fruit of labor, and could never have existed if labor had not *first* existed; that labor can exist without capital, but that capital could never have existence without labor. Hence, they hold that labor is the superior—greatly the superior—of capital.

They do not deny that there is, and probably always will be, *a* relation between labor and capital. The error, as they hold, is in assuming that the *whole* labor of the world exists within that relation. A few men own capital; and that few avoid labor themselves, and with their capital, hire or buy another few to labor for them. A large majority belong to neither class—neither work for others, nor have others work for them. Even in all our Slave States, except South Carolina, a majority of the whole people, of all colors, are neither slaves nor masters. In these free States, a large majority are neither *hirers* nor hired. Men, with their families —wives, sons, and daughters—work for themselves, on their farms, in their houses and in their shops, taking the whole product to themselves, and asking no favor of capital on the one hand, nor of hirelings or slaves on the other. It is not forgotten that a considerable number of persons mingle their own labor with capital —that is, labor with their own hands, and also buy slaves or hire freemen to labor for them; but this is only a *mixed*, and not a *distinct*, class. No principle stated is disturbed by the existence of this mixed class.

Again, as has already been said, the opponents of the "*mud-sill*" theory insist that there is not, of necessity, any such thing as the free hired laborer being fixed to that condition for life. There is demonstration for saying this. Many independent men, in this assembly, doubtless, a few years ago were hired laborers. And their case is almost, if not quite, the general rule. The prudent, penniless beginner in the world labors for wages awhile, saves a surplus with which to buy tools or land for himself; then labors on his own account another while, and at length hires another new beginner to help him. This, say its advocates, is *free* labor—the just and generous and prosperous system which opens the way for all, gives hope to all, and energy and progress and improvement of condition to all. If any continue through life in the condition of the hired laborer, it is not the fault of the system, but because of either a dependent nature which prefers it, or of improvidence, folly, or singular misfortune. I have said this much about the elements of labor generally, as introductory to the consideration of a new phase which that element is in process of assuming. The old general rule was that *educated* people did not perform manual labor. They managed to eat their bread, leaving the toil of producing it to the uneducated. This was not an insupportable evil to the working bees, so long as the class of drones remained very small. But *now*, especially in these free States, nearly all are educated—quite too nearly all to leave the labor of the uneducated in any way adequate to the support of the whole. It follows from this that henceforth educated people too must labor. Otherwise education itself would become a positive and intolerable evil. No community can sustain, in idleness, more than a small per centage of its numbers. The great majority must labor at something useful—something productive. From these premises the problem springs, "How can *labor* and *education* be the most satisfactorily combined?"

By the "*mud-sill*" theory it is assumed that labor and education are incompatible, and any practical combination of them impossible. According to that theory, a blind horse upon a tread-mill is a perfect illustration of what a laborer should be—all the better for being blind, that he can not tread out of place, or kick understandingly. According to that theory, the educating of laborers is not only useless, but pernicious and dangerous. In fact, it is, in some sort, deemed a misfortune that laborers should have heads at all. Those same heads are regarded as explosive materials, only to be safely kept in damp places, as far as possible from that peculiar sort of fire which ignites them. A Yankee who could invent a strong-*handed* man, without a head, would secure the everlasting gratitude of the "*mud-sill*" advocates.

But free labor says, "No." Free labor argues that, as the Author of man makes every individual with one head, and one pair of hands, it was probably intended that heads and hands should co-operate as friends, and that that particular head should direct and control that particular pair of hands. As each man has one mouth to be fed, and one pair of hands to furnish food, it was probably intended that that particular pair of hands should feed that particular mouth—that each head is the natural guardian, director and protector of the hands and mouth inseparably connected with it; and that being so, every head should be cultivated and improved, by whatever will add to its capacity for performing its charge. In one word, free labor insists on universal education.

I have so far stated the opposite theories of "*mud-sill*" and "free labor," without declaring any preference of my own between them. On an occasion like this, I ought not to declare any; I suppose, however, I shall not be mistaken, in assuming as a fact, that the people of Wisconsin prefer free labor, with its natural companion, education.

This leads to the further reflection that no other human occupation opens so wide a field for the profitable and agreeable combination of labor with cultivated thought as agriculture.

I know nothing so pleasant to the mind, as the discovery of anything which is at once *new* and *valuable*—nothing which so lightens and sweetens toil as the hopeful pursuit of such discovery. And how vast and how varied a field is agriculture for such discovery. The mind, already trained to thought in the country school, or higher school, cannot fail to find it an exhaustless source of profitable enjoyment. Every blade of grass is a study; and to produce two where there was but one, is both a profit and a pleasure. And not grass alone, but soils, seeds and seasons; hedges, ditches and fences; draining, droughts, and irrigation; plowing, hoeing and harrowing; reaping, mowing and threshing;—saving crops; pests of crops; diseases of crops, and what will prevent or cure them; implements, utensils and machines, their relative merits, and how to improve them; hogs, horses and cattle; sheep, goats and poultry; trees, shrubs, fruits and flowers; the thousand things of which these are specimens, each a world of study within itself.

In all this, book-learning is available. A capacity and taste for reading, gives access to whatever has already been discovered by others. It is the key, or one of the keys, to the already solved problems. And not only so, it gives a relish and facility for successfully pursuing the yet unsolved ones. The rudiments of science are available and highly valuable. Some knowledge of botany assists in dealing with the vegetable world—with all growing crops; chemistry assists in the analysis of soils, selection and application of manures, and in numerous other ways. The mechanical branches of natural philosophy are ready helps in almost everything, but especially in reference to implements and machinery.

The thought occurs that education—cultivated thought—can best be combined with agricultural labor, or any labor, on the principle of *thorough* work—that careless, half performed, slovenly work, makes no place for such combination. And thorough work, again, renders sufficient the smallest quantity of ground to each man. And this, again, conforms to what must occur in a world less inclined to wars, and more devoted to the arts of peace, than heretofore. Population must increase rapidly, more rapidly than in former times—and ere long the most valuable of all arts will be the art of deriving a comfortable subsistence from the smallest area of soil. No community whose every member possesses this art, can ever be the victim of oppression in any of its forms. Such community will be alike independent of crowned kings, money kings, and land kings.

But, according to your programme the awarding of premiums awaits the closing of this address. Considering the deep interest necessarily pertaining to that performance, it would be no wonder if I am already heard with some impatience. I will detain you but a moment longer. Some of you will be successful, and such will need but little philosophy to take them home in cheerful spirits; others will be dissatisfied, and will be in a less happy mood. To such let me say, "Lay it not too much to heart." Let them adopt the maxim, "Better luck next time," and then, by renewed exertion, make that better luck for themselves.

And, by the successful and the unsuccessful, let it be remembered, that while occasions like the present bring their sober and durable benefits; the exultations and mortifications of them are but temporary; that the victor will soon be the vanquished, if he relax in his exertion; and that the vanquished this year may be the victor the next, in spite of all competition.

It is said an Eastern monarch once charged his wise men to invent him a sentiment to be ever in view, and which should be true and appropriate in all times and situations. They presented him the words, "*And this, too, shall pass away.*" How much it expresses! How chastening in the hour of pride; how consoling in the depths of affliction! "And this, too, shall pass away." And yet, let us hope, it is not *quite* true. Let us hope, rather, that by the best cultivation of the physical world, beneath and around us, and the intellectual and moral worlds within us, we shall secure an individual, social, and political prosperity and happiness, whose course shall be onward and upward, and which, while the earth endures, shall not pass away.

The basic text of this address is from the Chicago Daily Press and Tribune, *October 1, 1859, collated with the brochure reprinted from the volume of official pro-*

ceedings of the Wisconsin State Agricultural Society for 1859-60. (See Lincoln on Agriculture, *Lincoln Fellowship of Wisconsin, 1943, Historical Bulletin No. 1.) That the text preserved in the volume of "official proceedings" is less accurate than that in the* Daily Press and Tribune *is indicated by comparison with an extant page of the original manuscript owned by The Wisconsin State Historical Society. The story of the disposition of the manuscript is that Lincoln gave it to some unknown individual who handed it out a page at a time to the farmer listeners and others who heard the speech.*

Although this address has been discussed in "Lincoln's Development as a Writer," a note may not be amiss on one portion of it that may seem strange in the twentieth century—Lincoln's puzzlement over the problem of mechanics presented by the steam plow. Although the problem was effectively solved within a few years and steam plows became widely used in the flat open prairie country long before the day of gasoline tractors, the first popular reception of the idea was much like that of the steamboat. Theorists opined that it would not work. Lincoln, although not overly sanguine, at least recognized its possibilities.

WRITTEN BY LINCOLN IN THE AUTOGRAPH ALBUM OF MARY DELAHAY. DECEMBER 7, 1859

Dear Mary

With pleasure I write my name in your Album. Ere long some younger man will be more happy to confer *his* name upon *you*. Don't allow it, Mary, until fully assured that he is worthy of the happiness. Dec. 7—1859

Your friend
A. Lincoln

This expression of sentiment penned for the daughter of Mark W. Delahay, an old Illinois crony, lawyer, and editor, who had migrated to Kansas and was carrying on Republican activity in the state, was written during a speaking tour which took Lincoln to Kansas in the first week of December, 1859.

LETTER TO WILLIAM KELLOGG
DECEMBER 11, 1859

Springfield, Ills. Dec. 11, 1859

Hon. William Kellogg.
My dear Sir:

I have been a good deal relieved this morning by a sight of Greeley's letter to you, published in the Tribune. Before seeing it, I much feared you had, in changing interviews between Douglas & Greeley, stated what you *believed*, but did not certainly *know* to be true; and that it might be untrue, and our enemies would get an advantage of you. However, as G. admits the interviews, I think it will not hurt you that he denies conversing with D. about his re-election to the Senate. G. I think, will not tell a falsehood; and I think he will scarcely deny that he had the interviews with D. in order to assure himself from D's own lips, better than he could from his public acts & declarations, whether to try to bring the Republican party to his support generally, including his re-election to the Senate. What else could the interviews be for? Why immediately followed in the Tribune the advice that all anti-Lecompton democrats should be re-elected? The world will not consider it anything that D's reelection to the Senate was not specifically talked of by him and G.

Now, mark, I do not charge that G. was corrupt in this. I do not think he was, or is. It was his judgment that the course he took was the best way of serving the Republican cause. For this reason, and for the further reason, that he is now pulling straight with us, I think, if I were you, I would not pursue him further than necessary to my own justification. If I were you I would however be greatly tempted [to?] ask him if he really thinks D.'s advice to his friends to vote for a Lecompton & Slave code man, is very "*plucky*"

Please excuse what I have said in the way of unsolicited avice [*sic*]. I believe you will not doubt the sincerity of my friendship for you.

Yours very truly
A. Lincoln

Kellogg was a Republican politician from Canton, Illinois, who was elected to Congress. Something over a year later he was to cause Lincoln considerable political embarrassment. (See "Letter to William Kellogg," December 11, 1860, and note.) Horace Greeley's anti-slavery sentiment was often stronger than his Republicanism and practical results probably dictated his support of Douglas against Lincoln in the preceding campaign. Lincoln's attitude here is typical of his lack of personal animosity and his wish to place the general party welfare above other considerations. Of course, he recognized the power that Greeley wielded as editor of the New York Tribune.

LETTER TO G. W. DOLE, G. S. HUBBARD, AND W. H. BROWN. DECEMBER 14, 1859

Springfield, Dec. 14, 1859

Messrs. Dole, Hubbard & Brown—
Gent.

Your favor of the 12th. is at hand, and it gives me pleasure to be able to answer it. It is not my intention to take part in any of the rivalries for the Gubernatorial nomination; but the fear of being misunderstood upon that subject, ought not to deter me from doing justice to Mr. Judd, and preventing a wrong being done to him by the use of my name in connection with alledged wrongs to me.

In answer to your first question as to whether Mr. Judd was guilty of any unfairness to me at the time of Senator Trumbull's election, I answer unhesitatingly in the negative. Mr. Judd owed no political allegiance to any party whose candidate I was. He was in the Senate, holding over, having been elected by a democratic constituency. He never was in any caucus of the friends who sought to make me U. S. Senator—never gave me any promises or pledges to support me—and subsequent events have greatly tended to prove the wisdom, politically, of Mr. Judd's course. The election of Judge Trumbull strongly tended to sustain and preserve the position of that portion of the Democrats who condemned the repeal of the Missouri Compromise, and left them in a position of joining with us in forming the Republican party, as was done at the Bloomington Convention in 1856

During the canvass of 1858 for the Senatorship my belief was, and still is, that I had no more sincere and faithful friend than Mr. Judd—certainly none whom I trusted more. His position as Chairman of the State Central Committee, led to my greater intercourse with him, and to my giving him a larger share of my confidence, than with, or, to almost any other friend; and I have never suspected that that confidence was, to any degree, misplaced.

My relations with Mr. Judd, since the organization of the Republican party, in our State, in 1856, and especially since the adjournment of the Legislature in Feb. 1857, have been so very intimate, that I deem it an impossibility that he could have been dealing treacherously with me. He has also, at all times, appeared equally true and faithful to the party. In his position as Chairman of the Committee, I believe he did all that any man could have done. The best of us are liable to commit errors, which become apparent by subsequent developement; but I do not know of a single error, even, committed by Mr. Judd, since he and I have acted together politically.

I had occasionally heard these insinuations against Mr. Judd, before the receipt of your letter; and in no instance have I hesitated to pronounce them wholly unjust, to the full extent of my knowledge and belief. I have been, and still am, very anxious to take no part between the many friends, all good and true, who are mentioned as candidates for a Republican Gubernatorial nomination; but I can not feel that my own honor is quite clear, if I remain silent, when I hear any one of them assailed about matters of which I believe I know more than his assailants.

I take pleasure in adding that of all the avowed friends I had in the canvass of last year, I do not suspect any of having acted treacherously to me, or to our cause; and that there is not one of them in whose honesty, honor, and integrity I, to-day, have greater confidence than I have in those of Mr. Judd.

I dislike to appear before the public, in this matter; but you are at liberty to make such use of this letter as you may think justice requires.

Yours very truly
A. Lincoln

As Lincoln indicated his willingness that it should be, this letter was made public in the Chicago Daily Press and Tribune, *January 30, 1860. The persons addressed were prominent Chicago business men and Republicans. George W. Dole is often confused by Lincoln students with William P. Dole, who became Commissioner of Indian Affairs under Lincoln—a position which George W. Dole could hardly have held considering the fact that he died in 1860. George W. Dole had been a director of the State Bank as early as 1835, postmaster in 1851, a trustee of the Illinois Savings Institution in 1855, and one of the governors of the city hospital in 1859. Gurdon S. Hubbard was a native of Vermont who went to Chicago as an employee of the American Fur Company in 1818 and later became Chicago's first lumber dealer, first underwriter, and one of the first meat packers. As a member of the Illinois Legislature, he introduced a bill for the construction of the Illinois and Michigan Canal and various bills promoting construction of railroads in different parts of the state. William H. Brown moved to Kaskaskia, Illinois, from Connecticut in 1817, edited the* Illinois Intelligencer *at Vandalia (1820), and later went to Chicago as cashier of the State Bank (1835). He is listed in later Chicago directories as banker and lawyer. His interest in Chicago history led to his election as the first president of the Chicago Historical Society.*

LETTER TO J. W. FELL
INCLOSING AUTOBIOGRAPHY. DECEMBER 20, 1859

Springfield, Dec. 20. 1859

J. W. Fell, Esq
My dear Sir:

Herewith is a little sketch, as you requested. There is not much of it, for the reason, I suppose, that there is not much of me. If anything be made out of it, I wish it to be modest, and not to go beyond the materials. If it were thought necessary to incorporate any thing from any of my speeches, I suppose there would be no objection. Of course it must not appear to have been written by myself.

Yours very truly
A. Lincoln

I was born Feb. 12, 1809, in Hardin County, Kentucky. My parents were both born in Virginia, of undistinguished families—second families, perhaps I should say. My mother, who died in my tenth year, was of a family of the name of Hanks, some of whom now reside in Adams, and others in Macon Counties, Illinois. My paternal grandfather, Abraham Lincoln, emigrated from Rockingham County, Virginia, to Kentucky, about 1781 or 2, where, a year or two later, he was killed by indians, not in battle, but by stealth, when he was laboring to open a farm in the forest. His ancestors, who were Quakers, went to Virginia from Berks County, Pennsylvania. An effort to identify them with the New-England family of the same name ended in nothing more definite, than a similarity of Christian names in both families, such as Enoch, Levi, Mordecai, Solomon, Abraham, and the like.

My father, at the death of his father, was but six years of age; and he grew up, litterally [*sic*] without education. He removed from Kentucky to what is now Spencer County, Indiana, in my eighth year. We reached our new home about the time the State came into the Union. It was a wild region, with many bears and other wild animals, still in the woods. There I grew up. There were some schools, so called; but no qualification was ever required of a teacher beyond "readin, writin, and cipherin" to the Rule of Three. If a straggler supposed to understand latin happened to sojourn in the neighborhood, he was looked upon as a wizzard [*sic*]. There was absolutely nothing to excite ambition for education. Of course when I came of age I did not know much. Still somehow, I could read, write, and cipher to the Rule of Three; but that was all. I have not been to school since. The little advance I now have upon this store of education, I have picked up from time to time under the pressure of necessity.

I was raised to farm work, which I continued till I was twenty-two. At twenty one I came to Illinois, and passed the first year in Macon County. Then I got to New-Salem (at that time in Sangamon, now in Menard County, where I remained a year as a sort of Clerk in a store. Then came the Black-Hawk war; and I was elected a Captain of Volunteers—a success which gave me more pleasure than any I have had since. I went the campaign, was elated, ran for the Legislature the same year (1832) and was beaten—the only time I ever have been beaten by the people. The next, and three succeeding biennial elections, I was elected to the Legislature. I was not a candidate afterwards. During this Legislative period I had studied law, and removed to Springfield to practise it. In 1846 I was once elected to the lower House of

Congress. Was not a candidate for re-election. From 1849 to 1854, both inclusive, practiced law more assiduously than ever before. Always a whig in politics, and generally on the whig electoral tickets, making active canvasses—I was losing interest in politics, when the repeal of the Missouri Compromise aroused me again. What I have done since then is pretty well known.

If any personal description of me is thought desirable, it may be said, I am, in height, six feet, four inches, nearly; lean in flesh, weighing on an average one hundred and eighty pounds; dark complexion, with coarse black hair, and grey eyes—no other marks or brands recollected.

Yours very truly
A. Lincoln.

Hon J W. Fell.

Fell was a Bloomington, Illinois, Republican who had been associated with Lincoln in Whig politics from the thirties. A native son of Pennsylvania, while on a visit back home in 1858, he observed Lincoln's prestige among Pennsylvania Republicans and began thinking of Lincoln's presidential possibilities. At his suggestion, Lincoln prepared the autobiography to be sent to Joseph J. Lewis of Westchester, who used it in preparing an extended article on Lincoln for the Chester County Times, *February 11, 1860. The article, reprinted in various newspapers in following months, became the first widely read biographical sketch of Lincoln.*

FRAGMENT:
THE CONSTITUTION AND THE UNION [1860?]

All this is not the result of accident. It has a philosophical cause. Without the *Constitution* and the *Union*, we could not have attained the result; but even these, are not the primary cause of our great prosperity. There is something back of these, entwining itself more closely about the human heart. That something, is the principle of "Liberty to all"—the principle that clears the *path* for all—gives *hope* to all—and, by consequence, *enterprize*, and *industry* to all.

The *expression* of that principle, in our Declaration of Independence, was most happy, and fortunate. *Without* this, as well as *with* it, we could have declared our independence of Great Brittain [*sic*]; but *without* it, we could not, I think, have secured our free government, and consequent prosperity. No oppressed people will *fight*, and *endure*, as our fathers did, without the promise of something better, than a mere change of masters.

The assertion of that *principle*, at *that time*, was *the* word, "*fitly spoken*" which has proved an "apple of gold" to us. The *Union*, and the *Constitution*, are the *picture* of *silver*, subsequently framed around it. The picture was made, not to *conceal*, or *destroy* the apple; but to *adorn*, and *preserve* it. The *picture* was made *for* the apple—*not* the apple for the picture.

So let us act, that neither *picture*, or *apple*, shall ever be blurred, or broken.

That we may so act, we must study, and understand the points of danger.

This fragment contains one of Lincoln's most famous literary analogies, figuring the apple of gold in the picture of silver (Proverbs, 25:11) *as the principle of the Declaration of Independence framed by the Union and the Constitution. This figurative expression is, of course, simply what Lincoln had always insisted, in all kinds of expressions, to be the* raison d'être *of the United States. (Compare the central theme of "The Perpetuation of Our Political Institutions," 1838, and the "Gettysburg Address.")*

According to Paul M. Angle's note in New Letters and Papers of Lincoln, *the fragment was possibly used in Lincoln's New England speeches, on the tour which followed the "Address at Cooper Institute"; or possibly written later, after December 30, 1860, when Lincoln received from Alexander H. Stephens of Georgia a letter urging that "a word 'fitly spoken' by you now would indeed be like 'apples of gold in pictures of silver.'" The first possibility seems more likely, as Stephens may have read in the newspapers a quotation from one of the speeches in which Lincoln had used the figure, and in writing to his old friend may have made the allusion for its ironical emphasis.*

LETTER TO M. W. PACKARD
FEBRUARY 10, 1860

Springfield, Feb 10—1860

M. W. Packard, Esq
Dear Sir:

William Florville, a colored barber here, owns four lots in Bloomington, on which I have been paying the taxes for him several years, but which I forgot [to?] do, though under promise, when I was at Bloomington last. Will you please collect the ten dollars fee we spoke of, add enough of your own money, pay all taxes due, and send me the receipt, or receipts? If you will I shall be greatly obliged; and besides, will return you the money you advanced by the first mail.

William Thomas, Larrimore, and others there know about these lots.

Yours truly
A. Lincoln

LETTER TO O. P. HALL, J. R. FULLINWIDER, AND U. F. CORRELL. FEBRUARY 14, 1860

Springfield, Feb. 14. 1860

Messrs. O. P. Hall
J. R. Fullinwider & U. F. Correll.
Gentlemen.

Your letter, in which among other things, you ask "what I meant when I said this Union could not stand half slave and half free—and also what I meant when I said a house divided against itself could not stand" is received, and I very cheerfully answer it as plainly as I may be able. You misquote, to some material extent, what I did say; which induces me to think you have not, very carefully read the speech in which the expressions occur which [seem?] to puzzle you to understand. For this reason and because the language I used is as plain as I can make it, I now quote at length the whole paragraph in which the expressions which puzzle you occur. It is as follows: "We are now far into the fifth year since a policy was initiated with the avowed object, and confident promise of putting an end to slavery agitation. Under the operation of that policy that agitation has not only not ceased, but constantly augmented. I believe it will not cease until a crisis shall have been reached, and passed. A house divided against itself can not stand. I believe this government can not endure *permanently*, half slave, and half free. I do not expect the

Union to be dissolved; I do not expect the house to fall; but I do expect it will cease to be divided. It will become all one thing, or all the other. Either the opponents of slavery will arrest the further spread of it, and place it where the public mind shall rest in the belief that it is in course of ultimate extinction; or it's advocates will push it forward till it will become alike lawful in all the states, old as well as new, North, as well as South."

That is the whole paragraph; and it puzzles me to make my meaning plainer. Look over it carefully, and conclude I meant all I said and did not mean anything I did not say, and you will have my meaning. Douglas attacked me upon this, saying it was a declaration of war between the slave and the free states. You will perceive I said no such thing, and I assure you I thought of no such thing.

If I had said "I believe this government can not *last always*, half slave and half free" would you understand it any better than you do? "Endure permanently" and "last always" have exactly the same meaning.

If you, or any of you, will state to me some meaning which you suppose I had, I can, and will instantly tell you whether that was my meaning.

Yours very truly
A. Lincoln

The three men addressed in this letter were all farmers who lived in the eastern part of Sangamon County near Mechanicsburg, Illinois. Correll was a Democrat, Fullinwider a Republican, and Hall of unidentified political allegiance. Apparently they were neighbors and friends who, arguing politics early in the year of the presidential election and specifically discussing Lincoln's possibility as a candidate, could come to no agreement on Lincoln's famous pronouncement in the "House Divided Speech." Lincoln's painstaking answer to their question indicates his concern that the electorate should not misunderstand him to mean—as Douglas had charged, and as one suspects the Democrat Correll prob-

ably maintained—that he favored a permanent separation of the slave from the free states.

ADDRESS AT COOPER INSTITUTE, NEW YORK. FEBRUARY 27, 1860

Mr. President and fellow citizens of New York:—

The facts with which I shall deal this evening are mainly old and familiar; nor is there anything new in the general use I shall make of them. If there shall be any novelty, it will be in the mode of presenting the facts, and the inferences and observations following that presentation.

In his speech last autumn, at Columbus, Ohio, as reported in "The New-York Times," Senator Douglas said:

"Our fathers, when they framed the Government under which we live, understood this question just as well, and even better, than we do now."

I fully indorse this, and I adopt it as a text for this discourse. I so adopt it because it furnishes a precise and an agreed starting point for a discussion between Republicans and that wing of the Democracy headed by Senator Douglas. It simply leaves the inquiry: *"What was the understanding those fathers had of the question mentioned?"*

What is the frame of government under which we live?

The answer must be: "The Constitution of the United States." That Constitution consists of the original, framed in 1787, (and under which the present government first went into operation,) and twelve subsequently framed amendments, the first ten of which were framed in 1789.

Who were our fathers that framed the Constitution? I suppose the "thirty-nine" who signed the original instrument may be fairly called our fathers who framed that part of the present

Government. It is almost exactly true to say they framed it, and it is altogether true to say they fairly represented the opinion and sentiment of the whole nation at that time. Their names, being familiar to nearly all, and accessible to quite all, need not now be repeated.

I take these "thirty-nine," for the present, as being "our fathers who framed the Government under which we live."

What is the question which, according to the text, those fathers understood "just as well, and even better than we do now?"

It is this: Does the proper division of local from federal authority, or anything in the Constitution, forbid our *Federal Government* to control as to slavery in *our Federal Territories*?

Upon this, Senator Douglas holds the affirmative, and Republicans the negative. This affirmation and denial form an issue; and this issue—this question—is precisely what the text declares our fathers understood "better than we."

Let us now inquire whether the "thirty-nine," or any of them, ever acted upon this question; and if they did, how they acted upon it—how they expressed that better understanding?

In 1784, three years before the Constitution—the United States then owning the Northwestern Territory, and no other, the Congress of the Confederation had before them the question of prohibiting slavery in that Territory; and four of the "thirty-nine" who afterward framed the Constitution, were in that Congress, and voted on that question. Of these, Roger Sherman, Thomas Mifflin, and Hugh Williamson voted for the prohibition, thus showing that, in their understanding, no line dividing local from federal authority, nor anything else, properly forbade the Federal Government to control as to slavery in federal territory. The other of the four—James M'Henry—voted against the prohibition, showing that, for some cause, he thought it improper to vote for it.

In 1787, still before the Constitution, but while the Convention was in session framing it, and while the Northwestern Territory still was the only territory owned by the United States, the same question of prohibiting slavery in the territory again came before the Congress of the Confederation; and two more of the "thirty-nine" who afterward signed the Constitution, were in that Congress, and voted on the question. They were William Blount and William Few; and they both voted for the prohibition —thus showing that, in their understanding, no line dividing local from federal authority, nor anything else, properly forbids the Federal Government to control as to slavery in Federal territory. This time the prohibition became a law, being part of what is now well known as the Ordinance of '87.

The question of federal control of slavery in the territories, seems not to have been directly before the Convention which framed the original Constitution; and hence it is not recorded that the "thirty-nine," or any of them, while engaged on that instrument, expressed any opinion on that precise question.

In 1789, by the first Congress which sat under the Constitution, an act was passed to enforce the Ordinance of '87, including the prohibition of slavery in the Northwestern Territory. The bill for this act was reported by one of the "thirty-nine," Thomas Fitzsimmons, then a member of the House of Representatives from Pennsylvania. It went through all its stages without a word of opposition, and finally passed both branches without yeas and nays, which is equivalent to an unanimous passage. In this Congress there were sixteen of the thirty-nine fathers who framed the original Constitution. They were John Langdon, Nicholas Gilman, Wm. S. Johnson, Roger Sherman, Robert Morris, Thos. Fitzsimmons, William Few, Abraham Baldwin, Rufus King, William Paterson, George Clymer, Richard Bassett, George Read, Pierce Butler, Daniel Carroll, James Madison.

This shows that, in their understanding, no line dividing local from federal authority, nor anything in the Constitution, properly forbade Congress to prohibit slavery in the federal territory; else both their fidelity to correct principle, and their oath to support the Constitution, would have constrained them to oppose the prohibition.

Again, George Washington, another of the "thirty-nine," was then President of the United States, and, as such approved and signed the bill; thus completing its validity as a law, and thus showing that, in his understanding, no line dividing local from federal authority, nor anything in the Constitution, forbade the Federal Government, to control as to slavery in federal territory.

No great while after the adoption of the original Constitution, North Carolina ceded to the Federal Government the country now constituting the State of Tennessee; and a few years later Georgia ceded that which now constitutes the States of Mississippi and Alabama. In both deeds of cession it was made a condition by the ceding States that the Federal Government should not prohibit slavery in the ceded country. Besides this, slavery was then actually in the ceded country. Under these circumstances, Congress, on taking charge of these countries, did not absolutely prohibit slavery within them. But they did interfere with it—take control of it—even there, to a certain extent. In 1798, Congress organized the Territory of Mississippi. In the act of organization, they prohibited the bringing of slaves into the Territory, from any place without the United States, by fine, and giving freedom to slaves so brought. This act passed both branches of Congress without yeas and nays. In that Congress were three of the "thirty-nine" who framed the original Constitution. They were John Langdon, George Read and Abraham Baldwin. They all, probably, voted for it. Certainly they would have placed their opposition to it upon record, if, in their understanding, any line dividing local from federal authority, or anything in the Constitution, properly forbade the Federal Government to control as to slavery in federal territory.

In 1803, the Federal Government purchased the Louisiana country. Our former territorial acquisitions came from certain of our own States; but this Louisiana country was acquired from a foreign nation. In 1804, Congress gave a territorial organization to that part of it which now constitutes the State of Louisiana. New Orleans, lying within that part, was an old and comparatively large city. There were other considerable towns and settlements, and slavery was extensively and thoroughly intermingled with the people. Congress did not, in the Territorial Act, prohibit slavery; but they did interfere with it—take control of it—in a more marked and extensive way than they did in the case of Mississippi. The substance of the provision therein made, in relation to slaves, was:

First. That no slave should be imported into the territory from foreign parts.

Second. That no slave should be carried into it who had been imported into the United States since the first day of May, 1798.

Third. That no slave should be carried into it, except by the owner, and for his own use as a settler; the penalty in all the cases being a fine upon the violator of the law, and freedom to the slave.

This act also was passed without yeas and nays. In the Congress which passed it, there were two of the "thirty-nine." They were Abraham Baldwin and Jonathan Dayton. As stated in the case of Mississippi, it is probable they both voted for it. They would not have allowed it to pass without recording their opposition to it, if, in their understanding, it violated either the line properly dividing local from federal authority, or any provision of the Constitution.

In 1819-20, came and passed the Missouri question. Many votes were taken, by yeas and nays, in both branches of Congress, upon the various phases of the general question. Two of the "thirty-nine"—Rufus King and Charles Pinckney—were members of that Congress. Mr. King steadily voted for slavery prohibition and against all compromises, while Mr. Pinckney as steadily voted against slavery prohibition and against all compromises. By this, Mr. King showed that, in his understanding, no line dividing local from federal authority, nor anything in the Constitution, was violated by Congress prohibiting slavery in federal territory; while Mr. Pinckney, by his votes, showed that, in his understanding, there was some sufficient reason for opposing such prohibition in that case.

The cases I have mentioned are the only acts of the "thirty-nine," or of any of them, upon the direct issue, which I have been able to discover.

To enumerate the persons who thus acted, as being four in 1784, two in 1787, seventeen in 1789, three in 1798, two in 1804, and two in 1819-20—there would be thirty of them. But this would be counting John Langdon, Roger Sherman, William Few, Rufus King, and George Read each twice, and Abraham Baldwin, three times. The true number of those of the "thirty-nine" whom I have shown to have acted upon the question, which, by the text, they understood better than we, is twenty-three, leaving sixteen not shown to have acted upon it in any way.

Here, then, we have twenty-three out of our thirty-nine fathers 'who framed the government under which we live," who have, upon their official responsibility and their corporal oaths, acted upon the very question which the text affirms they "understood just as well, and even better than we do now;" and twenty-one of them—a clear majority of the whole "thirty-nine"—so acting upon it as to make them guilty of gross political impropriety and wilful perjury, if, in their understanding, any proper division between local and federal authority, or anything in the Constitution they had made themselves, and sworn to support, forbade the Federal Government to control as to slavery in the federal territories. Thus the twenty-one acted; and, as actions speak louder than words, so actions, under such responsibility, speak still louder.

Two of the twenty-three voted against Congressional prohibition of slavery in the federal territories, in the instances in which they acted upon the question. But for what reasons they so voted is not known. They may have done so because they thought a proper division of local from federal authority, or some provision or principle of the Constitution, stood in the way; or they may, without any such question, have voted against the prohibition, on what appeared to them to be sufficient grounds of expediency. No one who has sworn to support the Constitution can conscientiously vote for what he understands to be an unconstitutional measure, however expedient he may think it; but one may and ought to vote against a measure which he deems constitutional, if, at the same time, he deems it inexpedient. It, therefore, would be unsafe to set down even the two who voted against the prohibition, as having done so because, in their understanding, any proper division of local from federal authority, or anything in the Constitution, forbade the Federal Government to control as to slavery in federal territory.

The remaining sixteen of the "thirty-nine," so far as I have discovered, have left no record of their understanding upon the direct question of federal control of slavery in the federal territories. But there is much reason to believe that their understanding upon that question would not have appeared different from that of their twenty-three compeers, had it been manifested at all.

For the purpose of adhering rigidly to the text, I have purposely omitted whatever understanding may have been manifested by any person, however distinguished, other than the thirty-nine fathers who framed the original Constitution; and, for the same reason, I have also omitted whatever understanding may have been manifested by any of the "thirty-nine" even, on any other phase of the general question of slavery. If we should look into their acts and declarations on those other phases, as the foreign slave trade, and the morality and policy of slavery generally, it would appear to us that on the direct question of federal control of slavery in federal territories, the sixteen, if they had acted at all, would probably have acted just as the twenty-three did. Among that sixteen were several of the most noted anti-slavery men of those times—as Dr. Franklin, Alexander Hamilton and Gouverneur Morris—while there was not one now known to have been otherwise, unless it may be John Rutledge, of South Carolina.

The sum of the whole is, that of our thirty-nine fathers who framed the original Constitution, twenty-one—a clear majority of the whole—certainly understood that no proper division of local from federal authority, nor any part of the Constitution, forbade the Federal Government to control slavery in the federal territories; while all the rest probably had the same understanding. Such, unquestionably, was the understanding of our fathers who framed the original Constitution; and the text affirms that they understood the question "better than we."

But, so far, I have been considering the understanding of the question manifested by the framers of the original Constitution. In and by the original instrument, a mode was provided for amending it; and, as I have already stated, the present frame of "the Government under which we live" consists of that original, and twelve amendatory articles framed and adopted since. Those who now insist that federal control of slavery in federal territories violates the Constitution, point us to the provisions which they suppose it thus violates; and, as I understand, that all fix upon provisions in these amendatory articles, and not in the original instrument. The Supreme Court, in the Dred Scott case, plant themselves upon the fifth amendment, which provides that no person shall be deprived of "life, liberty or property without due process of law;" while Senator Douglas and his peculiar adherents plant themselves upon the tenth amendment, providing that "the powers not delegated to the United States by the Constitution" "are reserved to the States respectively, or to the people."

Now, it so happens that these amendments were framed by the first Congress which sat under the Constitution—the identical Congress which passed the act already mentioned, enforcing the prohibition of slavery in the Northwestern Territory. Not only was it the same Congress, but they were the identical, same individual men who, at the same session, and at the same time within the session, had under consideration, and in progress toward maturity, these Constitutional amendments, and this act prohibiting slavery in all the territory the nation then owned. The Constitutional amendments were introduced before, and passed after the act enforcing the Ordinance of '87; so that, during the whole pendency of the act to enforce the Ordinance, the Constitutional amendments were also pending.

The seventy-six members of that Congress, including sixteen of the framers of the original Constitution, as before stated, were pre-eminently our fathers who framed that part of "the Government under which we live," which is now claimed as forbidding the Federal Government to control slavery in the federal territories.

Is it not a little presumptuous in any one at this day to affirm that the two things which that Congress deliberately framed, and carried to maturity at the same time, are absolutely inconsistent with each other? And does not such affirmation become impudently absurd when coupled with the other affirmation from the same mouth, that those who did the two things, alleged to be inconsistent, understood whether they really were inconsistent better than we—better than he who affirms that they are inconsistent?

It is surely safe to assume that the thirty-nine framers of the original Constitution, and the seventy-six members of the Congress which framed the amendments thereto, taken together, do certainly include those who may be fairly called "our fathers who framed the Government under which we live." And so assuming, I defy any man to show that any one of them ever, in his whole life, declared that, in his understanding, any proper division of local from federal authority, or any part of the Constitution, forbade the Federal Government to control as to slavery in the federal territories. I go a step further. I defy any one to show that any living man in the whole world ever did, prior to the beginning of the present century, (and I might almost say prior to the beginning of the last half of the present century,) declare that, in his understanding, any proper division of local from federal authority, or any part of the Constitution, forbade the Federal Government to control as to slavery in the federal territories. To those who now so declare, I give, not only "our fathers who framed the Government under which we live," but with them all other living men within the century in which it was framed, among whom to search, and they shall not be able to find the evidence of a single man agreeing with them.

Now, and here, let me guard a little against being misunderstood. I do not mean to say we are bound to follow implicitly in whatever our fathers did. To do so, would be to discard all the lights of current experience—to reject all progress—all improvement. What I do say is, that if we would supplant the opinions and policy of our fathers in any case, we should do so upon evidence so conclusive, and argument so clear, that even their great authority, fairly considered and weighed, cannot stand; and most surely not in a case whereof we ourselves declare they understood the question better than we.

If any man at this day sincerely believes that a proper division of local from federal authority, or any part of the Constitution, forbids the Federal Government to control as to slavery in the federal territories, he is right to say so, and to enforce his position by all truthful evidence and fair argument which he can. But he has no right to mislead others, who have less access to history, and less leisure to study it, into the false belief that "our fathers who framed the Government under which we live" were of the same opinion—thus substituting falsehood and deception for truthful evidence and fair argument. If any man at this day sincerely believes "our fathers who framed the Government under which we live," used and applied principles, in other cases, which ought to have led them to understand that a proper division of local from federal authority or some part of the Constitution, forbids the Federal Government to control as to slavery in the federal territories, he is right to say so. But he should, at the same time, brave the responsibility of declaring that, in his opinion, he understands their principles better than they did themselves; and especially should he not shirk that responsibility by asserting that they "understood the question just as well, and even better, than we do now."

But enough! *Let all who believe that "our fathers, who framed the Government under which we live, understood this question just as well, and even better, than we do now," speak as they spoke, and act as they acted upon it. This is all Republicans ask—all Republicans desire—in relation to slavery. As those fathers marked it, so let it be again marked, as an evil not to be extended, but to be tolerated and protected only because of and so far as its actual presence among us makes that toleration and protection a necessity. Let all the guaranties those fathers gave it, be, not grudgingly, but fully and fairly, maintained.* For this Republicans contend, and with this, so far as I know or believe, they will be content.

And now, if they would listen—as I suppose they will not—I would address a few words to the Southern people.

I would say to them:— You consider yourselves a reasonable and a just people; and I consider that in the general qualities of reason and justice you are not inferior to any other people. Still, when you speak of us Republicans, you do so only to denounce us as reptiles, or, at the best, as no better than outlaws. You will grant a hearing to pirates or murderers, but nothing like it to "Black Republicans." In all your contentions with one another, each of you deems an unconditional condemnation of "Black Republicanism" as the first thing to be attended to. Indeed, such condemnation of us seems to be an indispensable prerequisite—license, so to speak—among you to be admitted or permitted to speak at all. Now, can you, or not, be prevailed upon to pause and to consider whether this is quite just to us, or even to yourselves? Bring forward your charges and specifications, and then be patient long enough to hear us deny or justify.

You say we are sectional. We deny it. That makes an issue; and the burden of proof is upon you. You produce your proof; and what is it? Why, that our party has no existence in your section—gets no votes in your section. The fact is substantially true; but does it prove the issue? If it does, then in case we should, without change of principle, begin to get votes in your section, we should thereby cease to be sectional. You cannot escape this conclusion; and yet, are you willing to abide by it? If you are, you will probably soon find that we have ceased to be sectional, for we shall get votes in your section this very year. You will then begin to discover, as the truth plainly is, that your proof does not touch the issue. The fact that we get no votes in your section, is a fact of your making, and not of ours. And if there be fault in that fact, that fault is primarily yours, and remains until you show that we repel you by some wrong principle or practice. If we do repel you by any wrong principle or practice, the fault is ours; but this brings you to where you ought to have started—to a discussion of the right or wrong of our principle. If our principle, put in practice, would wrong your section for the benefit of ours, or for any other object, then our principle, and we with it, are sectional, and are justly opposed and denounced as such. Meet us, then, on the question of whether our principle, put in practice, would wrong your section; and so meet it as if it were possible that something may be said on our side. Do you accept the challenge? No! Then you really believe that the principle which "our fathers who framed the Government under which we live" thought so clearly right as to adopt it, and indorse it again and again, upon their official oaths, is in fact so clearly wrong as to demand your condemnation without a moment's consideration.

Some of you delight to flaunt in our faces the warning against sectional parties given by Washington in his Farewell Address. Less than eight years before Washington gave that warning, he had, as President of the United States, approved and signed an act of Congress, enforcing the prohibition of slavery in the Northwestern Territory, which act embodied the policy of the Government upon that subject up to and at the very moment he penned that warning; and about one year after he penned it, he wrote LaFayette that he considered that prohibition a wise measure, expressing in the same connection his hope that we should at some time have a confederacy of free States.

Bearing this in mind, and seeing that sectionalism has since arisen upon this same subject, is that warning a weapon in your hands against us, or in our hands against you? Could Washington himself speak, would he cast the blame of that sectionalism upon us, who sustain his policy, or upon you who repudiate it? We respect that warning of Washington, and we commend it to you, together with his example pointing to the right application of it.

But you say you are conservative—eminently conservative—while we are revolutionary, destructive, or something of the sort. What is conservatism? Is it not adherence to the old and tried, against the new and untried? We stick to, contend for, the identical old policy on the point in controversy which was adopted by "our fathers who framed the Government under which we live;" while you with one accord reject, and scout, and spit upon that old policy, and insist upon substituting something new. True, you disagree among yourselves as to what that substitute shall be. You are divided on new propositions and plans, but you are unanimous in rejecting and denouncing the old policy of the fathers. Some of you are for reviving the foreign slave trade; some for a Congressional Slave-Code for the Territories; some for Congress forbidding the Territories to prohibit Slavery within their limits; some for maintaining Slavery in the Territories through the judiciary; some for the "gur-reat pur-rinciple" that "if one man would enslave another, no third man should object," fantastically called "Popular Sovereignty;" but never a man among you is in favor of federal prohibition of slavery in federal territories, according to the practice of "our fathers who framed the Government under which we live." Not one of all your various plans can show a precedent or an advocate in the century within which our Government originated. Consider, then, whether your claim of conservatism for yourselves, and your charge of destructiveness against us, are based on the most clear and stable foundations.

Again, you say we have made the slavery question more

prominent than it formerly was. We deny it. We admit that it is more prominent, but we deny that we made it so. It was not we, but you, who discarded the old policy of the fathers. We resisted, and still resist, your innovation; and thence comes the greater prominence of the question. Would you have that question reduced to its former proportions? Go back to that old policy. What has been will be again, under the same conditions. If you would have the peace of the old times, readopt the precepts and policy of the old times.

You charge that we stir up insurrections among your slaves. We deny it; and what is your proof? Harper's Ferry! John Brown!! John Brown was no Republican; and you have failed to implicate a single Republican in his Harper's Ferry enterprise. If any member of our party is guilty in that matter, you know it or you do not know it. If you do know it, you are inexcusable for not designating the man and proving the fact. If you do not know it, you are inexcusable for asserting it, and especially for persisting in the assertion after you have tried and failed to make the proof. You need not be told that persisting in a charge which one does not know to be true, is simply malicious slander.

Some of you admit that no Republican designedly aided or encouraged the Harper's Ferry affair, but still insist that our doctrines and declarations necessarily lead to such results. We do not believe it. We know we hold to no doctrine, and make no declaration, which were not held to and made by "our fathers who framed the Government under which we live." You never dealt fairly by us in relation to this affair. When it occurred, some important State elections were near at hand, and you were in evident glee with the belief that, by charging the blame upon us, you could get an advantage of us in those elections. The elections came, and your expectations were not quite fulfilled. Every Republican man knew that, as to himself at least, your charge was a slander, and he was not much inclined by it to cast his vote in your favor. Republican doctrines and declarations are accompanied with a continual protest against any interference whatever with your slaves, or with you about your slaves. Surely, this does not encourage them to revolt. True, we do, in common with "our fathers, who framed the Government under which we live," declare our belief that slavery is wrong; but the slaves do not hear us declare even this. For anything we say or do, the slaves would scarcely know there is a Republican party. I believe they would not, in fact, generally know it but for your misrepresentations of us, in their hearing. In your political contests among yourselves, each faction charges the other with sympathy with Black Republicanism; and then, to give point to the charge, defines Black Republicanism to simply be insurrection, blood and thunder among the slaves.

Slave insurrections are no more common now than they were before the Republican party was organized. What induced the Southampton insurrection, twenty-eight years ago, in which, at least three times as many lives were lost as at Harper's Ferry? You can scarcely stretch your very elastic fancy to the conclusion that Southampton was "got up by Black Republicanism." In the present state of things in the United States, I do not think a general, or even a very extensive slave insurrection is possible. The indispensable concert of action cannot be attained. The slaves have no means of rapid communication; nor can incendiary freemen, black or white, supply it. The explosive materials are everywhere in parcels; but there neither are, nor can be supplied, the indispensable connecting trains.

Much is said by Southern people about the affection of slaves for their masters and mistresses; and a part of it, at least, is true. A plot for an uprising could scarcely be devised and communicated to twenty individuals before some one of them, to save the life of a favorite master or mistress, would divulge it. This is the rule; and the slave revolution in Hayti was not an exception to it, but a case occurring under peculiar circumstances. The gunpowder plot of British history, though not connected with slaves, was more in point. In that case, only about twenty were admitted to the secret; and yet one of them, in his anxiety to save a friend, betrayed the plot to that friend, and, by consequence, averted the calamity. Occasional poisonings from the kitchen, and open or stealthy assassinations in the field, and local revolts extending to a score or so, will continue to occur as the natural results of slavery; but no general insurrection of slaves, as I think, can happen in this country for a long time. Whoever much fears, or much hopes for such an event, will be alike disappointed.

In the language of Mr. Jefferson, uttered many years ago, "It is still in our power to direct the process of emancipation, and deportation, peaceably, and in such slow degrees, as that the evil will wear off insensibly; and their places be, *pari passu*, filled up by free white laborers. If, on the contrary, it is left to force itself on, human nature must shudder at the prospect held up."

Mr. Jefferson did not mean to say, nor do I, that the power of emancipation is in the Federal Government. He spoke of Virginia; and, as to the power of emancipation, I speak of the slave-holding States only. The Federal Government, however, as we insist, has the power of restraining the extension of the institution—the power to insure that a slave insurrection shall never occur on any American soil which is now free from slavery.

John Brown's effort was peculiar. It was not a slave insurrection. It was an attempt by white men to get up a revolt among slaves, in which the slaves refused to participate. In fact, it was so absurd that the slaves, with all their ignorance, saw plainly enough it could not succeed. That affair, in its philosophy, corresponds with the many attempts, related in history, at the assassination of kings and emperors. An enthusiast broods over the oppression of a people till he fancies himself commissioned by Heaven to liberate them. He ventures the attempt, which ends in little else than his own execution. Orsini's attempt on Louis Napoleon, and John Brown's attempt at Harper's Ferry were, in their philosophy, precisely the same. The eagerness to cast blame on old England in the one case, and on New England in the other, does not disprove the sameness of the two things.

And how much would it avail you, if you could, by the use of John Brown, Helper's Book, and the like, break up the Republican organization? Human action can be modified to some extent, but human nature cannot be changed. There is a judgment and a feeling against slavery in this nation, which cast at least a million and a half of votes. You cannot destroy that judgment and feeling—that sentiment—by breaking up the political organization which rallies around it. You can scarcely scatter and disperse an army which has been formed into order in the face of your heaviest fire; but if you could, how much would you gain by forcing the sentiment which created it out of the peaceful channel of the ballot-box, into some other channel? What would that other channel probably be? Would the number of John Browns be lessened or enlarged by the operation?

But you will break up the Union rather than submit to a denial of your Constitutional rights.

That has a somewhat reckless sound; but it would be palliated, if not fully justified, were we proposing, by the mere force of numbers, to deprive you of some right, plainly written down in the Constitution. But we are proposing no such thing.

When you make these declarations, you have a specific and well-understood allusion to an assumed Constitutional right of yours, to take slaves into the federal territories, and to hold them there as property. But no such right is specifically written in the Constitution. That instrument is literally silent about any such right. We, on the contrary, deny that such a right has any existence in the Constitution, even by implication.

Your purpose, then, plainly stated, is that you will destroy the Government, unless you be allowed to construe and enforce the Constitution as you please, on all points in dispute between you and us. You will rule or ruin in all events.

This, plainly stated, is your language. Perhaps you will say the Supreme Court has decided the disputed Constitutional question in your favor. Not quite so. But waiving the lawyer's distinction between dictum and decision, the Court have decided the question for you in a sort of way. The Court have substantially said, it is your Constitutional right to take slaves into the federal territories, and to hold them there as property. When I say the decision was made in a sort of way, I mean it was made in a divided Court, by a bare majority of the Judges, and they not quite agreeing with one another in the reasons for making it; that it is so made as that its avowed supporters disagree with one another about its meaning, and that it was mainly based upon a mistaken statement of fact—the statement in the opinion that "the right of property in a slave is distinctly and expressly affirmed in the Constitution."

An inspection of the Constitution will show that the right

of property in a slave is not "*distinctly* and *expressly* affirmed" in it. Bear in mind, the Judges do not pledge their judicial opinion that such right is *impliedly* affirmed in the Constitution; but they pledge their veracity that it is "*distinctly* and *expressly*" affirmed there—"distinctly," that is, not mingled with anything else—"expressly," that is, in words meaning just that, without the aid of any inference, and susceptible of no other meaning.

If they had only pledged their judicial opinion that such right is affirmed in the instrument by implication, it would be open to others to show that neither the word "slave" nor "slavery" is to be found in the Constitution, nor the word "property" even, in any connection with language alluding to the things slave, or slavery; and that wherever in that instrument the slave is alluded to, he is called a "person;"—and wherever his master's legal right in relation to him is alluded to, it is spoken of as "service or labor which may be due,"—as a debt payable in service or labor. Also, it would be open to show, by contemporaneous history, that this mode of alluding to slaves and slavery, instead of speaking of them, was employed on purpose to exclude from the Constitution the idea that there could be property in man.

To show all this, is easy and certain.

When this obvious mistake of the Judges shall be brought to their notice, is it not reasonable to expect that they will withdraw the mistaken statement, and reconsider the conclusion based upon it?

And then it is to be remembered that "our fathers, who framed the Government under which we live"—the men who made the Constitution—decided this same Constitutional question in our favor, long ago—decided it without division among themselves, when making the decision; without division among themselves about the meaning of it after it was made, and, so far as any evidence is left, without basing it upon any mistaken statement of facts.

Under all these circumstances, do you really feel yourselves justified to break up this Government unless such a court decision as yours is, shall be at once submitted to as a conclusive and final rule of political action? But you will not abide the election of a Republican president! In that supposed event, you say, you will destroy the Union; and then, you say, the great crime of having destroyed it will be upon us! That is cool. A highwayman holds a pistol to my ear, and mutters through his teeth, "Stand and deliver, or I shall kill you, and then you will be a murderer!"

To be sure, what the robber demanded of me—my money—was my own; and I had a clear right to keep it; but it was no more my own than my vote is my own; and the threat of death to me, to extort my money, and the threat of destruction to the Union, to extort my vote, can scarcely be distinguished in principle.

A few words now to Republicans. *It is exceedingly desirable that all parts of this great Confederacy shall be at peace, and in harmony, one with another. Let us Republicans do our part to have it so. Even though much provoked, let us do nothing through passion and ill temper. Even though the southern people will not so much as listen to us, let us calmly consider their demands, and yield to them if, in our deliberate view of our duty, we possibly can.* Judging by all they say and do, and by the subject and nature of their controversy with us, let us determine, if we can, what will satisfy them.

Will they be satisfied if the Territories be unconditionally surrendered to them? We know they will not. In all their present complaints against us, the Territories are scarcely mentioned. Invasions and insurrections are the rage now. Will it satisfy them, if, in the future, we have nothing to do with invasions and insurrections? We know it will not. We so know, because we know we never had anything to do with invasions and insurrections; and yet this total abstaining does not exempt us from the charge and the denunciation.

The question recurs, what will satisfy them? Simply this: We must not only let them alone, but we must somehow, convince them that we do let them alone. This, we know by experience, is no easy task. We have been so trying to convince them from the very beginning of our organization, but with no success. In all our platforms and speeches we have constantly protested our purpose to let them alone; but this has had no tendency to convince them. Alike unavailing to convince them, is the fact that they have never detected a man of us in any attempt to disturb them.

These natural, and apparently adequate means all failing, what will convince them? This, and this only: cease to call slavery *wrong*, and join them in calling it *right*. And this must be done thoroughly—done in *acts* as well as in *words*. Silence will not be tolerated—we must place ourselves avowedly with them. Senator Douglas's new sedition law must be enacted and enforced, suppressing all declarations that slavery is wrong, whether made in politics, in presses, in pulpits, or in private. We must arrest and return their fugitive slaves with greedy pleasure. We must pull down our Free State constitutions. The whole atmosphere must be disinfected from all taint of opposition to slavery, before they will cease to believe that all their troubles proceed from us.

I am quite aware they do not state their case precisely in this way. Most of them would probably say to us, "Let us alone, do nothing to us, and say what you please about slavery." But we do let them alone—have never disturbed them—so that, after all, it is what we say, which dissatisfies them. They will continue to accuse us of doing, until we cease saying.

I am also aware they have not, as yet, in terms, demanded the overthrow of our Free-State Constitutions. Yet those Constitutions declare the wrong of slavery, with more solemn emphasis, than do all other sayings against it; and when all these other sayings shall have been silenced, the overthrow of these Constitutions will be demanded, and nothing be left to resist the demand. It is nothing to the contrary, that they do not demand the whole of this just now. Demanding what they do, and for the reason they do, they can voluntarily stop nowhere short of this consummation. Holding, as they do, that slavery is morally right, and socially elevating, they cannot cease to demand a full national recognition of it, as a legal right, and a social blessing.

Nor can we justifiably withhold this, on any ground save our conviction that slavery is wrong. If slavery is right, all words, acts, laws, and constitutions against it, are themselves wrong, and should be silenced, and swept away. If it is right, we cannot justly object to its nationality—its universality; if it is wrong, they cannot justly insist upon its extension—its enlargement. All they ask, we could readily grant, if we thought slavery right; all we ask, they could as readily grant, if they thought it wrong. Their thinking it right, and our thinking it wrong, is the precise fact upon which depends the whole controversy. Thinking it right, as they do, they are not to blame for desiring its full recognition, as being right; but, thinking it wrong, as we do, can we yield to them? Can we cast our votes with their view, and against our own? In view of our moral, social, and political responsibilities, can we do this?

Wrong as we think slavery is, we can yet afford to let it alone where it is, because that much is due to the necessity arising from its actual presence in the nation; but can we, while our votes will prevent it, allow it to spread into the National Territories, and to overrun us here in these Free States? If our sense of duty forbids this, then let us stand by our duty, fearlessly and effectively. Let us be diverted by none of those sophistical contrivances wherewith we are so industriously plied and belabored—contrivances such as groping for some middle ground between the right and the wrong, vain as the search for a man who should be neither a living man nor a dead man—such as a policy of "don't care" on a question about which all true men do care—such as Union appeals beseeching true Union men to yield to Disunionists, reversing the divine rule, and calling, not the sinners, but the righteous to repentance—such as invocations to Washington, imploring men to unsay what Washington said, and undo what Washington did.

Neither let us be slandered from our duty by false accusations against us, nor frightened from it by menaces of destruction to the Government nor of dungeons to ourselves. LET US HAVE FAITH THAT RIGHT MAKES MIGHT, AND IN THAT FAITH, LET US, TO THE END, DARE TO DO OUR DUTY AS WE UNDERSTAND IT.

The text of this address is from the revised and annotated edition published by the Young Men's Republican Union under the editorship of Charles C. Nott and Cephas Brainerd in September, 1860. Lincoln authorized the text and checked the editorial emendations.

The following "Preface" prepared by Nott and Brainerd requires no further explanation:

"This edition of Mr. Lincoln's address has been prepared and published by the Young Men's Republican Union of New York, to exemplify its wisdom, truthfulness, and learning. No one who has not actually attempted to verify its details can understand the patient research and historical labor which it embodies. The history of our earlier politics is scattered through numerous journals, statutes, pamphlets, and letters; and these are defective in completeness and accuracy of statement, and in indices and tables of contents. Neither can any one who has not travelled over this precise ground appreciate the accuracy of every trivial detail, or the self-denying impartiality with which Mr. Lincoln has turned from the testimony of 'the Fathers,' on the general question of slavery, to present the single question which he discusses. From the first line to the last—from his premises to his conclusion, he travels with swift, unerring directness which no logician ever excelled—an argument complete and full, without the affectation of learning, and without the stiffness which usually accompanies dates and details. A single, easy, simple sentence of plain Anglo-Saxon words contains a chapter of history that, in some instances, has taken days of labor to verify and which must have cost the author months of investigation to acquire. And, though the public should justly estimate the labor bestowed on the facts which are stated, they cannot estimate the greater labor involved on those which are omitted—how many pages have been read—how many works examined—what numerous statutes, resolutions, speeches, letters, and biographies have been looked through. Commencing with this address as a political pamphlet, the reader will leave it as an historical work—brief, complete, profound, impartial, truthful—which will survive the time and the occasion that called

it forth, and be esteemed hereafter, no less for its intrinsic worth than its unpretending modesty.
"New York, September, *1860"*

In preparing the revised edition for publication, Nott and Brainerd made numerous minor changes and submitted them for Lincoln's approval. Lincoln's "Letter to Charles C. Nott," May 31, 1860, containing Lincoln's reply to the suggested emendations, corroborates Herndon's testimony that Lincoln was "inflexible" if anyone "volunteered to recommend or even suggest a change of language which involved a change of sentiment." Nott's letter explaining his editorial labors and complimenting Lincoln's address is as follows:

"69 Wall St., New York
"May 23, 1860

"Dear Sir:

"I enclose a copy of your address in New York.

"We (the Young Men's Rep. Union) design to publish a new edition in larger type and better form, with such notes and references as will best attract readers seeking information. Have you any memoranda of your investigations which you would approve of inserting?

"You and your Western friends, I think, underrate this speech. It has produced a greater effect here than any other single speech. It is the real platform in the Eastern States, and must carry the conservative element in New York, New Jersey, and Pennsylvania.

"Therefore I desire that it should be as nearly perfect as may be. Most of the emendations are trivial and do not affect the substance—all are merely suggested for your judgment.

"I cannot help adding that this speech is an extraordinary example of condensed English. After some experience in criticizing for Reviews, I find hardly anything to touch and nothing to omit. It is the only one I know of which I cannot shorten, *and—like a good*

arch—moving one word tumbles a whole sentence down.

"Finally—it being a bad and foolish thing for a candidate to write letters, and you having doubtless more to do of that than is pleasant or profitable, we will not add to your burden in that regard, but if you will let any friend who has nothing to do, advise us as to your wishes, in this or any other matter, we will try to carry them out.

"Respectfully,

"Charles C. Nott

"To Hon. Abraham Lincoln."

LETTER TO MARK W. DELAHAY MARCH 16, 1860

Springfield, Ills—Mar—16, 1860

Dear Delahay.

I have just returned from the East. Before leaving, I received your letter of Feb. 6; and on my return I find those of the 17th. & 19th. with Genl. Lane's note inclosed in one of them.

I sincerely wish you could be elected one of the first Senators for Kansas; but how to help you I do not know. If it were permissable [*sic*] for me to interfere, I am not personally acquainted with a single member of your Legislature. If my known friendship for you could be of any advantage, that friendship was abundantly manifested by me last December while in Kansas. If any member had written me, as you say some have Trumbull, I would very readily answer him. I shall write Trumbull on the subject at this sitting.

I understood, while in Kansas, that the State Legislature will not meet until the State is admitted. Was that the right understanding?

As to your kind wishes for myself, allow me to say I can not enter the ring on the money basis—first, because, in the main, it is wrong; and secondly, I have not, and can not get, the money. I say, in the main, the use of money is wrong; but for certain objects, in a political contest, the use of some, is both right, and indispensable. With me, as with yourself, this long struggle has been one of great pecuniary loss. I now distinctly say this. If you shall be appointed a delegate to Chicago, I will furnish one hundred dollars to bear the expences [*sic*] of the trip.

Present my respects to Genl. Lane; and say to him, I shall be pleased to hear from him at any time.

Your friend, as ever
A. Lincoln—

P. S. I have not yet taken the newspaper slip to the Journal. I shall do that to-morrow; and then send you the paper as requested.

A. L

Delahay's distant relationship to Lincoln (Delahay's mother was a Hanks) and his early association with Lincoln in Illinois provided a friendship and political alliance that some of Lincoln's biographers have deprecated because of Delahay's personal shortcomings. The fact that Lincoln trusted his friend's political principles, in spite of shady personal traits, is obvious, although one may read in this letter some misgivings on Lincoln's part as to the propriety of financing Delahay's trip to Chicago. In his allusion to Delahay's "pecuniary loss" in the struggle, Lincoln probably had in mind the fact that Delahay's newspaper office had been destroyed by a proslavery mob.

LETTER TO F. C. HERBURGER
APRIL 7, 1860

Springfield, Ills. April 7, 1860

F. C. Herburger Secy &c
Dear Sir

Yours of March 14th addressed to me at Chicago, and seeking to arrange with me to Lecture for the Harrison Literary Institute, has been received. I regret to say I can not make such arrangement. I am not a professional lecturer—have never got up but one lecture; and that, I think, rather a poor one. Besides, what time I can spare from my own business this season, I shall be compelled to give to politics.

Respectfully yours,
A. Lincoln

Lincoln wrote almost identical letters to Herburger and John M. Carson, Secretary and Chairman, respecttively, of the Committee on Lectures of the Harrison Literary Institute, which was presumably in Chicago but about which the editor has been able to learn nothing. Another invitation to lecture had to be declined in the interest of politics.

LETTER TO LYMAN TRUMBULL
APRIL 29, 1860

Springfield, April 29. 1860

Hon: L. Trumbull:
My dear Sir:

Yours of the 24th. was duly received; and I have postponed answering it, hoping by the result at Charleston, to know who is to lead our adversaries, before writing. But Charleston hangs fire, and I wait no longer.

As you request, I will be entirely frank. The taste *is* in my mouth a little; and this, no doubt, disqualifies me, to some extent, to form correct opinions. You may confidently rely, however, that by no advice or consent of mine, shall my pretentions [*sic*] be pressed to the point of endangering our common cause.

Now, as to my opinions about the chances of others in Illinois. I think neither Seward nor Bates can carry Illinois if Douglas shall be on the track; and that either of them can, if he shall not be. I rather think McLean could carry it with D. on or off—in other words, I think McLean is stronger in Illinois, taking all sections of it, than either S. or B; and I think S. the weakest of the three. I hear no objection to McLean, except his age; but that objection seems to occur to every one; and it is possible it might leave him no stronger than the others. By the way, if we should nominate him, how would we save to ourselves the chance of filling his vacancy in the Court? Have him hold on up to the moment of his inaugeration [*sic*]? Would that course be no drawback upon us in the canvass?

Recurring to Illinois, we want something here quite as much as, and which is harder to get than, the electoral vote—the Legislature. And it is exactly in this point that Seward's nomination would be hard upon us. Suppose he should gain us a thousand votes in Winnebago, it would not compensate for the loss of fifty in Edgar.

A word now for your own special benefit. You better write no letters which can possibly be distorted into opposition, or quasi opposition to me. There are men on the constant watch for such things out of which to prejudice my peculiar friends against you. While I have no more suspicion of you than I have of my best friend living, I am kept in a constant struggle against suggestions of this sort. I have hesitated some to write this paragraph, lest you should suspect I do it for my own benefit, and not for yours; but on reflection I conclude you will not suspect me.

Let no eye but your own see this—not that there is anything wrong, or even ungenerous, in it; but it would be misconstrued.

Your friend as ever

A. Lincoln

LETTER TO GEORGE ASHMUN
MAY 23, 1860

Springfield. Ills. May 23. 1860

Hon: George Ashmun:
President of the Republican National Convention.
Sir:

I accept the nomination tendered me by the convention over which you presided, and of which I am formally apprised in the letter of yourself and others, acting as a committee of the convention, for that purpose.

The declaration of principles and sentiments, which accompanies your letter, meets my approval; and it shall be my care not to violate or disregard it, in any part.

Imploring the assistance of Divine Providence, and with due regard to the views and feelings of all who were represented in the Convention; to the rights of all the states, and territories, and people of the nation; to the inviolability of the Constitution, and the perpetual union, harmony, and prosperity of all, I am most happy to co-operate for the practical success of the principles declared by the Convention.

Your obliged friend, and fellow citizen
A. Lincoln

LETTER TO SAMUEL HAYCRAFT AND AUTOBIOGRAPHY. MAY 28, 1860

Springfield, Ills. May 28. 1860

Hon. Sam. Haycraft
Dear Sir:

Your recent letter, without date, is received. Also the copy of your speech on the contemplated Daniel Boone Monument, which I have not yet had time to read. In the main you are right about my history. My father was Thomas Lincoln, and Mrs. Sally Johnston, was his second wife. You are mistaken about my mother—her maiden name was Nancy Hanks. I was not born at Elizabethtown; but my mother's first child, a daughter, two years older than myself, and now long since deceased, was. I was born Feb. 12. 1809, near where Hogginsville [Hodgenville?] now is, then in Hardin County. I do not think I ever saw you, though I very well know who you are—so well that I recognized your hand-writing, on opening your letter, before I saw the signature. My recollection is that Ben. Helm was first Clerk, that you succeeded him, that Jack Thomas and William Farleigh graduated in the same office, and that your handwritings were all very similar. Am I right?

My father has been dead near ten years; but my step-mother (Mrs. Johnson [*sic*]) is still living.

I am really very glad of your letter, and shall be pleased to receive another at any time.

Yours very truly
A. Lincoln

LETTER TO CHARLES C. NOTT
MAY 31, 1860

Springfield, Ills., May 31, 1860

Charles C. Nott, Esq.
My dear Sir:

Yours of the 23rd, accompanied by a copy of the speech delivered by me at the Cooper Institute, and upon which you have made some notes for emendations, was received some days ago. Of course I would not object to, but would be pleased rather, with a more perfect edition of that speech.

I did not preserve memoranda of my investigations; and I could not now re-examine, and make notes, without an expenditure of time which I can not bestow upon it. Some of your notes I do not understand.

So far as it is intended merely to improve in grammar, and elegance of composition, I am quite agreed; but I do not wish the sense changed, or modified, to a hair's breadth. And you, not having studied the particular points so closely as I have, can not be quite sure that you do not change the sense when you do not intend it. For instance, in a note at bottom of first page, you propose to substitute "Democrats" for "Douglas." But what I am saying there is *true* of Douglas, and is not true of "Democrats" generally; so that the proposed substitution would be a very considerable blunder. Your proposed insertion of "residences" though it would do little or no harm, is not at all necessary to the sense I was trying to convey. On page 5 your proposed grammatical change would certainly do no harm. The "*impudently absurd*" I stick to. The striking out "he" and inserting "we" turns the sense exactly wrong. The striking out "upon it" leaves the sense too general and incomplete. The sense is "act as they acted *upon that question*"—not as they acted generally.

After considering your proposed changes on page 7, I do

not think them material, but I am willing to defer to you in relation to them.

On page 9, striking out "to us" is probably right. The word "lawyer's" I wish retained. The word "Courts" struck out twice, I wish reduced to "Court" and retained. "Court" as a collection more properly governs the plural "have" as I understand. "The" preceding "Court," in the latter case, must also be retained. The words "quite," "as," and "or" on the same page, I wish retained. The italicising, and quotation marking, I have no objection to.

As to the note at bottom, I do not think any too much is admitted. What you propose on page 11 is right. I return your copy of the speech, together with one printed here, under my own hasty supervising. That at New York was printed without any supervision by me. If you conclude to publish a new edition, allow me to see the proof-sheets.

And now thanking you for your very complimentary letter, and your interest for me generally, I subscribe myself.

Your friend and servant,

A. Lincoln

For the student interested in Lincoln's writings this letter is of particular note. Herndon's statement that Lincoln would take no corrections which involved a change in meaning or sentiment is fully borne out, though he is ready to acquiesce in so far as corrections of grammar are concerned. In the matter of grammar, however, Lincoln was able to set his editors straight on a point or two!

SHORT AUTOBIOGRAPHY WRITTEN FOR THE CAMPAIGN OF 1860. JUNE [1?], 1860

Abraham Lincoln was born February 12, 1809, then in Hardin, now in the more recently formed county of La Rue, Kentucky. His father, Thomas, and grandfather, Abraham, were born in Rockingham County, Virginia, whither their ancestors had come from Berks County, Pennsylvania. His lineage has been traced no farther back than this. The family were originally Quakers, though in later times they have fallen away from the peculiar habits of that people. The grandfather, Abraham, had four brothers—Isaac, Jacob, John, and Thomas. So far as known, the descendants of Jacob and John are still in Virginia. Isaac went to a place near where Virginia, North Carolina, and Tennessee join; and his descendants are in that region. Thomas came to Kentucky, and after many years died there, whence his descendants went to Missouri. Abraham, grandfather of the subject of this sketch, came to Kentucky, and was killed by Indians about the year 1784. He left a widow, three sons, and two daughters. The eldest son, Mordecai, remained in Kentucky till late in life, when he removed to Hancock County, Illinois, where soon after he died, and where several of his descendants still remain. The second son, Josiah, removed at an early day to a place on Blue River, now within Hancock County, Indiana, but no recent information of him or his family has been obtained. The eldest sister, Mary, married Ralph Crume, and some of her descendants are now known to be in Breckenridge County, Kentucky. The second sister, Nancy, married William Brumfield, and her family are not known to have left Kentucky, but there is no recent information from them. Thomas, the youngest son, and father of the present subject, by the early death of his father, and very narrow circumstances of his mother, even in childhood was a wandering laboring-boy, and grew up literally without education. He never did more in the way of writing than to bunglingly write his own name. Before he was grown he passed one year as a hired hand with his uncle Isaac on Watauga, a branch of the Holston River. Getting back into Kentucky, and having reached his twenty-eighth year, he married Nancy Hanks—mother of the present subject—in the year 1806. She also was born in Virginia; and relatives of hers of the name of Hanks, and of other names, now reside in Coles, in Macon, and in Adams counties, Illinois, and also in Iowa. The present subject has no brother or sister of the whole or half blood. He had a sister, older than himself, who was grown and married, but died many years ago, leaving no child; also a brother, younger than himself, who died in infancy. Before leaving Kentucky, he and his sister were sent, for short periods, to A B C schools, the first kept by Zachariah Riney, and the second by Caleb Hazel.

At this time his father resided on Knob Creek, on the road from Bardstown, Kentucky, to Nashville, Tennessee, at a point three or three and a half miles south or southwest of Atherton's Ferry, on the Rolling Fork. From this place he removed to what is now Spencer County, Indiana, in the autumn of 1816, Abraham then being in his eighth year. This removal was partly on account of slavery, but chiefly on account of the difficulty in land titles in Kentucky. He settled in an unbroken forest, and the clearing away of surplus wood was the great task ahead. Abraham, though very young, was large of his age, and had an ax put into his hands at once; and from that till within his twenty-third year he was almost constantly handling that most useful instrument—less, of course, in plowing and harvesting seasons. At this place Abraham took an early start as a hunter, which was never much improved afterward. A few days before the completion of his eighth year, in the absence of his father, a flock of wild turkeys approached the new log cabin, and Abraham with a rifle-gun, standing inside, shot through a crack and killed one of them. He has never since pulled a trigger on any larger game. In the autumn of 1818 his mother died; and a year afterward his father married Mrs. Sally Johnston, at Elizabethtown, Kentucky, a widow with three children of her first marriage. She proved a good and kind mother to Abraham, and is still living in Coles County, Illinois. There were no children of this second marriage. His father's residence continued at the same place in Indiana till 1830. While here Abraham went to A B C schools by littles, kept successively by Andrew Crawford,—Sweeney, and Azel W. Dorsey. He does not remember any other. The family of Mr. Dorsey now resides in Schuyler County, Illinois. Abraham now thinks that the aggregate of all his schooling did not amount to one year. He was never in a college or academy as a student, and never inside of a college or academy building till since he had a law license. What he has in the way of education he has picked up. After he was twenty-three and had separated from his father, he studied English grammar—imperfectly, of course, but so as to speak and write as well as he now does. He studied and nearly mastered the six books of Euclid since he was a member of Congress. He regrets his want of education, and does what he can to supply the want. In his tenth year he was kicked by a horse, and apparently killed for a time. When he was nineteen, still residing in Indiana, he made his first trip upon a flatboat to New Orleans. He was a hired hand merely, and he and a son of the owner, without other assistance, made the trip. The nature of part of the "cargo-load," as it was called, made it necessary for them to linger and trade along the sugar-coast; and one night they were attacked by seven negroes with intent to kill and rob them. They were hurt some in the mêlée, but succeeded in driving the negroes from the boat, and then "cut cable," "weighed anchor," and left.

March 1, 1830, Abraham having just completed his twenty-first year, his father and family, with the families of the two daughters and sons-in-law of his stepmother, left the old homestead in Indiana and came to Illinois. Their mode of conveyance was wagons drawn by ox-teams, and Abraham drove one of the teams. They reached the county of Macon, and stopped there some time within the same month of March. His father and family settled a new place on the north side of the Sangamon River, at the junction of the timberland and prairie, about ten miles westerly from Decatur. Here they built a log cabin, into which they removed, and made sufficient of rails to fence ten acres of ground, fenced and broke the ground, and raised a crop of sown corn upon it the same year. These are, or are supposed to be, the rails about which so much is being said just now, though these are far from being the first or only rails ever made by Abraham.

The sons-in-law were temporarily settled in other places in the county. In the autumn all hands were greatly afflicted with ague and fever, to which they had not been used, and by which they were greatly discouraged, so much so that they determined on leaving the county. They remained, however, through the succeeding winter, which was the winter of the very celebrated "deep snow" of Illinois. During that winter Abraham, together with his stepmother's son, John D. Johnston, and John Hanks, yet residing in Macon County, hired themselves to Denton Offutt to take a flatboat from Beardstown, Illinois, to New Orleans; and for that purpose were to join him—Offutt—at Springfield, Illinois, so soon as the snow should go off. When it did go off, which was about the first of March, 1831, the county was so flooded as to make traveling by land impracticable; to obviate which difficulty they purchased a large canoe, and came down the Sangamon River in it. This is the time and the manner of Abraham's first entrance into Sangamon County. They found Offutt at Springfield, but learned from him that he had failed in getting a boat at Beardstown. This led to their hiring themselves to him for twelve dollars per month each, and getting the timber out of the trees and building a boat at Old Sangamon town on the Sangamon River, seven miles northwest of Springfield, which boat they took to New Orleans, substantially upon the old contract.

During this boat-enterprise acquaintance with Offutt, who was previously an entire stranger, he conceived a liking for Abraham, and believing he could turn him to account, he contracted with him to act as clerk for him, on his return from New Orleans, in charge of a store and mill at New Salem, then in Sangamon, now in Menard County. Hanks had not gone to New Orleans, but having a family, and being likely to be detained from home longer than at first expected, had turned back from St. Louis. He is the same John Hanks who now engineers the "rail enterprise" at Decatur, and is a first cousin to Abraham's mother. Abraham's father, with his own family and others mentioned, had, in pursuance of their intention, removed from Macon to Coles County. John D. Johnston, the stepmother's son, went to them, and Abraham stopped indefinitely and for the first time, as it were, by himself at New Salem, before mentioned. This was in July, 1831. Here he rapidly made acquaintances and friends. In less than a year Offutt's business was failing—had almost failed—when the Black Hawk war of 1832 broke out. Abraham joined a volunteer company, and, to his own surprise, was elected captain of it. He says he has not since had any success in life which gave him so much satisfaction. He went to the campaign, served near three months, met the ordinary hardships of such an expedition, but was in no battle. He now owns, in Iowa, the land upon which his own warrants for the service were located. Returning from the campaign, and encouraged by his great popularity among his immediate neighbors, he the same year ran for the legislature, and was beaten,—his own precinct, however, casting its votes 277 for and 7 against him—and that, too, while he was an avowed Clay man, and the precinct the autumn afterward giving a majority of 115 to General Jackson over Mr. Clay. This was the only time Abraham was ever beaten on a direct vote of the people. He was now without means and out of business, but was anxious to remain with his friends who had treated him with so much generosity, especially as he had nothing elsewhere to go to. He studied what he should do—thought of learning the blacksmith trade—thought of trying to study law—rather thought he could not succeed at that without a better education. Before long, strangely enough, a man offered to sell, and did sell, to Abraham and another as poor as himself, an old stock of goods, upon credit. They opened as merchants; and he says that was *the* store. Of course they did nothing but get deeper and deeper in debt. He was appointed postmaster at New Salem—the office being too insignificant to make his politics an objection. The store winked out. The surveyor of Sangamon offered to depute to Abraham that portion of his work which was within his part of the county. He accepted, procured a compass and chain, studied Flint and Gibson a little, and went at it. This procured bread, and kept soul and body together. The election of 1834 came, and he was then elected to the legislature by the highest vote cast for any candidate. Major John T. Stuart, then in full practice of the law, was also elected. During the canvass, in a private conversation he encouraged

Abraham [to] study law. After the election he borrowed books of Stuart, took them home with him, and went at it in good earnest. He studied with nobody. He still mixed in the surveying to pay board and clothing bills. When the legislature met, the law-books were dropped, but were taken up again at the end of the session. He was reelected in 1836, 1838, and 1840. In the autumn of 1836 he obtained a law license, and on April 15, 1837, removed to Springfield, and commenced the practice—his old friend Stuart taking him into partnership. March 3, 1837, by a protest entered upon the "Illinois House Journal" of that date, at pages 817 and 818, Abraham, with Dan Stone, another representative of Sangamon, briefly defined his position on the slavery question; and so far as it goes, it was then the same that it is now. The protest is as follows:

"Resolutions upon the subject of domestic slavery having passed both branches of the General Assembly at its present session, the undersigned hereby protest against the passage of the same.

"They believe that the institution of slavery is founded on both injustice and bad policy, but that the promulgation of Abolition doctrines tends rather to increase than abate its evils.

"They believe that the Congress of the United States has no power under the Constitution to interfere with the institution of slavery in the different States.

"They believe that the Congress of the United States has no power, under the Constitution, to abolish slavery in the District of Columbia, but that the power ought not to be exercised unless at the request of the people of the District.

"The difference between these opinions and those contained in the above resolutions is their reason for entering this protest.

"Dan Stone,
"A Lincoln,
"Representatives from the County of Sangamon."

In 1838 and 1840, Mr. Lincoln's party voted for him as Speaker, but being in the minority he was not elected. After 1840 he declined a reelection to the legislature. He was on the Harrison electoral ticket in 1840, and on that of Clay in 1844, and spent much time and labor in both those canvasses. In November, 1842, he was married to Mary, daughter of Robert S. Todd, of Lexington, Kentucky. They have three living children, all sons, one born in 1843, one in 1850, and one in 1853. They lost one, who was born in 1846.

In 1846 he was elected to the lower House of Congress, and served one term only, commencing in December, 1847, and ending with the inauguration of General Taylor, in March 1849. All the battles of the Mexican war had been fought before Mr. Lincoln took his seat in Congress, but the American army was still in Mexico, and the treaty of peace was not fully and formally ratified till the June afterward. Much has been said of his course in Congress in regard to this war. A careful examination of the "Journal" and "Congressional Globe" shows that he voted for all the supply measures that came up, and for all the measures in any way favorable to the officers, soldiers, and their families, who conducted the war through: with the exception that some of these measures passed without yeas and nays, leaving no record as to how particular men voted. The "Journal" and "Globe" also show him voting that the war was unnecessarily and unconstitutionally begun by the President of the United States. This is the language of Mr. Ashmun's amendment, for which Mr. Lincoln and nearly or quite all other Whigs of the House of Representatives voted.

Mr. Lincoln's reasons for the opinion expressed by this vote were briefly that the President had sent General Taylor into an inhabited part of the country belonging to Mexico, and not to the United States, and thereby had provoked the first act of hostility, in fact the commencement of the war; that the place, being the country bordering on the east bank of the Rio Grande, was inhabited by native Mexicans, born there under the Mexican government, and had never submitted to, nor been conquered by, Texas or the United States, nor transferred to either by treaty; that although Texas claimed the Rio Grande as her boundary, Mexico had never recognized it, and neither Texas nor the United States had ever enforced it; that there was a broad desert between that and the country over which Texas had actual control; that the country where hostilities commenced, having once belonged to Mexico, must remain so until it was somehow legally transferred, which had never been done.

Mr. Lincoln thought the act of sending an armed force among the Mexicans was unnecessary, inasmuch as Mexico was in no way molesting or menacing the United States or the people thereof; and that it was unconstitutional, because the power of levying war is vested in Congress, and not in the President. He thought the principal motive for the act was to divert public attention from the surrender of "Fifty-four, forty, or fight" to Great Britain, on the Oregon boundary question.

Mr. Lincoln was not a candidate for reelection. This was determined upon and declared before he went to Washington, in accordance with an understanding among Whig friends, by which Colonel Hardin and Colonel Baker had each previously served a single term in this same district.

In 1848, during his term in Congress, he advocated General Taylor's nomination for the presidency, in opposition to all others, and also took an active part for his election after his nomination, speaking a few times in Maryland, near Washington, several times in Massachusetts, and canvassing quite fully his own district in Illinois, which was followed by a majority in the district of over 1500 for General Taylor.

Upon his return from Congress he went to the practice of the law with greater earnestness than ever before. In 1852 he was upon the Scott electoral ticket, and did something in the way of canvassing, but owing to the hopelessness of the cause in Illinois he did less than in previous presidential canvasses.

In 1854 his profession had almost superseded the thought of politics in his mind, when the repeal of the Missouri Compromise aroused him as he had never been before.

In the autumn of that year he took the stump with no broader practical aim or object than to secure, if possible, the reelection of Hon. Richard Yates to Congress. His speeches at once attracted a more marked attention than they had ever before done. As the canvass proceeded he was drawn to different parts of the State outside of Mr. Yates's district. He did not abandon the law, but gave his attention by turns to that and politics. The State agricultural fair was at Springfield that year, and Douglas was announced to speak there.

In the canvass of 1856 Mr. Lincoln made over fifty speeches, no one of which, so far as he remembers, was put in print. One of them was made at Galena, but Mr. Lincoln has no recollection of any part of it being printed; nor does he remember whether in that speech he said anything about a Supreme Court decision. He may have spoken upon that subject, and some of the newspapers may have reported him as saying what is now ascribed to him, but he thinks he could not have expressed himself as represented.

Campaign biographies were beginning to be announced by publishers as "authorized" by Lincoln. (See "Letter to Samuel Galloway," June 19, 1860.) Lincoln prepared this sketch in third person with the understanding that it would be followed explicitly in a biography to be written by John L. Scripps. The original manuscript is in the Robert Lincoln Collection in the Library of Congress, which is unavailable to students until 1947 by reason of the stipulation in the bequest.

LETTER TO SAMUEL GALLOWAY
JUNE 19, 1860

Especially Confidential

Springfield, Ills. June 19. 1860

Hon: Saml. Galloway:
My dear Sir

Your very kind letter of the 15th. is received. Messrs. Follett, Foster & Co's Life of me is *not* by my authority; and I have scarcely been so much astounded by any thing, as by their public announcement that it is authorized by me. They have fallen into some strange misunderstanding. I certainly knew they contemplated publishing a biography; and I certainly did not object to their doing so, *upon their own responsibility*. I even took pains to facilitate them. But, at the same time, I made myself tiresome, if not hoarse, with repeating to Mr. Howard, their only agent seen by me, my protest that I *authorized nothing*—would be *responsible for nothing*. How, they could so misunderstand me, passes comprehension. As a matter, *wholly my own*, I would authorize no biography, without *time*, and *opertunity* [*sic*] to carefully examine and consider every word of it; and, in this case, in the nature of things, I can have no such time and opertunity [*sic*]. But, in my present position, when, by the lessons of the past, and the united voice of all discreet friends I can neither write or speak a word for the public, how dare I to send forth, by my authority, a volume of hundreds of pages, for adversaries to make points upon without end. Were I to do so, the Convention would have a right to re-assemble, and substitute another name for mine.

For these reasons, I would not look at the proof sheets. I am determined to maintain the position of of [*sic*] truly saying I never saw the proof sheets, or any part of their work, before it's publication.

Now, do not mistake me. I feel great Kindness for Messrs F. F. & Co—do not think they have intentionally done wrong. There may be nothing wrong in their proposed book. I sincerely hope there will not. I barely suggest that you, or any of the friends there, on the party account, look it over, & exclude what you may think would embarrass the party—bearing in mind, at all times, that I *authorize nothing*—will be *responsible* for *nothing*.

Your friend, as ever

A. Lincoln

The biography referred to in this letter is the one written by William Dean Howells, who was at the time an editorial writer on the Ohio State Journal *at Columbus. Howells had access to a copy of the sketch Lincoln wrote for Scripps, which was given to James Q. Howard, an agent sent to Springfield by Howells for the purpose of collecting material. Lincoln later read and corrected a copy of Howells's book belonging to Samuel C. Parks, which has been published in facsimile by The Abraham Lincoln Association (1938).*

LETTER TO ABRAHAM JONAS JULY 21, 1860

Confidential

Springfield, Ills. July 21. 1860

Hon. A. Jonas
My dear Sir

Yours of the 20th. is received. I suppose as good, or even better, men than I may have been in American, or Know-Nothing lodges; but in point of fact, I never was in one, at Quincy, or elsewhere. I was never in Quincy but one day and two nights, while Know-Nothing lodges were in existence, and you were with me that day and both those nights. I had never been there before in my life; and never afterwards, till the joint debate with Douglas in 1858. It was in 1854, when I spoke in some Hall there, and after the speaking, you, with others, took me to an oyster saloon, passed an hour there, and you walked with me to, and parted with me at, the Quincy-House, quite late at night. I left by stage for Naples before day-light in the morning, having come in by the same route, after dark, the evening previous to the speaking, when I found you waiting at the Quincy House to meet me. A few days after I was there, Richardson, as I understood, started this same story about my having been in a Know-Nothing lodge. When I heard of the charge, as I did soon after, I taxed my recollection for some incident which could have suggested it; and I remembered that on parting with you the last night, I went to the Office of the Hotel to take my stage passage for the morning, was told that no stage office for that line was kept there, and that I must see the driver, before retiring, to insure his calling for me in the morning; and a servant was sent with me to find the driver, who after taking me a square or two, stopped me, and stepped perhaps a dozen steps farther, and in my hearing called to some one, who answered him apparently from the upper part of a building, and promised to call with the stage for me at the Quincy House. I returned and went to bed; and before day the stage called and took me. This is all.

That I never was in a Know-Nothing lodge in Quincy, I should expect, could be easily proved, by respectable men, who were always in the lodges and never saw me there.

An affidavit of one or two such would put the matter at rest.

And now, a word of caution. Our adversaries think they can gain a point, if they could force me to openly deny the charge, by which some degree of offence would be given to the Americans. For this reason, it must not publicly appear that I am paying any attention to the charge.

Yours truly
A. Lincoln

Abraham Jonas of Jonas & Asbury, attorneys, Quincy, Illinois, was an English Jew, a prominent Mason, and a political organizer among the Jews. His friendship with Lincoln was of long standing, and hence Lincoln felt that he could be trusted to handle the delicate political matter referred to. Lincoln had repeatedly and publicly expressed his opposition to Know-Nothing principles, but he did not wish to antagonize the Know-Nothings who had "fused" with other dissidents in forming the Republican party.

LETTER TO GEORGE LATHAM
JULY 22, 1860

Springfield Ills July 22. 1860.

My dear George

I have scarcely felt greater pain in my life than on learning yesterday from Bob's letter, that you had failed to enter Harvard University. And yet there is very little in it, if you will allow no feeling of *discouragement* to seize, and prey upon you. It is a *certain* truth, that you *can* enter, and graduate in, Harvard University; and having made the attempt, you *must* succeed in it. '*Must*' is the word.

I know not how to aid you, save in the assurance of one of mature age, and much severe experience, that you *can* not fail, if you resolutely determine, that you *will* not.

The President of the institution, can scarcely be other than a kind man; and doubtless he would grant you an interview, and point out the readiest way to remove, or overcome, the obstacles which have thwarted you.

In your temporary failure there is no evidence that you may not yet be a better scholar, and a more successful man in the great struggle of life, than many others, who have entered college more easily.

Again I say let no feeling of discouragement prey upon you, and in the end you are sure to succeed.

With more than a common interest I subscribe myself

Very truly your friend

A. Lincoln

Here Lincoln writes to a school friend of his son Robert. George and Robert attended Exeter together, and in March, 1860, had accompanied Lincoln from Exeter to Concord, where Lincoln had a speaking en-

gagement on his New England tour. The following year George was a member of the Presidential party on the way to Washington. A remarkable glimpse into Lincoln's inner self is revealed in this letter. More succinctly and poignantly than any other statement, it reveals the quality of spirit which underlies all that Lincoln achieved.

LETTER TO CHARLES C. NOTT SEPTEMBER 22, 1860

Springfield, Ills., Sept. 22, 1860.

Charles C. Nott, Esq.,
My dear Sir:

Yours of the 17th was duly received. The 250 copies have not yet arrived. I am greatly obliged to you for what you have done, and what you propose to do.

The "Abraham Baldwin letter" in substance was that I could not find the Journal of the Confederation Congress for the session at which was passed the Ordinance of 1787—and that in stating Mr. Baldwin had voted for its passage, I had relied on a communication of Mr. Greeley over his own signature, published in the New York *Weekly Tribune* of October 15, 1859. If you will turn to that paper, you will there see that Mr. Greeley apparently copies from the Journal, and places the name of Mr. Baldwin among those of the men who voted for the measure.

Still, if the Journal itself shows differently, of course it is right.

Yours very truly,
A. Lincoln.

LETTER TO MRS. M. J. GREEN
SEPTEMBER 22, 1860

Springfield, Ills. Sep. 22. 1860

Mrs. M. J. Green
My Dear Madam.

Your kind congratulatory letter, of August, was received in due course—and should have been answered sooner. The truth is I have never corresponded much with ladies; and hence I post-pone writing letters to them, as a business which I do not under-stand. I can only say now I thank you for the good opinion you express of me, fearing, at the same time, I may not be able to maintain it through life.

Yours very truly
A. Lincoln.

LETTER TO MISS GRACE BEDELL
OCTOBER 19, 1860

Private

Springfield, Ills. Oct 19. 1860

Miss. Grace Bedell
My dear little Miss.

Your very agreeable letter of the 15th. is received.

I regret the necessity of saying I have no daughters. I have three sons—one seventeen, one nine, and one seven, years of age. They, with their mother, constitute my whole family.

As to the whiskers, having never worn any, do you not think

people would call it a piece of silly affection [*sic*] if I were to begin it now—?

Your very sincere well-wisher
A. Lincoln.

The communication which called forth this letter is as interesting as Lincoln's reply:

"NY
"Westfield Chatauqua Co
"Oct 15, 1860

"Hon A B Lincoln
"Dear Sir

"My father has just home from the fair and brought home your picture and Mr. Hamlin's. I am a little girl only eleven years old, but want you should be President of the United States very much so I hope you wont think me very bold to write to such a great man as you are. Have you any little girls about as large as I am if so give them my love and tell her to write to me, if you cannot answer this letter. I have got 4 [?] brothers and part of them will vote for you anyway and if you will let your whiskers grow I will try and get the rest of them to vote for you you would look a great deal better for your face is so thin. All the ladies like whiskers and they would tease their husbands to vote for you and then you would be President. My father is agoing to vote for you to but I will try and get every one to vote for you that I can think that rail fence around your picture makes it look very pretty I have got a little baby sister she is nine weeks old and is just as cunning as can be. When you direct your letter diret [sic] *to Grace Bedell Westfield Chatauqua County New York.*

"I must not write any more answer this letter right off Good bye

"Grace Bedell"

LETTER TO GEORGE T. M. DAVIS
OCTOBER 27, 1860

Private & confidential.

Springfield, Ills. Oct. 27. 1860

Geo. T. M. Davis, Esq
My dear Sir:

Mr. Dubois has shown me your letter of the 20th.; and I promised him to write you. What is it I could say which would quiet alarm? Is it that no interference by the government, with slaves or slavery within the states, is intended? I have said this so often already, that a repetition of it is but mockery, bearing an appearance of weakness, and cowardice, which perhaps should be avoided. Why do not uneasy men *read* what I have already said? and what our *platform* says? If they will not read, or heed, then, would they read, or heed, a repetition of them? Of course the declaration that there is no intention to interfere with slaves or slavery, in the states, with all that is fairly implied in such declaration, is true; and I should have no objection to make, and repeat the declaration a thousand times, if there were no danger of encouraging bold bad men to believe they are dealing with one who can be scared into anything.

I have some reason to believe the Sub-National Committee, at the Astor House, may be considering this question; and if their judgment should be different from mine, mine might be modified by theirs.

Yours very truly
A. Lincoln.

George Turnbull Moore Davis was a well-to-do New York business man at the time this letter was written. In early life he had worked on the staff of the Louisville Courier Journal *and practiced law in Alton,*

Illinois, where he was one of the defenders of the pioneer abolitionists associated with Elijah P. Lovejoy, who was killed defending his press in 1837. At the close of the Mexican War—in which he volunteered, rose to the rank of Colonel, and acted as General Quitman's Secretary of State during his Governorship of Mexico City—he became chief clerk in the War Department at Washington. From Washington he went to New York and entered business. He became connected with several Western railroads, and was, at his death in 1888, vice-president of the Adirondack Railroad. (Autobiography of the Late Colonel George T. M. Davis, *pp. 390-91.)*

LETTER TO H. J. RAYMOND
NOVEMBER 28, 1860

Private & Confidential

Springfield, Ills. Nov. 28. 1860

Hon. H. J. Raymond
My dear Sir

Yours of the 14th. was received in due course. I have delayed so long to answer it, because my reasons for not coming before the public in any form just now, had substantially appeared in your paper (The Times), and hence I feared they were not deemed sufficient by you, else you would not have written me as you did.

I now think we have a demonstration in favor of my view. On the 20th. Inst. Senator Trumbull made a short speech which I suppose you have both seen and approved. Has a single newspaper, heretofore against us, urged that speech [upon its readers] with a purpose to quiet public anxiety? Not one, so far as I know. On the contrary the Boston Courier, and it's class, hold me responsible for the speech, and endeavor to inflame the North with the belief that it foreshadows an abandonment of Republican ground by the incoming administration; while the Washington Constitution, and it's class hold the same speech up to the South as an open declaration of war against them.

This is just as I expected, and just what would happen with any declaration I could make. These political fiends are not half sick enough yet. "Party malice" and not "public good" possesses them entirely. "They seek a sign, and no sign shall be given them." At least such is my present feeling and purpose.

[Signature cut off]

Raymond was editor of the New York Times *and had been Seward's staunch supporter for the nomination. Upon Lincoln's election, he felt that a statement should be issued to clarify the intentions of the newly-elected President. Lincoln's policy of saying nothing is fully explained here, and was held to strictly until his inauguration.*

Raymond's note on the manuscript specifies that "the signature was cut off to oblige a friend with an autograph."

LETTER TO WILLIAM KELLOGG
DECEMBER 11, 1860

Private & Confidential

Springfield, Ills, Dec. 11. 1860

Hon. William Kellogg.
My dear Sir—

Entertain no proposition for a compromise in regard to the *extension* of slavery. The instant you do, they have us under again; all our labor is lost, and sooner or later must be done over. Douglas is sure to be again trying to bring in his "Pop. Sov." Have none of it. The tug has to come & better now than later.

You know I think the fugitive slave clause of the constitution ought to be enforced—to put it in the mildest form, ought not to be resisted. In haste

Yours as ever
A. Lincoln

In spite of Lincoln's insistence, Kellogg proceeded in the following February to introduce a Compromise Bill to amend the Constitution so that slaves could be taken into any territory south of 36° 30′. Kellogg's closeness to Lincoln politically occasioned much speculation that Lincoln was leaning toward compromise, but Kellogg stated his sole responsibility on the floor of the House of Representatives. For a detailed account of Kellogg's association with Lincoln, see "The Recollections of William Pitt Kellogg," edited by Paul M. Angle, in The Abraham Lincoln Quarterly.

LETTER TO JOHN D. DEFREES DECEMBER 18, 1860

Confidential

Springfield Ills. Dec. 18. 1860

Hon. Jno. D. Defrees.
My dear Sir

Yours of the 15th. is received. I am sorry any republican inclines to dally with Pop. Sov. of any sort. It acknowledges that slavery has equal rights with liberty, and surrenders all we have contended for. Once fastened on us as a settled policy, filibustering for all South of us, and making slave states of it, follows in spite of us, with an early Supreme Court decision, holding our free-state constitutions to be unconstitutional.

Would Scott or Stephens go into the Cabinet? And if yes, on what terms? Do they come to me? or I go to them? or are we to lead off in open hostility to each other?

Yours truly
A. Lincoln

Defrees was a native of South Bend, Indiana, where he edited a newspaper until 1854. Politician and Republican party man, he was appointed government printer by Lincoln, March 23, 1861. The well-known incident of his tilt with Lincoln over the diction of Lincoln's first "Message to Congress in Special Session" has been told in "Lincoln's Development as a Writer."

LETTER TO A. H. STEPHENS
DECEMBER 22, 1860

For your own eye only

Springfield, Ills. Dec. 22. 1860

Hon. A. H. Stephens—
My dear Sir

Your obliging answer to my short note is just received, and for which please accept my thanks. I fully appreciate the present peril the country is in, and the weight of responsibility on me.

Do the people of the South really entertain fears that a Republican administration would, *directly*, or *indirectly*, interfere with their slaves, or with them, about their slaves? If they do, I wish to assure you, as once a friend, and still, I hope, not an enemy, that there is no cause for such fears.

The South would be in no more danger in this respect, than it was in the days of Washington. I suppose, however, this does not meet the case. You think slavery is *right*, and ought to be extended; while we think it is *wrong* and ought to be restricted. That I suppose is the rub. It certainly is the only substantial difference between us.

Yours very truly
A. Lincoln

At the time of this letter Stephens was still supporting the Union, but when Georgia seceded on January 17, 1861—in spite of Stephens's efforts—his loyalty went with his State.

FAREWELL ADDRESS AT SPRINGFIELD, ILLINOIS FEBRUARY 11, 1861

My Friends:

No one, not in my situation, can appreciate my feeling of sadness at this parting. To this place, and the kindness of these people, I owe everything. Here I have lived a quarter of a century, and have passed from a young to an old man. Here my children have been born, and one is buried. I now leave, not knowing when or whether ever I may return, with a task before me greater than that which rested upon Washington. Without the assistance of that Divine Being who ever attended him, I cannot succeed. With that assistance, I cannot fail. Trusting in Him who can go with me, and remain with you, and be everywhere for good, let us confidently hope that all will yet be well. To His care commending you, as I hope in your prayers you will commend me, I bid you an affectionate farewell.

The text of this address is from the Complete Works of Abraham Lincoln. *The manuscript is purported to be in the Robert Lincoln Collection in the Library of Congress. According to Nicolay's account in* Abraham Lincoln: A History, *Vol. III, p. 291 n., it was written out on the train after the departure from Springfield, partly by Lincoln and partly by Nicolay from Lincoln's dictation.*

In view of Lincoln's general style, most of the differences between this version and the versions printed in newspapers at the time seem to be differences which Lincoln would have brought about in writing it out. This version tends to enhance the alliterative sequences and to strengthen the rhythm pattern, both of which are apparent even in the newspaper versions. This is entirely in keeping with Lincoln's usual practice.

Of the several newspaper versions, two are interesting for purposes of comparison. The first is the version which was published in the Illinois State Journal, *February 12, 1861, and the second is the version of a contemporary broadside, published by the American News Company of New York, which is in all but a few marks of punctuation identical with the version which appeared in* Harper's Weekly *and various eastern newspapers. The two versions are as follows:*

"Friends:

"No one who has never been placed in a like position, can understand my feelings at this hour, nor the oppressive sadness I feel at this parting. For more than a quarter of a century I have lived among you, and during all that time I have received nothing but kindness at your hands. Here I have lived from my youth until now I am an old man. Here the most sacred ties of earth were assumed; here all my children were born; and here one of them lies buried. To you, dear friends, I owe all that I have, all that I am. All the strange, chequered past seems

to crowd now upon my mind. To-day I leave you; I go to assume a task more difficult than that which devolved upon general Washington. Unless the great God who assisted him, shall be with and aid me, I must fail. But if the same omniscient mind, and Almighty arm that directed and protected him, shall guide and support me, I shall not fail, I shall succeed. Let us all pray that the God of our fathers may not forsake us now. To him I commend you all—permit me to ask that with equal security and faith, you all will invoke His wisdom and guidance for me. With these few words I must leave you—for how long I know not. Friends, one and all, I must now bid you an affectionate farewell."

"My Friends:

"No one not in my position can appreciate the sadness I feel at this parting. To this people I owe all that I am. Here I have lived more than a quarter of a century; here my children were born, and here one of them lies buried. I know not how soon I shall see you again. A duty devolves upon me which is, perhaps, greater than that which devolved upon any other man since the days of Washington. He never would have succeeded except for the aid of Divine Providence, upon which he at all times relied. I feel that I cannot succeed without the same Divine aid which sustained him, and on the same Almighty Being I place my reliance for support, and I hope you, my friends, will all pray that I may receive that Divine assistance without which I cannot succeed, but with which success is certain. Again I bid you an affectionate farewell."

SPEECH AT INDIANAPOLIS, INDIANA FEBRUARY 11, 1861

Fellow-Citizens of the State of Indiana:

I am here to thank you much for this magnificent welcome, and still more for the very generous support given by your State to that political cause which I think is the true and just cause of the whole country and the whole world. Solomon says, "There is a time to keep silence," and when men wrangle by the month with no certainty that they mean the same thing while using the same word, it perhaps were as well if they would keep silence. The words "coercion" and "invasion" are much used in these days, and often with some temper and hot blood. Let us make sure, if we can, that we do not misunderstand the meaning of those who use them. Let us get the exact definitions of these words, not from dictionaries, but from the men themselves, who certainly deprecate the things they would represent by the use of the words. What, then, is "coercion?" What is "invasion?" Would the marching of an army into South Carolina, without the consent of her people, and with hostile intent toward them be invasion? I certainly think it would; and it would be "coercion" also if the South Carolinians were forced to submit. *But if the United States should merely hold and retake its own forts and other property, and collect the duties on foreign importations, or even withhold the mails from places where they were habitually violated, would any or all these things be "invasion" or "coercion?"* Do our professed lovers of the Union, but who spitefully resolve that they will resist coercion and invasion, understand that such things as these on the part of the United States would be coercion or invasion of a State? If so, their idea of means to preserve the object of their great affection would seem to be exceedingly thin and airy. If sick, the little pills of the homeopathist would be much too large for it to swallow. In their view, the Union, as a family relation, would seem to be no regular marriage, but rather a sort of free-love arrangement, to be maintained only on passional attraction. By the way, in what consists the special sacredness of a State? I speak not of the position assigned to a State in the Union by the Constitution, for that by the bond we all recognize. That position, however, a State cannot carry out of the Union with it. I speak of that assumed primary right of a State to rule all which is less than itself, and to ruin all which is larger than itself. If a State and a county, in a given case, should be equal in extent of territory and equal in number of inhabitants, in what, as a matter of principle, is the State better than the county? Would an exchange of names be an exchange of rights? Upon principle, on what rightful principle, may a State, being no more than one-fiftieth part of the nation in soil and population, break up the nation and then coerce a proportionably larger subdivision of itself in the most arbitrary way? What mysterious right to play tyrant is conferred on a district of country with its people by merely calling it a State? Fellow-citizens, I am not asserting anything. I am merely asking questions for you to consider. And now allow me to bid you farewell.

ADDRESS TO GERMANS AT CINCINNATI, OHIO FEBRUARY 12, 1861

Mr. Chairman:

I thank you and those whom you represent, for the compliment you have paid me, by tendering me this address. In so far as there is an allusion to our present national difficulties, which expresses, as you have said, the views of the gentlemen present, I shall have to beg pardon for not entering fully upon the questions which the address you have now read suggests.

I deem it my duty—a duty which I owe to my constituents—to you, gentlemen, that I should wait until the last moment, for a development of the present national difficulties, before I express myself decidedly what course I shall pursue. I hope, then, not to be false to anything that you have to expect of me.

I agree with you, Mr. Chairman, that the working men are the basis of all governments, for the plain reason that they are the more numerous, and as you added that those were the sentiments of the gentlemen present, representing not only the working class, but citizens of other callings than those of the mechanic, I am happy to concur with you in these sentiments, not only for the native-born citizens, but also of the Germans and foreigners from other countries.

Mr. Chairman, I hold that while man exists, it is his duty to improve not only his own condition, but to assist in ameliorating mankind; and therefore, without entering upon the details of the question, I will simply say that I am for those means which will give the greatest good to the greatest number.

In regard to the Homestead law, I have to say that in so far as the Government lands can be disposed of, I am in favor of cutting up the wild lands into parcels, so that every poor man may have a home.

In regard to the Germans and foreigners, I esteem them no better than other people, nor any worse. It is not my nature, when I see a people borne down by the weight of their shackles—the oppression of tyranny—to make their life more bitter by heaping upon them greater burdens; but rather would I do all in my power to raise the yoke, than to add anything that would tend to crush them.

Inasmuch as our country is extensive and new, and the countries of Europe are densely populated, if there are any abroad who desire to make this the land of their adoption, it is not in my heart to throw aught in their way, to prevent them from coming to the United States.

Mr. Chairman, and Gentlemen, I will bid you an affectionate farewell.

The correspondent of the New York Daily Tribune *gives the circumstances of this address as follows: "In the evening, Mr. Lincoln submitted to a public reception, which he prolonged further than his friends would have desired, but which was less severe than that at Indianapolis. During the evening a German club visited the hotel in a torchlight procession. Mr. Lincoln was addressed on behalf of the Club by Fred Oberline, esq., and Mr. Lincoln replied as follows": [Address].*

ADDRESS TO THE SENATE OF NEW JERSEY
FEBRUARY 21, 1861

Mr. President and Gentlemen of the Senate of the State of New-Jersey:

I am very grateful to you for the honorable reception of which I have been the object. I cannot but remember the place that New-Jersey holds in our early history. In the early Revolutionary struggle, few of the States among the old Thirteen had more of the battle-fields of the country within their limits than old New-Jersey. May I be pardoned if, upon this occasion, I mention that away back in my childhood, the earliest days of my being able to read, I got hold of a small book, such a one as few of the younger members have ever seen, "Weems' Life of Washington." I remember all the accounts there given of the battle fields and struggles for the liberties of the country, and none fixed themselves upon my imagination so deeply as the struggle here at Trenton, New-Jersey. The crossing of the river; the contest with the Hessians; the great hardships endured at that time, all fixed themselves on my memory more than any single revolutionary event; and you all know, for you have all been boys, how these early impressions last longer than any others. I recollect thinking then, boy even though I was, that there must have been something more than common that those men struggled for. I am exceedingly anxious that that thing which they struggled for; that something even more than National Independence; that something that held out a great promise to all the people of the world to all time to come; I am exceedingly anxious that this Union, the Constitution, and the liberties of the people shall be perpetuated in accordance with the original idea for which that struggle was made, and I shall be most happy indeed if I shall be an humble instrument in the hands of the Almighty, and of this, his almost chosen people, for perpetuating the object of that great struggle. You give me this reception, as I understand, without distinction of party. I learn that this body is composed of a majority of gentlemen who, in the exercise of their best judgment in the choice of a Chief Magistrate, did not think I was the man. I understand, nevertheless, that they came forward here to greet me as the constitutional President of the United States—as citizens of the United States, to meet the man who, for the time being, is the representative man of the nation, united by a purpose to perpetuate the Union and liberties of the people. As such, I accept this reception more gratefully than I could do did I believe it was tendered to me as an individual.

ADDRESS TO THE ASSEMBLY OF NEW JERSEY
FEBRUARY 21, 1861

Mr. Speaker and Gentlemen:

I have just enjoyed the honor of a reception by the other branch of this Legislature, and I return to you and them my thanks for the reception which the people of New-Jersey have given, through their chosen representatives, to me, as the representative, for the time being, of the majesty of the people of the United States. I appropriate to myself very little of the demonstrations of respect with which I have been greeted. I think little should be given to any man, but that it should be a manifestation of adherence to the Union and the Constitution. I understand myself to be received here by the representatives of the people of

New-Jersey, a majority of whom differ in opinion from those with whom I have acted. This manifestation is therefore to be regarded by me as expressing their devotion to the Union, the Constitution and the liberties of the people. You, Mr. Speaker, have well said that this is a time when the bravest and wisest look with doubt and awe upon the aspect presented by our national affairs. Under these circumstances, you will readily see why I should not speak in detail of the course I shall deem it best to pursue. It is proper that I should avail myself of all the information and all the time at my command, in order that when the time arrives in which I must speak officially, I shall be able to take the ground which I deem the best and safest, and from which I may have no occasion to swerve. I shall endeavor to take the ground I deem most just to the North, the East, the West, the South, and the whole country. I take it, I hope, in good temper—certainly with no malice toward any section. I shall do all that may be in my power to promote a peaceful settlement of all our difficulties. The man does not live who is more devoted to peace than I am. None who would do more to preserve it. But it may be necessary to put the foot down firmly. And if I do my duty, and do right, you will sustain me, will you not? (Loud cheers, and cries of "Yes," "Yes," "We will.") Received, as I am, by the members of a Legislature the majority of whom do not agree with me in political sentiments, I trust that I may have their assistance in piloting the ship of State through this voyage, surrounded by perils as it is; for, if it should suffer wreck now, there will be no pilot ever needed for another voyage.

Gentlemen, I have already spoken longer than I intended, and I must beg leave to stop here.

ADDRESS IN INDEPENDENCE HALL, PHILADELPHIA FEBRUARY 22, 1861

Mr. Cuyler:

I am filled with deep emotion at finding myself standing here, in this place, where were collected together the wisdom, the patriotism, the devotion to principle, from which sprang the institutions under which we live. You have kindly suggested to me that in my hands is the task of restoring peace to the present distracted condition of the country. I can say in return, Sir, that all the political sentiments I entertain have been drawn, so far as I have been able to draw them, from the sentiments which originated and were given to the world from this hall. I have never had a feeling politically that did not spring from the sentiments embodied in the Declaration of Independence. I have often pondered over the dangers which were incurred by the men who assembled here, and framed and adopted that Declaration of Independence. I have pondered over the toils that were endured by the officers and soldiers of the army who achieved that Independence. I have often inquired of myself what great principle or idea it was that kept this Confederacy so long together. It was not the mere matter of the separation of the Colonies from the motherland; but that sentiment in the Declaration of Independence which gave liberty, not alone to the people of this country, but, I hope, to the world, for all future time. It was that which gave promise that in due time the weight would be lifted from the shoulders of all men. This is a sentiment embodied in the Declaration of Independence. Now, my friends, can this country be saved upon that basis? If it can, I will consider myself one of the happiest men in the world, if I can help to save it. If it cannot be saved upon that principle, it will be truly awful. But if this country cannot be saved without giving up that principle, I was about to say I would rather be assassinated on this spot than surrender it. Now, in my view of the present aspect of affairs, there need be no bloodshed or war.

There is no necessity for it. I am not in favor of such a course, and I may say, in advance, that there will be no bloodshed unless it be forced upon the Government, and then it will be compelled to act in self-defense.

My friends, this is wholly an unexpected speech, and I did not expect to be called upon to say a word when I came here. I supposed it was merely to do something toward raising the flag. I may, therefore, have said something indiscreet. (Cries of "No, no") I have said nothing but what I am willing to live by and, if it be the pleasure of Almighty God, die by.

The New York Daily Tribune's *account of the circumstances attending this address runs in part as follows: "At 7 o'clock Mr. Lincoln was escorted to the Hall, and there received by Theodore Cuyler, who warmly welcomed him to its venerable walls in the hour of national peril and distress, when the great work achieved by the wisdom and patriotism of our fathers seems threatened by instant ruin. Mr. Lincoln responded as follows": [Address].*

"Mr. Lincoln concluded amid great applause. The members of the City Council paid their respects to him, and the procession moved directly toward the platform erected in front of the State-House . . .

"Mr. Benton of the Select Council made a brief address inviting Mr. Lincoln to raise the flag.

"Mr. Lincoln replied in a patriotic speech, stating a cheerful compliance with the request. He alluded to the original flag of thirteen stars, saying that the number had increased as time rolled on, and we became a happy, powerful people, each star adding to its prosperity. The future is in the hands of the people. It was on such an occasion we could reason together, reaffirm our devotion to the country, and the principles of the Declaration of Independence. Let us make up our minds that when-

ever we do put a new star upon our banner, it shall be a fixed one, never to be dimmed by the horrors of war, but brightened by the contentment and prosperity of peace. Let us go on to extend the area of our usefulness, add star upon star until their light shall shine over five hundred millions of a free and happy people. [Lincoln's estimates on prospective population, both here and in the "Message to Congress," December 1, 1862, were natural enough at the time. Immigration was rapid and unrestricted, the birthrate high, and the average increase per decade for several decades past indicated Lincoln's figure as entirely probable within a century.]

"Mr. Lincoln then threw off his overcoat in an off-hand, easy manner, the backwoodsian style of which caused many good-natured remarks.

"The Rev. Mr. Clark addressed the Throne of Grace in an impressive prayer, many spectators uncovering themselves, when the flag was rolled up in a man-of-war style, then adjusted, a signal fired, and, amid the most excited enthusiasm, the President elect hoisted the national ensign. A stiff breeze caught the folded bunting and threw it out boldly to the winds. Cheer followed cheer, until hoarseness prevented continuance."

FIRST INAUGURAL ADDRESS
MARCH 4, 1861

Fellow-citizens of the United States:

In compliance with a custom as old as the government itself, I appear before you to address you briefly, and to take, in your presence, the oath prescribed by the Constitution of the United States, to be taken by the President "before he enters on the execution of his office."

I do not consider it necessary at present for me to discuss

those matters of administration about which there is no special anxiety or excitement.

Apprehension seems to exist among the people of the Southern States, that by the accession of a Republican Administration, their property, and their peace, and personal security, are to be endangered. There has never been any reasonable cause for such apprehension. Indeed, the most ample evidence to the contrary has all the while existed, and been open to their inspection. It is found in nearly all the published speeches of him who now addresses you. I do but quote from one of those speeches when I declare that "I have no purpose, directly or indirectly, to interfere with the institution of slavery in the States where it exists. I believe I have no lawful right to do so, and I have no inclination to do so." Those who nominated and elected me did so with full knowledge that I had made this, and many similar declarations, and had never recanted them. And more than this, they placed in the platform, for my acceptance, and as a law to themselves, and to me, the clear and emphatic resolution which I now read:

"*Resolved*, That the maintenance inviolate of the rights of the States, and especially the right of each State to order and control its own domestic institutions according to its own judgment exclusively, is essential to that balance of power on which the perfection and endurance of our political fabric depend; and we denounce the lawless invasion by armed force of the soil of any State or Territory, no matter under what pretext, as among the gravest of crimes."

I now reiterate these sentiments: and in doing so, I only press upon the public attention the most conclusive evidence of which the case is susceptible, that the property, peace and security of no section are to be in any wise endangered by the now incoming Administration. I add too, that all the protection which, consistently with the Constitution and the laws, can be given, will be cheerfully given to all the States when lawfully demanded, for whatever cause—as cheerfully to one section as to another.

There is much controversy about the delivering up of fugitives from service or labor. The clause I now read is as plainly written in the Constitution as any other of its provisions:

"No person held to service or labor in one State, under the laws thereof, escaping into another, shall, in consequence of any law or regulation therein, be discharged from such service or labor, but shall be delivered up on claim of the party to whom such service or labor may be due."

It is scarcely questioned that this provision was intended by those who made it, for the reclaiming of what we call fugitive slaves; and the intention of the law-giver is the law. All members of Congress swear their support to the whole Constitution—to this provision as much as to any other. To the proposition, then, that slaves whose cases come within the terms of this clause, "shall be delivered up," their oaths are unanimous. Now, if they would make the effort in good temper, could they not, with nearly equal unanimity, frame and pass a law, by means of which to keep good that unanimous oath?

There is some difference of opinion whether this clause should be enforced by national or by state authority; but surely that difference is not a very material one. If the slave is to be surrendered, it can be of but little consequence to him, or to others, by which authority it is done. And should any one, in any case, be content that his oath shall go unkept, on a merely unsubstantial controversy as to *how* it shall be kept?

Again, in any law upon this subject, ought not all the safeguards of liberty known in civilized and humane jurisprudence to be introduced, so that a free man be not, in any case, surrendered as a slave? And might it not be well, at the same time to provide by law for the enforcement of that clause in the Constitution which guarantees that "the citizens of each State shall be entitled to all privileges and immunities of citizens in the several States"?

I take the official oath to-day, with no mental reservations, and with no purpose to construe the Constitution or laws, by any hypercritical rules. And while I do not choose now to specify particular acts of Congress as proper to be enforced, I do suggest that it will be much safer for all, both in official and private stations, to conform to, and abide by, all those acts which stand unrepealed, than to violate any of them, trusting to find impunity in having them held to be unconstitutional.

It is seventy-two years since the first inauguration of a President under our national Constitution. During that period fifteen different and greatly distinguished citizens, have, in succession, administered the executive branch of the government. They have conducted it through many perils; and, generally, with great success. Yet, with all this scope for [of] precedent, I now enter upon the same task for the brief constitutional term of four years, under great and peculiar difficulty. A disruption of the Federal Union, heretofore only menaced, is now formidably attempted.

I hold, that in contemplation of universal law, and of the Constitution, the Union of these States is perpetual. Perpetuity is implied, if not expressed, in the fundamental law of all national governments. It is safe to assert that no government proper, ever had a provision in its organic law for its own termination. Continue to execute all the express provisions of our national Constitution, and the Union will endure forever—it being impossible to destroy it, except by some action not provided for in the instrument itself.

Again, if the United States be not a government proper, but an association of States in the nature of contract merely, can it, as a contract, be peaceably unmade, by less than all the parties who made it? One party to a contract may violate it—break it, so to speak; but does it not require all to lawfully rescind it?

Descending from these general principles, we find the proposition that, in legal contemplation, the Union is perpetual, confirmed by the history of the Union itself. The Union is much older than the Constitution. It was formed in fact, by the Articles of Association in 1774. It was matured and continued by the Declaration of Independence in 1776. It was further matured and the faith of all the then thirteen States expressly plighted and engaged that it should be perpetual, by the Articles of Confederation in 1778. And finally, in 1787, one of the declared objects for ordaining and establishing the Constitution, was "*to form a more perfect Union.*"

But if [the] destruction of the Union, by one, or by a part only, of the States, be lawfully possible, the Union is *less* perfect than before the Constitution, having lost the vital element of perpetuity.

It follows from these views that no State, upon its own mere motion, can lawfully get out of the Union,—that *resolves* and *ordinances* to that effect are legally void, and that acts of violence, within any State or States, against the authority of the United States, are insurrectionary or revolutionary, according to circumstances.

I therefore consider that in view of the Constitution and the laws, the Union is unbroken; and to the extent of my ability I shall take care, as the Constitution itself expressly enjoins upon me, that the laws of the Union be faithfully executed in all the States. Doing this I deem to be only a simple duty on my part; and I shall perform it, so far as practicable, unless my rightful masters, the American people, shall withhold the requisite means, or, in some authoritative manner, direct the contrary. I trust this will not be regarded as a menace, but only as the declared purpose of the Union that it will constitutionally defend and maintain itself.

In doing this there needs to be no bloodshed or violence; and there shall be none, unless it be forced upon the national authority. The power confided to me will be used to hold, occupy, and possess the property and places belonging to the government, and to collect the duties and imposts; but beyond what may be necessary for these objects, there will be no invasion—no using of force against or among the people anywhere. Where hostility to the United States, in any interior locality, shall be so great and so universal, as to prevent competent resident citizens from holding the Federal offices, there will be no attempt to force obnoxious strangers among the people for that object. While the strict legal right may exist in the government to enforce the exercise of these offices, the attempt to do so would be so irritating, and so nearly impracticable with all, that I deem it better to forego, for the time, the uses of such offices.

The mails, unless repelled, will continue to be furnished in all parts of the Union. So far as possible, the people everywhere shall have that sense of perfect security which is most favorable to calm thought and reflection. The course here indicated will be followed, unless current events and experience shall show a modification or change to be proper; and in every case and exigency my best discretion will be exercised according to circumstances actually existing, and with a view and a hope of a peaceful solution of the national troubles, and the restoration of fraternal sympathies and affections.

That there are persons in one section or another who seek to destroy the Union at all events, and are glad of any pretext to do it, I will neither affirm or deny; but if there be such, I need address no word to them. To those, however, who really love the Union, may I not speak?

Before entering upon so grave a matter as the destruction of our national fabric, with all its benefits, its memories and its hopes, would it not be wise to ascertain precisely why we do it? Will you hazard so desperate a step, while there is any possibility that any portion of the ills you fly from have no real existence? Will you, while the certain ills you fly to, are greater than all the real ones you fly from? Will you risk the commission of so fearful a mistake?

All profess to be content in the Union, if all constitutional rights can be maintained. Is it true, then, that any right, plainly written in the Constitution, has been denied? I think not. Happily the human mind is so constituted, that no party can reach to the audacity of doing this. Think, if you can, of a single instance in which a plainly written provision of the Constitution has ever been denied. If, by the mere force of numbers, a majority should deprive a minority of any clearly written constitutional right, it might, in a moral point of view, justify revolution—certainly would, if such a right were a vital one. But such is not our case. All the vital rights of minorities, and of individuals, are so plainly assured to them, by affirmations and negations, guarantees and prohibitions, in the Constitution, that controversies never arise concerning them. But no organic law can ever be framed with a provision specifically applicable to every question which may occur in practical administration. No foresight can anticipate, nor any document of reasonable length contain express provisions for all possible questions. Shall fugitives from labor be surrendered by national or by State authority? The Constitution does not expressly say. *May* Congress prohibit slavery in the territories? The Constitution does not expressly say. *Must* Congress protect slavery in the territories? The Constitution does not expressly say.

From questions of this class spring all our constitutional controversies, and we divide upon them into majorities and minorities.

If the minority will not acquiesce, the majority must, or the government must cease. There is no other alternative; for continuing the government, is acquiescence on one side or the other. If a minority, in such case, will secede rather than acquiesce, they make a precedent which, in turn, will divide and ruin them; for a minority of their own will secede from them whenever a majority refuses to be controlled by such minority. For instance, why may not any portion of a new confederacy, a year or two hence, arbitrarily secede again, precisely as portions of the present Union now claim to secede from it? All who cherish disunion sentiments, are now being educated to the exact temper of doing this.

Is there such perfect identity of interests among the States to compose a new Union, as to produce harmony only, and prevent renewed secession?

Plainly, the central idea of secession, is the essence of anarchy. A majority, held in restraint by constitutional checks and limitations, and always changing easily with deliberate changes of popular opinions and sentiments is the only true sovereign of a free people. Whoever rejects it, does, of necessity, fly to anarchy or to despotism. Unanimity is impossible; the rule of a minority, as a permanent arrangement, is wholly inadmissible; so that, rejecting the majority principle, anarchy or despotism in some form is all that is left.

I do not forget the position assumed by some, that constitutional questions are to be decided by the Supreme Court; nor do I deny that such decisions must be binding in any case, upon the parties to a suit, as to the object of that suit, while they are also entitled to very high respect and consideration in all parallel cases by all other departments of the government. And while it is obviously possible that such decision may be erroneous in any given case, still the evil effect following it, being limited to that particular case, with the chance that it may be over-ruled, and never become a precedent for other cases, can better be borne than could the evils of a different practice. At the same time, the candid citizen must confess that if the policy of the government upon vital questions, affecting the whole people, is to be irrevocably fixed by decisions of the Supreme Court, the instant they are made, in ordinary litigation between parties, in personal actions, the people will have ceased to be their own rulers, having to that extent practically resigned their government into the hands of that eminent tribunal. Nor is there in this view any assault upon the court or the judges. It is a duty from which they may not shrink, to decide cases properly brought before them; and it is no fault of theirs if others seek to turn their decisions to political purposes.

One section of our country believes slavery is *right*, and ought to be extended, while the other believes it is *wrong*, and ought not to be extended. This is the only substantial dispute. The fugitive slave clause of the Constitution, and the law for the suppression of the foreign slave trade, are each as well enforced, perhaps, as any law can ever be in a community where the moral sense of the people imperfectly supports the law itself. The great body of the people abide by the dry legal obligation in both cases, and a few break over in each. This, I think, cannot be perfectly cured; and it would be worse in both cases *after* the separation of the sections, than before. The foreign slave trade, now imperfectly suppressed, would be ultimately revived without restriction, in one section; while fugitive slaves, now only partially surrendered, would not be surrendered at all, by the other.

Physically speaking, we cannot separate. We cannot remove our respective sections from each other, nor build an impassable wall between them. A husband and wife may be divorced, and go out of the presence, and beyond the reach of each other; but the different parts of our country cannot do this. They cannot but remain face to face; and intercourse, either amicable or hostile, must continue between them. Is it possible, then, to make that intercourse more advantageous or more satisfactory, *after* separation than *before*? Can aliens make treaties easier than friends can make laws? Can treaties be more faithfully enforced between aliens than laws can among friends? Suppose you go to war, you cannot fight always; and when, after much loss on both sides, and no gain on either, you cease fighting, the identical old questions, as to terms of intercourse, are again upon you.

This country, with its institutions, belongs to the people who inhabit it. Whenever they shall grow weary of the existing government, they can exercise their *constitutional* right of amending it, or their *revolutionary* right to dismember or overthrow it. I cannot be ignorant of the fact that many worthy and patriotic citizens are desirous of having the national Constitution amended. While I make no recommendation of amendments, I fully recognize the rightful authority of the people over the whole subject to be exercised in either of the modes prescribed in the instrument itself; and I should under existing circumstances favor rather than oppose a fair opportunity being afforded the people to act upon it.

I will venture to add that to me the Convention mode seems preferable, in that it allows amendments to originate with the people themselves, instead of only permitting them to take or reject propositions, originated by others, not especially chosen for the purpose, and which might not be precisely such as they would wish to either accept or refuse. I understand a proposed amendment to the Constitution, which amendment, however, I have not seen, has passed Congress, to the effect that the federal government shall never interfere with the domestic institutions of the States, including that of persons held to service. To avoid misconstruction of what I have said, I depart from my purpose not to speak of particular amendments, so far as to say that holding such a provision to now be implied constitutional law, I have no objection to its being made express and irrevocable.

The Chief Magistrate derives all his authority from the people, and they have conferred none upon him to fix terms for the separation of the States. The people themselves can do this also if they choose; but the executive, as such, has nothing to do with it. His duty is to administer the present government, as it came to his hands, and to transmit it, unimpaired by him, to his successor.

Why should there not be a patient confidence in the ultimate justice of the people? Is there any better or equal hope, in the world? In our present differences, is either party without faith of being in the right? If the Almighty Ruler of nations, with his eternal truth and justice, be on your side of the North or on yours of the South, that truth, and that justice, will surely prevail, by the judgment of this great tribunal, the American people.

By the frame of the government under which we live, this same people have wisely given their public servants but little power for mischief; and have, with equal wisdom, provided for the return of that little to their own hands at very short intervals.

While the people retain their virtue and vigilance, no administration, by any extreme of wickedness or folly, can very seriously injure the government in the short space of four years.

My countrymen, one and all, think calmly and *well*, upon this whole subject. Nothing valuable can be lost by taking time. If there be an object to *hurry* any of you, in hot haste, to a step which you would never take *deliberately*, that object will be frustrated by taking time; but no good object can be frustrated by it. Such of you as are now dissatisfied, still have the old Constitution unimpaired, and, on the sensitive point, the laws of your own framing under it; while the new administration will have no immediate power, if it would, to change either. If it were admitted that you who are dissatisfied, hold the right side in the dispute, there still is no single good reason for precipitate action. Intelligence, patriotism, Christianity, and a firm reliance on Him, who has never yet forsaken this favored land, are still competent to adjust, in the best way, all our present difficulty.

In *your* hands, my dissatisfied fellow countrymen, and not in *mine*, is the momentous issue of civil war. The government will not assail *you*. You can have no conflict, without being yourselves the aggressors. *You* have no oath registered in Heaven to destroy the government, while *I* shall have the most solemn one to "preserve, protect and defend" it.

I am loth to close. We are not enemies, but friends. We must not be enemies. Though passion may have strained, it must not break our bonds of affection. The mystic chords of memory, stretching from every battle-field, and patriot grave, to every living heart and hearth-stone, all over this broad land, will yet swell the chorus of the Union, when again touched, as surely they will be, by the better angels of our nature.

As most students of Lincoln know, this address was written in Springfield late in January, 1861. According to William H. Herndon's account Lincoln "locked himself up in a room upstairs over a store across the street from the State House" and wrote the address, using only four references: "Henry Clay's great speech delivered in 1850, Andrew Jackson's proclamation against Nullification, a copy of the Constitution . . . [and] Webster's reply to Hayne."

This first draft was finished and several copies printed for Lincoln before he left Springfield for Washington. The subsequent revisions of several passages make an interesting study, especially in the light of Lincoln's usual inflexibility in the face of suggestions as to changes in language which involved a change in sentiment. Lincoln wished to be completely firm and unequivocal in his language, but he did not wish to fan the flames of secession. Hence, he adopted for this most important utterance some changes in language suggested by O. H. Browning and W. H. Seward. Even here, however, Herndon's statement of Lincoln's inflexibility is not disproved by the adoptions, for in no instance does any suggestion which Lincoln adopted actually involve a change of sentiment.

For a comparative study of the revisions in this address the reader should consult Louis A. Warren's article in Lincoln Lore, *No. 358 and No. 359. The most significant revision is the concluding paragraph in which Lincoln accepted a suggestion from Seward and revised it in his own way. For convenience in making comparison, Seward's suggested close is given as in the facsimile of the original. It will be observed that Lincoln adopted Seward's first choice of diction more often than his final suggestion:*

"I close. We are not we must not be aliens or enemies but ~~countrym~~ fellow countrymen and brethren. Although passion has strained our bonds of affection too hardly they must not ~~be broken they will not~~ I am sure they will not be broken. The mystic chords of memory which proceeding from ~~every ba~~ so many battle fields and ~~patriot~~ so many patriot graves ~~br~~ pass through all the hearts and ~~hearths~~ all the hearths in this broad continent

of ours will yet ~~harmo~~ again harmonize in their ancient music when ~~touched as they surely~~ breathed upon ~~again~~ by the ~~better angel~~ guardian angel of the nation."

Two similar "final" copies of the address are in existence, made up of passages clipped from the first printing and pasted on sheets of paper, with the revised passages written in between and in the margins. In one of these copies the revised passages appear in Nicolay's handwriting. This was the copy prepared for and delivered to the press. In the other copy, from which Lincoln read at the inaugural ceremony, the revised passages are partly in Lincoln's handwriting. After the ceremony Lincoln turned this reading copy over to Crosby Stuart Noyes of the Washington Star, *and from it the* Star *printed the speech on the day it was delivered. A few unimportant variants in the two copies are indicated in the present text, and the punctuation of the concluding paragraph follows (to the extent of two additional commas) the paragraph in Lincoln's handwriting rather than the press copy.*

REPLY TO SECRETARY SEWARD'S MEMORANDUM APRIL 1, 1861

Executive Mansion, April 1, 1861.

Hon. W. H. Seward.
My dear Sir:

Since parting with you I have been considering your paper dated this day, and entitled "Some Thoughts for the President's Consideration." The first proposition in it is, "*First*, We are at the end of a month's administration, and yet without a policy either domestic or foreign."

At the beginning of that month, in the inaugural, I said: "The power confided to me will be used to hold, occupy, and possess the property and places belonging to the government, and to collect the duties and imposts." This had your distinct approval at the time; and, taken in connection with the order I immediately gave General Scott, directing him to employ every means in his power to strengthen and hold the forts, comprises the exact domestic policy you now urge, with the single exception that it does not propose to abandon Fort Sumter.

Again, I do not perceive how the reinforcement of Fort Sumter would be done on a slavery or a party issue, while that of Fort Pickens would be on a more national and patriotic one.

The news received yesterday in regard to St. Domingo certainly brings a new item within the range of our foreign policy; but up to that time we have been preparing circulars and instructions to ministers and the like, all in perfect harmony, without even a suggestion that we had no foreign policy.

Upon your closing propositions—that "whatever policy we adopt, there must be an energetic prosecution of it.

"For this purpose it must be somebody's business to pursue and direct it incessantly.

"Either the President must do it himself, and be all the while active in it, or

"Devolve it on some member of his cabinet. Once adopted, debates on it must end, and all agree and abide"—I remark that if this must be done, I must do it. When a general line of policy is adopted, I apprehend there is no danger of its being changed without good reason, or continuing to be a subject of unnecessary debate; still, upon points arising in its progress I wish, and suppose I am entitled to have, the advice of all the cabinet.

Your obedient servant,

A. Lincoln.

LETTER TO COLONEL E. E. ELLSWORTH
APRIL 15, 1861

Washington, April 15. 1861

Col. E. E. Ellsworth
My dear Sir:

Ever since the beginning of our acquaintance, I have valued you highly as a person [*sic*] friend, and at the same time (without much capacity of judging) have had a very high estimate of your military talent. Accordingly I have been, and still am anxious for you to have the best position in the military which can be given you, consistently with justice and proper courtesy towards the older officers of the army. I can not incurr [*sic*] the risk of doing them injustice, or a discurtesy [*sic*]; but I do say they would personally oblige me, if they could, and would place you in some position, or in some service, satisfactory to yourself.

Your Obt. Servt.
A. Lincoln

Ellsworth had been a student of law in Lincoln's office and had accompanied him to Washington as a personal friend and quasi bodyguard. He organized a volunteer regiment of Zouaves that achieved fame for martial appearance and precise drill. During the occupation of Alexandria, Virginia, he became one of the early casualties of the war (the only casualty on this occasion), when he was shot by a hotel proprietor whose Confederate flag Ellsworth was personally removing from the building. Lincoln's admiration for him is fully expressed in the succeeding letter written to Ellsworth's parents.

LETTER TO COLONEL E. E. ELLSWORTH'S PARENTS. MAY 25, 1861

Washington D. C. May 25. 1861.

To the Father and Mother of Col. Elmer E. Ellsworth:
My dear Sir and Madam,

In the untimely loss of your noble son, our affliction here, is scarcely less than your own. So much of promised usefulness to one's country, and of bright hopes for one's self and friends, have rarely been so suddenly dashed, as in his fall. In size, in years, and in youthful appearance, a boy only, his power to command men, was surpassingly great. This power, combined with a fine intellect, an indomitable energy, and a taste altogether military, constituted in him, as seemed to me, the best natural talent, in that department, I ever knew.

And yet he was singularly modest and deferential in social intercourse. My acquaintance with him began less than two years ago; yet through the latter half of the intervening period, it was as intimate as the disparity of our ages, and my engrossing engagements, would permit. To me, he appeared to have no indulgences or pastimes; and I never heard him utter a profane, or an intemperate word. What was conclusive of his good heart, he never forgot his parents. The honors he labored for so laudably, and, in the sad end, so gallantly gave his life, he meant for them, no less than for himself.

In the hope that it may be no intrusion upon the sacredness of your sorrow, I have ventured to address you this tribute to the memory of my young friend, and your brave and early fallen child.

May God give you that consolation which is beyond all earthly power.

Sincerely your friend in a common affliction—

A. Lincoln

MESSAGE TO CONGRESS IN SPECIAL SESSION
JULY 4, 1861

Fellow-Citizens of the Senate and House of Representatives:

Having been convened on an extraordinary occasion, as authorized by the Constitution, your attention is not called to any ordinary subject of legislation.

At the beginning of the present presidential term, four months ago, the functions of the Federal Government were found to be generally suspended within the several States of South Carolina, Georgia, Alabama, Mississippi, Louisiana, and Florida, excepting only those of the Post Office Department.

Within these States all the forts, arsenals, dockyards, custom-houses, and the like, including the movable and stationary property in and about them, had been seized, and were held in open hostility to this Government, excepting only Forts Pickens, Taylor, and Jefferson, on and near the Florida coast, and Fort Sumter, in Charleston harbor, South Carolina. The forts thus seized had been put in improved condition, new ones had been built, and armed forces had been organized and were organizing, all avowedly with the same hostile purpose.

The forts remaining in the possession of the Federal Government in and near these States were either besieged or menaced by warlike preparations, and especially Fort Sumter was nearly surrounded by well-protected hostile batteries, with guns equal in quality to the best of its own, and outnumbering the latter as perhaps ten to one. A disproportionate share of the Federal muskets and rifles had somehow found their way into these States, and had been seized to be used against the Government. Accumulations of the public revenue, lying within them, had been seized for the same object. The Navy was scattered in distant seas, leaving but a very small part of it within the immediate reach of the Government. Officers of the Federal Army and Navy had resigned in great numbers; and of those resigning, a large proportion had taken up arms against the Government. Simultaneously, and in connection with all this, the purpose to sever the Federal Union was openly avowed. In accordance with this purpose, an ordinance had been adopted in each of these States, declaring the States, respectively, to be separated from the National Union. A formula for instituting a combined government of these States had been promulgated; and this illegal organization in the character of confederate States, was already invoking recognition, aid, and intervention, from foreign Powers.

Finding this condition of things, and believing it to be an imperative duty upon the incoming Executive to prevent, if possible, the consummation of such attempt to destroy the Federal Union, a choice of means to that end became indispensable. This choice was made, and was declared in the inaugural address. The policy chosen looked to the exhaustion of all peaceful measures, before a resort to any stronger ones. It sought only to hold the public places and property not already wrested from the Government, and to collect the revenue, relying for the rest on time, discussion, and the ballot-box. It promised a continuance of the mails, at Government expense, to the very people who were resisting the Government; and it gave repeated pledges against any disturbance to any of the people, or any of their rights. Of all that which a President might constitutionally and justifiably do in such a case, everything was forborne, without which it was believed possible to keep the government on foot.

On the 5th of March, (the present incumbent's first full day in office,) a letter of Major Anderson, commanding at Fort Sumter, written on the 28th of February, and received at the War Department on the 4th of March, was, by that Department, placed in his hands. This letter expressed the professional opinion of the writer, that reinforcements could not be thrown into that fort within the time for his relief, rendered necessary by the limited supply of provisions, and with a view of holding possession of the same, with a force of less than twenty thousand good and well disciplined men. This opinion was concurred in by all the officers of his command, and their *memoranda* on the subject were made inclosures of Major Anderson's letter. The whole was immediately laid before Lieutenant General Scott, who at once concurred with Major Anderson in opinion. On reflection, however, he took full time, consulting with other officers, both of the Army and the Navy, and, at the end of four days, came reluctantly, but decidedly, to the same conclusion as before. He also stated at the same time that no such sufficient force was then at the control of the Government, or could be raised and brought to the ground within the time when the provisions in the fort would be exhausted. In a purely military point of view, this reduced the duty of the Administration in the case, to the mere matter of getting the garrison safely out of the fort.

It was believed, however, that to so abandon that position, under the circumstances, would be utterly ruinous; that the *necessity* under which it was to be done would not be fully understood; that by many it would be construed as a part of a *voluntary* policy; that at home it would discourage the friends of the Union, embolden its adversaries, and go far to insure to the latter a recognition abroad; that, in fact, it would be our national destruction consummated. This could not be allowed. Starvation was not yet upon the garrison; and ere it would be reached *Fort Pickens* might be reinforced. This last would be a clear indication of *policy*, and would better enable the country to accept the evacuation of Fort Sumter as a military *necessity*. An order was at once directed to be sent for the landing of the troops from the steamship Brooklyn into Fort Pickens. This order could not go by land, but must take the longer and slower route by sea. The first return news from the order was received just one week before the fall of Fort Sumter. The news itself was that the officer commanding the Sabine, to which vessel the troops had been transferred from the Brooklyn, acting upon some *quasi* armistice of the late Administration, (and of the existence of which the present Administration, up to the time the order was dispatched, had only too vague and uncertain rumors to fix attention,) had refused to land the troops. To now reinforce Fort Pickens before a crisis would be reached at Fort Sumter was impossible—rendered so by the near exhaustion of provisions in the latter-named fort. In precaution against such a conjuncture, the Government had a few days before commenced preparing an expedition, as well adapted as might be, to relieve

Fort Sumter, which expedition was intended to be ultimately used or not, according to circumstances. The strongest anticipated case for using it was now presented; and it was resolved to send it forward. As had been intended in this contingency, it was also resolved to notify the Governor of South Carolina that he might expect an attempt would be made to provision the fort; and that, if the attempt should not be resisted, there would be no effort to throw in men, arms, or ammunition, without further notice, or in case of an attack upon the fort. This notice was accordingly given; whereupon the fort was attacked and bombarded to its fall, without even awaiting the arrival of the provisioning expedition.

It is thus seen that the assault upon and reduction of Fort Sumter was in no sense a matter of self defense on the part of the assailants. They well knew that the garrison in the fort could by no possibility commit aggression upon them. They knew—they were expressly notified—that the giving of bread to the few brave and hungry men of the garrison was all which would on that occasion be attempted, unless themselves, by resisting so much, should provoke more. They knew that this Government desired to keep the garrison in the fort, not to assail them, but merely to maintain visible possession, and thus to preserve the Union from actual and immediate dissolution—trusting, as hereinbefore stated, to time, discussion, and the ballot-box, for final adjustment; and they assailed and reduced the fort for precisely the reverse object—to drive out the visible authority of the Federal Union, and thus force it to immediate dissolution. That this was their object, the Executive well understood; and having said to them in the inaugural address, "You can have no conflict without being yourselves the aggressors," he took pains not only to keep this declaration good, but also to keep the case so free from the power of ingenious sophistry that the world should not be able to misunderstand it. By the affair at Fort Sumter, with its surrounding circumstances, that point was reached. Then and thereby the assailants of the Government began the conflict of arms, without a gun in sight or in expectancy to return their fire, save only the few in the fort, sent to that harbor years before for their own protection, and still ready to give that protection in whatever was lawful. In this act, discarding all else, they have forced upon the country the distinct issue, "immediate dissolution or blood."

And this issue embraces more than the fate of these United States. It presents to the whole family of man the question, whether a constitutional republic, or democracy—a Government of the people by the same people—can or cannot maintain its territorial integrity against its own domestic foes. It presents the question, whether discontented individuals, too few in numbers to control administration, according to organic law, in any case, can always, upon the pretenses made in this case, or on any other pretenses, or arbitrarily, without any pretense, break up their Government, and thus practically put an end to free government upon the earth. It forces us to ask: "Is there, in all republics, this inherent and fatal weakness?" "Must a Government, of necessity, be too *strong* for the liberties of its own people, or too *weak* to maintain its own existence?"

So viewing the issue, no choice was left but to call out the war power of the Government; and so to resist force employed for its destruction, by force for its preservation.

The call was made, and the response of the country was most gratifying, surpassing in unanimity and spirit the most sanguine expectation. Yet none of the States commonly called slave States, except Delaware, gave a regiment through regular State organization. A few regiments have been organized within some others of those States by individual enterprise, and received into the Government service. Of course, the seceded States, so called, (and to which Texas had been joined about the time of the inauguration,) gave no troops to the cause of the Union. The border States, so called, were not uniform in their action, some of them being almost *for* the Union, while in others—as Virginia, North Carolina, Tennessee, and Arkansas—the Union sentiment was nearly repressed and silenced. The course taken in Virginia was the most remarkable—perhaps the most important. A convention, elected by the people of that State to consider this very question of disrupting the Federal Union, was in session at the capital of Virginia when Fort Sumter fell. To this body the people had chosen a large majority of *professed* Union men. Almost immediately after the fall of Sumter, many members of that majority went over to the original disunion minority, and, with them, adopted an ordinance for withdrawing the State from the Union. Whether this change was wrought by their great approval of the assault upon Sumter, or their great resentment at the Government's resistance to that assault, is not definitely known. Although they submitted the ordinance, for ratification, to a vote of the people, to be taken on a day then somewhat more than a month distant, the convention and the Legislature, (which was also in session at the same time and place,) with leading men of the State, not members of either, immediately commenced acting as if the State were already out of the Union. They pushed military preparations vigorously forward all over the State. They seized the United States armory at Harper's Ferry, and the navy-yard at Gosport, near Norfolk. They received—perhaps invited—into their State large bodies of troops, with their warlike appointments, from the so-called seceded States. They formally entered into a treaty of temporary alliance and cooperation with the so-called "Confederate States," and sent members to their congress at Montgomery; and, finally, they permitted the insurrectionary government to be transferred to their capital at Richmond.

The people of Virginia have thus allowed this giant insurrection to make its nest within her borders; and this Government has no choice left but to deal with it *where* it finds it. And it has the less regret, as the loyal citizens have in due form claimed its protection. Those loyal citizens this Government is bound to recognize and protect as being Virginia.

In the border States, so called—in fact, the Middle States —there are those who favor a policy which they call "armed neutrality;" that is, an arming of those States to prevent the Union forces passing one way, or the disunion the other, over their soil. This would be disunion completed. Figuratively speaking, it would be the building of an impassable wall along the line of separation—and yet not quite an impassable one; for, under the guise of neutrality, it would tie the hands of the Union men, and freely pass supplies from among them to the insurrectionists, which it could not do as an open enemy. At a stroke it would take all the trouble off the hands of secession, except only what proceeds from the external blockade. It would do for the disunionists that which of all things they most desire—feed them well and give them disunion without a struggle of their own. It recognizes no fidelity to the Constitution, no obligation to maintain the Union; and while very many who have favored it are doubtless loyal citizens, it is, nevertheless, very injurious in effect.

Recurring to the action of the Government, it may be stated that at first a call was made for seventy-five thousand militia; and rapidly following this a proclamation was issued for closing the ports of the insurrectionary districts by proceedings in the nature of a blockade. So far all was believed to be strictly legal. At this point the insurrectionists announced their purpose to enter upon the practice of privateering.

Other calls were made for volunteers to serve for three years, unless sooner discharged, and also for large additions to the regular Army and Navy. These measures, whether strictly legal or not, were ventured upon under what appeared to be a popular demand and a public necessity; trusting then as now that Congress would readily ratify them. It is believed that nothing has been done beyond the constitutional competency of Congress.

Soon after the first call for militia, it was considered a duty to authorize the commanding general in proper cases, according to his discretion, to suspend the privilege of the writ of *habeas corpus*, or, in other words, to arrest and detain, without resort to the ordinary processes and forms of law, such individuals as he might deem dangerous to the public safety. This authority has purposely been exercised but very sparingly. Nevertheless, the legality and propriety of what has been done under it are questioned, and the attention of the country has been called to the proposition that one who is sworn to "take care that the laws be faithfully executed" should not himself violate them. Of course some consideration was given to the questions of power and propriety before this matter was acted upon. The whole of the laws which were required to be faithfully executed were being resisted, and failing of execution in nearly one third of the States. Must they be allowed to finally fail of execution, even had it been perfectly clear that by the use of the means necessary to their execution some single law, made in such extreme tenderness of the citizen's liberty, that practically it relieves more of the guilty than of the innocent, should to a very limited extent be violated?

To state the question more directly: are all the laws *but one* to go unexecuted, and the Government itself go to pieces, lest that one be violated? Even in such a case, would not the official oath be broken if the government should be overthrown, when it was believed that disregarding the single law would tend to preserve it? But it was not believed that this question was presented. It was not believed that any law was violated. The provision of the Constitution that "the privilege of the writ of *habeas corpus* shall not be suspended unless when, in cases of rebellion or invasion, the public safety may require it," is equivalent to a provision—is a provision—that such privilege may be suspended when, in case of rebellion or invasion, the public safety *does* require it. It was decided that we have a case of rebellion, and that the public safety does require the qualified suspension of the privilege of the writ which was authorized to be made. Now, it is insisted that Congress, and not the Executive, is vested with this power. But the Constitution itself is silent as to which or who is to exercise the power; and as the provision was plainly made for a dangerous emergency, it cannot be believed the framers of the instrument intended that in every case the danger should run its course until Congress could be called together; the very assembling of which might be prevented, as was intended in this case, by the rebellion.

No more extended argument is now offered, as an opinion, at some length, will probably be presented by the Attorney General. Whether there shall be any legislation upon the subject, and if any, what, is submitted entirely to the better judgment of Congress.

The forbearance of this Government had been so extraordinary, and so long continued, as to lead some foreign nations to shape their action as if they supposed the early destruction of our national Union was probable. While this, on discovery, gave the Executive some concern, he is now happy to say that the sovereignty and rights of the United States are now everywhere practically respected by foreign Powers; and a general sympathy with the country is manifested throughout the world.

The reports of the Secretaries of the Treasury, War, and the Navy, will give the information in detail deemed necessary and convenient for your deliberation and action; while the Executive and all the Departments will stand ready to supply omissions, or to communicate new facts considered important for you to know.

It is now recommended that you give the legal means for making this contest a short and a decisive one; that you place at the control of the Government, for the work, at least four hundred thousand men, and $400,000,000. That number of men is about one tenth of those of proper ages within the regions where, apparently, *all* are willing to engage; and the sum is less than a twenty-third part of the money value owned by the men who seem ready to devote the whole. A debt of $600,000,000 *now*, is a less sum per head than was the debt of our Revolution when we came out of that struggle; and the money value in the country now bears even a greater proportion to what it was *then*, than does the population. Surely each man has as strong a motive *now* to *preserve* our liberties, as each had *then* to *establish* them.

A right result, at this time, will be worth more to the world than ten times the men and ten times the money. The evidence reaching us from the country leaves no doubt that the material for the work is abundant, and that it needs only the hand of legislation to give it legal sanction, and the hand of the executive to give it practical shape and efficiency. One of the greatest perplexities of the Government is to avoid receiving troops faster than it can provide for them. In a word, the people will save their Government if the Government itself will do its part only indifferently well.

It might seem, at first thought, to be of little difference whether the present movement at the South be called "secession" or "rebellion." The movers, however, well understand the difference. At the beginning they knew they could never raise their treason to any respectable magnitude by any name which implies *violation* of law. They knew their people possessed as much of moral sense, as much of devotion to law and order, and as much pride in, and reverence for, the history and Government of their common country, as any other civilized and patriotic people. They knew they could make no advancement directly in the teeth of these strong and noble sentiments. Accordingly they commenced by an insidious debauching of the public mind. They invented an ingenious sophism, which, if conceded, was followed by perfectly logical steps, through all the incidents, to the complete destruction of the Union. The sophism itself is, that any State of the Union may, *consistently* with the national Constitution, and therefore *lawfully* and *peacefully*, withdraw from the Union without the consent of the Union or of any other State. The little disguise that the supposed right is to be exercised only for just cause, themselves to be the sole judge of its justice, is too thin to merit any notice.

With rebellion thus sugar-coated they have been drugging the public mind of their section for more than thirty years, and until at length they have brought many good men to a willingness to take up arms against the Government the day *after* some assemblage of men have enacted the farcical pretense of taking their State out of the Union, who could have been brought to no such thing the day *before.*

This sophism derives much, perhaps the whole, of its currency from the assumption that there is some omnipotent and sacred supremacy pertaining to a *State*—to each State of our Federal Union. Our States have neither more nor less power than that reserved to them in the Union by the Constitution—no one of them ever having been a State *out* of the Union. The original ones passed into the Union even *before* they cast off their British colonial dependence; and the new ones each came into the Union directly from a condition of dependence, excepting Texas. And even Texas, in its temporary independence, was never designated a State. The new ones only took the designation of States on coming into the Union, while that name was first adopted for the old ones in and by the Declaration of Independence. Therein the "United Colonies" were declared to be "free and independent States;" but, even then, the object plainly was not to declare their independence of *one another*, or of the *Union*, but directly the contrary, as their mutual pledge, and their mutual action, before, at the time, and afterwards, abundantly show. The express plighting of faith by each and all of the original thirteen in the Articles of Confederation, two years later, that the Union shall be perpetual, is most conclusive. Having never been States, either in substance or in name, *outside* of the

Union, whence this magical omnipotence of "State rights," asserting a claim of power to lawfully destroy the Union itself? Much is said about the "sovereignty" of the States; but the word, even, is not in the national Constitution; nor, as is believed, in any of the State constitutions. What is "sovereignty," in the political sense of the term? Would it be far wrong to define it "a political community, without a political superior"? Tested by this, no one of our States, except Texas, ever was a sovereignty. And even Texas gave up the character on coming into the Union; by which act she acknowledged the Constitution of the United States and the laws and treaties of the United States made in pursuance of the Constitution to be, for her, the supreme law of the land. The States have their *status* in the Union, and they have no other legal *status*. If they break from this, they can only do so against law and by revolution. The Union, and not themselves separately, procured their independence and their liberty. By conquest, or purchase, the Union gave each of them whatever of independence and liberty it has. The Union is older than any of the States, and, in fact, it created them as States. Originally some dependent colonies made the Union, and, in turn, the Union threw off their old dependence for them, and made them States, such as they are. Not one of them ever had a State constitution independent of the Union. Of course, it is not forgotten that all the new States framed their constitutions before they entered the Union; nevertheless, dependent upon, and preparatory to, coming into the Union.

Unquestionably the States have the powers and rights reserved to them in and by the national Constitution; but among these, surely, are not included all conceivable powers, however mischievous or destructive; but, at most, such only as were known in the world, at the time, as governmental powers; and certainly a power to destroy the Government itself had never been known as a governmental—as a merely administrative power. This relative matter of national power and State rights, as a principle, is no other than the principle of *generality* and *locality*. Whatever concerns the whole should be confided to the whole—to the General Government; while whatever concerns *only* the State should be left exclusively to the State. This is all there is of original principle about it. Whether the National Constitution in defining boundaries between the two has applied the principle with exact accuracy, is not to be questioned. We are all bound by that defining, without question.

What is now combated, is the position that secession is *consistent* with the Constitution—is *lawful* and *peaceful*. It is not contended that there is any express law for it; and nothing should ever be implied as law which leads to unjust or absurd consequences. The nation purchased with money the countries out of which several of these States were formed: is it just that they shall go off without leave and without refunding? The nation paid very large sums (in the aggregate, I believe, nearly a hundred millions) to relieve Florida of the aboriginal tribes: is it just that she shall now be off without consent, or without making any return? The nation is now in debt for money applied to the benefit of these so-called seceding States in common with the rest: is it just either that creditors shall go unpaid, or the remaining States pay the whole? A part of the present national debt was contracted to pay the old debts of Texas: is it just that she shall leave and pay no part of this herself?

Again: if one State may secede, so may another; and when all shall have seceded, none is left to pay the debts. Is this quite just to creditors? Did we notify them of this sage view of ours when we borrowed their money? If we now recognize this doctrine by allowing the seceders to go in peace, it is difficult to see what we can do if others choose to go, or to extort terms upon which they will promise to remain.

The seceders insist that our Constitution admits of secession. They have assumed to make a national constitution of their own, in which, of necessity, they have either *discarded* or *retained* the right of secession, as they insist it exists in ours. If they have discarded it, they thereby admit that, on principle, it ought not to be in ours. If they have retained it, by their own construction of ours they show that, to be consistent, they must secede from one another whenever they shall find it the easiest way of settling their debts, or effecting any other selfish or unjust object. The principle itself is one of disintegration, and upon which no Government can possibly endure.

If all the States, save one, should assert the power to *drive* that one out of the Union, it is presumed the whole class of seceder politicians would at once deny the power, and denounce the act as the greatest outrage upon State rights. But suppose that precisely the same act, instead of being called "driving the one out," should be called "the seceding of the others from that one:" it would be exactly what the seceders claim to do; unless, indeed, they make the point that the one, because it is a minority, may rightfully do what the others, because they are a majority, may not rightfully do. These politicians are subtile and profound on the rights of minorities. They are not partial to that power which made the Constitution, and speaks from the preamble, calling itself "We, the People."

It may well be questioned whether there is, to-day, a majority of the legally-qualified voters of any State, except perhaps South Carolina, in favor of disunion. There is much reason to believe that the Union men are the majority in many, if not in every other one, of the so-called seceded States. The contrary has not been demonstrated in any one of them. It is ventured to affirm this even of Virginia and Tennessee; for the result of an election held in military camps, where the bayonets are all on one side of the question voted upon, can scarcely be considered as demonstrating popular sentiment. At such an election, all that large class who are at once *for* the Union, and *against* coercion, would be coerced to vote against the Union.

It may be affirmed, without extravagance, that the free institutions we enjoy have developed the powers and improved the condition of our whole people, beyond any example in the world. Of this we now have a striking and an impressive illustration. So large an army as the government has now on foot was never before known without a soldier in it but who had taken his place there of his own free choice. But more than this: there are many single regiments whose members, one and another, possess full practical knowledge of all the arts, sciences, professions, and whatever else, whether useful or elegant, is known in the world; and there is scarcely one from which there could not be selected a President, a Cabinet, a Congress, and perhaps a court, abundantly competent to administer the Government itself! Nor do I say this is not true also in the army of our late friends, now adversaries, in this contest; but if it is, so much better the reason why the Government which has conferred such benefits on both them and us should not be broken up. Whoever, in any section, proposes to abandon such a Government, would do well to consider, in deference to what principle it is that he does it; what better he is likely to get in its stead; whether the substitute will give, or be intended to give, so much of good to the people? There are some foreshadowings on this subject. Our adversaries have adopted some declarations of independence, in which, unlike the good old one, penned by Jefferson, they omit the words "all men are created equal." Why? They have adopted a temporary national constitution, in the preamble of which, unlike our good old one, signed by Washington, they omit "We, the People," and substitute "We, the deputies of the sovereign and independent States." Why? Why this deliberate pressing out of view the rights of men and the authority of the people?

This is essentially a people's contest. On the side of the Union, it is a struggle for maintaining in the world that form and substance of government whose leading object is to elevate the condition of men; to lift artificial weights from all shoulders; to clear the paths of laudable pursuit for all; to afford all an unfettered start and a fair chance in the race of life. Yielding to partial and temporary departures, from necessity, this is the leading object of the Government for whose existence we contend.

I am most happy to believe that the plain people understand and appreciate this. It is worthy of note, that while in this the Government's hour of trial, large numbers of those in the Army and Navy who have been favored with the offices have resigned and proved false to the hand which had pampered them, not one common soldier or common sailor is known to have deserted his flag.

Great honor is due to those officers who remained true, despite the example of their treacherous associates; but the greatest honor, and most important fact of all, is the unanimous firmness of the common soldiers and common sailors. To the last man, so far as known, they have successfully resisted the traitorous efforts of those whose commands, but an hour before, they obeyed as absolute law. This is the patriotic instinct of plain people. They understand, without an argument, that the destroying the Government which was made by Washington means no good to them.

Our popular government has often been called an experiment. Two points in it our people have already settled—the successful *establishing* and the successful *administering* of it. One still remains—its successful *maintenance* against a formidable internal attempt to overthrow it. It is now for them to demonstrate to the world that those who can fairly carry an election can also suppress a rebellion; that ballots are the rightful and peaceful successors of bullets; and that when ballots have fairly and constitutionally decided, there can be no successful appeal back to bullets; that there can be no successful appeal except to ballots themselves, at succeeding elections. Such will be a great lesson of peace; teaching men that what they cannot take by an election, neither can they take by a war; teaching all the folly of being the beginners of a war.

Lest there be some uneasiness in the minds of candid men as to what is to be the course of the Government towards the southern States *after* the rebellion shall have been suppressed, the Executive deems it proper to say, it will be his purpose then, as ever, to be guided by the Constitution and the laws; and that he probably will have no different understanding of the powers and duties of the Federal Government relatively [relative?] to the rights of the States and the people, under the Constitution than that expressed in the inaugural address.

He desires to preserve the Government, that it may be administered for all, as it was administered by the men who made it. Loyal citizens everywhere have the right to claim this of their Government, and the Government has no right to withhold or neglect it. It is not perceived that, in giving it, there is any coercion, any conquest, or any subjugation, in any just sense of those terms.

The Constitution provides, and all the States have accepted the provision, that "the United States shall guaranty to every State in this Union a republican form of Government." But if a State may lawfully go out of the Union, having done so, it may also discard the republican form of Government; so that to prevent its going out is an indispensable *means* to the *end* of maintaining the guarantee mentioned; and when an end is lawful and obligatory, the indispensable means to it are also lawful and obligatory.

It was with the deepest regret that the Executive found the duty of employing the war power in defense of the Government forced upon him. He could but perform this duty, or surrender the existence of the Government. No compromise by public servants could in this case be a cure; not that compromises are not often proper, but that no popular Government can long survive a marked precedent that those who carry an election can only save the Government from immediate destruction by giving up the main point upon which the people gave the election. The people themselves, and not their servants, can safely reverse their own deliberate decisions.

As a private citizen, the Executive could not have consented that these institutions shall perish; much less could he, in betrayal of so vast and so sacred a trust as these free people have confided to him. He felt that he had no moral right to shrink, or even to count the chances of his own life, in what might follow. In full view of his great responsibility, he has, so far, done what he has deemed his duty. You will now, according to your own judgment, perform yours. He sincerely hopes that your views and your action may so accord with his as to assure all faithful citizens who have been disturbed in their rights of a certain and speedy restoration to them, under the Constitution and the laws.

And having thus chosen our course, without guile and with pure purpose, let us renew our trust in God, and go forward without fear and with manly hearts.

Abraham Lincoln.

July 4, 1861.

The text of this message is from the Congressional Globe. *Although the editor was able to locate the official manuscripts of the other messages and proclamations in the National Archives or the Library of Congress, he failed to find any trace of the manuscript of this one.*

PROCLAMATION OF A NATIONAL FAST-DAY AUGUST 12, 1861

By the President of the United States of America:

A PROCLAMATION.

Whereas a joint Committee of both Houses of Congress has waited on the President of the United States, and requested him to "recommend a day of public humiliation, prayer and fasting, to be observed by the people of the United States with religious solemnities, and the offering of fervent supplications to Almighty God for the safety and welfare of these States, His blessings on their arms, and a speedy restoration of peace":—

And whereas it is fit and becoming in all people, at all times, to acknowledge and revere the Supreme Government of God; to bow in humble submission to His chastisements; to confess and deplore their sins and transgressions in the full conviction that the fear of the Lord is the beginning of wisdom; and to pray, with all fervency and contrition, for the pardon of their past offences, and for a blessing upon their present and prospective action:

And whereas, when our own beloved Country, once, by the blessing of God, united, prosperous and happy, is now afflicted with faction and civil war, it is peculiarly fit for us to recognize the hand of God in this terrible visitation, and in sorrowful remembrance of our own faults and crimes as a nation and as individuals, to humble ourselves before Him and to pray for His mercy,—to pray that we may be spared farther punishment, though most justly deserved; that our arms may be blessed and made effectual for the reestablishment of law, order and peace, throughout the wide extent of our country; and that the inestimable boon of civil and religious liberty, earned under His guidance and blessing, by the labors and sufferings of our fathers, may be restored in all its original excellence:—

Therefore, I, Abraham Lincoln, President of the United States, do appoint the last Thursday in September next, as a day of humiliation, prayer and fasting for all the people of the nation. And I do earnestly recommend to all the People, and especially to all ministers and teachers of religion of all denominations, and to all heads of families, to observe and keep that day according to their several creeds and modes of worship, in all humility and with all religious solemnity, to the end that the united prayer of the nation may ascend to the Throne of Grace, and bring down plentiful blessings upon our Country.

[L. S.] In testimony whereof, I have hereunto set my hand, and caused the Seal of the United States to be affixed, this 12th day of August A.D. 1861, and of the Independence of the United States of America the 86th.

By the President: Abraham Lincoln.

William H. Seward,
Secretary of State

LETTER TO GOVERNOR BERIAH MAGOFFIN AUGUST 24, 1861

Washington D. C August 24. 1861

To His Excellency
B. Magoffin
Governor of the State of Kentucky
Sir:

Your letter of the 19th. Inst. in which you "*urge the removal from the limits of Kentucky of the military force now organized, and in camp within said State*" is received.

I may not possess full and precisely accurate knowledge upon this subject; but I believe it is true that there is a military force in camp within Kentucky, acting by authority of the United States, which force is not very large, and is not now being augmented.

I also believe that some arms have been furnished to this force by the United States.

I also believe that this force consists exclusively of Kentuckians, having their camp in the immediate vicinity of their own homes, and not assailing, or menacing, any of the good people of Kentucky.

In all I have done in the premises, I have acted upon the urgent solicitation of many Kentuckians, and in accordance with what I believed, and still believe, to be the wish of a majority of all the Union-loving people of Kentucky

While I have conversed on this subject with many eminent men of Kentucky, including a large majority of her Members of Congress, I do not remember that any one of them, or any other person, except your Excellency and the bearers of your Excellency's letter, has urged me to remove the military force from Kentucky, or to disband it. One other very worthy citizen of Kentucky did solicit me to have the augmenting of the force suspended for a time.

Taking all the means within my reach to form a judgment, I do not believe it is the popular wish of Kentucky that this force shall be removed beyond her limits; and, with this impression, I must respectfully decline to so remove it.

I most cordially sympathize with your Excellency, in the wish to preserve the peace of my own native State, Kentucky; but it is with regret I search, and can not find, in your not very short letter, any declaration, or intimation, that you entertain any desire for the preservation of the Federal Union.

Your Obedient Servant,

A. Lincoln

Governor Beriah Magoffin consistently attempted to take Kentucky into the Confederacy but was thwarted by the majority of Union members in the two branches of the Kentucky Legislature. Lincoln's irony is at its best here.

LETTER TO O. H. BROWNING SEPTEMBER 22, 1861

Private & Confidential.

Executive Mansion
Washington Sept 22d 1861.

Hon. O. H. Browning
My dear Sir

Yours of the 17th is just received; and coming from you, I confess it astonishes me. That you should object to my adhering to a law, which you had assisted in making, and presenting to me, less than a month before, is odd enough. But this is a very small part. Genl. Fremont's proclamation, as to confiscation of property, and the liberation of slaves, is *purely political,* and not within the range of *military* law, or necessity. If a commanding General finds a necessity to seize the farm of a private owner, for a pasture, and encampment, or a fortification, he has the right to do so, and to so hold it, as long as the necessity lasts; and this is within military law, because within military necessity. But to say the farm shall no longer belong to the owner, or his heirs forever; and this as well when the farm is not needed for military purposes as when it is, is purely political, without the savor of military law about it. And the same is true of slaves. If the General needs them, he can seize them, and use them; but when the need is past, it is not for him to fix their permanent future condition. That must be settled according to laws made by law-makers, and not by military proclamations. The proclamation in the point in question, is simply "dictatorship." It assumes that the general may do *anything* he pleases—confiscate the lands and free the slaves of *loyal* people, as well as of disloyal ones. And going the whole figure I have no doubt would be more popular with some thoughtless people, than that which has been done! But I cannot assume this reckless position, nor allow others to assume it on my responsibility. You speak of it as being the only means of *saving* the government. On the contrary it is itself the surrender of the government. Can it be pretended that it is any longer the Government of the U. S.—any government of Constitution and laws,—wherein a General, or a President, may make permanent rules of property by proclamation?

I do not say Congress might not with propriety pass a law, on the point, just such as General Fremont proclaimed. I do not say I might not, as a member of Congress, vote for it. What I object to is, that I as President, shall expressly or impliedly seize and exercise the permanent legislative functions of the government.

So much as to principle. Now as to policy. No doubt the thing was popular in some quarters, and would have been more so if it had been a general declaration of emancipation. The Kentucky Legislature would not budge till that proclamation was modified; and Gen. Anderson telegraphed me that on the news of Gen. Fremont having actually issued deeds of manumission, a whole company of our Volunteers threw down their arms and disbanded. I was so assured, as to think it probable, that the very arms we had furnished Kentucky would be turned against us. I think to lose Kentucky is nearly the same as to lose the whole game. Kentucky gone, we can not hold Missouri, nor, as I think, Maryland. These all against us, and the job on our hands is too large for us. We would as well consent to separation at once, including the surrender of this capitol. On the contrary, if you will give up your restlessness for new positions, and back me manfully on the grounds upon which you and other kind friends gave me the election, and have approved in my public documents, we shall go through triumphantly.

You must not understand I took my course on the proclamation *because* of Kentucky. I took the same ground in a private letter to General Fremont before I heard from Kentucky.

You think I am inconsistent because I did not also forbid Gen. Fremont to shoot men under the proclamation. I understand that part to be within military law; but I also think, and so privately wrote Gen. Fremont, that it is impolitic in this, that our adversaries have the power, and will certainly exercise it, to shoot as many of our men as we shoot of theirs. I did not say this in the public letter, because it is a subject I prefer not to discuss in the hearing of our enemies.

There has been no thought of removing Gen. Fremont on any ground connected with his proclamation; and if there has been any wish for his removal on any ground, our mutual friend Sam Glover can probably tell you what it was. I hope no real necessity for it exists on any ground.

Suppose you write to Hurlbut and get him to resign.

Your friend as ever

A. Lincoln

Browning, a lawyer of Quincy, Illinois, and one of Lincoln's oldest and most trusted political associates, was Senator from Illinois. He had written to Lincoln, quizzing Lincoln's action in countermanding General Frémont's proclamation freeing slaves in the area under his command.

This letter was apparently dictated to Nicolay, in whose handwriting the manuscript is, but several emendations and the signature are in Lincoln's hand.

LETTER TO MAJOR [G. D.?] RAMSAY OCTOBER 17, 1861

Executive Mansion
Oct. 17, 1861

Majr. Ramsay
My dear Sir

The lady—bearer of this—says she has two sons who want work. Set them at it, if possible. Wanting to work is so rare a merit, that it should be encouraged

Yours truly

A. Lincoln

The difficulty involved in reading Lincoln's script has usually resulted in the word merit *which appears in this letter being transcribed as* want. *Lincoln's* a *and* e *are often identical, his* i *undotted (hence* ri *appearing here as nearly like* n *as can be), and his* w *and* m *so nearly alike as to be difficult of determining. The word may as well end* ant *as* erit, *but since Lincoln rarely if ever begins an initial* w *with an upstroke of the pen, the editor has decided that the first letter is* m, *and hence that the word is* merit, *though he is ready to grant other Lincoln students the reading of* want.

ANNUAL MESSAGE TO CONGRESS
DECEMBER 3, 1861

Fellow-citizens of the Senate and House of Representatives:

In the midst of unprecedented political troubles, we have cause of great gratitude to God for unusual good health, and most abundant harvests.

You will not be surprised to learn that, in the peculiar exigencies of the times, our intercourse with foreign nations has been attended with profound solicitude, chiefly turning upon our own domestic affairs.

A disloyal portion of the American people have, during the whole year, been engaged in an attempt to divide and destroy the Union. A nation which endures factious domestic division, is exposed to disrespect abroad; and one party, if not both, is sure, sooner or later, to invoke foreign intervention.

Nations, thus tempted to interfere, are not always able to resist the counsels of seeming expediency, and ungenerous ambition, although measures adopted under such influences seldom fail to be unfortunate and injurious to those adopting them.

The disloyal citizens of the United States who have offered the ruin of our country, in return for the aid and comfort which they have invoked abroad, have received less patronage and encouragement than they probably expected. If it were just to suppose, as the insurgents have seemed to assume, that foreign nations, in this case, discarding all moral, social, and treaty obligations, would act solely, and selfishly, for the most speedy restoration of commerce, including, especially, the acquisition of cotton, those nations appear, as yet, not to have seen their way to their object more directly, or clearly, through the destruction, than through the preservation, of the Union. If we could dare to believe that foreign nations are actuated by no higher principle than this, I am quite sure a sound argument could be made to show them that they can reach their aim more readily, and easily, by aiding to crush this rebellion, than by giving encouragement to it.

The principal lever relied on by the insurgents for exciting foreign nations to hostility against us, as already intimated, is the embarrassment of commerce. Those nations, however, not improbably, saw from the first, that it was the Union which made as well our foreign, as our domestic, commerce. They can scarcely have failed to perceive that the effort for disunion produces the existing difficulty; and that one strong nation promises more durable peace, and a more extensive, valuable and reliable commerce, than can the same nation broken into hostile fragments.

It is not my purpose to review our discussions with foreign states; because whatever might be their wishes, or dispositions, the integrity of our country, and the stability of our government, mainly depend, not upon them, but on the loyalty, virtue, patriotism, and intelligence of the American people. The correspondence itself, with the usual reservations, is herewith submitted.

I venture to hope it will appear that we have practised prudence, and liberality towards foreign powers, averting causes of irritation; and, with firmness, maintaining our own rights and honor.

Since, however, it is apparent that here, as in every other state, foreign dangers necessarily attend domestic difficulties, I recommend that adequate and ample measures be adopted for maintaining the public defences on every side. While, under this general recommendation, provision for defending our sea-coast line readily occurs to the mind, I also, in the same connexion, ask the attention of Congress to our great lakes and rivers. It is believed that some fortifications and depots of arms and munitions, with harbor and navigation improvements, all at well selected points upon these, would be of great importance to the national defence and preservation. I ask attention to the views of the Secretary of War, expressed in his report, upon the same general subject.

I deem it of importance that the loyal regions of East Tennessee and western North Carolina should be connected with Kentucky, and other faithful parts of the Union, by railroad. I therefore recommend, as a military measure, that Congress provide for the construction of such road, as speedily as possible. Kentucky, no doubt, will co-operate, and, through her legislature, make the most judicious selection of a line. The northern terminus must connect with some existing railroad; and whether the route shall be from Lexington, or Nicholasville, to the Cumberland Gap; or from Lebanon to the Tennessee line, in the direction of Knoxville; or on some still different line, can easily be determined. Kentucky and the general government co-operating, the work can be completed in a very short time; and when done, it will be not only of vast present usefulness, but also a valuable permanent improvement, worth its cost in all the future.

Some treaties, designed chiefly for the interests of commerce, and having no grave political importance, have been negotiated, and will be submitted to the Senate for their consideration.

Although we have failed to induce some of the commercial powers to adopt a desirable melioration of the rigor of maritime war, we have removed all obstructions from the way of this humane reform, except such as are merely of temporary and accidental occurrence.

I invite your attention to the correspondence between her Britannic Majesty's minister accredited to this government, and the Secretary of State, relative to the detention of the British ship Perthshire in June last, by the United States steamer Massachusetts, for a supposed breach of the blockade. As this detention was occasioned by an obvious misapprehension of the facts, and as justice requires that we should commit no belligerent act not founded in strict right, as sanctioned by public law, I recommend that an appropriation be made to satisfy the reasonable demand of the owners of the vessel for her detention.

I repeat the recommendation of my predecessor, in his annual message to Congress in December last, in regard to the disposition of the surplus which will probably remain after satisfying the claims of American citizens against China, pursuant to the awards of the commissioners under the act of the 3rd of March, 1859. If, however, it should not be deemed advisable to carry that recommendation into effect, I would suggest that authority be given for investing the principal, over the proceeds of the surplus referred to, in good securities, with a view to the satisfaction of such other just claims of our citizens against China as are not unlikely to arise hereafter in the course of our extensive trade with that Empire.

By the act of the 5th of August last, Congress authorized the President to instruct the commanders of suitable vessels to defend themselves against, and to capture pirates. This authority has been exercised in a single instance only. For the more effectual protection of our extensive and valuable commerce, in the eastern seas especially, it seems to me that it would also be advisable to authorize the commanders of sailing vessels to re-capture any prizes which pirates might make of United States vessels and their cargoes, and the consular courts, now established by law in eastern countries, to adjudicate the cases, in the event that this should not be objected to by the local authorities.

If any good reason exists why we should persevere longer in withholding our recognition of the independence and sovereignty of Hayti and Liberia, I am unable to discern it. Unwilling, however, to inaugurate a novel policy in regard to them without the approbation of Congress, I submit for your consideration the expediency of an appropriation for maintaining a chargé d'affaires near each of those new states. It does not admit of doubt that important commercial advantages might be secured by favorable commercial treaties with them.

The operations of the treasury during the period which has

elapsed since your adjournment have been conducted with signal success. The patriotism of the people has placed at the disposal of the government the large means demanded by the public exigencies. Much of the national loan has been taken by citizens of the industrial classes, whose confidence in their country's faith, and zeal for their country's deliverance from present peril, have induced them to contribute to the support of the government the whole of their limited acquisitions. This fact imposes peculiar obligations to economy in disbursement and energy in action.

The revenue from all sources, including loans, for the financial year ending on the 30th June, 1861, was eighty six million, eight hundred and thirty five thousand, nine hundred dollars, and twenty seven cents, ($86,835,900.27,) and the expenditures for the same period, including payments on account of the public debt, were eighty four million, five hundred and seventy eight thousand, eight hundred and thirty four dollars and forty seven cents, ($84,578,834.47;) leaving a balance in the treasury, on the 1st July, of two million, two hundred and fifty seven thousand, sixty five dollars and eighty cents, ($2,257,065.80.) For the first quarter of the financial year, ending on the 30th September, 1861, the receipts from all sources, including the balance of first of July, were $102,532,509.27, and the expenses $98,239,733.09; leaving a balance on the 1st October, 1861, of $4,292,776.18.

Estimates for the remaining three quarters of the year, and for the financial year 1863, together with his views of ways and means for meeting the demands contemplated by them, will be submitted to Congress by the Secretary of the Treasury. It is gratifying to know that the expenditures made necessary by the rebellion are not beyond the resources of the loyal people, and to believe that the same patriotism which has thus far sustained the government will continue to sustain it till peace and union shall again bless the land.

I respectfully refer to the report of the Secretary of War for information respecting the numerical strength of the Army, and for recommendations having in view an increase of its efficiency and the well-being of the various branches of the service intrusted to his care. It is gratifying to know that the patriotism of the people has proved equal to the occasion, and that the number of troops tendered greatly exceeds the force which Congress authorized me to call into the field.

I refer with pleasure to those portions of his report which make allusion to the creditable degree of discipline already attained by our troops, and to the excellent sanitary condition of the entire army.

The recommendation of the secretary for an organization of the militia upon a uniform basis, is a subject of vital importance to the future safety of the country, and is commended to the serious attention of Congress.

The large addition to the regular Army, in connection with the defection that has so considerably diminished the number of its officers, gives peculiar importance to his recommendation for increasing the corps of cadets to the greatest capacity of the Military Academy.

By mere omission, I presume, Congress has failed to provide chaplains for hospitals occupied by volunteers. This subject was brought to my notice, and I was induced to draw up the form of a letter, one copy of which, properly addressed, has been delivered to each of the persons, and at the dates respectively named and stated, in a schedule, containing also the form of the letter, marked A, and herewith transmitted.

These gentlemen, I understand, entered upon the duties designated, at the times respectively stated in the schedule, and have labored faithfully therein ever since. I therefore recommend that they be compensated at the same rate as chaplains in the army. I further suggest that general provision be made for chaplains to serve at hospitals, as well as with regiments.

The report of the Secretary of the Navy presents in detail the operations of that branch of the service, the activity and energy which have characterized its administration, and the results of measures to increase its efficiency and power. Such have been the additions, by construction and purchase, that it may almost be said a navy has been created and brought into service since our difficulties commenced.

Besides blockading our extensive coast, squadrons larger than ever before assembled under our flag have been put afloat and performed deeds which have increased our naval renown.

I would invite special attention to the recommendation of the Secretary for a more perfect organization of the Navy by introducing additional grades in the service.

The present organization is defective and unsatisfactory, and the suggestions submitted by the Department will, it is believed, if adopted, obviate the difficulties alluded to, promote harmony, and increase the efficiency of the Navy.

There are three vacancies on the bench of the Supreme Court—two by the decease of Justices Daniel and McLean, and one by the resignation of Justice Campbell. I have so far forborne making nominations to fill these vacancies for reasons which I will now state. Two of the outgoing judges resided within the States now overrun by revolt; so that if successors were appointed in the same localities, they could not now serve upon their circuits; and many of the most competent men there probably would not take the personal hazard of accepting to serve, even here, upon the supreme bench. I have been unwilling to throw all the appointments northward, thus disabling myself from doing justice to the South on the return of peace; although I may remark that to transfer to the North one which has heretofore been in the South, would not, with reference to territory and population, be unjust.

During the long and brilliant judicial career of Judge McLean his circuit grew into an empire—altogether too large for any one judge to give the courts therein more than a nominal attendance—rising in population from one million four hundred and seventy thousand and eighteen in 1830, to six million one hundred and fifty-one thousand four hundred and five in 1860.

Besides this, the country generally has outgrown our present judicial system. If uniformity was at all intended, the system requires that all the States shall be accommodated with circuit courts, attended by supreme judges, while, in fact, Wisconsin, Minnesota, Iowa, Kansas, Florida, Texas, California, and Oregon, have never had any such courts. Nor can this well be remedied without a change of the system; because the adding of judges to the Supreme Court, enough for the accommodation of all parts of the country, with circuit courts, would create a court altogether too numerous for a judicial body of any sort. And the evil, if it be one, will increase as new States come into the Union. Circuit courts are useful, or they are not useful. If useful, no State should be denied them; if not useful, no State should have them. Let them be provided for all, or abolished as to all.

Three modifications occur to me, either of which, I think, would be an improvement upon our present system. Let the Supreme Court be of convenient number in every event. Then, first, let the whole country be divided into circuits of convenient size, the supreme judges to serve in a number of them corresponding to their own number, and independent circuit judges be provided for all the rest. Or, secondly, let the supreme judges be relieved from circuit duties, and circuit judges provided for all the circuits. Or, thirdly, dispense with circuit courts altogether, leaving the judicial functions wholly to the district courts and an independent Supreme Court.

I respectfully recommend to the consideration of Congress the present condition of the Statute laws, with the hope that Congress will be able to find an easy remedy for many of the inconveniences and evils which constantly embarrass those engaged in the practical administration of them. Since the organization of the government, Congress has enacted some five thousand acts and joint resolutions, which fill more than six thousand closely printed pages, and are scattered through many volumes. Many of these acts have been drawn in haste and without sufficient caution, so that their provisions are often obscure in themselves, or in conflict with each other, or at least so doubtful as to render it very difficult for even the best informed persons to ascertain precisely what the statute law really is.

It seems to me very important that the statute laws should be made as plain and intelligible as possible, and be reduced to as small a compass as may consist with the fullness and precision of the will of the legislature and the perspicuity of its language. This, well done, would, I think, greatly facilitate the labors of those whose duty it is to assist in the administration of the laws, and would be a lasting benefit to the people, by placing before them, in a more accessible and intelligible form, the laws which so deeply concern their interests and their duties.

I am informed by some whose opinions I respect, that all

the acts of Congress now in force, and of a permanent and general nature, might be revised and rewritten, so as to be embraced in one volume (or at most, two volumes) of ordinary and convenient size. And I respectfully recommend to Congress to consider of the subject, and, if my suggestion be approved, to devise such plan as to their wisdom shall seem most proper for the attainment of the end proposed.

One of the unavoidable consequences of the present insurrection is the entire suppression, in many places, of all the ordinary means of administering civil justice by the officers and in the forms of existing law. This is the case, in whole or in part, in all the insurgent States; and as our armies advance upon and take possession of parts of those States, the principal evil becomes more apparent. There are no courts nor officers to whom the citizens of other States may apply for the enforcement of their lawful claims against citizens of the insurgent States; and there is a vast amount of debt constituting such claims. Some have estimated it as high as two hundred million dollars, due, in large part, from insurgents, in open rebellion, to loyal citizens who are, even now, making great sacrifices in the discharge of their patriotic duty to support the government.

Under these circumstances, I have been urgently solicited to establish, by military power, courts to administer summary justice in such cases. I have thus far declined to do it, not because I had any doubt that the end proposed—the collection of the debts—was just and right in itself, but because I have been unwilling to go beyond the pressure of necessity in the unusual exercise of power. But the powers of Congress I suppose are equal to the anomalous occasion, and therefore I refer the whole matter to Congress, with the hope that a plan may be devised for the administration of justice in all such parts of the insurgent States and Territories as may be under the control of this government, whether by a voluntary return to allegiance and order or by the power of our arms. This, however, not to be a permanent institution, but a temporary substitute, and to cease as soon as the ordinary courts can be reestablished in peace.

It is important that some more convenient means should be provided, if possible, for the adjustment of claims against the government, especially in view of their increased number by reason of the war. It is as much the duty of government to render prompt justice against itself, in favor of citizens, as it is to administer the same, between private individuals. The investigation and adjudication of claims, in their nature belong to the judicial department; besides, it is apparent that the attention of Congress will be more than usually engaged, for some time to come, with great national questions. It was intended, by the organization of the Court of Claims mainly to remove this branch of business from the Halls of Congress; but while the court has proved to be an effective and valuable means of investigation, it in great degree fails to effect the object of its creation, for want of power to make its judgments final.

Fully aware of the delicacy, not to say the danger, of the subject, I commend to your careful consideration whether this power of making judgments final may not properly be given to the court, reserving the right of appeal on questions of law to the Supreme Court, with such other provisions as experience may have shown to be necessary.

I ask attention to the report of the Postmaster General, the following being a summary statement of the condition of the department:

The revenue from all sources during the fiscal year ending June 30, 1861, including the annual permanent appropriation of seven hundred thousand dollars ($700,000) for the transportation of "free mail matter," was nine million, forty nine thousand, two hundred and ninety six dollars and forty cents ($9,049,296.40,) being about two per cent. less than the revenue for 1860.

The expenditures were thirteen million, six hundred and six thousand, seven hundred and fifty nine dollars and eleven cents ($13,606,759.11) showing a decrease of more than eight per cent. as compared with those of the previous year, and leaving an excess of expenditure over the revenue for the last fiscal year of four million, five hundred and fifty seven thousand, four hundred and sixty two dollars and seventy one cents ($4,557,462.71)

The gross revenue for the year ending June 30, 1863, is estimated at an increase of four per cent. on that of 1861, making eight million, six hundred and eighty three thousand dollars ($8,683,000) to which should be added the earnings of the department in carrying free matter, viz: seven hundred thousand dollars ($700,000.) making nine million, three hundred and eighty three thousand dollars ($9,383,000.)

The total expenditures for 1863 are estimated at $12,528,000, leaving an estimated deficiency of $3,145,000, to be supplied from the treasury, in addition to the permanent appropriation.

The present insurrection shows, I think, that the extension of this District across the Potomac river, at the time of establishing the capital here, was eminently wise, and consequently that the relinquishment of that portion of it which lies within the State of Virginia was unwise and dangerous. I submit for your consideration the expediency of regaining that part of the District, and the restoration of the original boundaries thereof, through negotiations with the State of Virginia.

The report of the Secretary of the Interior, with the accompanying documents, exhibits the condition of the several branches of the public business pertaining to that department. The depressing influences of the insurrection have been especially felt in the operations of the Patent and General Land Offices. The cash receipts from the sales of public lands during the past year have exceeded the expenses of our land system only about $200,000. The sales have been entirely suspended in the southern States, while the interruptions to the business of the country, and the diversion of large numbers of men from labor to military service, have obstructed settlements in the new States and Territories of the northwest.

The receipts of the Patent Office have declined in nine months about $100,000, rendering a large reduction of the force employed necessary to make it self sustaining.

The demands upon the Pension Office will be largely increased by the insurrection. Numerous applications for pensions, based upon the casualties of the existing war, have already been made. There is reason to believe that many who are now upon the pension rolls and in receipt of the bounty of the government, are in the ranks of the insurgent army, or giving them aid and comfort. The Secretary of the Interior has directed a suspension of the payment of the pensions of such persons upon proof of their disloyalty. I recommend that Congress authorize that officer to cause the names of such persons to be stricken from the pension rolls.

The relations of the government with the Indian tribes have been greatly disturbed by the insurrection, especially in the southern superintendency and in that of New Mexico. The Indian country south of Kansas is in the possession of insurgents from Texas and Arkansas. The agents of the United States appointed since the 4th of March for this superintendency have been unable to reach their posts, while the most of those who were in office before that time have espoused the insurrectionary cause, and assume to exercise the powers of agents by virtue of commissions from the insurrectionists. It has been stated in the public press that a portion of those Indians have been organized as a military force, and are attached to the army of the insurgents. Although the government has no official information upon this subject, letters have been written to the Commissioner of Indian Affairs by several prominent chiefs, giving assurance of their loyalty to the United States, and expressing a wish for the presence of federal troops to protect them. It is believed that upon the repossession of the country by the federal forces the Indians will readily cease all hostile demonstrations, and resume their former relations to the government.

Agriculture, confessedly the largest interest of the nation, has, not a department, nor a bureau, but a clerkship only, assigned to it in the government. While it is fortunate that this great interest is so independent in its nature as to not have demanded and extorted more from the government, I respectfully ask Congress to consider whether something more cannot be given voluntarily with general advantage.

Annual reports exhibiting the condition of our agriculture, commerce, and manufactures would present a fund of information of great practical value to the country. While I make no suggestion as to details, I venture the opinion that an agricultural and statistical bureau might profitably be organized.

The execution of the laws for the suppression of the African slave trade, has been confided to the Department of the Interior.

It is a subject of gratulation that the efforts which have been made for the suppression of this inhuman traffic, have been recently attended with unusual success. Five vessels being fitted out for the slave trade have been seized and condemned. Two mates of vessels engaged in the trade, and one person in equipping a vessel as a slaver, have been convicted and subjected to the penalty of fine and imprisonment, and one captain, taken with a cargo of Africans on board his vessel, has been convicted of the highest grade of offence under our laws, the punishment of which is death.

The Territories of Colorado, Dakotah [*sic*] and Nevada, created by the last Congress, have been organized, and civil administration has been inaugurated therein under auspices especially gratifying, when it is considered that the leaven of treason was found existing in some of these new countries when the federal officers arrived there.

The abundant natural resources of these Territories, with the security and protection afforded by organized government, will doubtless invite to them a large immigration when peace shall restore the business of the country to its accustomed channels. I submit the resolutions of the legislature of Colorado, which evidence the patriotic spirit of the people of the Territory. So far the authority of the United States has been upheld in all the Territories, as it is hoped it will be in the future. I commend their interests and defence to the enlightened and generous care of Congress.

I recommend to the favorable consideration of Congress the interests of the District of Columbia. The insurrection has been the cause of much suffering and sacrifice to its inhabitants, and as they have no representative in Congress, that body should not overlook their just claims upon the government.

At your late session a joint resolution was adopted authorizing the President to take measures for facilitating a proper representation of the industrial interests of the United States at the exhibition of the industry of all nations to be holden at London in the year 1862. I regret to say I have been unable to give personal attention to this subject,—a subject at once so interesting in itself, and so extensively and intimately connected with the material prosperity of the world. Through the Secretaries of State and of the Interior a plan, or system, has been devised, and partly matured, and which will be laid before you.

Under and by virtue of the act of Congress entitled "An act to confiscate property used for insurrectionary purposes," approved August 6, 1861, the legal claims of certain persons to the labor and service of certain other persons have become forfeited; and numbers of the latter, thus liberated, are already dependent on the United States, and must be provided for in some way. Besides this, it is not impossible that some of the States will pass similar enactments for their own benefit respectively, and by operation of which persons of the same class will be thrown upon them for disposal. In such case I recommend that Congress provide for accepting such persons from such States, according to some mode of valuation, in lieu, *pro tanto*, of direct taxes, or upon some other plan to be agreed on with such States respectively; that such persons, on such acceptance by the general government, be at once deemed free; and that, in any event, steps be taken for colonizing both classes, (or the one first mentioned, if the other shall not be brought into existence,) at some place, or places, in a climate congenial to them. It might be well to consider, too, whether the free colored people already in the United States could not, so far as individuals may desire, be included in such colonization.

To carry out the plan of colonization may involve the acquiring of territory, and also the appropriation of money beyond that to be expended in the territorial acquisition. Having practiced the acquisition of territory for nearly sixty years, the question of constitutional power to do so is no longer an open one with us. The power was questioned at first by Mr. Jefferson, who, however, in the purchase of Louisiana, yielded his scruples on the plea of great expediency. If it be said that the only legitimate object of acquiring territory is to furnish homes for white men, this measure effects that object; for the emigration of colored men leaves additional room for white men remaining or coming here. Mr. Jefferson, however, placed the importance of procuring Louisiana more on political and commercial grounds than on providing room for population.

On this whole proposition, including the appropriation of money with the acquisition of territory, does not the expediency amount to absolute necessity—that, without which the government itself cannot be perpetuated? The war continues. In considering the policy to be adopted for suppressing the insurrection, I have been anxious and careful that the inevitable conflict for this purpose shall not degenerate into a violent and remorseless revolutionary struggle. I have, therefore, in every case, thought it proper to keep the integrity of the Union prominent as the primary object of the contest on our part, leaving all questions which are not of vital military importance to the more deliberate action of the legislature.

In the exercise of my best discretion I have adhered to the blockade of the ports held by the insurgents, instead of putting in force, by proclamation, the law of Congress enacted at the late session, for closing those ports. So, also, obeying the dictates of prudence, as well as the obligations of law, instead of transcending, I have adhered to the act of Congress to confiscate property used for insurrectionary purposes. If a new law upon the same subject shall be proposed, its propriety will be duly considered.

The Union must be preserved, and hence, all indispensable means must be employed. We should not be in haste to determine that radical and extreme measures, which may reach the loyal as well as the disloyal, are indispensable.

The inaugural address at the beginning of the Administration, and the message to Congress at the late special session, were both mainly devoted to the domestic controversy out of which the insurrection and consequent war have sprung. Nothing now occurs to add or subtract, to or from, the principles or general purposes stated and expressed in those documents.

The last ray of hope for preserving the Union peaceably, expired at the assault upon Fort Sumter; and a general review of what has occurred since may not be unprofitable. What was painfully uncertain then, is much better defined and more distinct now; and the progress of events is plainly in the right direction. The insurgents confidently claimed a strong support from north of Mason and Dixon's line; and the friends of the Union were not free from apprehension on the point. This, however, was soon settled definitely and on the right side. South of the line, noble little Delaware led off right from the first. Maryland was made to *seem* against the Union. Our soldiers were assaulted, bridges were burned, and railroads torn up, within her limits; and we were many days, at one time, without the ability to bring a single regiment over her soil to the capital. Now, her bridges and railroads are repaired and open to the government; she already gives seven regiments to the cause of the Union and none to the enemy; and her people, at a regular election, have sustained the Union, by a larger majority, and a larger aggregate vote than they ever before gave to any candidate, or any question. Kentucky, too, for some time in doubt, is now decidedly, and, I think, unchangeably, ranged on the side of the Union. Missouri is comparatively quiet; and I believe cannot again be overrun by the insurrectionists. These three States of Maryland, Kentucky, and Missouri, neither of which would promise a single soldier at first, have now an aggregate of not less than forty thousand in the field, for the Union; while, of their citizens, certainly not more than a third of that number, and they of doubtful whereabouts, and doubtful existence, are in arms against it. After a somewhat bloody struggle of months, winter closes on the Union people of western Virginia, leaving them masters of their own country.

An insurgent force of about fifteen hundred, for months dominating the narrow peninsular region, constituting the counties of Accomac and Northampton, and known as eastern shore of Virginia, together with some contiguous parts of Maryland, have laid down their arms; and the people there have renewed their allegiance to, and accepted the protection of, the old flag. This leaves no armed insurrectionist north of the Potomac, or east of the Chesapeake.

Also we have obtained a footing at each of the isolated points, on the southern coast, of Hatteras, Port Royal, Tybee Island, near Savannah, and Ship Island; and we likewise have some general accounts of popular movements, in behalf of the Union, in North Carolina and Tennessee.

These things demonstrate that the cause of the Union is advancing steadily and certainly southward.

Since your last adjournment, Lieutenant General Scott has

retired from the head of the army. During his long life, the nation has not been unmindful of his merit; yet, on calling to mind how faithfully, ably and brilliantly he has served the country, from a time far back in our history, when few of the now living had been born, and thenceforward continually, I cannot but think we are still his debtors. I submit, therefore, for your consideration, what further mark of recognition is due to him, and to ourselves, as a grateful people.

With the retirement of General Scott came the executive duty of appointing, in his stead, a general-in-chief of the army. It is a fortunate circumstance that neither in council nor country was there, so far as I know, any difference of opinion as to the proper person to be selected. The retiring chief repeatedly expressed his judgment in favor of General McClellan for the position; and in this the nation seemed to give a unanimous concurrence. The designation of General McClellan is therefore in considerable degree, the selection of the Country as well as of the Executive; and hence there is better reason to hope there will be given him, the confidence, and cordial support thus, by fair implication, promised, and without which, he cannot, with so full efficiency, serve the country.

It has been said that one bad general is better than two good ones; and the saying is true, if taken to mean no more than that an army is better directed by a single mind, though inferior, than by two superior ones, at variance, and cross-purposes with each other.

And the same is true, in all joint operations wherein those engaged, *can* have none but a common end in view, and *can* differ only as to the choice of means. In a storm at sea, no one on board *can* wish the ship to sink; and yet, not unfrequently, all go down together, because too many will direct, and no single mind can be allowed to control.

It continues to develop that the insurrection is largely, if not exclusively, a war upon the first principle of popular government—the rights of the people. Conclusive evidence of this is found in the most grave and maturely considered public documents, as well as in the general tone of the insurgents. In those documents we find the abridgement of the existing right of suffrage and the denial to the people of all right to participate in the selection of public officers, except the legislative boldly advocated, with labored arguments to prove that large control of the people in government, is the source of all political evil. Monarchy itself is sometimes hinted at as a possible refuge from the power of the people.

In my present position, I could scarcely be justified were I to omit raising a warning voice against this approach of returning despotism.

It is not needed, not fitting here, that a general argument should be made in favor of popular institutions; but there is one point, with its connexions, not so hackneyed as most others, to which I ask a brief attention. It is the effort to place *capital* on an equal footing with, if not above *labor*, in the structure of government. It is assumed that labor is available only in connexion with capital; that nobody labors unless somebody else, owning capital, somehow by the use of it, induces him to labor. This assumed, it is next considered whether it is best that capital shall *hire* laborers, and thus induce them to work by their own consent, or *buy* them, and drive them to it without their consent. Having proceeded so far, it is naturally concluded that all laborers are either *hired* laborers, or what we call slaves. And further it is assumed that whoever is once a hired laborer, is fixed in that condition for life.

Now, there is no such relation between capital and labor as assumed; nor is there any such thing as a free man being fixed for life in the condition of a hired laborer. Both these assumptions are false, and all inferences from them are groundless. Labor is prior to, and independent of, capital. Capital is only the fruit of labor, and could never have existed if labor had not first existed. Labor is the superior of capital, and deserves much the higher consideration. Capital has its rights, which are as worthy of protection as any other rights. Nor is it denied that there is, and probably always will be, a relation between labor and capital, producing mutual benefits. The error is in assuming that the whole labor of community exists within that relation. A few men own capital, and that few avoid labor themselves, and, with their capital, hire or buy another few to labor for them. A large majority belong to neither class—neither work for others, nor have others working for them. In most of the southern states, a majority of the whole people of all colors are neither slaves nor masters; while in the northern a large majority are neither hirers nor hired. Men with their families—wives, sons, and daughters—work for themselves, on their farms, in their houses, and in their shops, taking the whole product to themselves, and asking no favors of capital on the one hand, nor of hired laborers or slaves on the other. It is not forgotten that a considerable number of persons mingle their own labor with capital—that is, they labor with their own hands, and also buy or hire others to labor for them; but this is only a mixed, and not a distinct class. No principle stated is disturbed by the existence of this mixed class.

Again: as has already been said, there is not, of necessity, any such thing as the free hired laborer being fixed to that condition for life. Many independent men everywhere in these States, a few years back in their lives, were hired laborers. The prudent, penniless beginner in the world, labors for wages awhile, saves a surplus with which to buy tools or land for himself; then labors on his own account another while, and at length hires another new beginner to help him. This is the just, and generous, and prosperous system, which opens the way to all—gives hope to all, and consequent energy, and progress, and improvement of condition to all. No men living are more worthy to be trusted than those who toil up from poverty—none less inclined to take, or touch, aught which they have not honestly earned. Let them beware of surrendering a political power which they already possess, and which, if surrendered, will surely be used to close the door of advancement against such as they, and to fix new disabilities and burdens upon them, till all of liberty shall be lost.

From the first taking of our national census to the last are seventy years; and we find our population at the end of the period eight times as great as it was at the beginning. The increase of those other things which men deem desirable has been even greater. We thus have at one view, what the popular principle applied to government, through the machinery of the States and the Union, has produced in a given time; and also what, if firmly maintained, it promises for the future. There are already among us those, who, if the Union be preserved, will live to see it contain two hundred and fifty millions. The struggle *of* to-day, is not altogether for to-day—it is for a vast future also. With a reliance on Providence, all the more firm and earnest, let us proceed in the great task which events have devolved upon us.

Abraham Lincoln

December 3, 1861

LETTER TO MRS. SUSANNAH WEATHERS DECEMBER 4, 1861

Executive Mansion,
Washington, Dec. 4 1861.

My dear Madam

I take great pleasure in acknowledging the receipt of your letter of Nov. 26; and in thanking you for the present by which it was accompanied. A pair of socks so fine, and soft, and warm, could hardly have been manufactured in any other way than the old Kentucky fashion. Your letter informs me that your maiden name was Crume, and that you were raised in Washington County, Kentucky, by which I infer that an uncle of mine by marriage was a relative of yours. Nearly, or quite sixty years ago, Ralph Crume married Mary Lincoln, a sister of my father, in Washington County, Kentucky.

Accept my thanks, and believe me

Very truly
Your friend
A. Lincoln.

Mrs. Susannah Weathers
Rossville, Clinton Co. Ind.

TELEGRAM TO GENERAL D. C. BUELL
JANUARY 4, 1862

Washington, D. C. Jan. 4. 1862

Brig. Gen. Buell
Louisville, Ky.

Have arms gone forward for East-Tennessee? Please tell me the progress and condition of the movement in that direction. Answer.

A. Lincoln

LETTER TO GENERAL D. C. BUELL
JANUARY 6, 1862

Executive Mansion,
Washington, January 6, 1862.

Brig. Gen. Buell
My dear Sir

Your despatch of yesterday has been received, and it disappoints and distresses me. I have shown it to Gen. McClellan, who says he will write you to-day. I am not competent to criticise your views, and therefore what I offer is merely in justification of myself. Of the two, I would rather have a point on the Railroad south of Cumberland Gap, than Nashville, first, because it cuts a great artery of the enemies' communication, which Nashville does not, and secondly because it is in the midst of loyal people, who would rally around it, while Nashville is not. Again, I cannot see why the movement on East Tennessee would not be a diversion in your favor, rather than a disadvantage, assuming that a movement towards Nashville is the main object.

But my distress is that our friends in East Tennessee are being hanged and driven to despair, and even now I fear, are thinking of taking rebel arms for the sake of personal protection. In this we lose the most valuable stake we have in the South. My despatch, to which yours is an answer, was sent with the knowledge of Senator Johnson and Representative Maynard of East Tennessee, and they will be upon me to know the answer, which I cannot safely show them. They would despair—possibly resign to go and save their families somehow, or die with them.

I do not intend this to be an order in any sense, but merely, as intimated before, to show you the grounds of my anxiety.

Yours very Truly,
A. Lincoln

LETTER TO GENERAL A. E. BURNSIDE
JANUARY 28, 1862

Executive Mansion,
Washington, January 28, 1862

Major Gen. Burnside
My dear Sir

Gen. Humphreys is now with me saying that you told him that you had strongly urged upon me, his, Gen. H's promotion, and that I in response had used such strong language, that you were sure his name would be sent to the Senate. I remember nothing of your speaking to me; or I to you, about Gen. H. still this is far from conclusive that nothing was said. I will now thank you to drop me a note, saying what you think is right and just about Gen. Humphreys.

Yours as ever
A. Lincoln

LETTER TO GENERAL G. B. McCLELLAN APRIL 9, 1862

Washington, April 9. 1862

Major General McClellan.
My dear Sir.

Your despatches complaining that you are not properly sustained, while they do not offend me, do pain me very much.

Blencker's [*sic*] Division was withdrawn from you before you left here; and you knew the pressure under which I did it, and, as I thought, acquiesced in it—certainly not without reluctance.

After you left, I ascertained that less than twenty thousand unorganized men, without a single field battery, were all you designed to be left for the defence of Washington, and Manassas Juntion [*sic*] and part of this even, was to go to Gen. Hooker's old position. General Banks' corps, once designed for Manassas Junction, was diverted, and tied up on the line of Winchester and Strausburg [*sic*], and could not leave it without again exposing the upper Potomac, and the Baltimore and Ohio Railroad. This presented, (or would present, when McDowell and Sumner should be gone) a great temptation to the enemy to turn back from the Rappahonock [*sic*], and sack Washington. My explicit order that Washington should, by the judgment of *all* the commanders of Army corps, be left entirely secure, had been neglected. It was precisely this that drove me to detain McDowell.

I do not forget that I was satisfied with your arrangement to leave Banks at Mannassas [*sic*] Junction; but when that arrangement was broken up, and *nothing* was substituted for it, of course I was not satisfied. I was constrained to substitute something for it myself. And now allow me to ask "Do you really think I should permit the line from Richmond, *via* Mannassas [*sic*] Junction, to this city to be entirely open, except what resistence [*sic*] could be presented by less than twenty thousand unorganized troops?" This is a question which the country will not allow me to evade.

There is a curious mystery about the *number* of the troops now with you. When I telegraphed you on the 6th. saying you had over a hundred thousand with you, I had just obtained from the Secretary of War, a statement, taken as he said, from your own returns, making 108.000 then with you, and *en route* to you. You now say you will have but 85,000, when all *en route* to you shall have reached you. How can this discrepancy of 23.000 be accounted for?

As to Gen. Wool's command, I understand it is doing for you precisely what a like number of your own would have to do, if that command was away.

I suppose the whole force which has gone forward for you, is with you by this time; and if so, I think it is the precise time for you to strike a blow. By delay the enemy will relatively gain upon you—that is, he will gain faster, by *fortifications* and *re-inforcements*, than you can by re-inforcements alone.

And, once more let me tell you, it is indispensable to *you* that you strike a blow. *I* am poweless [*sic*] to help this. You will do me the justice to remember I always insisted, that going down the Bay in search of a field, instead of fighting at or near Mannassas [*sic*], was only shifting, and not surmounting, a difficulty—that we would find the same enemy, and the same, or equal, intrenchments, at either place. The country will not fail to note—is now noting—that the present hesitation to move upon an intrenched enemy, is but the story of Manassas repeated.

I beg to assure you that I have never written you, or spoken to you, in greater kindness of feeling than now, nor with a fuller purpose to sustain you, so far as in my most anxious judgment, I consistently can. *But you must act.*

Yours very truly
A. Lincoln

Lincoln's numerous letters and telegrams to McClellan—represented by this and several of the most interesting ones written between this date and Novem-

ber 5, 1862, when Lincoln removed McClellan from command of the Union Army—reveal Lincoln's constant dissatisfaction with McClellan's inaction. The consensus of military opinion in later years has sustained Lincoln's views for the most part and has rated McClellan as an efficient organizer, but a poor commander for offensive action. Some students have felt that Lincoln meddled too much with strategy and interfered too often with the plans of his commanders. It should be noted, however, that there was little inclination on Lincoln's part to interfere with those generals who got results. The contrast between his letters to Grant and those to McClellan is obvious; although Lincoln sometimes disagreed with Grant, as he admits in the letter written July 13, 1863, he kept the matter to himself.

LETTER TO THE SENATE AND HOUSE OF REPRESENTATIVES. APRIL 16, 1862

Fellow Citizens of the Senate, and House of Representatives.

The Act entitled "An Act for the release of certain persons held to service, or labor in the District of Columbia" has this day been approved, and signed.

I have never doubted the constitutional authority of Congress to abolish slavery in this District; and I have ever desired to see the national capital freed from the institution in some satisfactory way. Hence there has never been; in my mind, any question upon the subject, except the one of expediency, arising in view of all the circumstances. If there be matters within and above this act, which might have taken a course or shape, more satisfactory to my judgment, I do-not attempt to specify them. I am gratified that the two principles of compensation, and colonization, are both recognized, and practically applied in the act.

In the matter of compensation, it is provided that claims may be presented within ninety days from the passage of the act "but not thereafter"; and there is no saving for minors, femes-covert, insane, or absent persons. I presume this is an omission by mere over-sight, and I recommend that it be supplied by an amendatory or supplemental act.

Abraham Lincoln

April 16, 1862.

LETTER TO GENERAL G. B. McCLELLAN
MAY 9, 1862

Head-quarters, Department of Va.
Fort Monroe, Va. May 9 1862.

Major General McClellan
My dear Sir

I have just assisted the Secretary of War in framing the part of a despatch to you relating to army corps, which despatch of course will have reached you long before this will. I wish to say a few words to you privately on this subject. I ordered the army corps organization not only on the unanimous opinion of the twelve generals whom you had selected and assigned as Generals of Division but also on the unanimous opinion of every *military man* I could get an opinion from, and every modern military book, yourself only excepted. Of course I did not, on my own judgment pretend to understand the subject. I now think it indispensable for you to know how your struggle against it is received in quarters which we cannot entirely disregard. It is looked upon as merely an effort to pamper one or two pets and to persecute and degrade their supposed rivals. I have no word from Sumner Heintzlman [*sic*] or Keyes—the commanders of these corps are of course the three highest officers with you, but I am constantly told that you have no consultation or communication with them;

that you consult and communicate with no body but Gen. Fitz John Porter and perhaps Gen Franklin. I do not say these complaints are true or just, but at all events it is proper you should know of their existence. Do the Commanders of Corps disobey your orders in anything?

When you relieved Gen Hamilton of his command the other day, you thereby lost the confidence of at least one of your best friends in the Senate. And here let me say, not as applicable to you personally, that Senators and Representatives speak of me in their places as they please without question; and that officers of the army must cease addressing insulting letters to them for taking no greater liberty with them. But to return. Are you strong enough—are you strong enough even with my help—to set your foot upon the necks of Sumner Heintzleman [*sic*] and Keyes all at once? This is a practical and very serious question for you.

The success of your army and the cause of the country are the same; and of course I only desire the good of the cause.

Yours truly
A Lincoln

The text of this letter has been edited from a contemporary copy, made on the same day Lincoln wrote the letter at Fort Monroe, and now among the Papers of Edward M. Stanton in the Library of Congress. The editor has not been able to locate the original manuscript.

TELEGRAM TO GENERAL G. B. McCLELLAN
MAY 28, 1862

Washington City, D. C.
May 28, 1862. 8.40 P. M.

Maj. Gen. McClellan

I am very glad of Gen. F. J. Porter's victory. Still, if it was a total rout of the enemy, I am puzzled to know why the Richmond and Fredericksburg Railroad was not seized. Again, as you say you have *all* the Railroads but the Richmond and Fredericksburg, I am puzzled to see how, lacking that, you can have any, except the scrap from Richmond to West Point. The scrap of the Virginia Central from Richmond to Hanover Junction, without more, is simply nothing.

That the whole force of the enemy is concentrating in Richmond, I think can not be certainly known to you or me. Saxton, at Harper's Ferry, informs us that a large force (supposed to be Jackson's and Ewells) forced his advance from Charleston to-day. Gen. King telegraphs us from Fredericksburg that contrabands give certain information that fifteen thousand left Hanover Junction Monday morning to re-inforce Jackson. I am painfully impressed with the importance of the struggle before you;· and I shall aid you all I can consistently with my view of due regard to all points.*

A. Lincoln

* A last phrase, which Lincoln deleted, reads as follows: "but I must be the Judge as to the *duty*, of the government in this respect."

TELEGRAM TO GENERAL G. B. McCLELLAN
JUNE 28, 1862

Washington City, D. C. June 28—1862.

Major Gen. McClellan

Save your Army at all events. Will send re-inforcements as fast as we can. Of course they can not reach you to-day, to-morrow, or next day. I have not said you were ungenous [*sic*] for saying you needed re-inforcements. I thought you were ungenerous in assuming that I did not send them as fast as I could. I feel any misfortune to you and your Army quite as keenly as you feel it yourself. If you have had a drawn battle, or a repulse, it is the price we pay for the enemy not being in Washington. We protected Washington, and the enemy concentrated on you; had we stripped Washington, he would have been upon us before the troops sent could have got to you. Less than a week ago you notified us that re-inforcements were leaving Richmond to come in front of us. It is the nature of the case, and neither you or the government that is to blame. Please tell at once the present condition and aspect of things.

A. Lincoln

P. S.

Gen. Pope thinks if you fall back, it would be much better towards York River, than towards the James. As Pope now has charge of the Capital, please confer with him through the telegraph.

A. L.

TELEGRAM TO GENERAL G. B. McCLELLAN
JULY 1, 1862

Executive Mansion,
Washington, July 1 1862.

Major Genl. McClellan—

It is impossible to re-inforce you for your present emergency. If we had a million of men we could not get them to you in time. We have not the men to send. If you are not strong enough to face the enemy you must find a place of security, and wait, rest, and repair. Maintain your ground if you can; but save the Army at all events, even if you fall back to Fortress-Monroe. We still have strength enough in the country, and will bring it out.

A. Lincoln

LETTER TO GENERAL G. B. McCLELLAN
JULY 2, 1862

Washington, D. C., July 2, 1862.

Major Gen. McClellan

Your despatch of Tuesday morning induces me to hope your Army is having some rest. In this hope, allow me to reason with you a moment. When you ask for fifty thousand men to be promptly sent you, you surely labor under some gross mistake of fact. Recently you sent papers showing your disposal of forces, made last spring, for the defence of Washington, and advising a return to that plan. I find it included in, and about Washington seventyfive thousand men. Now please be assured, I have not men enough to fill that very plan by fifteen thousand. All of Fremont in the valley, all of Banks, all of McDowell, not with you, and all in Washington, taken together do not exceed, if they reach sixty thousand. With Wool and Dix added to those mentioned, I have not, outside of your Army, seventyfive thousand men East of the mountains. Thus, the idea of sending you fifty thousand, or any other considerable force promptly, is simply absurd. If in your frequent mention of responsibility, you have the impression that I blame you for not doing more than you can, please be relieved of such impression. I only beg that in like manner, you will not ask impossibilities of me. If you think you are not strong enough to take Richmond just now, I do not ask you to try just now. Save the Army, material and personal; and I will strengthen it for the offensive again, as fast as I can. The governors of eighteen states offer me a new levy of three hundred thousand, which I accept.

A. Lincoln

TELEGRAM TO GENERAL G. B. McCLELLAN JULY 3, 1862

Washington City, D. C. July 3, 1862.

Major Genl. McClellan

Yours of 5.30. yesterday is just received. I am satisfied that yourself, officers and men have done the best you could. All accounts say better fighting was never done. Ten thousand thanks for it.

On the 28th. we sent Gen. Burnside an order to send all the force he could spare, to you. We then learned that you had requested him to go to Goldsborough, upon which, we said to him our order was intended for your benefit, and we did not wish to be in conflict with your views. We hope you will have help from him soon. To-day we have ordered Gen. Hunter to send you all he can spare. At last advices Halleck thinks he can not send reinforcements, without endangering all he has gained.*

A. Lincoln

TELEGRAM TO GENERAL G. B. McCLELLAN
JULY 5, 1862

Washington City, D. C. July 5. 1862.

Major Genl. McClellan

A thousand thanks for the relief your two despatches of 12 & 1 P. M. yesterday give me. Be assured the heroism and skill of yourself, officers, and men, are, and forever will be appreciated. If you can hold your present position, we shall "*hive*" the enemy yet.

A. Lincoln

LETTER TO GENERAL G. B. McCLELLAN
JULY 13, 1862

Executive Mansion,
Washington, July 13 1862.

Major General McClellan

My dear Sir—

I am told that over 160-000 men have gone into your Army on the Peninsula. When I was with you the other day we made

* The last sentence as it stands is written above the following sentence, which Lincoln deleted: "I repeat what I have twice before said, 'save the Army, at all events.'"

out 86,500 remaining, leaving 73,500 to be accounted for. I believe 23,500 will cover all the killed, wounded and missing in all your battles and skirmishes, leaving 50-000 who have left otherwise. Not more than 5000 of these have died, leaving 45-000 of your Army still alive, and not with it. I believe half, or two thirds of them are fit for duty to-day. Have you any more perfect knowledge of this than I have? If I am right, and you had these men with you, you could go into Richmond in the next three days. How can they be got to you? and how can they be prevented from getting away in such numbers for the future?

A. Lincoln

LETTER TO CUTHBERT BULLITT
JULY 28, 1862

(*Private.*)

Washington, D. C., July 28, 1862.

Cuthbert Bullitt, Esq.,
New Orleans, Louisiana.
Sir:

The copy of a letter addressed to yourself by Mr. Thomas J. Durant has been shown to me. The writer appears to be an able, a dispassionate, and an entirely sincere man. The first part of the letter is devoted to an effort to show that the secession ordinance of Louisiana was adopted against the will of a majority of the people. This is probably true, and in that fact may be found some instruction. Why did they allow the ordinance to go into effect? Why did they not assert themselves? Why stand passive and allow themselves to be trodden down by a minority? Why did they not hold popular meetings and have a convention of their own to express and enforce the true sentiment of the State? If preorganization was against them then, why not do this now that the United States army is present to protect them? The paralysis—the dead palsy—of the government in this whole struggle is, that this class of men will do nothing for the government, nothing for themselves, except demanding that the government shall not strike its open enemies, lest they be struck by accident!

Mr. Durant complains that in various ways the relation of master and slave is disturbed by the presence of our army, and he considers it particularly vexatious that this, in part, is done under cover of an act of Congress, while constitutional guaranties are suspended on the plea of military necessity. The truth is, that what is done and omitted about slaves is done and omitted on the same military necessity. It is a military necessity to have men and money; and we can get neither in sufficient numbers or amounts if we keep from or drive from our lines slaves coming to them. Mr. Durant cannot be ignorant of the pressure in this direction, nor of my efforts to hold it within bounds till he and such as he shall have time to help themselves.

I am not posted to speak understandingly on all the police regulations of which Mr. Durant complains. If experience shows any one of them to be wrong, let them be set right. I think I can perceive in the freedom of trade which Mr. Durant urges that he would relieve both friends and enemies from the pressure of the blockade. By this he would serve the enemy more effectively than the enemy is able to serve himself. I do not say or believe that to serve the enemy is the purpose of Mr. Durant, or that he is conscious of any purpose other than national and patriotic ones. Still, if there were a class of men who, having no choice of sides in the contest, were anxious only to have quiet and comfort for themselves while it rages, and to fall in with the victorious side at the end of it without loss to themselves, their advice as to the mode of conducting the contest would be precisely such as his is. He speaks of no duty—apparently thinks of none—resting upon Union men. He even thinks it injurious to the Union cause that they should be restrained in trade and passage without taking sides. They are to touch neither a sail nor a pump, but to be merely passengers—deadheads at that—to be carried snug and dry throughout the storm, and safely landed right side up. Nay, more: even a mutineer is to go untouched, lest these sacred passengers receive an accidental wound. Of course the rebellion will never be suppressed in Louisiana if the professed Union men there will neither help to do it nor permit the government to do it without their help. Now, I think the true remedy is very different from what is suggested by Mr. Durant. It does not lie in rounding the rough angles of the war, but in removing the necessity for the war. The people of Louisiana who wish protection to person and property have but to reach forth their hands and take it. Let them in good faith reinaugurate the national authority, and set up a State government conforming thereto under the Constitution. They know how to do it, and can have the protection of the army while doing it. The army will be withdrawn so soon as such State government can dispense with its presence; and the people of the State can then, upon the old constitutional terms, govern themselves to their own liking. This is very simple and easy.

If they will not do this—if they prefer to hazard all for the sake of destroying the government, it is for them to consider whether it is probable I will surrender the government to save them from losing all. If they decline what I suggest, you scarcely need to ask what I will do. What would you do in my position? Would you drop the war where it is? Or would you prosecute it in future with elder-stalk squirts charged with rose-water? Would you deal lighter blows rather than heavier ones? Would you give up the contest, leaving any available means unapplied? I am in no boastful mood. I shall not do more than I can, and I shall do all I can, to save the government, which is my sworn duty as well as my personal inclination. I shall do nothing in malice. What I deal with is too vast for malicious dealing.

Yours truly,
A. Lincoln.

LETTER TO JOHN M. CLAY
AUGUST 9, 1862

Executive Mansion,
Washington, August 9, 1862

Mr. John M. Clay.
My dear Sir:

The snuff-box you sent, with the accompanying note, was received yesterday. Thanks for this *memento* of your great and patriotic father. Thanks also for the assurance that, in these days of dereliction, you remain true to his principles. In the concurrent sentiment of your venerable mother, so long the partner of his bosom and his honors, and lingering now, where he *was*, but for the call to rejoin him where he *is*, I recognize his voice, speaking as it ever spoke, for the Union, the Constitution, and the freedom of mankind.

Your Obt. Servt.
A. Lincoln

LETTER TO HORACE GREELEY
AUGUST 22, 1862

Executive Mansion,
Washington, August 22, 1862.

Hon. Horace Greeley:
Dear Sir.

I have just read yours of the 19th. addressed to myself through the New-York Tribune. If there be in it any statements, or assumptions of fact, which I may know to be erroneous, I do not, now and here, controvert them. If there be in it any inferences which I may believe to be falsely drawn, I do not now and here, argue against them. If there be perceptable [*sic*] in it an impatient and dictatorial tone, I waive it in deference to an old friend, whose heart I have always supposed to be right.

As to the policy I "seem to be pursuing" as you say, I have not meant to leave any one in doubt.

I would save the Union. I would save it the shortest way under the Constitution. The sooner the national authority can be restored; the nearer the Union will be "the Union as it was."* If there be those who would not save the Union, unless they could at the same time *save* slavery, I do not agree with them. If there be those who would not save the Union unless they could at the same time *destroy* slavery, I do not agree with them. My paramount object in this struggle *is* to save the Union, and is *not* either to save or to destroy slavery. If I could save the Union without freeing *any* slave I would do it, and if I could save it by freeing *all* the slaves, I would do it; and if I could save it by freeing some and leaving others alone I would also do that. What I do about slavery, and the colored race, I do because I believe it helps to save the Union; and what I forbear, I forbear because I do *not* believe it would help to save the Union. I shall do *less* whenever I shall believe what I am doing hurts the cause, and I shall do *more* whenever I shall believe doing more will help the cause. I shall try to correct errors when shown to be errors; and I shall adopt new views so fast as they shall appear to be true views.

I have here stated my purpose according to my view of *official* duty; and I intend no modification of my oft-expressed *personal* wish that all men everywhere could be free.

Yours,
A. Lincoln.

Lincoln wrote this public letter in answer to a communication entitled "The Prayer of Twenty Millions"

* At this point Lincoln deleted a sentence which stood as follows: "Broken eggs can never be mended, and the longer the breaking proceeds the more will be broken."

addressed to Lincoln by Greeley in his paper the New York Tribune. *It was characteristic of Greeley to presume that his views were those of a majority of the people. The "Prayer" expressed the opinion that Lincoln might have dealt the rebellion a staggering blow in its infancy by holding out the threat of emancipation in his "Inaugural Address" and that a rigid execution of laws passed by Congress—especially the confiscation measure—would go far toward concluding the war. The people were lost and uncertain as to where the administration was taking the country because Lincoln himself seemed not to know. Lincoln seized the opportunity not so much to answer Greeley as to explain to the supposed "Twenty Millions" what he was trying to do.*

TELEGRAM TO GENERAL G. B. McCLELLAN SEPTEMBER 15, 1862

Washington, D. C., Sep. 15, 2:45 1862.

Major General McClellan.

Your despatches of to-day received. God bless you, and all with you. Destroy the rebel army, if possible.

A. Lincoln

TESTIMONIAL FOR DOCTOR ISACHAR ZACHARIE
SEPTEMBER 22, 1862

Dr. Zacharie has operated on my feet with great success, and considerable addition to my comfort.

A. Lincoln

Sep. 22, 1862.

LETTER TO JOHN ROSS
SEPTEMBER 25, 1862

Executive Mansion,
Washington, Sept. 25, 1862.

John Ross
Principal Chief of the Cherokee Nation
Sir.

Your letter of the 16th. Inst. was received two days ago. In the multitude of cares claiming my constant attention I have been unable to examine and determine the exact treaty relations between the United States and the Cherokee Nation. Neither have I been able to investigate and determine the exact state of facts claimed by you as constituting a failure of treaty obligation on our part, excusing the Cherokee Nation for making a treaty with a portion of the people of the United States in open rebellion against the government thereof. This letter therefore, must not be understood to decide anything upon these questions. I shall, however, cause a careful investigation of them to be made. Meanwhile the Cherokee people remaining practically loyal to the federal Union will receive all the protection which can be given them consistently with the duty of the government to the whole country. I sincerely hope the Cherokee country may not again be over-run by the enemy; and I shall do all I consistently can to prevent it.

Your Obt. Servt.
A. Lincoln.

MEDITATION ON THE DIVINE WILL
SEPTEMBER [30?], 1862

The will of God prevails. In great contests each party claims to act in accordance with the will of God. Both may be, and one must be, wrong. God cannot be for and against the same thing at the same time. In the present civil war it is quite possible that God's purpose is something different from the purpose of either party; and yet the human instrumentalities, working just as they do, are of the best adaptation to effect his purpose. I am almost ready to say that this is probably true; that God wills this contest, and wills that it shall not end yet. By his mere great power on the minds of the now contestants, he could have either saved or destroyed the Union without a human contest. Yet the contest began. And, having begun, he could give the final victory to either side any day. Yet the contest proceeds.

According to Nicolay and Hay's account in Abraham Lincoln: A History, *the meditation "was not written to be seen of men." Finding the piece of paper on which it was written, John Hay made a copy and thus preserved the text as printed in the* Complete Works of Abraham Lincoln. *When one reviews the disappointments which*

Lincoln had experienced in the repeated failures of General McClellan during preceding months, the drift of Lincoln's thought in this piece is more than adequately accounted for.

REMARKS TO THE ARMY OF THE POTOMAC AT FREDERICK, MARYLAND. OCTOBER 4, 1862

Fellow Citizens:

I see myself surrounded by soldiers, and a little further off I note the citizens of this good city of Frederick, anxious to hear something from me. I can only say, as I did five minutes ago, it is not proper for me to make speeches in my present position. I return thanks to our soldiers for the good service they have rendered, for the energies they have shown, the hardships they have endured, and the blood they have so nobly shed for this dear Union of ours; and I also return thanks not only to the soldiers, but to the good citizens of Maryland, and to all good men and women in this land, for their devotion to our glorious cause. I say this without any malice in my heart to those who have done otherwise. May our children and our children's children, to a thousand generations, continue to enjoy the benefits conferred upon us by a united country, and have cause yet to rejoice under those glorious institutions bequeathed us by Washington and his compeers. Now, my friends, soldiers and citizens, I can only say once more, farewell.

LETTER TO GENERAL G. B. McCLELLAN OCTOBER 13, 1862

Executive Mansion,
Washington, D.C., October 13, 1862.

Major-General McClellan.
My dear Sir:

You remember my speaking to you of what I called your over-cautiousness. Are you not over-cautious when you assume that you cannot do what the enemy is constantly doing? Should you not claim to be at least his equal in prowess, and act upon the claim? As I understand, you telegraphed General Halleck that you cannot subsist your army at Winchester unless the railroad from Harper's Ferry to that point be put in working order. But the enemy does now subsist his army at Winchester, at a distance nearly twice as great from railroad transportation as you would have to do without the railroad last named. He now wagons from Culpeper Court House, which is just about twice as far as you would have to do from Harper's Ferry. He is certainly not more than half as well provided with wagons as you are. I certainly should be pleased for you to have the advantage of the railroad from Harper's Ferry to Winchester, but it wastes all the remainder of autumn to give it to you, and in fact ignores the question of time, which cannot and must not be ignored. Again, one of the standard maxims of war, as you know, is to "operate upon the enemy's communications as much as possible without exposing your own." You seem to act as if this applies against you, but cannot apply in your favor. Change positions with the enemy, and think you not he would break your communication with Richmond within the next twenty-four hours? You dread his going into Pennsylvania; but if he does so in full force, he gives up his communications to you absolutely, and you have nothing to do but to follow and ruin him. If he does so with less than full force, fall upon and beat what is left behind all the easier. Exclusive of the water-line, you are now nearer Richmond than the enemy is by the route that you can and he must take. Why can you not reach there before him, unless you admit that he is more than your equal on a march? His route is the arc of a circle, while yours is the chord. The roads are as good on yours as on his. You know I desired, but did not order, you to cross the Potomac below, instead of above, the Shenandoah and Blue Ridge. My idea was that this would at once menace the enemy's communications, which I would seize if he would permit.

If he should move northward, I would follow him closely, holding his communications. If he should prevent our seizing his communications and move toward Richmond, I would press closely to him, fight him if a favorable opportunity should present, and at least try to beat him to Richmond on the inside track. I say "try"; if we never try, we shall never succeed. If he makes a stand at Winchester, moving neither north nor south, I would fight him there, on the idea that if we cannot beat him when he bears the wastage of coming to us, we never can when we bear the wastage of going to him. This proposition is a simple truth, and is too important to be lost sight of for a moment. In coming to us he tenders us an advantage which we should not waive. We should not so operate as to merely drive him away. As we must beat him somewhere or fail finally, we can do it, if at all, easier near to us than far away. If we cannot beat the enemy where he now is, we never can, he again being within the intrenchments of Richmond.

Recurring to the idea of going to Richmond on the inside track, the facility of supplying from the side away from the enemy is remarkable, as it were, by the different spokes of a wheel extending from the hub toward the rim, and this whether you move directly by the chord or on the inside arc, hugging the Blue Ridge more closely. The chord-line, as you see, carries you by Aldie, Hay Market, and Fredericksburg; and you see how turnpikes, railroads, and finally the Potomac, by Aquia Creek, meet you at all points from Washington; the same, only the lines lengthened a little, if you press closer to the Blue Ridge part of the way.

The gaps through the Blue Ridge I understand to be about

the following distances from Harper's Ferry, to wit: Vestal's 5 miles; Gregory's, 13; Snicker's, 18; Ashby's, 28; Manassas, 38; Chester, 45; and Thornton's, 53. I should think it preferable to take the route nearest the enemy, disabling him to make an important move without your knowledge, and compelling him to keep his forces together for dread of you. The gaps would enable you to attack if you should wish. For a great part of the way you would be practically between the enemy and both Washington and Richmond, enabling us to spare you the greatest number of troops from here. When at length running for Richmond ahead of him enables him to move this way, if he does so, turn and attack him in rear. But I think he should be engaged long before such point is reached. It is all easy if our troops march as well as the enemy, and it is unmanly to say they cannot do it. This letter is in no sense an order.

Yours truly,
A. Lincoln.

TELEGRAM TO GENERAL G. B. McCLELLAN OCTOBER 24, 1862

Washington City, D. C. Oct. 24. 1862

Majr. Genl. McClellan

I have just read your despatch about sore tongued and fatigued horses.

Will you pardon me for asking what the horses of your army have done since the battle of Antietam that fatigue anything?

A. Lincoln

TELEGRAM TO GENERAL G. B. McCLELLAN OCTOBER 27, 1862

Executive Mansion,
Washington, Oct. 27, 1862

Majr. Gen. McClellan.

Yours of yesterday received. Most certainly I intend no injustice to any; and if I have done any, I deeply regret it. To be told after more than five weeks total inaction of the Army, and during which period we had sent to that Army every fresh horse we possibly could, amounting in the whole to 7918 that the cavalry horses were too much fatigued to move, presented a very cheerless, almost hopeless, prospect for the future; and it may have forced something of impatience into my despatches. If not recruited, and rested then, when could they ever be? I suppose the river is rising, and I am glad to believe you are crossing.

A. Lincoln

LETTER TO GENERAL CARL SCHURZ NOVEMBER 10, 1862

"Private & Confidential"

Executive Mansion,
Washington, Nov. 10, 1862.

Gen. Schurz.
My dear Sir

Yours of the 8th. was, to-day, read to me by Mrs. S. We have lost the elections; and it is natural that each of us will believe, and say, it has been because his peculiar view was not made sufficiently prominent. I think I know what it was, but I may be mistaken. Three main causes told the whole story. 1. The democrats were left in a majority by our friends going to the war. 2. The democrats observed this & determined to re-instate themselves in power, and 3. Our newspaper's, by vilifying and disparaging the administration, furnished them all the weapons to do it with. Certainly, the ill-success of the war had much to do with this.

You give a different set of reasons. If you had not made the following statements, I should not have suspected them to be true. "The defeat of the administration is the administrations own fault." (Opinion) "It admitted its professed opponents to its counsels" (Asserted as a fact) "It placed the Army, now a great power in this Republic, into the hands of it's enemys [*sic*]" (Asserted as a fact) "In all personal questions, to be hostile to the party of the Government, seemed, to be a title to consideration." (Asserted as a fact) "If to forget the great rule, that if you are true to your friends, your friends will be true to you, and that you make your enemies stronger by placing them upon an equality with your friends." "Is it surprising that the opponents of the administration should have got into their hands the government of the principal states, after they have had for a long time the principal management of the war, the great business of the national government."

I can not dispute about the matter of opinion. On the the [*sic*] three matters (stated as facts) I shall be glad to have your evidence upon them when I shall meet you. The plain facts, as they appear to me, are these. The administration came into power, very largely in a minority of the popular vote. Nothwithstanding this, it distributed to it's party friends as nearly all the civil patronage as any administration ever did. The war came. The administration could not even start in this, without assistance outside of it's party. It was mere nonsense to suppose a minority could put down a majority in rebellion. Mr. Schurz (now Gen. Schurz) was about here then & I do not recollect that he then considered all who were not republicans, were enemies of the government, and that none of them must be appointed to to [*sic*] military positions. He will correct me if I am mistaken. It so happened that very few of our friends had a military education or were of the profession of arms. It would have been a question whether the war should be conducted on military knowledge, or on political affinity, only that our own friends (I think Mr. Schurz included) seemed to think that such a question was inadmissable [*sic*]. Accordingly I have scarcely appointed a democrat to a command, who was not urged by many republicans and opposed by none. It was so as to McClellan. He was first brought forward by the Republican Governor of Ohio, & claimed, and contended for at the same time by the Republican Governor of Pennsylvania. I received recommendations from the republican delegations in Congress, and I believe every one of them recommended a majority of democrats. But, after all many Republicans were appointed; and I mean no disparagement to them when I say I do not see that their superiority of success has been so marked as to throw great suspicion on the good faith of those who are not Republicans.

Yours truly,
A. Lincoln

Schurz was an intellectual and political leader among the German-American population which had swelled so rapidly in the years following the German Revolution of 1848. Lincoln had cultivated their support even to the extent of subsidizing a German language newspaper, 1859-60, and in fact all over the North a large percentage of them had joined the Republican party.

Lincoln's ironical treatment of Schurz's criticism of administration policy in appointing Democrats to important commands was prompted by the fact that Republicans in general and Schurz in particular had displayed little evidence of their superior military ability.

LETTER TO SAMUEL TREAT
NOVEMBER 19, 1862

Private

Executive Mansion,
Washington, Nov. 19, 1862.

Judge S. Treat
St. Louis, Mo.
My dear Sir

Your very patriotic and judicious letter, addressed to Judge Davis, in relation to the Mississippi, has been left with me by him for perusal. You do not estimate the value of the object you press, more highly than it is estimated here. It is now the object of particular attention. It has not been neglected, as you seem to think, because the West was divided into different Military Departments. The cause is much deeper. The country will not allow us to send our whole Western force down the Mississippi, while the enemy sacks Louisville and Cincinnati. Possibly it would be better if the country would allow this, but it will not. I confidently believed, last September that we could end the war by allowing the enemy to go to Harrisburg and Philadelphia, only that we could not keep down mutiny, and utter demoralization among the Pennsylvanians. And this, though very unhandy sometimes, is not at all strange. I presume if an army was starting to-day for New-Orleans, and you confidently believed that St. Louis would be sacked in consequence, you would be in favor of stopping such army.

We are compelled to watch all these things.

With great respect
Your Obt. Servt
A. Lincoln.

Samuel Treat, United States Judge at St. Louis, was impatient that General Grant had not moved to free the Mississippi as rapidly as Treat and other residents of St. Louis desired.

LETTER TO GENERAL CARL SCHURZ
NOVEMBER 24, 1862

Executive Mansion,
Washington, Nov. 24., 1862.

Gen. Carl Schurz
My dear Sir

I have just received, and read, your letter of the 20th. The purport of it is that we lost the late elections, and the administration is failing, because the war is unsuccessful; and that I must not flatter myself that I am not justly to blame for it. I certainly know that if the war fails, the administration fails, and that I *will* be blamed for it, whether I deserve it or not. And I ought to be blamed, if I could do better. You think I could do better; therefore you blame me already. I think I could not do better; therefore I blame you for blaming me. I understand you *now* to be willing to accept the help of men, who are not republicans, provided they have "heart in it." Agreed. I want no others. But who is to be the judge of hearts, or of "heart in it"? If I must discard my own judgment, and take yours, I must also take that of others; and by the time I should reject all I should be advised to reject, I should have none left, republicans, or others—not even yourself. For, be assured, my dear Sir, there are men who have "heart in it" that think you are performing your part as poorly as you think I am performing mine. I certainly have been dissatisfied with the slowness of Buell and McClellan; but before I relieved them I had great fears I should not find successors to them, who would do better; and I am sorry to add, that I have seen little since to relieve those fears. I do not clearly see the prospect of any more rapid movements. I fear we shall at last find out that the difficulty is in our case, rather than in particular generals. I wish to disparage no one—certainly not those who sympathize with me; but I must say I need success more than I need sympathy, and that I have not seen the so much greater evidence of getting success from my sympathizers, than from those who are denounced as the contrary. It does seem to me that in the field the two classes have been very much alike, in what they have done, and what they have failed to do. In sealing their faith with their blood, Baker, and Lyon, and Bohlen, and Richardson, republicans, did all that men could do; but did they any more than Kearny, and Stevens, and Reno, and Mansfield, none of whom were republicans, and some, at least of whom, have been bitterly, and repeatedly, denounced to me as secession sympathizers? I will not perform the ungrateful task of comparing cases of failure.

In answer to your question "Has it not been publicly stated in the newspapers, and apparently proved as a fact, that from the commencement of the war, the enemy was continually supplied with information by some of the confidential subordinates of as important an officer as Adjutant General Thomas?" I must say "no" so far as my knowledge extends. And I add that if you can give any tangible evidence upon that subject, I will thank you to come to the City and do so.

Very truly your friend

A. Lincoln

ANNUAL MESSAGE TO CONGRESS DECEMBER 1, 1862

Fellow-citizens of the Senate and House of Representatives:

Since your last annual assembling another year of health and bountiful harvests has passed. And while it has not pleased the Almighty to bless us with a return of peace, we can but press on, guided by the best light He gives us, trusting that in His own good time, and wise way, all will yet be well.

The correspondence touching foreign affairs which has taken place during the last year is herewith submitted, in virtual compliance with a request to that effect, made by the House of Representatives near the close of the last session of Congress.

If the condition of our relations with other nations is less gratifying than it has usually been at former periods, it is certainly more satisfactory than a nation so unhappily distracted as we are might reasonably have apprehended. In the month of June last there were some grounds to expect that the maritime Powers which, at the beginning of our domestic difficulties, so unwisely and unnecessarily, as we think, recognized the insurgents as a belligerent, would soon recede from that position, which has proved only less injurious to themselves than to our own country. But the temporary reverses which afterwards befell the national arms, and which were exaggerated by our own disloyal citizens abroad have hitherto delayed that act of simple justice.

The civil war, which has so radically changed for the moment, the occupations and habits of the American people, has necessarily disturbed the social condition, and affected very deeply the prosperity of the nations with which we have carried on a commerce that has been steadily increasing throughout a period of half a century. It has, at the same time, excited political ambitions and apprehensions which have produced a profound agitation throughout the civilized world. In this unusual agitation we have forborne from taking part in any controversy between foreign states, and between parties or factions in such states. We have attempted no propagandism, and acknowledged no revolution. But we have left to every nation the exclusive conduct and management of its own affairs. Our struggle has been, of course, contemplated by foreign nations with reference less to its own merits, than to its supposed, and often exaggerated effects and consequences resulting to those nations themselves. Nevertheless, complaint on the part of this government, even if it were just, would certainly be unwise.

The treaty with Great Britain for the suppression of the slave trade has been put into operation with a good prospect of complete success. It is an occasion of special pleasure to acknowledge that the execution of it, on the part of her Majesty's government has been marked with a jealous respect for the authority of the United States, and the rights of their moral and loyal citizens.

The convention with Hanover for the abolition of the stade dues has been carried into full effect, under the act of Congress for that purpose.

A blockade of three thousand miles of sea-coast could not be established, and vigorously enforced, in a season of great commercial activity like the present, without committing occasional mistakes, and inflicting unintentional injuries upon foreign nations and their subjects.

A civil war occurring in a country where foreigners reside and carry on trade under treaty stipulations, is necessarily fruitful of complaints of the violation of neutral rights. All such collisions tend to excite misapprehensions, and possibly to produce mutual reclamations between nations which have a common interest in preserving peace and friendship. In clear cases of these kinds I have, so far as possible, heard and redressed complaints which have been presented by friendly powers. There is still, however, a large and an augmenting number of doubtful cases upon which the government is unable to agree with the governments whose protection is demanded by the claimants. There are, moreover, many cases in which the United States, or their citizens, suffer wrongs from the naval or military authorities of foreign nations, which the governments of those states are not at once prepared to redress. I have proposed to some of the foreign states, thus interested, mutual conventions to examine and adjust such complaints. This proposition has been made especially to Great Britain, to France, to Spain, and to Prussia. In each case it has been kindly received, but has not yet been formally adopted.

I deem it my duty to recommend an appropriation in behalf of the owners of the Norwegian bark Admiral P. Tordenskiold, which vessel was, in May, 1861, prevented by the commander of the blockading force off Charleston from leaving that port with cargo, notwithstanding a similar privilege had, shortly before, been granted to an English vessel. I have directed the Secretary of State to cause the papers in the case to be communicated to the proper committees.

Applications have been made to me by many free Americans of African descent to favor their emigration, with a view to such colonization as was contemplated in recent acts of Congress. Other parties, at home and abroad—some from interested motives, others upon patriotic considerations, and still others influenced by philanthropic sentiments—have suggested similar measures; while, on the other hand, several of the Spanish-American republics have protested against the sending of such colonies to their respective territories. Under these circumstances, I have declined to move any such colony to any state, without first obtaining the consent of its government, with an agreement on its part to receive and protect such emigrants in all the rights of freemen; and I have, at the same time, offered to the several states situated within the tropics, or having colonies there, to negotiate with them, subject to the advice and consent of the Senate, to favor the voluntary emigration of persons of that class to their respective territories, upon conditions which shall be equal, just, and humane. Liberia and Hayti are, as yet, the only countries to which colonists of African descent from here, could go with certainty of being received and adopted as citizens; and I regret to say such persons, contemplating colonization do not seem so willing to migrate to those countries as to some others, nor so willing as I think their interest demands. I believe, however, opinion among them, in this respect, is improving; and that, ere long, there will be an augmented, and considerable migration to both these countries, from the United States.

The new commercial treaty between the United States and the Sultan of Turkey has been carried into execution.

A commercial and consular treaty has been negotiated, subject to the Senate's consent, with Liberia; and a similar negotiation is now pending with the republic of Hayti. A considerable improvement of our national commerce is expected to result from these measures.

Our relations with Great Britain, France, Spain, Portugal, Russia, Prussia, Denmark, Sweden, Austria, the Netherlands, Italy, Rome, and the other European states, remain undisturbed. Very favorable relations also continue to be maintained with Turkey, Morocco, China and Japan.

During the last year there has not only been no change of our previous relations with the independent states of our own continent, but, more friendly sentiments than have heretofore existed, are believed to be entertained by these neighbors, whose safety and progress, are so intimately connected with our own. This statement especially applies to Mexico, Nicaragua, Costa Rica, Honduras, Peru, and Chile.

The commission under the convention with the republic of New Granada closed its session, without having audited and passed upon, all the claims which were submitted to it. A proposition is pending to revive the convention, that it may be able to do more complete justice. The joint commission between the United States and the republic of Costa Rica has completed its labors and submitted its report.

I have favored the project for connecting the United States with Europe by an Atlantic telegraph, and a similar project to extend the telegraph from San Francisco, to connect by a Pacific telegraph with the line which is being extended across the Russian empire.

The Territories of the United States, with unimportant exceptions, have remained undisturbed by the civil war, and they are exhibiting such evidence of prosperity as justifies an expectation that some of them will soon be in a condition to be organized as States, and be constitutionally admitted into the federal Union.

The immense mineral resources of some of those Territories

ought to be developed as rapidly as possible. Every step in that direction would have a tendency to improve the revenues of the government, and diminish the burdens of the people. It is worthy of your serious consideration whether some extraordinary measures to promote that end cannot be adopted. The means which suggests itself as most likely to be effective, is a scientific exploration of the mineral regions in those Territories, with a view to the publication of its results at home and in foreign countries—results which cannot fail to be auspicious.

The condition of the finances will claim your most diligent consideration. The vast expenditures incident to the military and naval operations required for the suppression of the rebellion, have hitherto been met with a promptitude, and certainty, unusual in similar circumstances, and the public credit has been fully maintained. The continuance of the war, however, and the increased disbursements made necessary by the augmented forces now in the field, demand your best reflections as to the best modes of providing the necessary revenue, without injury to business and with the least possible burdens upon labor.

The suspension of specie payments by the banks, soon after the commencement of your last session, made large issues of United States notes unavoidable. In no other way could the payment of the troops, and the satisfaction of other just demands, be so economically, or so well provided for. The judicious legislation of Congress, securing the receivability of these notes for loans and internal duties, and making them a legal tender for other debts, has made them an universal currency; and has satisfied, partially, at least, and for the time, the long felt want of an uniform circulating medium, saving thereby to the people, immense sums in discounts and exchanges.

A return to specie payments, however, at the earliest period compatible with due regard to all interests concerned, should ever be kept in view. Fluctuations in the value of currency are always injurious, and to reduce these fluctuations to the lowest possible point will always be a leading purpose in wise legislation. Convertibility, prompt and certain convertibility into coin, is generally acknowledged to be the best and surest safeguard against them; and it is extremely doubtful whether a circulation

Meserve No. 85. A photograph made by Mathew B. Brady on February 9, 1864. Mr. Robert Todd Lincoln stated to Frederick Hill Meserve that he considered this to be the best photograph of his father. It is the most widely known of all the portraits of Lincoln, as it appears on the five-dollar bill.

of United States notes, payable in coin, and sufficiently large for the wants of the people, can be permanently, usefully and safely maintained.

Is there, then, any other mode in which the necessary provision for the public wants can be made, and the great advantages of a safe and uniform currency secured?

I know of none which promises so certain results, and is, at the same time, so unobjectionable, as the organization of banking associations, under a general act of Congress, well guarded in its provisions. To such associations the government might furnish circulating notes, on the security of United States bonds deposited in the treasury. These notes, prepared under the supervision of proper officers, being uniform in appearance and security, and convertible always into coin, would at once protect labor against the evils of a vicious currency, and facilitate commerce by cheap and safe exchanges.

A moderate reservation from the interest on the bonds would compensate the United States for the preparation and distribution of the notes and a general supervision of the system, and would lighten the burden of that part of the public debt employed as securities. The public credit, moreover, would be greatly improved, and the negotiation of new loans greatly facilitated by the steady market demand for government bonds which the adoption of the proposed system would create.

It is an additional recommendation of the measure, of considerable weight, in my judgment, that it would reconcile, as far as possible, all existing interests, by the opportunity offered to existing institutions to reorganize under the act, substituting only the secured uniform national circulation for the local and various circulation, secured and unsecured, now issued by them.

The receipts into the treasury from all sources, including loans and balance from the preceding year, for the fiscal year ending on the 30th June, 1862, were $583,885,247.06, of which sum $49,056,397.62 were derived from customs; $1,795,331.73 from the direct tax; from public lands, $152,203.77; from miscellaneous sources, $931,787.64; from loans in all forms, $529,692,460.50. The remainder, $2,257,065.80, was the balance from last year.

The disbursements during the same period were for congressional, executive, and judicial purposes, $5,939,009.29; for foreign intercourse, $1,339,710.35; for miscellaneous expenses, including the mints, loans, post office deficiencies, collection of revenue, and other like charges, $14,129,771.50; for expenses under the Interior Department, $3,102,985.52; under the War Department, $394,368,407.36; under the Navy Department, $42,674,569.69; for interest on public debt, $13,190,324.45; and for payment of public debt, including reimbursement of temporary loan, and redemptions, $96,096,922.09; making an aggregate of $570,841,700.25, and leaving a balance in the treasury on the first day of July, 1862, of $13,043,546.81.

It should be observed that the sum of $96,096,922.09, expended for reimbursements and redemption of public debt, being included also in the loans made, may be properly deducted, both from receipts and expenditures, leaving the actual receipts for the year $487,788,324.97; and the expenditures, $474,744,778.16.

Other information on the subject of the finances will be found in the report of the Secretary of the Treasury, to whose statements and views I invite your most candid and considerate attention.

The reports of the Secretaries of War, and of the Navy, are herewith transmitted. These reports, though lengthy, are scarcely more than brief abstracts of the very numerous and extensive transactions and operations conducted through those departments. Nor could I give a summary of them here, upon any principle, which would admit of its being much shorter than the reports themselves. I therefore content myself with laying the reports before you, and asking your attention to them.

It gives me pleasure to report a decided improvement in the financial condition of the Post Office Department, as compared with several preceding years. The receipts for the fiscal year 1861 amounted to $8,349,296.40, which embraced the revenue from all the States of the Union for three quarters of that year. Notwithstanding the cessation of revenue from the so-called seceded States during the last fiscal year, the increase of the correspondence of the loyal States has been sufficient to produce a revenue during the same year of $8,299,820.90, being only $50,000 less than was derived from all the States of the Union during the previous year. The expenditures show a still more favorable result. The amount expended in 1861 was $13,606,759.11. For the last year the amount has been reduced to $11,125,364.13, showing a decrease of about $2,481,000 in the expenditures as compared with the preceding year and about $3,750,000 as compared with the fiscal year 1860. The deficiency in the department for the previous year was $4,551,966.98. For the last fiscal year it was reduced to $2,112,814.57. These favorable results are in part owing to the cessation of mail service in the insurrectionary States, and in part to a careful review of all expenditures in that department in the interest of economy. The efficiency of the postal service, it is believed, has also been much improved. The Postmaster General has also opened a correspondence, through the Department of State, with foreign governments, proposing a convention of postal representatives for the purpose of simplifying the rates of foreign postage, and to expedite the foreign mails. This proposition, equally important to our adopted citizens, and to the commercial interests of this country, has been favorably entertained, and agreed to, by all the governments from whom replies have been received.

I ask the attention of Congress to the suggestions of the Postmaster General in his report respecting the further legislation required, in his opinion, for the benefit of the postal service.

The Secretary of the Interior reports as follows in regard to the public lands:

"The public lands have ceased to be a source of revenue. From the 1st July, 1861, to the 30th September, 1862, the entire cash receipts from the sale of lands were $137,476.26—a sum much less than the expenses of our land system during the same period. The homestead law, which will take effect on the 1st of January next, offers such inducements to settlers, that sales for cash cannot be expected, to an extent sufficient to meet the expenses of the General Land Office, and the cost of surveying and bringing the land into market."

The discrepancy between the sum here stated as arising from the sales of the public lands, and the sum derived from the same source as reported from the Treasury Department, arises, as I understand, from the fact that the periods of time, though apparently, were not really, coincident at the beginning point—the Treasury report including a considerable sum now, which had previously been reported from the Interior—sufficiently large to greatly overreach the sum derived from the three months now reported upon by the Interior, and not by the Treasury.

The Indian tribes upon our frontiers have, during the past year, manifested a spirit of insubordination, and, at several points, have engaged in open hostilities against the white settlements in their vicinity. The tribes occupying the Indian country south of Kansas, renounced their allegiance to the United States, and entered into treaties with the insurgents. Those who remained loyal to the United States were driven from the country. The chief of the Cherokees has visited this city for the purpose of restoring the former relations of the tribe with the United States. He alleges that they were constrained, by superior force, to enter into treaties with the insurgents, and that the United States neglected to furnish the protection which their treaty stipulations required.

In the month of August last the Sioux Indians, in Minnesota, attacked the settlements in their vicinity with extreme ferocity, killing, indiscriminately, men, women, and children. This attack was wholly unexpected, and, therefore, no means of defence had been provided. It is estimated that not less than eight hundred persons were killed by the Indians, and a large amount of property was destroyed. How this outbreak was induced is not definitely known, and suspicions, which may be unjust, need not to be stated. Information was received by the Indian bureau, from different sources, about the time hostilities were commenced, that a simultaneous attack was to be made upon the white settlements by all the tribes between the Mississippi River and the Rocky mountains. The State of Minnesota has suffered great injury from this Indian war. A large portion of her territory has been depopulated, and a severe loss has been sustained by the destruction of property. The people of that State manifest much anxiety for the removal of the tribes beyond the limits of the State as a guarantee against future hostilities. The Commissioner of Indian Affairs will furnish full details. I submit for your especial consideration whether our Indian system shall not be remodelled. Many wise and good men have impressed me with the belief that this can be profitably done.

I submit a statement of the proceedings of commissioners, which shows the progress that has been made in the enterprise of constructing the Pacific railroad. And this suggests the earliest completion of this road, and also the favorable action of Congress upon the projects now pending before them for enlarging the capacities of the great canals in New York and Illinois, as being of vital and rapidly increasing importance to the whole nation, and especially to the vast interior region hereinafter to be noticed at some greater length. I propose having prepared and laid before you at an early day some interesting and valuable statistical information upon this subject. The military and commercial importance of enlarging the Illinois and Michigan canal, and improving the Illinois River, is presented in the report of Colonel Webster to the Secretary of War, and now transmitted to Congress. I respectfully ask attention to it.

To carry out the provisions of the act of Congress of the 15th of May last, I have caused the Department of Agriculture of the United States to be organized.

The commissioner informs me that within the period of a few months this department has established an extensive system of correspondence and exchanges, both at home and abroad, which promises to effect highly beneficial results in the development of a correct knowledge of recent improvements in agriculture, in the introduction of new products, and in the collection of the agricultural statistics of the different States.

Also, that it will soon be prepared to distribute largely seeds, cereals, plants and cuttings, and has already published, and liberally diffused, much valuable information in anticipation of a more elaborate report, which will in due time be furnished, embracing some valuable tests in chemical science now in progress in the laboratory.

The creation of this department was for the more immediate benefit of a large class of our most valuable citizens; and I trust that the liberal basis upon which it has been organized will not only meet your approbation, but that it will realize, at no distant day, all the fondest anticipations of its most sanguine friends, and become the fruitful source of advantage to all our people.

On the twenty-second day of September last a proclamation was issued by the Executive, a copy of which is herewith submitted.

In accordance with the purpose expressed in the second paragraph of that paper, I now respectfully recall your attention to what may be called "compensated emancipation."

A nation may be said to consist of its territory, its people, and its laws. The territory is the only part which is of certain durability. "One generation passeth away, and another generation cometh, but the earth abideth forever." It is of the first importance to duly consider, and estimate, this ever-enduring part. That portion of the earth's surface which is owned and inhabited by the people of the United States, is well adapted to be the home of one national family; and it is not well adapted for two, or more. Its vast extent, and its variety of climate and productions, are of advantage, in this age, for one people, whatever they might have been in former ages. Steam, telegraphs, and intelligence, have brought these, to be an advantageous combination for one united people.

In the inaugural address I briefly pointed out the total inadequacy of disunion, as a remedy for the differences between the people of the two sections. I did so in language which I cannot improve, and which, therefore, I beg to repeat:

"One section of our country believes slavery is *right*, and ought to be extended, while the other believes it is *wrong*, and ought not to be extended. This is the only substantial dispute. The fugitive slave clause of the Constitution, and the law for the suppression of the foreign slave trade, are each as well enforced, perhaps, as any law can ever be in a community where the moral sense of the people imperfectly supports the law itself. The great body of the people abide by the dry legal obligation in both cases, and a few break over in each. This, I think, cannot be perfectly cured; and it would be worse in both cases *after* the separation of the sections, than before. The foreign slave trade, now imperfectly suppressed, would be ultimately revived without restriction in one section; while fugitive slaves, now only partially surrendered, would not be surrendered at all by the other.

"Physically speaking, we cannot separate. We cannot remove our respective sections from each other, nor build an impassable wall between them. A husband and wife may be divorced, and go out of the presence, and beyond the reach of each other; but the different parts of our country cannot do this. They cannot but remain face to face; and intercourse, either amicable or hostile, must continue between them. Is it possible, then, to make that intercourse more advantageous, or more satisfactory, *after* separation than *before*? Can aliens make treaties, easier than friends can make laws? Can treaties be more faithfully enforced between aliens, than laws can among friends? Suppose you go to war, you cannot fight always; and when, after much loss on both sides, and no gain on either, you cease fighting, the identical old questions, as to terms of intercourse, are again upon you."

There is no line, straight or crooked, suitable for a national boundary, upon which to divide. Trace through, from east to west, upon the line between the free and slave country, and we shall find a little more than one-third of its length are rivers, easy to be crossed, and populated, or soon to be populated, thickly upon both sides; while nearly all its remaining length are merely surveyor's lines, over which people may walk back and forth without any consciousness of their presence. No part of this line can be made any more difficult to pass, by writing it down on paper, or parchment, as a national boundary. The fact of separation, if it comes, gives up, on the part of the seceding section, the fugitive slave clause, along with all other constitutional obligations upon the section seceded from, while I should expect no treaty stipulation would be ever made to take its place.

But there is another difficulty. The great interior region, bounded east by the Alleghanies, north by the British dominions, west by the Rocky Mountains, and south by the line along which the culture of corn and cotton meets, and which includes part of Virginia, part of Tennessee, all of Kentucky, Ohio, Indiana, Michigan, Wisconsin, Illinois, Missouri, Kansas, Iowa, Minnesota, and the Territories of Dakota, Nebraska, and part of Colorado, already has above ten millions of people, and will have fifty millions within fifty years, if not prevented by any political folly or mistake. It contains more than one third of the country owned by the United States—certainly more than one million of square miles. Once half as populous as Massachusetts already is, it would have more than seventy-five millions of people. A glance at the map shows that, territorially speaking, it is the great body of the republic. The other parts are but marginal borders to it, the magnificent region sloping west from the Rocky Mountains to the Pacific, being the deepest and also the richest in undeveloped resources. In the production of provisions, grains, grasses, and all which proceed from them, this great interior region is naturally one of the most important in the world. Ascertain from the statistics the small proportion of the region which has, as yet, been brought into cultivation, and also the large and rapidly increasing amount of its products, and we shall be overwhelmed with the magnitude of the prospect presented. And yet this region has no sea-coast, touches no ocean anywhere. As part of one nation, its people now find, and may forever find, their way to Europe by New York, to South America and Africa by New Orleans, and to Asia by San Francisco. But separate our common country into two nations, as designed by the present rebellion, and every man of this great interior region is thereby cut off from some one or more of these outlets, not, perhaps, by a physical barrier, but by embarrassing and onerous trade regulations.

And this is true, *wherever* a dividing, or boundary line, may be fixed. Place it between the now free and slave country, or place it south of Kentucky, or north of Ohio, and still the truth remains, that none south of it, can trade to any port or place north of it, and none north of it, can trade to any port or place south of it, except upon terms dictated by a government foreign to them. These outlets, east, west, and south, are indispensable to the well-being of the people inhabiting, and to inhabit, this vast interior region. *Which* of the three may be the best, is no proper question. All, are better than either, and all, of right, belong to that people, and to their successors forever. True to themselves, they will not ask *where* a line of separation shall be, but will vow, rather, that there shall be no such line. Nor are the marginal regions less interested in these communications to, and through them, to the great outside world. They, too, and each of them, must have access to this Egypt of the West, without paying toll at the crossing of any national boundary.

Our national strife springs not from our permanent part; not from the land we inhabit; not from our national homestead. There is no possible severing of this, but would multiply, and not mitigate, evils among us. In all its adaptations and aptitudes, it demands union, and abhors separation. In fact, it would, ere long, force reunion, however much of blood and treasure the separation might have cost.

Our strife pertains to ourselves—to the passing generations of men; and it can, without convulsion, be hushed forever with the passing of one generation.

In this view, I recommend the adoption of the following resolution and articles amendatory to the Constitution of the United States:

"*Resolved by the Senate and House of Representatives of the United States of America in Congress assembled*, (two-thirds of both Houses concurring,) That the following articles be proposed to the legislatures (or conventions) of the several States as amendments to the Constitution of the United States, all or any of which articles when ratified by three fourths of the said legislatures (or conventions) to be valid as part or parts of the said Constitution, viz:

"Article —.

"Every State, wherein slavery now exists, which shall abolish the same therein, at any time, or times, before the first day of January, in the year of our Lord one thousand and nine hundred, shall receive compensation from the United States, as follows, to wit:

"The President of the United States shall deliver to every such State, bonds of the United States, bearing interest at the rate of —— percent, per annum, to an amount equal to the aggregate sum of ———— for each slave shown to have been therein, by the eighth census of the United States, said bonds to be delivered to such State by instalments, or in one parcel, at the completion of the abolishment, accordingly as the same shall have been gradual, or at one time, within such State; and interest shall begin to run upon any such bond, only from the proper time of its delivery as aforesaid. Any State having received bonds as aforesaid, and afterwards reintroducing or tolerating slavery therein, shall refund to the United States the bonds so received, or the value thereof, and all interest paid thereon.

"Article —.

"All slaves who shall have enjoyed actual freedom by the chances of the war, at any time before the end of the rebellion, shall be forever free; but all owners of such, who shall not have been disloyal, shall be compensated for them, at the same rates as is provided for States adopting abolishment of slavery, but in such way, that no slave shall be twice accounted for.

"Article —.

"Congress may appropriate money, and otherwise provide, for colonizing free colored persons, with their own consent, at any place or places without the United States."

I beg indulgence to discuss these proposed articles at some length. Without slavery the rebellion could never have existed; without slavery it could not continue.

Among the friends of the Union there is great diversity of sentiment, and of policy, in regard to slavery, and the African race amongst us. Some would perpetuate slavery; some would abolish it suddenly, and without compensation; some would abolish it gradually, and with compensation; some would remove the freed people from us, and some would retain them with us; and there are yet other minor diversities. Because of these diversities, we waste much strength in struggles among ourselves. By mutual concession we should harmonize, and act together. This would be compromise; but it would be compromise among the friends, and not with the enemies of the Union. These articles are intended to embody a plan of such mutual concessions. If the plan shall be adopted, it is assumed that emancipation will follow, at least, in several of the States.

As to the first article, the main points are: first, the emancipation; secondly, the length of time for consummating it—thirty-seven years; and thirdly, the compensation.

The emancipation will be unsatisfactory to the advocates of perpetual slavery; but the length of time should greatly mitigate their dissatisfaction. The time spares both races from the evils of sudden derangement—in fact, from the necessity of any derangement—while most of those whose habitual course of thought will be disturbed by the measure will have passed away before its consummation. They will never see it. Another class will hail the prospect of emancipation, but will deprecate the length of time. They will feel that it gives too little to the now living slaves. But it really gives them much. It saves them from the vagrant destitution which must largely attend immediate emancipation in localities where their numbers are very great; and it gives the inspiring assurance that their posterity shall be free forever. The plan leaves to each State, choosing to act under it, to abolish slavery now, or at the end of the century, or at any intermediate time, or by degrees, extending over the whole or any part of the period; and it obliges no two States to proceed alike. It also provides for compensation, and generally the mode of making it. This, it would seem, must further mitigate the dissatisfaction of those who favor perpetual slavery, and especially of those who are to receive the compensation. Doubtless some of those who are to pay, and not to receive will object. Yet the measure is both just and economical. In a certain sense the liberation of slaves is the destruction of property—property acquired by descent, or by purchase, the same as any other property. It is no less true for having been often said, that the people of the South are not more responsible for the original introduction of this property, than are the people of the North; and when it is remembered how unhesitatingly we all use cotton and sugar, and share the profits of dealing in them, it may not be quite safe to say, that the South has been more responsible than the North for its continuance. If then, for a common object, this property is to be sacrificed is it not just that it be done at a common charge?

And if, with less money, or money more easily paid, we can preserve the benefits of the Union by this means, than we can by the war alone, is it not also economical to do it? Let us consider it then. Let us ascertain the sum we have expended in the war since compensated emancipation was proposed last March, and consider whether, if that measure had been promptly accepted, by even some of the slave States, the same sum would not have done more to close the war, than has been otherwise done. If so the measure would save money, and in that view, would be a prudent and economical measure. Certainly it is not so easy to pay *something* as it is to pay *nothing*; but it is easier to pay a *large* sum than it is to pay a *larger* one. And it is easier to pay any sum *when* we are able, than it is to pay it *before* we are able. The war requires large sums, and requires them at once. The aggregate sum necessary for compensated emancipation, of course, would be large. But it would require no ready cash; nor the bonds even, any faster than the emancipation progresses. This might not, and probably would not, close before the end of the thirty-seven years. At that time we shall probably have a hundred millions of people to share the burden, instead of thirty-one millions, as now. And not only so, but the increase of our population may be expected to continue for a long time after that period, as rapidly as before; because our territory will not have become full. I do not state this inconsiderately. At the same ratio of increase which we have maintained, on an average, from our first national census, in 1790, until that of 1860, we should, in 1900, have a population of 103,208,415. And why may we not continue that ratio far beyond that period? Our abundant room—our broad national homestead—is our ample resource. Were our territory as limited as are the British Isles, very certainly our population could not expand as stated. Instead of receiving the foreign born, as now, we should be compelled to send part of the native born away. But such is not our condition. We have two millions nine hundred and sixty-three thousand square miles. Europe has three millions and eight hundred thousand, with a population averaging seventy-three and one-third persons to the square mile. Why may not our country, at some time, average as many? Is it less fertile? Has it more waste surface, by mountains, rivers, lakes, deserts, or other causes? Is it inferior to Europe in any natural advantage? If, then, we are, at some time, to be as populous as Europe, how soon? As to when this *may* be, we can judge by the past and the present; as to when it *will* be, if ever, depends much on whether we maintain the Union. Several of our States are already above the average of Europe—seventy three and a third to the square mile. Massachusetts has 157; Rhode Island, 133; Connecticut, 99; New York and New Jersey, each, 80; Also two other great States, Pennsylvania and Ohio, are not far below, the former having 63, and the latter 59. The States already above the European average, except New York, have increased in as rapid a ratio, since passing that point, as ever before; while no one of them is equal to some other parts of our country in natural capacity for sustaining a dense population.

Taking the nation in the aggregate, and we find its population and ratio of increase, for the several decennial periods, to be as follows:—

1790	3,929,827						
1800	5,305,937	35.02	per	cent.	ratio	of	increase.
1810	7,239,814	36.45	"	"	"	"	"
1820	9,638,131	33.13	"	"	"	"	"
1830	12,866,020	33.49	"	"	"	"	"
1840	17,069,453	32.67	"	"	"	"	"
1850	23,191,876	35.87	"	"	"	"	"
1860	31,443,790	35.58	"	"	"	"	"

This shows an average decennial increase of 34.60 per cent. in population through the seventy years from our first, to our last census yet taken. It is seen that the ratio of increase, at no one of these seven periods, is either two per cent. below, or two per cent. above, the average; thus showing how inflexible, and, consequently, how reliable, the law of increase, in our case, is. Assuming that it will continue, gives the following results:—

1870	42,323,341
1880	56,967,216
1890	76,677,872
1900	103,208,415
1910	138,918,526
1920	186,984,335
1930	251,680,914

These figures show that our country *may* be as populous as Europe now is, at some point between 1920 and 1930—say about 1925—our territory, at seventy-three and a third persons to the square mile, being of capacity to contain 217,186,000.

And we *will* reach this, too, if we do not ourselves relinquish the chance, by the folly and evils of disunion, or by long, and exhausting war springing from the only great element of national discord among us. While it cannot be foreseen exactly how much one huge example of secession, breeding lesser ones indefinitely, would retard population, civilization, and prosperity, no one can doubt that the extent of it would be very great and injurious.

The proposed emancipation would shorten the war, perpetuate peace, insure this increase of population, and proportionately the wealth of the country. With these, we should pay all the emancipation would cost, together with our other debt, easier than we should pay our other debt, without it. If we had allowed our old national debt to run at six per cent. per annum, simple interest, from the end of our revolutionary struggle until today, without paying anything on either principal or interest, each man of us would owe less upon that debt now, than each owed upon it then; and this because our increase of men, through the whole period, has been greater than six per cent.; has run faster than the interest upon the debt. Thus, time alone relieves a debtor nation, so long as its population increases faster than unpaid interest accumulates on its debt.

This fact would be no excuse for delaying payment of what is justly due; but it shows the great importance of time in this connexion—the great advantage of a policy by which we shall not have to pay until we number a hundred millions, what, by a different policy, we would have to pay now, when we number but thirty one millions. In a word, it shows that a dollar will be much harder to pay for the war, than will be a dollar for emancipation on the proposed plan. And then the latter will cost no blood, no precious life. It will be a saving of both.

As to the second article, I think it would be impracticable to return to bondage the class of persons therein contemplated. Some of them, doubtless, in the property sense, belong to loyal owners; and hence, provision is made in this article for compensating such.

The third article relates to the future of the freed people. It does not oblige, but merely authorizes, Congress to aid in colonizing such as may consent. This ought not to be regarded as objectionable, on the one hand, or on the other, in so much as it comes to nothing, unless by the mutual consent of the people to be deported, and the American voters, through their representatives in Congress.

I cannot make it better known than it already is, that I strongly favor colonization. And yet I wish to say there is an objection urged against free colored persons remaining in the country, which is largely imaginary, if not sometimes malicious.

It is insisted that their presence would injure, and displace white labor and white laborers. If there ever could be a proper time for mere catch arguments, that time surely is not now. In times like the present, men should utter nothing for which they would not willingly be responsible through time and in eternity. Is it true, then, that colored people can displace any more white labor, by being free, than by remaining slaves? If they stay in their old places, they jostle no white laborers; if they leave their old places, they leave them open to white laborers. Logically, there is neither more nor less of it. Emancipation, even without deportation, would probably enhance the wages of white labor, and, very surely, would not reduce them. Thus, the customary amount of labor would still have to be performed; the freed people would surely not do more than their old proportion of it, and very probably, for a time, would do less, leaving an increased part to white laborers, bringing their labor into greater demand, and, consequently, enhancing the wages of it. With deportation, even to a limited extent, enhanced wages to white labor is mathematically certain. Labor is like any other commodity in the market—increase the demand for it, and you increase the price of it. Reduce the supply of black labor, by colonizing the black laborer out of the country, and, by precisely so much, you increase the demand for, and wages of, white labor.

But it is dreaded that the freed people will swarm forth, and cover the whole land? Are they not already in the land? Will liberation make them any more numerous? Equally distributed among the whites of the whole country, and there would be but one colored to seven whites. Could the one, in any way, greatly disturb the seven? There are many communities now, having more than one free colored person, to seven whites; and this, without any apparent consciousness of evil from it. The District of Columbia, and the States of Maryland and Delaware, are all in this condition. The district has more than one free colored to six whites; and yet, in its frequent petitions to Congress, I believe it has never presented the presence of free colored persons as one of its grievances. But why should emancipation south, send the freed people north? People, of any color, seldom run, unless there be something to run from. *Heretofore* colored people, to some extent, have fled north from bondage; and *now*, perhaps, from both bondage and destitution. But if gradual emancipation and deportation be adopted, they will have neither to flee from. Their old masters will give them wages at least until new laborers can be procured; and the freed men, in turn, will gladly give their labor for the wages, till new homes can be found for them, in congenial climes, and with people of their own blood and race. This proposition can be trusted on the mutual interests involved. And, in any event, cannot the north decide for itself, whether to receive them?

Again, as practice proves more than theory, in any case, has there been any irruption of colored people northward, because of the abolishment of slavery in this District last spring?

What I have said of the proportion of free colored persons to the whites, in the District, is from the census of 1860, having no reference to persons called contrabands, nor to those made free by the act of Congress abolishing slavery here.

The plan consisting of these articles is recommended, not but that a restoration of the national authority would be accepted without its adoption.

Nor will the war, nor proceedings under the proclamation of September 22, 1862, be stayed because of the *recommendation* of this plan. Its timely *adoption*, I doubt not, would bring restoration and thereby stay both.

And, notwithstanding this plan, the recommendation that Congress provide by law for compensating any State which may adopt emancipation, before this plan shall have been acted upon, is hereby earnestly renewed. Such would be only an advance part of the plan, and the same arguments apply to both.

This plan is recommended as a means, not in exclusion of, but additional to, all others for restoring and preserving the national authority throughout the Union. The subject is presented exclusively in its economical aspect. The plan would, I am confident, secure peace more speedily, and maintain it more permanently, than can be done by force alone; while all it would cost, considering amounts, and manner of payment, and times of payment, would be easier paid than will be the additional cost of the war, if we rely solely upon force. It is much—very much—that it would cost no blood at all.

The plan is proposed as permanent constitutional law. It cannot become such without the concurrence of, first, two thirds of Congress, and, afterwards, three-fourths of the States. The requisite three-fourths of the States will necessarily include seven of the Slave States. Their concurrence, if obtained, will give assurance of their severally adopting emancipation, at no very distant day, upon the new constitutional terms. This assurance would end the struggle now, and save the Union forever.

I do not forget the gravity which should characterize a paper addressed to the Congress of the nation by the Chief Magistrate of the nation. Nor do I forget that some of you are my seniors, nor that many of you have more experience than I, in the conduct of public affairs. Yet I trust that in view of the great responsibility resting upon me, you will perceive no want of respect yourselves, in any undue earnestness I may seem to display.

Is it doubted, then, that the plan I propose, if adopted, would shorten the war, and thus lessen its expenditure of money and of blood? Is it doubted that it would restore the national authority and national prosperity, and perpetuate both indefinitely? Is it doubted that we here—Congress and Executive—can secure its adoption? Will not the good people respond to a united, and earnest appeal from us? Can we, can they, by any other means, so certainly, or so speedily, assure these vital objects? We can succeed only by concert. It is not "can *any* of us *imagine* better?" but, "can we *all* do better?" Object whatsoever is possible, still the question recurs, "can we do better?" The dogmas of the quiet past, are inadequate to the stormy present. The occasion is piled high with difficulty, and we must rise—with the occasion. As our case is new, so we must think anew, and act anew. We must disenthrall ourselves, and then we shall save our country.

Fellow-citizens, *we* cannot escape history. We of this Congress and this administration, will be remembered in spite of ourselves. No personal significance, or insignificance, can spare one or another of us. The fiery trial through which we pass, will light us down, in honor or dishonor, to the latest generation. We *say* we are for the Union. The world will not forget that we say this. We know how to save the Union. The world knows we do know how to save it. We—even *we here*—hold the power, and bear the responsibility. In *giving* freedom to the *slave*, we *assure* freedom to the *free*—honorable alike in what we give, and what we preserve. We shall nobly save, or meanly lose, the last best hope of earth. Other means may succeed; this could not fail. The way is plain, peaceful, generous, just—a way which, if followed, the world will forever applaud, and God must forever bless.

Abraham Lincoln.

December 1, 1862.

LETTER TO MISS FANNY McCULLOUGH
DECEMBER 23, 1862

Executive Mansion,
Washington, December 23., 1862.

Dear Fanny

It is with deep grief that I learn of the death of your kind and brave Father; and, especially, that it is affecting your young heart beyond what is common in such cases. In this sad world of ours, sorrow comes to all; and, to the young, it comes with bitterest agony, because it takes them unawares. The older have learned to ever expect it. I am anxious to afford some alleviation of your present distress. Perfect relief is not possible, except with time. You can not now realize that you will ever feel better. Is not this so? And yet it is a mistake. You are sure to be happy again. To know this, which is certainly true, will make you some less miserable now. I have had experience enough to know what I say; and you need only to believe it, to feel better at once. The memory of your dear Father, instead of an agony, will yet be a sad sweet feeling in your heart, of a purer, and holier sort than you have known before.

Please present my kind regards to your afflicted Mother.

Miss. Fanny McCullough.

Your sincere friend,

A. Lincoln.

Fanny was the daughter of Colonel William McCullough of the 4th Illinois Cavalry. A resident of Bloomington, Illinois, and a long-time friend of Lincoln's, McCullough had seen military service in the Black Hawk War and early in the Civil War helped to organize the 4th Illinois Cavalry. For an account of his gallant death, see Carl Sandburg, Abraham Lincoln: The War Years, *Vol. I, p. 617.*

FINAL EMANCIPATION PROCLAMATION JANUARY 1, 1863

A PROCLAMATION.

Whereas, on the twentysecond day of September, in the year of our Lord one thousand eight hundred and sixty two a proclamation was issued by the President of the United States, containing, among other things, the following, to wit:

"That on the first day of January, in the year of our Lord one thousand eight hundred and sixty-three, all persons held as slaves within any state, or designated part of a state, the people whereof shall then be in rebellion against the United States, shall be then, thenceforward and forever free; and the Executive Government of the United States, including the military and naval authority thereof, will recognize and maintain the freedom of such persons, and will do no act or acts to repress such persons, or any of them, in any efforts they may make for their actual freedom.

"That the executive will, on the first day of January aforesaid, by proclamation, designate the states and parts of states, if any, in which the people thereof, respectively, shall then be in rebellion against the United States, and the fact that any state, or the people thereof, shall on that day be in good faith represented in the Congress of the United States by members chosen thereto, at elections wherein a majority of the qualified voters of such state shall have participated, shall, in the absence of strong countervailing testimony, be deemed conclusive evidence that such state, and the people thereof, are not then in rebellion against the United States."

Now, therefore I, Abraham Lincoln President of the United States, by virtue of the power in me vested as Commander-in-Chief, of the Army and Navy of the United States in time of actual armed rebellion against authority and government of the United States, and as a fit and necessary war measure for suppressing said rebellion, do on this first day of January, in the year of our Lord one thousand eight hundred and sixty three, and in accordance with my purpose so to do publicly proclaimed for the full period of one hundred days, from the day first above mentioned, order and designate as the States and parts of States wherein the people thereof respectively, are this day in rebellion against the United States, the following, to wit

Arkansas, Texas, Louisiana, (except the Parishes of St. Bernard, Plaquemine, Jefferson, St. Johns, St. Charles, St. James,

Ascension, Assumption, Terrebonne, Lafourche, St. Mary, St. Martin, and Orleans, including the City of New-Orleans) Mississippi, Alabama, Florida, Georgia, South-Carolina, North-Carolina, and Virginia, (except the forty-eight counties designated as West Virginia and also the counties of Berkeley, Accomac, Northampton, Elizabeth City, York, Princess-Ann, and Norfolk, including the cities of Norfolk & Portsmouth; and which excepted parts are for the present left precisely as if this proclamation were not issued.

And by virtue of the power and for the purpose aforesaid I do order and declare that all persons held as slaves within said designated States, and parts of States are and henceforward shall be free; and that the Executive government of the United States, including the military and naval authorities thereof, will recognize and maintain the freedom of said persons.

And I hereby enjoin upon the people so declared to be free to abstain from all violence, unless in necessary self-defense; and I recommend to them that in all cases when allowed, they labor faithfully for reasonable wages.

And I further declare and make known, that such persons of suitable condition, will be received into the armed service of the United States to garrison forts, positions, stations and other places, and to man vessels of all sorts in said service.

And upon this act sincerely believed to be an act of justice, warranted by the Constitution upon military necessity, I invoke the considerate judgment of mankind, and the gracious favor of Almighty God.

In witness whereof, I have hereunto set my hand and caused the seal of the United States to be affixed

[L. S.] Done at the city of Washington, this first day of January, in the year of our Lord one thousand eight hundred and sixty three, and of the Independence of the United States of America the eighty-seventh.

By the President: Abraham Lincoln

William H. Seward,
Secretary of State

The original draft of the "Emancipation Proclamation" was prepared by Lincoln and submitted to the Cabinet on July 22, 1862. A number of changes were made, and the preliminary proclamation was issued on September 22, 1862, stipulating January 1, 1863, as the date on which emancipation would go into effect. The final version which appears in the text contains only minor changes in wording.

LETTER TO GENERAL J. A. McCLERNAND JANUARY 22, 1863

Executive Mansion,
Washington, January 22, 1863.

Major Gen. McClernand
My dear Sir:

Yours of the 7th. was received yesterday. I need not recite, because you remember the contents. The charges, in their nature, are such that I must know as much about the facts involved, as you can. I have too many *family* controversies, (so to speak) already on my hands, to voluntarily, or so long as I can avoid it, take up another. You are now doing well—well for the country, and well for yourself—much better than you could possibly be, if engaged in open war with Gen. Halleck. Allow me to beg, that for your sake, for my sake, & for the country's sake, you give your whole attention to the better work.

Your success upon the Arkansas, was both brilliant and valuable, and is fully appreciated by the country and government.

Yours truly
A. Lincoln

McClernand was another Black Hawk War veteran and an Illinois Democrat whose support of the war effort Lincoln cherished and whose advancement was not entirely due to his military ability by any means. Lincoln advanced him over Sherman under Grant's command, and Sherman accepted with good grace, recognizing the political motives involved. McClernand made a number of military mistakes and Grant was obliged to remove him from command.

LETTER TO GENERAL JOSEPH HOOKER
JANUARY 26, 1863

Executive Mansion,
Washington, January 26, 1863.

Major-General Hooker:
General.

I have placed you at the head of the Army of the Potomac. Of course I have done this upon what appear to me to be sufficient reasons. And yet I think it best for you to know that there are some things in regard to which, I am not quite satisfied with you. I believe you to be a brave and skilful soldier, which, of course, I like. I also believe you do not mix politics with your profession, in which you are right. You have confidence in yourself, which is a valuable, if not an indispensable quality. You are ambitious, which, within reasonable bounds, does good rather than harm. But I think that during Gen. Burnside's command of the Army, you have taken counsel of your ambition, and thwarted him as much as you could, in which you did a great wrong to the country, and to a most meritorious and honorable brother officer. I have heard, in such a way as to believe it, of your recently saying that both the Army and the Government needed a Dictator. Of course it was not *for* this, but in spite of it, that I have given you the command. Only those generals who gain successes, can set up dictators. What I now ask of you is military success, and I will risk the dictatorship. The government will support you to the utmost of it's ability, which is neither more nor less than it has done and will do for all commanders. I much fear that the spirit which you have aided to infuse into the Army, of criticizing their Commander, and withholding confidence from him, will now turn upon you. I shall assist you as far as I can, to put it down. Neither you, nor Napoleon, if he were alive again, could get any good out of an army, while such a spirit prevails in it.

And now, beware of rashness. Beware of rashness, but with energy, and sleepless vigilance, go forward, and give us victories.

Yours very truly
A. Lincoln.

LETTER TO GOVERNOR ANDREW JOHNSON
MARCH 26, 1863

Private

Executive Mansion,
Washington, March 26., 1863.

Hon. Andrew Johnson
My dear Sir:

I am told you have at least *thought* of raising a negro military force. In my opinion the country now needs no specific thing so much as some man of your ability, and position, to go to this work. When I speak of your position, I mean that of an eminent citizen of a slave-state, and himself a slave-holder. The colored population is the great *available* and yet *unavailed of*, force for restoring the Union. The bare sight of fifty thousand armed, and drilled black soldiers on the banks of the Mississippi, would end the rebellion at once. And who doubts that we can present that sight, if we but take hold in earnest? If you *have* been thinking of it please do not dismiss the thought.

Yours truly
A. Lincoln

LETTÊR TO GENERAL JOSEPH HOOKER
MAY 7, 1863

Head-quarters, Army of the Potomac,
May. 7 1863.

Major General Hooker.
My dear Sir

The recent movement of your army is ended without effecting it's object, except perhaps some important breakings of the enemies [*sic*] communications. What next? If possible I would be very glad of another movement early enough to give us some benefit from the fact of the enemies [*sic*] communications being broken. But neither for this reason or any other, do I wish anything done in desperation or rashness. An early movement would also help to supersede the bad moral effect of the recent one, which is sure to be considerably injurious. Have you already in your mind a plan wholly, or partially formed? If you have, prosecute [*sic*] it without interference from me. If you have not, please inform me, so that I, incompetent as I may be, can try [to?] assist in the formation of some plan for the Army.

Yours as ever
A Lincoln

LETTER TO ISAAC N. ARNOLD
MAY 26, 1863

Private & confidential

Executive Mansion,
Washington, May 26., 1863.

Hon. I. N. Arnold.
My dear Sir:

Your letter advising me to dismiss Gen. Halleck is received. If the public believe, as you say, that he has driven Fremont, Butler, and Sigel from the service, they believe what I know to be false; so that if I was to yield to it, it would only be to be instantly beset by someother [*sic*] demand based on another falsehood equally gross. You know yourself that Fremont was relieved at his own request, before Halleck could have had anything to do with it —went out near the end of June, while Halleck only came in near the end of July. I know equally well that no wish of Halleck's had any thing to do with the removal of Butler or Sigel. Sigel, like Fremont, was relieved at his own request, pressed upon me almost constantly for six months, and upon complaints that could have been made as justly by almost any Corps commander in the army, and more justly by some. So much for the way they got out. Now a word as to their not getting back. In the early Spring, Gen. Fremont sought active service again; and, as it seemed to me, sought it in a very good and reasonable spirit. But he holds the highest rank in the Army, except McClellan, so that I could not well offer him a subordinate command. Was I to displace Hooker, or Hunter, or Rosecrans, or Grant, or Banks? If not, what was I to do? And similar to this, is the case of both the others. One month after Gen. Butler's return, I offered him a position in which I thought and still think, he could have done himself the highest credit, and the country the greatest service, but he declined it. When Gen. Sigel was relieved, at his own request as I have said, of course I had to put another in command of his corps. Can I instantly thrust that other out to put him in again?

And now my good friend, let me turn your eyes upon another point. Whether Gen. Grant shall or shall not consummate the capture of Vicksburg, his campaign from the beginning of this month up to the twenty second day of it, is one of the most brilliant in the world. His corps commanders & Division commanders, in part, are McClernand, McPherson, Sherman, Steele, Hovey, Blair, & Logan. And yet taking Gen. Grant and these seven of his generals, and you can scarcely name one of them that has not been constantly denounced and opposed by the same men who are now so anxious to get Halleck out, and Fremont & Butler & Sigel in. I believe no one of them went through the Senate easily, and certainly one failed to get through at all. I am compelled to take a more impartial and unprejudiced view of things. Without claiming to be your superior, which I do not, my position enables me to understand my duty in all these matters better than you possibly can, and I hope you do not yet doubt my integrity.

Your friend, as ever

A. Lincoln

Arnold was a member of Congress from Illinois and a trusted friend to whom Lincoln felt a confidential explanation was due when he could not follow Arnold's advice.

TELEGRAM TO GENERAL JOSEPH HOOKER JUNE 5, 1863

Washington, D. C., June 5. 1863

Major General Hooker

Yours of to-day was received an hour ago. So much of professional military skill is requisite to answer it, that I have turned the task over to Gen. Halleck. He promises to perform it with his utmost care. I have but one idea which I think worth suggesting to you, and that is in case you find Lee coming to the North of the Rappahannock, I would by no means cross to the South of it. If he should leave a rear force at Fredericksburg, tempting you to fall upon it, it would fight in intrenchments, and have you at disadvantage, and so, man for man, worst you at that point, while his main force would in some way be getting an advantage of you Northward. In one word, I would not take any risk of being entangled upon the river, like an ox jumped half over a fence, and liable to be torn by dogs, front and rear, without a fair chance to gore one way or kick the other. If Lee would come to my side of the river, I would keep on the same side & fight him, or act on the defence, according as might be my estimate of his strength relatively [*sic*] to my own. But these are mere suggestions which I desire to be controlled by the judgment of yourself and Gen. Halleck.

A. Lincoln

LETTER TO ERASTUS CORNING AND OTHERS JUNE 12, 1863

Executive Mansion,
Washington, June 12, 1863.

Hon. Erastus Corning and Others.
Gentlemen:

Your letter of May 19, inclosing the resolutions of a public meeting held at Albany, New York, on the 16th of the same month, was received several days ago.

The resolutions, as I understand them, are resolvable into two propositions—first, the expression of a purpose to sustain the cause of the Union, to secure peace through victory, and to support the administration in every constitutional and lawful measure to suppress the rebellion; and, secondly, a declaration of censure upon the administration for supposed unconstitutional action, such as the making of military arrests. And from the two propositions a third is deduced, which is that the gentlemen composing the meeting are resolved on doing their part to maintain our common government and country, despite the folly or wickedness, as they may conceive, of any administration. This position is eminently patriotic, and as such I thank the meeting, and congratulate the nation for it. My own purpose is the same; so that the meeting and myself have a common object, and can have no difference, except in the choice of means or measures for effecting that object.

And here I ought to close this paper, and would close it, if there were no apprehension that more injurious consequences than any merely personal to myself might follow the censures systematically cast upon me for doing what, in my view of duty, I could not forbear. The resolutions promise to support me in every constitutional and lawful measure to suppress the rebellion; and I have not knowingly employed, nor shall knowingly employ, any other. But the meeting, by their resolutions, assert and argue that certain military arrests, and proceedings following them, for which I am ultimately responsible, are unconstitutional. I think they are not. The resolutions quote from the Constitution the definition of treason, and also the limiting safeguards and guarantees therein provided for the citizen on trials for treason, and on his being held to answer for capital or otherwise infamous crimes, and in criminal prosecutions his right to a speedy and public trial by an impartial jury. They proceed to resolve "that these safeguards of the rights of the citizen against the pretensions of arbitrary power were intended more especially for his protection in times of civil commotion." And, apparently to demonstrate the proposition, the resolutions proceed: "They were secured substantially to the English people after years of protracted civil war, and were adopted into our Constitution at the close of the revolution." Would not the demonstration have been better if it could have been truly said that these safeguards had been adopted and applied during the civil wars and during our revolution, instead of after the one and at the close of the other? I, too, am devotedly for them after civil war, and before civil war, and at all times, "except when, in cases of rebellion or invasion, the public safety may require" their suspension. The resolutions proceed to tell us that these safeguards "have stood the test of seventy-six years of trial under our republican system, under circumstances which show that while they constitute the foundation of all free government, they are the elements of the enduring stability of the republic." No one denies that they have so stood the test up to the beginning of the present rebellion, if we except a certain occurrence at New Orleans hereafter to be mentioned; nor does any one question that they will stand the same test much longer after the rebellion closes. But these provisions of the Constitution have no application to the case we have in hand, because the arrests complained of were not made for treason—that is, not for the treason defined in the Constitution, and upon the conviction of which the punishment is death—nor yet were they made to hold persons to answer for any capital or otherwise infamous crimes; nor were the proceedings following, in any constitutional or legal sense, "criminal prosecutions." The arrests were made on totally different grounds, and the proceedings following accorded with the grounds of the arrests. Let us consider the real case with which we are dealing, and apply to it the parts of the Constitution plainly made for such cases.

Prior to my installation here it had been inculcated that any State had a lawful right to secede from the national Union, and that it would be expedient to exercise the right whenever the devotees of the doctrine should fail to elect a president to their own liking. I was elected contrary to their liking; and, accordingly, so far as it was legally possible, they had taken seven States out of the Union, had seized many of the United States forts, and had fired upon the United States flag, all before I was inaugurated, and, of course, before I had done any official act whatever. The rebellion thus begun soon ran into the present civil war; and, in certain respects, it began on very unequal terms between the parties. The insurgents had been preparing for it more than thirty years, while the government had taken no steps to resist them. The former had carefully considered all the means which could be turned to their account. It undoubtedly was a well-pondered reliance with them that in their own unrestricted effort to destroy Union, Constitution and law, all together, the government would, in great degree, be restrained by the same Constitution and law from arresting their progress. Their sympathizers pervaded all departments of the government and nearly all communities of the people. From this material, under cover of "liberty of speech," "liberty of the press," and "*habeas corpus*," they hoped to keep on foot amongst us a most efficient corps of spies, informers, suppliers, and aiders and abettors of their cause in a thousand ways. They knew that in times such as they were inaugurating, by the Constitution itself the "*habeas corpus*" might be suspended; but they also knew they had friends who would make a question as to who was to suspend it; meanwhile their spies and others might remain at large to help on their cause. Or if, as has happened, the Executive should suspend the writ without ruinous waste of time, instances of arresting innocent persons might occur, as are always likely to occur in such cases; and then a clamor could be raised in regard to this, which might be at least of some service to the insurgent cause. It needed no very keen perception to discover this part of the enemy's programme, so soon as by open hostilities their machinery was fairly put in motion. Yet, thoroughly imbued with a reverence for the guaranteed rights of individuals, I was slow to adopt the strong measures which by degrees I have been forced to regard as being within the exceptions of the Constitution, and as indispensable to the public safety. Nothing is better known to history than that courts of justice are utterly incompetent to such cases. Civil courts are organized chiefly for trials of individuals, or, at most, a few individuals acting in concert—and this in quiet times, and on charges of crimes well defined in the law. Even in times of peace bands of horse-thieves and robbers frequently grow too numerous and powerful for the ordinary courts of justice. But what comparison, in numbers, have such bands ever borne to the insurgent sympathizers even in many of the loyal States? Again, a jury too frequently has at least one member more ready to hang the panel than to hang the traitor. And yet again, he who dissuades one man from volunteering, or induces one soldier to desert, weakens the Union cause as much as he who kills a Union soldier in battle. Yet this dissuasion or inducement may be so conducted as to be no defined crime of which any civil court would take cognizance.

Ours is a case of rebellion—so called by the resolutions before me—in fact, a clear, flagrant, and gigantic case of rebellion; and the provision of the Constitution that "the privilege of the writ of *habeas corpus* shall not be suspended unless when, in cases of rebellion or invasion, the public safety may require it," is the provision which specially applies to our present case. This provision plainly attests the understanding of those who made the Constitution that ordinary courts of justice are inadequate to "cases of rebellion"—attests their purpose that, in such cases, men may be held in custody whom the courts, acting on ordinary rules, would discharge. *Habeas corpus* does not discharge men who are proved to be guilty of defined crime; and its suspension is allowed by the Constitution on purpose that men may be arrested and held who cannot be proved to be guilty of defined crime, "when, in cases of rebellion or invasion, the public safety may require it."

This is precisely our present case—a case of rebellion wherein the public safety does require the suspension. Indeed, arrests by process of courts and arrests in cases of rebellion do not proceed

Meserve No. 100. A photograph made by Alexander Gardner on Monday, April 10, 1865. Mr. Truman H. Bartlett, the author and sculptor, acquired it from Mr. Gardner in 1874, who then stated that only one print was made from the large broken negative before it was considered valueless and destroyed, and that it was the last photograph made on that day. No later photographs were made of the President in life. This single print is in the Meserve Collection.

altogether upon the same basis. The former is directed at the small percentage of ordinary and continuous perpetration of crime, while the latter is directed at sudden and extensive uprisings against the government, which, at most, will succeed or fail in no great length of time. In the latter case arrests are made not so much for what has been done, as for what probably would be done. The latter is more for the preventive and less for the vindictive than the former. In such cases the purposes of men are much more easily understood than in cases of ordinary crime. The man who stands by and says nothing when the peril of his government is discussed, cannot be misunderstood. If not hindered, he is sure to help the enemy; much more if he talks ambiguously—talks for his country with "buts," and "ifs" and "ands." Of how little value the constitutional provision I have quoted will be rendered if arrests shall never be made until defined crimes shall have been committed, may be illustrated by a few notable examples: General John C. Breckinridge, General Robert E. Lee, General Joseph E. Johnston, General John B. Magruder, General William B. Preston, General Simon B. Buckner, and Commodore Franklin Buchanan, now occupying the very highest places in the rebel war service, were all within the power of the government since the rebellion began, and were nearly as well known to be traitors then as now. Unquestionably if we had seized and held them, the insurgent cause would be much weaker. But no one of them had then committed any crime defined in the law. Every one of them, if arrested, would have been discharged on *habeas corpus* were the writ allowed to operate. In view of these and similar cases, I think the time not unlikely to come when I shall be blamed for having made too few arrests rather than too many.

By the third resolution the meeting indicate their opinion that military arrests may be constitutional in localities where rebellion actually exists, but that such arrests are unconstitutional in localities where rebellion or insurrection does not actually exist. They insist that such arrests shall not be made "outside of the lines of necessary military occupation and the scenes of insurrection." Inasmuch, however, as the Constitution itself makes no such distinction, I am unable to believe that there is any such constitutional distinction. I concede that the class of arrests complained of can be constitutional only when, in cases of rebellion or invasion, the public safety may require them; and I insist that in such cases they are constitutional wherever the public safety does require them, as well in places to which they may prevent the rebellion extending, as in those where it may be already prevailing; as well where they may restrain mischievous interference with the raising and supplying of armies to suppress the rebellion, as where the rebellion may actually be; as well where they may restrain the enticing men out of the army, as where they would prevent mutiny in the army; equally constitutional at all places where they will conduce to the public safety, as against the dangers of rebellion or invasion. Take the particular case mentioned by the meeting. It is asserted in substance, that Mr. Vallandigham was, by a military commander, seized and tried "for no other reason than words addressed to a public meeting in criticism of the course of the administration, and in condemnation of the military orders of the general." Now, if there be no mistake about this, if this assertion is the truth and the whole truth, if there was no other reason for the arrest, then I concede that the arrest was wrong. But the arrest, as I understand, was made for a very different reason. Mr. Vallandigham avows his hostility to the war on the part of the Union; and his arrest was made because he was laboring, with some effect, to prevent the raising of troops, to encourage desertions from the army, and to leave the rebellion without an adequate military force to suppress it. He was not arrested because he was damaging the political prospects of the administration or the personal interests of the commanding general, but because he was damaging the army, upon the existence and vigor of which the life of the nation depends. He was warring upon the military, and this gave the military constitutional jurisdiction to lay hands upon him. If Mr. Vallandigham was not damaging the military power of the country, then his arrest was made on mistake of fact, which I would be glad to correct on reasonably satisfactory evidence.

I understand the meeting whose resolutions I am considering to be in favor of suppressing the rebellion by military force—by armies. Long experience has shown that armies cannot be maintained unless desertion shall be punished by the severe penalty of death. The case requires, and the law and the Constitution sanction, this punishment. Must I shoot a simple-minded soldier boy who deserts, while I must not touch a hair of a wily agitator who induces him to desert? This is none the less injurious when effected by getting a father, or brother, or friend into a public meeting, and there working upon his feelings till he is persuaded to write the soldier boy that he is fighting in a bad cause, for a wicked administration of a contemptible government, too weak to arrest and punish him if he shall desert. I think that, in such a case, to silence the agitator and save the boy is not only constitutional, but withal a great mercy.

If I be wrong on this question of constitutional power, my error lies in believing that certain proceedings are constitutional when, in cases of rebellion or invasion, the public safety requires them, which would not be constitutional when, in absence of rebellion or invasion, the public safety does not require them: in other words, that the Constitution is not in its application in all respects the same in cases of rebellion or invasion involving the public safety, as it is in times of profound peace and public security. The Constitution itself makes the distinction, and I can no more be persuaded that the government can constitutionally take no strong measures in time of rebellion, because it can be shown that the same could not be lawfully taken in time of peace, than I can be persuaded that a particular drug is not good medicine for a sick man because it can be shown to not be good food for a well one. Nor am I able to appreciate the danger apprehended by the meeting, that the American people will by means of military arrests during the rebellion lose the right of public discussion, the liberty of speech and the press, the law of evidence, trial by jury, and *habeas corpus* throughout the indefinite peaceful future which I trust lies before them, any more than I am able to believe that a man could contract so strong an appetite for emetics during temporary illness as to persist in feeding upon them during the remainder of his healthful life.

In giving the resolutions that earnest consideration which you request of me, I cannot overlook the fact that the meeting speak as "Democrats." Nor can I, with full respect for their known intelligence, and the fairly presumed deliberation with which they prepared their resolutions, be permitted to suppose that this occurred by accident, or in any way other than that they preferred to designate themselves "Democrats" rather than "American citizens." In this time of national peril I would have preferred to meet you upon a level one step higher than any party platform, because I am sure that from such more elevated position we could do better battle for the country we all love than we possibly can from those lower ones where, from the force of habit, the prejudices of the past, and selfish hopes of the future, we are sure to expend much of our ingenuity and strength in finding fault with and aiming blows at each other. But since you have denied me this, I will yet be thankful for the country's sake that not all Democrats have done so. He on whose discretionary judgment Mr. Vallandigham was arrested and tried is a Democrat, having no old party affinity with me, and the judge who rejected the constitutional view expressed in these resolutions, by refusing to discharge Mr. Vallandigham on *habeas corpus*, is a Democrat of better days than these, having received his judicial mantle at the hands of President Jackson. And still more, of all those Democrats who are nobly exposing their lives and shedding their blood on the battle-field, I have learned that many approve the course taken with Mr. Vallandigham, while I have not heard of a single one condemning it. I cannot assert that there are none such. And the name of President Jackson recalls an instance of pertinent history. After the battle of New Orleans, and while the fact that the treaty of peace had been concluded was well known in the city, but before official knowledge of it had arrived, General Jackson still maintained martial or military law. Now that it could be said the war was over, the clamor against martial law, which had existed from the first, grew more furious. Among other things, a Mr. Louaillier published a denunciatory newspaper article. General Jackson arrested him. A lawyer by the name of Morel procured the United States Judge Hall to order a writ of *habeas corpus* to release Mr. Louaillier. General Jackson arrested both the lawyer and the judge. A Mr. Hollander ventured to say of some part of the matter that "it was a dirty trick." General Jackson arrested him. When the officer undertook to serve the writ of *habeas corpus,* General Jackson took it from him, and sent him away with a copy. Holding the judge in custody a few days, the general sent him beyond the limits of his encampment, and set him at liberty with an order to remain till the ratification of peace should be regularly announced, or until the British should have left the southern coast. A day or two more elapsed, the ratification of the treaty of peace was regularly announced, and the judge and others were fully liberated. A few days more, and the judge called General Jackson into court and fined him $1000 for having arrested him and the others named. The general paid the fine, and then the matter rested for nearly thirty years, when Congress refunded principal and interest. The late Senator Douglas, then in the House of Representatives, took a leading part in the debates in which the constitutional question was much discussed. I am not prepared to say whom the journals would show to have voted for the measure.

It may be remarked—first, that we had the same Constitution then as now; secondly, that we then had a case of invasion, and now we have a case of rebellion; and, thirdly, that the permanent right of the people to public discussion, the liberty of speech and of the press, the trial by jury, the law of evidence, and the *habeas corpus,* suffered no detriment whatever by that conduct of General Jackson, or its subsequent approval by the American Congress.

And yet, let me say that, in my own discretion, I do not know whether I would have ordered the arrest of Mr. Vallandigham. While I cannot shift the responsibility from myself, I hold that, as a general rule, the commander in the field is the better judge of the necessity in any particular case. Of course I must practise a general directory and revisory power in the matter.

One of the resolutions expresses the opinion of the meeting that arbitrary arrests will have the effect to divide and distract those who should be united in suppressing the rebellion, and I am specifically called on to discharge Mr. Vallandigham. I regard this as, at least, a fair appeal to me on the expediency of exercising a constitutional power which I think exists. In response to such appeal I have to say, it gave me pain when I learned that Mr. Vallandigham had been arrested (that is, I was pained that there should have seemed to be a necessity for arresting him), and that it will afford me great pleasure to discharge him so soon as I can by any means believe the public safety will not suffer by it.

I further say that, as the war progresses, it appears to me, opinion and action, which were in great confusion at first, take shape and fall into more regular channels, so that the necessity for strong dealing with them gradually decreases. I have every reason to desire that it should cease altogether, and far from the least is my regard for the opinions and wishes of those who, like the meeting at Albany, declare their purpose to sustain the government in every constitutional and lawful measure to suppress the rebellion. Still, I must continue to do so much as may seem to be required by the public safety.

A. Lincoln.

Corning was an influential, wealthy Democrat of New York. The resolutions passed by the Albany Democratic Convention had equivocated to an extent in maintaining absolute loyalty to the Union while at the same time criticizing Lincoln for permitting the arrest of the notorious Copperhead, Clement L. Vallandigham, member of Congress from Ohio.

TELEGRAM TO GENERAL JOSEPH HOOKER JUNE 14, 1863

Washington, June 14. 1863. 5.50 P. M.

Major General Hooker.

So far as we can make out here the enemy have Milroy surrounded at Winchester, and Tyler at Martinsburg. If they could hold out a few days, could you help them? If the head of Lee's army is at Martinsburg, and the tail of it on the Plank road between Fredericksburg & Chancellorsville, the animal must be very slim somewhere. Could you not break him?

A. Lincoln.

RESPONSE TO A SERENADE
JULY 7, 1863

Fellow-citizens:

I am very glad indeed to see you to-night, and yet I will not say I thank you for this call, but I do most sincerely thank Almighty God for the occasion on which you have called. How long ago is it—eighty odd years—since on the Fourth of July for the first time in the history of the world a nation by its representatives, assembled and declared as a self-evident truth that "all men are created equal." That was the birthday of the United States of America. Since then the Fourth of July has had several peculiar recognitions. The two most distinguished men in the framing and support of the Declaration were Thomas Jefferson and John Adams—the one having penned it and the other sustained it the most forcibly in debate—the only two of the fifty-five who sustained it being elected President of the United States. Precisely fifty years after they put their hands to the paper it pleased Almighty God to take both from the stage of action. This was indeed an extraordinary and remarkable event in our history. Another President, five years after, was called from this stage of existence on the same day and month of the year; and now, on this last Fourth of July just passed, when we have a gigantic Rebellion, at the bottom of which is an effort to overthrow the principle that all men are created equal, we have the surrender of a most powerful position and army on that very day, and not only so, but in a succession of battles in Pennsylvania, near to us, through three days, so rapidly fought that they might be called one great battle on the 1st, 2d, and 3d of the month of July; and on the 4th the cohorts of those who opposed the declaration that all men are created equal, "turned tail" and ran. Gentlemen, this is a glorious theme, and the occasion for a speech, but I am not prepared to make one worthy of the occasion. I would like to speak in terms of praise due to the many brave officers and soldiers who have fought in the cause of the Union and liberties of the country from the beginning of the war. There are trying occasions, not only in success, but for the want of success. I dislike to mention the name of one single officer, lest I might do wrong to those I might forget. Recent events bring up glorious names, and particularly prominent ones, but these I will not mention. Having said this much, I will now take the music.

The germ idea which Lincoln rounded out to full figure in the "Gettysburg Address," may be observed in this speech in an undeveloped, casual statement, made only a few days after the battle. It is of interest to observe that the significance of the date and event were beginning this early to assume the symbolism in Lincoln's mind which he poetically expanded four months later in his metaphor of birth and death.

LETTER TO GENERAL U. S. GRANT
JULY 13, 1863

Executive Mansion,
Washington, July 13, 1863.

Major General Grant
My dear General

I do not remember that you and I ever met personally. I write this now as a grateful acknowledgment for the almost inestimable service you have done the country. I wish to say a word further. When you first reached the vicinity of Vicksburg, I thought you should do, what you finally did—march the troops across the neck, run the batteries with the transports, and thus go below; and I never had any faith, except a general hope that you knew better than I, that the Yazoo Pass expedition, and the like, could succeed. When you got below, and took Port-Gibson, Grand Gulf, and vicinity, I thought you should go down the river and join Gen. Banks; and when you turned Northward East of the Big Black, I feared it was a mistake. I now wish to make the personal acknowledgment that you were right, and I was wrong.

Yours very truly
A. Lincoln

DRAFT OF LETTER TO GENERAL G. G. MEADE JULY 14, 1863

Executive Mansion,
Washington, July 14, 1863.

Major-General Meade:

I have just seen your despatch to General Halleck, asking to be relieved of your command because of a supposed censure of mine. I am very, very grateful to you for the magnificent success you gave the cause of the country at Gettysburg; and I am sorry now to be the author of the slightest pain to you. But I was in such deep distress myself that I could not restrain some expression of it. I have been oppressed nearly ever since the battles at Gettysburg by what appeared to be evidences that yourself and General Couch and General Smith were not seeking a collision with the enemy, but were trying to get him across the river without another battle. What these evidences were, if you please, I hope to tell you at some time when we shall both feel better. The case, summarily stated, is this: You fought and beat the enemy at

Gettysburg, and, of course, to say the least, his loss was as great as yours. He retreated, and you did not, as it seemed to me, pressingly pursue him; but a flood in the river detained him till, by slow degrees, you were again upon him. You had at least twenty thousand veteran troops directly with you, and as many more raw ones within supporting distance, all in addition to those who fought with you at Gettysburg, while it was not possible that he had received a single recruit, and yet you stood and let the flood run down, bridges be built, and the enemy move away at his leisure without attacking him. And Couch and Smith! The latter left Carlisle in time, upon all ordinary calculation, to have aided you in the last battle at Gettysburg, but he did not arrive. At the end of more than ten days, I believe twelve, under constant urging, he reached Hagerstown from Carlisle, which is not an inch over fifty-five miles, if so much, and Couch's movement was very little different.

Again, my dear general, I do not believe you appreciate the magnitude of the misfortune involved in Lee's escape. He was within your easy grasp, and to have closed upon him would, in connection with our other late successes, have ended the war. As it is, the war will be prolonged indefinitely. If you could not safely attack Lee last Monday, how can you possibly do so south of the river, when you can take with you very few more than two thirds of the force you then had in hand? It would be unreasonable to expect, and I do not expect [that], you can now effect much. Your golden opportunity is gone, and I am distressed immeasurably because of it.

I beg you will not consider this a prosecution or persecution of yourself. As you had learned that I was dissatisfied, I have thought it best to kindly tell you why.

[*Indorsement on the Envelop*]

To General Meade, never sent or signed.

As printed in the Complete Works of Abraham Lincoln, *this letter contains the indorsement on the envelope as indicated at the end of the letter. The original manuscript has not been available to the editor.*

LETTER TO GENERAL H. W. HALLECK JULY 29, 1863

Executive Mansion,
Washington, July 29, 1863.

Major General Halleck

Seeing General Meade's despatch of yesterday to yourself, causes me to fear that he supposes the government here is demanding of him to bring on a general engagement with Lee as soon as possible. I am claiming no such thing of him. In fact, my judgement is against it; which judgement, of course, I will yield if yours and his are the contrary. If he could not safely engage Lee at Williamsport, it seems absurd to suppose he can safely engage him now, when he has scarcely more than two-thirds of the force he had at Williamsport, while it must be that Lee has been reinforced. True, I desired Gen. Meade to pursue Lee across the Potomac, hoping, as has proved true, that he would thereby clear the Baltimore and Ohio Rail Road, and get some advantage by harrassing [*sic*] him on his retreat. These being past I am unwilling he should now get into a general engagement on the impression that we here are pressing him; and I shall be glad for you to so inform him, unless your own judgement is against it.

Yours truly
A. Lincoln.

The manuscript of this letter is in John Hay's handwriting, emended and signed by Lincoln's hand. The probability that Lincoln dictated the contents is indicated by the fact that the word "caused" is emended in

Lincoln's hand to "causes." The failure to keep tenses parallel would have been a natural error in dictating. Hay's Diary makes this probability seem a certainty with the following comment under July 29, 1863: "The President today wrote a letter to General Halleck..." The entire entry summarizes the letter. It seems improbable that so short a letter would have been written out by Lincoln, then recopied by Hay and revised and signed by Lincoln. The importance of these facts to the whole picture of Hay's function as secretary to Lincoln is that they seem to establish fairly well that some of the letters in Hay's handwriting were dictated by Lincoln. Hay's later testimony concerning his function as secretary to Lincoln did not mention the fact that many of the letters which he or one of the other White House secretaries penned were dictated by Lincoln, particularly in the very busy summer and fall of 1863.

LETTER TO GENERAL N. P. BANKS
AUGUST 5, 1863

Executive Mansion,
Washington, August 5, 1863.

My dear General Banks

Being a poor correspondent is the only apology I offer for not having sooner tendered my thanks for your very successful, and very valuable military operations this year. The final stroke in opening the Mississippi never should, and I think never will, be forgotten.

Recent events in Mexico, I think, render early action in Texas more important than ever. I expect, however, the General-in-Chief, will address you more fully upon this subject.

Governor Boutwell read me to-day that part of your letter to him, which relates to Louisiana affairs. While I very well know what I would be glad for Louisiana to do, it is quite a different thing for me to assume direction of the matter. I would be glad for her to make a new constitution recognizing the emancipation proclamation, and adopting emancipation in those parts of the state to which the proclamation does not apply. And while she is at it, I think it would not be objectionable for her to adopt some practical system by which the two races could gradually live themselves out of their old relation to each other, and both come out better prepared for the new. Education for young blacks should be included in the plan. After all, the power, or element, of "contract" may be sufficient for this probationary period; and, by it's simplicity, and flexibility, may be the better.

As an anti-slavery man I have a motive to desire emancipation, which pro-slavery men do not have; but even they have strong enough reason to thus place themselves again under the shield of the Union, and to thus perpetually hedge against the recurrence of the scenes through which we are now passing.

Gov. Shepley has informed me that Mr. Durant is now taking a registry, with a view to the election of a Constitutional Convention in Louisiana. This, to me, appears proper. If such convention were to ask my views, I could present little else than what I now say to you. I think the thing should be pushed forward, so that if possible, it's mature work may reach here by the meeting of Congress.

For my own part I think I shall not, in any event, retract the emancipation proclamation; nor, as executive, ever return to slavery any person who is free by the terms of that proclamation, or by any of the acts of Congress.

If Louisiana shall send members to Congress, then admission to seats will depend, as you know, upon the respective Houses, and not upon the President.

If these views can be of any advantage in giving shape, and impetus, to action there, I shall be glad for you to use them prudently for that object. Of course you will confer with intelligent and trusty citizens of the State, among whom I would suggest Messrs. Flanders, Hahn, and Durant; and to each of whom I now think I may send copies of this letter. Still it is perhaps better to not make the letter generally public.

Yours very truly
A. Lincoln.

Banks's military operations in Louisiana were heartily condemned by regular army men as incompetent, and he was referred to as a "political general." Lincoln's opinion of him was high for the very reason that Banks recognized his function in restoring political life in the area of his command as equal to his military function. He once commented on his relative failure and success by observing that "the President gave me too much to do—more than any other major-general in the army." This letter confirms his comment to a large degree.

LETTER TO MARY TODD LINCOLN
AUGUST 8, 1863

Executive Mansion,
Washington, August 8, 1863.

My dear Wife:

All as well as usual, and no particular trouble anyway. I put the money into the Treasury at five per cent., with the privilege of withdrawing it any time upon thirty days' notice. I suppose you are glad to learn this. Tell dear Tad poor "Nanny Goat" is lost, and Mrs. Cuthbert and I are in distress about it. The day you left, Nanny was found resting herself and chewing her little cud on the middle of Tad's bed; but now she's gone! The gardener kept complaining that she destroyed the flowers, till it was concluded to bring her down to the White House. This was done, and the second day she had disappeared and has not been heard of since. This is the last we know of poor "Nanny."

The weather continues dry and excessively warm here. Nothing very important occurring. The election in Kentucky has gone very strongly right. Old Mr. Wickliffe got ugly, as you know: ran for governor, and is terribly beaten. Upon Mr. Crittenden's death, Brutus Clay, Cassius's brother, was put on the track for Congress, and is largely elected. Mr. Menzies, who, as we thought, behaved very badly last session of Congress, is largely beaten in the district opposite Cincinnati, by Green Clay Smith, Cassius Clay's nephew. But enough.

Affectionately,
A. Lincoln.

LETTER TO GENERAL J. A. McCLERNAND
AUGUST 12, 1863

Executive Mansion,
Washington, August 12, 1863.

Major General McClernand:
My dear Sir:

Our friend, William G. Greene, has just presented a kind letter in regard to yourself, addressed to me by our other friends, Yates, Hatch, and Dubois. I doubt whether your present position is more painful to you than to myself. Grateful for the patriotic stand so early taken by you in the life-and-death struggle of the nation, I have done whatever has appeared practicable to advance you and the public interest together. No charges, with a view to a trial, have been preferred against you by any one; nor do I suppose any will be. All there is, so far as I have heard, is Gen. Grant's statement of his reason for relieving you. And even this I have not seen or sought to see; because it is a case, as appears to me, in which I could do nothing without doing harm. Gen.

Grant and yourself have been conspicuous in our most important successes; and for me to interfere, and thus magnify a breach between you, could not but be of evil effect. Better leave it where the law of the case has placed it. For me to force you back upon Gen. Grant, would be forcing him to resign. I can not give you a new command, because we have no forces except such as already have commanders. I am constantly pressed by those who *scold* before they *think*, or without thinking at all, to give commands respectively to Fremont, McClellan, Butler, Sigel, Curtis, Hunter, Hooker, and perhaps others; when, all else out of the way, I have no commands to give them. This is now your case, which, as I have before said, pains me, not less than it does you.

My belief is that the permanent estimate of what a general does in the field, is fixed by the "cloud of witnesses" who have been with him in the field; and that relying on them, he who has the right needs not to fear.

Your friend as ever
A. Lincoln

LETTER TO J. H. HACKETT
AUGUST 17, 1863

Executive Mansion,
Washington, August 17, 1863.

My dear Sir:

Months ago I should have acknowledged the receipt of your book, and accompanying kind note, and I now have to beg your pardon for not having done so.

For one of my age I have seen very little of the Drama. The first presentation of Falstaff I ever saw was yours here last winter or spring. Perhaps the best compliment I can pay is, to say, as I truly can, I am very anxious to see it again. Some of Shakespeare's Plays I have never read, whilst others I have gone over perhaps as frequently as any unprofessional reader. Among the latter are Lear, Richard Third, Henry Eighth, Hamlet, and especially Macbeth. I think nothing equals Macbeth. It is wonderful. Unlike you gentlemen of the profession, I think the soliloquy in Hamlet commencing "O, my offense is rank," surpasses that commencing "To be or not to be." But pardon this small attempt at criticism. I should like to hear you pronounce the opening speech of Richard the Third.

Will you not soon visit Washington again? If you do, please call and let me make your personal acquaintance.

Yours truly,
A. Lincoln.

James H. Hackett, Esq.

Hackett was a well-known Shakespearean actor of the era, whose appearances in Washington gave Lincoln much pleasure. Upon receiving this letter from the President, he published it in a broadside which carried the notation, "Printed not for publication but for private distribution only, and its convenient perusal by personal friends." Subsequently it came to the attention of the unfriendly press, and Lincoln's venture into Shakespearean criticism became the object of ridicule; whereupon Hackett apologized to the President and received the letter dated November 2, 1863, in reply. Lincoln's preference for the King's soliloquy in Hamlet *was possibly due to its theme of conscience and moral conflict.*

LETTER TO JAMES C. CONKLING
AUGUST 26, 1863

Executive Mansion,
Washington, August 26, 1863.

Hon. James C. Conkling
My Dear Sir.

Your letter inviting me to attend a mass-meeting of unconditional Union-men, to be held at the Capitol of Illinois, on the 3d day of September, has been received.

It would be very agreeable to me, to thus meet my old friends, at my own home; but I can not, just now, be absent from here, so long as a visit there, would require.

The meeting is to be of all those who maintain unconditional devotion to the Union; and I am sure my old political friends will thank me for tendering, as I do, the nation's gratitude to those other noble men, whom no partizan malice, or partizan hope, can make false to the nation's life.

There are those who are dissatisfied with me. To such I would say: You desire peace; and you blame me that we do not have it. But how can we attain it? There are but three conceivable ways. First, to suppress the rebellion by force of arms. This I am trying to do. Are you for it? If you are, so far we are agreed. If you are not for it, a second way is to give up the Union. I am against this. Are you for it? If you are, you should say so plainly. If you are not for *force*, nor yet for *dissolution*, there only remains some imaginable *compromise*. I do not believe any compromise, embracing the maintenance of the Union, is now possible. All I learn, leads to a directly opposite belief. The strength of the rebellion, is its military—its army. That army dominates all the country, and all the people, within its range. Any offer of terms made by any man or men within that range, in opposition to that army, is simply nothing for the present; because such man or men, have no power whatever to enforce their side of a compromise, if one were made with them. To illustrate. Suppose refugees from the South, and peace men of the North, get together in convention, and frame and proclaim a compromise embracing a restoration of the Union; in what way can that compromise be used to keep Lee's army out of Pennsylvania? Meade's army can keep Lee's army out of Pennsylvania; and, I think, can ultimately drive it out of existence. But no paper compromise, to which the controllers of Lee's army are not agreed, can at all affect that army. In an effort at such compromise we should waste time, which the enemy would improve to our disadvantage; and that would be all. A compromise, to be effective, must be made either with those who control the rebel army, or with the people first liberated from the domination of that army, by the success of our own army. Now allow me to assure you, that no word or intimation, from that rebel army, or from any of the men controlling it, in relation to any peace compromise, has ever come to my knowledge or belief. All charges and insinuations to the contrary, are deceptive and groundless. And I promise you, that if any such proposition shall hereafter come, it shall not be rejected, and kept a secret from you. I freely acknowledge myself the servant of the people, according to the bond of service—the United States Constitution; and that, as such, I am responsible to them.

But to be plain, you are dissatisfied with me about the negro. Quite likely there is a difference of opinion between you and myself upon that subject. I certainly wish that all men could be free, while I suppose you do not. Yet I have neither adopted, nor proposed any measure, which is not consistent with even your view, provided you are for the Union. I suggested compensated emancipation; to which you replied you wished not to be taxed to buy negroes. But I had not asked you to be taxed to buy negroes, except in such way, as to save you from greater taxation to save the Union exclusively by other means.

You dislike the emancipation proclamation; and, perhaps, would have it retracted. You say it is unconstitutional—I think differently. I think the constitution invests its Commander-in-chief, with the law of war, in time of war. The most that can be said, if so much, is, that slaves are property. Is there—has there ever been—any question that by the law of war, property, both of enemies and friends, may be taken when needed? And is it not needed whenever taking it, helps us, or hurts the enemy? Armies, the world over, destroy enemie's property when they can not use it; and even destroy their own to keep it from the enemy. Civilized belligerents do all in their power to help themselves, or hurt the enemy, except a few things regarded as barbarous or cruel. Among the exceptions are the massacre of vanquished foes, and non-combatants, male and female.

But the proclamation, as law, either is valid, or is not valid. If it is not valid, it needs no retraction. If it is valid, it can not be retracted, any more than the dead can be brought to life. Some of you profess to think its retraction would operate favorably for the Union. Why better *after* the retraction, than *before* the issue? There was more than a year and a half of trial to suppress the rebellion before the proclamation issued, the last one hundred days of which passed under an explicit notice that it was coming, unless averted by those in revolt, returning to their allegiance. The war has certainly progressed as favorably for us, since the issue of the proclamation as before. I know, as fully as one can know the opinions of others, that some of the commanders of our armies in the field who have given us our most important successes believe the emancipation policy and the use of the colored troops constitute the heaviest blow yet dealt to the Rebellion, and that at least one of these important successes could not have been achieved when it was but for the aid of black soldiers. Among the commanders holding these views are some who have never had any affinity with what is called abolitionism or with the Republican party policies but who held them purely as military opinions. I submit these opinions as being entitled to some weight against the objections often urged that emancipation and arming the blacks are unwise as military measures and were not adopted as such in good faith.

You say you will not fight to free negroes. Some of them seem willing to fight for you; but, no matter. Fight you, then, exclusively to save the Union. I issued the proclamation on purpose to aid you in saving the Union. Whenever you shall have conquered all resistance to the Union, if I shall urge you to continue fighting, it will be an apt time, then, for you to declare you will not fight to free negroes.

I thought that in your struggle for the Union, to whatever extent the negroes should cease helping the enemy, to that extent it weakened the enemy in his resistance to you. Do you think differently? I thought that whatever negroes can be got to do as soldiers, leaves just so much less for white soldiers to do, in saving the Union. Does it appear otherwise to you? But negroes, like other people, act upon motives. Why should they do any thing for us, if we will do nothing for them? If they stake their lives for us, they must be prompted by the strongest motive—even the promise of freedom. And the promise being made, must be kept.

The signs look better. The Father of Waters again goes unvexed to the sea. Thanks to the great Northwest for it. Nor yet wholly to them. Three hundred miles up, they met New England, Empire, Key-stone, and Jersey, hewing their way right and left. The Sunny South too, in more colors than one, also lent a hand. On the spot, their part of the history was jotted down in black and white. The job was a great national one; and let none be banned who bore an honorable part in it. And while those who have cleared the great river may well be proud, even that is not all. It is hard to say that anything has been more bravely, and well done, than at Antietam, Murfreesboro, Gettysburg, and on many fields of lesser note. Nor must Uncle Sam's web-feet be forgotten. At all the watery margins they have been present. Not only on the deep sea, the broad bay, and the rapid river, but also up the narrow muddy bayou, and wherever the ground was a little damp, they have been, and made their tracks. Thanks to all. For the great republic—for the principle it lives by, and keeps alive —for man's vast future—thanks to all.

Peace does not appear so distant as it did. I hope it will come soon, and come to stay; and so come as to be worth the keeping in all future time. It will then have been proved that, among free men, there can be no successful appeal from the ballot to the bullet; and that they who take such appeal are sure to lose their case, and pay the cost. And then, there will be some black men who can remember that, with silent tongue, and clenched teeth, and steady eye, and well-poised bayonet, they have helped mankind on to this great consummation; while, I fear, there will be some white ones, unable to forget that, with malignant heart, and deceitful speech, they strove to hinder it.

Still, let us not be over-sanguine of a speedy final triumph. Let us be quite sober. Let us diligently apply the means, never doubting that a just God, in his own good time, will give us the rightful result.

Yours very truly
A. Lincoln.

The manuscript of this letter appears to have been copied from Lincoln's first draft by one of the official secretaries who did a good deal of copy work at the White House, and whose hand appears in certain pages of the official manuscripts of the Messages to Congress. A number of emendations, as well as the close and signature, are in Lincoln's hand. The style and content declare Lincoln's composition beyond any doubt. The last three sentences of the seventh paragraph were added by means of a telegram. Hay's Diary records on August 23, 1863, that Lincoln "went into the Library to write a letter to Conkling." In a letter to Nicolay dated September 11, 1863, Hay refers to the letter again, calling it "a great thing" but disparaging its "hideously bad rhetoric."

There is some slight appearance that the secretary, either consciously or unconsciously, imitated Lincoln's handwriting in superficial matters such as capital letters. If he were copying from Lincoln's first draft, this would be readily understandable. The fact is worth notice chiefly because of the allegation that John Hay often imitated Lincoln's handwriting in official letters. Such superficial similarities to Lincoln's handwriting as are found in this letter and the "Letter to General H. W. Halleck," September 19, 1863, may have been the basis for assumptions that Hay indulged in imitating Lincoln's handwriting; but close study of the manuscripts does not anywhere indicate deliberate imitation, and eliminates in the editor's opinion the possibility that John Hay was the secretary who penned them. For further discussion of this problem, see the note on "Letter to Mrs. Bixby," November 21, 1864.

LETTER TO JAMES C. CONKLING
AUGUST 27, 1863

Private

War Department,
Washington City, D. C. Aug. 27 1863.

My dear Conkling

I can not leave here now. Herewith is a letter instead. You are one of the best public readers. I have but one suggestion. Read it very slowly.

And now God bless you, and all good Union-men.

Yours as ever
A. Lincoln

Lincoln could not leave Washington to make a speech, but he could write a letter embodying all he wished to say, and his good friend Conkling could read it to the rally of Union supporters which was to be held in Springfield, Illinois. This short note refers, of course, to the preceding letter of August 26, and was inclosed with it.

LETTER TO GENERAL H. W. HALLECK SEPTEMBER 19, 1863

Executive Mansion,
Washington, Sepbr. 19, 1863.

Major General Halleck:

By Gen Meade's despatch to you of yesterday, it appears that he desires your views, and those of the Government, as to whether he shall advance upon the enemy. I am not prepared to order, or even advise an advance in this case, wherein I know so little of particulars, and wherein he, in the field, thinks the risk is so great and the promise of advantage so small. And yet the case presents matter for very serious consideration in another aspect. These two armies confront each other across a small river, substantially midway between the two Capitals, each defending its own Capital, and menacing the other. Gen. Meade estimates the enemy's infantry in front of him at not less than forty thousand. Suppose we add fifty per cent. to this for cavalry, artillery, and extra-duty men stretching as far as Richmond, making the whole force of the enemy sixty thousand, Gen. Meade, as shown by the returns, has with him, and between him and Washington, of the same classes of well men, over ninety thousand. Neither can bring the whole of his men into a battle, but each can bring as large a per centage in as the other. For a battle, then, Gen Meade has three men to Gen. Lee's two. Yet, it having been determined that choosing ground and standing on the defensive gives so great advantage that the three cannot safely attack the two, the three are left simply standing on the defensive also. If the enemy's sixty thousand are sufficient to keep our ninety thousand away from Richmond, why, by the same rule, may not forty thousand of ours keep their sixty thousand away from Washington, leaving us fifty thousand to put to some other use? Having practically come to the mere defensive, it seems to be no economy at all to employ twice as many men for that object as are needed. With no object, certainly, to mislead myself, I can perceive no fault in this statement, unless we admit we are not the equal of the enemy, man for man. I hope you will consider it.

To avoid misunderstanding, let me say that to attempt to fight the enemy slowly back into his entrenchments at Richmond, and there to capture him, is an idea I have been trying to repudiate for quite a year. My judgment is so clear against it, that I would scarcely allow the attempt to be made, if the General in command should desire to make it. My last attempt upon Richmond was to get McClellan, when he was nearer there than the enemy was, to run in ahead of him. Since then I have constantly desired the Army of the Potomac to make Lee's army, and not Richmond, its objective point. If our army cannot fall upon the enemy and hurt him where he is, it is plain to me it can gain nothing by attempting to follow him over a succession of intrenched lines into a fortified city.

Yours truly,
A. Lincoln

PROCLAMATION FOR THANKSGIVING
OCTOBER 3, 1863

By the President of the United States of America.

A PROCLAMATION.

The year that is drawing toward its close, has been filled with the blessings of fruitful fields and healthful skies. To these bounties, which are so constantly enjoyed that we are prone to forget the source from which they come, others have been added, which are of so extraordinary a nature, that they cannot fail to penetrate and soften even the heart which is habitually insensible to the ever watchful providence of Almighty God. In the midst of a civil war of unequaled magnitude and severity, which has sometimes seemed to foreign States to invite and provoke their aggression, peace has been preserved with all nations, order has been maintained, the laws have been respected and obeyed, and harmony has prevailed everywhere except in the theatre of military conflict; while that theatre has been greatly contracted by the advancing armies and navies of the Union. Needful diversions of wealth and of strength from the fields of peaceful industry to the national defence, have not arrested the plough, the shuttle or the ship; the axe has enlarged the borders of our settlements, and the mines, as well of iron and coal as of the precious metals, have yielded even more abundantly than heretofore. Population has steadily increased, notwithstanding the waste that has been made in the camp, the siege and the battle-field; and the country, rejoicing in the consciousness of augmented strength and vigor, is permitted to expect continuance of years with large increase of freedom. No human counsel hath devised nor hath any mortal hand worked out these great things. They are the gracious gifts of the Most High God, who, while dealing with us in anger for our sins, hath nevertheless remembered mercy. It has seemed to me fit and proper that they should be solemnly, reverently, and gratefully acknowledged as with one heart and one voice by the whole American People. I do therefore invite my fellow citizens in every part of the United States, and also those who are at sea and those who are sojourning in foreign lands, to set apart and observe the last Thursday of November next, as a day of Thanksgiving and Praise to our beneficent Father who dwelleth in the Heavens. And I recommend to them that while offering up the ascriptions justly due to Him for such singular deliverances and blessings, they do also, with humble penitence for our national perverseness and disobedience, commend to His tender care all those who have become widows, orphans, mourners, or sufferers in the lamentable civil strife in which we are unavoidably engaged, and fervently implore the interposition of the Almighty Hand to heal the wounds of the nation and to restore it as soon as may be consistent with the Divine purposes to the full enjoyment of peace, harmony, tranquillity, and Union.

In testimony whereof, I have hereunto set my hand and caused the Seal of the United States to be affixed.

Done at the City of Washington, this Third day of [L. S.] October, in the year of our Lord one thousand eight hundred and sixty-three, and of the Independence of the United States the Eighty-eighth.

By the President: Abraham Lincoln

William H. Seward,
Secretary of State.

Although Lincoln had issued an earlier "Proclamation for Thanksgiving," July 15, 1863, designating August 6 as the day of observance, this is the proclamation which set the precedent for our national holiday. The second observance of the last Thursday in November was proclaimed by Lincoln in the proclamation dated October 20, 1864. In the following year, President Andrew Johnson, perhaps at Secretary Seward's suggestion, designated the third observance of the day. Seward wrote President Johnson's proclamation, and in view of the supposition of Daniel Kilham Dodge in Abraham Lincoln: Master of Words, *that Seward had a hand in the composition of Lincoln's proclamations, an interesting comparison can be made between them. Most notable is the absence from Seward's proclamation of the very characteristics which Dodge cites as evidence of Seward's possible authorship of Lincoln's proclamations. Where Lincoln's proclamations (see also those of August 12, 1861, and October 20, 1864) employ doubling of words and phrases quite liberally, Seward's (Johnson's) proclamation employs it but sparsely. Other characteristics of Lincoln's proclamations are likewise notably absent from Seward's composition. The numerous characteristic Lincoln phrases—"In the midst of a Civil War," "peace has been preserved with all nations," "large increase of freedom," "fit and proper,"—in this proclamation of October 3, 1863, as well as in the others, leave little ground for supposing*

Seward's authorship when they are compared with an indubitable bit of Seward's writing.

The Proclamation of November, 1865, as preserved in the manuscript of the first draft, entirely in Seward's handwriting, is as follows:

"By the P. of the U.S.

"A PROCLAMATION.

*"Almighty God our Heavenly Father has been pleased to vouchsafe to us as a people another year of that national life which is an indispensable condition of peace security and progress. That year has moreover been crowned with many peculiar blessings. The civil war that so recently closed among us has not been anywhere reopened. Domestic tranquility has improved, sentiments of conciliation have largely prevailed, and affections of loyalty and fraternity have been widely revived. Our fields have yielded quite abundently [*sic*] and our mining industry has been richly rewarded while our commerce has resumed its customary activity in foreign seas. These great national blessings demand a national acknowledgement. Now Therefore I Andrew Johnson President of the U.S. do hereby set apart and appoint Thursday the ____ day of November next to be observed everywhere in the several states and territories of the United States by the people thereof as a day of Thanksgiving and Praise [Prayer?] to Almighty God with due remembrance that in his temple doth every man speak of His Honor. I recommend also that on the same solemn occasion they do humbly and devoutly implore him to grant to our national councils and to our whole people that divine wisdom which alone can lead us [or?] any nation into the ways of all good. In offering this national thanksgiving and supplication let us remember that we have the divine assurance that the Lord remarks a King's praise. The Lord shall give strength to*

his People and the Lord shall give to his People the blessings of peace."

(From the original owned by The Abraham Lincoln Book Shop, Chicago, by courtesy of Mr. Ralph G. Newman.)

TELEGRAM TO GENERAL G. G. MEADE
OCTOBER 8, 1863

Washington, D. C., Oct. 8. 1863

Major General Meade
Army of Potomac

I am appealed to in behalf of August Blittersdorf, at Mitchells Station, Va. to be shot to-morrow, as a deserter. I am unwilling for any boy under eighteen to be shot; and his father affirms that he is yet under sixteen. Please answer. His Regt. or Co. not given me.

A Lincoln

LETTER TO GENERAL H. W. HALLECK
OCTOBER 16, 1863

Executive Mansion,
Washington, Oct. 16., 1863.

Major General Halleck

I do not believe Lee can have over sixty thousand effective men. Longstreet's corps would not be sent away, to bring an equal force back upon the same road; and there is no other direction for them to have come from. Doubtless, in making the present movement Lee gathered in all available scraps, and added them to Hills & Ewell's corps; but that is all. And he made the movement in the belief that *four* corps had left Gen. Meade; and Gen. Meade's apparently avoiding a collision with him has confirmed him in that belief. If Gen. Meade can now attack him on a field no worse than equal for us, and will do so with all the skill and courage, which he, his officers and men possess, the honor will be his if he succeeds, and the blame may be mine if he fails.

Yours truly,
A. Lincoln

LETTER TO J. H. HACKETT
NOVEMBER 2, 1863

(*Private.*)

Executive Mansion,
Washington, November 2, 1863.

James H. Hackett.
My dear Sir:

Yours of October 22 is received, as also was in due course that of October 3. I look forward with pleasure to the fulfilment of the promise made in the former.

Give yourself no uneasiness on the subject mentioned in that of the 22d.

My note to you I certainly did not expect to see in print; yet I have not been much shocked by the newspaper comments upon it. Those comments constitute a fair specimen of what has occurred to me through life. I have endured a great deal of ridicule without much malice; and have received a great deal of kindness, not quite free from ridicule. I am used to it.

Yours truly,
A. Lincoln.

LETTER TO E. M. STANTON, SECRETARY OF WAR NOVEMBER 11, 1863

Executive Mansion,
Washington, Nov. 11, 1863.

Hon. Secretary of War.
My dear Sir:

I personally wish Jacob R. Freese, of New-Jersey, to be appointed a Colonel for a colored regiment—and this regardless of whether he can tell the exact shade of Julius Caesars hair.

Yours truly
A. Lincoln

Freese was a former resident of Illinois of whom Lincoln later wrote, "I have enjoyed much of his friendship," but whose attachment for Lincoln was something less than constant. (For details see Carl Sandburg, Abraham Lincoln: The War Years, *Vol. III, p. 452.) Lincoln's relationship with Secretary Stanton, as suggested by this as well as other notes of similar humor, seems to have been far more informal, if not more agreeable, than that enjoyed by other members of the Cabinet.*

ADDRESS DELIVERED AT THE DEDICATION OF THE CEMETERY AT GETTYSBURG NOVEMBER 19, 1863

Four score and seven years ago our fathers brought forth on this continent, a new nation, conceived in Liberty, and dedicated to the proposition that all men are created equal.

Now we are engaged in a great civil war, testing whether that nation, or any nation so conceived and so dedicated, can long endure. We are met on a great battle-field of that war. We have come to dedicate a portion of that field, as a final resting place for those who here gave their lives that that nation might live. It is altogether fitting and proper that we should do this.

But, in a larger sense, we can not dedicate—we can not consecrate—we can not hallow—this ground. The brave men, living and dead, who struggled here, have consecrated it, far above our poor power to add or detract. The world will little note, nor long remember what we say here, but it can never forget what they did here. It is for us the living, rather, to be dedicated here to the unfinished work which they who fought here have thus far so nobly advanced. It is rather for us to be here dedicated to the great task remaining before us—that from these honored dead we take increased devotion to that cause for which they gave the last full measure of devotion—that we here highly resolve that these dead shall not have died in vain—that this nation, under God, shall have a new birth of freedom—and that government of the people, by the people, for the people, shall not perish from the earth.

Abraham Lincoln.

November 19, 1863.

The text is that of the final manuscript, known as "the Bliss copy," which Lincoln prepared for Colonel

Alexander Bliss, for publication as a lithograph facsimile in Autographed Leaves of Our Country's Authors *(1864). In all, there are five extant manuscripts of this address. Two of them have the honor of being considered the "original" draft, authorities being divided as to which of the two was penned first. For purposes of comparison, both of these are given below. W. E. Barton in* Lincoln at Gettysburg *holds the twenty-nine line manuscript (the first of the two printed below) to have been the "original" and the thirty-three line manuscript (the second printed below) to have been the second draft. Dr. Louis A. Warren in* Lincoln Lore, *No. 182, holds the opposite opinion.*

Except for the corrections, there are only minor differences between the two, and it seems likely that one was copied from the other. Assuming this, however, one becomes involved in difficulties as to which *was copied. In either case, Lincoln was apparently dissatisfied enough to consider further changes, and the changes seem to the editor not to present conclusive evidence of priority of composition. Other evidence presented by Barton seems to make probable the order in which they are here given. Reproduced with Lincoln's emendations, they are as follows:*

FIRST (?) DRAFT

Executive Mansion,
Washington, _______, 186_.

"Four score and seven years ago our fathers brought forth, upon this continent, a new nation, conceived in liberty, and dedicated to the proposition that 'all men are created equal'

"Now we are engaged in a great civil war, testing whether that nation, or any nation so conceived, and so dedicated, can long endure. We are met on a great battle field of that war. We have come to dedicate a portion of it, as a final resting place for those who died here, that

the nation might live. This we may, in all propriety do. But, in a larger sense, we can not dedicate—we can not consecrate—we can not hallow, this ground—The brave men, living and dead, who struggled here, have hallowed it, far above our poor power to add or detract. The world will little note, nor long remember what we say here; while it can never forget what they did *here.*

we here be dedicated

"It is rather for us, the living, ~~to stand here~~, to the great task remaining before us—that, from these honored dead we take increased devotion to that cause for which they here, gave the last full measure of devotion—that we here highly resolve these dead shall not have died in vain; that the nation, shall have a new birth of freedom, and that government of the people by the people for the people, shall not perish from the earth."

SECOND (?) DRAFT

"Four score and seven years ago our fathers brought forth, upon this continent, a new nation, conceived in Liberty, and dedicated to the proposition that all men are created equal.

"Now we are engaged in a great civil war, testing whether that nation, or any nation, so conceived, and so dedicated, can long endure. We are met here on a great

have come

battle-field of that war. We ~~are met~~ to dedicate a portion

a for

of it as ~~the~~ final resting place ~~of~~ those who here gave their lives that that nation might live. It is altogether fitting and proper that we should do this.

"But in a larger sense we can not dedicate—we can not consecrate—we can not hallow this ground. The brave men, living and dead, who struggled here, have

poor

consecrated it far above our power to add or detract. The world will little note, nor long remember, what we

say here, but can never forget what they did here. It is for us, the living, rather to be dedicated here to
work
the unfinished^which they have, thus far, so nobly carried on. It is rather for us to be here dedicated to the
us
great task remaining before^—that from these honored dead we take increased devotion to that cause for which they here gave ~~gave~~ the last full measure of devotion—that we here highly resolve that these dead shall not have died in vain; that this nation shall have a new birth of freedom; and that this government of the people, by the people, for the people, shall not perish from the earth."

LETTER TO EDWARD EVERETT
NOVEMBER 20, 1863

Executive Mansion,
Washington, Nov. 20, 1863.

Hon. Edward Everett.
My dear Sir:

Your kind note of to-day is received. In our respective parts yesterday, you could not have been excused to make a short address, nor I a long one. I am pleased to know that, in your judgment, the little I did say was not entirely a failure. Of course I knew Mr. Everett would not fail; and yet, while the whole discourse was eminently satisfactory, and will be of great value, there were passages in it which trancended [*sic*] my expectation. The point made against the theory of the general government being only an agency, whose principals are the States, was new to me, and, as I think, is one of the best arguments for the national supremacy. The tribute to our noble women for their angel-ministering to the suffering soldiers, surpasses, in its way, as do the subjects of it, whatever has gone before.

Our sick boy, for whom you kindly enquire, we hope is past the worst.

Your Obt. Servt.
A. Lincoln

In the letter to which Lincoln was replying, Everett had written, "I should be glad if I could flatter myself that I came as near the central idea of the occasion in two hours as you did in two minutes." The central theme of Everett's address is, in fact, almost identical with Lincoln's theme, and the parallel may in part have been the result of the fact that Everett had sent Lincoln a copy of his address printed in advance of the occasion. But, as has been pointed out in the note on the "Response to a Serenade," July 7, 1863, Lincoln had anticipated the theme at the very time of the victory at Gettysburg.

PROCLAMATION OF AMNESTY AND RECONSTRUCTION. DECEMBER 8, 1863

By The President of the United States of America:

A PROCLAMATION.

Whereas, in and by the Constitution of the United States, it is provided that the President "shall have power to grant reprieves and pardons for offences against the United States, except in cases of impeachment;" and

Whereas a rebellion now exists whereby the loyal State governments of several States have for a long time been subverted, and many persons have committed and are now guilty of treason against the United States; and

Whereas, with reference to said rebellion and treason, laws have been enacted by Congress, declaring forfeitures and confiscation of property and liberation of slaves, all upon terms and conditions therein stated, and also declaring that the President was thereby authorized at any time thereafter, by proclamation, to extend to persons who may have participated in the existing rebellion, in any State or part thereof, pardon and amnesty, with such exceptions and at such times and on such conditions as he may deem expedient for the public welfare; and

Whereas the congressional declaration for limited and conditional pardon accords with well-established judicial exposition of the pardoning power; and

Whereas, with reference to said rebellion, the President of the United States has issued several proclamations, with provisions in regard to the liberation of slaves; and

Whereas it is now desired by some persons heretofore engaged in said rebellion to resume their allegiance to the United States, and to reinaugurate loyal State governments within and for their respective States; therefore,

I, Abraham Lincoln, President of the United States, do proclaim, declare, and make known to all persons who have, directly or by implication, participated in the existing rebellion, except as hereinafter excepted, that a full pardon is hereby granted to them and each of them, with restoration of all rights of property, except as to slaves, and in property cases where rights of third parties shall have intervened, and upon the condition that every such person shall take and subscribe an oath, and thenceforward keep and maintain said oath inviolate; and which oath shall be registered for permanent preservation, and shall be of the tenor and effect following, to wit:

"I, ———, do solemnly swear, in presence of Almighty God, that I will henceforth faithfully support, protect and defend the Constitution of the United States, and the union of the States thereunder; and that I will, in like manner, abide by and faithfully support all acts of Congress passed during the existing rebellion with reference to slaves, so long and so far as not repealed, modified or held void by Congress, or by decision of the Supreme Court; and that I will, in like manner, abide by and faithfully support all proclamations of the President made during the existing rebellion having reference to slaves, so long and so far as not modified or declared void by decision of the Supreme Court. So help me God."

The persons excepted from the benefits of the foregoing provisions are all who are, or shall have been, civil or diplomatic officers or agents of the so-called confederate government; all who have left judicial stations under the United States to aid the rebellion; all who are, or shall have been, military or naval officers of said so-called confederate government above the rank of colonel in the army, or of lieutenant in the navy; all who left seats in the United States Congress to aid the rebellion; all who resigned commissions in the army or navy of the United States, and afterwards aided the rebellion; and all who have engaged in any way in treating colored persons or white persons, in charge of such, otherwise than lawfully as prisoners of war, and which persons may have been found in the United States service, as soldiers, seamen, or in any other capacity.

And I do further proclaim, declare, and make known that whenever, in any of the States of Arkansas, Texas, Louisiana, Mississippi, Tennessee, Alabama, Georgia, Florida, South Carolina, and North Carolina, a number of persons, not less than one-tenth in number of the votes cast in such State at the Presidential election of the year of our Lord one thousand eight hundred and sixty, each having taken the oath aforesaid and not having since violated it, and being a qualified voter by the election law of the State existing immediately before the so-called act of secession, and excluding all others, shall re-establish a State government which shall be republican, and in no wise contravening said oath, such shall be recognized as the true government of the State, and the State shall receive thereunder the benefits of the constitutional provision which declares that "The United States shall guaranty to every State in this union a republican form of government, and shall protect each of them against invasion; and, on application of the legislature, or the executive, (when the legislature cannot be convened,) against domestic violence."

And I do further proclaim, declare, and make known that any provision which may be adopted by such State government in relation to the freed people of such State, which shall recognize and declare their permanent freedom, provide for their education, and which may yet be consistent, as a temporary arrangement, with their present condition as a laboring, landless, and homeless class, will not be objected to by the national Executive. And it is suggested as not improper, that, in constructing a loyal State government in any State, the name of the State, the boundary, the subdivisions, the constitution, and the general code of laws, as before the rebellion, be maintained, subject only to the modifications made necessary by the conditions hereinbefore stated, and such others, if any, not contravening said conditions, and which may be deemed expedient by those framing the new State government.

To avoid misunderstanding, it may be proper to say that this proclamation, so far as it relates to State governments, has no reference to States wherein loyal State governments have all the while been maintained. And for the same reason, it may be proper to further say that whether members sent to Congress from any State shall be admitted to seats, constitutionally rests exclusively with the respective Houses, and not to any extent with the Executive. And still further, that this proclamation is intended to present the people of the States wherein the national authority has been suspended, and loyal State governments have been subverted, a mode in and by which the national authority and loyal State governments may be re-established within said States, or in any of them; and, while the mode presented is the best the Executive can suggest, with his present impressions, it must not be understood that no other possible mode would be acceptable.

[L. S.] Given under my hand at the city of Washington, the 8th day of December, A. D. one thousand eight hundred and sixty-three, and of the independence of the United States of America the eighty-eighth.

By the President: Abraham Lincoln.

William H. Seward,
Secretary of State.

LETTER TO CRAFTS J. WRIGHT AND C. K. HAWKES JANUARY 7, 1864

Executive Mansion,
Washington, Jany. 7, 1864.

Gentlemen:

You have presented me a plan for getting cotton and other products, from within the rebel lines, from which you think the United States will derive some advantage. Please carefully and considerately, answer me the following questions.

1. If now, without any new order or rule, a rebel should come into our lines with cotton, and offer to take the oath of Dec. 8th. what do you understand would be done with him and his cotton?

2. How will the physical difficulty, and danger, of getting cotton from within the rebel lines be lessened by your plan? or how will the owners motive to surmount that difficulty and danger, be heightened by it?

3. If your plan be adopted, *where* do you propose putting the cotton &c. into market? how assure the government of your good faith in the business? and how be compensated for your services?

Very Respectfully
A. Lincoln

Messrs. Crafts J. Wright &
C. K. Hawkes.

The editor has been unable to identify the individuals, or possibly the firm, to whom Lincoln wrote this letter. Lincoln's interest in getting cotton, which was badly needed by the North, was tempered by his suspicion of the proposed plan.

LETTER TO GENERAL N. P. BANKS
JANUARY 31, 1864

Executive Mansion,
Washington, January 31, 1864.

Major General Banks

Yours of the 22nd. Inst. is just received. In the proclamation of Dec. 8, and which contains the oath that you say some loyal people wish to avoid taking, I said:

"And still further, that this proclamation is intended to present the people of the States wherein the national authority has been suspended, and loyal State governments have been subverted, a mode in and by which the national authority and loyal State governments may be re-established within said States, or in any of them; and, while the mode presented is the best the Executive can suggest, with his present impressions, it must not be understood that no other possible mode would be acceptable."

And Speaking of this in the message, I said:

"Saying that reconstruction will be accepted if presented in a specified way, it is not said it will never be accepted in any other way."

These things were put into these documents on purpose that some conformity to circumstances should be admissable [*sic*]; and when I have, more than once, said to you in my letters that available labor already done should not be thrown away, I had in mind the very class of cases you now mention. So you see it is not even a modification of anything I have heretofore said when I tell you that you are at liberty to adopt any rule which shall admit to vote any unquestionably loyal free-state men and none others. And yet I do wish they would all take the oath

Yours truly,
A Lincoln

This letter is one of several written to General Banks during December, 1863, and January, 1864, conveying advice and instructions for setting up the new government in Louisiana. It illustrates perfectly Lincoln's attitude toward the problem—giving Banks absolute freedom of action to effect the establishment of a government of loyal Union men. The election which ensued on February 22 resulted in the election of Michael Hahn as Governor, and the first step in restoring a key state to the Union was achieved.

LETTER TO E. M. STANTON, SECRETARY OF WAR MARCH 1, 1864

Executive Mansion,
Washington, March 1, 1864.

Hon. Sec. of War—
My dear Sir:

A poor widow, by the name of Baird, has a son in the Army, that for some offence has been sentenced to serve a long time without pay, or at most, with very little pay. I do not like this punishment of withholding pay—it falls so very hard upon poor families. After he has been serving in this way for several months, at the tearful appeal of the poor mother, I made a direction that he be allowed to enlist for a new term, on the same conditions as others. She now comes, and says she can not get it acted upon. Please do it.

Yours truly
A Lincoln

LETTER TO GOVERNOR MICHAEL HAHN
MARCH 13, 1864

Private

Executive Mansion,
Washington, March 13., 1864.

Hon. Michael Hahn
My dear Sir:

I congratulate you on having fixed your name in history as the first-free-state Governor of Louisiana Now you are about to have a Convention which, among other things, will probably define the elective franchise. I barely suggest for your private consideration, whether some of the colored people may not be let in—as, for instance, the very intelligent, and especially those who have fought gallantly in our ranks They would probably help, in some trying time to come, to keep the jewel of liberty within the family of freedom. But this is only a suggestion, not to the public, but to you alone

Yours truly
A. Lincoln

LETTER TO E. M. STANTON, SECRETARY OF WAR
MARCH 15, 1864

Executive Mansion,
Washington, March 15, 1864.

Hon. Sec. of War
My dear Sir

Please see the gallant Drummer-boy, Robert H. Hendershot, whose history is briefly written on the fine drum presented him which he now carries. He must have a chance, and if you can find any situation suitable to him, I shall be obliged.

Yours truly
A. Lincoln

Robert Henry Hendershot, born in Cambridge, Michigan, December 11, 1850, was barely twelve years old when he gained fame for his daring at the battle of Fredericksburg on December 12, 1862. "When he (the boy) found that the Captain would not permit him to remain in the boat, he begged the privilege of pushing the boat off, and the request was granted. Whereupon, instead of remaining on shore, he clung to the stern of the boat, and, submerged to the waist in water, he crossed the Rappahannock. Soon as he landed, a fragment of a shell struck his old drum and knocked it to pieces. Picking up a musket, he went in search of rebel relics, and obtained a secesh flag, a clock, a knife, and a bone ring. On opening a back door in one of the rebel houses, he found a rebel wounded in the hand, and ordered him to surrender. He did so and was taken by the boy soldier to the Seventh Michigan . . ." For a full account of Hendershot's action at Fredericksburg and later at the battle of Murfreesboro, see Frank Moore, The Civil War in Song and Story 1860-1865, *pp. 245-6.*

MEMORANDUM FOR MRS. S. W. HUNT
APRIL 11, 1864

Executive Mansion,
Washington, April 11, 1864.

Whom it may concern

I know nothing on the subject of the attached letter, except as therein stated. Neither do I personally know Mrs. Hunt. She has, however, from the beginning of the war, been constantly represented to me as an open, and somewhat influential friend of the Union. It has been said to me, (I know not whether truly) that her husband is in the rebel army, that she avows her purpose to not live with him again, and that she refused to see him when she had an opportunity during one of John Morgan's raids into Kentucky. I would not offer her, or any wife, a temptation to a permanent separation from her husband; but if she shall avow that her mind is already, independently and fully made up to such separation, I shall be glad for the property sought by her letter, to be delivered to her, upon her taking the oath of December 8, 1863

A. Lincoln

Mrs. Sallie Ward Hunt, an acquaintance of Mrs. Lincoln's in Kentucky, who was separated from her husband Daniel Hunt not merely by conditions of war but by choice, had written to Mrs. Lincoln hoping through her influence to get "valuable personal effects" being held by Federal authorities in New Orleans. Lincoln sent her letter together with this note to one of his "confidential advisers in Kentucky." (William H. Townsend, Lincoln and His Wife's Home Town, *p. 349.)*

ADDRESS AT A SANITARY FAIR IN BALTIMORE APRIL 18, 1864

Ladies and Gentlemen—

Calling to mind that we are in Baltimore, we can not fail to note that the world moves. Looking upon these many people, assembled here, to serve, as they best may, the soldiers of the Union, it occurs at once that three years ago the same soldiers could not so much as pass through Baltimore. The change from then till now, is both great, and gratifying. Blessings on the brave men who have wrought the change, and the fair women who strive to reward them for it.

But Baltimore suggests more than could happen within Baltimore. The change within Baltimore is part only of a far wider change. When the war began, three years ago, neither party, nor any man, expected it would last till now. Each looked for the end, in some way, long ere to-day. Neither did any anticipate that domestic slavery would be much affected by the war. But here we are; the war has not ended, and slavery has been much affected —how much needs not now to be recounted. So true is it that man proposes, and God disposes.

But we can see the past, though we may not claim to have directed it; and seeing it, in this case, we feel more hopeful and confident for the future.

The world has never had a good definition of the word liberty, and the American people, just now, are much in want of one. We all declare for liberty; but in using the same *word* we do not all mean the same *thing*. With some the word liberty may mean for each man to do as he pleases with himself, and the product of his labor; while with others the same word may mean for some men to do as they please with other men, and the product of other men's labor. Here are two, not only different, but incompatable [*sic*] things, called by the same name—liberty. And it follows that each of the things is, by the respective parties, called by two different and incompatable [*sic*] names—liberty and tyranny.

The shepherd drives the wolf from the sheep's throat, for which the sheep thanks the shepherd as a *liberator*, while the wolf denounces him for the same act as the destroyer of liberty, especially as the sheep was a black one. Plainly the sheep and the wolf are not agreed upon a definition of the word liberty; and precisely the same difference prevails to-day among us human creatures, even in the North, and all professing to love liberty. Hence we behold the processes by which thousands are daily passing from under the yoke of bondage, hailed by some as the advance of liberty, and bewailed by others as the destruction of all liberty. Recently, as it seems, the people of Maryland have been doing something to define liberty; and thanks to them that, in what they have done, the wolf's dictionary, has been repudiated.

It is not very becoming for one in my position to make speeches at great length; but there is another subject upon which I feel that I ought to say a word. A painful rumor, true I fear, has reached us of the massacre, by the rebel forces, at Fort Pillow, in the West end of Tennessee, on the Mississippi river, of some three hundred colored soldiers and white officers, who had just been overpowered by their assailants. There seems to be some anxiety in the public mind whether the government is doing it's duty to the colored soldier, and to the service, at this point. At the beginning of the war, and for some time, the use of colored troops was not contemplated; and how the change of purpose was wrought, I will not now take time to explain. Upon a clear conviction of duty I resolved to turn that element of strength to account; and I am responsible for it to the American people, to the Christian world, to history, and on my final account, to God. Having determined to use the negro as a soldier, there is no way but to give him all the protection given to any other soldier. The difficulty is not in stating the principle, but in practically applying it. It is a mistake to suppose the government is indiffent [*sic*] to this matter, or is not doing the best it can in regard to it. We do not to-day *know* that a colored soldier, or white officer commanding colored soldiers, has been massacred by the rebels when made a prisoner. We fear it, believe it, I may say, but we do not know it. To take the life of one of their prisoners, on the assumption that they murder ours, when it is short of certainty that they do murder ours, might be too serious, too cruel a mistake. We are having the Fort-Pillow affair thoroughly investigated; and such investigation will probably show conclusively how the truth is. If, after all that has been said, it shall turn out that there has been no massacre at Fort-Pillow, it will be almost safe to say there has been none, and will be none elsewhere. If there has been the massacre of three hundred there, or even the tenth part of three hundred, it will be conclusively proved; and being so proved, the retribution shall as surely come. It will be matter of grave consideration in what exact course to apply the retribution; but in the supposed case, it must come.

The Women's Central Association of Relief, a forerunner of our modern Red Cross organization, conducted fairs to raise money for medical supplies and services to the wounded and sick soldiers. Lincoln's address on this occasion and later at Philadelphia was scheduled to promote attendance. Crowds were large, and much merchandise donated by those who could not make a cash contribution was sold.

LETTER TO GENERAL U. S. GRANT
APRIL 30, 1864

Executive Mansion
Washington, April 30. 1864.

Lieutenant General Grant.

Not expecting to see you again before the Spring campaign opens, I wish to express, in this way, my entire satisfaction with what you have done up to this time, so far as I understand it. The particulars of your plans I neither know or seek to know. You are vigilant and self-reliant; and, pleased with this, I wish not to obtrude any constraints or restraints upon you. While I am very anxious that any great disaster, or capture of our men in great numbers, shall be avoided, I know these points are less likely to escape your attention than they would be mine. If there is anything wanting which is within my power to give, do not fail to let me know it.

And now with a brave army, and a just cause, may God sustain you.

Yours very truly
A. Lincoln

SPEECH AT A SANITARY FAIR IN PHILADELPHIA JUNE 16, 1864

I suppose that this toast was intended to open the way for me to say something.

War, at the best, is terrible, and this war of ours, in its magnitude and in its duration, is one of the most terrible. It has deranged business, totally in many localities, and partially in all localities. It has destroyed property and ruined homes; it has produced a national debt and taxation unprecedented, at least in this country; it has carried mourning to almost every home, until it can almost be said that the "heavens are hung in black."

Yet the war continues, and several relieving coincidents have accompanied it from the very beginning which have not been known, as I understand, or have any knowledge of, in any former wars in the history of the world. The Sanitary Commission, with all its benevolent labors; the Christian Commission, with all its Christian and benevolent labors; and the various places, arrangements, so to speak, and institutions, have contributed to the comfort and relief of the soldiers. You have two of these places in this city—the Cooper Shop and Union Volunteer Refreshment Saloons. And lastly, these fairs, which, I believe, began only last August, if I mistake not, in Chicago, then at Boston, at Cincinnati, Brooklyn, New York, and Baltimore, and those at present held at St. Louis, Pittsburgh, and Philadelphia. The motive and object that lie at the bottom of all these are most worthy; for, say what you will, after all, the most is due to the soldier who takes his life in his hands and goes to fight the battles of his country. In what is contributed to his comfort when he passes to and fro, and in what is contributed to him when he is sick and wounded, in whatever shape it comes, whether from the fair and tender hand of woman, or from any other source, it is much, very much. But I think that there is still that which is of as much value to him in the continual reminders he sees in the newspapers that while he is absent he is yet remembered by the loved ones at home. Another view of these various institutions, if I may so call them, is worthy of consideration, I think. They are voluntary contributions, given zealously and earnestly, on top of all the disturbances of business, of all the disorders, of all the taxation, and of all the burdens that the war has imposed upon us, giving proof that the national resources are not at all exhausted, and that the national spirit of patriotism is even firmer and stronger than at the commencement of the war.

It is a pertinent question, often asked in the mind privately, and from one to the other, when is the war to end. Surely I feel as deep an interest in this question as any other can; but I do not wish to name a day, a month, or a year, when it is to end. I do not wish to run any risk of seeing the time come without our being ready for the end, for fear of disappointment because the time had come and not the end. We accepted this war for an object, a worthy object, and the war will end when that object is attained. Under God, I hope it never will end until that time. Speaking of the present campaign, General Grant is reported to have said, "I am going through on this line if it takes all summer." This war has taken three years; it was begun or accepted upon the line of restoring the national authority over the whole national domain, and for the American people, as far as my knowledge enables me to speak, I say we are going through on this line if it takes three years more.

My friends, I did not know but that I might be called upon to say a few words before I got away from here, but I did not know it was coming just here. I have never been in the habit of making predictions in regard to the war, but I am almost tempted to make one. If I were to hazard it, it is this: That Grant is this evening, with General Meade and General Hancock, and the brave officers and soldiers with him, in a position from whence he will never be dislodged until Richmond is taken; and I have but one single proposition to put now, and perhaps I can best put it in the form of an interrogative. If I shall discover that General Grant and the noble officers and men under him can be greatly facilitated in their work by a sudden pouring forward of men and assistance, will you give them to me? Are you ready to march? [Cries of "Yes".] Then I say, Stand ready, for I am watching for the chance. I thank you, gentlemen.

LETTER TO WILLIAM DENNISON & OTHERS, A COMMITTEE OF THE NATIONAL UNION CONVENTION. JUNE 27, 1864

Executive Mansion,
Washington, June 27, 1864.

Hon. William Dennison & others, a
Committee of the National Union Convention.
Gentlemen:

Your letter of the 14th. Inst. formally notifying me that I have been nominated by the convention you represent for the Presidency of the United States for four years from the fourth of March next has been received. The nomination is gratefully accepted, as the resolutions of the convention, called the platform, are heartily approved. While the resolution in regard to the supplanting of republican government upon the Western continent is fully concurred in, there might be misunderstanding were I not to say that the position of the government, in relation to the action of France in Mexico, as assumed through the State Department, and approved and indorsed by the convention, among the measures and acts of the Executive, will be faithfully maintained, so long as the state of facts shall leave that position pertinent and applicable. I am especially gratified that the soldier and the seaman were not forgotten by the convention, as they forever must and will be remembered by the grateful country for whose salvation they devote their lives.

Thanking you for the kind and complimentary terms in which you have communicated the nomination and the proceedings of the convention, I subscribe myself

Your Obt. Servt
Abraham Lincoln.

LETTER TO HORACE GREELEY
JULY 15, 1864

Executive Mansion,
Washington, July 15, 1864.

Hon. Horace Greeley
My dear Sir

Yours of the 13th is just received; and I am disappointed that you have not already reached here with those Commissioners, if they would consent to come, on being shown my letter to you of the 9th Inst. Show that and this to them; and if they will come on the terms stated in the former, bring them. I not only intend a sincere effort for peace, but I intend that you shall be a personal witness that it is made.

Yours truly
A. Lincoln

The fiasco of Greeley's "peace mission" occupies a full chapter in Nicolay and Hay, Abraham Lincoln: A History. *This letter was carried to Greeley by John Hay, who acted as Lincoln's personal emissary, accompanying Greeley to Niagara where Greeley had reported two Confederate Commissioners to be waiting to negotiate peace terms. Greeley had made much ado about the administration's indifference to Confederate overtures for peace, and Lincoln's action forced him to produce the facts. Apparently suspicious that he had overstepped his facts in insisting that the Confederacy was trying to make peace, Greeley went with Hay reluctantly. The "Confederate Commissioners" were found to be without authority to negotiate, and the affair ended, as Lincoln feared it would, in no achievement whatsoever.*

ADDRESS TO THE 164th OHIO REGIMENT
AUGUST 18, 1864

Soldiers:

You are about to return to your homes and your friends, after having, as I learn, performed in camp a comparatively short term of duty in this great contest. I am greatly obliged to you, and to all who have come forward at the call of their country. I wish it might be more generally and universally understood what the country is now engaged in. We have, as all will agree, a free Government, where every man has a right to be equal with every other man. In this great struggle, this form of Government and every form of human right is endangered if our enemies succeed. There is more involved in this contest than is realized by every one. There is involved in this struggle the question whether your children and my children shall enjoy the privileges we have enjoyed. I say this in order to impress upon you, if you are not already so impressed, that no small matter should divert us from our great purpose. There may be some inequalities in the practical application of our system. It is fair that each man shall pay taxes in exact proportion to the value of his property; but if we should wait before collecting a tax to adjust the taxes upon each man in exact proportion with every other man, we should never collect any tax at all. There may be mistakes made sometimes; things may be done wrong while the officers of the Government do all they can to prevent mistakes. But I beg of you, as citizens of this great Republic, not to let your minds be carried off from the great work we have before us. This struggle is too large for you to be diverted from it by any small matter. When you return to your homes rise up to the height of a generation of men worthy of a free Government, and we will carry out the great work we have commenced. I return to you my sincere thanks, soldiers, for the honor you have done me this afternoon.

ADDRESS TO THE 166th OHIO REGIMENT AUGUST 22, 1864

I suppose you are going home to see your families and friends. For the service you have done in this great struggle in which we are engaged I present you sincere thanks for myself and the country. I almost always feel inclined, when I happen to say anything to soldiers, to impress upon them in a few brief remarks the importance of success in this contest. It is not merely for to-day, but for all time to come that we should perpetuate for our children's children this great and free government, which we have enjoyed all our lives. I beg you to remember this, not merely for my sake, but for yours. I happen temporarily to occupy this big White House. I am a living witness that any one of your children may look to come here as my father's child has. It is in order that each one of you may have through this free government which we have enjoyed, an open field and a fair chance for your industry, enterprise and intelligence: that you may all have equal privileges in the race of life, with all its desirable human aspirations. It is for this the struggle should be maintained, that we may not lose our birthright—not only for one, but for two or three years. The nation is worth fighting for, to secure such an inestimable jewel.

LETTER TO MRS. ELIZA P. GURNEY
SEPTEMBER 4, 1864

Executive Mansion,
Washington, September 4., 1864.

Eliza P. Gurney.
My esteemed friend.

I have not forgotten—probably never shall forget—the very impressive occasion when yourself and friends visited me on a Sabbath forenoon two years ago. Nor has your kind letter, written nearly a year later, ever been forgotten. In all, it has been your purpose to strengthen my reliance on God. I am much indebted to the good Christian people of the country for their constant prayers and consolations; and to no one of them, more than to yourself. The purposes of the Almighty are perfect, and must prevail, though we erring mortals may fail to accurately perceive them in advance. We hoped for a happy termination of this terrible war long before this; but God knows best, and has ruled otherwise. We shall yet acknowledge His wisdom and our own error therein. Meanwhile we must work earnestly in the best light He gives us, trusting that so working still conduces to the great ends He ordains. Surely He intends some great good to follow this mighty convulsion, which no mortal could make, and no mortal could stay.

Your people—the Friends—have had, and are having, a very great trial. On principle, and faith, opposed to both war and oppression, they can only practically oppose oppression by war. In this hard dilemma, some have chosen one horn, and some the other. For those appealing to me on conscientious grounds, I have done, and shall do, the best I could and can, in my own conscience, under my oath to the law. That you believe this I doubt not; and believing it, I shall still receive, for our country and myself, your earnest prayers to our Father in heaven.

Your sincere friend
A. Lincoln.

LETTER TO GENERAL U. S. GRANT
SEPTEMBER 22, 1864

Executive Mansion,
Washington, Sep. 22, 1864.

Lieut. General Grant

I send this as an explanation to you, and to do justice to the Secretary of War. I was induced, upon pressing application, to authorize agents of one of the Districts of Pennsylvania to recruit in one of the prisoner depots in Illinois; and the thing went so far before it came to the knowledge of the Secretary of War that in my judgment it could not be abandoned without greater evil than would follow it's going through. I did not know, at the time, that you had protested against that class of thing being done; and I now say that while this particular job must be completed, no other of the sort, will be authorized, without an understanding with you, if at all. The Secretary of War is wholly free of any part of this blunder

Yours truly
A. Lincoln

LETTER TO HENRY W. HOFFMAN
OCTOBER 10, 1864

Executive Mansion,
Washington, October 10, 1864.

Hon. Henry W Hoffman
My dear Sir:

A convention of Maryland has framed a new constitution for the State; a public meeting is called for this evening, at Baltimore, to aid in securing its ratification by the people; and you ask a word from me, for the occasion. I presume the only feature of the instrument, about which there is serious controversy, is that which provides for the extinction of slavery. It needs not to be a secret, and I presume it is no secret, that I wish success to this provision. I desire it on every consideration. I wish all men to be free. I wish the material prosperity of the already free which I feel sure the extinction of slavery would bring. I wish to see, in process of disappearing, that only thing which ever could bring this nation to civil war. I attempt no argument. Argument upon the question is already exhausted by the abler, better posted, and more immediately interested sons of Maryland herself. I only add that I shall be gratified exceedingly if the good people of the State shall by their votes, ratify the new constitution.

Yours truly
A. Lincoln

As John Hay records in his Diary, the manuscript shows that Hay erased Lincoln's phrase "better posted" and wrote in "better informed." The text restores Lincoln's wording.

RESPONSE TO A SERENADE
OCTOBER 19, 1864

I am notified that this is a compliment paid me by the loyal Marylanders, resident in this District. I infer that the adoption of the new Constitution for the State, furnishes the occasion; and that, in your view, the extirpation of slavery constitutes the chief merit of the new constitution. Most heartily do I congratulate you, and Maryland, and the nation, and the world, upon this event. I regret that it did not occur two years sooner, which I am sure would have saved to the nation more money than would have met all the private loss incident to the measure. But it has come at last, and I sincerely hope it's friends may fully realize all their anticipations of good from it; and that it's opponents may, by it's effects, be agreeably and profitably disappointed.

A word upon another subject. Something said by the Secretary of State, in his recent speech at Auburn, has been construed by some into a threat that, if I shall be beaten at the election, I will, between then and the end of my constitutional term, do what I may be able to ruin the government.

Others regard the fact that the Chicago Convention adjourned, not *sine die*, but to meet again, if called to do so by a particular individual, as the intimation of a purpose that if their nominee shall be elected, he will at once seize control of the government. I hope the good people will permit themselves to suffer no uneasiness on either point. I am struggling to maintain the government, not to overthrow it. I am struggling especially to prevent others from overthrowing it. I therefore say, that if I shall live, I shall remain President until the fourth of next march; and that whoever shall be constitutionally elected therefor in November, shall be duly installed as President on the fourth of March; and that in the interval I shall do my utmost that whoever is to hold the helm for the next voyage, shall start with the best possible chance to save the ship.

This is due to the people both on principle, and under the Constitution. Their will, constitutionally expressed, is the ultimate law for all. If they should deliberately resolve to have immediate peace even at the loss of their country, and their liberty, I know not the power or the right to resist them. It is their own business, and they must do as they please with their own. I believe, however, they are still resolved to preserve their country and their liberty; and in this, in office or out of it, I am resolved to stand by them.

I may add that in this purpose to save the country and its liberties, no classes of people seem so nearly unanimous as the soldiers in the field and the sailors afloat. Do they not have the hardest of it? Who should quail when they do not? God bless the soldiers and seamen, with all their brave commanders.

PROCLAMATION OF THANKSGIVING OCTOBER 20, 1864

By The President of the United States of America:

A PROCLAMATION.

It has pleased Almighty God to prolong our national life another year, defending us with his guardian care against unfriendly designs from abroad, and vouchsafing to us in His mercy many and signal victories over the enemy, who is of our own household. It has also pleased our Heavenly Father to favor as well our citizens in their homes as our soldiers in their camps and our sailors on the rivers and seas with unusual health. He has largely augmented our free population by emancipation and by immigration, while he has opened to us new sources of wealth, and has crowned the labor of our working men in every department of industry with abundant rewards. Moreover, he has been pleased to animate and inspire our minds and hearts with fortitude, courage and resolution sufficient for the great trial of civil war into which we have been brought by our adherence as a nation to the cause of Freedom and Humanity, and to afford to us reasonable hopes of an ultimate and happy deliverance from all our dangers and afflictions.

Now, therefore, I, Abraham Lincoln, President of the United States, do, hereby, appoint and set apart the last Thursday in November next as a day which I desire to be observed by all my fellow-citizens wherever they may then be as a day of Thanksgiving and Praise to Almighty God the beneficent Creator and Ruler of the Universe. And I do farther recommend to my fellow-citizens aforesaid that on that occasion they do reverently humble themselves in the dust, and from thence offer up penitent and fervent prayers and supplications to the Great Disposer of events for a return of the inestimable blessings of Peace, Union, and Harmony throughout the land, which it has pleased him to assign as a dwelling place for ourselves and for our posterity throughout all generations.

In testimony whereof, I have hereunto set my hand and caused the seal of the United States to be affixed.

[L. S.] Done at the city of Washington this twentieth day of October, in the year of our Lord one thousand eight hundred and sixty four, and of the Independence of the United States the eighty-ninth.

By the President: Abraham Lincoln

William H. Seward
Secretary of State

TELEGRAM TO GENERAL P. H. SHERIDAN
OCTOBER 22, 1864

Executive Mansion
Washington, Oct. 22, 1864

Major General Sheridan.

With great pleasure I tender to you and your brave army, the thanks of the Nation, and my own personal admiration and gratitude, for the months operations in the Shenandoah Valley; and especially for the splendid work of October 19, 1864.

Your Obt. Servt.
Abraham Lincoln.

RESPONSE TO A SERENADE
NOVEMBER 10, 1864

(Nov. 10 1864)

It has long been a grave question whether any government, not *too* strong for the liberties of its people, can be strong *enough* to maintain its own existence in great emergencies.

On this point the present rebellion brought our republic to a severe test; and a presidential election occurring in regular course during the rebellion added not a little to the strain. If the loyal people, *united*, were put to the utmost of their strength by the rebellion, must they not fail when *divided*, and partially paralized [*sic*], by a political war among themselves?

But the election was a necessity.

We can not have free government without elections; and if the rebellion could force us to forego, or postpone a national election, it might fairly claim to have already conquered and ruined us. The strife of the election is but human-nature practically applied to the facts of the case. What has occurred in this case, must ever recur in similar cases. Human-nature will not change. In any future great national trial, compared with the men of this, we shall have as weak, and as strong; as silly and as wise; as bad and good. Let us, therefore, study the incidents of this, as philosophy to learn wisdom from, and none of them as wrongs to be revenged.

But the election, along with its incidental, and undesirable strife, has done good too. It has demonstrated that a people's government can sustain a national election, in the midst of a great civil war. Until now it has not been known to the world that this was a possibility. It shows also how *sound*, and how *strong* we still are. It shows that, even among candidates of the same party, he who is most devoted to the Union, and most opposed to treason, can receive most of the people's votes. It shows also, to the extent yet known, that we have more men now, than we had when the war began. Gold is good in its place; but living, brave, patriotic men, are better than gold.

But the rebellion continues; and now that the election is over, may not all, having a common interest, re-unite in a common effort, to save our common country? For my own part I have striven, and shall strive to avoid placing any obstacle in the way. So long as I have been here I have not willingly planted a thorn in any man's bosom.

While I am deeply sensible to the high compliment of a re-election; and duly grateful, as I trust, to Almighty God for having directed my countrymen to a right conclusion, as I think, for their own good, it adds nothing to my satisfaction that any other man may be disappointed or pained by the result.

May I ask those who have not differed with me, to join with me, in this same spirit towards those who have?

And now, let me close by asking three hearty cheers for our brave soldiers and seamen and their gallant and skilful commanders.

LETTER TO GENERAL W. S. ROSECRANS NOVEMBER 19, 1864

Executive Mansion,
Washington, Nov 19th, 1864

Major General Rosecrans.

A Major Wolf, as it seems was under sentence, in your Department, to be executed in retaliation for the murder of a Major Wilson; and I, without any particular knowledge of the facts, was induced, by appeals for mercy, to order the suspension of his execution until further order. Understanding that you so desire, this letter places the case again within your control, with the remark only that I wish you to do nothing merely for revenge, but that what you may do, shall be solely done with reference to the security of the future.

Yours truly,
A. Lincoln

The manuscript of this letter is not in the handwriting of Lincoln nor in that of one of his secretaries, but is signed by Lincoln. From the endorsement on the back and from circumstances indicated in the letter, it may be concluded that a clerk from the War Department brought Lincoln the papers relating to Major Wolf, took down Lincoln's dictated reply, and secured his signature before returning to the office. The letter is not imposing at first glance, but is a splendid example, especially in the adroit final sentence, of the care with which Lincoln phrased a difficult idea, even in haste. Apparently General Rosecrans did not wish to assume responsibility for deciding that "the security of the future" demanded Wolf's execution, for the Confederate officer's life was spared.

Major Wolf returned to his farm in Fulton County, Arkansas, where he lived for many years proud in the distinction of having been, as he phrased it, "recalled to life."

LETTER TO MRS. BIXBY
NOVEMBER 21, 1864

Executive Mansion,
Washington, Nov. 21, 1864.

Dear Madam,—

I have been shown in the files of the war Department a statement of the Adjutant General of Massachusetts, that you are the mother of five sons who have died gloriously on the field of battle.

I feel how weak and fruitless must be any word of mine which should attempt to beguile you from the grief of a loss so overwhelming. But I cannot refrain from tendering to you the consolation that may be found in the thanks of the Republic they died to save.

I pray that our Heavenly Father may assuage the anguish of your bereavement, and leave you only the cherished memory of the loved and lost, and the solemn pride that must be yours, to have laid so costly a sacrifice upon the altar of Freedom.

Yours, very sincerely and respectfully,
A. Lincoln

Mrs. Bixby.

(For more detailed discussion of the question of the authorship of this letter, the reader may consult the editor's article, "Who Wrote the 'Letter to Mrs. Bixby'?" in the Lincoln Herald, *February, 1943, and a forthcoming book by F. Lauriston Bullard and Edward C. Stone entitled* Lincoln Wrote the Bixby Letter, a Detective

Story, *which the editor has been privileged to read in manuscript and which will provide the most complete account of all available evidence on the composition of the letter.)*

As is well known to most students of Lincoln, the purported facsimiles of this letter have been judged to be forgeries, and the original manuscript has never been found. Furthermore, the opinion has been somewhat widely held that Lincoln never wrote the letter at all. In his book, Across the Busy Years, *Nicholas Murray Butler relates that "John Hay told [John] Morley that he had himself written the Bixby letter and that this was the reason why it could not be found among Lincoln's papers and why no original copy of it had ever been forthcoming." Dr. Butler goes even beyond this to maintain that: "As a matter of fact, Abraham Lincoln wrote very few letters that bore his signature. John G. Nicolay wrote almost all of those which were official, while John Hay wrote almost all of those which were personal. Hay was able to imitate Lincoln's handwriting and signature in well-nigh perfect fashion."*

If one admits the possibility that John Hay told Morley that he had written the letter, there is still the question of what he may have meant when he used the word wrote. *Did he mean simply that he had* penned *the letter, or that he had* composed *it?*

In a letter written from Paris on September 5, 1866, Hay answered Herndon's specific inquiry concerning the letters which Lincoln wrote as President, in the following language: "He wrote very few letters. He did not read one in fifty that he received. At first we tried to bring them to his notice, but at last he gave the whole thing over to me, and signed without reading them the letters I wrote in his name. He wrote perhaps half-a-dozen a week himself—not more." (From a photostatic copy in possession of the editor. The complete letter is printed in The Hidden Lincoln, *edited by Emanuel Hertz.)*

This statement may be considered generally true.

After 1861 Lincoln wrote as few letters as he could. Hay's estimate of "half-a-dozen a week" amply covers the really significant letters, of which there are rarely that many in a single week. There are, however, several inadequacies and inaccuracies in the statement as a whole. When Hay states that "he gave the whole thing over to me," he hardly does justice to Nicolay or the other secretaries, who, as numerous manuscripts show, penned many of Lincoln's letters. Furthermore, when Hay states that Lincoln "signed without reading them the letters which I wrote in his name," he presumes quite a bit. If he had looked over a number of such letters as he did pen for Lincoln, he would have found some with corrections and emendations written in by Lincoln before he signed them. Then, too, Hay's statement implies that all the letters thus signed by Lincoln were composed by Hay himself. This is demonstrably not the case in the "Letter to General H. W. Halleck," July 29, 1863, which is in phraseology and style distinctly Lincoln's, and is emended and corrected as well as signed in Lincoln's handwriting, though penned by Hay. Some letters Lincoln apparently dictated to Hay, others to Nicolay, and still others to secretaries who relieved and assisted them from time to time. And often Lincoln emended them before signing his name. Finally, Hay's statement fails to take into account the many letters he did write in his own person (and in his own handwriting!) and signed with his own name as the President's Secretary.

Another interesting example of how loosely Hay used the word wrote *is contained in two references in his Diary to Lincoln's "Response to a Serenade," November 9, 1864. The first of these is as follows: "The President answered from the window with rather unusual dignity and effect and we came home. [Added later: 'I wrote the speech and sent it to Hanscum.']" (Tyler Dennett, editor,* Lincoln and the Civil War in the Diaries and Letters of John Hay, *p. 236). This statement might readily be misinterpreted, if detached from its setting, to mean that Hay had composed the "Response," when as a matter of fact he merely penned what Lincoln had said, perhaps polishing a bit according to his own light. It is interesting that this speech as printed in the* Complete Works of Abraham Lincoln *is far inferior to the "Response" delivered the following evening, November 10, 1864, which Lincoln took the trouble to write out himself. Hay's second comment is as follows: "The speeches of the President at the last two serenades are very highly spoken of. The first I wrote after the fact, to prevent the 'loyal Pennsylvanians' getting a swing at it themselves" (Dennett, p. 239).*

Furthermore, it is a curiously interesting fact concerning the two letters which Hay states in his Diary that he "wrote" (implying definitely composed*), that one is omitted from the first edition of the* Complete Works of Abraham Lincoln *(1894) and the other is so utterly without personal style and without significance as to be of little worth. Of the first of these two letters Hay notes: "Today I induced the President to sign a letter to Col. Rowland approving his proposed National Rifle Corps. I think Rowland himself rather a humbug but his idea is a good one" (Dennett, p. 104). This "induced the President to sign" sounds far different from the tone of Hay's statement to Herndon and probably indicates far more accurately the limit to which Hay's authority and function as Secretary extended. The second of these letters is the "Letter to G. H. Boker," October 26, 1863, which may be consulted in the* Complete Works *as an example of the colorless and inconsequential style of Hay's compositions as Secretary to the President, most of which Hay signed in his own name with the notation "A.P.S." appended.*

In regard to the specific question of Hay's ability to imitate Lincoln's handwriting "in well-nigh perfect fashion," one must doubt Dr. Butler's belief. That there can be no large number of letters in which this was done, or even attempted, is certain. Hay could not have had the time to imitate Lincoln's scrawl in any number of letters. To attempt such a task would have entailed an enormous amount of labor beyond his required duties as secretary. The business of imitating handwriting (forging *is the less polite word for it) is no easy task for an expert, and Hay certainly had his hands full without undertaking such an utterly useless task. Also, the editor has never seen among the several hundred Lincoln manuscripts which he has studied either in the original or in photostatic copy any letter in which Lincoln's handwriting is open to suspicion of being an imitation by Hay. Furthermore, the editor has queried a number of authorities who know more about Lincoln manuscripts than he does, and not one of them has ever admitted having seen such a letter. In only one instance known to the editor is there even a bare possibility that Hay may have been attempting to imitate Lincoln's handwriting, and the similarity is so slight that it would seem most likely a matter of coincidence rather than imitation—and that is the "Telegram to Mrs. Lincoln," December 21, 1862 (original in the Brown University Library). The similarities do not extend beyond the likeness of a few capital letters and some slight likeness in the signature.*

In another instance Hay had an opportunity to imitate Lincoln's handwriting when there might have been real point to doing so. In the "Letter to Henry W. Hoffman," October 10, 1864, as already noted, Lincoln originally wrote the phrase "better posted." After Lincoln had finished the letter, Hay carefully "scraped out" the word posted, *as he records in his Diary, and wrote in the word* informed. *The emendation is plainly in Hay's hand with no appearance whatever of an attempt to imitate. In short, if there is any evidence that Hay ever attempted to imitate Lincoln's handwriting it has not been discovered.*

We may conclude concerning Hay's function as Secretary to President Lincoln, therefore, that Dr. Butler is probably incorrect in stating that Hay could and did imitate Lincoln's handwriting. Further, we may conclude that Dr. Butler is correct in his belief that as one of Lincoln's secretaries Hay wrote a good many letters, but incorrect in believing that many of the better letters were composed by Hay. Concerning Hay's statement to Herndon we may conclude that it is in certain particulars inadequate, inaccurate, and incorrect.

When the manuscript of the Bixby letter is produced we may know what Hay had to do with it, if anything, but since the original has been sought diligently for more than half a century, one must doubt that it is now in existence. In view of these circumstances, we can best rely on the circumstantial evidence surrounding the composition of the letter and the internal evidence of style, both of which point conclusively to Lincoln's authorship. In regard to the evidence of style, it should be pointed out that until someone produces an example of Hay's writing that sounds *sufficiently like Lincoln to merit the comparison, there is simply no ground for supposing that he could, or even had any desire to, write so. The editor has yet to find in Hay's letters any evidence that Hay imitated Lincoln or any other writer as to style. Some of Hay's poetry is imitative, but his letters are invariably in his own idiom. If anyone will read aloud a few of the better known lyrical passages which have been discussed in "Lincoln's Development as a Writer," then procure a copy of W. R. Thayer's* Life and Letters of John Hay *and read a few of Hay's compositions, and finally read the "Letter to Mrs. Bixby," his conclusion is very likely to be emphatic on the ground of style alone.*

In conclusion, however, if Hay's personal testimony can be accepted (in spite of the fact that in 1885 he wrote Richard Watson Gilder: "Can you remember things? I have to rely exclusively on documents. I would not trust my recollection in the slightest matter of historical interest"), there is Hay's letter to William E.

Chandler, which has been called to the editor's attention by Messrs. F. Lauriston Bullard and Edward C. Stone. In this letter written in 1904, Hay specifies as follows: "The letter of Mr. Lincoln to Mrs. Bixby is genuine, is printed in our edition of his Works, and has been frequently re-published; but the engraved copy of Mr. Lincoln's alleged manuscript, which is so extensively sold, is, in my opinion, a very ingenious forgery."

STORY WRITTEN FOR NOAH BROOKS DECEMBER [6?] 1864

THE PRESIDENT'S LAST, SHORTEST, AND BEST SPEECH.

On Thursday of last week two ladies from Tennessee came before the President asking the release of their husbands held as prisoners of war at Johnson's Island. They were put off till friday, when they came again; and were again put off to Saturday. At each of the interviews one of the ladies urged that her husband was a religious man. On Saturday the President ordered the release of the prisoners, and then said to this lady "You say your husband is a religious man; tell him when you meet him, that I say I am not much of a judge of religion, but that, in my opinion, the religion that sets men to rebel and fight against their government, because, as they think, that government does not sufficiently help *some* men to eat their bread in the sweat of *other* men's faces, is not the sort of religion upon which people can get to heaven."

A. Lincoln—

Lincoln sent for Brooks, who was then correspondent for a California paper, wrote out this news story, headline and all, on a piece of white pasteboard, and asked Brooks to have it printed in the Washington Daily Chronicle, *with the comment: "Don't wait to send it to California in your correspondence. I've a childish desire to see it in print right away." It appeared on the morning of December 7.*

Three months later, in the "Second Inaugural Address," Lincoln was to reiterate, more mildly, this same view.

ANNUAL MESSAGE TO CONGRESS DECEMBER 6, 1864

Fellow-citizens of the Senate and House of Representatives:

Again the blessings of health and abundant harvests claim our profoundest gratitude to Almighty God.

The condition of our foreign affairs is reasonably satisfactory.

Mexico continues to be a theatre of civil war. While our political relations with that country have undergone no change, we have, at the same time, strictly maintained neutrality between the belligerents.

At the request of the states of Costa Rica and Nicaragua, a competent engineer has been authorized to make a survey of the River San Juan and the port of San Juan. It is a source of much satisfaction that the difficulties which for a moment excited some political apprehensions, and caused a closing of the interoceanic transit route, have been amicably adjusted, and that there is a good prospect that the route will soon be reopened with an increase of capacity and adaptation. We could not exaggerate either the commercial or the political importance of that great improvement.

It would be doing injustice to an important South American state not to acknowledge the directness, frankness, and cordiality with which the United States of Colombia have entered into intimate relations with this government. A claims convention has been constituted to complete the unfinished work of the one which closed its session in 1861.

The new liberal constitution of Venezuela having gone into effect with the universal acquiescence of the people, the government under it has been recognized, and diplomatic intercourse with it has opened in a cordial and friendly spirit. The long-deferred Aves Island claim has been satisfactorily paid and discharged.

Mutual payments have been made of the claims awarded by the late joint commission for the settlement of claims between the United States and Peru. An earnest and cordial friendship continues to exist between the two countries, and such efforts as were in my power have been used to remove misunderstanding and avert a threatened war between Peru and Spain.

Our relations are of the most friendly nature with Chile, the Argentine Republic, Bolivia, Costa Rica, Paraguay, San Salvador, and Hayti.

During the past year no differences of any kind have arisen with any of those republics, and, on the other hand, their sympathies with the United States are constantly expressed with cordiality and earnestness.

The claim arising from the seizure of the cargo of the brig Macedonian in 1821 has been paid in full by the government of Chile.

Civil war continues in the Spanish part of San Domingo, apparently without prospect of an early close.

Official correspondence has been freely opened with Liberia, and it gives us a pleasing view of social and political progress in that Republic. It may be expected to derive new vigor from American influence, improved by the rapid disappearance of slavery in the United States.

I solicit your authority to furnish to the republic a gunboat at moderate cost, to be reimbursed to the United States by instalments. Such a vessel is needed for the safety of that state against the native African races; and in Liberian hands it would be more effective in arresting the African slave trade than a squadron in our own hands. The possession of the least organized naval force would stimulate a generous ambition in the republic, and the confidence which we should manifest by furnishing it would win forbearance and favor towards the colony from all civilized nations.

The proposed overland telegraph between America and Europe, by the way of Behring's Straits and Asiatic Russia, which was sanctioned by Congress at the last session, has been undertaken, under very favorable circumstances, by an association of American citizens, with the cordial good-will and support as well of this government as of those of Great Britain and Russia. Assurances have been received from most of the South American States of their high appreciation of the enterprise, and their readiness to co-operate in constructing lines tributary to that world-encircling communication. I learn, with much satisfaction, that the noble design of a telegraphic communication between the eastern coast of America and Great Britain has been renewed with full expectation of its early accomplishment.

Thus it is hoped that with the return of domestic peace the country will be able to resume with energy and advantage its former high career of commerce and civilization.

Our very popular and estimable representative in Egypt died in April last. An unpleasant altercation which arose between the temporary incumbent of the office and the government of the Pacha resulted in a suspension of intercourse. The evil was promptly corrected on the arrival of the successor in the consulate, and our relations with Egypt, as well as our relations with the Barbary powers, are entirely satisfactory.

The rebellion which has so long been flagrant in China, has at last been suppressed, with the co-operating good offices of this government, and of the other western commercial states. The judicial consular establishment there has become very difficult and onerous, and it will need legislative revision to adapt it to the extension of our commerce, and to the more intimate intercourse which has been instituted with the government and people of that vast empire. China seems to be accepting with hearty good-will the conventional laws which regulate commercial and social intercourse among the western nations.

Owing to the peculiar situation of Japan, and the anomalous form of its government, the action of that empire in performing treaty stipulations is inconstant and capricious. Nevertheless, good progress has been effected by the western powers, moving with enlightened concert. Our own pecuniary claims have been allowed, or put in course of settlement, and the inland sea has been reopened to commerce. There is reason also to believe that these proceedings have increased rather than diminished the friendship of Japan towards the United States.

The ports of Norfolk, Fernandina, and Pensacola have been opened by proclamation. It is hoped that foreign merchants will now consider whether it is not safer and more profitable to themselves, as well as just to the United States, to resort to these and other open ports, than it is to pursue, through many hazards, and at vast cost, a contraband trade with other ports which are closed, if not by actual military occupation, at least by a lawful and effective blockade.

For myself, I have no doubt of the power and duty of the Executive, under the law of nations, to exclude enemies of the human race from an asylum in the United States. If Congress should think that proceedings in such cases lack the authority of law, or ought to be further regulated by it, I recommend that provision be made for effectually preventing foreign slave traders from acquiring domicile and facilities for their criminal occupation in our country.

It is possible that, if it were a new and open question, the maritime powers, with the lights they now enjoy, would not concede the privileges of a naval belligerent to the insurgents of the United States, destitute, as they are, and always have been, equally of ships-of-war and of ports and harbors. Disloyal emissaries have been neither less assiduous nor more successful during the last year than they were before that time in their efforts, under favor of that privilege, to embroil our country in foreign wars. The desire and determination of the governments of the maritime states to defeat that design are believed to be as sincere as, and cannot be more earnest than our own. Nevertheless, unforeseen political difficulties have arisen, especially in Brazilian and British ports, and on the northern boundary of the

United States, which have required, and are likely to continue to require, the practice of constant vigilance, and a just and conciliatory spirit on the part of the United States as well as of the nations concerned and their governments.

Commissioners have been appointed under the treaty with Great Britain on the adjustment of the claims of the Hudson's Bay and Puget's Sound Agricultural Companies, in Oregon, and are now proceeding to the execution of the trust assigned to them.

In view of the insecurity of life and property in the region adjacent to the Canadian border, by reason of recent assaults and depredations committed by inimical and desperate persons, who are harbored there, it has been thought proper to give notice that after the expiration of six months, the period conditionally stipulated in the existing arrangement with Great Britain, the United States must hold themselves at liberty to increase their naval armament upon the lakes, if they shall find that proceeding necessary. The condition of the border will necessarily come into consideration in connection with the question of continuing or modifying the rights of transit from Canada through the United States, as well as the regulation of imposts, which were temporarily established by the reciprocity treaty of the 5th of June, 1854.

I desire, however, to be understood, while making this statement, that the Colonial authorities of Canada are not deemed to be intentionally unjust or unfriendly towards the United States; but, on the contrary, there is every reason to expect that, with the approval of the imperial government, they will take the necessary measures to prevent new incursions across the border.

The act passed at the last session for the encouragement of emigration has, so far as was possible, been put into operation. It seems to need amendment which will enable the officers of the government to prevent the practice of frauds against the immigrants while on their way and on their arrival in the ports, so as to secure them here a free choice of avocations and places of settlement. A liberal disposition towards this great national policy is manifested by most of the European States, and ought to be reciprocated on our part by giving the immigrants effective national protection. I regard our emigrants as one of the principal replenishing streams which are appointed by Providence to repair the ravages of internal war, and its wastes of national strength and health. All that is necessary is to secure the flow of that stream in its present fullness, and to that end the government must, in every way, make it manifest that it neither needs nor designs to impose involuntary military service upon those who come from other lands to cast their lot in our country.

The financial affairs of the government have been successfully administered during the last year. The legislation of the last session of Congress has beneficially affected the revenues, although sufficient time has not yet elapsed to experience the full effect of several of the provisions of the acts of Congress imposing increased taxation.

The receipts during the year, from all sources, upon the basis of warrants signed by the Secretary of the Treasury, including loans and the balance in the treasury on the first day of July, 1863, were $1,394,796,007.62; and the aggregate disbursements, upon the same basis, were $1,298,056,101.89, leaving a balance in the treasury, as shown by warrants, of $96,739,905.73.

Deduct from these amounts the amount of the principal of the public debt redeemed, and the amount of issues in substitution therefor, and the actual cash operations of the treasury were: receipts, $884,076,646.57; disbursements, $865,234,087.86; which leaves a cash balance in the treasury of $18,842,558.71.

Of the receipts, there were derived from customs, $102,316,152.99; from lands, $588,333.29; from direct taxes, $475,648.96; from internal revenue, $109,741,134.10; from miscellaneous sources, $47,511,448.10; and from loans applied to actual expenditures, including former balances, $623,443,929.13.

There were disbursed, for the civil service, $27,505,599.46; for pensions and Indians, $7,517,930.97; for the War Department, $690,791,842.97; for the Navy Department, $85,733,292.77; for interest of the public debt, $53,685,421.69;—making an aggregate of $865,234,087.86, and leaving a balance in the treasury of $18,842,558.71, as before stated.

For the actual receipts and disbursements for the first quarter, and the estimated receipts and disbursements for the three remaining quarters of the current fiscal year, and the general operations of the treasury in detail, I refer you to the report of the Secretary of the Treasury. I concur with him in the opinion that the proportion of moneys required to meet the expenses consequent upon the war derived from taxation should be still further increased; and I earnestly invite your attention to this subject, to the end that there may be such additional legislation as shall be required to meet the just expectations of the Secretary.

The public debt on the first day of July last, as appears by the books of the treasury, amounted to $1,740,690,489.49. Probably, should the war continue for another year, that amount may be increased by not far from five hundred millions. Held as it is, for the most part, by our own people, it has become a substantial branch of national though private, property. For obvious reasons, the more nearly this property can be distributed among all the people the better. To favor such general distribution, greater inducements to become owners might, perhaps, with good effect, and without injury, be presented to persons of limited means. With this view, I suggest whether it might not be both competent and expedient for Congress to provide that a limited amount of some future issue of public securities might be held by any bona-fide purchaser exempt from taxation, and from seizure for debt, under such restrictions and limitations as might be necessary to guard against abuse of so important a privilege. This would enable every prudent person to set aside a small annuity against a possible day of want.

Privileges like these would render the possession of such securities, to the amount limited, most desirable to every person of small means who might be able to save enough for the purpose. The great advantage of citizens being creditors as well as debtors, with relation to the public debt, is obvious. Men readily perceive that they cannot be much oppressed by a debt which they owe to themselves.

The public debt on the first day of July last, although somewhat exceeding the estimate of the Secretary of the Treasury made to Congress at the commencement of the last session, falls short of the estimate of that officer made in the preceding December, as to its probable amount at the beginning of this year, by the sum of $3,995,097.31. This fact exhibits a satisfactory condition and conduct of the operations of the treasury.

The national banking system is proving to be acceptable to capitalists and to the people. On the twenty-fifth day of November five hundred and eighty-four national banks had been organized, a considerable number of which were conversions from State banks. Changes from State systems to the national system are rapidly taking place, and it is hoped that, very soon, there will be in the United States, no banks of issue not authorized by Congress, and no bank-note circulation not secured by the government. That the government and the people will derive great benefit from this change in the banking systems of the country can hardly be questioned. The national system will create a reliable and permanent influence in support of the national credit, and protect the people against losses in the use of paper money. Whether or not any further legislation is advisable for the suppression of State bank issues, it will be for Congress to determine. It seems quite clear that the treasury cannot be satisfactorily conducted unless the government can exercise a restraining power over the bank-note circulation of the country.

The report of the Secretary of War and the accompanying documents will detail the campaigns of the armies in the field since the date of the last annual message, and also the operations of the several administrative bureaus of the War Department during the last year. It will also specify the measures deemed essential for the national defence, and to keep up and supply the requisite military force.

The report of the Secretary of the Navy presents a comprehensive and satisfactory exhibit of the affairs of that Department and of the naval service. It is a subject of congratulation and laudable pride to our countrymen that a navy of such vast proportions has been organized in so brief a period, and conducted with so much efficiency and success.

The general exhibit of the navy, including vessels under construction on the 1st of December, 1864, shows a total of 671 vessels, carrying 4,610 guns, and 510,396 tons, being an actual increase during the year, over and above all losses by shipwreck or in battle, of 83 vessels, 167 guns, and 42,427 tons.

The total number of men at this time in the naval service, including officers, is about 51,000.

There have been captured by the navy during the year 324 vessels, and the whole number of naval captures since hostilities commenced is 1,379, of which 267 are steamers.

The gross proceeds arising from the sale of condemned prize property, thus far reported, amount to $14,396,250.51. A large amount of such proceeds is still under adjudication and yet to be reported.

The total expenditures of the Navy Department of every description, including the cost of the immense squadrons that have been called into existence from the 4th of March, 1861, to the 1st of November, 1864, are $238,647,262.35.

Your favorable consideration is invited to the various recommendations of the Secretary of the Navy, especially in regard to a navy yard and suitable establishment for the construction and repair of iron vessels, and the machinery and armature for our ships, to which reference was made in my last annual message.

Your attention is also invited to the views expressed in the report in relation to the legislation of Congress at its last session in respect to prize on our inland waters.

I cordially concur in the recommendation of the Secretary as to the propriety of creating the new rank of vice-admiral in our naval service.

Your attention is invited to the report of the Postmaster General for a detailed account of the operations and financial condition of the Post Office Department.

The postal revenues for the year ending June 30, 1864, amounted to $12,438,253.78 and the expenditures to $12,664,786.20; the excess of expenditures over receipts being $206,652.42.

The views presented by the Postmaster-General on the subject of special grants by the government in aid of the establishment of new lines of ocean mail steamships, and the policy he recommends for the development of increased commercial intercourse with adjacent and neighboring countries, should receive the careful consideration of Congress.

It is of noteworthy interest that the steady expansion of population, improvement and governmental institutions over the new and unoccupied portions of our country have scarcely been checked, much less impeded or destroyed, by our great civil war, which at first glance would seem to have absorbed almost the entire energies of the nation.

The organization and admission of the State of Nevada has been completed in conformity with law, and thus our excellent system is firmly established in the mountains, which once seemed a barren and uninhabitable waste between the Atlantic States and those which have grown up on the coast of the Pacific Ocean.

The territories of the Union are generally in a condition of prosperity and rapid growth. Idaho and Montana, by reason of their great distance and the interruption of communication with them by Indian hostilities, have been only partially organized; but it is understood that these difficulties are about to disappear, which will permit their governments, like those of the others, to go into speedy and full operation.

As intimately connected with, and promotive of, this material growth of the nation, I ask the attention of Congress to the valuable information and important recommendations relating to the public lands, Indian affairs, the Pacific railroad, and mineral discoveries contained in the report of the Secretary of the Interior, which is herewith transmitted, and which report also embraces the subjects of patents, pensions and other topics of public interest pertaining to his department.

The quantity of public land disposed of during the five quarters ending on the 30th of September last was 4,221,342 acres, of which 1,538,614 acres were entered under the homestead law. The remainder was located with military land warrants, agricultural scrip certified to States for railroads, and sold for cash. The cash received from sales and location fees was $1,019,446.

The income from sales during the fiscal year, ending June 30, 1864, was $678,007.21, against $136,077.95 received during the preceding year. The aggregate number of acres surveyed during the year has been equal to the quantity disposed of; and there is open to settlement about 133,000,000 acres of surveyed land.

The great enterprise of connecting the Atlantic with the Pacific States by railways and telegraph lines has been entered upon with a vigor that gives assurance of success, notwithstanding the embarrassments arising from the prevailing high prices of materials and labor. The route of the main line of the road has been definitely located for one hundred miles westward from the initial point at Omaha City, Nebraska, and a preliminary location of the Pacific railroad of California has been made from Sacramento eastward to the great bend of the Truckee River, in Nevada.

Numerous discoveries of gold, silver and cinnabar mines have been added to the many heretofore known and the country occupied by the Sierra Nevada and Rocky Mountains, and the subordinate ranges, now teems with enterprising labor, which is richly remunerative. It is believed that the product of the mines of precious metals in that region has, during the year, reached, if not exceeded, one hundred millions in value.

It was recommended in my last annual message that our Indian system be remodelled. Congress, at its last session, acting upon the recommendation, did provide for reorganizing the system in California, and it is believed that under the present organization the management of the Indians there will be attended with reasonable success. Much yet remains to be done to provide for the proper government of the Indians in other parts of the country to render it secure for the advancing settler, and to provide for the welfare of the Indian. The Secretary reiterates his recommendations, and to them the attention of Congress is invited.

The liberal provisions made by Congress for paying pensions to invalid soldiers and sailors of the republic, and to the widows, orphans, and dependent mothers of those who have fallen in battle, or died of disease contracted, or of wounds received in the service of their country, have been diligently administered. There have been added to the pension rolls, during the year ending the 30th day of June last, the names of 16,770 invalid soldiers, and of 271 disabled seamen; making the present number of army invalid pensioners 22,767, and of navy invalid pensioners 712.

Of widows, orphans, and mothers, 22,198 have been placed on the army pension rolls, and 248 on the navy rolls. The present number of army pensioners of this class is 25,433, and of navy pensioners, 793. At the beginning of the year the number of Revolutionary pensioners was 1,430; only twelve of them were soldiers, of whom seven have since died. The remainder are those who, under the law, receive pensions because of relationship to revolutionary soldiers. During the year ending the 30th of June, 1864, $4,504,616.92 have been paid to pensioners of all classes.

I cheerfully commend to your continued patronage the benevolent institutions of the District of Columbia, which have hitherto been established or fostered by Congress, and respectfully refer, for information concerning them, and in relation to the Washington aqueduct, the Capitol, and other matters of local interest, to the report of the Secretary.

The Agricultural Department, under the supervision of its present energetic and faithful head, is rapidly commending itself to the great and vital interest it was created to advance. It is peculiarly the people's department, in which they feel more directly concerned than in any other. I commend it to the continued attention and fostering care of Congress.

The war continues. Since the last annual message all the important lines and positions then occupied by our forces have been maintained, and our arms have steadily advanced, thus liberating the regions left in rear; so that Missouri, Kentucky, Tennessee, and parts of other States have again produced reasonably fair crops.

The most remarkable feature in the military operations of the year is General Sherman's attempted march of three hundred miles, directly through the insurgent region. It tends to show a great increase of our relative strength that our General-in-Chief should feel able to confront and hold in check every active force of the enemy, and yet to detach a well-appointed large army to move on such an expedition. The result not yet being known, conjecture in regard to it is not here indulged.

Important movements have also occurred during the year

to the effect of moulding society for durability in the Union. Although short of complete success, it is much in the right direction, that twelve thousand citizens in each of the States of Arkansas and Louisiana have organized loyal State governments with free constitutions, and are earnestly struggling to maintain and administer them. The movements in the same direction, more extensive, though less definite in Missouri, Kentucky and Tennessee, should not be overlooked. But Maryland presents the example of complete success. Maryland is secure to Liberty and Union for all the future. The genius of rebellion will no more claim Maryland. Like another foul spirit, being driven out, it may seek to tear her, but it will woo her no more.

At the last session of Congress a proposed amendment of the Constitution abolishing slavery throughout the United States, passed the Senate, but failed for lack of the requisite two-thirds vote in the House of Representatives. Although the present is the same Congress, and nearly the same members, and without questioning the wisdom or patriotism of those who stood in opposition, I venture to recommend the reconsideration and passage of the measure at the present session. Of course the abstract question is not changed; but an intervening election shows, almost certainly, that the next Congress will pass the measure if this does not. Hence there is only a question of *time* as to when the proposed amendment will go to the States for their action. And as it is to so go, at all events, may we not agree that the sooner the better? It is not claimed that the election has imposed a duty on members to change their views or their votes, any further than, as an additional element to be considered, their judgment may be affected by it. It is the voice of the people now, for the first time, heard upon the question. In a great national crisis, like ours, unanimity of action among those seeking a common end is very desirable—almost indispensable. And yet no approach to such unanimity is attainable, unless some deference shall be paid to the will of the majority, simply because it is the will of the majority. In this case the common end is the maintenance of the Union; and, among the means to secure that end, such will, through the election, is most clearly declared in favor of such constitutional amendment.

The most reliable indication of public purpose in this country is derived through our popular elections. Judging by the recent canvass and its result, the purpose of the people, within the loyal States, to maintain the integrity of the Union, was never more firm, nor more nearly unanimous, than now. The extraordinary calmness and good order with which the millions of voters met and mingled at the polls, give strong assurance of this. Not only all those who supported the Union ticket, so called, but a great majority of the opposing party also, may be fairly claimed to entertain, and to be actuated by, the same purpose. It is an unanswerable argument to this effect, that no candidate for any office whatever, high or low, has ventured to seek votes on the avowal that he was for giving up the Union. There have been much impugning of motives, and much heated controversy as to the proper means and best mode of advancing the Union cause; but on the distinct issue of Union or no Union, the politicians have shown their instinctive knowledge that there is no diversity among the people. In affording the people the fair opportunity of showing, one to another and to the world, this firmness and unanimity of purpose, the election has been of vast value to the national cause.

The election has exhibited another fact not less valuable to be known—the fact that we do not approach exhaustion in the most important branch of national resources—that of living men. While it is melancholy to reflect that the war has filled so many graves, and carried mourning to so many hearts, it is some relief to know that, compared with the surviving, the fallen have been so few. While corps, and divisions, and brigades, and regiments have formed, and fought, and dwindled, and gone out of existence, a great majority of the men who composed them are still living. The same is true of the naval service. The election returns prove this. So many voters could not else be found. The States regularly holding elections, both now and four years ago, to wit, California, Connecticut, Delaware, Illinois, Indiana, Iowa, Kentucky, Maine, Maryland, Massachusetts, Michigan, Minnesota, Missouri, New Hampshire, New Jersey, New York, Ohio, Oregon, Pennsylvania, Rhode Island, Vermont, West Virginia, and Wisconsin cast 3,982,011 votes now, against 3,870,222 cast then; showing an aggregate now of 3,982,011. To this is to be added 33,762 cast now in the new States of Kansas and Nevada, which States did not vote in 1860, thus swelling the aggregate to 4,015,773, and the net increase during the three years and a half of war to 145,551. A table is appended showing particulars. To this again should be added the number of all soldiers in the field from Massachusetts, Rhode Island, New Jersey, Delaware, Indiana, Illinois, and California, who, by the laws of those States, could not vote away from their homes, and which number cannot be less than 90,000. Nor yet is this all. The number in organized Territories is triple now what it was four years ago, while thousands, white and black, join us as the national arms press back the insurgent lines. So much is shown, affirmatively and negatively, by the election. It is not material to inquire *how* the increase has been produced, or to show that it would have been *greater* but for the war, which is probably true. The important fact remains demonstrated, that we have *more* men *now* than we had when the war *began*; that we are not exhausted, nor in process of exhaustion; that we are *gaining* strength, and may, if need be, maintain the contest indefinitely. This as to men. Material resources are now more complete and abundant than ever.

The national resources, then, are unexhausted, and, as we believe, inexhaustible. The public purpose to re-establish and maintain the national authority is unchanged, and, as we believe, unchangeable. The manner of continuing the effort remains to choose. On careful consideration of all the evidence accessible it seems to me that no attempt at negotiation with the insurgent leader could result in any good. He would accept nothing short of severance of the Union—precisely what we will not and cannot give. His declarations to this effect are explicit and oft-repeated. He does not attempt to deceive us. He affords us no excuse to deceive ourselves. He cannot voluntarily reaccept the Union; we cannot voluntarily yield it. Between him and us the issue is distinct, simple, and inflexible. It is an issue which can only be tried by war, and decided by victory. If we yield, we are beaten; if the Southern people fail him, he is beaten. Either way, it would be the victory and defeat following war. What is true, however, of him who heads the insurgent cause, is not necessarily true of those who follow. Although he cannot reaccept the Union, they can. Some of them, we know, already desire peace and reunion. The number of such may increase. They can, at any moment, have peace simply by laying down their arms and submitting to the national authority under the Constitution. After so much, the government could not, if it would, maintain war against them. The loyal people would not sustain or allow it. If questions should remain, we would adjust them by the peaceful means of legislation, conference, courts, and votes, operating only in constitutional and lawful channels. Some certain, and other possible, questions are, and would be, beyond the Executive power to adjust; as, for instance, the admission of members into Congress, and whatever might require the appropriation of money. The Executive power itself would be greatly diminished by the cessation of actual war. Pardons and remissions of forfeitures, however, would still be within Executive control. In what spirit and temper this control would be exercised can be fairly judged of by the past.

A year ago general pardon and amnesty, upon specified terms, were offered to all, except certain designated classes; and, it was, at the same time, made known that the excepted classes were still within contemplation of special clemency. During the year many availed themselves of the general provision, and many more would, only that the signs of bad faith in some led to such precautionary measures as rendered the practical process less easy and certain. During the same time also special pardons have been granted to individuals of the excepted classes, and no voluntary application has been denied. Thus, practically, the door has been, for a full year, open to all, except such as were not in condition to make free choice—that is, such as were in custody or under constraint. It is still so open to all. But the time may come—probably will come—when public duty shall demand that it be closed; and that, in lieu, more rigorous measures than heretofore shall be adopted.

In presenting the abandonment of armed resistance to the national authority on the part of the insurgents, as the only indispensable condition to ending the war on the part of the government, I retract nothing heretofore said as to slavery. I repeat the declaration made a year ago, that "while I remain in my present position I shall not attempt to retract or modify the emancipation proclamation, nor shall I return to slavery any person who is free by the terms of that proclamation, or by any of the Acts of Congress." If the people should, by whatever mode or means, make it an Executive duty to re-enslave such persons, another, and not I, must be their instrument to perform it.

In stating a single condition of peace, I mean simply to say that the war will cease on the part of the government, whenever it shall have ceased on the part of those who began it.

Abraham Lincoln

December 6, 1864

LETTER TO GENERAL W. T. SHERMAN DECEMBER 26, 1864

(Original sent by Gen. Logan)

Executive Mansion,
Washington, December 26, 1864.

My dear General Sherman

Many, Many thanks for your Christmas gift, the capture of Savannah.

When you were about leaving Atlanta for the Atlantic coast, I was *anxious*, if not fearful; but feeling that you were the better judge, and remembering that "nothing risked, nothing gained," I did not interfere. Now, the undertaking being a success, the honor is all yours; for I believe none of us went further than to acquiesce. And taking the work of Gen. Thomas into the count, as it should be taken, it is indeed a great success. Not only does it afford the obvious and immediate military advantages; but, in showing to the world that your army could be divided, putting the stronger part to an important new service, and yet leaving enough to vanquish the old opposing force of the whole—Hood's army—it brings those who sat in darkness to see a great light. But what next I suppose it will be safe if I leave Gen. Grant and yourself to decide.

Please make my grateful acknowledgments to your whole army—officers and men.

Yours very truly
A. Lincoln

The superscription and the signature of this manuscript are in Lincoln's handwriting. Presumably the original went directly to General Sherman (as indicated in the superscription) without the knowledge of Secretary Stanton, and this certified copy was sent to the War Department for the Secretary's files.

LETTER TO GENERAL U. S. GRANT
JANUARY 19, 1865

Executive Mansion,
Washington, Jan. 19, 1865.

Lieut. General Grant:

Please read and answer this letter as though I was not President, but only a friend. My son, now in his twenty second year, having graduated at Harvard, wishes to see something of the war before it ends. I do not wish to put him in the ranks, nor yet to give him a commission, to which those who have already served long, are better entitled, and better qualified to hold. Could he, without embarrassment to you, or detriment to the service; go into your military family with some nominal rank, I, and not the public, furnishing his necessary means? If no, say so without the least hesitation, because I am as anxious, and as deeply interested, that you shall not be encumbered as you can be yourself.

Yours truly
A. Lincoln

TERMS FOR GENERAL R. E. LEE'S CAPITULATION MARCH 3, 1865

March 3, 1865

Lieutenant General Grant

The President directs me to say to you that he wishes you to have no conference with General Lee unless it be for the capitulation of Gen. Lee's army, or on some minor, and purely, military matter. He instructs me to say that you are not to decide, discuss, or confer upon any political question. Such questions the President holds in his own hands; and will submit them to no military conferences or conventions. Meantime you are to press to the utmost, your military advantages.

Edwin M. Stanton
Secretary of War

The manuscript of this item is in Lincoln's handwriting, but bears Stanton's signature. Lincoln drew up the terms to be forwarded through the proper channels of the War Department.

SECOND INAUGURAL ADDRESS
MARCH 4, 1865

At this second appearing to take the oath of the presidential office, there is less occasion for an extended address than there was at the first. Then a statement, somewhat in detail, of a course to be pursued, seemed fitting and proper. Now, at the expiration of four years, during which public declarations have been constantly called forth on every point and phase of the great contest which still absorbs the attention, and engrosses the energies of the nation, little that is new could be presented. The progress of our arms, upon which all else chiefly depends, is as well known to the public as to myself; and it is, I trust, reasonably satisfactory and encouraging to all. With high hope for the future, no prediction in regard to it is ventured.

On the occasion corresponding to this four years ago, all thoughts were anxiously directed to an impending civil war. All dreaded it—all sought to avert it. While the inaugeral [*sic*] address was being delivered from this place, devoted altogether to *saving* the Union without war, insurgent agents were in the city seeking to *destroy* it without war—seeking to dissole [*sic*] the Union, and divide effects, by negotiation. Both parties deprecated war; but one of them would *make* war rather than let the nation survive; and the other would *accept* war rather than let it perish. And the war came.

One eighth of the whole population were colored slaves, not distributed generally over the Union, but localized in the Southern part of it. These slaves constituted a peculiar and powerful interest. All knew that this interest was, somehow, the cause of the war. To strengthen, perpetuate, and extend this interest was the object for which the insurgents would rend the Union, even by war; while the government claimed no right to do more than to restrict the territorial enlargement of it. Neither party expected for the war, the magnitude, or the duration, which it has already attained. Neither anticipated that the *cause* of the conflict might cease with, or even before, the conflict itself should cease. Each looked for an easier triumph, and a result less fundamental and astounding. Both read the same Bible, and pray to the same God; and each invokes His aid against the other. It may seem strange that any men should dare to ask a just God's assistance in wringing their bread from the sweat of other men's faces; but let us judge not that we be not judged. The prayers of both could not be answered; that of neither has been answered fully. The Almighty has his own purposes. "Woe unto the world because of offences! for it must needs be that offences come; but woe to that man by whom the offence cometh!" If we shall suppose that American Slavery is one of those offences which, in the providence of God, must needs come, but which, having continued through His appointed time, He now wills to remove, and that He gives to both North and South, this terrible war, as the woe due to those by whom the offence came, shall we discern therein any departure from those divine attributes which the believers in a Living God always ascribe to Him? Fondly do we hope—fervently do we pray—that this mighty scourge of war may speedily pass away. Yet, if God wills that it continue, until all the wealth piled by the bond-man's two hundred and fifty years of unrequited toil shall be sunk, and until every drop of blood drawn with the lash, shall be paid by another drawn with the sword, as was said three thousand years ago, so still it must be said "the judgments of the Lord, are true and righteous altogether"

With malice toward none; with charity for all; with firmness in the right, as God gives us to see the right, let us strive on to finish the work we are in; to bind up the nation's wounds; to care for him who shall have borne the battle, and for his widow, and his orphan—to do all which may achieve and cherish a just and lasting peace, among ourselves, and with all nations.

LETTER TO THURLOW WEED
MARCH 15, 1865

Executive Mansion,
Washington, March 15, 1865.

Thurlow Weed, Esq
My dear Sir.

Every one likes a compliment. Thank you for yours on my little notification speech, and on the recent Inaugeral [*sic*] Address. I expect the latter to wear as well as—perhaps better than—anything I have produced; but I believe it is not immediately popular. Men are not flattered by being shown that there has been a difference of purpose between the Almighty and them. To deny it, however, in this case, is to deny that there is a God governing the world. It is a truth which I thought needed to be told; and as whatever of humiliation there is in it, falls most directly on myself, I thought others might afford for me to tell it.

Yours truly
A. Lincoln

ADDRESS TO THE 140th INDIANA REGIMENT
MARCH 17, 1865

Fellow Citizens—

It will be but a very few words that I shall undertake to say. I was born in Kentucky, raised in Indiana and lived in Illinois. And now I am here, where it is my business to care equally for the good people of all the States. I am glad to see an Indiana regiment on this day able to present the captured flag to the Governor of Indiana. I am not disposed, in saying this, to make a distinction between the States, for all have done equally well. There are but few views or aspects of this great war upon which I have not said or written something whereby my own opinions might be known. But there is one—the recent attempt of our erring brethren, as they are sometimes called—to employ the negro to fight for them. I have neither written nor made a speech on that subject, because that was their business, not mine; and if I had a wish upon the subject I had not the power to introduce it, or make it effective. The great question with them was, whether the negro, being put into the army, would fight for them. I do not know, and therefore cannot decide. They ought to know better than we. I have in my lifetime heard many arguments why the negroes ought to be slaves; but if they fight for those who would keep them in slavery it will be a better argument than any I have yet heard. He who will fight for that ought to be a slave. They have concluded at last to take one out of four of the slaves, and put them in the army; and that one out of the four who will fight to keep the others in slavery ought to be a slave himself unless he is killed in a fight. While I have often said that all men ought to be free, yet I would allow those colored persons to be slaves who want to be; and next to them those white persons who argue in favor of making other people slaves. I am in favor of giving an opportunity to such white men to try it on for themselves. I will say one thing in regard to the negro being employed to fight for them. I do know he cannot fight and stay at home and make bread too—and as one is about as important as the other to them, I don't care which they do. I am rather in favor of having them try them as soldiers. They lack one vote of doing that, and I wish I could send my vote over the river so that I might cast it in favor of allowing the negro to fight. But they cannot fight and work both. We must now see the bottom of the enemy's resources. They will stand out as long as they can, and if the negro will fight for them, they must allow him to fight. They have drawn upon their last branch of resources. And we can now see the bottom. I am glad to see the end so near at hand. I have said now more than I intended, and will therefore bid you goodby.

TELEGRAM TO GENERAL U. S. GRANT
APRIL 2, 1865

Head Quarters Armies of the United States,
City-Point, April, 2, 8/15 P.M. 1865.

Lieut. General Grant.

Allow me to tender to you, and all with you, the nations grateful thanks for this additional, and magnificent success. At your kind suggestion, I think I will visit you to-morrow.

A. Lincoln

LAST PUBLIC ADDRESS
APRIL 11, 1865

We meet this evening, not in sorrow, but in gladness of heart. The evacuation of Petersburg and Richmond, and the surrender of the principal insurgent army, give hope of a righteous and speedy peace whose joyous expression can not be restrained. In the midst of this, however, He from whom all blessings flow, must not be forgotten. A call for a national thanksgiving is being prepared, and will be duly promulgated. Nor must those whose harder part gives us the cause of rejoicing, be overlooked. Their honors must not be parcelled out with others. I myself was near the front, and had the high pleasure of transmitting much of the good news to you; but no part of the honor, for plan or execution, is mine. To Gen. Grant, his skilful officers, and brave men, all belongs. The gallant Navy stood ready, but was not in reach to take active part.

By these recent successes the re-inauguration of the national authority—reconstruction—which has had a large share of thought from the first, is pressed much more closely upon our attention. It is fraught with great difficulty. Unlike a case of a war between independent nations, there is no authorized organ for us to treat with. No one man has authority to give up the rebellion for any other man. We simply must begin with, and mould from, disorganized and discordant elements. Nor is it a small additional embarrassment that we, the loyal people, differ among ourselves as to the mode, manner, and means of reconstruction.

As a general rule, I abstain from reading the reports of attacks upon myself, wishing not to be provoked by that to which I can not properly offer an answer. In spite of this precaution, however, it comes to my knowledge that I am much censured for some supposed agency in setting up, and seeking to sustain, the new State government of Louisiana. In this I have done just so much as, and no more than, the public knows. In the Annual Message of Dec. 1863 and accompanying Proclamation, I presented *a* plan of re-construction (as the phrase goes) which, I promised, if adopted by any State, should be acceptable to, and sustained by, the Executive government of the nation. I distinctly stated that this was not the only plan which might possibly be acceptable; and I also distinctly protested that the Executive claimed no right to say when, or whether members should be admitted to seats in Congress from such States. This plan was, in advance, submitted to the then Cabinet, and distinctly approved by every member of it. One of them suggested that I should then, and in that connection, apply the Emancipation Proclamation to the theretofore excepted parts of Virginia and Louisiana; that I should drop the suggestion about apprenticeship for freed-people, and that I should omit the protest against my own power, in regard to the admission of members to Congress; but even he approved every part and parcel of the plan which has since been employed or touched by the action of

Louisiana. The new constitution of Louisiana, declaring emancipation for the whole State, practically applies the Proclamation to the part previously excepted. It does not adopt apprenticeship for freed-people; and it is silent, as it could not well be otherwise, about the admission of members to Congress. So that, as it applies to Louisiana, every member of the Cabinet fully approved the plan. The message went to Congress, and I received many commendations of the plan, written and verbal; and not a single objection to it, from any professed emancipationist, came to my knowledge, until after the news reached Washington that the people of Louisiana had begun to move in accordance with it. From about July 1862, I had corresponded with different persons, supposed to be interested, seeking a reconstruction of a State government for Louisiana. When the message of 1863, with the plan before mentioned, reached New-Orleans, Gen. Banks wrote me that he was confident the people, with his military co-operation, would reconstruct, substantially on that plan. I wrote him, and some of them to try it; they tried it, and the result is known. Such only has been my agency in getting up the Louisiana government. As to sustaining it, my promise is out, as before stated. But, as bad promises are better broken than kept, I shall treat this as a bad promise, and break it, whenever I shall be convinced that keeping it is adverse to the public interest. But I have not yet been so convinced.

I have been shown a letter on this subject, supposed to be an able one, in which the writer expresses regret that my mind has not seemed to be definitely fixed on the question whether the seceded States, so called, are in the Union or out of it. It would perhaps, add astonishment to his regret, were he to learn that since I have found professed Union men endeavoring to make that question, I have *purposely* forborne any public expression upon it. As appears to me that question has not been, nor yet is, a practically material one, and that any discussion of it, while it thus remains practically immaterial, could have no effect other than the mischievous one of dividing our friends. As yet, whatever it may hereafter become, that question is bad, as the basis of a controversy, and good for nothing at all—a merely pernicious abstraction.

We all agree that the seceded States, so called, are out of their proper practical relation with the Union; and that the sole object of the government, civil and military, in regard to those States is to again get them into that proper practical relation. I believe it is not only possible, but in fact, easier to do this, without deciding, or even considering, whether these States have ever been out of the Union, than with it. Finding themselves safely at home, it would be utterly immaterial whether they had ever been abroad. Let us all join in doing the acts necessary to restoring the proper practical relations between these States and the Union; and each forever after, innocently indulge his own opinion whether, in doing the acts, he brought the States from without, into the Union, or only gave them proper assistance, they never having been out of it.

The amount of constituency, so to speak, on which the new Louisiana government rests, would be more satisfactory to all, if it contained fifty, thirty, or even twenty thousand, instead of only about twelve thousand, as it does. It is also unsatisfactory to some that the elective franchise is not given to the colored man. I would myself prefer that it were now conferred on the very intelligent, and on those who serve our cause as soldiers. Still the question is not whether the Louisiana government, as it stands, is quite all that is desirable. The question is, "Will it be wiser to take it as it is, and help to improve it; or to reject, and disperse it?" "Can Louisiana be brought into proper practical relation with the Union *sooner* by *sustaining*, or by *discarding* her new State government?"

Some twelve thousand voters in the heretofore slave-state of Louisiana have sworn allegiance to the Union, assumed to be the rightful political power of the State, held elections, organized a State government, adopted a free-state constitution, giving the benefit of public schools equally to black and white, and empowering the Legislature to confer the elective franchise upon the colored man. Their Legislature has already voted to ratify the constitutional amendment recently passed by Congress, abolishing slavery throughout the nation. These twelve thousand persons are thus fully committed to the Union, and to perpetual freedom in the state—committed to the very things, and nearly all the things the nation wants—and they ask the nations recognition and it's assistance to make good their committal. Now, if we reject, and spurn them, we do our utmost to disorganize and disperse them. We in effect say to the white men "You are worthless, or worse—we will neither help you, nor be helped by you." To the blacks we say "This cup of liberty which these, your old masters, hold to your lips, we will dash from you, and leave you to the chances of gathering the spilled and scattered contents in some vague and undefined when, where, and how." If this course, discouraging and paralyzing both white and black, has any tendency to bring Louisiana into proper practical relations with the Union, I have, so far, been unable to perceive it. If, on the contrary, we recognize, and sustain the new government of Louisiana the converse of all this is made true. We encourage the hearts, and nerve the arms of the twelve thousand to adhere to their work, and argue for it, and proselyte for it, and fight for it, and feed it, and grow it, and ripen it to a complete success. The colored man too, in seeing all united for him, is inspired with vigilance, and energy, and daring, to the same end. Grant that he desires the elective franchise, will he not attain it sooner by saving the already advanced steps toward it, than by running backward over them? Concede that the new government of Louisiana is only to what it should be as the egg is to the fowl, we shall sooner have the fowl by hatching the egg than by smashing it? Again, if we reject Louisiana, we also reject one vote in favor of the proposed amendment to the national Constitution. To meet this proposition, it has been argued that no more than three fourths of those States which have not attempted secession are necessary to validly ratify the amendment. I do not commit myself against this, further than to say that such a ratification would be questionable, and sure to be persistently questioned; while a ratification by three-fourths of all the States would be unquestioned and unquestionable.

I repeat the question. "Can Louisiana be brought into proper practical relation with the Union *sooner* by *sustaining* or by *discarding* her new State Government?

What has been said of Louisiana will apply generally to other States. And yet so great peculiarities pertain to each state, and such important and sudden changes occur in the same state; and, withal, so new and unprecedented is the whole case, that no exclusive, and inflexible plan can safely be prescribed as to details and colatterals [*sic*]. Such exclusive, and inflexible plan, would surely become a new entanglement. Important principles may, and must, be inflexible.

In the present "*situation*" as the phrase goes, it may be my duty to make some new announcement to the people of the South. I am considering, and shall not fail to act, when satisfied that action will be proper.

Upon returning to Washington after Appomattox, Lincoln found the city in an uproar of celebration. On the night of April 10, a crowd came to serenade, expecting to be addressed as they had been many times before. Lincoln declined but promised to prepare a speech for the following night if they would return.

One suspects that many were disappointed in that audience on the next night, for Lincoln spoke not in the vein of celebration but of heavy conviction. The problems of reconstruction were vast and he was far ahead of his audience in thinking of the future. Congress had not approved of reconstruction as carried out under Lincoln's war powers in Louisiana. There was not enough punishment in it to suit some of the more radical members. It is clear from Lincoln's analysis of the problem in this Address that he is beginning the attempt to educate the public to the task ahead, in order that he may get support for his program in Congress, now that his war powers are nearing their termination.

TELEGRAM TO GENERAL GODFREY WEITZEL APRIL 12, 1865

"Cypher"

Office U. S. Military Telegraph,
War Department,
Washington, D. C. April 12, 1865.

Major General Weitzel
Richmond, Va

I have just seen Judge Campbell's letter to you of the 7th. He assumes as appears to me that I have called the insurgent Legislature of Virginia together, as the rightful Legislature of the State, to settle all differences with the United States. I have done no such thing. I spoke of them not as a Legislature, but as "the gentlemen who have *acted* as the Legislature of Virginia in support of the rebellion." I did this on purpose to exclude the assumption that I was recognizing them as a *rightful* body. I dealt with them as men having power *de facto* to do a specific thing to wit, "to withdraw the Virginia troops, and other support from resistance to the General Government," for which in the paper handed Judge Campbell I promised a specific equivalent, to wit, a remission to the people of the State, except in certain cases, the confiscation of their property. I meant this and no more. In as much however as Judge Campbell misconstrues this and is still pressing for an armistice, contrary to the explicit statement of the paper I gave him; and particularly as Gen. Grant has since captured the Virginia troops, so that giving a consideration for their withdrawal is no longer applicable, let my letter to you, and the paper to Judge Campbell both be withdrawn or countermanded and he be notified of it. Do not now allow them to assemble; but if any have come allow them safe-return to their homes.

A. Lincoln

This is the last piece of writing of any consequence which Lincoln did. Reconstruction was under way. Misunderstandings were already beginning to complicate the process. In his usual, calm way Lincoln analyzes the circumstances and gets on with the job, to the practical end of restoring Virginia to the Union. To leave him thus, rather than with his "Last Public Address," seems appropriate.

SOURCES AND BIBLIOGRAPHY

SOURCES AND BIBLIOGRAPHY

SOURCES OF TEXT

TO THE PEOPLE OF SANGAMO COUNTY: POLITICAL ANNOUNCEMENT—March 9, 1832. *Sangamo Journal*, March 15, 1832

ANNOUNCEMENT OF POLITICAL VIEWS IN *Sangamo Journal*—June 13, 1836. *Sangamo Journal*, June 18, 1836

LETTER TO COLONEL ROBERT ALLEN—June 21, 1836. Original, Illinois State Historical Library

LETTER TO MISS MARY OWENS—December 13, 1836. Photostat, Lincoln Memorial University

SPEECH IN THE ILLINOIS LEGISLATURE—January 11, 1837. *Sangamo Journal*, January 28, 1837

LETTER TO MISS MARY OWENS—May 7, 1837. Photostat, The Abraham Lincoln Association

LETTER TO MISS MARY OWENS—August 16, 1837. Photostat, The Abraham Lincoln Association

THE PERPETUATION OF OUR POLITICAL INSTITUTIONS: ADDRESS DELIVERED BEFORE THE YOUNG MEN'S LYCEUM OF SPRINGFIELD, ILLINOIS—January 27, 1838. *Sangamo Journal*, February 3, 1838

LETTER TO MRS. O. H. BROWNING—April 1, 1838. Photostat, Lincoln Memorial University

THE SUB-TREASURY: SPEECH AT A POLITICAL DISCUSSION IN THE HALL OF THE HOUSE OF REPRESENTATIVES AT SPRINGFIELD, ILLINOIS—December [26], 1839. Pamphlet, Fish 518 [February ? 1840]; *Sangamo Journal*, March 6, 1840

LETTER TO JOHN T. STUART—January 20, 1841. Photostat, The Abraham Lincoln Association

LETTER TO JOHN T. STUART—January 23, 1841. Photostat, The Abraham Lincoln Association

LETTER TO JOSHUA F. SPEED—June 19, 1841. Original owned by Mr. Oliver R. Barrett

LETTER TO MISS MARY SPEED—September 27, 1841. Photostat, The Abraham Lincoln Association

LETTER TO JOSHUA F. SPEED—January 3, 1842. Original owned by Mr. Oliver R. Barrett

LETTER TO JOSHUA F. SPEED—February 3, 1842. Original owned by Mr. Oliver R. Barrett

EULOGY ON BENJAMIN FERGUSON—February 8, 1842. *Sangamo Journal*, February 11, 1842

LETTER TO JOSHUA F. SPEED—February 13, 1842. Original owned by Mr. Oliver R. Barrett

TEMPERANCE ADDRESS DELIVERED BEFORE THE SPRINGFIELD WASHINGTON TEMPERANCE SOCIETY—February 22, 1842. *Sangamo Journal*, March 26, 1842

LETTER TO JOSHUA F. SPEED—February 25, 1842. Original owned by Mr. Oliver R. Barrett

LETTER TO JOSHUA F. SPEED—February 25, 1842. Original owned by Mr. Oliver R. Barrett

LETTER TO JOSHUA F. SPEED—March 27, 1842. Original owned by Mr. Oliver R. Barrett

LETTER TO JOSHUA F. SPEED—July 4, 1842. Original owned by Mr. Oliver R. Barrett

A LETTER FROM THE LOST TOWNSHIPS—August 27, 1842. *Sangamo Journal*, September 2, 1842

CORRESPONDENCE ABOUT THE LINCOLN-SHIELDS DUEL—September 17, 1842. *Sangamo Journal*, October 14, 1842

MEMORANDUM OF INSTRUCTIONS TO E. H. MERRYMAN, LINCOLN'S SECOND —September 19, 1842. *Sangamo Journal*, September 17, 1842

LETTER TO JOSHUA F. SPEED—October 5, 1842. Original owned by Mr. Oliver R. Barrett

LETTER TO JAMES S. IRWIN—November 2, 1842. Original owned by Mr. Oliver R. Barrett

LETTER TO SAMUEL D. MARSHALL—November 11, 1842. Original, Chicago Historical Society

LETTER TO JOSHUA F. SPEED—March 24, 1843. Original, Illinois State Historical Library

LETTER TO JOSHUA F. SPEED—May 18, 1843. Original owned by Mr. Oliver R. Barrett

LETTER TO WILLIAMSON DURLEY—October 3, 1845. Original, Illinois State Historical Library

LETTER TO HENRY E. DUMMER—November 18, 1845. Original, Chicago Historical Society

LETTER TO B. F. JAMES—February 9, 1846. Photostat, The Abraham Lincoln Association

REMARKABLE CASE OF ARREST FOR MURDER—April 15, 1846. *Quincy Whig*, April 15, 1846

LETTER TO ANDREW JOHNSTON—April 18, 1846. Nicolay and Hay, editors, *Complete Works of Abraham Lincoln*, 1905

RELIGIOUS VIEWS: LETTER TO THE EDITOR OF THE *Illinois Gazette*—August 11, 1846. *Illinois Gazette*, Lacon, Illinois, August 15, 1846

LETTER TO ANDREW JOHNSTON—September 6, 1846. Original, Historical Society of Pennsylvania

MY CHILDHOOD HOME I SEE AGAIN—1846. Original, The Library of Congress

THE BEAR HUNT—[1846]. Original, Pierpont Morgan Library

LETTER TO JOSHUA F. SPEED—October 22, 1846. Original owned by Mr. Oliver R. Barrett

LETTER TO WILLIAM H. HERNDON—December 12, 1847. Original, Illinois State Historical Library

RESOLUTIONS IN THE UNITED STATES HOUSE OF REPRESENTATIVES—December 22, 1847. *Congressional Globe*, Thirtieth Congress, First Session, 1848

THE WAR WITH MEXICO: SPEECH IN THE UNITED STATES HOUSE OF REPRESENTATIVES—January 12, 1848. *Congressional Globe*, Appendix, Thirtieth Congress, First Session, New Series, 1847-8

LETTER TO WILLIAM H. HERNDON—February 1, 1848. Nicolay and Hay, editors, *Complete Works of Abraham Lincoln*, 1905

LETTER TO WILLIAM H. HERNDON—February 2, 1848. Original owned by Mr. Oliver R. Barrett

LETTER TO WILLIAM H. HERNDON—February 15, 1848. Photostat, Harvard University Library

LETTER TO USHER F. LINDER—March 22, 1848. Original, Illinois State Historical Library

LETTER TO DAVID LINCOLN—March 24, 1848. Photostat, The Abraham Lincoln Association

LETTER TO DAVID LINCOLN—April 2, 1848. Photostat, The Abraham Lincoln Association

LETTER TO MARY TODD LINCOLN—April 16, 1848. Original owned by Mr. Oliver R. Barrett

LETTER TO MARY TODD LINCOLN—June 12, 1848. Photostat, The Abraham Lincoln Association

LETTER TO MARY TODD LINCOLN—July 2, 1848. Photostat, The Abraham Lincoln Association

LETTER TO WILLIAM H. HERNDON—July 11, 1848. Original owned by Mr. Oliver R. Barrett

THE PRESIDENTIAL QUESTION: SPEECH IN THE UNITED STATES HOUSE OF REPRESENTATIVES—July 27, 1848. *Congressional Globe*, Appendix, Thirtieth Congress, First Session, New Series, 1847-8

LETTERS TO THOMAS LINCOLN AND JOHN D. JOHNSTON—December 24, 1848. Photostat, The Abraham Lincoln Association

LETTER TO WILLIAM H. HERNDON—January 5, 1849. Photostat, The Abraham Lincoln Association

LETTER TO C. U. SCHLATER—January 5, 1849. Photostat, The Abraham Lincoln Association

LETTER TO C. R. WELLES—February 20, 1849. Original, Illinois State Historical Library

LETTER TO JOSHUA F. SPEED—February 20, 1849. Original, Maine Historical Society

LETTER TO ABRAM BALE—February 22, 1850. Original, Illinois State Historical Library

LETTER TO JOHN D. JOHNSTON—Janury 12, 1851. Original owned by Mr. Oliver R. Barrett

LETTER TO ANDREW MC CALLEN—July 4, 1851. Original owned by Mr. Oliver R. Barrett

LETTER TO JOHN D. JOHNSTON—November 4, 1851. Nicolay and Hay, editors, *Complete Works of Abraham Lincoln*, 1905

LETTER TO JOHN D. JOHNSTON—November 9, 1851. Original, Maine Historical Society

LETTER TO JOHN D. JOHNSTON—November 25, 1851. Photostat, The Abraham Lincoln Association

EULOGY ON HENRY CLAY DELIVERED IN THE STATE HOUSE AT SPRINGFIELD, ILLINOIS—July 6, 1852. *Illinois Journal*, July 21, 1852

FRAGMENTS: ON SLAVERY—[July 1, 1854?]. Originals owned by Mr. Oliver R. Barrett

LETTER TO J. M. PALMER—September 7, 1854. Original owned by Mr. Oliver R. Barrett

THE 14TH SECTION: AN EDITORIAL IN THE *Illinois Journal*—September 11, 1854. *Illinois Journal*, September 11, 1854

THE REPEAL OF THE MISSOURI COMPROMISE AND THE PROPRIETY OF ITS RESTORATION: SPEECH AT PEORIA, ILLINOIS, IN REPLY TO SENATOR

DOUGLAS—October 16, 1854. *Illinois Journal*, October 21, 23, 24, 25, 26, 27, 28, 1854

LETTER TO E. B. WASHBURNE—December 14, 1854. Original, Illinois State Historical Library

LETTER TO E. B. WASHBURNE—February 9, 1855. Original, Illinois State Historical Library

LETTER TO OWEN LOVEJOY—August 11, 1855. Original, Henry E. Huntington Library

LETTER TO GEORGE ROBERTSON—August 15, 1855. Original, The Library of Congress

LETTER TO JOSHUA F. SPEED—August 24, 1855. Photostat, The Abraham Lincoln Association

LETTER TO ISHAM REAVIS—November 5, 1855. Photostat, The Abraham Lincoln Association

LETTER TO R. P. MORGAN—February 13, 1856. Facsimile, *Buffalo, Rochester and Pittsburg Rw. Employees' Magazine*, February, 1916

FRÉMONT, BUCHANAN, AND THE EXTENSION OF SLAVERY: SPEECH DELIVERED AT KALAMAZOO, MICHIGAN—August 27, 1856. *Detroit Daily Advertiser*, August 29, 1856

LETTER TO JULIAN M. STURTEVANT—September 27, 1856. Photostat, The Abraham Lincoln Association

SECTIONALISM—[October 1?], 1856. Photostat, The Abraham Lincoln Association

THE DRED SCOTT DECISION: SPEECH AT SPRINGFIELD, ILLINOIS—June 26, 1857. *Illinois State Journal*, June 29, 1857, and Pamphlet Reprint, Oakleaf 818

LETTER TO E. B. WASHBURNE—April 26, 1858. Original, Illinois State Historical Library

LETTER TO E. B. WASHBURNE—May 15, 1858. Original, Illinois State Historical Library

LETTER TO JEDIAH F. ALEXANDER—May 15, 1858. Photostat, The Abraham Lincoln Association

LETTER TO E. B. WASHBURNE—May 27, 1858. Original, Illinois State Historical Library

LETTER TO SAMUEL WILKINSON—June 10, 1858. Original, Illinois State Historical Library

A HOUSE DIVIDED: SPEECH DELIVERED AT SPRINGFIELD, ILLINOIS, AT THE CLOSE OF THE REPUBLICAN STATE CONVENTION—June 16, 1858. *Illinois Journal*, June 18, 1858; *Political Debates*, Columbus: Follett, Foster and Company, 1860

LETTER TO JOSEPH MEDILL—June 25, 1858. Photostat, The Abraham Lincoln Association

LETTER TO JAMES W. SOMERS—June 25, 1858. Photostat, The Abraham Lincoln Association

SPEECH IN REPLY TO DOUGLAS AT CHICAGO, ILLINOIS—July 10, 1858. *Chicago Daily Press and Tribune*, July 12, 1858; *Political Debates,* Columbus: Follett, Foster and Company, 1860

SPEECH IN REPLY TO DOUGLAS AT SPRINGFIELD, ILLINOIS—July 17, 1858. *Illinois State Journal*, July 20, 1858; *Political Debates,* Columbus: Follett, Foster and Company, 1860

LETTER TO JOHN MATHERS—July 20, 1858. Facsimile, *Jacksonville Daily Journal*, Jacksonville, Illinois, February 13, 1909

LETTER TO HENRY ASBURY—July 31, 1858. Original owned by Mr. Oliver R. Barrett

FRAGMENT: ON SLAVERY—[August 1, 1858?]. Facsimile, The Lincoln National Life Foundation

LETTER TO HENRY E. DUMMER—August 5, 1858. Original, Chicago Historical Society

FIRST DEBATE, AT OTTAWA, ILLINOIS—August 21, 1858. *Political Debates,* Columbus: Follett, Foster and Company, 1860; *The Lincoln Douglas Debates,* editor, E. E. Sparks, 1908

FRAGMENT: SPEECH AT EDWARDSVILLE, ILLINOIS—September 11, 1858. *Alton Courier*, Alton, Illinois, September 16, 1858

LETTER TO M. P. SWEET—September 16, 1858. Original, Illinois State Historical Library

VERSES: TO ROSA—September 28, 1858. Photostat, The Abraham Lincoln Association

VERSES: TO LINNIE—September 30, 1858. Photostat, The Abraham Lincoln Association

FRAGMENT: ON SLAVERY—[October 1, 1858?]. Photostat, The Abraham Lincoln Association

LETTER TO J. N. BROWN—October 18, 1858. Original, Henry E. Huntington Library

LAST SPEECH IN SPRINGFIELD, ILLINOIS, IN THE CAMPAIGN OF 1858—[October 30, 1858]. Original owned by Mr. Oliver R. Barrett

LETTER TO HENRY ASBURY—November 19, 1858. Original owned by Mr. Oliver R. Barrett

LETTER TO DOCTOR C. H. RAY—November 20, 1858. Original owned by Mr. Oliver R. Barrett

NOTES OF AN ARGUMENT—[December ?], 1858. Original owned by Mr. Oliver R. Barrett

LETTER TO JAMES T. THORNTON—December 2, 1858. Photostat, The Abraham Lincoln Association

LETTER TO LYMAN TRUMBULL—December 11, 1858. Photostat, The Abraham Lincoln Association

LETTER TO H. L. PIERCE AND OTHERS—April 6, 1859. Original, Brown University Library

LETTER TO T. J. PICKETT—April 16, 1859. Original owned by Mr. Oliver R. Barrett

LETTER TO SALMON PORTLAND CHASE—June 9, 1859. Original, The Historical Society of Pennsylvania

LETTER TO SALMON PORTLAND CHASE—June 20, 1859. Original, The Historical Society of Pennsylvania

AGRICULTURE: ANNUAL ADDRESS BEFORE THE WISCONSIN STATE AGRICULTURAL SOCIETY AT MILWAUKEE, WISCONSIN—September 30, 1859. *Chicago Daily Press and Tribune*, October 1, 1859

WRITTEN BY LINCOLN IN THE AUTOGRAPH ALBUM OF MARY DELAHAY—December 7, 1859. Photostat, The Abraham Lincoln Association

LETTER TO WILLIAM KELLOGG—December 11, 1859. Original owned by Mr. Oliver R. Barrett

LETTER TO G. W. DOLE, G. S. HUBBARD, AND W. H. BROWN—December 14, 1859. Original, Chicago Historical Society

LETTER TO J. W. FELL INCLOSING AUTOBIOGRAPHY—December 20, 1859. Photostat, The Abraham Lincoln Association

FRAGMENT: THE CONSTITUTION AND THE UNION—[1860?]. Original owned by Mr. Oliver R. Barrett

LETTER TO M. W. PACKARD—February 10, 1860. Original, Illinois State Historical Library

LETTER TO O. P. HALL, J. R. FULLINWIDER, AND U. F. CORRELL—February 14, 1860. Original, The University of Chicago Library

ADDRESS AT COOPER INSTITUTE, NEW YORK—February 27, 1860. Revised edition, Charles C. Nott and Cephas Brainerd, editors, 1860

LETTER TO MARK W. DELAHAY—March 16, 1860. Photostat, The Abraham Lincoln Association

LETTER TO F. C. HERBURGER—April 7, 1860. Original owned by Mr. Oliver R. Barrett

LETTER TO LYMAN TRUMBULL—April 29, 1860. Photostat, The Abraham Lincoln Association

LETTER TO GEORGE ASHMUN—May 23, 1860. Photostat, The Abraham Lincoln Association

LETTER TO SAMUEL HAYCRAFT AND AUTOBIOGRAPHY—May 28, 1860. Photostat, The Abraham Lincoln Association

LETTER TO CHARLES C. NOTT—May 31, 1860. G. H. Putnam, *Abraham Lincoln: The People's Leader*, 1909

SHORT AUTOBIOGRAPHY WRITTEN FOR THE CAMPAIGN OF 1860—June [1?], 1860. Nicolay and Hay, editors, *Complete Works of Abraham Lincoln*, 1905

LETTER TO SAMUEL GALLOWAY—June 19, 1860. Original, Illinois State Historical Library

LETTER TO ABRAHAM JONAS—July 21, 1860. Photostat, The Abraham Lincoln Association

LETTER TO GEORGE LATHAM—July 22, 1860. Photostat, The Abraham Lincoln Association

LETTER TO CHARLES C. NOTT—September 22, 1860. G. H. Putnam, *Abraham Lincoln: The People's Leader*, 1909

LETTER TO MRS. M. J. GREEN—September 22, 1860. Photostat, The Abraham Lincoln Association

LETTER TO MISS GRACE BEDELL—October 19, 1860. Photostat, The Abraham Lincoln Association

LETTER TO GEORGE T. M. DAVIS—October 27, 1860. Original, Illinois State Historical Library

LETTER TO H. J. RAYMOND—November 28, 1860. Original, Illinois State Historical Library

LETTER TO WILLIAM KELLOGG—December 11, 1860. Original owned by Mr. Oliver R. Barrett

LETTER TO JOHN D. DEFREES—December 18, 1860. Photostat, The Abraham Lincoln Association

LETTER TO A. H. STEPHENS—December 22, 1860. Photostat, The Abraham Lincoln Association

FAREWELL ADDRESS AT SPRINGFIELD, ILLINOIS—February 11, 1861. Nicolay and Hay, editors, *Complete Works of Abraham Lincoln*, 1905

SPEECH AT INDIANOPOLIS, INDIANA—February 11, 1861. *Cincinnati Daily Commercial*, February 13, 1861; *New York Daily Tribune*, February 13, 1861

ADDRESS TO GERMANS AT CINCINNATI, OHIO—February 12, 1861. *New York Daily Tribune*, February 16, 1861

ADDRESS TO THE SENATE OF NEW JERSEY—February 21, 1861. *New York Daily Tribune*, February 22, 1861

ADDRESS TO THE ASSEMBLY OF NEW JERSEY—February 21, 1861. *New York Daily Tribune*, February 22, 1861; *Illinois State Journal*, February 22, 1861

ADDRESS IN INDEPENDENCE HALL, PHILADELPHIA—February 22, 1861. *New York Daily Tribune*, February 23, 1861

FIRST INAUGURAL ADDRESS—March 4, 1861. Photostat of final proofsheets, The Lincoln National Life Foundation

REPLY TO SECRETARY SEWARD'S MEMORANDUM—April 1, 1861. Nicolay and Hay, editors, *Complete Works of Abraham Lincoln*, 1905

LETTER TO COLONEL E. E. ELLSWORTH—April 15, 1861. Photostat, The Abraham Lincoln Association

LETTER TO COLONEL E. E. ELLSWORTH'S PARENTS—May 25, 1861. Facsimile, F. H. Meserve, *Lincoln's Ellsworth Letter*, privately printed, New York, 1916

MESSAGE TO CONGRESS IN SPECIAL SESSION—July 4, 1861. *Congressional Globe*, Appendix, Thirty-Seventh Congress, First Session

PROCLAMATION OF A NATIONAL FAST-DAY—August 12, 1861. Original, The National Archives

LETTER TO GOVERNOR BERIAH MAGOFFIN—August 24, 1861. Original, Illinois State Historical Library

LETTER TO O. H. BROWNING—September 22, 1861. Original, Illinois State Historical Library

LETTER TO MAJOR [G. D. ?] RAMSAY—October 17, 1861. Original owned by Mr. Oliver R. Barrett

ANNUAL MESSAGE TO CONGRESS—December 3, 1861. Original, Division of Manuscripts, The Library of Congress, and for missing pages *Congressional Globe*, Appendix, Thirty-Seventh Congress, Second Session

LETTER TO MRS. SUSANNAH WEATHERS—December 4, 1861. Original owned by Mr. Oliver R. Barrett

TELEGRAM TO GENERAL D. C. BUELL—January 4, 1862. Photostat, The Abraham Lincoln Association

LETTER TO GENERAL D. C. BUELL—January 6, 1862. Original owned by Mr. Oliver R. Barrett

LETTER TO GENERAL A. E. BURNSIDE—January 28, 1862. Original, Illinois State Historical Library

LETTER TO GENERAL G. B. MC CLELLAN—April 9, 1862. Original, Drexel Institute of Technology

LETTER TO THE SENATE AND HOUSE OF REPRESENTATIVES—April 16, 1862. Original owned by Mr. Oliver R. Barrett

LETTER TO GENERAL G. B. MC CLELLAN—May 9, 1862. Photostat, The Abraham Lincoln Association

TELEGRAM TO GENERAL G. B. MC CLELLAN—May 28, 1862. Original, Brown University Library

TELEGRAM TO GENERAL G. B. MC CLELLAN—June 28, 1862. Original, Illinois State Historical Library

TELEGRAM TO GENERAL G. B. MC CLELLAN—July 1, 1862. Original, The New York Public Library

LETTER TO GENERAL G. B. MC CLELLAN—July 2, 1862. Original, Illinois State Historical Library

TELEGRAM TO GENERAL G. B. MC CLELLAN—July 3, 1862. Original, Illinois State Historical Library

TELEGRAM TO GENERAL G. B. MC CLELLAN—July 5, 1862. Original, Illinois State Historical Library

LETTER TO GENERAL G. B. MC CLELLAN—July 13, 1862. Original, Illinois State Historical Library

LETTER TO CUTHBERT BULLITT—July 28, 1862. Nicolay and Hay, editors, *Complete Works of Abraham Lincoln,* 1905

LETTER TO JOHN M. CLAY—August 9, 1862. Photostat, The Abraham Lincoln Association

LETTER TO HORACE GREELEY—August 22, 1862. Original, Wadsworth Atheneum, Hartford, Connecticut

TELEGRAM TO GENERAL G. B. MC CLELLAN—September 15, 1862. Original, Illinois State Historical Library

TESTIMONIAL FOR DOCTOR ISACHAR ZACHARIE—September 22, 1862. Original owned by Mr. Oliver R. Barrett

LETTER TO JOHN ROSS—September 25, 1862. Photostat, The Abraham Lincoln Association

MEDITATION ON THE DIVINE WILL—September [30?], 1862. Nicolay and Hay, editors, *Complete Works of Abraham Lincoln,* 1905

REMARKS TO THE ARMY OF THE POTOMAC AT FREDERICK, MARYLAND—October 4, 1862. *New York Daily Tribune,* October 6, 1862

LETTER TO GENERAL G. B. MC CLELLAN—October 13, 1862. Nicolay and Hay, editors, *Complete Works of Abraham Lincoln,* 1905

TELEGRAM TO GENERAL G. B. MC CLELLAN—October 24, 1862. Original, Illinois State Historical Library

TELEGRAM TO GENERAL G. B. MC CLELLAN—October 27, 1862. Original, Illinois State Historical Library

LETTER TO GENERAL CARL SCHURZ—November 10, 1862. Photostat, The Abraham Lincoln Association

LETTER TO SAMUEL TREAT—November 19, 1862. Original, Missouri Historical Society, St. Louis, Missouri

LETTER TO GENERAL CARL SCHURZ—November 24, 1862. Photostat, The Abraham Lincoln Association

ANNUAL MESSAGE TO CONGRESS—December 1, 1862. Original, The National Archives, Records of the United States Senate

LETTER TO MISS FANNY MC CULLOUGH—December 23, 1862. Photostat, The Abraham Lincoln Association

FINAL EMANCIPATION PROCLAMATION—January 1, 1863. Photostat, The Abraham Lincoln Association

LETTER TO GENERAL J. A. MC CLERNAND—January 22, 1863. Original, Illinois State Historical Library

LETTER TO GENERAL JOSEPH HOOKER—January 26, 1863. Photostat, The Abraham Lincoln Association

LETTER TO GOVERNOR ANDREW JOHNSON—March 26, 1863. Original, Pierpont Morgan Library

LETTER TO GENERAL JOSEPH HOOKER—May 7, 1863. Photostat, The Abraham Lincoln Association

LETTER TO ISAAC N. ARNOLD—May 26, 1863. Original, Chicago Historical Society

TELEGRAM TO GENERAL JOSEPH HOOKER—June 5, 1863. Original, Illinois State Historical Library

LETTER TO ERASTUS CORNING AND OTHERS—June 12, 1863. Nicolay and Hay, editors, *Complete Works of Abraham Lincoln*, 1905

TELEGRAM TO GENERAL JOSEPH HOOKER—June 14, 1863. Original, Alfred J. Stern.

RESPONSE TO A SERENADE—July 7, 1863. *New York Daily Tribune*, July 8, 1863; *New York Herald*, July 8, 1863; *New York Times*, July 8, 1863

LETTER TO GENERAL U. S. GRANT—July 13, 1863. Original, Historical Society of Pennsylvania

DRAFT OF LETTER TO GENERAL G. G. MEADE—July 14, 1863. Nicolay and Hay, editors, *Complete Works of Abraham Lincoln*, 1905

LETTER TO GENERAL H. W. HALLECK—July 29, 1863. Original, Illinois State Historical Library

LETTER TO GENERAL N. P. BANKS—August 5, 1863. Original, Illinois State Historical Library

LETTER TO MARY TODD LINCOLN—August 8, 1863. Nicolay and Hay, editors, *Complete Works of Abraham Lincoln*, 1905

LETTER TO GENERAL J. A. MC CLERNAND—August 12, 1863. Original, Illinois State Historical Library

LETTER TO J. H. HACKETT—August 17, 1863. Broadside printed by Hackett

LETTER TO JAMES C. CONKLING—August 26, 1863. Original, Illinois State Historical Library

LETTER TO JAMES C. CONKLING—August 27, 1863. Original, Illinois State Historical Library

LETTER TO GENERAL H. W. HALLECK—September 19, 1863. Original, Illinois State Historical Library

PROCLAMATION FOR THANKSGIVING—October 3, 1863. Original, The National Archives

TELEGRAM TO GENERAL G. G. MEADE—October 8, 1863. Original, Illinois State Historical Library

LETTER TO GENERAL H. W. HALLECK—October 16, 1863. Original owned by Mr. Oliver R. Barrett

LETTER TO J. H. HACKETT—November 2, 1863. Nicolay and Hay, editors, *Complete Works of Abraham Lincoln*, 1905

LETTER TO E. M. STANTON, SECRETARY OF WAR—November 11, 1863. Photostat, The Abraham Lincoln Association

ADDRESS DELIVERED AT THE DEDICATION OF THE CEMETERY AT GETTYSBURG—November 19, 1863. Facsimiles in W. E. Barton, *Lincoln at Gettysburg*, 1930

LETTER TO EDWARD EVERETT—November 20, 1863. Original, Massachusetts Historical Society

PROCLAMATION OF AMNESTY AND RECONSTRUCTION—December 8, 1863. Original, The National Archives

LETTER TO CRAFTS J. WRIGHT AND C. K. HAWKES—January 7, 1864. Original, Illinois State Historical Library

LETTER TO GENERAL N. P. BANKS—January 31, 1864. Original, Illinois State Historical Library

LETTER TO E. M. STANTON, SECRETARY OF WAR—March 1, 1864. Stanton Papers, The Library of Congress

LETTER TO GOVERNOR MICHAEL HAHN—March 13, 1864. Original owned by Mr. Roger W. Barrett

LETTER TO E. M. STANTON, SECRETARY OF WAR—March 15, 1864. Photostat, The Abraham Lincoln Association

MEMORANDUM FOR MRS. S. W. HUNT—April 11, 1864. Original owned by Mr. Oliver R. Barrett

ADDRESS AT A SANITARY FAIR IN BALTIMORE—April 18, 1864. Original, The Rosenbach Company

LETTER TO GENERAL U. S. GRANT—April 30, 1864. Photostat, The Abraham Lincoln Association

SPEECH AT A SANITARY FAIR IN PHILADELPHIA—June 16, 1864. Nicolay and Hay, editors, *Complete Works of Abraham Lincoln*, 1905

LETTER TO WILLIAM DENNISON & OTHERS, A COMMITTEE OF THE NATIONAL

UNION CONVENTION—June 27, 1864. Photostat, The Abraham Lincoln Association

LETTER TO HORACE GREELEY—July 15, 1864. Original owned by Mr. Oliver R. Barrett

ADDRESS TO THE 164TH OHIO REGIMENT—August 18, 1864. *New York Times*, August 19, 1864; *New York Daily Tribune*, August 19, 1864

ADDRESS TO THE 166TH OHIO REGIMENT—August 22, 1864. *New York Herald*, August 23, 1864

LETTER TO MRS. ELIZA P. GURNEY—September 4, 1864. Original, Atlantic City Free Public Library

LETTER TO GENERAL U. S. GRANT—September 22, 1864. Original, Louis J. Kolb Collection

LETTER TO HENRY W. HOFFMAN—October 10, 1864. Photostat, Maryland Historical Society

RESPONSE TO A SERENADE—October 19, 1864. Photostat, Illinois State Historical Library

PROCLAMATION OF THANKSGIVING—October 20, 1864. Original, The National Archives

TELEGRAM TO GENERAL P. H. SHERIDAN—October 22, 1864. Photostat, The Abraham Lincoln Association

RESPONSE TO A SERENADE—November 10, 1864. Photostat, The Abraham Lincoln Association

LETTER TO GENERAL W. S. ROSECRANS—November 19, 1864. Original owned by Mr. Oliver R. Barrett

LETTER TO MRS. BIXBY—November 21, 1864. *Boston Transcript*, November 25, 1864

STORY WRITTEN FOR NOAH BROOKS—December [6?], 1864. Facsimile, Carl Sandburg, *Abraham Lincoln: The War Years*, 1939

ANNUAL MESSAGE TO CONGRESS—December 6, 1864. Original, The National Archives, Records of the United States Senate, Thirty-Eighth Congress, Second Session

LETTER TO GENERAL W. T. SHERMAN—December 26, 1864. Copy, Stanton Papers, The Library of Congress

LETTER TO GENERAL U. S. GRANT—January 19, 1865. Original, The Grand Rapids Art Gallery

TERMS FOR GENERAL R. E. LEE'S CAPITULATION—March 3, 1865. Original, Louis J. Kolb Collection

SECOND INAUGURAL ADDRESS—March 4, 1865. Photostat, The Abraham Lincoln Association

LETTER TO THURLOW WEED—March 15, 1865. Photostat, The Abraham Lincoln Association

ADDRESS TO THE 140TH INDIANA REGIMENT—March 17, 1865. *New York Herald,* March 18, 1865

TELEGRAM TO GENERAL U. S. GRANT—April 2, 1865. Original owned by Mr. Oliver R. Barrett

LAST PUBLIC ADDRESS—April 11, 1865. Photostat, The Abraham Lincoln Association

TELEGRAM TO GENERAL GODFREY WEITZEL—April 12, 1865. Original owned by Mr. Oliver R. Barrett

WORKS CITED IN THE NOTES

ANGLE, PAUL M. *Lincoln: 1854-1861, Being the Day-by-Day Activities of Abraham Lincoln from January 1, 1854, to March 4, 1861.* Springfield, Illinois, 1933.

—— "The Record of a Friendship," *Journal of the Illinois State Historical Society,* Vol. XXXI, No. 2, June, 1938.

—— (collaborator. Work cited under SANDBURG).

—— (editor. Work cited under KELLOGG).

—— (editor. Work cited under LINCOLN).

ANONYMOUS. *History of Gallatin, Saline, Hamilton, Franklin, and Williamson Counties, Illinois.* Chicago, 1887.

BARRETT, ROGER W. (editor. Work cited under LINCOLN).

BARTON, WILLIAM E. *Lincoln at Gettysburg.* Indianapolis, Indiana, 1930.

BASLER, ROY P. "The Authorship of the 'Rebecca' Letters," *The Abraham Lincoln Quarterly,* Vol. II, No. 2, June, 1942.

—— "Who Wrote the 'Letter to Mrs. Bixby'?," *Lincoln Herald,* Vol. XLV, No. 1, February, 1943.

BEVERIDGE, ALBERT J. *Abraham Lincoln: 1809-1858,* 2 vols. Boston and New York, 1928.

BUTLER, NICHOLAS MURRAY. *Across the Busy Years; Recollections and Reflections,* 2 vols. New York, 1939-40.

CLARK, LEON PIERCE. *Lincoln; a Psychobiography.* New York, 1933.

DAVIS, GEORGE T. M. *Autobiography of the Late Colonel George T. M. Davis.* New York, 1891.

DENNETT, TYLER (editor. Work cited under HAY).

DODGE, DANIEL KILHAM. *Abraham Lincoln: Master of Words.* New York, 1924.

—— *Abraham Lincoln: The Evolution of His Literary Style.* The University Studies, University of Illinois, Vol. I, No. 1, May, 1900.

FEDERAL WRITERS PROJECT. *Washington, City and Capital.* Washington, 1937.

HAY, JOHN. *Lincoln and the Civil War in the Diaries and Letters of John Hay*, edited by Tyler Dennett. New York, 1939.

HERNDON, WILLIAM H. *The Hidden Lincoln: From the Letters and Papers of William H. Herndon*, edited by Emanuel Hertz. New York, 1938.

—— and JESSE WILLIAM WEIK. *Herndon's Lincoln: The True Story of a Great Life*, 3 vols. Chicago, 1889.

HERTZ, EMANUEL (editor. Work cited under HERNDON).

KELLOGG, WILLIAM PITT. "The Recollections of William Pitt Kellogg," edited by Paul M. Angle, *The Abraham Lincoln Quarterly*, Vol. III, No. 7, September, 1945.

KINCAID, ROBERT L. *Joshua Fry Speed: Lincoln's Most Intimate Friend.* Harrogate, Tennessee, 1943.

LINCOLN, ABRAHAM. *A Strange Affair*, edited by Roger W. Barrett. Peoria, Illinois, 1933.

—— *Complete Works of Abraham Lincoln*, edited by John G. Nicolay and John Hay, 12 vols. New York, 1905.

—— *Lincoln on Agriculture: Address, Wisconsin State Agricultural Society, State Fair, Milwaukee, September 30, 1859.* Reprinted from Proceedings of the Society, 1859, Lincoln Fellowship of Wisconsin Historical Bulletin No. 1. Madison, Wisconsin, 1943.

—— *New Letters and Papers of Lincoln*, edited by Paul M. Angle. Boston and New York, 1930.

LINN, JAMES WEBER. "Such Were His Words," *Abraham Lincoln Association Papers, Delivered before the Members of the Abraham Lincoln Association at Springfield, Illinois, on February 11, 12, 1939.* Springfield, Illinois, 1940.

MOORE, FRANK. *The Civil War in Song and Story 1860-1865.* New York, 1889.

NICOLAY, JOHN G., and JOHN HAY. *Abraham Lincoln: A History*, 10 vols. New York, 1890.

—— (editas. Work cited under LINCOLN).

O'BYRNE, MICHAEL C. *History of LaSalle County, Illinois*, 3 vols. Chicago, 1924.

PALMER, JOHN M. (editor). *The Bench and Bar of Illinois*, 2 vols. Chicago, 1899.

PEASE, THEODORE CALVIN. *Frontier State: 1818-1848.* Springfield, Illinois, 1918.

PETERSEN, WILLIAM F. *Lincoln-Douglas: The Weather as Destiny.* Springfield, Illinois, 1943.

[PHILLIPS, DAVID LYMAN]. *Biographies of the State Officers.* Springfield, Illinois, 1883.

PRATT, HARRY E. "Lincoln—Author of the Letters by 'A Conservative,'" *Bulletin of the Abraham Lincoln Association*, No. 50, December, 1937.

—— *The Personal Finances of Abraham Lincoln*. Springfield, Illinois, 1943.

SANDBURG, CARL. *Abraham Lincoln: The Prairie Years*, 2 vols. New York, 1926.

—— *Abraham Lincoln: The War Years*, 4 vols. New York, 1939.

—— and PAUL M. ANGLE. *Mary Lincoln: Wife and Widow*. New York, 1932.

SEYMOUR, GLEN H. "'Conservative'—Another Lincoln Pseudonym?" *Journal of the Illinois State Historical Society*, Vol. XXIX, No. 2, July, 1936.

SHUTES, MILTON HENRY. *Lincoln and the Doctors: A Medical Narrative of the Life of Abraham Lincoln*. New York, 1933.

SPEED, JOSHUA F. *Reminiscences of Abraham Lincoln and Notes of a Visit to California*. Louisville, Kentucky, 1884.

TARBELL, IDA M. *In the Footsteps of the Lincolns*. New York, 1924.

THAYER, W. R. *Life and Letters of John Hay*, 2 vols. Boston and New York, 1915.

TOWNSEND, WILLIAM H. *Lincoln and His Wife's Home Town*. Indianapolis, Indiana, 1929.

VAN HOESEN, H. B. *The Humor of Lincoln and the Seriousness of His Biographers*. Books at Brown, Published by the Friends of the Library of Brown University, Vol. III, No. 2, 3, December, 1944, March, 1945.

WARREN, LOUIS A. "Gettysburg Addresses in Autograph," *Lincoln Lore*, No. 182, October 3, 1932.

—— "Original Draft of the First Inaugural," *Lincoln Lore*, No. 358, No. 359, February 17, 24, 1936.

INDEX

INDEX

"A House Divided: Speech Delivered at Springfield, Illinois," 19, 21, 23-27, 32, 40, 332n., 372-381, 515-516; replies to Douglas's criticism of, 391-396, 423-424, 425n., 446, 449.
"A Letter from the Lost Townships," 72n., 148-154.
A Strange Affair, 182n.
Able, Bennett, 62.
Able, Mrs. Bennett, 62.
Abolitionism, Douglas charges Lincoln with, 430-435, 437, 438; Lincoln's reply, 442-445.
Abraham Lincoln Association, The, 557n.
Abraham Lincoln Quarterly, The, 154n.
Adams, Charles Francis, Jr., 2.
Adams, John, 489, 709.
Adams, John Quincy, 105, 108, 231n., 268, 348.
"Address at a Sanitary Fair in Baltimore," 748-750.
"Address at Cooper Institute," 17, 19, 20, 22, 32-33, 514n., 517-536, 536-539n.
"Address before the Springfield Scott Club," 18.
"Address before the Wisconsin Agricultural Society," 31, 39, 493-505n.
"Address Delivered at the Dedication of the Cemetery at Gettysburg," 9, 12, 29, 35, 40, 41-44, 47, 490n., 710n., 734-737n.
"Address in Independence Hall, Philadelphia," 577-578.
"Address to Germans at Cincinnati, Ohio," 572-573.
"Address to the Assembly of New Jersey," 575-576.
"Address to the 140th Indiana Regiment," 794-796.
"Address to the 164th Ohio Regiment," 755-756.
"Address to the 166th Ohio Regiment," 756-757.
"Address to the Senate of New Jersey," 574-575.
Aesop's *Fables*, 5.
African slave trade, suppression of, 628, 667.
"Agriculture: Annual Address before the Wisconsin State Agricultural Society at Milwaukee," 31, 39, 493-505n.
Agriculture Department, report on, 627, 675, 784.
Albany, N. Y., Democratic Convention at, 699, 708.
Albert, Prince, 231n.
Aldie, Va., 658.
Alexander, Jediah F., letter to, 369, 370n.
Alexander the Great, 83.
Alexandria, Va., 592n.
Allen, Charles, 320.
Allen, G. T., 327.
Allen, Robert, 148, 161, 168; letter to, 59-60, 60n.
Allen, ——, 226.
Allison, John, 234, 235.
Alton, Ill., 160, 172, 352n., 563n.-564n.; last debate at, 29.
Alton Courier, 474n.
American Colonization Society, 275, 276.
American Fur Company, 509n.
American News Company, 569n.
Amnesty and reconstruction, proclamation of, 738-741, 743.
Anderson, Robert, 595-596, 614.
André, John, 315.

Angle, Paul M., 282n.; *Lincoln: 1854-1861*, 486n.; and Carl Sandburg, *Mary Lincoln: Wife and Widow*, 120-121n., 228n.; ed., *New Letters and Papers of Lincoln*, 230n., 258n., 372n., 514n.; ed., "The Recollections of William Pitt Kellogg," 566n.; "The Record of a Friendship," 172n.
"Annual Message to Congress" (December 3, 1861), 39, 616-635.
"Annual Message to Congress" (December 1, 1862), 38, 39-40, 666-688.
"Annual Message to Congress" (December 8, 1863), 797.
"Annual Message to Congress" (December 6, 1864), 773-789.
Antietam, battle of, 659, 723.
Appomattox, Va., surrender at, 801n.
Arabian Nights, 5.
Army of the Potomac, remarks to, 656.
Arnold, Isaac N., 696-697, 697n.
Arnold, Matthew, 42.
Articles of Association, 582.
Articles of Confederation, 284, 492, 582, 603.
Asbury, Henry, letters to, 425-426, 426n., 482.
Ashby's Gap, Va., 659.
Ashmun, George, 217, 553; letter to, 543-544.
Atchison, David R., 348.
Atherton's Ferry (Ky.), 548.
Atlanta, Ga., 789.
Auburn, N. Y., 760.
Autobiography, *see* "Short Autobiography Written for the Campaign of 1860," *and* "Letter to J. W. Fell Inclosing Autobiography."
Autographed Leaves of Our Country's Authors, 735n.

Baird, Mrs., 744.
Baker & Van Bergen, 148.
Baker, Edward D., 118, 165-166, 167, 168, 171, 174n., 218, 248, 253, 256, 257n., 382, 554, 665.
Baker, Ezra, 69.
Baker, Palmer, 327.
Baldwin, Abraham, 519, 520, 521, 560.
Bale, Abram, letter to, 258, 258n.
Baltimore, Md., 249, 748, 752, 759; address at Sanitary Fair at, 748-750n.
Baltimore American, 239.
Baltimore and Ohio Railroad, 638, 713.
Baltimore Convention, 238.
Bank of Illinois, 8, 64-72, 72n., 510n.
Banks, Nathaniel P., 638, 646, 696, 711, 798; letters to, 714-716n., 743-744n.
Bardstown, Ky., 548.
Barrett, Joseph H., 36.
Barrett, Oliver R., 163, 381n., 426n.
Barrett, Roger W., 182n.
Barry, ——, 108-110.
Barton, W. E., *Lincoln at Gettysburg*, 735n.
Basler, Roy P., "The Authorship of the 'Rebecca' Letters," 154n.; "Who Wrote the 'Letter to Mrs. Bixby'?," 766n.
Bassett, Richard, 519.
Bates, Edward, 542.
Beardstown, Ill., 172, 337n., 368, 427, 550.
Beck, Mrs., 168.
Bedell, Grace, letter to, 561-562n.
Bell, James, & Co., 148, 197-198.
Bell, John, 255.
Belleville, Ill., 257n.
Benton, —— 578n.
Beveridge, Albert J., *Abraham Lincoln: 1809-1858*, 72n., 85n., 154n., 185n., 201n., 277n.
Birdsall, ——, 239.
Bishop, ——, 218, 221, 222, 223.
Bixby, Mrs. Lydia, letter to, 34-36, 725n., 766-772n.
Black Hawk War, 242, 511, 551, 689n., 693n.
Blackstone's *Commentaries*, 2, 6.
Blair, Francis P., 697.

Blenker, Louis, 638.
Blittersdorf, August, 731.
Bloomington, Ill., 329, 338n., 345n., 413, 414, 418, 514, 689n.; "Lost Speech" at, 21.
Blount, William, 519.
Bohlen, Henry, 665.
Boker, G. H., letter to, 769n.
Bolivar, Simon, 266.
Bonaparte, Napoleon, 77, 83, 266, 321, 694.
Book of Common Prayer, The, 37.
Boonville, Mo., 168.
Boston, Mass., 99, 230, 752.
Boutwell, George S., 715.
Brainerd, Cephas, 536n.-539n.
Branson, ——, 148.
Breckinridge, John C., 164n., 703.
Bright, Jesse D., 348.
Brooklyn, N. Y., 752.
Brooks, Noah, story written for, 772-773n.
Brooks, Preston S., 416.
Broome, Mrs., 226.
Brown, James N., letter to, 478-479, 480n.
Brown, John, opinion of, 529-532.
Brown University Library, 770n.
Brown, W. H., letter to, 507-510n.
Browning, Mrs. O. H., letter to, 85-88, 89n.
Browning, O. H., 88, 89n., 256, 257n., 393, 435, 589n.; letter to, 613-615n.
Brumfield, Nancy (Lincoln), 547.
Brumfield, William, 547.
Buchanan, Franklin, 703.
Buchanan, James, 22, 25, 231n., 339-345, 347, 348, 351, 368, 371, 372n., 374, 377, 387, 408, 410, 425, 449, 457, 465.
Buckner, A. H., 69.
Buckner, Simon B., 703.
Buell, D. C., 664; letter to, 636-637; telegram to, 636.
Bullard, F. Lauriston and Edward C. Stone, *Lincoln Wrote the Bixby Letter, a Detective Story,* 766-767n., 772n.
Bullitt, Cuthbert, 16; letter to, 648-650.
Bunyan's *The Pilgrim's Progress,* 5.
Burke, Edmund, 40.
Burnet, David G., 213n.
Burns, Robert, 6.
Burnside, A. E., 646, 693; letter to, 637.
Butler, Benjamin F., 696, 697, 718.
Butler, Nicholas Murray, *Across the Busy Years,* 767n., 770n.-771n.
Butler, Pierce, 519.
Butler, William, 115, 146, 161, 163n., 166n., 168.
Butterfield, Justin, 257n.

Caesar, Julius, 16, 83, 111, 733.
Calhoun, John, 6, 102, 282, 348, 389.
Cambridge, Mich., 746n.
Campbell, John A., 622, 802.
Campbell, Thomas, 475, 475n.
Cannan & Harlan, 167.
Capital and labor, views on, 22, 31-32, 39, 500-503, 633-634.
Carlin, Thomas, 151.
Carlisle, Pa., 712.
Carpenter, Milton, 150, 151.
Carroll, Daniel, 519.
Carson, John M., 541n.
Carter, Nick, 195.
Cartwright, Peter, 13, 186-187, 188-189n.
Carusi, Louis, 230-231n.
Cass, Lewis, 15, 235, 237, 238, 240, 242-247, 250n., 351, 466; Nicholson letter, 472-473.
Chancellorsville, Va., 709.
Chandler, William E., 771n., 772n.
Channing, William Ellery, 8.
Charleston Courier, 218.
Charleston, Ill., 123, 225, 261, 480n.
Charleston, S. C., 99, 487, 542, 643, 668.
Chase, Salmon P., 378, 430, 434, 453, 466; letters to, 491-493.
Cherokee Indians, treaty relations with, 654, 674.
Chester County (Pa.) Times, 512n.

Chester Gap, Va., 659.
Chicago, Alton & St. Louis R. R., 338n.
Chicago American, The, 115.
Chicago & M. Rd., 338n.
Chicago Daily Press and Tribune, 370, 384n., 483n., 504-505n., 506, 509n.
Chicago Democrat, 326n.
Chicago Democratic Convention (1864), 760-761.
Chicago Historical Society, 510n.
Chicago, Ill., 245-246, 325, 366, 367, 413, 415, 418, 480n., 509 n., 541, 752; speech in reply to Douglas at, 28, 385-404.
Chicago Journal, 367n.
Chicago Times, 383n.
Chitty's *Pleadings,* 2.
Christian Commission, 751.
Christy, Samuel C., 69.
Cicero, 40.
Cincinnati, O., 329, 663, 752; address to Germans at, 572-574n.
Cincinnati Platform, 399, 420, 459.
Clark, Beverly L., 233.
Clark, Leon Pierce, *Lincoln; a Psychobiography,* 62n.
Clark, ——, 579n.
Clary's Grove, 117, 119.
Clay, Brutus, 717.
Clay, Cassius, 218, 717.
Clay, Henry, 14, 18, 23, 169-170, 185, 218, 239, 248, 264-278n., 287, 322, 331, 421, 422, 429, 460, 471, 551, 553, 589n.; Mendenhall speech, 479, 480n.; eulogy on, 264-277.
Clay, John M., letter to, 651.
Cleveland, O., 238.
Clinton, Ill., 451, 454.
Clymer, George, 519.
Codding, Ichabod, 462.
Coercion and invasion, attitude on, 571-572.
Coleridge, S. T., 9.
Collingsworth, James, 214n.
Colonization of freed slaves, 685-688.
Columbus, Christopher, 472.
Columbus, O., 517; Douglas's speech at, 32.
Compensated emancipation, 676-688, 721.
"Concluding Speech," *see* "Last Speech in the Campaign of 1858."
Condorcet, Marquis de, 9.
Confederate Peace Commissioners, 754-755n.
Congress, annual message to (1861), 39, 616-635; annual message to (1862), 38, 39-40, 666-688; annual message to (1863), 797; annual message to (1864), 773-789; message to in special session (1861), 594-609.
Congress of the Federation, 518-519.
Congressional Globe, 609n.
Conkling, James C., letters to, 35, 720-724n., 725, 725n.
Constitution, U. S., 32-33, 81, 103, 244, 271, 272, 281, 284, 285, 287, 305, 307, 311, 313, 314, 318, 333, 345, 351, 355, 356, 357, 358, 373, 375, 376, 378, 390, 393, 395, 396, 403, 416, 419, 421, 431, 436, 439, 450, 453, 455, 484, 491, 492, 513, 513-514n., 517, 518-526, 532, 533, 543, 552, 572, 575, 576, 579-588, 594, 600-609, 614, 629, 640, 649, 650, 651, 652, 676-677, 679, 687, 700-703, 705, 707, 721, 738-739, 741, 760, 761, 785, 788, 800.
Constitutional Convention, 715.
Cook, Burton C., 327.
Cooper Institute, address at, 517-539n., 545-546; *see also* "Address at Cooper Institute."
Cooper Shop and Union Volunteer Refreshment Saloons, 752.
Corning, Erastus, and Others, letter to, 699-708n.
Corning, Erastus, letter to, 36.
Correll, U. F., letter to, 515-517n.
"Correspondence About the Lincoln-Shields Duel," 156-158.
Corydon, Ind., 225.
Couch, Darius N., 711, 712.
Crawford, Andrew, 549.

Crittenden, John J., 221, 256, 257n., 717.
Crume, Mary (Lincoln), 547, 635.
Crume, Ralph, 547, 635.
Crume, Susannah, *see* Weathers, Susannah (Crume).
Culpeper Court House, 657.
Curtis, Benjamin R., 354, 357, 378.
Curtis, Samuel R., 718.
Cuthbert, John, 93n.
Cuthbert, Mrs., 716.
Cuyler, Theodore, 577-578n.

Daily National Intelligencer, 231n.
Daniel, Peter V., 622.
Danites, 486, 487n.
Davidson, W. H., 69.
Davis, David I., 328, 663.
Davis, Eliza Julia (Speed), 123, 142.
Davis, George T. M., 218; letter to, 563-564n.
Davis, Walter, 252, 253n.
Dayton, Jonathan, 521.
Dayton, William L., 343, 347.
Decatur Convention, 280n.
Declaration of Independence, 28, 40, 42, 43, 81, 103, 284, 285, 291, 309, 314, 315, 358, 359, 360-362, 390, 401-403, 422, 423, 437, 443, 445, 460, 462, 472, 479, 489-490n., 513, 513-514n., 577, 578n., 582, 603, 607, 709-710.
Defoe's *Robinson Crusoe,* 5.
Defrees, John D., 38; letter to, 566-567n.
Delahay, Mark W., 172, 506n.; letter to, 539-540n.
Delahay, Mary, 505.
Democracy, *see* Political philosophy.
Demosthenes, 40.
Dennett, Tyler, ed., *Lincoln and the Civil War in the Diaries and Letters of John Hay,* 768n.
Dennison, William, and Others, A Committee of the National Union Convention, letter to, 753-754.
Detroit Daily Advertiser, 345n.
Detroit, Mich., 250n.
Dilworth's *A New Guide to the English Tongue,* 3.
"Discoveries, Inventions and Improvements," lecture, 30-31.
Dodge, Daniel Kilham, *Abraham Lincoln: Master of Words,* 36, 729n.; *Abraham Lincoln: The Evolution of his Literary Style,* 26-27.
Dole, G. W., G. S. Hubbard, and W. H. Brown, letter to, 507-510n.
Dole, W. P., 509n.
Doniphan, Alexander W., 218.
Dorman, Mrs. Rebecca, 165n.
Dorman, William, 164.
Dorsey, Azel W., 549.
Douglas, Stephen A., 18, 20, 22, 23, 24, 25, 26, 27, 28, 29, 30, 47, 90, 104, 106, 107, 108, 110, 283, 287, 288, 290, 295, 298, 304, 305, 316, 318-323, 324-325n., 332n., 335, 340, 342, 350, 351, 352, 354, 355, 356, 359-365n., 366-371n., 377, 379, 380, 383n., 385-400, 402, 404n., 406, 407, 409-415, 417, 418-423, 425, 426n.,469-473, 475, 481, 482, 483, 486, 487, 506, 507, 507n., 516, 516n., 517, 518, 524, 535, 542, 545, 555, 557, 565-566, 707; debate at Ottawa, 428-469n.; speech at Columbus, Ohio, 32.
Douglass, Frederick, 430, 433, 434, 438.
Dred Scott decision, 22, 24, 27, 28; speech on, 346n., 352-365n., 373, 375, 376, 377, 378, 384, 396, 397, 399, 402, 417, 418, 420, 421, 436-438, 448, 451, 453, 454, 458, 460, 461, 470, 473, 524.
Dubois, Jesse K., 563, 717.
Dumbolton, J. A., 231n.
Dummer, Henry E., 337; letters to, 171-172n., 427.
Dunbar, Alexander P., 221, 223.
Duncan, Garnett, 257.
Durant, Thomas J., 648-650, 715, 716.
Durley, Williamson, letter to, 169-171n.

Eastham, Marvelous, 142.
Education, 1-5, 511, 548, 549, 551; views on, 2, 56, 501-504, 559.
Edwards, Cyrus, 256, 257n.
Edwards, N. W., 59.
Edwardsville, Ill., speech at, 469-474n.
Elections during war, views on, 763-764.
Ellsworth, E. E., letter to, 592-592n.
Ellsworth's (E. E.) Parents, letter to, 34-35, 593.
Emancipation, compensated, 676-688, 721.
"Emancipation Proclamation," 36, 689-692n., 715, 721-722, 789, 797-798.
Emerson, Ralph W., 8.
Emigration Act, operation of, 777-778.
English Bill, 405n.
Euclid, 489, 490n.; Lincoln's study of, 43, 549.
"Eulogy on Benjamin Ferguson," 128-129n.
"Eulogy on Henry Clay Delivered in the State House at Springfield, Illinois," 18, 264-277, 278n.
Evening Mirror, 185n.
Everett, Edward, letter to, 737-738n.
Everett, ——, 145-146.
Ewell, Richard S., 643, 732.
Exeter Academy, 559n.-560n.

Falstaff, Sir John, 86.
"Farewell Address at Springfield, Illinois," 12, 29, 41, 46, 568-570n.
Farmington, Ill., 121, 372n.
Farnsworth, John F., 437.
Fell, Jesse W., 20; letter to, inclosing autobiography, 510-512n.
Ferguson, Benjamin, eulogy on, 10, 128-129n.
Few, William, 519, 521.
Figures of speech, employment of, 24-28.
Filisola, Vincente, 214n.
Fillmore, Millard, 341.
"Final Emancipation Proclamation," 689-692n.
"First Debate at Ottawa, Illinois," 28-29, 428-469n.
"First Inaugural Address," 29, 39, 41, 48, 576-577, 579-590n., 595.
Fish, Daniel, 112n.
Fisher, Archibald, 117, 119, 120, 175-184n.
Fitzsimmons, Thomas, 519.
Flanders, Benjamin F., 716.
Flint, Abel, 551.
Florida War, cost of, 107.
Florville, William, 514.
Flournoy, Thomas S., 216n.
Follet, Foster and Company, 381n., 483n., 555.
Forbes & Hill, 164.
Ford, Allen N., 188n.
Ford, Thomas, 150.
Ford's *History of Illinois*, 459.
Foreign affairs, report on, 773-777.
Foreign and domestic policy, 590-591, 617, 619, 667-669.
Fort Jefferson, 594.
Fort Monroe, 642n., 645.
Fort Pickens, 591, 594, 596.
Fort Pillow, 749-750.
Fort Sumter, 591, 594, 596-599, 630.
Fort Taylor, 594.
Fort Wayne, Ind., 245-246.
"Fragment: On Slavery," 427.
"Fragment: On Slavery," 477-478.
"Fragment: Speech at Edwardsville," 469-474.
"Fragment: The Constitution and the Union," 513.
"Fragments: On Slavery," 278-279.
Francis, Mrs. Simeon, 126n.
Francis, Simeon, 155n.
Franklin, Benjamin, 436.
Franklin, William B., 642.
Frederick, Md., 656.
Fredericksburg, Va., 643, 698, 709; battle of, 746n.
Freeport Heresy, 27, 426n.
Freeport, Ill., 426n.
Freese, Jacob R., 16, 733.
"Frémont, Buchanan, and the Exten-

sion of Slavery: Speech at Kalamazoo, Michigan," 22, 339-345.
Frémont, John C., 22, 339-345, 347, 348, 613-615, 645, 696, 697, 718.
French Indemnities, cost of, 108, 110.
French Revolution, 266.
Fry, Nelson, 197-198.
Fugitive Slave Law, 312, 431, 444, 462, 491-493.
Fullinwider, J. R., letter to, 515-517n.
Fulton, Ill., 367.

Gaines, John P., 222, 248.
Galena Advertiser, 351n.
Galena, Ill., 325n., 351n.;, 367, 555.
Galloway, Samuel, letter to, 555n., 555-557n.
Galloway, ——, 120.
Garrison, William Lloyd, 8.
General Assembly of Illinois, Lincoln's resolutions on slavery in, 552.
General Ticket System, 115-116n.
Germon, ——, 231n.
Gettysburg, Pa., 711-712, 738n.; battle of, 43, 723; *see also* "Address Delivered at the Dedication of the Cemetery at Gettysburg."
Gibson, Robert, 551.
Giddings, Joshua R., 284, 430, 433, 434, 438.
Gilder, Richard W., 771n.
Gilman, Nicholas, 519.
Gilman, W. S., 69.
Gilmore, Dr., 119-120, 179, 180.
Glover, Sam, 615.
Goddard, Dr., 150.
Godfrey, Benjamin, 69.
Godwin, William, 9; *Political Justice,* 10.
Graham, Mentor, 4, 5, 6.
Grand Gulf, Miss., 711.
Grant, Ulysses S., 640n., 664n., 693n., 696, 697, 717-718, 752, 753, 790, 802; letters to, 710-711, 750-751, 758, 790-791n.; telegram to, 796.
Grayson, P. W., 214n.
Greeley, Horace, 35, 506-507n., 560; letters to, 651-653n., 754-755n.
Green, Mrs. M. J., letter to, 561.
Green, Robert R., 69.
Greene, William G., 717.
Greenleaf's *Evidence,* 2.
Greenville Advocate, 370n.
Greenville, Ill., 370.
Gregory's Gap, Va., 659.
Grigg, John, 255n.
Grimshaw's *History of the United States,* 5.
Gurney, Mrs. Eliza P., letter to, 757-758.

Hackett, J. H., letters to, 45, 718-719n., 732.
Hagerstown, Md., 712.
Haggard, Linnie, verses to, 477.
Haggard, Rosa, verses to, 476.
Hahn, Michael, 716, 744n.; letter to, 745.
Hall, Bell & Co. *v.*, 148, 167.
Hall, O. P., J. R. Fullinwider, and U. F. Correll, letter to, 515-517n.
Halleck, Henry W., 647, 657, 692, 696, 697, 698, 711; letters to, 713-714n., 724n., 726-727, 731-732, 768n.
Haman, 334.
Hamburg, financial system of, 93n.
Hamilton, Alexander, 234, 436.
Hamilton, Richard I., 69.
Hamilton, Schuyler, 642.
Hancock, Winfield S., 753.
Hanks, Chapman, 262.
Hanks, Dennis, 262n.
Hanks, Elizabeth (Johnston), 262n.
Hanks, John, 550.
Hanover, abolition of the stade dues, 667.
Hanover Junction, Va., 643.
Hanscomb ("Hanscum"), S. P., 768n.
Hardiman, B., 214n.
Hardin, John J., 168, 172, 173, 174n., 248, 382, 554.

Harlan, Justin, 167.
Harper, Walter, & Co., 229.
Harper's Ferry, W. Va., 529, 530, 531, 532, 599, 643, 657, 659.
Harper's Weekly, 569n.
Harrington, ——, 110.
Harrington, ——, 231n.
Harris, Thomas L., 280.
Harris, ——, 97.
Harrisburg, Pa., 663.
Harrison Literary Institute, 541, 541n.
Harrison, Quinn, 189n.
Harrison, William Henry, 152, 222, 241-242, 269, 348, 552-553.
Hart, Ellis, 120.
Harvard University, 559, 790.
Harvey, William, 167.
Haskell, William P., 218, 222, 248.
Hatch, Ozias M., 483, 717.
Hawkes, C. K., letter to, 742-742n.
Hawkins, ——, 97.
Hay, John, 713n.-714n., 724n.-725n., 755n., 759n., 767n.-772n.; *see also* Nicolay and Hay.
Hay Market, Va., 658.
Haycraft, Samuel, letter to, and autobiography, 544.
Hayne, Robert Y., 26, 589n.
Hazel, Caleb, 548.
Heintzelman, Samuel P., 641.
Hendershot, Robert H., 745, 746n.
Hennepin, Ill., 171n.
Henning, Fanny, *see* Speed, Fanny (Henning).
Henry, Anson G., 113-114.
Henry, John, 382-383.
Henry, Patrick, 271.
Hentz, Caroline Lee, 6.
Herburger, F. C., 491n.; letter to, 541-541n.
Herndon, Uncle Billy, 128.
Herndon, William H., 6, 8, 12, 15, 47, 62n., 85n., 215n., 223n., 227n., 367, 381n., 537n., 546n., 588n., 589n., 767n., 771n.; letters to, 199, 217-218, 219n., 220-221, 232, 232n., 252-253.
Hertz, Emanuel, ed., *The Hidden Lincoln,* 189n., 767n.
Hewett, Mary, 230.
Hickox, Virgil, 117, 119, 120, 258.
Hickox's mill, 178.
Hill, Ambrose P., 732.
Hoffman, Henry W., letter to, 759, 770n.
Hollander, ——, 706.
Homestead Law, 573.
Hood, John B., 790.
Hood, P. H., & Co., 229.
Hooker, Joseph, 638, 696, 718; letters to, 35, 693-694, 695; telegrams to, 36, 698, 708-709.
Hooper, Johnson Jones, 11.
"House Divided Speech," *see* "A House Divided."
Hovey, Alvin P., 697.
Howard, James Q., 556, 556n.
Howard ——, 231n.
Howells, William D., 556, 557n.
Hubbard, G. S., 507-509, 509-510n.
Hudson's Bay and Puget's Sound Agricultural Companies, 777.
Hull, Dr., 384.
Hull, William, 241-242, 250n.
Humor, character of, 15-17, 57n.-58n., 89n., 323n., 468-469n.
Humphreys, Andrew A., 637.
Hunt, Daniel, 747n.
Hunt, Mrs. S. W., memorandum for, 747, 747n.
Hunter, David, 646, 696, 718.
Hurlbut, Stephen A., 615.
Hurst, Charles R., 165, 167, 169, 197-198.

Illinois College, 346n.
Illinois Gazette, letter to, 13, 188n.
Illinois House Journal, Lincoln's resolution on slavery in, 552.
Illinois Intelligencer, 510n.
Illinois Legislature (General Assembly), Lincoln a candidate for General Assembly, 53ff.; resolutions in, 552; speech in, 63-72.
Illinois Savings Institution, 509n.

Illinois State Journal, 278n., 282n., 324n., 381n., 481n., 540, 569n.
Illinois State Register, criticism of Lincoln's humor, 15, 113n., 368.
Inaugural Addresses, *see* "First Inaugural Address" *and* "Second Inaugural Address."
Independence Hall, address in, 577-579n.
Independence, Mo., 365n.
Indian tribes, relations of government with, 627, 654-655, 674-675, 783.
Indiana, 140th Regiment, address to, 794-796.
Indianapolis, Ind., speech at, 571-572, 574n.
Interior Department, report on operations of, 626, 673-674, 782-783.
Internal Improvement Convention, 61.
Irwin, James S., 167; letter to, 163-164n.
Irwin, John, 148, 167.
Iverson, Alfred, 239, 240.

Jackson, Andrew, 23, 103, 105, 238, 240-241, 268, 269, 348, 356-357, 397, 398, 419, 459, 551, 589n., 706.
Jackson, Thomas J., 643.
Jacksonville Daily Journal, 425n.
Jacksonville, Ill., 53, 145, 160, 164n., 186, 425n.
James, B. F., letter to, 173-174.
James, ——, 218.
Jarvis, ——, 418.
Jay, John, 436.
Jefferson, Thomas, 6, 105, 234, 272, 275, 284, 285, 418, 419, 436, 447, 449, 459, 474n., 488-489, 489n.-490n., 531, 607, 629, 709.
Jenkins, A. M., 69.
Jesus, 98.
Jewett, ——, 167.
Johnson, Andrew, 729n.; letter to, 694-695.
Johnson, Reverdy, 637.
Johnson, William S., 519.
Johnston, Abram, 262n., 263.
Johnston, Andrew, 11, 181n., 193n.; letters to, 184-185n., 189-190.
Johnston, John D., 550; letters to, 250-252n., 259, 261-262, 263-264.
Johnston, Joseph E., 703.
Jonas, Abraham, letter to, 557-558n.
Jonesboro, Ill., 432.
Journal of the Illinois State Historical Society, 172n.
Judas, 98.
Judd, Norman B., 327, 508-509.

Kalamazoo, Mich., speech at, 339-345n.
Kansas Constitutional Convention, 353.
Kansas-Nebraska Bill, 17, 18, 20, 24, 27, 281-282, 293, 298, 310, 312, 313, 316, 317, 318, 319-322, 335, 341, 345, 350, 353, 359, 373-375, 377-378, 387, 393, 398-399, 416, 422, 429, 430, 452, 453, 466, 467, 471.
Kaskaskia, Ill., 510n.
Kearny, Philip, 665.
Kellogg, William, 368; letters to, 506-507n., 565-566n.
Kelso, Jack, 6.
Kentucky Preceptor, The, 3.
Keyes, Erasmus D., 641.
Keys, James W., 117, 119.
Kincaid, Robert L., *Joshua Fry Speed: Lincoln's Most Intimate Friend,* 121n.
King James Bible, 5, 45.
King, Rufus, 519, 521.
King, William R., 343, 348.
King, ——, 643.
Kirkham's *Grammar,* 3, 4.
Knob Creek (Ky.), 548.
Know-Nothings, Lincoln's attitude toward, 21, 328-329, 335-336, 557-558n.
Knox, William, "Mortality," 11-12, 185n.
Knoxville, Tenn., 618.

Labor and capital, views on, 22, 31-32, 39, 500-503, 573, 633-634.
Lacon, Ill., 173.
LaFayette, Marquis de, 528.
La Harp, Ill., 225.
Lamborn, Josiah, 104, 110, 111, 118.
Land Office appointment, 256-257n.
Lane, James H., 539, 540.
Lane, John, 164-165n.
Langdon, John, 519, 521.
Langford, James P., 120.
Larrimore, ——, 515.
"Last Debate at Alton, Illinois," 29.
"Last Public Address," 796-801n., 803n.
"Last Speech in the Campaign of 1858," 12, 23-24, 29, 480-481n.
Latham, George, letter to, 559-560n.
Latshaw, ——, 223.
Lavely, William, 118.
Law, advice on study of, 2, 337; philosophy of, 70-72n., 483-484.
Lebanon, Ky., 618.
Lecompton Constitution, 371-372n., 375, 390, 399, 404n., 408, 409-413, 456-457, 487, 487n.
Lecture on "Discoveries, Inventions and Improvements," 30-31, 491n.
Lee, Robert E., 36, 698, 703, 712, 713, 721, 731; terms for Lee's capitulation, 791-791n.
Letter writing, 34-36.
Lewis, Joseph J., 512n.
Lewiston, Ill., 119, 179.
Lexington, Ky., 225, 226, 228, 229, 268, 331n., 618.
Liberty, definition of, 748-750.
Library of Congress, 609n., 642n.
Lincoln, Abraham (Lincoln's grandfather), 224, 510-511, 547.
Lincoln, Abraham (son of Mordecai), 225.
Lincoln, David, letters to, 224, 224-225.
Lincoln, Eddy, 226, 227.
Lincoln Fellowship of Wisconsin, 505n.
Lincoln Herald, 766n.
Lincoln, Ill., 351n.
Lincoln, Isaac (brother of Lincoln's grandfather), 225, 547.
Lincoln, Jacob (brother of Lincoln's grandfather), 225, 547.
Lincoln, John (uncle), 225, 547.
Lincoln, Josiah (uncle), 225, 547.
Lincoln Lore, 589n.
Lincoln, Mary (Todd), 10, 114n., 120, 120n., 126n., 131n., 159n., 160n., 168, 169, 198, 336, 553, 747n.; letters to, 226-228n., 228-229, 229-230, 716-717; telegram to, 770n.
Lincoln, Mordecai (uncle), 225, 547.
Lincoln, Mordecai (son of Mordecai), 225.
Lincoln, Nancy (Hanks), 510, 548.
Lincoln, Robert, 198, 227, 229, 555n., 559-560n., 569, 790-791.
Lincoln, Sarah (Bush Johnston), 252n., 259, 261-262n., 263-264, 548.
Lincoln, Thomas (father), 225, 252n., 259, 511, 547-548; and John D. Johnston, letters to, 250-252n.
Lincoln, Thomas (son of Josiah), 225, 547.
Lincoln, Thomas (uncle), 225.
Lincoln, Thomas Todd ("Tad"), 716.
Linder, Usher F., 15, 63, 69, 72n.; letter to, 221-223n.
Linn, James Weber, "Such Were His Words" (*Abraham Lincoln Association Papers,* 1940), 85n.
Linn, W., 69, 97.
Lockridge, John, 145, 148, 165.
Logan & Lincoln, 12.
Logan, John A., 697.
Logan, Stephen T., 116, 118, 163, 164, 219.
Longstreet, Augustus Baldwin, 11.
Longstreet, James, 731.
"Lost Speech," 21, 345n.
Lost Townships, 148-154n., 156n., 158, 159; letter from, 148-156n.
Louaillier, ——, 706.

Louisiana government, recognition of, 797-801.
Louisville Courier Journal, 563n.
Louisville, Ky., 120, 123n., 146, 333, 663.
Lovejoy, Elijah P., 564n.
Lovejoy, Owen, 430, 434, 442; letter to, 328-330n.
Lowell, James R., 8.
Lyceum Address, 76-85n.
Lyon, Nathaniel, 665.

McCallen, Andrew, letter to, 260, 260n.
McClane, Robert M., 249.
McClellan, George B., 35, 632, 636, 656n., 662, 664, 696, 718, 727; letters to, 638-640n., 641-642, 645-646, 647-648, 657-659; telegrams to, 643, 644, 645, 646-647, 647, 653, 659, 660.
McClernand, J. A., letters to, 692-693n., 697, 717-718.
McCullough, Fanny, letter to, 34, 688-689.
McCullough, Mrs. William, 689.
McCullough, William, 688-689n.
McDowell, Irvin, 638, 646.
McDowell, James, 224, 225.
Mace, Daniel, 378.
McGaughey, Edward W., 256, 257n.
McHenry, James, 518.
McIntosh, lynching, 78.
McKinley, ——, 384.
McKnight, ——, 226.
McLaughlin, Robert K., 69.
McLean, John, 354, 378, 542, 622.
McPherson, James B., 697.
Madison, James, 105, 234, 436, 440, 447, 449, 519.
Magoffin, Beriah, letter to, 611-612n.
Magruder, John B., 703.
Maine boundary question, 110.
Mallory, ——, 120.
Mammon, 359.
Manassas Junction, Va., 638-639.
Manassas Gap, Va., 659.
Mangum, Willie P., 348.
Mansfield, Joseph K., 665.
Marion, Francis, 315.
Marshall, Samuel D., 248; letter to, 164-165n.
Martinsburg, Va., 708-709.
Maryland, new constitution for, 759-761.
Matheny, James H., 430, 434, 435.
Mather, Thomas, 69.
Mathers, John, letter to, 424-425n.
Matteson, Joel A., 326-328.
Maxcy, Jim, 117-119.
May, William L., 118.
Maynard, Horace, 637.
Meade, G. G., 713, 721, 726, 732, 753; draft of letter to, 711-712; telegram to, 731.
Mechanicsburg, Ill., 516n.
Medill, Joseph, 370; letter to, 382-384n.
"Meditation on the Divine Will," 655.
Melancholia, 63n., 114n.
"Memorandum for Mrs. S. W. Hunt", 747, 747n.
"Memorandum of Instructions to E. H. Merryman, Lincoln's Second," 159-160.
Menzies, ——, 717.
Merryman, E. H., 118, 156n., 158n., 159n., 160-162.
"Message to Congress in Special Session," 38-39, 594-609.
Messages to Congress, style of, 38-41.
Metaphor, employment of, 24-28.
Mexican War, 14, 199-214n., 217-218, 220-223, 247-248, 382-383, 434, 445-446, 553.
Mifflin, Thomas, 518.
Military strategy, 638-639, 641, 642, 644-645, 646, 647-648, 653, 657-659, 694, 695, 698, 711-712, 713, 726-727, 731-732.
Miller, Jacob W., 242-243.
Milroy, ——, 708.
Milwaukee, Wis., agricultural society, address at, 493-504.
Missouri Compromise, 19, 20, 21, 30, 281-282, 283-323, 330, 332n.,

333, 334, 350, 416, 417, 422, 429, 467, 481, 508, 512, 554.
Mitchell's Station, Va., 731.
Mob law, opinion on, 77-81.
Moffett, Thomas, 167.
Molly (Mary Todd Lincoln), 120.
Montgomery, Ala., 599.
Moore, Frank, *The Civil War in Song and Story*, 746n.
Morgan, John, 747.
Morgan *Journal*, 173.
Morgan, R. P., letter to, 16, 338, 338n.
Morley, John, 767n.
Mormons, 352-353, 365-366n.
Morris, Robert, 519.
Morrison, James L. D., 248, 256, 257n., 327.
Mt. Sterling, Ill., 164n.
Mudsill theory, 500-503.
Murfreesboro, Tenn., battle of, 723, 746n.
Muscatine, Iowa, 483n.
"My Childhood Home I See Again," 11, 185n., 190-193.
Myers, ——, 117, 120, 175, 176, 179, 180.

Nasby, Petroleum V., 16.
Nashville, Tenn., 243, 548, 636-637.
National Bank, contrasted with Sub-Treasury, 90-113n., 397, 459; report on, 780.
Navy Department, report on operations of, 621-622, 672, 780-781.
Nebraska Bill, *see* Kansas-Nebraska Bill.
Necessity, doctrine of, 9, 13.
Negro military force, attitude toward organization of, 694-695.
Negro soldiers, attitude toward, 722-724, 749-750.
Nelson, Samuel, 378.
New Jersey, address to Assembly of, 575-576.
New Jersey, address to Senate of, 574-575.
New Orleans, La., 285, 549, 663, 691, 700, 706, 747n., 798.
New Salem, Ill., 6, 7, 60n., 258, 337, 433, 551.
New York Daily Tribune, 507n., 573n., 578n., 651.
New York, N. Y., 99, 546, 569n.
New York Times, 517, 565n.
New York Weekly Tribune, 560.
Newman, Ralph G., 731n.
Newton, ——, 229.
Niagara Falls, N. Y., 755n.
Nicholasville, Ky., 618.
Nicholson, A. O. P., 243.
Nicolay and Hay, *Abraham Lincoln: A History*, 569n., 655 n., 755n.; editors, *Complete Works of Abraham Lincoln*, 18, 36, 57n., 113n., 131n., 252n., 277n., 284n., 324n., 351-352n., 569n.
Nicolay, John G., 569n., 590n., 615n., 724n., 767n., 768n.
Niles' National (or *Weekly*) *Register*, 206, 218, 243.
Norfolk, Va., 599, 691, 776.
"Notes of an Argument," 483-484.
Nott, Charles C., 536-539n.; letters to, 545-546, 560.
Noyes, Crosby S., 590n.

Oberline, Fred, 574n.
O'Byrne, M. C., *History of LaSalle County, Illinois*, 486n.
Offutt, Denton, 550, 551.
Ohio, 164th Regiment, address to, 755-756.
Ohio, 166th Regiment, address to, 756-757.
Ohio State Journal, 556n.
Ordinance of 1787, 524.
Osgood, Uri, 327.
Otis, James, 271.
Ottawa, Ill., 432, 480n.; debate at, 428-468.
Owens, Mary, letters to, 60-62, 63n., 73-74, 74n., 75-76, 89n., 228n.; affair with, 114n.

Packard, M. W., letter to, 514-515.
Paine, Thomas, 6.
Palmer, John M., letter to, 279-280n.

Palmer, John M., *The Bench and Bar of Illinois*, 260n., 261n.
Paris, France, 767n.
Parker, John, 226, 229.
Parker, Theodore, 8.
Parks, Samuel C., 557n.
Parrington, V. L., *Main Currents in American Thought*, 25.
Party allegiance, indecision concerning, 328-330n.
Patent office, report on, 626.
Paterson, William, 519.
Peace, attitude on, 723-724.
Pease, Theodore Calvin, *The Frontier State*, 112n.-113n.
Peay, Mrs. Peachy W., 123.
Pekin, Ill., 172, 173.
Pell, ——, 231n.
Pendleton, John S., 216n.
Pensacola, Fla., port of, 776.
Pension office, report on, 626-627, 783-784.
Peoria, Ill., 119, 324n., 480n.; speech at, 282n., 283-325n., 332n.
Peoria Register, 115.
Petersburg, Ill., 258.
Petersburg, Va., 796.
Petersen, William F., *Lincoln-Douglas: The Weather as Destiny*, 62n., 114n.
Pharaoh, 277.
Philadelphia, Pa., 228, 663; speech at a Sanitary Fair in, 751-753.
Phillips, D. L., *Biographies of the State Officers*, 486n.
Phillips, ——, 321.
Pickett, T. J., letter to, 490, 491n.
Pierce, Franklin, 18, 25, 343, 351, 377, 449, 465.
Pierce, H. L., letter to, 488-489.
Pierson, Edward L., 69.
Pinckney, Charles, 521.
Piqua, O., 245-246.
Pittsburgh, Pa., 752.
Poe, Edgar Allan, "The Raven," 184, 185n.
Political institutions, *see* "The Perpetuation of Our Political Institutions."
Political philosophy, 8, 21, 28, 29-30, 42-43, 58-59, 81, 85n., 330-331, 400-403, 427, 473-474, 488-489, 501-504, 513, 525, 526, 577-578, 580-588, 598, 606, 607, 608, 609, 632, 755-757.
Polk, James K., 14, 201n.-202n., 222, 238, 240, 269, 287.
Pope, Alexander, quoted, 494.
Pope, John, 644.
Pope, Nathaniel, 255.
Popular sovereignty, 18, 28, 387, 388, 389, 408, 409, 421, 422, 447-449, 453, 472, 473, 528, 565-566.
Population, ratio of increase of, 682-683.
Port Gibson, Miss., 711.
Porter, Fitz-John, 642, 643.
Porter, William, 120.
Portsmouth, Va., 691.
Post Office Department, cost of, 108-110, 255n., 594; reports on, 625-626, 672-673, 781-782.
Pratt, Harry E., 7‡, 13, 113n.; *Personal Finances of Abraham Lincoln*, 165n.
Prentice, Charles, 69.
Presidential question, speech on, 233-250n.
Preston, William B., 216n., 703.
Price, ——, 97, 110.
"Proclamation for Thanksgiving," 727-729, 729n.
"Proclamation of Amnesty and Reconstruction," 738-741.
"Proclamation of a National Fast-Day," 610-611.
"Proclamation of Thanksgiving," 761-762.
Proclamations, style of, 36-38.
Proverbs, 513n.
Psychoanalysis of Lincoln, 62n.-63n., 114n.

Quakers, 547.
Quincy, Ill., 11, 156, 426, 558n., 615n.

Quincy Whig, 11, 181n., 329.
Quitman, John A., 564n.

Ramsay [G. D.?], letter to, 615.
Ramsey's *Life of Washington*, 5.
Randolph, Edmund, 234.
Ransdell, Wharton, 118, 182n.
Ranson, ——, 167.
Ray, Charles H., 367; letter to, 482-483n.
Raymond, H. J., letter to, 564-565n.
Reade, George, 519, 520, 521.
Reading, 5-6.
Reavis, Isham, letter to, 337, 337n.
"Rebecca" letters, 7, 7†, 10, 12, 15, 16, 154n., 155n., 158, 159, 159n.; *see also* "A Letter from the Lost Townships."
Rebellion, views on, 594-609, 616-617, 632, 680, 701-705, 707, 709, 738-741.
Reconstruction, 738-741, 797-801.
Reeder, Andrew H., 334.
Reeside, James, 109.
Religious views, 13, 41, 186-188, 655, 772, 793, 794.
"Religious Views: Letter to the Editor of the *Illinois Gazette*," 186-189n.
"Remarkable Case of Arrest for Murder," 175-184n.
"Remarks to the Army of the Potomac at Frederick, Maryland," 656.
Removal of Indians, cost of, 107-108.
Reno, Jesse L., 665.
"Reply to Secretary Seward's Memorandum," 590-591.
Republican National Convention (1860), 491, 493.
"Resolutions in the United States House of Representatives," 199-202n.
"Resolutions upon the Subject of Domestic Slavery," 552.
Responses to Serenades, 709-710, 738n., 760-761, 763-764, 768n.
Revolutionary War, 323.
Richardson, Israel B., 665.
Richardson, Mrs. W. A., 230.
Richardson, William A., 203, 208, 217, 230, 359, 557.
Richmond and Fredericksburg Railroad, 643.
Richmond *Enquirer*, 343.
Richmond, Va., 599, 638, 643, 644, 646, 648, 657-659, 726-727, 753, 796.
Rickard, Elizabeth, 163n.
Rickard, Sarah, 120, 128, 145, 163n.
Riley, John C., 69.
Riney, Zachariah, 548.
Rives, ——, 96.
Roberts, Edmund, 69.
Robertson, George, letters to, 21, 330n., 330-332n.
Robertson, George, *Scrap Book on Law and Politics, Men and Times*, 332n.
Rock Island, Ill., 490.
Rockingham, Va., 224.
Rollin, Charles, 6.
Rolling Fork (Ky.), 548.
Rosecrans, William S., 696; letters to, 36, 765, 765n.
Ross, John, letter to, 654-655.
Ross, Rev. Dr., 478.
Rossville, Ind., 635.
Rousseau, Jean Jacques, 9, 10.
Rowland, ——, 769n.
Rush, Richard, 348.
Rusk, T. J., 214n.
Rutledge, Ann, 62n.

St. Clair, Ill., 327.
St. Louis, Mo., 99, 122, 123n., 161, 218, 226, 251, 255, 275, 333, 663, 664n., 752; lynching of McIntosh at, 78-79.
San Francisco, Cal., 669, 678.
Sandburg, Carl, *Abraham Lincoln: The War Years*, quoted, 35, 733n.; *Abraham Lincoln: The Prairie Years*, 165n., 486n.; and Paul M. Angle, *Mary Lincoln: Wife and Widow*, 120n.-121n., 228n.

Sangamo Journal, 7, 7*, 10, 57n., 58, 112n., 115, 145, 148, 154n., 155n., 156n., 157, 158, 159, 161n., 181n.
Sangamon (Sangamo) County, internal improvements of, 53-55.
Sangamon (Sangamo) River, navigation of, 54-55.
Sanitary Commission, 751.
Santa Anna, Antonio Lopez de, 205, 206, 213n., 214n.
Savannah, Ga., 631, 789.
Saxton, Rufus, 643.
Schlater, C. U., letter to, 254.
Schurz, Carl, letters to, 660-662n., 664-665.
Schurz, Mrs. Carl, 660.
Scott, Dred, 352-365, 376, 396, 397, 418.
Scott, Winfield, 18, 212, 567, 591, 632.
Scott's *Lessons in Elocution,* 3.
Scripps, John L., 5, 555n.
Secession, views on, 33, 586, 595-609, 616-617, 648-650, 676-679, 683-684, 701.
"Second Inaugural Address," 12, 29, 41, 45, 46, 773n., 792-793.
"Sectionalism," 22, 347-351.
Self-government, attitude toward, 303-308, 314, 318.
Senate and House of Representatives, letter to, 640-641.
Seward, William H., 36, 37, 47, 542, 565n., 589n., 611, 691, 729, 729-730n., 741, 760, 762; reply to Seward's memorandum, 590-591.
Seymour, Glen H., "'Conservative'—Another Lincoln Pseudonym?," 7†.
Shakespeare, William, 6; comment on plays of, 718-719.
Shawneetown, Ill., 165n., 261n.
Shelbyville, Ky., 229.
Shelley, Percy Bysshe, 9.
Shepley, George F., 715.
Sheridan, Philip H., telegram to, 763.
Sherman, Roger, 518, 519, 521.
Sherman, William T., 693n., 697, 784, 790n.; letter to, 789-790.
Shields, Alexander, 182n.
Shields, James A., 64, 72n., 150, 151, 152, 153, 154n., 155n., 157, 158, 159, 160n.-161n., 161-162, 326-327, 359, 434, 441.
"Short Autobiography Written for the Campaign of 1860," 4, 547-555n.
Shutes, Milton Henry, *Lincoln and the Doctors,* 62n.
Sigel, Franz, 696, 697, 718.
Silliman letter, 375.
Sioux Indians, 674.
Slavery, abolition of in District of Columbia, 640-641; Emancipation Proclamation, 689-691, 721-722, 797-798; extension of, 283-323; extinction of, 330-331; proposed amendment for abolishment of, 785; resolutions in Illinois Legislature, 552; views on, 8, 19-22, 24, 29-30, 32-33, 122, 123n., 169-171, 278-279, 321-322, 332-336, 339-345, 347-351, 360, 363-365, 372-381, 392-394, 400, 427, 446-448, 458, 469-471, 473-474, 477-479, 500-501, 517-536, 552, 580-588, 652, 680, 688, 721, 795.
Smith, C. B., 236.
Smith, Charles F., 711-712.
Smith, Edgar, 65.
Smith, Green C., 717.
Smith, Truman, 216n.
Snicker's Gap, Va., 659n.
Solomon, 150, 571.
Somers, James W., letter to, 384.
South, attitude toward, 291-292, 443, 480-481, 500, 526-534, 567-568, 580-588, 594-609, 616, 648-650, 792-793.
South Bend, Ind., 567n.
Sovereignty, 601, 604.
"Speech at a Sanitary Fair in Philadelphia," 751-753.
"Speech at Indianapolis, Indiana," 571-572.

"Speech at Peoria, Illinois," 17-20, 282n., 283-325n., 332n.
Speech Delivered at Kalamazoo, Michigan, *see* "Frémont, Buchanan, and the Extension of Slavery: Speech at Kalamazoo, Michigan."
"Speech in Reply to Douglas at Chicago, Illinois," 28, 385-404.
"Speech in Reply to Douglas at Springfield, Illinois," 28, 405-424, 451.
"Speech in the Illinois Legislature," 63-72, 223n.
Speed, Fanny (Henning), 123, 130-131, 141-142, 143-144, 145, 147, 148, 162, 169, 198, 257, 336.
Speed, Joshua F., 10, 11, 12, 21, 120-122, 123n., 154n., 181n., 330n.; letters to, 116-120, 124-126n., 127-128, 130-131, 141-142n., 143-144, 144-146, 146-148, 161-163n., 165-166n., 167-169, 196-198, 256-257, 332-336n.; *Reminiscences of Abraham Lincoln,* 336n.
Speed, Mary, 89n., 123n.; letter to, 121-123, 336n.
Speed, William P., 124, 143, 197.
"Spot Resolutions," 14, 199-202n.
Springfield, Ill., 7, 41, 53, 60n., 61, 73, 113, 117-118, 122, 152, 156, 175, 176, 177, 179, 225, 258n., 278n., 316, 441, 451, 461-463, 550, 555, 569n., 588n., 589n., 725n.; farewell address at, 568-570; speech in reply to Douglas at, 405-424; last speech at, during campaign of 1858, 480-481; Dred Scott decision, speech at, 352-365.
Squatter sovereignty, 373, 387-388.
Stanton, Edwin M., 16, 642n., 758, 790n., 791; letters to, 733, 733n., 744, 745-746.
Stanton, Frederick P., 233.
Stanwood, ——, 231n.
State Bank, *see* Bank of Illinois.
States' rights, views on, 572, 580, 587, 594-609.
Steamboat *Lebanon,* 122.
Steele, Frederick, 697.
Stephens, Alexander H., 42, 215n.-261n., 219, 514n.; letter to, 567-568n.
Stevens, Isaac, 665.
Stillman's defeat, 242.
Stone, Dan, 8, 171n.; co-author of resolutions on slavery, 552.
Stone, Edward C., 772n.
Story's *Equity,* 2.
Story's *Equity Pleadings,* 2.
"Story Written for Noah Brooks," 772.
Stringfellow, Benjamin R., & Co., 335.
Strong, William, 227.
Strunk, ——, 326-327.
Stuart, John T., 6, 172n., 551, 552; letters to, 113-114, 115-116n.
Stuart, ——, 455.
Sturtevant, Julian M., letter to, 346.
Sub-Treasury, speech on, 90-113n.
Sumner, Charles, 42, 416.
Sumner, Edwin V., 638, 641.
Supreme Court, report on operations of, 622-625.
Swartwout, ——, 97, 110.
Sweeney, William, 549.
Sweet, M. P., 256, 257n.; letter to, 475.

Taney, Roger B., 25, 354, 357, 358, 360, 377, 378, 449, 451, 465.
Tarbell, Ida M., *In the Footsteps of the Lincolns,* 338n.
Taylor, Edmund D., 69.
Taylor, John, 69.
Taylor, Zachary, 15, 201, 210, 221, 222, 233-237, 240, 247-250n., 269, 553-554.
Tazewell Whig, 174n.
"Temperance Address Delivered before the Springfield Washington Temperance Society," 8, 10, 131-141.

"Testimonial for Doctor Isachar Zacharie," 654.
"Terms for General Lee's Capitulation," 791.
Texas, annexation of, 170-171.
Thayer, W. R., *Life and Letters of John Hay,* 771n.
"The Bear Hunt," 193-196.
"The Dred Scott Decision: Speech at Springfield, Illinois," 22, 352-365.
"The 14th Section; An Editorial in the *Illinois Journal,*" 281-282.
The National Archives, 609n.
"The Perpetuation of Our Political Institutions: Address before the Young Men's Lyceum of Springfield, Illinois," 4, 8, 9, 72n., 76-85n., 514n.
"The Presidential Question: Speech in the United States House of Representatives," 233-250n.
"The President's Last, Shortest, and Best Speech," *see* "Story Written for Noah Brooks."
"The Repeal of the Missouri Compromise and the Propriety of Its Restoration: Speech at Peoria, Illinois, in Reply to Senator Douglas," 283-325n.
"The Sub-Treasury: Speech at a Political Discussion in the Hall of the House of Representatives at Springfield, Illinois," 4, 90-113n.
"The War with Mexico: Speech in the United States House of Representatives," 14, 202-216n.
Thomas, George H., 789.
Thomas, Lorenzo, 665.
Thomas, William, 515.
Thoreau, Henry D., 8.
Thornton, James T., letter to, 337n., 485, 485n.
Thornton, J. W., 485-486n.
Thornton, W. F., 69.
Thornton's Gap, Va., 659.
Tilson, John, 69.
Todd, Ann, 125, 168.
Todd, Mary, *see* Lincoln, Mary (Todd).
Todd, Robert S., 553.
Toombs, Robert, 216n.
Tordenskiold, P., 668.
"To the People of Sangamo County," 4, 5.
Townsend, William H., *Lincoln and His Wife's Home Town,* 747n.
Trailor, Archibald, 117-120, 175-181, 182-184n.
Trailor, Henry, 117-120, 175-181, 182-184n.
Trailor, William, 117-120, 175-181, 182n.-184n.
Transportation, report on, 675.
Transylvania College, 332n.
Trapp, ——, 327.
Treasury Department, report on operations of, 619-620, 670-672, 778-780.
Treat, Samuel, letter to, 663, 664n.
Tremont, Ill., 174n.
Trenton, N. J., 574.
Trumbull, Lyman, 20, 280n., 326-328, 340, 374, 391, 412, 430, 434, 435, 441, 508, 539; letters to, 486-487, 542-543.
Tunstall, Warrich, 226.
Twain, Mark, 11.
Tyler, Daniel, 708.
Tyler, John, 152, 348.

Underwood, ——, 486-487.
Union, preservation of, 308-311, 315, 584, 630-631, 650, 652, 687-688, 699-708, 722, 734.
Urbana, Ill., 485n.-486n.
Usury, proposal for laws governing, 55-56, 57-58n.

Vallandigham, Clement L., 704, 706, 707, 708n.
Van Bergen, Peter, 148, 167.
Van Buren, Martin, 61, 91, 92, 105, 106, 107, 110, 111, 203, 239, 240, 244, 269.
Vandalia, Ill., 87, 510n.

Van Hoesen, H. B., *The Humor of Lincoln and the Seriousness of His Biographers,* 17, 57n.-58n.
"Verses: To Linnie," 477.
"Verses: To Rosa," 476.
Vestal's Gap, Va., 659.
Vicksburg, Miss., 697, 711; lynching at, 79.
Victoria, Queen, 231n.
Volney, C. F. C. de, 6.
Voltaire, 6, 275.

Wallace, William S., 168.
Walters, William, 165, 167, 168.
Wann, Daniel, 69.
War Department, report on operations of, 620-621, 672, 780.
War, effect on American society, 666-667; report on progress of, 784-785.
War of 1812, 250n., 270, 271.
Ward, Artemus, 16.
Warren, Louis A., *Lincoln Lore,* 735n.
Washburne, E. B., 20, 280n.; letters to, 325, 326-328, 366-367n., 370-371.
Washington Daily Chronicle, 773n.
Washington, D. C., 64, 246, 266, 297, 560n., 589n., 592n., 638, 644, 645, 646, 658-659, 719, 719n., 725n., 726, 729, 741, 762, 784, 798, 801n.
Washington, George, 46, 85, 103, 105-106, 141, 209, 215n., 234, 271, 436, 440, 447, 449, 519, 527, 568, 570n., 607, 608, 656; discussion of Farewell Address, 527-528.
Washington Star, 590n.
Washington Temperance Society, 129n.
Washington *Union,* Lincoln reads article in, 454-457.
Weathers, Mrs. Susannah (Crume), letter to, 635.
Webster, B. C., & Co., 167, 169.
Webster, Daniel, 26, 150, 248, 322, 421, 429, 589n.
Webster, Noah, 319.
Weed, Thurlow, letter to, 794.
Weems, Mason L., *Life of Washington,* 5, 574.
Weik, Jesse W., 47.
Weitzel, Godfrey, telegram to, 802.
Weldon, Lawrence, 384.
Welles, C. R., letter to, 254-255n.
Wentworth, John, 237-238, 325, 326n., 435.
Westfield, N. Y., 562n.
Whig, 175, 181n.
White, Horace, 381n.
White, Hugh L., 59.
White, ——, 231n.
Whiteside, John D., 156n., 157, 158n., 159n., 161-162.
Whitman, Walt, 8, 39.
Whitney, Henry C., 21.
Whittier, John G., 8.
Wickersham, Josiah, 117.
Wickliffe family, 226.
Wickliffe, Robert, 331n.
Wickliffe, ——, 717.
Widmer, John H., 2, 485, 485n.-486n.
Wiggins, Samuel, 65-72.
Wight, A. G. S., 69.
Wilkinson, Samuel, letter to, 371-372n.
Williams, Archibald, 329, 435.
Williamson, Elizabeth, 142.
Williamson, Hugh, 518.
Williamson, John, 142.
Williamsport, Va., 713.
Willis, N. P., 185n.
Wilmot, David, 288.
Wilmot Proviso, 235, 237, 242, 243, 288, 289, 293, 294, 295, 296, 297, 335.
Wilson, Charles L., 367, 367n., 368, 370.
Wilson, Edward M., 69.
Winchester, Ill., 433, 476, 476n., 477.
Winchester, Va., 657, 658, 708.
Wisconsin State Agricultural Society, address before, 493-504, 504n.-505n.

Wolf, Enoch O., 765, 765n.-766n.
Women's Central Association of Relief, 750n.
Woodbury, Levi, 93n.
Woodward, ——, 187.
Wool, John E., 639, 646.
Wordsworth, William, 9.
Wren, Aquilla, 69.
Wright, Crafts J., and C. K. Hawkes, letter to, 742.
Wright, Silas, 92.
"Written by Lincoln in the Autograph Album of Mary Delahay," 505.

Yates, Richard, 320, 462, 554, 717.
Yazoo Pass expedition, 711.
Yeatman, James E., 255.
Young & Brothers, 254.
Young, Brigham, 366n.
Young Men's Central Republican Union, 32, 536n.-539n.

Zacharie, Isachar, testimonial for, 654.

Executive Mansion,

Washington, January 26, 1863.

Major General Hooker:

General.

I have placed you at the head of the Army of the Potomac. Of course I have done this upon what appear to me to be sufficient reasons. And yet I think it best for you to know that there are some things in regard to which, I am not quite satisfied with you. I believe you to be a brave and a skilful soldier, which, of course, I like. I also believe you do not mix politics with your profession, in which you are right. You have confidence in yourself, which is a valuable, if not an indispensable quality. You are ambitious, which, within reasonable bounds, does good rather than harm. But I think that during Gen. Burnside's command of the Army, you have taken counsel of your ambition, and thwarted him as much as you could, in which you did a great wrong to the country, and to a most meritorious and honorable brother officer. I have heard, in such way as to believe it, of your recent-by saying that both the Army and the Government needed a Dictator. Of course it was not *for* this, but in spite of it, that I have given you the command. Only those generals who gain successes, can set up dictators. What I now ask of you is military success, and I will risk the dictatorship. The government will support you to the utmost of it's ability, which is neither more nor less than it has done and will do for all commanders. I much fear that the spirit which you have aided to infuse into the Army, of criticising their Commander, and withholding confidence from him, will now turn upon you. I shall assist you as far as I can, to put it down. Neither you, nor Napoleon, if he were alive again, ~~can~~ could get any good out of an army, while such a spirit prevails in it.

And now, beware of rashness— Beware of rashness, but with energy, and sleepless vigilance, go forward, and give us victories.

Yours very truly
A. Lincoln